CLASSROOM ASSESSMENT
Principles and Practice for Effective Standards-Based Instruction

CANADIAN EDITION

James H. McMillan, VIRGINIA COMMONWEALTH UNIVERSITY
Laurie-Ann M. Hellsten, UNIVERSITY OF SASKATCHEWAN
Don A. Klinger, QUEEN'S UNIVERSITY

Pearson Canada
Toronto

My work on this textbook is dedicated to my parents, who taught me the joy of reading; to my husband, Peter, and son, Braeden, for their support of my work; and to my mentor, Dr. W. Todd Rogers.

—L.H.

I would like to dedicate my work to my family, Marsha, Leisha, and Shayla and to my mentor, Dr. W. Todd Rogers.

—D.K.

Library and Archives Canada Cataloguing in Publication

McMillan, James H
　　Classroom assessment : principles and practice for effective standards-based instruction / James H. McMillan, Laurie Hellsten, Don Klinger.—1st Canadian ed.

Includes bibliographical references and index.
ISBN 978-0-205-57346-2

　　1. Educational tests and measurements.　2. Examinations.　I. Hellsten, Laurie, 1974–
　　II. Klinger, Don, 1960–　III. Title.

LB3051.M39 2010　　371.26　　C2009-904524-9

ISBN 978-0-205-57346-2

Vice-President, Editorial Director: Gary Bennett
Editor-in-Chief: Ky Pruesse
Editor, Humanities and Social Sciences: Joel Gladstone
Signing Representative: Duncan MacKinnon
Marketing Manager: Loula March
Associate Editor: Brian Simons
Production Editor: Melissa Hajek
Copy Editor: Caroline Kaiser
Proofreaders: Carol Anderson and Laura Neves
Production Coordinator: Sarah Lukaweski
Composition: Integra
Permissions and Photo Researcher: Jamie Whittla
Art Director: Julia Hall
Cover Design: Sandra Friesen
Cover Image: Getty Images

　　13　　17

Printed in Canada.

Contents

6   Objectively Scored Assessments of Knowledge and Simple Understanding   149

7   Selected-Response, Short-Answer, and Essay Items   183

8   Performance Assessments   217

Preface

It wasn't too long ago that we both began our graduate programs in measurement and assessment. Laurie had come from the field of physical education and Don had left a teaching position as a district coordinator of assessment and evaluation. Neither of us really envisioned what our measurement courses would require of us, and our previous experience was not adequate preparation for the complexities of measurement that we had previously taken for granted in our earlier experiences. Yet underlying this complexity were sound principles for assessment that continue to guide our ongoing efforts to improve our own assessment practices and understanding, and those of the teachers we wish to support. We have helped to revise this text with the intention of providing a more accurate reflection of the assessment practices and needs of teachers in Canadian schools and jurisdictions. Our intention is to have this book be directly relevant to teachers' instruction so that both teaching and student learning are enhanced.

There is a renewed interest in assessment, and our understanding of its role in our classroom continues to expand. The assessment field is evolving and much more emphasis is now placed on how *student assessment can be an integral part of teaching*, not something that's done after instruction to measure only what students have learned. System accountability is common throughout our education systems across the country, although not to the extent found in the USA. Our Canadian assessment practices continue to chart our own paths, both in terms of classroom and large-scale assessments and we have worked to highlight the assessment culture that currently exists in Canada. Finally, there is renewed interest in the importance of "scientific" research and "empirical data" as sources of knowledge about what works in education. These three influences—assessment as part of instruction, standards-based teaching, and data-driven evidence—form the foundation for this book. All are essential factors in understanding how classroom assessments can influence targeted student outcomes.

This book, then, is designed to provide prospective and practicing teachers with (1) a *concise presentation* of assessment principles that clearly and specifically relate to standards-based instruction, (2) *current research and new directions* in the assessment field, and (3) *practical and realistic* examples, suggestions, and case studies. We have tried to keep the writing *nontechnical, easy to understand, and interesting*.

The approach we have taken to meet these criteria is to build assessment into the instructional process, focusing on assessment concepts and principles that are essential for effective teacher decision making. The emphasis throughout is on helping teachers to understand the importance of establishing credible learning expectations, communicating these standards to students, and providing feedback to students on their progress. There is much less emphasis on technical measurement concepts that teachers rarely find useful, though there is extensive discussion of aspects of assessment that result in high quality and credibility, such as fairness, matching assessment to clearly and publicly stated standards, positive consequences, and practicality.

The book is organized by what teachers do before, during, and after an instructional segment, rather than by type of assessment technique. Thus, the chapter sequence reflects the steps teachers take in using assessment as part of instruction. Chapters 1 through 3 present the fundamental principles of assessment and instruction, with an emphasis on the importance of the teacher's professional judgment and decision making as integral to making useful and credible assessments. Chapter 4 summarizes assessment activities that occur before instruction begins, and Chapter 5 examines assessment that occurs during instruction. Chapters 6 through 10 discuss various types of assessments for different types of learning outcomes that are measured at the end of an instructional segment. Chapter 11 reviews the assessment of students with exceptionalities. Chapter 12 examines what teachers do with assessment information in the form of grading and reporting the results. Finally, Chapter 13 summarizes important information concerning the administration, interpretation, and use of large-scale assessments.

Several instructional aids have been included to facilitate understanding and applying the material. These include *cognitive maps* at the beginning of each chapter to provide graphic overviews; *boldface key terms*; *quotes from teachers* throughout to illustrate practical applications; *chapter summaries* to review essential ideas; *self-instructional review exercises*, with answers, to provide opportunities for practice and application; *suggestions for conducting action research*; extensive use of *examples, diagrams, charts, and tables*; *case studies for reflection*; and a *glossary* of key terms;

Several changes and additions have been made to ensure this edition reflects the Canadian perspective while also focusing on current conceptions of assessment:

- Examination of the nature and influence of large-scale provincial testing programs in Canada.

- Use of terms and language that are currently used in Canadian jurisdictions.

- Thorough treatment of assessment *for* and *as* learning.

- More emphasis on alignment of classroom assessments with standards and standards-based tests.

- Greater emphasis on student motivational and engagement consequences of different assessment and grading practices.

- More emphasis on student self-assessment.

- Expanded coverage of multiple-choice item formats.

- New section on student cheating.

- Expanded discussion of the nature of understanding (simple and deep), especially as related to performance assessments.

SUPPLEMENTS

Instructor's Manual. An instructor's manual is available with this Canadian edition. Its features include introductory comments, suggestions for instruction, and suggestions for assessment.

Test Item File. This carefully prepared test item file contains multiple-choice questions and short answer questions that are designed to test students' comprehension of the text.

Both the Instructor's Manual and Test Item File can be downloaded by instructors from a password-protected section of Pearson Education Canada's online catalogue (**vig.pearsoned.ca**). Navigate to the catalogue page for your textbook to view the list of those supplements that are available. Contact your local sales representative for further information.

CourseSmart. CourseSmart goes beyond traditional expectations—providing instant, online access to the textbooks and course materials you need at an average savings of 50%. With instant access from any computer and the ability to search your text, you'll find the content you need quickly, no matter where you are. And with online tools like highlighting and note-taking, you can save time and study efficiently. See all the benefits at www.coursesmart.com/students.

ACKNOWLEDGMENTS

Throughout the revision of this book, we have been fortunate to have the support of our colleagues, families, and teachers. They continue to keep us grounded and help us to ensure that we continue to walk the talk in our own practices. They have provided us the necessary guidance and inspiration as we endeavoured to make the text more applicable to Canadian educators. At the same time, we want to express our gratitude to the editorial team at Pearson, Brian Simons, Melissa Hajek, and of course Caroline Kaiser.

Certainly, we are also indebted to those classroom teachers who worked with James McMillan on the original text. These teachers provided quotations, practical examples, and suggestions. They include Steve Myran, Suzanne Nash, Steve Eliasek, Daphne Patterson, Craig Nunemaker, Judy Bowman, Jeremy Lloyd, Marc Bacon, Mary Carlson, Michelle Barrow, Margie Tully, Rixey Wilcher, Judith Jindrich, Dan Geary, Joshua Cole, Christy Davis, Elizabeth O'Brien, Beth Harvey, Rita Truelove, Rita Driscoll, Dodie Whitt, Joe Solomon, and Leslie Gross. Similarly, we are also thankful to those university professors who offered insightful and helpful comments and suggestions to the original book: For the first edition, Cheri Magill, Virginia Commonwealth University; H. D. Hoover, University of Iowa; Kathryn A. Alvestad, Calvert County Public Schools; John R. Bing, Salisbury State University; John Criswell, Edinboro University of Pennsylvania; George A. Johanson, Ohio University; Catherine McCartney, Bemidji State University; and

Anthony Truog, University of Wisconsin, Whitewater; for the second edition, Lyle C. Jensen, Baldwin-Wallace College; Cathleen D. Rafferty, Indiana State University; Gerald Dillashaw, Elon College; Daniel L. Kain, North Arizona University; Charles Eiszler, Central Michigan University; Betty Jo Simmons, Longwood College; for the third edition, Gyu-Pan Cho, University of Alabama; Saramma T. Mathew, Troy University; E. Michael Nussbaum, University of Nevada; and Kit Juniewicz, University of New England; and for the fourth edition, Sally Blake, University of Texas at El Paso; Roberta Devlin-Scherer, Seton Hall University; Carla Michele Gismondi Haser, Marymount University; Saramma T. Mathew, Troy University.

We would also like to thank those that reviewed this Canadian edition during the development process: Philip Allingham, Lakehead University; Alexa Okrainec, Brandon University; Susan Drake, Brock Univeristy; Iris Geva, Simon Fraser University; Nola Aitken, University of Lethbridge; Ajit Bedi, Memorial University; Sally Brenton-Haden, University of Alberta; and Willow Brown, University of Northern British Columbia.

We are also grateful for the enthusiastic assistance of Michelle Prytula who ensured that we stayed true to the Canadian classroom context.

Finally, we would also like to express our deep appreciation for W. Todd Rogers, who supervised both of us during our graduate work and continues to act as a mentor and friend.

Chapter 1
The Role of Assessment in Teaching

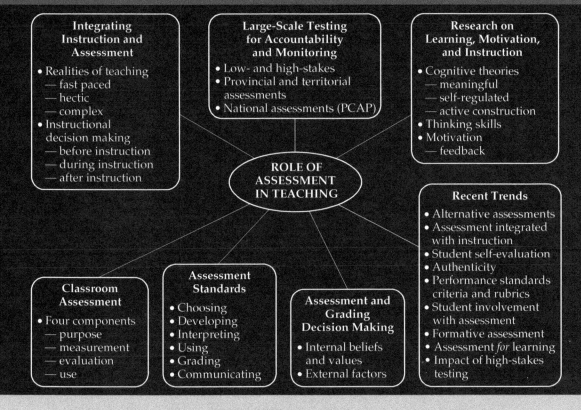

Integrating Instruction and Assessment
- Realities of teaching
  - fast paced
  - hectic
  - complex
- Instructional decision making
  - before instruction
  - during instruction
  - after instruction

Large-Scale Testing for Accountability and Monitoring
- Low- and high-stakes
- Provincial and territorial assessments
- National assessments (PCAP)

Research on Learning, Motivation, and Instruction
- Cognitive theories
  - meaningful
  - self-regulated
  - active construction
- Thinking skills
- Motivation
  - feedback

ROLE OF ASSESSMENT IN TEACHING

Recent Trends
- Alternative assessments
- Assessment integrated with instruction
- Student self-evaluation
- Authenticity
- Performance standards criteria and rubrics
- Student involvement with assessment
- Formative assessment
- Assessment *for* learning
- Impact of high-stakes testing

Classroom Assessment
- Four components
  - purpose
  - measurement
  - evaluation
  - use

Assessment Standards
- Choosing
- Developing
- Interpreting
- Using
- Grading
- Communicating

Assessment and Grading Decision Making
- Internal beliefs and values
- External factors

This book is about how teachers can use classroom assessments to improve student learning in contexts that include large-scale testing for accountability and monitoring. Over the past 20 years or so, research on teacher decision making, cognitive learning, student motivation, and other topics has changed what we know about the importance of assessment for effective teaching and learning. For example, one finding is that good teachers continually assess their students relative to learning goals and adjust their instruction based on this information. These teachers also help their students use this information to direct their own learning. Thus, the assessment of students not only documents what students know and can do, but also influences learning. Assessment that enhances learning is as important as assessment that documents learning. As a result of this research, new purposes, methods, and approaches to student assessment have been developed. These changes underscore a new understanding of the important role that assessment plays in instruction and learning.

In the past few years, large-scale testing for accountability and monitoring ("low- and high-stakes" testing) has had significant impacts on education at all levels. These two areas of influence have changed classroom assessment considerably: research on student learning and motivation, and teacher decision making, on the one hand, and large-scale testing on the other.

Dodie Whitt, an elementary teacher in a suburban school district, explains how her classroom assessments have changed over the past five years:

> I have seen assessments change a lot over the past five years. Assessments have moved from a more informal, performance-based portfolio, to formal pencil–paper tests. The reason for this is simple. SOLs, or "high-stakes" tests, require that children be prepared for standardized tests. They need to not only be prepared to show what they know on these tests, but they also need to possess test-taking skills. It seems that the only way to learn to take a standardized test is to actually take one, so we start as early as Kindergarten learning test format and simple test-taking skills. Please do not think, however, that formal assessments are the only types of assessments being used in classrooms today. I still do quite a bit of informal assessing, in part because of the developmental nature of children, but also because not all skills can be assessed with a pencil–paper test. I "kid-watch" to assess progress, I assign projects and writing assignments to assess progress, and I even use the assessments that come with textbook series. I feel that using different sorts of assessments will give a more accurate indication of the overall progress of the child. Just as children do not all learn the same way, they do not test the same way either. Providing students with a variety of ways to show what they know will give the best picture of what they really do understand. Formal standardized testing is just one part of the big picture when it comes to assessing children.

It is within this dynamic context that classroom assessment exists as a key element in what teachers do and what students learn. It is important to think about classroom assessment as a process that *supports and enhances student learning,* not something that merely documents what students know, understand, and can do. This means that teaching and assessment coexist in dynamic interaction, each feeding and influencing the other.

This chapter summarizes the research on teacher decision making to show how assessment is integrated with instruction and how teachers make decisions about their assessment and grading practices.

INTEGRATING INSTRUCTION AND ASSESSMENT
The Realities of Teaching

Classroom life is fast-paced, hectic, and complex. To illustrate this reality, I have summarized some of what Michelle Barrow does during a typical day in her grade 1 classroom. She has ten boys and eleven girls in her class, four of whom are from racial minority groups and six of whom are from single-parent families. As many as four of her students will participate in the gifted/talented program, and four students were retained from the previous year.

See how easy it is for you to get through this list of disparate tasks. Before school begins in the morning, Michelle

- reviews what was learned/taught the previous day
- goes over student papers to see who did or did not grasp concepts
- prepares a rough agenda for the day
- speaks with an aide about plans for the day
- puts journals on student desks

As soon as students enter the classroom, Michelle

- greets them at the door
- reminds them to put away their homework
- speaks with Brent about his expected behaviour for the day
- reminds Anthony about what he is to do if he becomes bothered or frustrated by others

During the morning, Michelle

- calls students to the table, to go over the reading assignment
- has Dawn read a column of words and then goes back and randomly points to words to see whether Dawn knows them or simply has memorized them
- comments to Lucy that she has really improved since the first day of school
- discusses with Kevin the importance of doing homework every night
- listens as Tim attempts to sound out each word and gradually blend the sounds together
- reminds Maggie that she is to be working in her journal, not visiting and talking with others
- gives Jason, Kory, and Kristen a vocabulary sheet to do because they have completed their journals
- observes students in learning centres before calling reading groups to tables
- verbally reinforces correct answers, gives each student a copy of the week's story, goes through the book, and points out action words
- calls up the low-level reading group and focuses on the letters "m" and "f"
- notices that Kevin has poor fine-motor skills and makes a mental note to send a message to his parents telling them that he should practise his handwriting
- checks on Anthony to see how many centres he has completed
- notices that students in the writing centre are not doing as they were instructed
- walks beside Anthony down the hall, verbally praising him for following directions

- notices that Sarah has some difficulty answering higher-level thinking questions
- makes a mental note to split the gifted group into two smaller groups

After lunch, Michelle's day continues as she

- begins the math lesson on beginning addition with a hippo counter
- walks behind Scott and gives the next problem to the class
- punches the cards of students who have followed directions
- notices that another table of students immediately stops talking and starts paying attention
- tells students to rewrite sloppy copies
- reminds Kevin and Brent to use guide lines on the paper
- praises and punches the cards of Sarah and a few other students for good handwriting and concentration
- notices that Tim is watching others and asks him if he needs help
- gives a five-minute warning for music time and notices students working more intensely
- looks over the students' writing while they're in music and arranges the papers into groups

After students leave for the day, Michelle continues to teach by

- grading student papers
- making sure materials are ready for the next day
- making notes in her markbook about notes sent home and how the day went
- checking portfolios to see progress
- calling some parents

Was it difficult to get through the list? If so, you have some empathy for the hectic nature of classrooms and the need to make many decisions quickly about students and instructional activities. Represented here is just a small sample of Michelle's actions, all of which are based on decisions that depend on how well she has assessed her students. How did she decide to discuss with Kevin the importance of homework? What evidence did she use to decide that she needed to check Dawn's reading? In each of these cases, Michelle had to conduct some kind of assessment of the student before making her decisions. The role of an effective teacher is to reach these decisions reflectively, based on evidence gathered through assessment, reasoning, and experience.

Each decision is based on information that Michelle has gathered through a multitude of student interactions and behaviour. Research indicates that a teacher may have as many as 1000 or even 1500 interactions with students each day (Billups & Rauth, 1987; Jackson, 1990). Often these interactions and decisions occur with incomplete or inaccurate information, making the job of teaching even more difficult.

Consider how the following aspects of Michelle's and other teachers' classrooms affect decision making (Doyle, 1986).

1. *Multi-dimensionality:* Teachers' choices are rarely simple. Many different tasks and events occur continuously, and students with different preferences and abilities must receive limited resources for different objectives. Waiting for one student to answer a question may negatively influence the motivation of another student. How can the teacher best assess these multiple demands and student responses to make appropriate decisions?

2. *Simultaneity:* Many things happen at once in classrooms. Good teachers monitor several activities at the same time. What does the teacher look and listen for so that the monitoring and responses to students are appropriate?

3. *Immediacy:* Because the pace of classrooms is rapid, there is little time for reflection. Decisions are made quickly. What should teachers focus on so that these quick decisions are the right ones that will help students learn?

4. *Unpredictability:* Classroom events often take unanticipated turns, and distractions are frequent. How do teachers evaluate and respond to these unexpected events?

5. *History:* After a few weeks, routines and norms are established for behaviour. What expectations for assessment does the teacher communicate to students?

In these complex environments, teachers must make some of their most important decisions about what and how much students have learned. Action is based on these decisions. Accurate and appropriate student assessment provides the information needed to help teachers make better decisions. In the classroom context, then, **assessment** is the gathering, interpretation, and use of information to aid teacher decision making. Assessment is an umbrella concept that encompasses different techniques, strategies, and uses.

Instructional Decision Making and Assessment

It is helpful to consider teacher decision making in the context of *when* decisions are made—before, during, or after instruction—and then to examine how assessment affects choices at each time. Pre-instructional decisions are needed to set learning goals, select appropriate teaching activities, and prepare learning materials. During instructional activities, decisions are made about the delivery and pace in presenting information, keeping the students' attention, controlling students' behaviour, and making adjustments in lesson plans. After instruction, teachers evaluate student learning, instructional activities, and themselves to determine what to teach next, to grade students, and to improve instruction. Table 1.1 presents examples of the types of questions teachers ask at these different points in the instructional process. Table 1.1 also offers examples of the type of assessment information needed to make these decisions.

Figure 1.1 illustrates further how assessment is involved in each stage of the instructional process. This figure shows how pre-instructional assessment provides information to transform learning expectations and outcomes into specific learning targets. You will usually

Table 1.1 Examples of Questions for Decision Making
and Assessment Information

When Decisions Are Made	Questions	Assessment Information
Before Instruction	How much do my students know?	Previous student achievement; test scores; observations of student performance
	Are my students motivated to learn?	Observations of student involvement and willingness to ask questions
	Are there any exceptional students? If so, what should I plan for them?	Student records; conference with a special education teacher
	What instructional activities should I plan? Are these activities realistic for these students?	Overall strengths and needs of students; comments from previous teachers; evaluations of previous teaching
	What homework assignments should I prepare?	Student progress and level of understanding
	What is acceptable evidence that students have attained desired proficiencies?	Which assessment methods will provide needed evidence
During Instruction	What type of feedback should I give to students?	Quality of student work; type of student
	What question should I ask?	Observation of student understanding
	How should a student response to a question be answered?	Potential for this student to know the answer
	Which students need my individual attention?	Performance on homework; observations of work in class
	What response to student inattention or disruption is best?	Effect of the student on others
	When should I stop this lesson?	Observation of student attention
After Instruction	How well have my students mastered the material?	Achievement test results in relation to a specified level
	Are students ready for the next unit?	Analysis of demonstrated knowledge
	What grades should the students receive?	Tests; quizzes; homework; class participation
	What comments should I make to parents?	Improvement; observations of behaviour
	How should I change my instruction?	Diagnosis of demonstrated learning; student evaluations

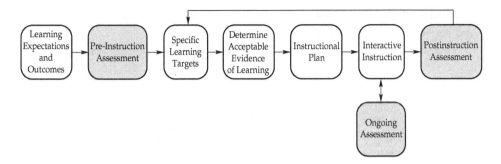

Figure 1.1 Relationship between Instruction and Assessment

be provided with provincial learning expectations and outcomes for a particular grade level or subject. These expectations are a starting point for developing more specific learning targets that take into account the characteristics and needs of the students, and your style and beliefs. Pre-instructional assessment is an absolutely essential step for effective instruction. If you can't identify what specific knowledge, skills, attitudes, and other learning targets are important, it is unlikely that you, students, or parents will know when they have been successful. In other words, you must determine what students should know, understand, and be able to do at the end of an instructional unit.

The next step in instructional decision making is to specify the evidence that is needed to document student learning. This evidence is identified *before* determining instructional plans because it should influence the nature of instruction. This approach to planning is known as "backward design" (McTighe & Wiggins, 2004; Wiggins, 1998; Wiggins & McTighe, 2005). It is called "backward" because conventional instructional planning typically considers assessment an activity that is done after instruction. But it is very helpful to think like an assessor before planning learning activities, since doing so helps accomplish a true integration of assessment and instruction.

Once acceptable evidence is identified, the teacher selects instructional strategies and activities to meet the targets. This is often operationalized as a lesson plan or instructional plan. It consists of what teachers will do and what they will have their students do for a specific period of time. During instruction, interaction between the teacher and students involves constantly making assessments about how to respond to students appropriately and keep them on task. During this time, assessment information is used to monitor learning, check for progress, and diagnose learning problems.

After instruction, teachers conduct more formal assessments of learning targets, which inform subsequent learning targets, instructional plans, and interactive instruction. Assessment at the end of an instructional unit also provides information for grading students, evaluating teaching, and evaluating curriculum and school programs.

Classroom assessments define what is really important in schooling. Regardless of publicly stated objectives or provincial outcomes, the nature of classroom assessments defines what students learn. Clearly, what is assessed and how it is assessed in the classroom deliver strong messages about what is valued.

The point is that assessment is not only an *add-on* activity that occurs after instruction is completed. Rather, assessment is integrally related to all aspects of teacher decision making and instruction. Michelle Barrow did assessment *before* instruction by reviewing the performance of students on the previous day's work to see who did and who did not grasp the concepts. She used this information to plan subsequent instruction. *During* instruction, Michelle constantly observed student work and responded, in order to provide appropriate feedback and to keep students on task. *After* instruction she graded papers, checked student progress, and made decisions about the focus of instruction for the next day.

CASE STUDY FOR REFLECTION

In a recent study, teachers were asked whether assessment drives instruction or instruction drives assessment. Here is what a few of them said:

> "I would say my plan determines my assessments. What I teach is what I assess."
>
> "I guess a little bit of both, but I guess assessment comes from your lesson plans. You can't have the test made up if you have some unforeseen circumstance and you don't get to teach something during the week. It wouldn't be fair to have that on the test."
>
> "In the remedial class, assessment somewhat dictated lesson plans."
>
> "Assessments absolutely drive lesson plans. I'll introduce it, assess what students know and how fast they pick it up, and then adjust my plans or write my plans accordingly."
>
> "What we teach determines the assessment."
>
> "It's both, really. For instance, the writing rubric sometimes comes first because I know a certain skill that I want to teach them. So I'll design whatever final product I want them to come up with. Then I'll do my lesson plan to lead up to that."

In the first of the case studies that will appear in each of the chapters, teacher comments are made about whether assessment drives instruction or instruction drives assessment (McMillan & Workman, 1999). From what these teachers said, is it apparent that assessment should drive instruction? How would you respond to this question?

With this introduction, we will now consider more specifically what is meant by such terms as *test* and *assessment* and how current conceptualizations enhance older definitions of *measurement* and *evaluation* to improve teaching and learning.

WHAT IS CLASSROOM ASSESSMENT?

Classroom assessment can be defined as the collection, evaluation, and use of information to help teachers make decisions that improve student learning. Conceptualized in this way, assessment is more than *testing* or *measurement*, which are familiar terms that have been used extensively in discussing how students are evaluated.

There are four essential components to implementing classroom assessment: purpose, measurement, evaluation, and use. These components are illustrated in Figure 1.2, with questions to ask yourself at each step. The figure shows the sequence of the components, beginning with identification of purpose.

Purpose

Whether done before, during, or after instruction, the first step in any assessment is to clarify the specific purpose or purposes of gathering the information. You need a clear vision of what the assessment will accomplish. Why are you doing the assessment? What will be gained by it? What teacher decision making is enhanced by the information gathered through the assessment process? We have traditionally thought about assessment as a way to measure what students have learned and to grade them. But other reasons for doing assessment need to be considered. For example, will your assessment be designed deliberately to improve student performance and not simply to provide an audit of it? Will the assessment provide specific feedback to students? Do the results of the assessment make it possible to track student progress in learning? Do the assessments motivate students to learn? Do they accurately communicate your expectations to students and what is most valued? Do they provide a realistic estimation of what students are able to do outside the classroom? Is the purpose to assess breadth or depth of student learning? You will need to consider these kinds of questions to fully integrate assessment with instruction.

Measurement

The term *measurement* has traditionally been defined as a systematic process of assigning numbers to behaviour or performance. It is used to determine how much of a trait, attribute, or characteristic an individual possesses. Thus, **measurement** is the process by which

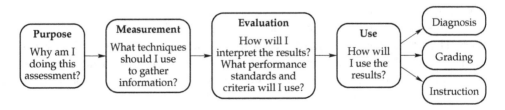

Figure 1.2 Components of Classroom Assessment

traits, characteristics, or behaviour are *differentiated*. The process of differentiation can be very formal and quantitative, such as using a thermometer to measure temperature, or it can consist of less formal processes, such as observation ("It's very hot today!"). Typically, measurement is used to assign numbers to describe attributes or characteristics of a person, object, or event. A variety of techniques can be used to measure a defined trait or learning target, such as tests, ratings, observations, and interviews.

Evaluation

Once measurement is used to gather information, you will need to place some degree of value on different numbers and observations, based on a specific frame of reference. This process is identified in Figure 1.2 as *evaluation*, the making of judgments about quality— how good the behaviour or performance is. **Evaluation** involves an *interpretation* of what has been gathered through measurement, in which value judgments are made about performance. For example, measurement often results in a percentage of items answered correctly. Evaluation is a judgment about what each percentage correct score means. Is 75 per cent correct good, average, or poor? Does 75 per cent indicate "proficiency"?

Teachers' professional judgments play a large role in evaluation. What is a "good" student paper to one teacher may be only an "adequate" paper to another teacher. Assessment is more than *correctness*; it is also about value.

An important determinant of how you evaluate a performance is the nature of the performance standards you employ. **Performance standards** are used to determine whether a performance is "good" or "bad." Increasingly, such standards refer to high, specific, and valued measurable results that indicate a specific level of performance.

Criteria also play an important part in the evaluation process. **Criteria** are the specific behaviours or dimensions that are evidence that the standard has been successfully attained. These criteria may be the most important influences on evaluation. They may be called *scoring criteria, scoring guidelines,* or *rubrics*. For example, take the standard that students know all the provincial capitals in Canada. The criteria are what the teacher uses to conclude that the student does, indeed, know the capitals. For one teacher, this may mean giving the students a map and having them write in the capital for each province; for another teacher, it may mean answering 20 multiple-choice questions correctly. Often teachers use criteria for scoring tests and papers without a clear standard. If only informally, teachers must have some type of criteria in mind to make assessment evaluations.

Both standards and criteria communicate to students the teacher's expectations of them. The nature of questions and feedback, the difficulty of assignments, and the rigour of the criteria tell students what the teacher believes they are capable of achieving. These expectations are important in motivating students and in setting a climate of academic achievement in the classroom.

As you can see, setting standards and criteria is a critical component of assessment, one that we will consider in much greater detail in Chapter 2.

Use

The final stage of implementing assessment is how the evaluations are used. The use of test scores and other information is closely tied to the decisions teachers must make to provide effective instruction, to the purposes of assessment, and to the needs of students and parents. As indicated in Figure 1.1, these decisions depend on *when* they are made; they can also be categorized into three major uses: diagnosis, grading, and instruction.

Diagnosis. Diagnostic decisions are made about individual students, as well as about group strengths, weaknesses, and needs. Typically, teachers gather information that will allow them to diagnose the specific area that needs further attention or an area in which progress is being made. The diagnosis includes an assessment of *why* a student may be having difficulty so that appropriate instructional activities can be prescribed. For example, teachers use homework diagnostically to determine the extent of student understanding and to identify students who do not understand the assignment. A pretest may be used to diagnose specific gaps in student knowledge that need to be targeted. Students are closely monitored to check motivation, understanding, and progress. Such *sizing-up* assessments are done at the beginning of the year to determine the abilities and interests of the students.

Grading. Grading decisions are based on measurement-driven information. Although most teachers must adhere to grading scales and definitions, great variability exists in what teachers use to determine grades, how they use grading to motivate students, and the standards they use to judge the quality of student work. Some teachers, for example, use grading to *control* and *motivate* (e.g., "This assignment will be graded"), and often teachers use completed work as a basis for giving privileges and otherwise rewarding students (e.g., "good" papers are posted for everyone to see). Grades and associated written comments also provide *feedback* to students and parents.

Instruction. Teachers constantly make instructional decisions, and good teachers are aware that they must continuously assess how students are doing in order to adjust their instruction appropriately. One type of decision, called a *process* instructional decision, is made almost instantaneously, such as deciding to end a lecture or ask a different type of question. *Planning* instructional decisions are made with more reflection; they might include changing student seating arrangements or grouping patterns, spending an extra day on a particular topic, or preparing additional worksheets for homework. Teachers should use credible measurement information with clear standards to evaluate student behaviour accurately.

An important aspect of teaching is *communicating expectations* to students, and assessments are used continuously during instruction to indicate what is expected of students. These expectations are communicated to students by the nature of the questions the teacher asks (e.g., are the questions easy or hard?), by how the teacher acknowledges student answers, by the type of feedback teachers give to students as they are completing assignments, and in many more subtle ways of responding to students. The nature of the tests teachers give and how they evaluate student answers communicate standards that students are expected to meet.

Finally, assessment processes can be used as instruction. For example, performance and authentic assessments are long term and provide opportunities for student learning. As we will see in later chapters, such assessments are useful as teaching tools, as well as methods to document student learning. As such, they educate and improve student performance, not merely audit it (Wiggins, 1998).

RESEARCH ON LEARNING, MOTIVATION, INSTRUCTION, AND CURRICULUM: IMPLICATIONS FOR ASSESSMENT

As summarized in Table 1.2, recent research on learning, motivation, instruction, and curriculum has important implications for the nature and use of classroom assessments. Effective instruction usually does much more than simply present information to students. Rather, good instruction provides an environment that engages the student in active learning that connects new information with existing knowledge. Contemporary cognitive theories show that learning is *meaningful* and *self-regulated* (Schunk, 2004). Learning is an ongoing process in which students actively receive, interpret, and relate information to what they already know, understand, and have experienced. Effective assessment, in turn, promotes this process (Phye, 1997a).

It is essential for students to develop thinking skills (e.g., skills in problem solving and decision making). Students need to be able to apply what they learn to real-world demands

Table 1.2 Linking Instruction and Assessment: Implications from Cognitive Learning Theory

Theory	Implications for Instruction/Assessment
Knowledge is constructed. Learning is a process of creating personal meaning from new information and prior knowledge.	• Encourage discussion of new ideas. • Encourage divergent thinking and multiple links and solutions, not just one right answer. • Encourage multiple modes of expression—for example, role play, simulations, debates, and explanations to others. • Emphasize critical thinking skills, such as the ability to analyze, compare, generalize, predict, and hypothesize. • Relate new information to personal experience and prior knowledge. • Apply information to a new situation.

(continued)

Table 1.2 (Continued)

Theory	Implications for Instruction/Assessment
People of all ages/abilities can think and solve problems. Learning isn't necessarily a linear progression of discrete skills.	• Engage all students in problem solving. • Don't make problem solving, critical thinking, or the discussion of concepts contingent on mastery of routine basic skills.
There is great variety in learning styles, attention spans, memory, developmental paces, and intelligences.	• Provide choices in tasks (not all reading and writing). • Provide choices in how to show mastery/competence. • Provide time to think about and do assignments. • Don't overuse timed tests. • Provide opportunity to revise and rethink. • Include concrete experiences (manipulatives and links to prior personal experience).
People perform better when they know the goal, see models, and know how their performance compares to the standard.	• Discuss goals; let students help define them (personal and class). • Provide a range of examples of student work; discuss characteristics. • Provide students with opportunities for self-evaluation and peer review. • Discuss criteria for judging performance. • Allow students to have input into standards.
It's important to know when to use knowledge, how to adapt it, and how to manage one's own learning.	• Give real-world opportunities (or simulations) to apply/adapt new knowledge. • Have students self-evaluate: think about how they learn well/poorly, set new goals, and discuss why they like certain work.
Motivation, effort, and self-esteem affect learning and performance.	• Motivate students with real-life tasks and connections to personal experiences. • Encourage students to see the connection between effort and results.
Learning has social components. Group work is valuable.	• Provide group work. • Incorporate heterogeneous groups. • Enable students to take on a variety of roles. • Consider group products and group processes.

Source: J.L. Herman, P.R. Aschbacher, & L. Winters, The National Center for Research on Evaluation, Standards and Student Testing (CRESST) (1992). *A Practical Guide to Alternative Assessment* (pp. 19–20). Alexandria, VA: Association for Supervision and Curriculum Development. Copyright © 1992 by The Regents of the University of California. Supported under the Institute of Education Sciences (IES), U.S. Department of Education.

and challenges, work with others to solve problems, and be self-regulated learners who have an awareness and willingness to explore new ideas and develop new skills. Instruction and curriculum, as well as assessment, need to be designed and delivered to enhance these skills.

Research on motivation suggests that teachers must constantly assess students and provide informative feedback. By providing specific and meaningful feedback to students and encouraging them to regulate their own learning, teachers encourage students to enhance their sense of self-efficacy and self-confidence, which are important determinants of motivation (Brookhart, 1997, 2004). Meaningful learning is intrinsically motivating because the content has relevance. The implication here is that assessment does not end with scoring and recording the results. Motivation is highly dependent on the nature of the feedback from the assessment. Thus, in keeping with the integration of assessment with instruction, feedback is an essential component of the assessment process.

As well, significant recent changes in curriculum theory have clear implications for classroom assessment. Due in part to the standards-based movement, curriculum is now based on the premise that all students can learn, that expectations for learning need to be high for all students, and that equal opportunity is essential. Curriculum needs to show students how learning is connected to the world outside of school.

Shepard (2000) has nicely illustrated the shared principles of contemporary curriculum theories, cognitive and constructivist learning theory, and recent trends in classroom assessment (Figure 1.3). Her overlapping circles signify that the changes from older behaviouristic theories of learning and motivation, curriculum designed for social efficiency, and principles derived from scientific measurement overlap to provide a new set of ideas to guide classroom assessment. Although the changes in principles of curriculum, learning, and motivation are now fairly well established, classroom assessment practices are only beginning to change. Furthermore, recent high-stakes or large-scale testing at some provincial levels has nudged many educators back toward behaviouristic and scientific (e.g., objective) measurement theories.

The research from cognitive learning and curriculum theories has laid the foundation for significant changes in classroom assessment. As we discover more about how students learn, we realize that assessment practices, as well as instructional practices, need to change in order to keep pace with this research.

RECENT TRENDS IN CLASSROOM ASSESSMENT

In the past two decades, some clear trends have emerged in classroom assessment. More established traditions of focusing assessment on "objective" testing at the *end* of instruction are being supplemented with (or sometimes replaced by) assessments *during* instruction called "alternative" assessments, which help teachers make moment-by-moment decisions. **Alternative assessments** include authentic assessment, performance assessment, portfolios, exhibitions, demonstrations, journals, and other forms of assessment that require the active construction of meaning, rather than the passive regurgitation of isolated facts. These assessments engage students in learning and require thinking skills, and therefore are consistent with cognitive theories of learning and motivation, as well as societal needs to prepare students for an increasingly complex workplace.

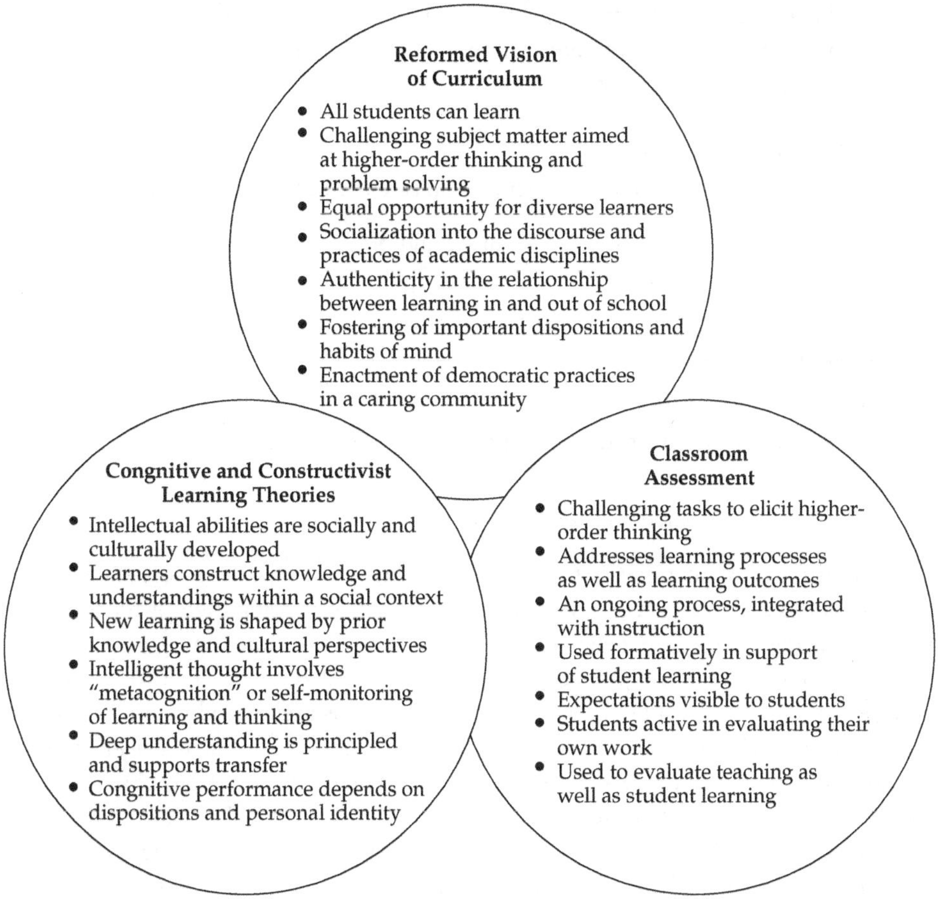

Figure 1.3 Shared Principles of Curriculum Theories, Psychological Theories, and Assessment Theory Characterizing an Emergent Constructivist Paradigm

Source: L.A. Shepard (2000). The role of assessment in a learning culture. *Educational Researcher,* 29(10), 4–14.

Another trend is the recognition that knowledge and skills should not be assessed in isolation. Rather, it is necessary to assess the application and the use of knowledge and skills together. More emphasis is now placed on assessing thinking skills and collaborative skills that are needed to work cooperatively with others. Newer forms of assessment provide opportunities for many "correct" answers, rather than a single right answer, and rely on multiple sources of information.

One of the most important advances in both instruction and assessment is the emphasis on **authenticity** (Wiggins, 1993, 1998). Authentic instruction and assessment focus on knowledge, thinking, and skills exhibited in real-life settings outside school that produce the student's best, rather than typical, performance. To accomplish this, students need multiple "authentic" opportunities to demonstrate the knowledge and skills, and continuous feedback. This kind of emphasis results in greater student motivation and improved achievement. In this way, authenticity effectively integrates instruction, assessment, and motivation. Consider the following characteristics of authentic instruction and assessment in light of what occurs in traditional classrooms (Borich & Tombari, 2004).

Authentic instruction and assessment emphasize the following:

- Students are assessed on what was taught and practised in ways that are consistent with assessment methods.

- The focus is on solving problems and accomplishing tasks like those done by professionals in the field.

- Standards or criteria for success are public; they are shared with the students.

- Assessment occurs over time, to provide meaningful feedback so students can improve.

- Learning and assessment contexts are similar to "real life."

Another important trend is to involve students in all aspects of assessment, from designing tasks and questions, to developing rubrics, to evaluating their own and others' work. Engaging students in developing assessment exercises, creating scoring criteria, applying criteria to student products, and performing self-assessment all help students understand how their own performance is evaluated. This understanding, in turn, facilitates student motivation and achievement. Students learn to confidently evaluate their performance, as well as the performance of other students. For example, if students are taught to internalize the key elements of what should be included in comprehending a short story, they are better able to monitor their progress toward achieving learning targets. Likewise, when students generate lists of the ways in which good essay answers differ from weak ones, they learn the criteria that determine high student performance. Thus, there is a change of emphasis from the teacher providing all assessment tasks and feedback to promoting student engagement in the assessment process. This is best accomplished through "a continuous flow of information about student achievement . . . to advance, not merely check on, student learning" (Stiggins, 2002, p. 761). That is, assessment *for* learning becomes as important as assessment *of* learning.

The distinction between assessment *of* learning and assessment *for* learning is critical for understanding the influences of recent theories of learning and motivation on the one hand (*for* learning), and external accountability testing on the other (*of* learning). These differences are summarized in Table 1.3. Note, too, that assessment *as* learning is also important.

Stiggins (2002, pp. 761–762) identifies eight ways that assessment *for* learning can be facilitated:

1. Understanding and articulating targets in advance of teaching/learning

2. Informing students about learning goals in terms that students understand, from the very beginning of the teaching and learning process

Table 1.3 Characteristics of Assessment *of* Learning, *for* Learning, and *as* Learning

Assessment *of* Learning	Assessment *for* Learning	Assessment *as* Learning
• Summative	• Formative	• Nature of assessment engages students in learning
• Certify learning	• Describes needs for future learning	• Fosters student self-monitoring of learning
• Conducted at the end of a unit; sporadic	• Conducted during a unit of instruction; ongoing	• Conducted during a unit of instruction
• Often uses normative scoring guidelines; ranks students	• Tasks allow teachers to modify instruction	• Emphasizes student knowledge of criteria used to evaluate learning
• Questions drawn from material studied	• Suggests corrective instruction	• Student selects corrective instruction
• General	• Specific	• Specific
• Used to report to parents	• Used to give feedback to students	• Fosters student self-monitoring
• Can decrease student motivation	• Enhances student motivation	• Enhances student motivation
• Highly efficient, superficial testing	• In-depth testing	• Testing teaches students
• Focus on reliability	• Focus on validity	• Focus on validity
• Delayed feedback	• Immediate feedback	• Immediate feedback
• Summary judgments	• Diagnostic	• Diagnostic

Source: Adapted from L.M. Earl (2003). *Assessment as learning: Using classroom assessment to maximize student learning.* Thousand Oaks, CA: Corwin Press; and P.G. LeMahieu & E.C. Reilly (2004). Systems of coherence and resonance: Assessment for education and assessment of education, in M. Wilson (Ed.), *Toward coherence between classroom assessment and accountability. 104th Yearbook of the National Society for the Study of Education.* Chicago: National Society for the Study of Education.

3. Becoming assessment literate and able to transform expectations into assessment exercises and scoring procedures that accurately reflect student achievement

4. Using classroom assessment to build students' confidence in themselves as learners and to help them take responsibility for their own learning

5. Translating classroom assessment results into frequent, descriptive feedback; providing students with specific insights as to how to improve

6. Continuously adjusting instruction based on the results of classroom assessment

7. Engaging students in regular self-assessment, with standards held constant so that students can watch themselves grow over time

8. Actively involving students in communicating with their teacher and parents about their achievement status and improvement

Student engagement in assessment is closely related to another recent trend: a greater emphasis on what is termed "formative" assessment. **Formative assessment** occurs when teachers obtain information about student understanding during instruction and provide feedback that includes correctives to help students learn. It involves both formal and informal methods of gathering information, with the sole purpose of improving student motivation and learning. In contrast, **summative assessment** documents what students have learned at the end of an instructional unit. Summative assessment is more formal and occurs after instruction is completed. Effective teaching requires the use of both formative and summative assessments. The greater emphasis on formative assessment in recent years, which integrates nicely with recent theories of motivation and cognition, suggests a continuing focus on improving student learning with assessments that are integrated with instruction.

These and other recent trends in classroom assessment are summarized in Table 1.4, with some arrows pointing back to indicate the influence of large-scale testing. These trends are not meant to suggest that what teachers have been doing for years is inappropriate or should necessarily be changed. Much of what we have learned about evaluating students from previous decades is very important and useful. For example, properly

Table 1.4 Recent Trends in Classroom Assessment

From	To
Sole emphasis on outcomes	Assessing of process
Isolated skills	Integrated skills
Isolated facts	Application of knowledge
Paper-and-pencil tasks	Authentic tasks
Decontextualized tasks	Contextualized tasks
A single correct answer ◄———————	Many correct answers
Secret standards	Public standards
Secret criteria	Public criteria
Individuals ◄———————	Groups
After instruction	During instruction
Little feedback	Considerable feedback
"Objective" tests ◄———————	Performance-based tests
Standardized tests	Informal tests
External evaluation	Student self-evaluation
Single assessments	Multiple assessments
Sporadic	Continual
Conclusive	Recursive
Assessment *of* learning ◄———————	Assessment *for* and *as* learning
Summative	Formative

constructed multiple-choice tests are excellent for efficiently and objectively assessing knowledge of a large content domain. A *balanced* approach to assessment is needed, in which appropriate techniques are administered and used in a credible way for decision making. Just because the assessment focuses on complex thinking skills or uses portfolios does not mean it is better or more credible. Assessment technique must be matched to purpose and must be conducted according to established quality standards. Some of the recent trends, such as making outcomes and criteria public, are helpful procedures regardless of the assessment employed, and they will improve traditional and newer types of measurement by engaging students in the entire assessment process.

THE INFLUENCE OF LARGE-SCALE ACCOUNTABILITY TESTING

Like it or not, it is abundantly clear that externally mandated large-scale accountability tests have a profound impact on teaching and classroom assessment. For most teachers, there is no escaping this reality. What you do in the classroom will be influenced by both the content and the nature of these tests.

Students, teachers, and administrators have always been held accountable, primarily at a local school or district level, and sometimes at the provincial level. In the last two decades, unprecedented provincial accountability policy initiatives have increased the pressure on schools to show positive results on provincially mandated tests. The first step toward this change was the shift from sporadic large-scale testing for system monitoring to annual testing programs that included all students from specific grades or courses. These tests were closely tied to provincial and territorial curricula having specified learning outcomes (more about these in Chapter 2). Accountability was tied to these outcomes in the form of "high-stakes" testing. **High-stakes tests** are ones that have important consequences. This is the case for tests that determine whether a student can graduate from high school and when school accreditation is tied to test scores. Province-wide (large-scale) high-stakes tests are now used to hold students, teachers, and schools accountable.

In 2002, the No Child Left Behind (NCLB) Act was passed in the United States, with federal-level pressure for demonstrating consistently improving student test scores. The heart of NCLB is to assure that states have "challenging" content standards and that there is extensive testing of the standards to hold schools accountable. By the 2005–2006 school year, states were required to test reading and mathematics annually in grades 3–11 (formerly in grades 10–12). Science tests were required by 2008–2009. To hold schools accountable with these tests, each state was required to establish a "starting point" target for the percentages of students that needed to be classified as "proficient" in 2002. Using a concept called adequate yearly progress (AYP), states will establish increasingly high percentages of students reaching the proficient level at each grade each year until 2014, when 100 per cent of students must be at the proficient level. What makes

AYP difficult is that it must be demonstrated for several subgroups of students (racial minorities and the learning disabled), as well as for the whole school. The implications of NCLB and AYP include increasing pressures that have resulted in increased high-stakes testing, educational sanctions, and in some cases, state takeover of schools.

Currently, no federal policies similar to NCLB and AYP exist in Canada, where education is a provincial/territorial jurisdiction rather than a federal jurisdiction. Nonetheless, large-scale provincial testing is increasing throughout Canada and is being used to serve accountability purposes. Administrators and local boards of education, as well as provincial-level policy makers, want these measures of student performance to be as high as possible. The public opinion of schools and of teachers may be influenced by the test results (private organizations provide public rankings of schools based on provincial assessment results). In fact, these tests are often the primary source of evidence used to judge our schools. The pressure is on, and administrators and teachers are reacting.

With these new accountability requirements, large-scale testing has significantly influenced what teachers do in the classroom, including what they do in the construction and use of their student assessments. There is a great amount of emphasis on "test prep," on "teaching to the test," on aligning classroom tests with large-scale tests, and on using classroom test formats like those used in the provincial assessments. Almost all of the large-scale tests include multiple-choice questions, and teachers are increasingly expected to use the same item format in their classroom assessments.

Teachers will be most effective by balancing the demands of large-scale tests with what they know about best practices of teaching and assessment that maximize student motivation and learning. Clearly, classroom assessment must be considered in the current climate, which emphasizes large-scale testing for the purposes of accountability and monitoring. One purpose of this book, then, is to incorporate these accountability/monitoring demands and influences with classroom assessment procedures that can enhance student learning. Unfortunately, for many, teaching to external outcomes and large-scale tests conflicts with classroom assessment methods that have changed to be more consistent with contemporary theories of learning and motivation. But here is the silver lining: classroom assessments, especially formative ones selected and implemented based on promoting student learning, rather than showing student performance, will result in higher provincial test results. The key is focusing on *how classroom assessments will maximize student motivation and learning*, rather than on what will result in the highest percentages of students judged at least proficient.

The first Teacher's Corner feature (below) shows what two Virginia teachers (one a Virginia regional "teacher of the year") think about the impact of high-stakes tests. Obviously, the influence is powerful. And such assessments, when used correctly, can improve student learning. While these teachers both work in the United States, teachers throughout Canada express similar thoughts in response to large-scale testing in their provinces.

TEACHERS' CLASSROOM-ASSESSMENT AND GRADING-PRACTICES DECISION MAKING

Every teacher makes many decisions about the types of assessments that will be used, when these assessments are used, and grading. Consistent with previous research, a recent survey of over 1000 teachers showed that these decisions result in highly individualized and idiosyncratic practices (McMillan, Workman, & Myran, 1998). Each teacher creates his or her own practices. This suggests that you too will develop your own assessment and grading practices.

To better understand the decision-making process teachers use, the author participated in a study in which in-depth, individual interviews were conducted with 28 teachers to investigate the reasons they gave for their assessment decisions (McMillan, 2003; McMillan & Workman, 1999). The results have interesting implications because of the strong connection between this decision-making process and instruction.

We found that two major sources of influence affect assessment and grading-practices decision making. One source lies within the teacher; it consists of beliefs and values about teaching (and learning more generally) that provide a basis for explaining how and why specific assessment and grading practices are used. A second source is external to the teacher; it consists of pressures that need to be considered, such as high-stakes testing. We found that these two sources of influence are in constant tension. Although internal beliefs and values that reflect a desire to enhance student learning are most influential, external pressures cause teachers to engage in certain practices that may not be in the best interests of student learning.

These influences are depicted in Figure 1.4, which shows the nature of the internal and external factors and how these factors are in tension with each other. Internal beliefs and values include a philosophy of teaching and learning, and assessment practices are consistent with that philosophy. For example, if teachers believe that all students can succeed and that individual differences among students should be accommodated, then they use

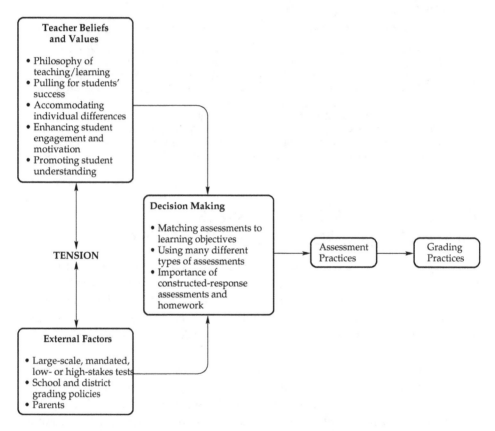

Figure 1.4 A Model of Teacher Assessment and Grading Practices Decision Making

multiple types of assessment to allow sufficient opportunities to show success. If teachers believe it is important to get students involved, engaged, and motivated, they may use performance assessments and give points for student participation and effort. To better understand how much students know and can do, most teachers rely on assessments in which students show their work.

External pressures include school or school district assessment and grading policies that must be followed, parental demands, and large-scale low- and high-stakes testing. Teachers want to collect assessment information that will show parents why specific grades were given. Externally mandated large-scale testing of students can be very influential, as well as a direct contradiction of teachers' internal beliefs and values. For example, if provincial testing consists of multiple-choice items covering a great amount of material and student performance will have important consequences, teachers feel pressure to use the same kinds of tests for classroom assessments. This may be in direct conflict with wanting to use performance assessments that are more engaging and informative about what students really understand.

Think about the model in Figure 1.4 in relation to your own beliefs and values and in relation to external pressures you may need to consider. Your decision making should consider these sources of influence so that the assessment and grading practices you implement reflect the relative importance of each. The most important question is this: To what extent are your assessment and grading practices consistent with principles of good instruction, and to what extent will the right kinds of student learning be enhanced?

ASSESSMENT STANDARDS FOR TEACHERS

Before closing this chapter, we want to familiarize you with important sets of assessment standards for teachers. In 1993, a joint advisory committee consisting of members from a variety of disciplines (including representatives from the Provincial and Territorial Ministries and Departments of Education, the Canadian Education Association, the Canadian School Boards Association, the Canadian Association for School Administrators, the Canadian Teachers Federation, the Canadian Guidance and Counselling Association, the Canadian Association of School Psychologists, the Canadian Council for Exceptional Children, the Canadian Psychological Association, and the Canadian Society for the Study of Education) published *Principles for Fair Student Assessment Practices for Education in Canada*. "This document is a set of principles and related guidelines generally accepted by professional organizations as indicative of fair assessment practice within the Canadian educational context" (*Principles for Fair Student Assessment Practices for Education in Canada*, 1993).

Part A of *Principles* is based on the conceptual framework provided in the American *Standards for Teacher Competence in Educational Assessment of Students* (1990) and is directed towards classroom assessment. *Principles* also indicates five specific areas of assessment knowledge or skills that a teacher should possess to perform assessment roles and responsibilities. Specifically, teachers should be skilled in the following:

1. developing and choosing methods for assessment
2. collecting assessment information
3. judging and scoring student performance
4. summarizing and interpreting results
5. reporting assessment findings

This document in its entirety is provided in Appendix B.

Four additional documents summarize important assessment knowledge and skills for teachers: the *Standards for Teacher Competence in Educational Assessment of Students* (Education Resources Information Center, 1990, www.eric.ed.gov/ERICWebPortal/ custom/portlets/recordDetails/detailmini.jsp?_nfpb=true&_&ERICExtSearch_ SearchValue_0=ED323186&ERICExtSearch_SearchType_0=no&accno=ED323186), the *Code of Professional Responsibilities in Educational Measurement* (National Council on Measurement in Education, 1995, www.natd.org/Code_of_Professional_ Responsibilities .html), *Principles and Indicators for Student Assessment Systems* (National Forum on Assessment, 1995, www.fairtest.org), and the *Student Evaluation Standards* (Gullickson, 2003). Appendix C summarizes the most recent standards, which were developed with the assistance of 16 major educational organizations and reflect an international consensus about assessment skills needed by teachers.

SUMMARY

This chapter introduced assessment as an integral part of teacher decision making and instruction. As a systematic method of collecting, interpreting, and using information, good assessment improves student learning. Major points in the chapter are the following:

- Assessment includes four major components: purpose, measurement, evaluation, and use.
- Measurement consists of differentiating behaviour and performance.
- Evaluation involves professional judgment of the value or worth of the measured performance.
- Recent research on learning, motivation, and instruction suggests the need to use more alternative forms of measurement, such

as performance assessments, portfolios, and authentic assessments.

- Student involvement in assessment promotes student engagement and achievement.
- The current trend is for more emphasis on formative assessment and assessment for learning, rather than of learning.
- Provincial accountability models use large-scale testing programs, which influence classroom assessments.
- Teacher assessment and grading decision making is influenced by internal beliefs and values and external factors.
- Professional standards have been developed to provide a framework for what teachers need to know about classroom assessment.

WHAT'S COMING

You have now been introduced to classroom assessment and some of the directions this assessment is taking. Provided here is an overview of the rest of this book—how it is organized, what you can expect, and how you can make the most of the application exercises at the end of each chapter.

The sequence of topics followed in the book reflects the steps teachers take in using assessment as part of instruction. The next two chapters present fundamental principles of any type of assessment. In Chapter 2 we consider how purpose is clarified through the development of appropriate learning targets. Chapter 3 reviews criteria that enhance the quality and credibility of assessments. With this background, methods of assessment are presented in the sequence teachers use when planning and delivering instruction. Single

chapters are devoted to assessment before and during instruction. Chapters 6–10 then present major methods of assessment, based on the different types of learning targets being assessed. These assessments are conducted at the end of a unit of instruction. In this book, the method of assessment follows from what needs to be assessed to emphasize that teachers first determine purpose and learning targets and then select and implement appropriate assessments. Chapter 11 focuses on issues concerning the assessment of students with special needs in inclusive settings. Chapter 12 examines what teachers do with assessment information in the form of grading and reporting information. The last chapter summarizes important information concerning the administration, interpretation, and use of standardized tests.

SELF-INSTRUCTIONAL REVIEW EXERCISES

Each chapter contains self-instructional exercises. They are intended to check your understanding of the content of the chapter. An answer key is provided (see Appendix A) to give you immediate feedback. Remember that you will learn the most if you don't look at the key before you answer the question.

1. What is the relationship between teacher decision making, complex classroom environments, and assessment?

2. What does it mean when we say that assessment is not an add-on activity?

3. What is the difference between a *test* and an *assessment?*

4. Refer to Table 1.1. Identify each of the following examples as pre-instructional assessment (pre), ongoing assessment (og), or postinstructional assessment (post).

   a. giving a pop quiz

   b. giving a cumulative final exam

   c. giving students praise for correct answers

   d. using homework to judge student knowledge

   e. reviewing student scores on last year's standardized test

   f. changing the lesson plan because of student inattention

   g. reviewing student files to understand the cultural backgrounds of students

5. Identify each of the following quotes as referring to one of the four components of classroom assessment: purpose (P), measurement (M), evaluation (E), and use (U).

   a. "Last week I determined that my students did not know very much about Confederation."

   b. "This year I want to see if I can assess student attitudes."

   c. "The test helped me to identify where students were weak."

d. "I like the idea of using performance-based assessments."

e. "I intend to combine several different assessments to determine the grade."

6. How do assessments communicate expectations for student learning?

7. Why, according to recent research on learning, is performance assessment well suited to effective instruction?

SUGGESTIONS FOR ACTION RESEARCH

At the end of each chapter are suggestions for action research. The intent of these suggestions is to help you apply what you are learning from the book to practical situations. By conducting this type of informal research, the principles and ideas presented will have greater relevance and meaning to you.

1. Investigate the time taken for assessment in the classroom by observing some classes. Compare your results to how much time the teacher believes is devoted to assessment. Also note in your observations the nature of teacher decision making. What kinds of decisions are made? How, specifically, does information from assessment contribute to this decision making?

2. Conduct an interview with a teacher or two and ask them some questions about assessment. For example, you could take Table 1.4 and ask the teachers if they believe the so-called recent trends are actually evident. You could ask about the relationship between assessment and teaching/learning to see the extent to which they are integrated. Use Figure 1.4 to ask about "internal" and "external" factors that affect their assessment, grading practices, and decision making.

3. Interview a school administrator about what teachers need to know about assessment. Ask about the assessment standards to get a perspective on the reasonableness of the standards.

Chapter 2
Learning Expectations and Outcomes

Curriculum
- Provincial and regional
- Content
- Performance
- Developmental
- Grade-level

Goals, Outcomes, and Objectives
- Educational goals
- Expectations or outcomes
- Objectives
- Criteria

Sources of Learning Expectations
- Bloom's taxonomy
- Revision of Bloom's taxonomy
- Standards documents
- Provincial and local

LEARNING EXPECTAIONS AND OUTCOMES

Types of Learning Expectations
- Knowledge and simple understanding
- Deep understanding and reasoning
- Skills
- Products
- Affect

Criteria for Selecting Learning Expectations and Outcomes
- Right number
- Comprehensive
- Reflects provincial goals
- Challenging yet feasible
- Consistent with learning

Good classroom assessment begins with appropriate *learning expectations and outcomes*. How else will you know what to teach, what to assess, and how to judge student performance? In Canada, the provincial and territorial governments are responsible for determining the expectations and outcomes to be included in the k–12 curriculum for each province, although these curricular expectations are often developed and revised in partnership with teachers. In this chapter we review the complex nature of learning expectations and outcomes, and present a framework that will help you to use them with your students. Clear, specific, and valued learning expectations are essential for effective classroom assessment.

WHAT ARE LEARNING EXPECTATIONS?

The answer to this question is not as obvious as it may seem. Your first reaction may be that a learning expectation is simply a clear description of what students should know and be able to do. You may think of an *expectation* as a goal, objective, competency, outcome, standard, or target. Yet each of these terms has come to mean something different, and it is important to review these differences so that you will understand how to develop credible assessments that ensure students have met these expectations.

Educational Goals

An **educational goal** is a very general statement of what students will know and be able to do. Goals are written to cover large blocks of instructional time, such as a unit, semester, or year, and indicate in broad terms what will be emphasized during that time period. Some educational goals require that students will be able to do the following:

- know how to think critically and solve problems
- work collaboratively with others
- understand the scientific method
- appreciate cultural differences
- develop an appreciation for fine arts
- learn to think independently
- become good citizens

Goals provide a starting point for more specific learning outcomes and expectations. By beginning with goals, you will have a general outline that can be validated by parents, teachers, and other school officials. In most school systems, educational goals are listed as defining the mission of the system, but these are usually too broad to be of much practical help in your classroom. Goals will also be found in provincial curriculum guides, textbooks, and teaching materials.

Expectations, Outcomes, and Objectives

Learning expectations, outcomes, and **objectives** are usually relatively specific statements of student performance that should be demonstrated at the end of an instructional unit. Gronlund uses the term *instructional objective* to mean "intended learning outcomes" (1995, p. 3). Educational jurisdictions in Canada refer primarily to expectations or outcomes, rather than objectives, although they are the same as what Gronlund describes. For example, the provincial curriculum documents in British Columbia use the term *prescribed learning outcomes*. In contrast, curriculum documents in Ontario use the terms *overall learning expectations* and *specific learning expectations*. Gronlund emphasizes that these instructional objectives (learning outcomes) should be stated in terms of specific, observable, and measurable student responses. This emphasis is based on a behavioural philosophy of teaching and learning. Learning outcomes are therefore sometimes referred to as behavioural, performance, or terminal outcomes. These types of learning outcomes are characterized by the use of action verbs, such as *add, state, define, list, contrast, design, categorize, count,* and *lift.* Action verbs are important because they indicate what the students actually do to demonstrate their learning. Here are some examples of learning outcomes.

The student will be able to do the following:

- summarize the main idea of the reading passage

- underline the verb and subject of each sentence

- write a title for the reading passage

- list five causes of the Northwest Rebellion

- identify on a map the location of each continent

- explain the process of photosynthesis

The degree of specificity used for learning outcomes can vary. Some are very specific, while others are more general. For example, highly precise behavioural objectives may include the following:

1. *Behaviour:* specific behaviour as indicated by action verbs

2. *Audience:* description of the students who are expected to demonstrate the behaviour (e.g., grade level or group)

3. *Criterion:* description of the criteria used to indicate whether the behaviour has been demonstrated (e.g., answering eight of ten questions correctly, or judgment of writing based on grammar, spelling, sentence construction, and organization)

4. *Condition:* circumstances, equipment, or materials used when demonstrating the behaviour (e.g., with or without class notes, open book, using graph paper, with a calculator)

When objectives are written to include these rules, they are highly specific, as in the following examples:

> From a standing-still position on a level, hard surface (condition), students (audience) will jump (behaviour) at least two feet (criterion).

> Given two hours in the library without notes (condition), students (audience) will identify (behaviour) five sources on the topic "national unity" (criterion).

Although such detailed learning expectations and outcomes are helpful in indicating what students will demonstrate, describing all of them in such detail is usually too time-consuming to develop and too confining for teachers. Hence, these expectations need to be written at an appropriate level of generality—not so narrow that they take much too long to write, and not so general that they provide little guidance for instruction. Ideally, expectations and outcomes should be stated in terms that are specific enough to inform teaching and assessment but not limit the flexibility of the teacher to modify instruction as needed. Outcomes that are too specific result in long lists of minutiae that are time-consuming to monitor and manage. Commonly, provincial curriculum documents contain both intermediate-level unit outcomes (overall learning expectations) and more specific learning outcomes (specific learning expectations) intended to guide instruction. The intermediate-level outcomes help keep the focus of student learning on the main under-standings, learning processes, attitudes, and other learning outcomes of the unit as a whole. Some examples of learning outcomes that are too specific, too broad, and at the right level of specificity are shown in Table 2.1.

Another approach is to state a goal or more general outcome and then state *examples* of specific outcomes that indicate the various types of student performances required. Here are some examples:

Overall Outcome	Understands the structure of federal government
Specific Outcomes	Explains what the concept of Parliament means
	Lists four functions of the governor general

Table 2.1 Specificity of Learning Outcomes

Too Specific	About Right	Too Broad
Given an article from the newspaper, the student will correctly identify ten statements that are facts and five statements that are opinions in less than ten minutes without the aid of any resource materials.	Students will state the difference between facts and opinions.	Students will learn how to think critically.
Based on reading the final statement of Louis Riel at his trial, the student will, without any aids, write four paragraphs in one hour that summarize, with at least 80 per cent accuracy, his defense of his actions.	Students will identify the major arguments used by Louis Riel to defend his actions in the speech he gave during his trial.	Summarize the last speech of Louis Riel.
The student, given grid paper, will analyze data on the frequency of student birthdays in each month and construct a bar graph in one hour in teams of two of the results that show the two most frequent and two least frequent months.	Given frequency data and grid paper, students will construct bar graphs of selected variables.	Students will construct bar graphs.

	Describes the purpose of the Cabinet
	Distinguishes between the Senate and the House of Commons
Overall Outcome	Knows the meaning of spelling words
Specific Outcome	Writes correct definitions for 80 per cent of the words
	Identifies correct antonyms for 50 per cent of the words
	Identifies correct synonyms for 70 per cent of the words
	Draws pictures that correctly illustrate 80 per cent of the words
	Writes sentences that include correct usage of 80 per cent of the words

Whether you focus on overall or specific learning expectations, or intermediate or detailed learning outcomes, the main point is to describe what students will know and be able to do and what constitutes sufficient evidence that students have learned—not what you will do to help students obtain the knowledge and skills identified. What you plan to do as a teacher may be called a **teaching objective** or *learning activity* and may include such things as lecturing for a certain amount of time, asking questions, putting students in groups, giving feedback to students individually, conducting experiments, using a map to show where certain countries are located, asking students to solve math problems on the board, having students read orally, and so on. These teaching objectives describe the activities students will be engaged in and how you can ensure that the activities occur as planned. Regardless of the specific labels, you will need to develop lesson plans that will include overall learning outcomes, more specific learning outcomes, teaching objectives, activities, materials needed, and plans for assessment of student learning. Table 2.2 illustrates a typical lesson plan as a backward design.

Table 2.2 Example of a Lesson Plan

Learning Expectation	Students will differentiate between vertebrate and invertebrate animals by correctly recalling the difference and naming examples of animals in each category.
Assessment	Without notes, students will be asked to recall the difference between invertebrate and vertebrate animals and give four examples of different types of animals in each category. Give the students a new set of animal pictures and have them apply their rules for group membership to sort the pictures.
Materials Needed	Textbook, eight copies of pictures and sketches of the anatomies of vertebrate and invertebrate animals, coloured pencils, and paper.

(continued)

Table 2.2 (Continued)

Instructional Activities	Set up groups of three or four students.
	Give each group a set of animal pictures and ask them to classify the pictures into two major groups.
	Monitor student work for 15 minutes.
	Ask students to indicate how the animals in each category are the same and how they are different.
	Emphasize the presence of a backbone as the major differentiating feature.
	Ask students to further classify vertebrate and invertebrate animals into additional categories.
	Ask students to draw concept maps of different types of animals, using different-coloured pencils.

Standards-Based Education

During the 1990s the idea of "standards" became ubiquitous and powerful in the United States, and, to a lesser extent, in Canada, fuelling reform by advocating specific high-level student outcomes. Although the standards movement mostly concerns what Canadian jurisdictions call student expectations or outcomes, the American reframing of how these outcomes would be judged was initiated in order to stress three points: (1) this is not business

Teacher's Corner

Dodie Whitt, an award-winning teacher, describes her approach to using learning outcomes to support her lesson planning.

> When I sit down to plan lessons for my students, the first place I look for student learning objectives is my curriculum guide. The other teachers on my grade-level team and I have worked together to create our own pacing guide, which takes the curriculum and maps it out for the year, so that we are sure to cover everything and so that we can pace our teaching and student learning as appropriate. I follow the pacing guide that we have created very closely, to ensure that all concepts and skills are taught. However, when I test the children each month on these concepts and skills, there are always a few who have not mastered what they have been taught. Although the pacing guide always keeps us moving ahead with learning, I know that it is my responsibility as the teacher to bring those children up to speed. So, I record the skills that need reinforcement and they become the targeted skills and concepts for small group lessons or for one-on-one instruction. I will also use these assessments to target those learners who have mastered all that has been taught and will provide these students with small group instruction geared toward enriching their learning. So, although most of my lessons are planned using the curriculum documents, it seems that assessments, and how my students perform on them, also play a huge role in determining what I teach and when I teach it.

as usual, not like "outcome-based" education; (2) standards apply to *all* students; and (3) student achievement goals are much higher than they were in the past. The intent was to frame the idea of standards in such a way that no one could refute its importance. This is how Popham describes it:

> *Standards*, of course, is a warmth-inducing word. Although perhaps not in the same league with *motherhood*, *democracy*, and *babies*, I suspect that standards ranks right up there with *oatmeal*, *honor*, and *excellence*. It's really tough not to groove on standards, especially if those standards are *high*. Everyone wants students to reach high standards. (2005, p. 108)

Standards-based education occurred first at the national level with content-oriented organizations, such as the National Council of Teachers of Mathematics or the Center for Civic Education. Today, all major subject-matter associations have **standards** that describe "what students should know and be able to do." Certainly, the evolution of curriculum in Canada has followed a different path. The result has been a difference in the terms used to describe expected learning. American educators will use terms such as *targets* and *standards*. Canadian jurisdictions most commonly use the terms *learning expectations* or *learning outcomes*. Perhaps an even more pronounced difference is the provincially developed curriculum that contains these learning outcomes. Curriculum in the United States is often developed by teachers or districts, resulting in different mechanisms for the development of "standards." Nevertheless, given the proximity of the United States and the influence of many American educational organizations, it is important to understand how American jurisdictions and organizations use these terms. There is a dizzying array of standards statements from which to choose, and there are different *types* of standards. We'll consider four of the most common (Table 2.3): content, performance, developmental, and grade-level standards.

Content standards (not to be confused with *curriculum* standards) are statements about what students should know, understand, and be able to do. Content standards describe "the knowledge and skills that students should attain" (Kendall & Marzano, 1997, p. 20). The

Table 2.3 Types of Educational Standards

Type of Standard	Description
Content	Desired outcomes for the content area
Performance	Desired proficiency levels for student skills; what students should be able to do
Developmental	Desired sequences of growth and change
Grade-level	Desired outcomes of a particular grade

Source: Adapted from M.W. Conley (2005). *Connecting standards and assessment through literacy.* Boston: Allyn & Bacon.

way in which content standards are presented differs depending on the source. One format, for example, may describe content as information:

> The periodic table describes the organization of the elements and their properties and trends.

More typically, a content standard includes a description of the nature of the knowledge:

> Students will demonstrate an understanding of the organization of the periodic table.

Content standards can also vary greatly in specificity. Note the generality of the following content standard:

> Students will understand how immigration has influenced Canadian society.

A more specific content standard would be the following:

> Students will compare the contributions of Socrates, Plato, and Aristotle to Greek life.

Content standards may also differ with respect to the nature of the learning or performance. Some standards use the term *knows* to describe student attainment, and others emphasize *understanding* or reasoning skills. As we will see, these important differences influence how students are assessed.

Developmental (age-appropriate) **standards** describe sequences of growth in learning over time. These standards may cover a single grade level or several grades. They are helpful because they provide **benchmarks** to monitor progress and record improvements in knowledge and skills. The focus is on what is developmentally appropriate. Standardized achievement tests provide scaled scores that may be used to document growth over several years, although there is ongoing debate as to the accuracy of such measures.

Grade-level standards are closely related, but they emphasize what students should know and be able to do *at each grade*. However, grade-level standards may not reflect what is developmentally appropriate. In the United States, these standards are the most important ones driving instruction to meet the demands of high-stakes accountability testing.

Content standards are largely analogous to what Canadian curriculum documents refer to as learning expectations or outcomes. Both emphasize what students can demonstrate after instruction. Provincial ministries of education do not directly refer to either developmental or grade-level standards as described in the American jurisdictions, although there is some overlap in the provincial curriculum documents. For example, most language arts curriculum documents describe learning outcomes using a developmental or spiralled trajectory.

A **performance standard** indicates the level of proficiency that must be demonstrated to indicate the degree to which content standards have been attained. The term is generally used the same way in both Canada and the United States. Performance standards address issues of attainment and quality. By indicating *degree* of attainment, performance standards are able to distinguish different levels of accomplishment. This is quite different from a behavioural objective (instructional outcome), which typically has a single level. In other words, a performance standard describes what students must *do* and how different levels of proficiency on the content standards result. As described by McTighe and Ferrara, performance standards "set expectations about how much students should know and how well students should perform" (1998, p. 34).

Ideally, the performance standard indicates what students must do, as well as different levels of performance. In reality, however, often what are called performance standards contain a description of what students must do but do not include levels of attainment. For example, consider the following:

> The student will understand the right of free speech.

A performance standard that contains a description of what the student must do to demonstrate this competency might be the following:

> Assess why immigrants came to Canada, the individual challenges they faced, and their contributions to Canada, giving historical reasons for the immigration of specific cultural groups to Canada. (adapted from the B.C. Ministry of Education, 2006, p. 93)

Performance standards can be combined with learning outcomes to describe both what the student should *know* and what the student should be able to *do*. For example,

What students should know: How to use various types of graphs, tables, timelines, and maps to obtain or to communicate information
What students should be able to do: Demonstrate proficiency using graphic information sources by

- comparing the advantages and disadvantages of various graphic forms of communication (e.g., graphs, tables, charts, maps, photographs, and sketches.
- interpreting scales and legends in graphs, tables, and maps.
- drawing conclusions from maps, tables, timelines, and graphs.
- comparing maps of early civilizations with modern maps of the same area.
- selecting an appropriate graphic form of communication for a specific purpose. (p. 109)

What is not indicated with this performance standard is any degree of attainment. To do this, you must establish criteria and then use descriptors of different levels with these criteria (e.g., not proficient, proficient, advanced, or complete, partial, or none).

Criteria

One of the most frustrating experiences for students is not knowing "what the teacher wants" or "how the teacher grades." Perhaps you can recall being in a class in which you did an assignment with little guidance from the teacher about how he or she would grade it. Once your assignment was returned with comments, your reaction might well have been, "If I had only known what the teacher was looking for, I could have provided it!" Essentially, this issue concerns the criteria the teacher uses for evaluating student work and whether students know, *in advance*, what those criteria are. Here is a poignant illustration of how a lack of clear criteria can be unfair. The following actually happened a few years ago to a sixth grader:

> [The student] was given the following problem to solve: "Three buses bring students to school. The first bus brings 9 students, the second bus brings 7 students, and the third bus brings 5 students. How many students in all do the buses bring? The student answered "21 kids," and the answer was marked wrong. After encouragement by my colleague the student asked the teacher "Why?" The reason was that the student said "kids" instead of "students." (Arter, 1996, p. VI-1:1)

Criteria, then, are clearly articulated and public descriptions of facets or dimensions of student performance that are used for judging the level of achievement. As pointed out in Chapter 1, criteria may be called *scoring criteria, rubrics, scoring rubrics*, or *scoring guidelines*. (The term *performance criteria* may also be used.) Although criteria have been promoted most for more recent alternative and performance assessments, the issue of how student responses will be evaluated lies at the heart of any type of assessment. The key component of criteria is making your professional judgments about student performance clear to others. All methods of assessment involve your professional judgment. If you use multiple-choice testing, judgment is used to prepare the items and decide which alternative is correct. In an essay test, judgment is involved in preparing the question and in reading and scoring answers. Clearly articulated criteria will help you in many ways, including the following:

- defining what you mean by "excellent," "good," or "average" work
- communicating instructional goals to parents
- communicating to parents, students, and others what constitutes excellence
- providing guidelines for making unbiased and consistent judgments
- documenting how judgments are made
- helping students evaluate their own work

When specifying criteria, summarize the dimensions of performance that are used to assign student work to a given level. The dimensions are what you consider to be essential qualities of the performance. They can be identified by asking yourself some questions: What are the attributes of good performance? How do I know when students have reached different levels of performance? What examples do I have of each level?

What do I look for when evaluating student work? Criteria are best developed by being clear about what constitutes excellence and proficiency in the performance area of interest. By identifying and prioritizing key elements, the most important aspects of the performance will be utilized.

Once the dimensions have been identified, you can develop a quantitative or qualitative scale to indicate different levels of performance. Label each level as "meets expectations," "exceeds expectations," "does not meet expectations," and so on. Examples of criteria for different types of performance are shown in Table 2.4. Many more examples are presented in Chapters 8 and 9.

Table 2.4 Examples of Performance Criteria

Making an Oral Presentation[1]

Excellent	Pupil consistently faces audience, stands straight, and maintains eye contact; voice projects well and clearly; pacing and tone variation appropriate; well organized, points logically and completely presented; brief summary at end
Good	Pupil usually faces audience, stands straight, and makes eye contact; voice projection good, but pace and clarity vary during talk; well organized but repetitive; occasional poor choice of words and incomplete summary
Fair	Pupil fidgety; some eye contact and facial expression change; uneven voice projection, not heard by all in room, some words slurred; loosely organized, repetitive, contains many incomplete thoughts; little summarization
Poor	Pupil's body movements distracting, little eye contact or voice change; words slurred, speaks in monotone, does not project voice beyond first few rows, no consistent or logical pacing; rambling presentation, little organization with no differentiation between major and minor points; no summary

Knows the Difference between Statements and Questions

More Than Adequate	Successfully identifies 20 of 25 sentences as statements or questions, lists 3 characteristics of statements and questions, generates 4 original examples of statements and questions
Adequate	Successfully identifies 18 of 25 sentences as statements or questions, lists 2 characteristics of statements and questions, generates 2 examples of statements and questions

(continued)

Table 2.4 (Continued)

Less Than Adequate	Successfully identifies fewer than 18 of 25 sentences as statements or questions, lists 1 or no characteristics of statements and questions, generates no examples of statements or questions
Estimation[2]	
Not Understanding	Makes unrealistic guesses, does not use strategies to refine estimates, cannot model or explain the specified strategy, cannot apply strategy, even with prompts
Developing Understanding	Refines guesser estimates by partitioning/comparing, etc., can model, explain, and apply a strategy when asked, has some strategies, others are not yet in place, uses estimation when appropriate
Understanding/ Applying	Makes realistic guesses or estimates, refines estimates to suggest a more exact estimate, uses estimation when appropriate, recognizes and readily uses a variety of strategies

[1] P.W. Airasian (2001). *Classroom assessment* (4th ed.). New York: McGraw-Hill, pp. 231–232. Reproduced with permission of the McGraw-Hill Companies.

[2] A. Beyer, et al., (1993). *Alternative assessment: Evaluating student performance in elementary mathematics*. Ann Arbor Public Schools. Palo Alto, CA: Dale Seymour Publications, p. 7. Used by permission of Pearson Education, Inc.

Although it is very helpful for students to know the criteria as communicated in a scoring rubric, it is even more helpful if they can see an example of a finished student product or performance and your evaluation of it. These examples are called **exemplars** or **anchors**. For example, if you have established four levels of performance, an exemplar of work at each level will make the criteria more clear. To emphasize once again, you should share the exemplars with students *before* they begin their work. This will help students to internalize the performance standards that you use and to know what constitutes excellence. The exemplars could be as simple as giving students examples of the type of math word problems that will be on a test and how their answers will be graded. Of course you don't want to give students something that they will memorize or copy, but you do need to give them a sense of the difficulty of the task.

Most, if not all, of your students will not be able to attain the highest level of performance. For example, we set a high performance standard for what constitutes a good play in football, but our expectations for middle school students differ from what we expect of professionals. In school you may have a high standard for a research paper, but your expectations of the students, because of their lack of previous learning, may not meet this high standard. If your expectations are not the same as your standards, either your standards will drop to accommodate most students, or your expectations will not be consistent with how students can really perform. In either case, you are not doing what is in the best interests of the students. If your standards are lowered, students may attain a false sense of competency; if your standards are too high, students may be frustrated at what they see as impossible demands. What you need to do is make high standards clear and then teach in a way that is consistent with realistic, yet challenging expectations. You want students to go the extra step, so be explicit with them about why the standards are high. Set high, obtainable standards for your students and provide the learning opportunities for them to meet these standards.

CASE STUDY FOR REFLECTION

Ms. Beckner decided to try a new way to assess her grade three students' science projects. She used a rubric with specific criteria, which both she and her students created. She wanted students to be aware of the different components that needed to be a part of their final presentation. She prepared the first two areas for the rubric:

Blast Off for an "A"

1. Students' science projects will result in an appropriate demonstration product, including an attractive visual display and a two-page report. (Examples of last year's projects in hallway.)

2. Students' two-page report with their project will clearly describe the scientific concept their project represents. (Examples on back table.)

Three other levels (Mission Control, Ground Crew, and Delayed Flight) were also identified, with two criteria for each. After the exemplars were prepared and put on display, Ms. Beckner discussed plans for science projects and asked her students to help her decide what a great science project might look like. Students' ideas were all put on the board, and from these, Ms. Beckner guided them through a selection process for two more criteria for an "A" science project. Through the use of good examples of previous student work, these students had a clearer idea of what the words *appropriate demonstration product* and *attractive visual display* in criterion 1 and *clearly describe* in criterion 2 actually meant. They also had internalized the assessment criteria by participating in the creation of some of them. After the projects were completed, Ms. Beckner found that her students not only scored better on their projects than in previous years, but they also enjoyed the process much more because they understood what was expected of them.

1. Does all this planning for assessment take away too much time from actual teaching of the content?

2. What are some problems that might arise when using student suggestions for determining criteria?

3. What did Ms. Beckner do right in coming up with the criteria?

4. What are some additional examples of criteria that could be used in this assignment?

Learning Targets

In this book, learning expectations and learning outcomes are defined by how the Canadian education system uses these terms. Combined with performance standards, criteria, and, where appropriate, rubrics, these result in the development of learning targets. A learning target includes *both* a description of what students should know, understand, and be able to do at the end of a unit of instruction (expectations or outcomes), and as much information as possible and feasible about the criteria for judging the level of performance demonstrated (see Figure 2.1). While learning targets are generally not part of the education lexicon in Canada, the notion of a target provides a valuable reminder that teachers need to consider both the expected learning and the expected demonstration of that learning.

The word *learning* conveys that expectations emphasize the importance of how students will *change*. Learning implies a focus on the demonstrated competence of students, not on what you do as a teacher. Change reflects the need to know more than what students know or can do at the end of instruction. Change requires knowledge of where students are in relation to the expectation before instruction, as well as at the end of instruction.

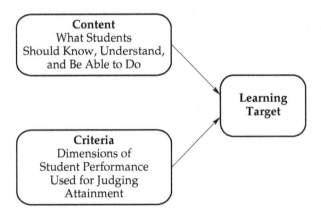

Figure 2.1 Components of Learning Targets

It is essential to include something about the criteria for judging levels of performance. Think for a moment about an expectation about shooting an arrow. The performance might be stated as "the student will hit the target with an arrow." But you need to communicate more than simply "hit the target." How far away is the target? How large is the target? Does it matter where the arrow hits the target? In other words, you need to indicate something about the dimensions of the performance that translate into qualitatively different levels of performance. Two teachers can state the same learning outcome, but if different criteria are used to evaluate the performance, then students in each class are actually learning something different.

A similar case can be made for learning subjects in school. The expectation that "students will know provincial capitals in Canada" means something different if students have to recall all 10 capitals from memory, rather than if they must correctly match half of the names of capitals with provinces. You must be able to articulate, as part of your learning target, the criteria you will use to judge performance. Remember, students should know these criteria *before* instruction. Describing criteria does not need to be done in a single sentence. It is easier, in fact, to think about targets as a description of what will be assessed and how it will be judged. These two aspects of the target can be separated into different sentences. For example, this sentence describes what students need to know:

■ Students will demonstrate an understanding of the effect of the sun on seasons, length of day, weather, and climate.

Information about criteria could be added with another sentence:

■ Students will demonstrate their understanding by correctly answering short-answer questions about each relationship.

If a matching test is used, try this description:

■ Students will demonstrate their understanding by correctly matching all effects with the four elements discussed.

In practice you would not be so wordy in describing the learning target. It is understood that "students will demonstrate," so you can simply say, "understand the effect of sun on the seasons, length of day, weather, and climate." The information about criteria can be shortened by simply referring to "matching" or "short answer."

Learning targets for units of instruction in Figure 2.2 include both what students should know or be able to do and some aspects of the criteria. Note that some are written as one sentence, and some are more detailed than others in aspects of criteria. The intent is not to worry about including specific aspects of criteria. Rather, you should be aware of the effect of the criteria on the learning that occurs and your evaluation of it. Throughout the text, the terms *learning expectations* or *learning outcomes* will be used rather than learning targets, reflecting the Canadian perspective. Nevertheless, do not forget that you will be expected to define the learning targets and performance levels for your students.

Students will be able to explain how various cultures are different and how cultures influence people's beliefs and lives by answering orally a comprehensive set of questions about cultural differences and their effects.

Students will demonstrate their knowledge of the parts of a plant by filling in words on a diagram of all parts studied.

Students will demonstrate their understanding of citizenship by correctly identifying whether previously unread statements about citizenship are true or false. A large number of items is used to sample most of the content learned.

Students will be able to explain why the Canadian Charter of Rights and Freedoms is important by writing an essay that indicates what would happen if we abolished the Charter. The papers will be graded holistically, looking for evidence of reasons, knowledge of the Charter, and organization.

Students will know the difference between components of sentences by correctly identifying verbs, adverbs, adjectives, nouns, and pronouns in seven of eight long, complex sentences.

Students will be able to multiply fractions by correctly computing eight of ten fraction problems. The problems are new to the students; some are similar to "challenge" questions in the book.

Figure 2.2 Examples of Unit Learning Expectations

TYPES OF LEARNING EXPECTATIONS AND OUTCOMES

How do you identify appropriate learning expectations for your students? Begin by realizing that many different kinds of learning expectations are appropriate because in most classrooms a variety of outcomes is stressed. The challenge is to organize and prioritize your expectations to reflect what is most important. To do this, think about a few categories that encompass typical types of learning expectations. In this book, categories described by Stiggins and Conklin (1992) are used because teachers view these categories as important, and because each type of expectation is clearly related to different approaches to assessment. The major categories of expectations (see Table 2.5) are introduced in this chapter, expanded on, and linked with specific kinds of assessment in subsequent chapters. Note that the categories are not presented as a hierarchy or in order. None of the categories is more important than any other. Each simply represents types of expectations that can be identified and used for assessment.

Knowledge and Simple Understanding Learning Expectations

Knowledge of subject matter is the foundation on which all other learning is based. As such, it represents what students need to *know* to solve problems and perform skills. This

Table 2.5 Types of Learning Expectations

Knowledge and simple understanding	Student mastery of substantive subject matter and procedures
Deep understanding and reasoning	Student ability to use knowledge to reason and solve problems
Skills	Student ability to demonstrate achievement-related skills, such as reading aloud, interpersonal interaction, speaking in a second language, operating equipment correctly and safely, conducting experiments, operating computers, and performing psychomotor behaviours
Products	Student ability to create achievement-related products, such as written reports, oral presentations, and art products
Affective	Student attainment of affective states, such as attitudes, values, interests, motivation, and self-efficacy

knowledge may be as simple as mastery of facts and information demonstrated through recall (e.g., remembering dates, events, places, definitions, and principles), or it may involve simple understanding (e.g., summarizing a paragraph, explaining charts, concept learning, or giving examples). *Knowing* usually refers to more than simple rote memory, even though some rote memorization may be needed. A student can *know* how to pronounce certain words by memorizing the links between letters and sounds, but it is also necessary to *understand* the meanings of the words.

Deep Understanding and Reasoning Learning Expectations

Recent advances in cognitive psychology and computer accessibility to information have resulted in increased attention to more sophisticated understanding and thinking skills. Such capabilities may be described with a number of different terms, including *problem solving, critical thinking, analysis, synthesis, comparing, intellectual skills, intellectual abilities, higher-order thinking skills,* and *judgment.* Research in cognitive psychology has shown that our ability to use knowledge to think about things is dependent on how we construct the knowledge and the demands that are placed on using the knowledge to reason and solve problems. This research has helped us to classify and understand what is termed "deep" understanding and the different reasoning processes that are used. Several reasoning frameworks are presented in Chapter 7. The challenge with these expectations is defining precisely what is meant by *reasoning, critical thinking, problem solving*, and so on. The frameworks will help you to formulate definitions that meet your needs.

Skill Learning Expectations

A skill is something that the student demonstrates, something that is done. Although, in one sense, recalling information and showing reasoning skills by answering questions is *doing* something, skill learning expectations involve a behaviour in which the knowledge, understanding, and reasoning are used overtly. For example, at one level students can demonstrate their knowledge of how a microscope works by recalling correct procedural steps, but skill is needed when the students use a microscope to demonstrate the steps to the teacher. It is like the difference between knowing how to manage classrooms by listing seven principles of classroom management, even analyzing case studies of classroom management, and actually being able to manage students in a classroom. Thus, in elementary school, students are expected to demonstrate reading skills and how to hold pencils to write; older students may be required to demonstrate oral presentation skills or speak in a foreign language. Most skills require procedural knowledge and reasoning to use the knowledge in an actual performance.

Product Learning Expectations

Products, like skills, are dependent on prior attainment of knowledge and reasoning expectations. Products are samples of student work that demonstrate the ability to use knowledge and reasoning in the creation of a tangible product, such as a term paper, report, artwork, or other project. Thus, products are used to demonstrate knowledge, understanding, reasoning, and skills. Performance-based assessments are examples of how product learning expectations are measured.

Affective Learning Expectations

This final category is broad, complex, and, to a certain extent, controversial. The term **affective** includes emotions and feelings, which are different from **cognitive** learning such as knowledge, reasoning, and skills. Affect can be described as being positive or negative, and most teachers hope that students will develop positive attitudes toward school subjects and learning, themselves as learners, other students, and school. Affect can also refer to motivational dispositions, values, and morals. Although most teachers believe that positive affect is an important outcome as well as a determinant of cognitive learning, many believe that schools should be concerned only with cognitive learning expectations. Because affective learning expectations are complex, they are difficult—but not impossible—to assess.

SOURCES OF LEARNING EXPECTATIONS AND OUTCOMES

The categories of learning expectations and outcomes just presented provide a start to identifying the focus of instruction and assessment (and provide the organizational structure of this book), but you will find other sources that are more specific about learning expectations and outcomes.

Bloom's Taxonomy of Objectives

Perhaps the best-known source for conceptualizing learning expectations and outcomes is the *Taxonomy of Educational Objectives I: Cognitive Domain* (Bloom, 1956). As implied in the title, this initial taxonomy covered cognitive learning objectives. Later publications of the taxonomy focused on the affective and psychomotor areas. Thus, "Bloom's taxonomy," as it has become known, consists of three domains—cognitive, affective, and psychomotor.

Bloom's taxonomy of the cognitive domain has received considerable attention and has been used to specify action verbs to accompany different types of cognitive learning (see Table 2.6; other domains are presented in later chapters). The cognitive domain contains six levels. Each level represents an increasingly complex type of cognition. Although the cognitive domain is often characterized as having "lower" and "higher" levels, only the knowledge level is considered by authors of the taxonomy to be lower; all other levels are higher. The first level, knowledge, describes several different types of knowledge. The remaining five levels are referred to as "intellectual abilities and skills."

Table 2.6 Bloom's Taxonomy of Educational Objectives: Cognitive Domain

Level	Illustrative Verbs
Knowledge: Recalling and remembering previously learned material, including specific facts, events, persons, dates, methods, procedures, concepts, principles, and theories	Names, matches, lists, recalls, selects, retells, states, defines, describes, labels, reproduces
Comprehension: Understanding and grasping the meaning of something; includes translation from one symbolic form to another (e.g., per cent into fractions), interpretation, explanation, prediction, inferences, restating, estimation, generalization, and other uses that demonstrate understanding	Explains, converts, interprets, paraphrases, predicts, estimates, rearranges, rephrases, summarizes

(continued)

Table 2.6 (Continued)

Level	Illustrative Verbs
Application: Using abstract ideas, rules, or generalized methods in novel, concrete situations	Changes, demonstrates, modifies, produces, solves, constructs, applies, uses, shows
Analysis: Breaking down a communication into constituent parts or elements and understanding the relationship among different elements	Distinguishes, compares, subdivides, diagrams, differentiates, relates, classifies, categorizes
Synthesis: Arranging and combining elements and parts into novel patterns or structures	Generates, combines, constructs, assembles, formulates, forecasts, projects, proposes, integrates
Evaluation: Judging the quality, worth, or value of something according to established criteria (e.g., determining the adequacy of evidence to support a conclusion)	Justifies, criticizes, decides, judges, argues, concludes, supports, defends, evaluates, verifies, confirms

Bloom's taxonomy can be very helpful when formulating specific learning outcomes, even though this categorization of cognitive tasks was created more than 50 years ago, and since that time there have been significant changes in the educational and psychological theories that formed the basis for the taxonomy. Current theories emphasize thinking processes, characterize the learner as an active information processor, and stress domain-specific thinking and learning. The taxonomy, in comparison, was based on a focus on objectives, the learner as an object and as a reactor in the learning situation, and broad, single organizing principles that cut across different domains (Tittle, Hecht, & Moore, 1993). The taxonomy is still valuable, however, in providing a comprehensive list of possible learning objectives with clear action verbs that operationalize the expectation.

Bloom's Revised Taxonomy of Objectives

Recently, a revision to Bloom's original taxonomy was proposed "to refocus educators' attention on the value of the original Handbook . . . and to incorporate new knowledge and thought into the framework" (Anderson & Krathwohl, 2001, pp. xxi–xxii). The revised taxonomy uses a two-dimensional model as a framework for identifying and writing learning objectives. The knowledge dimension, summarized in Table 2.7, includes four levels that describe different types of knowledge with a number of subcategories. The cognitive process dimension includes six major categories and numerous subcategories that describe increasingly complex thinking (Table 2.8). The reason for dividing the original single list into two dimensions is to create a matrix in which educators can identify the specific nature of the learning that is targeted.

Table 2.7 Knowledge Dimension of Revised Taxonomy

Major Types	Definition
Factual Knowledge	The basic elements students must know to be acquainted with a discipline or solve problems in it
Conceptual Knowledge	The interrelationships among the basic elements within a larger structure that enable them to function together
Procedural Knowledge	How to do something, methods of inquiry, and criteria for using skills, algorithms, techniques, and methods
Metacognitive Knowledge	Knowledge of cognition in general, as well as awareness and knowledge of one's own cognition

Source: Adapted from L. W. Anderson & D. R. Krathwohl (2001). *A taxonomy for learning, teaching, and assessing: A revision of Bloom's taxonomy of educational objectives.* Boston: Allyn and Bacon. Copyright © 2001 Pearson Education. Reprinted by permission of the publisher.

For each learning objective, a noun describes the type of knowledge and a verb indicates the level of cognitive processing that is needed. The advantage of this, according to the authors, is that teachers and administrators can be more precise than they could be with the older taxonomy. Figure 2.3 shows how an educational objective could be classified according to the two dimensions.

Table 2.8 Cognitive Process Dimension of New Taxonomy

Major Types	Definition
Remember	Retrieve relevant knowledge from long-term memory.
Understand	Construct meaning from instructional messages, including oral, written, and graphic communication.
Apply	Carry out or use a procedure in a given situation.
Analyze	Break material into its constituent parts and determine how the parts relate to one another and to an overall structure or pattern.
Evaluate	Make judgments based on criteria and standards.
Create	Put elements together to form a coherent or functional whole; reorganize elements into a new pattern or structure.

Source: Adapted from L. W. Anderson & D. R. Krathwohl (2001). *A taxonomy for learning, teaching, and assessing: A revision of Bloom's taxonomy of educational objectives.* Boston: Allyn and Bacon. Copyright © 2001 Pearson Education. Reprinted by permission of the publisher.

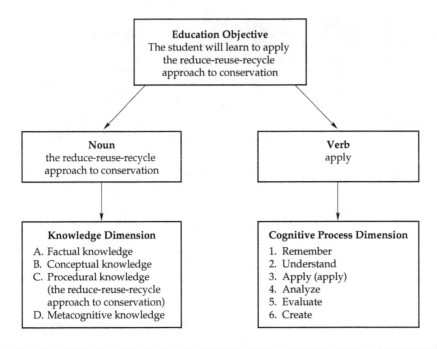

Figure 2.3 How an Objective (the Student Will Learn to Apply the Reduce-Reuse-Recycle Approach to Conservation) Is Classified in the Taxonomy Table

Source: Adapted from L. W. Anderson & D. R. Krathwohl, *A taxonomy for learning, teaching, and assessing: A revision of Bloom's taxonomy of educational objectives.* Boston: Allyn and Bacon. Copyright © 2001 Pearson Education. Reprinted by permission of the publisher.

Only time will tell if the new two-dimensional taxonomy will take hold. It is clear that a revised taxonomy was needed, but this version may be more complicated for teachers to work with and thus less practical. Further delineation of each of the dimensions will be incorporated in Chapters 6 and 7.

Professional Preparation

Throughout your professional preparation you have been exposed to essential principles and methods of different disciplines. As you master each discipline, you will be able to identify what is most important for learning. Perhaps you have heard that the best way to learn something is to teach it. Put yourself in the role of teacher even as you take courses. What specific knowledge is most important? What do you need to be able to do with the knowledge? What are *you* doing as a student? Do you *really know* the subject inside and out, so you can do more as a teacher than simply read notes or do exactly what the curriculum guide says? You will find that the quality of your assessments will follow from the depth of your understanding of what you teach. The more you understand, the better the assessments. It is also important to keep current with the professional literature in both the subjects you teach and education in general. This literature will keep you up to date and will give you many ideas about the kinds of learning expectations that are appropriate.

Textbooks

Most textbooks for students are accompanied by an instructor's guide or a teacher's edition that provides information to help you plan lessons, deliver appropriate instruction, and assess student learning. The teacher's edition typically includes "objectives" for each lesson.

Although the objectives in a teacher's edition can be useful, keep in mind that textbook authors tend to emphasize limited, lower-level objectives that are applicable to a wide range of different classes and locations. Furthermore, textbook objectives are rarely aligned with provincial curriculum. The objectives need to be reviewed in relation to your specific jurisdiction, teaching situation, and approach.

Three major criteria can be used to evaluate the appropriateness of textbook objectives (Brophy & Alleman, 1991). First, are the objectives stated with clear descriptions of what students will know or be able to do following instruction? Even if the behaviour is clearly stated, the textbook probably will not indicate what criteria should be used to complete the learning expectation. Second, are the objectives appropriate for your students? Have your students learned the prerequisite knowledge and skills? Is the level of learning that is required appropriate for your students? Third, do the objectives include most of the student expectations? How complete and comprehensive are the objectives? Are important areas overlooked? Using these three criteria, you can appraise the appropriateness and completeness of the objectives as a basis for your learning expectations. Most importantly, are the objectives contained explicitly or implicitly in the existing provincial curriculum?

Textbook publishers work to develop books that are linked to existing curriculum. Remember, though, that these judgments are from the publisher; the greater the match, the more likely a province or district will select the book as recommended, approved, or required.

Existing Lists of Standards

You will find it helpful to locate and review lists of standards that have already been developed. A number of sources can be used to locate these lists. Most methods of teaching textbooks, particularly those in each subject area, contain illustrative objectives as well as references that can be consulted. Yearbooks and handbooks in different disciplines sometimes contain objectives. Special reports and websites developed by professional groups, such as the National Council of Teachers of Mathematics, the Canadian Council of Teachers of English Language Arts, Council of Science Educators of Canada, Canadian Federation of Music Teachers' Associations, the British Columbia Social Studies Teachers' Association, and the Manitoba Physical Education Teachers' Association contain extensive lists of objectives that emphasize thinking skills and applications to real-life problems.

Provincial Curriculum

While several sources of learning outcomes and behavioural objectives are available (see Table 2.9), the most common sources in Canada are provincial curriculum documents. Provincial curriculum documents contain the educational goals and intermediate and specific learning expectations and outcomes for provincially mandated curriculum. Provinces set fairly specific outcomes for student learning, and curriculum is organized to focus on these learning outcomes. These documents are the primary sources for supporting your instruction; they identify the required learning expectations and outcomes within each program of study. While these documents describe the learning students will

---

Teacher's Corner

Rita Truelove

Rita is an eighth-grade science teacher who has been recognized for her teaching excellence. She has taught for 22 years.

As I plan a unit, I make sure that there is a "real life" connection to the objectives I want students to master. Science is not something that is done to students; it is something that students do. So I continually provide opportunities for my students to do science. In so doing, I find that objectives are met and the student walks away with a much richer understanding of the content.

An excellent source is the curriculum guides. Although these guides may present objectives at different levels of specificity, they are very helpful in their comprehensive nature of critical objectives.

Table 2.9 Strengths and Limitations of Different Sources for Establishing Learning Expectations

Source	Strengths	Limitations
Bloom's Taxonomy	Established; well known; comprehensive; contains action verbs; hierarchical design	Dated; based on behaviouristic learning theories; not consistent with recent cognitive theories of learning
Revision of Bloom's Taxonomy	Consistent with recent learning theory; contains action verbs	New; untested; may be overly complex
Professional Preparation	Focus on essentials of a discipline; personal experience	Difficult to translate into targets and keep up to date; may be confined to a specific type of target
Textbooks	Directly related to instruction; easily adapted	Tend to emphasize lower-level targets; lack criteria; need to be modified
Existing Lists of Objectives	Comprehensive; good ideas for targets	May not relate well to a local situation; need to be modified
Provinicial Curriculum	Comprehensive; tested; contains prescribed learning expectations and outcomes; often accompanied by instructional and assessment suggestions	Vary in the level of specificity; may need to be adapted to fit local contexts

Source: British Columbia Ministry of Education (2006). *Social studies K to 7: Integrated resource package.* Available at www.bced.gov.ba.ca/irp/ssk7.pdf; Ontario Ministry of Education (2005). *The Ontario curriculum: Mathematics.* Toronto: Queen's Printer for Ontario.

be expected to demonstrate, they do not generally attach levels of either importance or standards of performance to these learning expectations. Hence, these provincially developed outcomes may not be sufficient to support your teaching practice. Use your professional judgment to identify the most critical learning outcomes and the standards of performance you expect from your students.

Often these documents will include introductory information that provides further clarification of what student outcomes are expected. For example, Ontario's grades 1–8 mathematics guide states:

> Problem solving is central to learning mathematics. By learning to solve problems and by learning through problem solving, students are given numerous opportunities to connect mathematical ideas and to develop conceptual understanding. Problem solving forms the basis of effective mathematics programs and should be the mainstay of mathematical instruction. (Ontario Ministry of Education, 2005, p. 11)

Obviously, it is important for Ontario's teachers to focus on problem-solving learning expectations and outcomes. The actual overall and specific learning expectations make this more specific. The following is one of 14 Grade 5 mathematics standards.

Number Sense and Numeration

By the end of Grade 5, students will solve problems involving the multiplication and division of multi-digit whole numbers, and involving the addition and subtraction of decimal numbers to hundredths, using a variety of strategies. (p. 79)

CRITERIA FOR SELECTING LEARNING EXPECTATIONS AND OUTCOMES

After you have consulted the learning expectations and outcomes described in the provincial curriculum documents, and begun establishing your expectations and performance standards, you will need to make some choices about which outcomes are most important and which need more or less attention. The following criteria will help you judge the adequacy of your learning expectations and performance standards. They are summarized in Figure 2.4 in the form of a checklist.

1. Establish the right number of learning expectations. The number of different learning expectations will vary, depending on the length of the instructional segment and the complexity of the expectation. Obviously, the longer the instructional period, the more learning expectations are needed. As well, more complex learning expectations, such as those requiring reasoning, take more time. In general, these rules of thumb have been found appropriate: 40–60 expectations for a year; 8–12 for a unit; 1–3 for a single lesson. Hundreds of expectations for a year are clearly too many.

2. Establish comprehensive learning expectations. It is essential that the learning expectations represent all types of important learning from the instructional unit. Be careful not to overemphasize knowledge outcomes. Try to maintain a balance among the five areas (knowledge and simple understanding, deep understanding and reasoning, skills, products, and affect). Higher priority may be given to outcomes that

---

✓ Are there too many or too few learning expectations?
✓ Are all important types of learning included?
✓ Do your learning expectations reflect provincial curriculum and school goals?
✓ Will the expectations and performance standards challenge students to do their best work?
✓ Are the expectations consistent with research on learning and motivation?
✓ Are the expectations and performance standards established before instruction?

Figure 2.4 Checklist for Selecting Learning Expectations and Outcomes

integrate several of these areas. Rely heavily on provincial curriculum documents, but be prepared to clarify these to better meet the educational needs of your students.

3. Establish learning expectations that reflect provincial and school goals. Your expectations should be clearly related to more general provincial, district, and school learning goals. Priority may be given to expectations that focus on school improvement plans or restructuring efforts.

4. Establish learning expectations and performance standards that are challenging yet feasible. It is important to challenge students and seek the highest level of accomplishment for them. You need to have expectations that are neither too easy nor too hard. It is also important to assess the readiness of your students to meet these challenging expectations and performance standards. Do they have the necessary prerequisite skills and knowledge? Are they developmentally ready for the challenge? Do they have the needed motivation and attitudes? Will students see the expectations as too easy? As we will see in the next chapter, these questions need to be answered through proper assessment before your final selection of learning expectations, learning outcomes, performance standards, instructional activities, and your assessment of student learning.

5. Establish learning expectations and outcomes that are consistent with current principles of learning and motivation. Because learning outcomes are the basis for learning and instruction, what you expect will promote learning must be consistent with what we know about how learning occurs and what motivates students. For example, do the learning expectations and outcomes promote long-term retention in a meaningful way? Do the expectations reflect students' intrinsic interests and needs? Do the learning outcomes represent learning that will be applicable to life outside the classroom? Will the expectations and outcomes encourage a variety of instructional approaches and activities?

From year to year, you must revisit your learning expectations and performance standards and make appropriate modifications depending on changes in your students and provincial curriculum. It will also be helpful to develop and revise your criteria, with examples of student work that illustrate the different levels of performance.

SUMMARY

Learning expectations and outcomes—what students should know and be able to do and the criteria for judging student performance—are contrasted in this chapter with more traditional terms such as *goals* and *behavioural objectives*. The major points include the following:

■ Goals are broad statements about student learning.

■ Learning outcomes or behavioural objectives are specific statements that indicate what students should know and be able to do at the end of an instructional unit.

■ Expectations are the teacher's beliefs about what students are capable of achieving.

■ Goals, outcomes, and expectations focus on what students do, rather than on what the teacher does in instruction.

- It is not practical to write very specific behavioural objectives that include all aspects of the criteria and testing conditions.

- Criteria and rubrics are clearly stated dimensions of student performance that the teacher examines in making judgments about student proficiency. These criteria should be public and explained to students before each instructional unit.

- Exemplars and anchors are important examples that help students understand how teacher evaluations are made.

- Five types of learning expectations are introduced: knowledge and simple understanding, deep understanding and reasoning, skill, product, and affect.

- Sources for constructing learning expectations and outcomes include Bloom's taxonomy, the revision of Bloom's taxonomy, your professional preparation, textbooks, and most importantly, provincial and district learning outcomes.

- You should strive for the right number of comprehensive, challenging learning expectations that reflect school goals and are consistent with current principles of learning and motivation.

SELF-INSTRUCTIONAL REVIEW EXERCISES

1. Identify each of the following as a goal (G), learning outcome (LO), or expectation (E).
   a. My students will pass all their exams.
   b. Students will be familiar with global geography.
   c. It is unlikely that Tom will finish his test.
   d. Students will answer 10 of 12 questions about ancient Egypt in 15 minutes without the use of notes.

2. What does the term *criteria* have in common with learning outcomes? How is it different from what is contained in outcomes?

3. Suppose a teacher pulls out a graded paper that was handed in by a student from a previous year's class and distributes it to the class. What would the paper be called in relation to assessment?
   a. rubric
   b. anchor
   c. scoring criteria
   d. performance criteria

4. Give at least three reasons why using criteria that are shared with students before instruction is an effective teaching/learning tool for evaluating student work.

5. Why is it important to include criteria in learning expectations and outcomes?

6. Identify each of the following as a knowledge or simple understanding (K), deep understanding or reasoning (R), skill (S), product (P), or affect (A) expectation.
   a. shooting free throws
   b. recalling historical facts surrounding the development and cancellation of the Avro Arrow aircraft
   c. comparing vertebrates to invertebrates
   d. identifying the organs in a dissected frog
   e. working cooperatively with others
   f. building a three-dimensional structure from sticks and glue

7. Why may Bloom's original taxonomy of educational objectives not be the best source for identifying classroom learning expectations?

8. What are some examples of at least one learning expectation in each of the five areas (knowledge and simple understanding, deep understanding and reasoning, skills, products, and affect) that you could have students give about the content of this chapter?

9. What is the primary difference between learning outcomes and performance standards?

10. Give an example of a general and a specific learning outcome from your provincial curriculum.

SUGGESTIONS FOR ACTION RESEARCH

1. Obtain some examples of student work from teachers that demonstrate different levels of performance on the same assessment. How easy is it to see how the examples are different? See if the criteria you use to differentiate the examples are the same as the criteria the teacher used.

2. In small groups, generate some examples of student performance on the same learning target that would demonstrate qualitatively different levels of achievement concerning the content of this chapter or Chapter 1.

3. Examine textbook objectives and provincial learning outcomes in your area of expertise. How are they similar, and how are they different?

4. Interview a teacher and ask about using textbook objectives. How useful are these objectives? What determines whether the teacher will use them?

5. In a group of three or four other students, develop a scoring rubric that could be used for judging the performance of a student on an assignment, project, or test that was used in a school setting. Find or generate examples of student work that illustrate different levels of performance.

Chapter 3
High-Quality Classroom Assessment

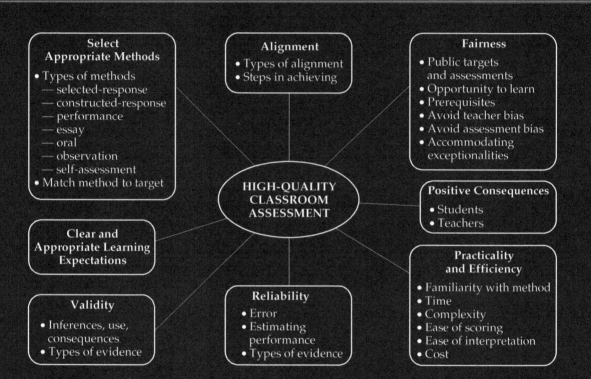

Select Appropriate Methods
- Types of methods
  - selected-response
  - constructed-response
  - performance
  - essay
  - oral
  - observation
  - self-assessment
- Match method to target

Alignment
- Types of alignment
- Steps in achieving

Fairness
- Public targets and assessments
- Opportunity to learn
- Prerequisites
- Avoid teacher bias
- Avoid assessment bias
- Accommodating exceptionalities

HIGH-QUALITY CLASSROOM ASSESSMENT

Positive Consequences
- Students
- Teachers

Clear and Appropriate Learning Expectations

Practicality and Efficiency
- Familiarity with method
- Time
- Complexity
- Ease of scoring
- Ease of interpretation
- Cost

Validity
- Inferences, use, consequences
- Types of evidence

Reliability
- Error
- Estimating performance
- Types of evidence

lassroom assessment consists of determining purpose and learning expectations related to standards, systematically obtaining information from students, interpreting the information collected, and using the information. In Chapter 2, we identified establishing learning expectations as the first step in conducting assessments. Once you have determined *what* to assess, you will probably be concerned with *how* to assess it. That is, what methods of data collection will you use to gather the information? Keep in mind several criteria that determine the quality and credibility of the assessment methods you choose. In this chapter, we review these criteria and suggest practical steps you can take to keep the quality of your assessments high.

WHAT IS HIGH-QUALITY CLASSROOM ASSESSMENT?

Obviously, classroom assessment must demonstrate principles and criteria so that its quality is high. Traditionally, assessment quality has been determined by the extent to which specific psychometric standards, such as validity and reliability, were met. These standards were originally derived for large-scale, published, standardized objective tests. However, for standardized tests the emphasis is on highly technical, statistically sophisticated standards. Thus, complex statistical procedures are used to provide estimates of validity, reliability, and measurement error. To interpret standardized tests properly, you must have a basic understanding of these properties.

But in most classrooms, such technical qualities have little relevance because the purpose of the assessment is different. This doesn't mean that the *ideas* of validity and reliability are not important criteria for classroom assessment. High-quality classroom assessment involves many other criteria as well, substituting technical types of validity and reliability with concerns about how the assessments influence learning and provide fair and credible reporting of student achievement. For teachers, the primary determinant of quality is how the information influences students. Thus, the focus is on the use and consequences of the results and what the assessments get students to do, rather than on a detailed inspection of the test itself. This means that judgments about quality are made *after* students' performance on the assessment is summarized and analyzed.

High-quality classroom assessments, then, are technically sound and provide results that demonstrate and improve targeted student learning. High-quality assessments also inform instructional decision making. As pointed out in Chapter 1, our understanding of learning and motivation, and our realization that much more is demanded of students than demonstrating simple knowledge, has changed how we define high-quality classroom assessments. The criteria of high-quality classroom assessment are presented in Figure 3.1. Each will be summarized in some detail.

Clear and appropriate learning expectations

Appropriateness of assessment methods

Validity

Reliability

Fairness

Positive consequences

Alignment

Practicality and efficiency

Figure 3.1 Criteria for Ensuring High-Quality Classroom Assessments

CLEAR AND APPROPRIATE LEARNING EXPECTATIONS

As discussed in Chapter 1, sound assessment begins with clear and appropriate learning expectations. Remember that the learning expectation includes both what students know and can do and the criteria for judging student performance. Are the expectations at the right level of difficulty to motivate students? Is there adequate balance among different types of expectations? Are the expectations consistent with your overall goals and the goals of the school and district? Are the expectations comprehensive, covering all major dimensions that you hope to change and need feedback about? Are the criteria for judging student performance clear?

APPROPRIATENESS OF ASSESSMENT METHODS

A number of different types of assessment methods can be used in the classroom. Although your ultimate choice of an assessment method will depend on how well all of the criteria in Figure 3.1 are met, the match between type of expectation and method is very important. Even though most expectations may be measured by several methods, certain methods measure some types of expectations better than other methods do. Once you have identified the targets, one of your first tasks is to match them with methods.

Types of Assessment Methods

Many different approaches or methods are used to assess students. We have categorized them in Table 3.1 according to the nature and characteristics of each method. A brief description of the methods is presented here to facilitate understanding about how the methods should be matched to expectations. The methods are covered in much more detail in later chapters.

Table 3.1 divides different methods of assessment into four major categories: selected-response, constructed-response, teacher observation, and student self-assessment. What distinguishes most classroom assessments is whether the items use selected-response or constructed-response formats. In the **selected-response** format, students are presented with a question that has two or more possible responses. Students then select an answer from the possible choices. Common selected-response items include multiple-choice, true/false, and matching. These kinds of items may also be called *objective*, referring to the way in which the answers are scored. A single correct or best answer is identified for each item, and scoring is simply a matter of checking to determine whether the correct choice was made. This feature makes it easy to score a large number of items efficiently by using scantron sheets and machines to read the answers (hence the term *machine-scorable* tests).

A **constructed-response** format requires students to create or produce their own answer in response to a question or task. Brief constructed-response items are those in which students provide very short, clearly delineated answers, such as filling in blanks, writing a few

Table 3.1 Different Assessment Methods

Selected-Response	Constructed-Response				Teacher Observation	Student Self-Assessment
	Brief Constructed-Response Items	*Performance Tasks*	*Essay Items*	*Oral Questioning*		*Self-Report Inventories*
• Multiple-choice • Binary-choice (e.g., true/false) • Matching • Interpretive	• Short answer • Completion • Label a diagram • "Show your work"	*Products* • Paper • Project • Poem • Portfolio • Video/audiotape • Spreadsheet • Web page • Exhibition • Reflection • Journal • Graph • Table • Illustration *Skills* • Speech • Demonstration • Dramatic reading • Debate • Enactment • Athletics • Keyboarding	• Restricted-response • Extended-response	• Informal questioning • Examinations • Conferences • Interviews	• Formal • Informal	• Attitude survey • Sociometric devices • Questionnaires • Inventories *Self-Evaluation* • Ratings • Portfolios • Conferences • Self-reflection • Evaluate others' performances

words or a sentence or two, or answering mathematics problems by showing how they arrived at their answers. Although many constructed-response assessments require considerable subjectivity in judging an answer, brief constructed-response items can be objectively scored because there is typically a single correct answer that is easily identified.

Performance assessments require students to construct a more extensive and elaborate answer or response. A well-defined task is identified, and students are asked to create, produce, or do something, often in settings that involve real-world application of knowledge and skills. Students demonstrate proficiency by providing an extended response. Performance formats are further differentiated into products and performances. The performance may result in a product, such as a painting, portfolio, paper, or exhibition, or it may consist of a performance, such as a speech, athletic skill, musical recital, or reading. (Many use the term *performance assessment* to refer to both performances and products, and others use *performance-based*.)

Essay items allow students to construct a response that is several sentences (restricted-response) to many paragraphs or pages in length (extended-response). Restricted-response essay items include limits on the content and nature of the answer, whereas extended-response items allow greater freedom in response.

Oral questioning is used continuously and informally during instruction to monitor student understanding. In a more formal format, oral questions are used to test or determine student understanding through interviews or conferences.

Teacher observations, like oral questions, are so common that we often don't think of them as assessment. But teachers *constantly* observe students informally to assess understanding and progress. Teachers watch students as they respond to questions, and listen to them as they speak with others. Often nonverbal communication, such as squinting, inattention, looks of frustration, and other cues, is more helpful than verbal feedback. Observation is used extensively as well in performance assessments, and other formal observational techniques are used to assess classroom climate, teacher effectiveness, and other dimensions of the classroom.

Student self-assessment refers to students' reporting on or evaluating themselves. In *self-evaluation of academic achievement*, students rate their own performance in relation to established standards and criteria. In *self-report inventories*, students are asked to complete a form or answer questions that reveal their attitudes and beliefs about themselves or other students. Examples of self-report instruments include attitude surveys, sociometric devices, self-concept questionnaires, interest inventories, and personality measures.

Matching Expectations with Methods

Table 3.2 presents the Matching Expectations with Methods Scorecard. This figure summarizes the relative strengths of different methods in measuring different expectations. Notice that several methods may be used for some expectations. This provides more flexibility in the assessments you use, but it also means there is no simple formula or one correct method.

Table 3.2 Matching Expectations with Methods Scorecard

Expectations	Assessment Methods					
	Selected-Response and Brief Constructed-Response	Essay	Performance	Oral Question	Observation	Student Self-Assessment
Knowledge and simple understanding	5	4	3	4	3	3
Deep understanding and reasoning	2	5	4	4	2	3
Skills	1	3	5	2	5	3
Products	1	1	5	2	4	4
Affect	1	2	4	4	4	5

Note: Higher numbers indicate better matches (e.g., 1 = poor, 5 = excellent).

The scorecard provides *general* guidelines about how well particular assessment methods measure each type of expectation. Remember that the numbers (1 = poor, 5 = excellent) represent the relative strength of the method to provide a high-quality assessment. Variations of what is presented in the table should be expected. For example, good selected-response items *can* provide a high-quality measure of reasoning, but such items are difficult and time-consuming to prepare. In assigning the numbers, we have considered both technical strengths and practical limitations. When each method is described in greater detail in later chapters, the variations will become more obvious. For now, however, the scorecard will provide both a good overview and some preliminary information for selecting appropriate methods.

Knowledge and Simple Understanding. Well-constructed selected-response and brief constructed-response items do a good job of assessing subject matter and procedural knowledge and simple understanding, particularly when students must recognize or remember isolated facts, definitions, spellings, concepts, and principles. The questions can be answered and scored quickly, so it is efficient for teachers. These formats also allow you to adequately sample a large amount of knowledge. Asking students questions orally about what they know is also an effective way to assess knowledge, but it takes much more time and the results are difficult to record. Advance planning is needed to prepare the questions and a method to record student responses. Thus, assessment by oral questioning is best when you are checking for mastery or understanding of a limited number of important facts, or when you are doing informal diagnostic assessment. This is usually done during instruction, to provide feedback about student progress.

Essays can be used effectively to assess knowledge and understanding when your objective is for students to learn large chunks or structures of related knowledge. For example, essays are effective in measuring whether students know the causes of World War II or the life cycles of different types of animals.

Using performance assessments presents some difficulties for determining what students know. Because performance assessments are time intensive for teachers and students, they are usually not the best choice for assessing vast amounts of knowledge. Much of the preparation for the performance often takes place outside of class, and the final paper or product typically does demonstrate that the student has mastered specific facts. When the performance involves a demonstration of a process or series of steps, knowledge of the process or steps can be assumed when they are demonstrated. However, performance assessments are very good for measuring student understanding that reflects more than surface knowledge.

Deep Understanding and Reasoning. Deep understanding and reasoning skills are best assessed in essays. Essays can focus directly on specific reasoning skills by asking students to compare, evaluate, critique, provide justification for, organize, integrate, defend, and solve problems. Time is provided to allow students to use reasoning before answering the question. Oral questions that require deep understanding and reasoning to be used for an answer are excellent. But they are also inefficient for systematic assessment of all students at the end of a unit.

Performance assessments are also effective in measuring deep understanding and reasoning skills. For example, by observing students demonstrate how to plan a budget for a family of four, you can draw inferences about how the student used all the information provided and balanced different priorities. Science projects illustrate the ability to interpret results and make conclusions.

Selected-response and brief constructed-response questions *can* be excellent methods for assessing certain aspects of deep understanding and reasoning. When an item demands more than simply recalling or recognizing a fact, reasoning may be needed. For example, if a question requires the student to interpret a chart, analyze a poem, or apply knowledge to solve a problem, thinking skills can be measured. However, constructing selected-response items that assess deep understanding and reasoning is very time-consuming.

Student self-evaluations of the reasoning they used in answering a question or solving a problem can help you diagnose learning difficulties. You can provide sample graded answers and then ask students to compare these to their responses. Students can also be involved in scoring teams that evaluate student answers.

Skills. Performance assessments are clearly the preferred method to determine systematically whether a student has mastered a skill. Whether the student is demonstrating how to shoot a basketball, give a persuasive speech, sing a song, speak a foreign language, or use a microscope, the skill is best assessed by observing the student perform the task. Informally, teachers use observation extensively to assess progress in demonstrating skills.

Selected-response and brief constructed-response tests and oral questioning can be used to assess student knowledge of skills, such as knowing the proper sequence of actions or recognizing the important dimensions of the skill. But this represents prerequisite knowledge and is not the same as measuring the extent to which the student can actually *do* a sequence of actions.

As with essays, student self-evaluations can focus students on how well their demonstration of a skill meets stated criteria. Student evaluations of others' demonstrations are also useful.

Products. The best way to assess student products is to have students complete them through a performance assessment. The best test of being able to write persuasively is to write a letter that argues for something; if you want students to be able to act, have them participate in a play.

Like skills, you can use objectively scored items, essay items, and oral questions to determine whether students know the components of the product or to evaluate different products. But there is no substitute for actually creating the product.

Student self-evaluations are very effective with performance assessment because students need to focus on the performance criteria and make judgments about their own performance in relation to the criteria. It is also effective to have students judge each others' performances.

Affect. Affective outcomes are best assessed by either observing students or using student self-reports. Remember that *affect* refers to attitudes, values, feelings, self-concept, interests, and other feelings and beliefs. Because these traits are complex, it is especially important to have clear learning expectations.

The most direct and efficient way to assess affect is to ask students directly, through self-report surveys and questionnaires. Direct oral questioning can be revealing if a good working relationship exists between teacher and student and if the atmosphere is conducive to honest sharing of feelings.

Observation can be effective in informally determining many affective traits (e.g., motivation and attitudes toward subjects and student self-concept are often apparent when the student shows negative feelings through body posture, a reluctance to interact with others, and withdrawal). Some performance assessments provide ample opportunities for teachers to observe affect, although like other observations, this is usually nonsystematic and inferences are required. Because you are both the observer and the one making the inference, be careful to avoid bias. Having clear learning expectations helps to prevent personal opinion or biases from clouding the assessments.

Make many choices to ensure that you match expectations to methods. As you learn about what it takes to do high-quality assessments with each of the methods, your matches will improve.

VALIDITY

What Is a Valid Assessment?

Classroom assessment is a process that includes gathering, interpreting, and using information. This conceptualization has important implications for how we define validity, a familiar concept at the heart of high-quality assessments. **Validity** is a characteristic that refers to the appropriateness of the inferences, uses, and consequences that result from the assessment. Validity is concerned with the soundness, trustworthiness, or legitimacy of the claims or inferences that are made on the basis of obtained scores. In other words, is the interpretation made from assessment results reasonable? Is the information gathered the right kind of evidence for the decision that needs to be made or the intended use? How sound is the interpretation of the information? Validity has to do with the consequences of the inferences, not the assessment itself. Thus, an inference or use is valid or invalid, not the assessment, test, instrument, or procedure used to gather information. Often we use the phrase "validity of the test," but it is more accurate to say "the validity of the interpretation, inference, or use of the results."

You may be familiar with a somewhat different definition of validity that defines the term as "the extent to which a test measures what it is supposed to measure." Although this notion is important to many decisions and uses, it suggests that validity is a characteristic that the instrument always possesses. In reality, the same test or instrument can be valid for one purpose and invalid for another. Actually, validity is always a matter of degree, depending on the situation. For example, a social studies test may have high validity for determining if students know the sequence of events leading to leading to Confederation, less validity for determining if students can reason, even less validity for determining if students can communicate effectively in writing, and virtually no validity for determining a student's mathematical ability. An assessment is not simply valid or invalid; it is valid to some degree in reference to specific inferences or uses.

How Is Validity Determined?

Validity is always determined by professional judgment. For classroom assessment, this judgment is made by the teacher. An analysis is done by accumulating evidence suggesting that an inference or use is appropriate, and whether the consequences of the interpretations and uses are reasonable and fair.

The process of determining validity is illustrated in Figure 3.2. Traditionally, the validity of an inference comes from one of three types of evidence: content-related, criterion-related, and construct-related evidence. However, these categories do not adequately address the consequences and uses of the results. Thus, we will consider how classroom teachers can use these three types of evidence, as well as consideration of consequences and uses, to make an overall judgment about the degree of validity of the assessment. Table 3.3 summarizes the major sources of information (evidence) that can be used to establish validity.

Content-Related Evidence. One feature of teaching that has important implications for assessment is that often a teacher is unable to assess everything that is taught or every instructional objective. Suppose you wanted to test for everything grade 6 students learn in a four-week unit about insects. Can you imagine how long the test would be and how much time students would take to complete the test? To assess in these situations, select a *sample* of what has been taught, and then use student achievement on this sample to make inferences about knowledge of the entire universe or domain of content, reasoning, and other objectives. That is, if a student correctly answers 85 per cent of the test items from a sample of the unit on insects, then you infer that the student knows 85 percent of the content of the entire unit. If your sample is judged to be representative of the universe or domain, then you have **content-related evidence** for validity. The inference from the test is that the student demonstrates knowledge about the unit.

Adequate sampling of content is determined by *your* professional judgment. This judgment process can be haphazard or it can be very systematic. In a superficial review of the expectation, objectives, and test, validity is based only on *appearance*. This is sometimes referred to as face validity. *Face validity* concerns whether, after superficial examination, a

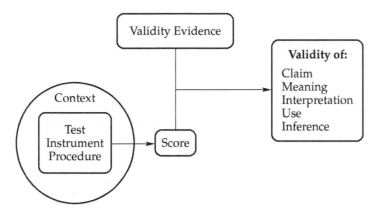

Figure 3.2 Determining Validity

Table 3.3 Sources of Information for Validity

Content-Related Evidence	The extent to which the assessment is representative of the domain of interest
Criterion-Related Evidence	The relationship between an assessment and another measure of the same trait
Construct-Related Evidence	The extent to which the assessment is a meaningful measure of an unobservable trait or characteristic

test seems to be a reasonable measure of the objectives and domain. Does the test, on the face of it, look like an adequate measure? Although it is important to avoid face *in*validity, the evidence should be more structured and systematic.

Once the complete domain of content and expectations is specified, the items on the test can be reviewed to ensure a match between the intended inferences and what is on the test. This process begins with clear learning expectations. Based on the expectations, a **test blueprint** or **table of specifications** is sometimes prepared, in order to further delineate what objectives you intend to assess and what is important from the content domain. The table of specifications is a two-way grid that shows the content and types of learning expectations represented in your assessment (Table 3.4). An alternative to the table of

Table 3.4 Format for a Table of Specifications[1]

Major Content Areas	Learning Expectation					
	Knowledge/ Simple Understanding	*Deep Understanding and Reasoning*	*Skills*	*Products*	*Affect*	*Totals*
1. (Topic)	No./%	No./%	No./%	No./%	No./%	No./%
2. (Topic)	No./%	No./%	No./%	No./%	No./%	No./%
3. (Topic)	No./%	No./%	No./%	No./%	No./%	No./%
4. (Topic)	No./%	No./%	No./%	No./%	No./%	No./%
•	•	•	•	•	•	•
•	•	•	•	•	•	•
•	•	•	•	•	•	•
N. (Topic)	•	•	•	•	•	•
Total no. of items/% of test	No./%	No./%	No./%	No./%	No./%	*Total no. of items/ 100%*

[1] The table is completed by indicating the number of test items (No.) and the percentage of items from each type of learning expectation for each topic. For example, if the topic were assessment, you might have reliability as one topic. If there were four knowledge items for reliability and this was 8 per cent of the test, then 4/8% would be included in the table under knowledge.

specifications is a complete, detailed list of learning objectives. Essentially, this list includes all of the cells that would be checked or completed in the table of specifications.

We want to emphasize that the goal of a blueprint is to make your professional judgment systematic so that you can improve the validity of the assessment. As illustrated in Table 3.5, your judgment determines what types of learning expectations will be assessed (knowledge and simple understanding, deep understanding and reasoning, skills, products, or affect), what areas of the content will be sampled, and how the assessment measures both content and type of learning. At this point, you are making decisions about the importance of different types of expectations, the content assessed, and how much of the assessment is measuring each expectation and area of content. If the assessment reflects an actual or modified table of specifications, then there is content-related evidence of validity.

Another consideration related to this type of evidence is the extent to which an assessment has *instructional* validity. **Instructional validity** is concerned with the match between what is taught and what is assessed. How closely does the test correspond to what has been covered in class and in assignments? Have students had the opportunity to learn what has been assessed? Again, *your* professional judgment is needed to ensure that what is assessed is consistent with what was taught. To check this, examine the table of specifications after teaching a unit to determine whether the emphasis in different areas or for different expectations is consistent with what you emphasized in class.

Criterion-Related Evidence. Another way to ensure appropriate inferences from assessments is to have evidence that a particular assessment is providing the same result as another assessment of the same thing. **Criterion-related evidence** provides such validity by relating an assessment to some other valued measure (criterion) that either provides an estimate of current performance (concurrent criterion-related evidence) or predicts future performance (predictive criterion-related evidence). Test developers and researchers use this approach to establish evidence that a test or other instrument is measuring the same

Table 3.5 Professional Judgments in Establishing Content-Related Evidence for Validity

Learning Expectations	Content	Instruction	Assessment
What learning expectations will be assessed? How much of the assessment will be done on each learning expectation area?	What content is most important? What topics will be assessed? How much of the assessment will be done in each topic?	What content and learning expectations have been emphasized in instruction?	Are assessments adequate samples of students' performance in each topic area and for each expectation?

trait, knowledge, or attitude by calculating a correlation coefficient to measure the relationship between the assessment and the criterion (see Chapter 13 for a discussion of correlation).

Classroom teachers do not conduct formal studies to obtain correlation coefficients that will provide evidence of validity, but they should employ the principle. The principle is that when you have two or more measures of the same thing, and these measures provide similar results, then you have established, albeit informally, criterion-related evidence. For example, if your assessment of a student's skill in using a microscope through observation coincides with the student's score on a quiz that tests steps in using microscopes, then you have criterion-related evidence that your inference about the skill of this student is valid. Similarly, if you are interested in the extent to which preparation by your students, as indicated by scores on a final exam in mathematics, predicts how well they will do next year, examine the grades of previous students and determine informally if students who scored high on your final exam are getting high grades and students who scored low on your final are getting low grades. If you find correlation, then an inference about predicting how your students will perform, based on their final exam, is valid. Based on this logic, you should conduct several assessments of the learning expectations; try not to rely on a single assessment.

Construct-Related Evidence. Psychologists refer to a *construct* as an unobservable trait or characteristic that a person possesses, such as intelligence, reading comprehension, honesty, self-concept, attitude, reasoning ability, learning style, and anxiety. These characteristics are not measured directly, in contrast to performance such as spelling or how many push-ups a person successfully completes. Rather, the characteristic is *constructed* to account for behaviour that can be observed. Whenever constructs are assessed, the validity of our interpretations depends on the extent of the **construct-related evidence** that is presented. This evidence can take many forms, any one of which is probably insufficient by itself.

The three types of construct-related evidence are theoretical, logical, and statistical. One important type of evidence derives from a clear theoretical explanation or definition of the characteristic so that its meaning is clear and not confused with any other construct. This is particularly important whenever you emphasize reasoning and affect expectations. For example, suppose you want to assess students' attitudes toward reading. What is your definition of *attitude*? Do you mean how much students *enjoy* reading, *value* reading, or *read* in their spare time? Are you interested in their *desire* to read or their perception of *ability* to read? None of these traits is necessarily correct as a measure of attitude, but you need to provide a clear definition that separates your construct from other similar but different constructs.

Logical analyses can be of several types. For some reasoning constructs, you can ask students to comment on what they were thinking when they answered the questions. Ideally, their thinking reveals an intended reasoning process. Another type of logical evidence comes from comparing the scores of groups that, as determined by other criteria, should respond differently. These groups can be before-being-taught and after-being-taught groups, age groups, or groups that have been identified by other means as being different on the construct.

Statistical procedures can be used to correlate scores from measures of the construct with scores from other measures of the same construct and measures of similar but different constructs. For example, self-concept of academic ability scores from one survey should be related to another measure of the same thing, but less related to measures of self-concept of physical ability. These statistical approaches are used for many standardized, published surveys and questionnaires. For a teacher, however, it will be most practical to use clear definitions and logical analyses as construct-related evidence.

Figure 3.3 summarizes suggestions for enhancing the validity of classroom assessments.

RELIABILITY

What Is a Reliable Score?

Like validity, the term *reliability* has been used for many years to describe an essential characteristic of sound assessment. **Reliability** is concerned with the consistency, stability, and dependability of the scores. Suppose Madame Lavoie is assessing her students' addition and subtraction skills. She decides to give the students a 20-mark quiz to determine their skills. Madame Lavoie examines the results, but she wants to be sure about the level of

---

- Ask others to judge the clarity of what you are assessing.
- Check to see if different ways of assessing the same thing give the same result.
- Sample a sufficient number of examples of what is being assessed.
- Prepare a detailed table of specifications.
- Ask others to judge the match between the assessment items and the objective of the assessment.
- Compare groups known to differ on what is being assessed.
- Compare scores taken before instruction to those taken after instruction.
- Compare predicted consequences to actual consequences.
- Compare scores on similar but different traits.
- Provide adequate time to complete the assessment.
- Ensure appropriate vocabulary, sentence structure, and item difficulty.
- Ask easy questions first.
- Use different methods to assess the same thing.
- Use the assessment *only* for intended purposes.

Figure 3.3 Suggestions for Enhancing Validity

CASE STUDY FOR REFLECTION

Ms. Pollard teaches middle-school mathematics. In a typical week, she gives several mini-quizzes for quick assessments of student understanding, and an end-of-week test. She also has a weekly problem-solving question. She checks homework, and she also collects a great deal of anecdotal evidence focused on student effort and achievement in daily work. Although Ms. Pollard is an experienced teacher, she wasn't sure how she should respond to her principal when asked about the "validity" of her classroom assessments.

Questions for Consideration

1. From the information she collects, what kind of validity evidence should she say she has obtained?
2. How should Ms. Pollard respond to the principal's query?
3. What possible pitfalls should she avoid so that her inferences about student learning will be valid?

performance before designing appropriate instruction, so she gives another quiz two days later on the same addition and subtraction skills. The results for some of her students are as follows:

Student	Addition		Subtraction	
	Quiz 1	Quiz 2	Quiz 1	Quiz 2
Rob	18	16	13	20
Carrie	10	12	18	10
Ryann	9	8	8	14
Felix	16	15	17	12

The addition quiz scores are fairly consistent. All four students scored within one or two points on the quizzes; students who scored high on the first quiz also scored high on the second quiz, and students who scored low did so on both quizzes. Consequently, the results for addition are reliable. For subtraction, on the other hand, there was considerable change in performance from the first to the second quiz. Students who scored high on the first quiz scored low on the second one, and students who scored low on the first quiz scored high on the second. For subtraction, then, the results are unreliable because they are inconsistent. The scores contradict one another.

So what does Madame Lavoie make of the mathematics scores? Her goal is to use the quiz to accurately determine the defined skill. She cannot know the *exact* level of the skills, but, as in the case of addition, she can get a fairly accurate picture with a reliable assessment. For subtraction, on the other hand, she cannot use these results alone to estimate the students' real or actual skill. More assessments are needed before she can be confident that the scores are reliable and thus provide a dependable result. But even the scores in addition are not without some degree of error. In fact, *all* assessments have error; they are never perfect measures of the trait or skill. Let's look at another example to illustrate this point.

Think about the difference between a measure of attitude toward science and time required to run a kilometre. The measure of attitude will have a relatively high degree of error, but the measure of time will be precise, with little error (highly reliable). This is because there are many more influences on how students answer questions about their attitudes (such as the student's mood that day, the heat in the room, poorly worded items, and fatigue) than there are on a timekeeper's ability to press the stopwatch and read the time elapsed. This doesn't mean that measuring time is without error, but the process will involve fewer errors than measuring attitudes.

Assessment Error

The concept of error in assessment is critical to understanding reliability. Conceptually, whenever we assess something, we get an *observed* score or result. This observed score is a product of what the *true* or *real* ability or skill is *plus* some degree of *error:*

Observed Score = True Score + Error

Reliability is directly related to error. It is not a matter of all or none, as if some results are reliable and others unreliable. Rather, for each assessment there is some *degree* of error. Thus, we think in terms of low, moderate, or high reliability. The error can also be positive or negative. That is, the observed score can be higher or lower than the true score, depending on the nature of the error. Sometimes you will know when a student's score is lower than it should be based on the students' behaviour at the time of the assessment. For example, if the student was sick, tired, in a bad mood, or distracted, the score may have negative error and underestimate the true score. This is obviously a subjective judgment, which is appropriate for many types of classroom assessment.

Figure 3.4 shows how different sources of error influence assessment results. Notice how reliability is influenced by factors within the student (internal sources of error), such as mood and physical condition, as well as external factors, such as the quality of the test, scoring errors, and test directions. The actual or true knowledge, reasoning, skill, or affect is captured to some extent by the assessment, but the internal and external sources of error also contribute to the score. In the end, you get an observed score that is made up of the actual or true performance plus some degree of error.

An important practical implication of knowing about error in testing is that small differences between scores of different students should be treated as if they were the same. Typically, your interpretation of a score of 75 should be the same as your interpretation of a

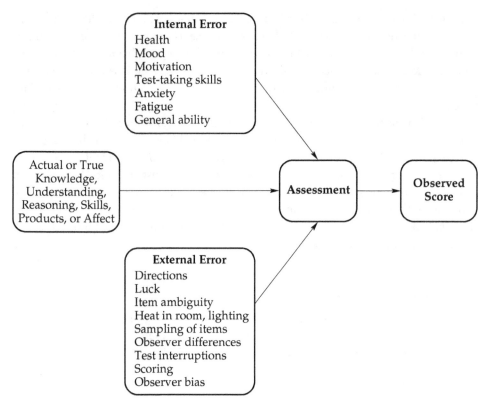

Figure 3.4 Sources of Error in Assessment

score of 77. These observed scores are so close that when we consider error that can be positive or negative, the true scores of the students should be considered equal (e.g., 75, plus or minus 3, or 77, plus or minus 3).

How Is Reliability Determined?

Reliability is determined by estimating the influence of various sources of error. If there is little error, then the reliability is high or strong. If there is a great deal of error, the reliability is low or weak. How, then, is this "amount of error" estimated? In large-scale and standardized testing, estimating error is done statistically with correlation procedures that produce reliability coefficients. These coefficients are then used to estimate the precise amount of random error that should be used in interpreting the results. This index is called the **standard error of measurement (SEM)**. It will be discussed in further detail in Chapter 13. In classroom assessment, there is rarely any statistical estimate of reliability (although software programs make this very easy for objective tests). Rather, in the classroom, reliability is determined by noting some sources of error, such as those in Figure 3.4, by using logic associated with different measures of the same thing, and by observing the consistency with which students answer questions on the same topic. For example, if Ms. Chan knows that Susan is distracted by a family problem and has difficulty concentrating, she concludes that a low score is being influenced by this problem. In other words, there is considerable error in Susan's observed performance. If different students score highest on different measures of the same skill, this lack of consistency points to low reliability. If one subgroup of students always scores well each time a quiz is given, whereas another subgroup always scores low, this consistency is logical evidence of good reliability.

Sources of Reliability Evidence

Like validity, making good judgments about reliability is based on using one or more sources of evidence to justify score interpretations. We will consider the five most common types of reliability evidence (summarized in Table 3.6).

Evidence Based on Stability. A stability estimate of reliability refers to consistency over time. It is produced by administering an assessment to a group, waiting for a specified amount of time (typically a week or more), and then administering the same assessment to the same group a second time. A correlation between the two sets of scores is calculated as an indicator or reliability. This type of estimate is also called **test-retest** reliability.

Evidence Based on Equivalent Forms. An estimate of equivalence is obtained by administering two forms of the same assessment to a group of students and correlating the scores. The approach is to generate two forms of an assessment that are equal in what is being measured. If the two forms are given at approximately the same time, as with our earlier example of Madame Lavoie's students, then an estimate of only equivalence is obtained. If there is a significant time delay between the administrations, then a stability feature is added, providing what is called an *equivalence and stability estimate*.

Table 3.6 Sources of Evidence in Estimating Reliability

Source of Evidence	Description
Stability	Scores from two administrations of the same assessment to the same group of individuals with a time interval between the assessments
Equivalence	Two forms of the same assessment given at about the same time
Internal Consistency	A single administration of the assessment
Scorer or Rater Consistency	Agreement between two or more scorers or raters on the same performances
Decision Consistency	Percentage of decisions that are the same

In classroom assessment, teachers rarely use equivalence evidence because it would be too time-consuming to make and administer two similar assessments of the same thing. However, from a logical standpoint, the *idea* of equivalence is relevant if students are offered make-up tests (which should be very similar to the original test) or if teachers want to use a pretest-posttest design to conduct some action research. Use logic to determine whether different assessments of the same trait show similar results (e.g., test scores being consistent with homework and quizzes). When students who score high on one assessment also score high on the others, and students who score low on one assessment score low on the others, there is overall consistency and good reliability.

Equivalent forms evidence is used extensively in standardized and large-scale assessment because several forms of the same test are needed to allow retakes and make-up testing. These estimates are statistical and are reported as reliability coefficients.

Evidence Based on Internal Consistency. Internal consistency evidence is based on the degree of homogeneity of the scores on items measuring the same trait.[1] Only a single form of the assessment is needed for this kind of evidence. This approach assumes that the scores of items measuring the same trait should give consistent results. Suppose a teacher has a 20-item test on the parts of a flower. If students who truly master this knowledge get all or almost all the items correct, whereas students who know nothing about flowers get all or almost all of the items wrong, then there would be internal consistency. In other words, are the items functioning together in a consistent manner?

From a practical standpoint, internal consistency evidence is relatively easy to obtain. There is no need to develop a second form, nor is it necessary to give the assessment more than once. There are some limitations, however. First, there needs to be a sufficient number of items. One rule of thumb is that five items are needed to measure a single trait or skill. Second, internal consistency is not appropriate for tests with a time limit (called "speeded" tests). Third, it is somewhat limiting if all you know is that students answer consistently *at one time*. Typically, teachers need to make inferences about student knowledge over time. After all, we want students to remember what they have learned, and we want them to retain skills over time; this is a more complete and accurate indication of student learning than what can be demonstrated within only a short time frame. This is consistent with using quizzes during a unit and then a larger, more comprehensive assessment at the end of the unit.

Evidence Based on Scorer or Rater Consistency. Whenever student responses need to be judged, rated, or scored, such as when teachers grade essays, writing samples, performance assessments, and portfolios, error can be contributed because of characteristics of the person doing the evaluation (e.g., halo effect, biases, fatigue, expectations, or other idiosyncrasies). To account for this kind of error, gather evidence concerning the extent to which two or more raters agree in their evaluations. For example, if two teachers score 20 student essays and give 15 of them the same score, then the percentage of agreement, 75 per cent, indicates rater consistency. You can also use correlations between two raters. Scorer or rater evidence is best when there is good variation in products to be judged, when the criteria for scoring are clear, and when there is training for the scorers or raters.

Evidence Based on Decision Consistency. A final kind of evidence is particularly important in making judgments about whether students are "meeting expectations" or whether they "pass." These kinds of decisions or classifications are used as the basis for reliability, rather than the scores themselves. Consistency is estimated as the percentage of same classifications on two or more administrations of the same test. For example, suppose a group of 20 students takes the same "minimum competency" test twice. On the first testing, 10 students were judged "competent" and 10 students were judged to be "not competent." On the second testing, all "competent" students were again classified as "competent," but only 8 of 10 "not competent" students were judged that way. Thus, of the 20 classifications, 18 matched, which can be converted to a percentage—90 per cent in this example. This approach can also be used in conjunction with rater consistency. Of the total number of decisions made, what percentage were the same?

Factors Influencing Reliability Estimates

Although a number of different sources of error will contribute to estimates of reliability, keep in mind a few factors that affect results. One important factor is the number of items in the assessment. The greater the number of items, the greater the reliability. The number of students also makes a difference—the higher the number of students, the stronger the reliability. Difficulty of items also affects reliability. The best reliability coefficients are obtained when items are neither too easy nor too hard. Carefully constructed items will improve reliability. Poorly worded or unclear items lead to poor reliability. The more objective the scoring, the greater the reliability. Typically, multiple-choice tests obtain better estimates of reliability than do constructed-response, performance, or portfolio assessments.

Figure 3.5 summarizes suggestions for developing and implementing highly reliable classroom assessments. The degree of reliability needed depends on the type of decision

- Use a sufficient number of items or tasks. (Other things being equal, longer tests are more reliable.)
- Use independent raters or observers who provide similar scores to the same performances.
- Construct items and tasks that clearly differentiate students on what is being assessed.
- Make sure the assessment procedures and scoring are as objective as possible.
- Continue assessment until results are consistent.
- Eliminate or reduce the influence of extraneous events or factors.
- Use shorter assessments more frequently than fewer long assessments.

Figure 3.5 Suggestions for Enhancing Reliability

that will be made on the basis of the results. Higher reliability is needed when the decision has important, lasting consequences for individual students (e.g., placement to receive special education services). When the decision is about groups and is less important (e.g., whether to repeat a part of a unit of instruction), the reliability does not need to be as high.

FAIRNESS

A *fair* assessment provides all students with an equal opportunity to demonstrate achievement and yields scores that are comparably valid from one person or group to another (Heubert & Hauser, 1999). We want to allow students to show us what they have learned from instruction. If some students have an advantage over others because of factors unrelated to what is being taught, then the assessment is not fair. Fair assessments are *unbiased* and *non-discriminatory*, uninfluenced by irrelevant or subjective factors. That is, neither the assessment task nor scoring is differentially affected by race, gender, ethnic background, exceptionality, or other factors unrelated to what is being assessed. Fairness is also evident in what students are told about the assessment and whether they have had the opportunity to learn what is being assessed. The following criteria, summarized in Figure 3.6, represent potential influences that determine whether an assessment is fair.

- Student knowledge of learning expectations and assessments
- Opportunity to learn
- Prerequisite knowledge and skills
- Avoiding student stereotyping
- Avoiding bias in assessment tasks and procedures
- Accommodating student exceptionalities

Figure 3.6 Key Components of Fairness

Student Knowledge of Learning Expectations and Assessments

How often have you taken a test and thought, "If I had only known the teacher was going to test *this* content, I would have studied it!"? In a fair assessment, it is clear what will and will not be tested. Your objective is not to fool or trick students or to outguess them on the assessment. Rather, be very clear and specific about the learning expectation—what is to be assessed and how it will be scored. And this is very important: both the content of the assessment and the scoring criteria should be *public*. Being public means that students know the content and scoring criteria before the assessment and often before instruction. When students know what will be assessed, they know what to study and focus on. By knowing the scoring criteria, students better understand the qualitative differences the teacher is looking for in student performance. One way to help students understand the assessment is to give them the assessment blueprint, sample questions, and examples of work completed by previous students and graded by the teacher.

When students know the learning expectations and scoring criteria in advance, they will probably be more intrinsically motivated to obtain true mastery, rather than mere performance. It helps to establish a *learning* goal orientation for students, in which the focus is on mastering a task, developing new skills, and improving competence and understanding. In contrast, when a *performance* goal orientation is established, in which students perform to get a grade, recognition, or reward, motivation is extrinsic and less intense, and students are not as engaged.

Opportunity to Learn

Opportunity to learn is concerned with sufficiency or quality of the time, resources, and conditions needed by students to demonstrate their achievement. It concerns the adequacy of instructional approaches and materials that are aligned with the assessment. Fair assessments are aligned with instruction that provides adequate time and opportunities for all students to learn. This is more than simply telling students, for example, that a test will cover certain chapters. Ample instructional time and resources are needed so that students are not penalized because of a lack of opportunity.

Prerequisite Knowledge and Skills

It is unfair to assess students on things that require prerequisite knowledge or skills that they do not possess. You need to have a good understanding of prerequisites that your students demonstrate. You also need to examine your assessments carefully to know what prerequisites are required. For example, suppose you want to test math reasoning skills. Your questions are based on short paragraphs that provide needed information. In this situation, math reasoning skills can be demonstrated only if students can read and understand the paragraphs. Thus, reading skills are prerequisites. If students do poorly on the assessment, their performance may have more to do with a lack of reading skills than with math reasoning.

Another type of prerequisite skill is concerned with test taking. Some students have better test-taking skills (test-wiseness) than others, such as knowing to read directions carefully, pacing, initially bypassing difficult items, checking answers, and eliminating wrong answers to multiple-choice items, rather than looking for the right answer. These skills are not difficult for students to learn, and you should make sure all students are familiar with them before you administer an assessment.

Avoiding Student Stereotyping

Stereotypes interfere with objectivity. It is your responsibility to judge each student on his or her performance on assessment tasks, not on how others who share characteristics of the student perform. Although you should not exclude personal feelings and intuitions about a student, you must separate these feelings from performance. Stereotypes are judgments about how groups of people will behave based on gender, race, socio-economic status, physical appearance, or other characteristics. It is impossible to avoid stereotypes completely because of our values, beliefs, preferences, and experiences with different kinds of people. However, we *can* control the influence of these prejudices.

Stereotypes can be based on groups of people; examples include "jocks have less motivation to do well," "boys do better in math," "students from a particular neighbourhood are more likely to have discipline problems," and "children with a single parent need extra help with homework." You can also label students with words such as *shy, gifted, smart, poor, learning disabled, leader,* and *at-risk.* These labels can affect your interactions and evaluations by establishing inappropriate expectations. The nature of teacher expectations is discussed in greater detail in the next chapter.

Avoiding Bias in Assessment Tasks and Procedures

Another source of bias is in the nature of the actual assessment task—the contents and process of the test, project, problem, or other task. For example, bias is present if the assessment distorts performance because of the student's ethnicity, gender, race, or religious background. Popham (2005) has identified two major forms of assessment bias: offensiveness and unfair penalization.

Offensiveness occurs if the content of the assessment offends, upsets, distresses, angers, or otherwise creates negative affect for particular students or a subgroup of students. This negative affect makes it less likely that the students will perform as well as they otherwise might, lowering the validity of the inferences. Offensiveness occurs most often when stereotypes of particular groups are present in the assessment. Suppose a test question portrayed a minority group in low-paying, low-status jobs and white groups in high-paying, high-status jobs. Students who are members of the minority group may understandably be offended by the question, mitigating their performance. Here is an example of a biased mathematics test question that may result in offensiveness:

> Amir Mahkmoot drives a taxicab. After deductions (e.g., gas, cab rental, etc.), he receives 45 cents per kilometre for each fare. Amir drove 270 kilometres on Tuesday. How much money did he make?

Unfair penalization is bias that creates a disadvantage for a student because of content that makes it more difficult for students from some groups to perform compared to students from other groups. That is, bias is evident when an unfair advantage or disadvantage is given to one group because of gender, socio-economic status, race, language, or other characteristic. Suppose you take an aptitude test that uses rural, farm-oriented examples. The questions deal with types of cows and pigs, winter wheat, and farm equipment. If you grew up in a suburban community, would you score as well as students who grew up on a farm? Similarly, will a student whose primary language is Chinese have an equal opportunity to demonstrate oral reading skills in English as students whose primary language is English? Do test items containing sports content unfairly give boys an advantage? Here is a reading comprehension test question that is biased due to unfair penalization:

> Write a persuasive essay about the advantages of hockey as a sport. Include in your essay comparisons of hockey with other types of sports, such as soccer, football, and basketball.

Teachers don't *deliberately* produce biased assessments. They are usually unconscious and unintended. For these reasons, you can minimize bias by having others review your assessments, looking specifically for the types of bias presented here. It can also be minimized by your own sensitivity when creating the assessments. Note that assessment tasks are not necessarily biased solely on the basis of differential performance by minority groups or other groups students may be members of. Cultural differences that are reflected in vocabulary, prior experiences, skills, and values may influence the assessment. These differences are especially important in our increasingly diverse society and classrooms. Consider the following examples of how cultural background influences assessment:

- Knowledge from the immediate environment of the student (e.g., large city, ethnic neighbourhood, rural, or coastal) provides a vocabulary and an indication of the importance or relevance of assessment tasks.
- Depending on the culture, rules for sharing beliefs, discussion, taking turns, and expressing opinions differ.

- Respect and politeness may be expressed differently by students from different backgrounds (e.g., not looking into another's eyes, silence, squinting as a way to say no, looking up or down when asked a question).

- Learning style differences—which are exhibited in preferences for learning alone or in a group, for learning by listening or reading, for reflective or impulsive responses, and in the ability to think analytically or globally—influence a student's confidence and motivation to complete assessment tasks.

The influence of these differences will be minimized to the extent that you first understand them and then utilize multiple assessments to allow all students to demonstrate their progress toward the learning expectation. If an assessment technique or approach is an advantage to one type of student, another technique may be a disadvantage to that type of student. By using different types of assessments, one provides a balance to the other. Students who are unable to respond well to one type of assessment will respond well to another type. This highlights an important principle of high-quality assessment—*never rely solely on one method of assessment*. This does not mean, however, that you should arbitrarily pick different methods. Select your assessments based on what will provide the fairest indication of student achievement for *all* your students.

Accommodating Students with Exceptionalities

Another type of assessment task bias that has received a lot of attention recently is the need to accommodate the special abilities of children with exceptionalities. An assessment is biased if performance is affected by a disability or other limiting characteristic when the student actually possesses the knowledge or skill being measured. In other words, when assessing students with exceptionalities, modify the assessment task so that the limiting characteristic is not a factor in the performance. For example, students with hearing loss may need written directions to complete an assessment that you give orally to other students. Chapter 11 deals with assessing students with exceptionalities in more detail.

POSITIVE CONSEQUENCES

The nature of classroom assessments has important consequences for teaching and learning. Ask yourself these questions: How will the assessment affect student motivation? Will students be more or less likely to be meaningfully involved? Will their motivation be intrinsic or extrinsic? How will the assessment affect how and what students study? How will it affect my teaching? How much time will the assessment take away from instruction? Will the results allow me to provide students with individualized feedback? What will the parents think about my assessments? High-quality assessments have consequences that will be positive for both you and your students.

Positive Consequences for Students

The most direct consequence of assessment is that students learn and study in a way that is consistent with your assessment task. If the assessment is a multiple-choice test to determine the students' knowledge of specific facts, then students will tend to memorize information. If the assessment calls for extended essays, students tend to learn the material in larger, related chunks, and they practice recall rather than recognition when studying. Assessments that require problem solving, such as performance-based assessments, encourage students to think and apply what they learn. A positive consequence is the appropriate match between the learning expectation and the assessment task.

Assessments also have clear consequences for student motivation. Student motivation is best thought of in the context of student learning as a "process whereby goal-directed activity is instigated and sustained" (Pintrich & Schunk, 2002, p. 5). Defined in this way, motivation involves three key elements: goals, making a commitment to put forth effort to learn, and putting forth continued effort to succeed. Students are motivated when they believe that their effort will result in meaningful success. In relation to assessment, think about how these factors are influenced. Does the nature of learning expectations determine whether success is meaningful? (Yes!) Do the types of test items influence student effort in studying and trying to learn? (Yes!) Does teacher feedback affect students' conceptions of whether they can succeed? (Yes!) Does the structure of the assessment determine whether students can show their best performance? (Yes!) Table 3.7 shows the

Table 3.7 Motivational Consequences That Result from Different Assessment Practices

Motivation *Decreased* by Assessments That:	Motivation *Increased* by Assessments That:
Are irrelevant to students' lives	Are relevant to students' lives
Are summative	Are designed around student interests
Are closed-ended	Are open-ended
Use feedback to manage students	Use immediate and specific feedback
Disclose or display student performance publicly	Are aligned with learning goals set by students
Emphasize quantity rather than quality	Show how mistakes are essential to learning
Compare students to each other	Use learning goals that incorporate specific performance standards
Are artificial and abstract	Are meaningful and authentic
Use tasks that only some students can be successful with	Use tasks that are challenging but attainable
Use long-term goals	Use short-term goals
Provide little and/or inaccurate attributional feedback (why they succeeded or failed)	Provide credible attributional feedback
Emphasize end products	Emphasize progress

positive and negative effects of classroom assessment practices on motivation. Obviously, we want positive motivational consequences. It is clear that the nature of the assessments affects this motivation. If students know what will be assessed and how it will be scored, and if they believe that the assessment will be fair, they are likely to be more motivated to learn.

Motivation also increases when the assessment tasks are relevant to the students' backgrounds and goals, challenging but possible, and structured to give students individualized feedback about their performance. What good is a high score on an easy test? Authentic assessments provide more active learning, which increases motivation. Giving students multiple assessments, rather than a single assessment, lessens fear and anxiety. When students are less apprehensive, risk taking, exploration, creativity, and questioning are enhanced.

Finally, the student–teacher relationship is influenced by the nature of assessment. When teachers construct assessments carefully and provide feedback to students, the relationship is strengthened. Conversely, if students have the impression that the assessment is sloppy, not matched with course objectives, designed to trick them (like some true/false questions we have all answered!), and provides little feedback, the relationship is weakened. How quickly do you return papers or tests to students? What types of comments do you write on papers or projects? Assessment affects the way students perceive the teacher and gives them an indication of how much the teacher cares about them and what they learn.

Positive Consequences for Teachers

Like students, teachers are affected by the nature of the assessments they give their students. Just as students learn depending on the assessment, teachers tend to teach to the test. Thus, if the assessment calls for memorization of facts, the teacher tends to teach lots of facts; if the assessment requires reasoning, then the teacher structures exercises and experiences that get students to think. The question, then, is how well your assessments encourage the teaching you want and what you want your students to learn.

There is often a trade-off between instructional time and the time needed for assessment. If your assessments require considerable time for preparation, administration, and scoring, then there is less time for instruction.

A goal of high-quality assessments is to lead to better information and decision making about students. Will the assessment help you make more valid judgments, or will it make judgments about students more difficult? As a result of assessment, are you likely to label students inappropriately?

Finally, assessments may influence how you are perceived by others. Are you comfortable with school administrators and parents reviewing and critiquing your assessments? What about the views of other teachers? How do your assessments fit with what you want to be as a professional?

ALIGNMENT

One of the most important features of large-scale testing in Canada has been the effort to align tests with learning expectations in the curriculum and instructional practice. **Alignment** is the degree of agreement among these different components. Obviously, it makes sense that what is taught is approximately the same as what is tested (instructional validity). The centralized control of education in each province certainly helps increase this alignment. But "degree of agreement" and "approximately the same" are a matter of ongoing debate because there are different types or levels of alignment.

With the large-scale testing that occurs in every province, at least four different questions can be asked (see, for example, American Educational Research Association [AERA], 2003):

- Does the test's content match the curricular content (topics and skills) as described by the learning expectations?

- Do the tests and learning expectations cover a comparable "range" or breadth of knowledge, and is there an appropriate "balance" of knowledge across the expectations?

- Does the level of cognitive demand or challenge called for in the learning expectations match that required for students to do well on the assessment?

- Does the test avoid adding material that is irrelevant to the learning expectation supposedly being assessed?

The first two questions are concerned primarily with whether test items correspond to a learning expectation, and whether the number of items in different areas matches the emphasis of different areas described by the learning expectations. Cognitive demand is a judgment about the nature of the mental skill required to answer the test item. For instance, does the item require simple understanding or deep understanding? Is it primarily a function of recall or application? The cognitive level is determined by the standard; then the item is matched to that level. Of course, what is simple understanding to one teacher might be deep understanding to another teacher. That's the nature of professional judgment, so some level of agreement among your colleagues is desirable.

For the purpose of aligning your instruction and classroom assessments with provincial learning outcomes and expectations, examine the curriculum and determine the nature of the cognitive skill demanded. You should also examine sample test items if they are available, but the curriculum documents are the most important source of information. Once you identify the cognitive skills embodied in the learning expectations listed in the curriculum documents, begin judging alignment with your instruction and classroom assessments. The type of judgment you make is represented in Figure 3.7. This continuum shows that the more easily made judgment (*primitive*) is insufficient to inform you about what to teach, how much to teach, and how to assess each area. This is because the alignment is based on a cursory review of the learning expectations and assessments as a whole. *Rough* alignment is a systematic way of simply checking for the presence of

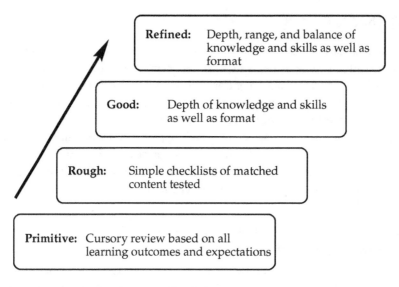

Figure 3.7 Types of Alignment Judgments

each expectation and matching assessment. *Good* alignment includes judgments about depth of knowledge and understanding. It also incorporates the item formats of provincial assessments. Ratings are more sophisticated and show the alignment by degree, rather than making a yes/ no judgment.

The *refined* approach includes matching the cognitive demand (*depth*) with the learning expectations, whether the *range* of what is covered in the curriculum is consistent with your instruction and assessment, and whether the degree of emphasis on different areas (*balance*) is appropriate. Of course, your classroom assessments must align with your specific learning objectives, theories of learning and motivation, instructional tasks given to students, assignments, questions asked, and criteria for scoring student work. Yes, this is a *lot* of alignment!

If you teach in a grade level and subject area that is assessed with a provincial test, be even more careful to address the learning expectations in the curriculum. Sample tests provide some guidance regarding the cognitive levels expected by the provincial tests. But simply tailoring your teaching and assessments to the provincial tests will not help students nearly as much as ensuring that your teaching and assessments provide a rich exploration of the curriculum. Consider the expectations of the provincial tests to be minimum expectations, and strive to help students move beyond these.

Figure 3.8 shows a series of steps that you can use to approach alignment systematically. Use simple ratings at each step so that the alignment is clear and in a format that can be shared with others. Your goal is to plan and implement instruction and classroom assessment that will document the attainment of important learning expectations listed in your provincial curriculum documents, providing more detail for these expectations as required. Finally, provide feedback to students that will promote and support their efforts to meet the standards of performance you have set for the learning expectations.

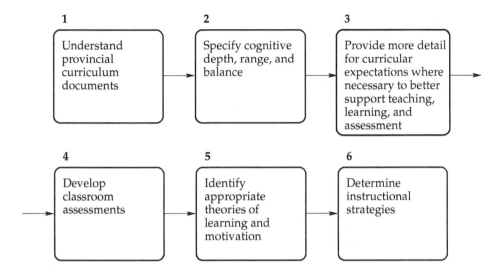

Figure 3.8 Steps in Achieving Alignment

PRACTICALITY AND EFFICIENCY

High-quality assessments are practical and efficient. It is important to balance these aspects of assessment with previously mentioned criteria. Time is a limited commodity for teachers. It may be best to use extensive performance assessments, but if these assessments take away too much from instruction, consider less time-consuming assessments. Essentially, ask yourself this question: Is the information obtained worth the resources and time required to obtain it? Other considerations include your familiarity with the method of assessment, the time required of students to complete the assessments, the complexity of administering them, the ease of scoring, the ease of interpretation, and cost. We'll consider each briefly.

Teacher Familiarity with the Method

Teachers need to know about the assessment methods they select. This includes knowledge of the strengths and limitations of the method, how to administer the assessment, how to score and properly interpret student responses, and the appropriateness of the method for given learning expectations. Teachers who use unfamiliar assessment methods risk time and resources for questionable results.

Time Required

Other things being equal, use the shortest assessment possible that provides credible results. In other words, gather only as much information as you need for the decision or other use of the results. The time required should include how long it takes to construct the assessment, how much time is needed for students to provide answers, and how long it takes to score the results. The time needed for each of these aspects of assessment is different for each method of assessment. Multiple-choice tests take a long time to prepare but a relatively short time for students to complete and for teachers to score. If you plan to use this format over and over for different groups of students, it is efficient to put in considerable time preparing the assessment, as long as you can use many of the same test items each semester or year. (Keep objective tests secure by not allowing students to keep their test; then you don't have to construct an entirely new test each time.) Essay tests, on the other hand, take less time to prepare, but a long time to score. Performance assessments are probably the most time intensive (in preparation, student response time, and scoring). For all types of assessments, reuse questions and tasks whenever possible.

Another consideration in planning time for assessment is reliability. The reliability of a test or other assessment is directly related to its length—the longer the test, the greater is its reliability. In general, assessments that take 30 or 40 minutes provide reliable results for a single score on a short unit. If separate scores are needed for subskills, more time may be needed. A general rule of thumb is that six to ten objective items are needed to provide a reliable assessment of a concept or specific skill.

Complexity of Administration

Practical and efficient assessments are easy to administer. The directions and procedures for administration are clear. Assessments that require long, complicated directions and set-up (like some performance assessments) are less efficient and may, because of student misunderstanding, have adverse effects on reliability and validity.

Ease of Scoring

Some methods of assessment, such as objective tests, are much easier to score than other methods, such as essays, papers, and oral presentations. Like other traits, scoring needs to match your method and purpose. In general, use the easiest method of scoring appropriate to the method and purpose of the assessment. Objective tests are easiest to score and contribute less scoring error to reliability. Scoring performance assessments, essays, papers, and the like is more difficult because more time is needed to ensure reliability. For these assessments, it is more practical to use rating scales and checklists rather than writing extended individualized evaluations.

Ease of Interpretation

Objective tests that report a single score are usually easiest to interpret; individualized written comments are more difficult to interpret. Many subjectively evaluated products are given a score or grade to enhance ease of interpretation. Provide sufficient information so that whatever interpretation is made is accurate. Often, grades or scores are applied too quickly, without enough thought and detailed feedback to students. This can be partially remedied by sharing a key with students and others that provides meaning to different scores or grades. Interpretation is easier if you can plan, before the assessment, how to use the results.

Cost

Because most classroom assessments are inexpensive, cost is relatively unimportant. It would certainly be unwise to use a more unreliable or invalid assessment just because it costs less. Some performance assessments are exceptions, because the cost of materials can be an important factor. Like other practical aspects, it is best to use the most economical assessment, other things being equal. But economy should be thought of in the long run, and unreliable, less expensive tests may eventually cost more in further assessment.

SUMMARY

High-quality classroom assessments provide reliable, valid, fair, and useful measures of student performance. Quality is enhanced when the assessments meet these important criteria:

- Match the method of assessment to learning expectations. Knowledge and simple understanding expectations are matched best with selected-response and brief constructed-response items, deep understanding and reasoning expectations with essays, and affective expectations with observation and student self-reports. Performance assessments are best for measuring deep understanding skills and products.

- Validity is the degree to which a score-based inference is appropriate, reasonable, and useful. Inferences are valid or invalid—not tests.

- Different types of evidence are used to establish the validity of classroom tests, the most important of which is content-related evidence.

- Whether face validity, a test blueprint, or instructional validity, the teacher's professional judgment is needed to ensure that there is adequate content-related evidence.

- Construct-related evidence is provided by theoretical, logical, and statistical analyses.

- Reliability is used to estimate the error in testing. It measures the degree of consistency when several items measure the same thing, and stability when the same measures are given across time.

- Different sources of error should be taken into consideration when interpreting test results.

- Sources of evidence for obtaining reliable scores include stability, equivalence, internal consistency, scorer or rater consistency, and decision consistency.

- Reliability is improved with increases in the spread of scores, number of items, number and heterogeneity of students, and with items that are clear and of medium difficulty.

- Assessment is fair if it is unbiased and provides students with a reasonable opportunity to demonstrate what they have learned.

- Fairness is enhanced by student knowledge of learning expectations before instruction, the opportunity to learn, the attainment of prerequisite knowledge and skills, unbiased assessment tasks and procedures, teachers who avoid stereotypes, and accommodating students with exceptionalities.

- Positive consequences for both teachers and students enhance the overall quality of assessment, particularly the effect of the assessments on student motivation and study habits. Assessments need to take into consideration the teacher's familiarity with the method, the time required, the complexity of administration, the ease of scoring and interpretation, and the cost to determine the assessment's practicality and efficiency.

SELF-INSTRUCTIONAL REVIEW EXERCISES

1. Should teachers be concerned about relatively technical features of assessments such as validity and reliability? Why or why not?

2. Match the description with the type of assessment.

   _____ **(1)** Based on verbal instructions

   _____ **(2)** Made up of questionnaires and surveys

   _____ **(3)** Selection or supply type

   _____ **(4)** Constructs unique response to demonstrate skill

   _____ **(5)** Either restricted- or extended-constructed response

   _____ **(6)** Used constantly by teachers informally

   a. Selected response

   b. Essay

   c. Performance

   d. Oral question

   e. Observation

   f. Self-assessment

3. For each of the following situations or questions, indicate which assessment method provides the best match (selected response, S; essay, E; performance, P; oral question, OR; observation, OB; and self-report, SR).

   a. Mrs. Matthews needs to check students to see if they are able to draw graphs correctly, like the example just demonstrated in class.

   b. Mr. Polonski wants to see if his students comprehend the story before moving to the next set of instructional activities.

   c. Ms. McDonald wants to find out how many spelling words her students know.

   d. Ms. Tanner wants to see how well her students can compare and contrast the Vietnam War with World War II.

   e. Mr. Johnson's objective is to enhance his students' self-efficacy and attitudes toward school.

   f. Mr. Lytle wants to know if his sailing clinic students can identify different parts of a sailboat.

4. Which of the following statements is correct, and why?

   a. Validity is impossible without strong reliability.

   b. A test can be reliable without being valid.

   c. A valid test is reliable.

5. Mr. Nelson asks the other math teachers in his high school to review his mid-term to see if the test items represent his learning expectations. Which type of evidence for validity is being used?

   a. content-related

   b. criterion-related

   c. instructional

   d. construct-related

6. The students in the following lists are rank ordered, based on their performance on two tests of the same content (highest score at the top, next highest score second, etc.) Do the results suggest a reliable assessment? Why or why not?

Test A	Test B
Germaine	Ryann
Cynthia	Robert
Ryann	Steve
Steve	Germaine
Robert	Cynthia

7. Which aspect of fairness is illustrated in each of the following assessment situations?

   a. Students complained because they were not told what to study for the test.

   b. Students studied the wrong way for the test (e.g., they memorized content).

   c. The teacher was unable to cover the last unit that was on the test.

   d. The story students read, the one they would be tested on, was about life in the Maritimes during winter. Students who had been to the Maritimes during winter showed better comprehension scores than students who had rarely even seen snow.

e. Students complained that most of what was taught was not on the test.

8. Is the following test item biased? Why or why not?

Ganesh Singh has decided to develop a family budget. He has $2000 to work with and decides to put $1000 into the mortgage, $300 into food, $200 into transportation, $300 into entertainment, $150 into utilities, and $50 into savings. What per cent of Ganesh's budget is being spent in each of the categories?

9. Why is it important for teachers to consider practicality and efficiency in selecting their assessments, as well as more technical aspects such as validity and reliability?

SUGGESTIONS FOR ACTION RESEARCH

1. Interview a teacher and ask about the types of assessments he or she uses. See if there is a match between the assessment methods and expectations consistent with Table 3.1. Also ask about validity and reliability. How does the teacher define these concepts, and how are they determined informally, if at all, by the teacher? How does the teacher account for error in testing? Finally, ask about additional criteria for making assessments fair and unbiased. Does the teacher make it clear to students what they will be tested on? Do all students have the same opportunity to do well?

2. Prepare a table of specifications for a test on this chapter. Include all the major expectation areas. Compare your table with those of other students to see how similar you are with respect to what you believe is most important to assess. Also include examples of test items.

3. Ask a group of high-, junior/middle-, or elementary-school students (depending on your interest) about what they see as fair, high-quality assessment. Ask them to generate some qualities that they believe contribute to good assessments, and then ask them specifically about each of the criteria in the chapter. Also, ask them how different kinds of assessments affect them; for example, do they study differently for essay and multiple-choice tests?

ENDNOTE

1. There are three common types of internal consistency estimates: split-half, Kuder-Richardson, and Coefficient Alpha. In the split-half method, the test items are divided into "equal" halves and each half is scored as a separate test. The two tests are then correlated. The Kuder-Richardson formulas (KR20 and KR21) are used for tests in which each item is scored dichotomously (e.g., right or wrong). You can think of KR approaches as the average of correlating the totals from all possible halves. This is the type of reliability that is calculated for teachers on most scoring software. The Coefficient Alpha is used when a scale has more than two possible responses, such as attitude surveys.

Chapter 4

Assessment *before* Instruction: Learning about Your Students

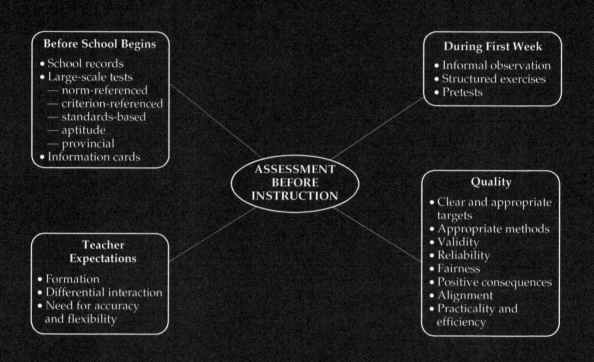

Before School Begins

- School records
- Large-scale tests
  — norm-referenced
  — criterion-referenced
  — standards-based
  — aptitude
  — provincial
- Information cards

During First Week

- Informal observation
- Structured exercises
- Pretests

ASSESSMENT BEFORE INSTRUCTION

Teacher Expectations

- Formation
- Differential interaction
- Need for accuracy and flexibility

Quality

- Clear and appropriate targets
- Appropriate methods
- Validity
- Reliability
- Fairness
- Positive consequences
- Alignment
- Practicality and efficiency

A hallmark of an effective teacher is being able to match instructional activities with the knowledge, skills, and affect that students bring to the classroom. Consequently, an important assessment process takes place before formal instruction. This occurs before the school year begins, continues for the first week or two of school, and occurs again when needed throughout the school year as new topics are introduced. You have set your general learning outcomes and expectations. You will need high-quality initial assessments before you can finalize more specific learning expectations, instructional activities, and subsequent assessments.

Important planning decisions are made before formal instruction begins. You can make these decisions thoughtfully and reflectively because there is less sense of urgency.

During this time, you can gather and process assessment information that will help you to make decisions concerning questions such as the following:

Do students have the content knowledge and intellectual skills to handle the material?

Are students likely to be interested in this content?

How can I plan for instruction that will motivate these particular students?

What are the implications of individual differences among the students?

Are some students likely to be far behind others? If so, how can I accommodate this?

Answers to these questions will allow you to base planning decisions concerning grouping, activities, content, and other instructional elements on current abilities, interests, and potential for learning. It is difficult to be responsive to students' strengths, weaknesses, and needs with appropriate individualization unless you *know* what those strengths, weaknesses, and needs are. Airasian (2005) uses the phrase "sizing-up assessment" to describe the kinds of information that teachers need to know about their students. He stresses the need to gather information about the knowledge, skills, dispositions, and more general characteristics of students so that the teacher can adequately plan instruction. Teachers must get to know not only the entire class, but also individuals. Effective instruction is not only targeted at the group; it is also tailored to each individual. Getting to know each student is a challenge for middle and junior/senior high school teachers, who may have 150 or more students each semester, especially if this kind of assessment needs to be done in the first week or so of school. In the end, however, knowing the academic strengths and weaknesses of your students, as well as their interests, attitudes, and backgrounds, will provide a foundation for designing effective instruction. Assessments made for planning purposes occur before the start of school, during the first few days or weeks, and throughout the year when you are beginning new instructional units. We consider each of these planning periods in this chapter.

BEFORE SCHOOL BEGINS: WHAT DO YOU KNOW ABOUT YOUR STUDENTS?

Before school starts, you will probably have some knowledge of the students you will be teaching. There certainly is no lack of available information. School records, standardized test scores, comments from other teachers, sibling performance, and other sources of information are readily available. The staff room may be the source of much discussion about students. Although disagreement exists about *how much* teachers should know about their students before they have them in class, you will probably know *something*. Teachers will use this information to plan instruction, but it may also influence their initial expectations about students' capabilities and may, in turn, determine how teachers interact with students. We will consider four major sources of information gathered before school begins—school records, norm-referenced standardized test scores, provincial large-scale testing results, and information cards—and we will examine how expectations may be formed from each source.

School Records

The major preclass systematic sources of information about students are school records. These records, often contained in a student's cumulative file, include report cards, written comments from other teachers, information about or from parents, inventories, results of standardized testing, attendance, health records, special placements, portfolios of student work, and other information. The specific types of information in school records depends on school policies and procedures.

Some teachers choose to examine information in these records before school begins, thinking that it is best to know as much as possible about the backgrounds of their students. Most teachers, however, do not want to know too much about their students from other sources. These teachers prefer to use their own interactions with the students as the primary pre-instruction source of information. They are wary of forming inappropriate expectations on the basis of other information.

Betty, an elementary teacher, expresses her viewpoint as follows:

> I usually look at the report cards at the beginning of the year . . . but I guess I like to form my own judgments of kids . . . and not really go by exactly what it says in here. . . . I would rather see for myself. (Davis, 1995, p. 187)

As indicated in Figure 4.1, using information in school records before meeting the students has both advantages and disadvantages. On the positive side, reviewing student

Advantages	Disadvantages
Provides additional information to help understand students	Information can be outdated
Helps teachers know students more quickly	Student changes may be overlooked
Previous accomplishments are not forgotten	Standardized test results may be misinterpreted
Provides long-range perspectives on the students	May prevent teachers from making an objective assessment
Prevents needless repetition of some assessments	First impressions may be inaccurate
Enhances grade-level and school-to-school transitions	May lead to inappropriate teacher expectations
Identifies specific areas in which teachers need to look or gather additional evidence	Teachers are unable to view students with a "clean slate"
Helps prevent inaccurate teacher expectations	Previous information may be biased, invalid, or unreliable
Allows instruction to begin more quickly	

Figure 4.1 Advantages and Disadvantages of Using School Records

records will help you get to know and understand your students more quickly. You can reinforce previous accomplishments and avoid repeating unnecessary material in class. School records can help you identify areas in which you should gather further information to more fully understand the students. Perhaps most importantly, school records can help you establish accurate and realistic expectations.

On the negative side, information in school records can be outdated or inaccurate, and recent changes in students may be overlooked. Such records may lead to inappropriate expectations, and teachers may have preconceived ideas that prevent students from changing old patterns of performance.

The advantages far outweigh the disadvantages as long as certain precautions are taken. Most of the disadvantages arise from inappropriate interpretations of the information. Because teachers need to know as much as possible about their students, information from a variety of sources provides them with a more complete picture than they are able to form on their own. For example, when grades, standardized test scores, and teacher comments point to the same conclusion, the inference you make about the student is more valid. You should also look for patterns of achievement that may occur over several years. Particularly in elementary school, prior knowledge of students will help provide smooth transitions from one grade to the next, especially when students move from one school to another.

An effective teacher should regard preclass information tentatively, combining it with his or her own observations and initial assessments of the students. Initial impressions should be treated as hypotheses that may be confirmed or disproved by subsequent assessments. Others' insights and previous student performance can augment your evaluations during the first few days of school so that instruction can begin as soon as possible. This information is helpful as long as you are able to resist forming rigid expectations.

Most teachers want to know about special student characteristics that will require instructional accommodations. It is important to know about serious physical or emotional difficulties. For example, if a student is on medication for hyperactivity, teachers need to know what the side effects are and what to do if the medication is not taken as prescribed. A student may have a physical challenge that will require certain classroom arrangements. You will also want to know if a student is receiving special services for a learning disability. It is also helpful to know of any difficult home situations that could affect student performance. At the very least, elementary teachers need to know who to contact at home, and who may be picking up or dropping off students.

Norm-Referenced Standardized Test Scores

Standardized tests have been frequently criticized as having few positive implications for teaching. Their critics argue that because of broad coverage and infrequent testing, heavy reliance on selected-response formats, encouragement to "teach to the test," cultural bias, and inappropriate ranking and comparison of students, the information from these tests is not very helpful.

Standardized test results, when used appropriately, can provide helpful information for instructional planning. The key is in understanding the scores that are reported and the limitations on how scores should be interpreted. As long as test results are not used as the *sole* criterion, scores can be used to form conclusions about the ability or prior achievement of students.

In this chapter, we consider standardized tests briefly in the context of instructional planning. Chapter 13 presents a more complete discussion of the nature of these tests and includes examples of the types of reports you are likely to see. Four different types of standardized tests may be used for classroom planning: norm-referenced achievement test batteries, aptitude tests, readiness tests, and large-scale provincial achievement tests.

Achievement Test Batteries. Norm-referenced achievement test batteries are the most common type of standardized test. They share characteristics of other types of large-scale standardized tests, including high technical quality, precise directions for administration, uniform scoring procedures, equivalent or comparable forms, and test manuals for interpretation of the scores. When standardized tests are **norm-referenced,** national samples of students have been used as the *norming* group for interpreting relative standing. Because these tests are designed to be used in different schools throughout the country, they tend to provide broad coverage of each content area to maximize potential usefulness in as many schools as possible. Thus, close inspection of the objectives and types of test items is needed to determine how well the test matches the emphasis in the provincial or local curriculum.

For a **test battery**, several individual tests are normed on the same national sample. This allows us to compare the scores of the different tests to determine students' strengths and weaknesses. Such comparisons are possible only when the tests have used the same national sample and cannot be done with different standardized tests that have different norming groups.

The results of test batteries are reported by objective or skill area. Some tests, such as the Canadian Test of Basic Skills and the Canadian Achievement Test, have *diagnostic* batteries. These batteries have more items in each area than the survey forms of the tests, which provides greater confidence when comparing achievement levels. Each battery is identified with a descriptive title, such as *reading comprehension, spelling, vocabulary, mathematics, sequencing, analogies,* and so on, but to ensure a match between what the battery purports to test and your instructional planning, examine the objectives and the type of test items that are used. (You won't be able to review items from the actual tests because they are secured.) With knowledge of the objectives and the nature of the items, particularly difficulty level, your interpretations of the scores are more accurate.

Two types of scores are reported for each student for standardized achievement tests. One type indicates how the student's performance compares to that of the norming group. The scores that indicate this relative standing are typically percentile rank, grade equivalent, or a type of standard score. We will consider the first two in this chapter and standard scores in Chapter 13. The second type of score indicates how many items a student answered correctly in each subscale or skill assessed, the per cent answered correctly, or an indication of mastery/nonmastery.

Percentile Rank.   The **percentile rank**, or *percentile score*, indicates the percentage of the *norm group* that is at or below the same raw score. In other words, the percentile score tells us the percentage of the norm group that the student outscored. The percentile score is based on the number of items answered correctly, but it does not indicate the *percentage* of items answered correctly. Thus, a student scoring at the 70th percentile did better on the test than 70 per cent of the norming group (70 per cent of the norming group scored below this student).

Because the percentile rank is calculated by comparison to the norming group, the nature and characteristics of this group determine the score. Thus, if the norming group is representative of the entire nation, a percentile score using this group will not be the same as a score determined by provincial norms. If the local community and school are stronger academically than the rest of the nation, the local norm percentile rank scores will be lower, even though the student answered the same number of items correctly.

Percentile scores are very useful in indicating relative strengths and weaknesses. If a student scores consistently higher in mathematics than in language arts, then we can conclude that the student is stronger in mathematics than language arts (at least as defined by the tests). However, this relative strength does not diagnose specific skills that should be addressed or remediated. This interpretation is dependent on the number of relevant items answered correctly, which is determined by the percentage correct and by inspecting the nature of the objectives measured by the test items.

Grade Equivalent. A grade equivalent score is commonly reported and commonly misinterpreted. There is a practical quality to expressing performance in relation to grade level, but this is easily misleading. **Grade equivalent (GE)** scores are expressed in terms of a year and month in school, assuming a 10-month school year. Thus, a 5.2 GE refers to grade 5, second month (some tests delete the decimal and report the score as 52). This means that the student's raw score on the test is the same as the median score that would be obtained by the norming group of students that is in the second month of grade 5. As with other norm-referenced measures, GEs indicate a student's standing in relation to the norming group. Consider Jack, a grade 3 student who has obtained a GE of 5.7 on his mathematics achievement test. Does this mean that Jack is achieving above grade level? Does it suggest that Jack could do as well as most other grade 5 students? Should he be promoted to grade 5? The answer to each of these questions is no. What we *can* say is that Jack has achieved about the same as students in the norming group who are in the seventh month of grade 5, if such students actually took the test. Compared to the other grade 3 students in the norming group, Jack is above average, but this does not tell us much about how he could do with grade 5 material or whether he should be in a different grade.

Aptitude Tests. Standardized **aptitude tests** measure a student's cognitive ability, potential, or capacity to learn. This ability is determined by both in-school and out-of-school experiences. Thus, aptitude tests are tied less specifically to what is taught in school than are achievement tests.

Aptitude tests provide a measure of current developed ability, not innate capacity that cannot change. This level of ability is helpful in planning instruction in two ways: knowing the general capabilities students bring to the class in different areas, and knowing the discrepancies between aptitude and achievement.

Understanding your students' general ability levels will help you design instructional experiences and group students appropriately. Suppose one class has an average aptitude score of 83 (below average) and another has a score of 120 (above average). Would you use the same teaching materials and approaches in each of these classes? Similarly, would you give the same assignments to individual students who differ widely in ability? Research in aptitude-treatment interactions suggests that student achievement is maximized when the method of instruction or learning activity matches the aptitude. For example, low-ability students may need remediation, and high-ability students would benefit most from enrichment activities. For cooperative learning, form groups that have mixed levels of aptitude.

Aptitude tests are also used for determining *expected* learning by examining any discrepancy between ability and achievement. If there is a large discrepancy and if other information is consistent, a student may be an underachiever. Some standardized test services (such as the Canadian Test of Basic Skills; see Chapter 13) provide a report that includes both aptitude and achievement test score results and presents predicted scores. This makes the determination of discrepancy easier.

Readiness Tests. Readiness tests are actually a specialized type of aptitude test. However, these tests, because of the high number of items from specific skill areas, can also be used diagnostically to determine the skills students need to improve to be successful in school. Thus, readiness tests both predict achievement and diagnose weaknesses.

Most readiness tests are used in early elementary grades and for reading. The tests help to identify particular skills and knowledge to plan instruction and to design remedial exercises. For example, the Boehm Test of Basic Concepts—Revised assesses student comprehension of the basic verbal concepts that are needed for comprehension of verbal communication (e.g., concepts such as many, smallest, and nearest). Reading readiness tests can help to identify skills that need to be mastered, such as visual discrimination of letters, auditory discrimination, recognition of letters and numbers, and following instructions. Readiness tests should not be used as the sole criterion for determining whether a child has the skills and knowledge to begin kindergarten or first grade. Scores from these tests should always be used with other information to provide a comprehensive evaluation of readiness.

Provincial Test Scores

Although all provinces have some form of large-scale achievement testing in place (Klinger, DeLuca, & Miller, 2008; Volante & Ben Jafaar, 2008), the tests are usually not truly standardized. Instead, they have standardized administration procedures. Furthermore, the extensiveness, subject matter, and grades tested by the large-scale assessments will differ. You may have access to the performances of your past and/or current students on tests such as the Ontario Secondary School Literacy Test or the Alberta Provincial Achievement Tests from the previous year. However, because most provincial testing programs in Canada were implemented for accountability and monitoring purposes (Volante & Ben Jafaar, 2008), the reported results are often general (e.g., the percentage of students in a specific class who "met or exceeded expectations") and not diagnostic in nature.

Current student scores that indicate performance at the end of the previous school year are meaningful if the interpretation takes into account several factors (see Figure 4.2). First, the scores are reported in categories or subscales, as well as for the total test, and the groupings of items refer to student performance in the corresponding domains of knowledge and skills. Although some test reports show results for each item, what is represented by the items as a group is important, not what individual items measure. The tests sample from the larger domains. Thus, you should generalize from the group of items to the standards they represent.

Second, the scores should be disaggregated, if possible, into groups of students. This allows you to specifically probe certain students to confirm what test scores suggest. In doing this, be cautious about using the average score, because this value is distorted by

1. Review the specific learning outcomes and expectations that were tested, along with sample items if possible, and know which learning outcomes and expectations are included in each subscale.
2. Determine the number of items that measure each learning outcome and expectation or set of learning outcomes and expectations; be wary of results based on just a few items.
3. Base your interpretation on how scores are verified by other data or observations.
4. Be wary of individual item scores, even if aggregated to the entire class.
5. Do not try to analyze each item for each student. What is most important is what is true for groups of students and learning outcomes and expectations that are represented by more than a few items.
6. Get some help aggregating results if a lot of paperwork or detailed item reports are distributed. Work with central office and school personnel to aggregate the data in a meaningful way.

Figure 4.2 Suggestions for Interpreting Current Students' Standards-Based Test Results from the End of the Previous Year

a few high or low scores. Third, consider possible sources of error or student motivation issues that could affect student performance. Fourth, be wary of comparing the percentage of items answered correctly for different subscales or domains. Because items differ in difficulty, such comparisons are usually unwarranted. Fifth, keep interpretations at the level of groups rather than individuals, unless there are unusually high or low scores. Finally, consider these and other assessments as barometers of student performance, which could be quite different with changes over the summer; always verify with other information.

The scores from these tests are reported by indicating how many items and/or the percentage of items that were answered correctly. The interpretation is based on what percentage correct indicates a satisfactory level of performance. This kind of interpretation is **criterion-referenced**. How students' performances compare to others is not emphasized. Some tests report whether "mastery" has been demonstrated. If pass–fail information is provided, be sure that you understand how it has been determined that a specific percentage correct of test items is reasonable. Difficult items, for instance, can make a relatively low percentage correct indicate a high level of performance.

Uses of Standardized Tests. We have mentioned the uses of different types of standardized and other large-scale tests for planning instruction before the beginning of the year and during the first week. These suggestions, and some others, are included in Figure 4.3. Remember that *results from this type of testing should never be used as the only source of information to make decisions about instruction*. Rather, use several sources of information to provide an accurate portrait of your students.

1. **Use results for identifying the level and range of student ability.** In conjunction with other information, these tests can provide objective evidence of the students' learning ability and achievement.

2. **Use differences between different subjects or skills to identify the students' relative strengths and weaknesses.** Focus instruction on improving weak areas, especially if the weak areas are consistent for a group of students. Use aptitude tests for ability, norm-referenced achievement tests to identify general strengths and weaknesses, criterion-referenced tests to identify specific strengths and weaknesses, and readiness tests to identify learning errors or deficiencies.

3. **Use results to provide an initial perspective of overall ability and achievement.** In conjunction with other information, use the results to establish realistic expectations. Do not form fatalistic expectations from low test scores or unrealistically high expectations from high test scores.

4. **Use test results to identify specific weaknesses in students that may be hindering progress.**

5. **Use results to identify discrepancies between ability and achievement.** Interpret with caution; verify with other evidence.

6. **Use results for modifying learning expectations.** Initial learning expectations can be modified by test results. If students are weak in an important area, new expectations can be established. Expectations that students have already met can be changed to the right level.

7. **Use results, with other evidence, for initial student grouping.**

8. **Use results to identify areas that need further investigation.** Standardized tests are like car temperature gauges—the scores can indicate that something is wrong, but further investigation is needed to confirm the nature of the problem. Check other records of a student's performance, speak with other teachers who have taught the student, closely observe the student's in-class performance, and ask the student to perform specific tasks that can confirm difficulties.

Figure 4.3 Suggestions for Using Standardized Tests for Instructional Planning

Information Cards

At the elementary level, teachers may keep some kind of information card or sheet that provides the students' new teachers with a summary of important information. These cards are especially helpful if they are targeted to placements in groups. For example, indicating the last reading or mathematics unit completed by a student gives the teacher a sense of where to begin instruction. Cards are a convenient way to communicate any special problems or circumstances that may be difficult to clarify in a cumulative folder. Often these cards are for teachers' eyes only and are not part of the cumulative folder. Teachers often review the cards and destroy them.

AFTER THE FIRST WEEK: NOW WHAT DO YOU KNOW ABOUT YOUR STUDENTS?

Once school has started, you will make more targeted pre-instructional assessments to learn about your students. The nature of these assessments varies considerably by grade level and general learning goals. At the elementary level, teachers are usually concerned about both academic and social dimensions; at the secondary level, teachers tend to focus on academic preparation, ability, and student interest in the subject. Teachers tend to view the information from these assessments as much more important than information gleaned from previously taken tests. The information comes mainly from two sources—informal observation and structured exercises—and is usually gathered during the first week of the year or semester.

Informal Observation

Most pre-instructional assessment consists of informal observation. During the first few days of school, teachers are constantly looking for any clues about the nature of their students. These observations are made from spontaneous student behaviour. The typical four steps involved are collecting information, interpreting the information, synthesizing the information, and naming the characteristic of the student the observation describes (Gordon, 1987).

During the first step, the teacher observes student appearance and behaviour. What type of clothes does the student wear? Is the student clean? Does the student talk with other students? What nonverbal cues are present? What kind of vocabulary does the student use? How well does the student speak? How does the student's face look? Is the student courteous? Does the student volunteer to answer questions? The process is more a matter of making careful mental notes of student actions, reactions, and interactions with other students than of looking for certain types of appearance or behaviour. Stiggins (2005) uses the term **personal communication** to describe forms of teacher–student interactions that provide pre-instructional information as well as information throughout the year. As with good physicians, experience helps effective teachers know what to attend to.

The second step is interpreting what has been observed. At this point, teachers make judgments about what the appearance or behaviour means. For example, a teacher may form the following tentative explanations:

> "David is always late to school and unprepared. I wonder if there is a situation at home that I need to know about?"

> "Ann is eager to answer almost every question with a smile. She is listening and motivated to learn and participate."

> "Yashar doesn't participate much and rarely looks directly at me when I speak to him. This may mean he has low self-esteem."

> "Ella does not interact much with the other students. Perhaps she is not well liked by them."

In each case, an interpretation is made from the observation. It is this interpretation that provides meaning.

Naturally, different teachers can observe the same behaviour and come up with different interpretations. In this sense, informal observations are *subjective*. That is, meaning is derived only by professional judgment of what is observed. Of course, observations can be *biased*, or heavily influenced by what the teacher wants to see or believe. Your own perspectives, preferences, and attitudes influence how you interpret your observations. Because each of us views the world differently, differences in interpretation can be expected. It is important to understand how your background may influence your interpretations, and you should obtain corroborating interpretations from different sources of information (e.g., another teacher or a more structured assessment).

In the third step, interpretations are synthesized into meaningful traits or characterizations of the students. This involves inductive thinking, whereby several separate interpretations are pulled together to form a tentative conclusion about the trait or characteristic (e.g., "Ryan is motivated," "Erin is from a dysfunctional home," "Josef is way behind on social skills"). At this point, be aware of the need to have a sufficient number of interpretations so that the synthesis provides an accurate description. It is also helpful to use others' interpretations to validate your own.

The fourth step is naming the trait or characteristic. This step is idiosyncratic, because your definitions of terms, such as *motivated, behind, uncooperative, easily distracted, talkative, able,* and so on, are not necessarily the same as others' definitions. Thus, how you characterize a student or class has meaning according to your definition of the trait. Furthermore, you will probably remember the more general name of the trait, which will influence subsequent interactions. That is, you are less likely to remember the specific behaviours and more likely to recall that the student was self-confident, lazy, shy, capable, and the like.

As shown in Figure 4.4, it is important to emphasize the cyclical nature of these informal observations. As you begin to make observations and interpretations, you will arrive at tentative syntheses. Then you will make further observations and interpretations to confirm or change these tentative conclusions.

Teacher's Corner

Rita Driscoll

As a language arts teacher, I always began assessment with the first day of school. The assignment for day one was to write a personal letter to me, including information about their families, past school experiences, sports, hobbies, and feelings about their interactions in school. These letters provided a wealth of information about each student that made planning instruction more effective. In reading the letters, I looked at elements of composition, spelling, vocabulary use, and focus on topic. This one assignment revealed to me not only needs for writing instruction but also personal connections that allowed me to get to know my students almost immediately. My feedback to the students was always in narrative form and usually with a personal question or two. It was the best way to quickly assess student writing and to determine a beginning point for instruction.

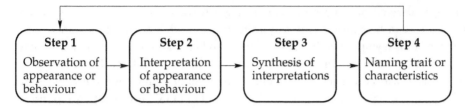

Figure 4.4 Steps in Informal Observation

Structured Exercises

A good approach to evaluating current student knowledge and skills is to design informal, structured exercises that will provide you with an opportunity to observe students in specific performance situations. These exercises are not like a formal pretest, but they are more structured than informal observation.

CASE STUDY FOR REFLECTION

Mr. Janzen has been a grade 7 teacher for five years and always feels overwhelmed for the first few weeks of each school term. He has often wondered how to better acquaint himself with his students' abilities and personality traits, which might positively affect his teaching and assessment practices. Mrs. Lai, in the classroom next door, has said that she often uses anecdotal records to help her with this identification process. Mr. Janzen wants to try this approach too. He has decided to keep notepads handy to jot down student behaviours, abilities, and insights throughout the day.

1. What are some foreseeable problems with this project that Mr. Janzen has not yet considered?

2. Should Mr. Janzen consider alternative ways to achieve this goal?

One approach is to design a class activity in which all the students participate. This could be a writing assignment, an oral presentation, or group work. For example, asking students to write about their summer vacation in class can help to identify language arts skills. Students can interview each other about their summer vacations and make short presentations to the class. You can use games to observe students' math skills. Ask students to read aloud. A common technique is to ask students to write information about themselves on cards, such as names of family members, hobbies, and interests. Any one of these demonstrations of knowledge or skills would be insufficient for instructional planning, but as you build a portrait of your students from many such observations—and combine this information with previous test scores, student records, and comments from other teachers—you will have a pretty accurate idea of your students' strengths and weaknesses by the end of the first week of school.

One aspect of successful structured exercises is to keep them *nonthreatening*. This is important for minimizing student anxiety, which may be high anyway at the beginning of the year. Obviously, it is best not to grade the exercise. In addition, arrange the conditions to be as comfortable as possible. Having a student read orally to a small group or only to you is probably less threatening than reading to the entire class. If students are able to work at their own pace, without strict time constraints, they are less likely to feel threatened. Avoid comparisons of students.

Pretests

During the first few days of school, some teachers ask students to complete a formal pretest of the content that will be covered. The pretest supposedly indicates what students know and don't know or what they can or cannot do. For several reasons, however, it is doubtful that the information from a pretest will be very helpful in planning instruction. First, at least in the fall, students have returned from vacation and probably have not thought too much about social studies, math, or other school subjects, and so their true knowledge may not be reflected on a surprise test. With some review, their knowledge would be much better. Second, it is hard to motivate students to do their best on such tests. What do they have to gain by trying hard to answer the questions? This is especially true for older students. Third, to be helpful diagnostically, the pretest would need to be fairly long and detailed, and it would be difficult to find time for such a test during the first week. Finally, presenting students with a pretest may not be the best way to start a class. Asking students what they know about something they will learn may be intimidating and create anxiety about the class (on the other hand, a pretest can communicate to students that the teacher is serious about learning). For these reasons, formal pretests are not used very often. The validity of the information is questionable, and the effect on the classroom environment and teacher–student relationships may be negative. If you use a pretest, do not grade it or average it into final grades.

Teacher's Corner

Cheri Magill, German Teacher

Pre-assessment was a very important part of my diagnosing the content knowledge of students taking German. When planning my first lessons for them I incorporated short diagnostic tests designed to let me know their degree of skill in manipulating specific sentence patterns, verb tenses, article forms, and declinations of nouns. This information, once analyzed, helped me identify what content to emphasize and what content I could safely ignore. Knowing that students could not, for example, correctly form the past tense of certain verbs was not enough. Further assessment was needed to determine exactly what stood in the way. Was it the meaning of the verb? Was it how to correctly form the participle? Was choosing and/or conjugating the correct helping verb the problem? Was word order an issue? Getting the data from student performance on these short diagnostic tests helped me assess their needs and better plan instruction at the appropriate level of difficulty for them.

To use a pretest successfully, keep it short and target it to specific knowledge and skills. Students need to be motivated to do their best work, and the teacher should make it clear to students that the purpose of a pretest is to help the teacher plan more effective instruction to help them learn more. The results may suggest the need for further diagnostic assessment.

Notice that the pretests helped Cheri assess student needs. The information was used with other assessments to plan instruction.

TEACHER EXPECTATIONS

Some teachers may not want to review student records or test scores because they want to avoid forming inappropriate expectations. This is a valid concern. The real issue, however, is not acquiring expectations or not, but forming *realistic, accurate* expectations that are flexible. **Teacher expectations** are beliefs about what students are capable of knowing or doing, and pre-instructional assessments are important in forming these beliefs. You will have expectations. They cannot be avoided. You should make sure they are as unbiased as possible and relevant to the subject matter to be taught.

Initial expectations are based on information about students before teachers meet them and during initial interactions, including attributes such as socio-economic status, previous test scores, appearance, race/ethnicity, name, language skills, and gender. These expectations influence subsequent interactions and whether pretests and structured exercises are administered to establish or confirm initial expectations. This information leads to the formation of confirmed expectations, which in turn influence student–teacher relationships and differential treatment. These interactions influence student expectations, which affect student performance. Student performance then feeds back to further confirm initial and subsequent expectations. This cycle is illustrated in Figure 4.5.

Teacher's Corner

Dodie Whitt

Pre-tests, actually, are quite essential to my planning, as they provide a great deal of information about what children in my class already know as well as what they need to know in order to gain mastery of a concept or skill. These tests, which can be as formal as a pencil–paper assessment or as informal as a series of questions administered individually, help me identify the students who already know the information about to be taught so that I can create lessons for them that challenge and enrich their learning. Pre-tests also help me identify those students who truly need direct instruction in order to learn and master certain skills. I like pre-testing my students because the information I gather from the tests enables me to create lessons that are geared toward teaching my students exactly what they need to know at their own individual level. Pretesting, as a result, also aids in differentiating curriculum.

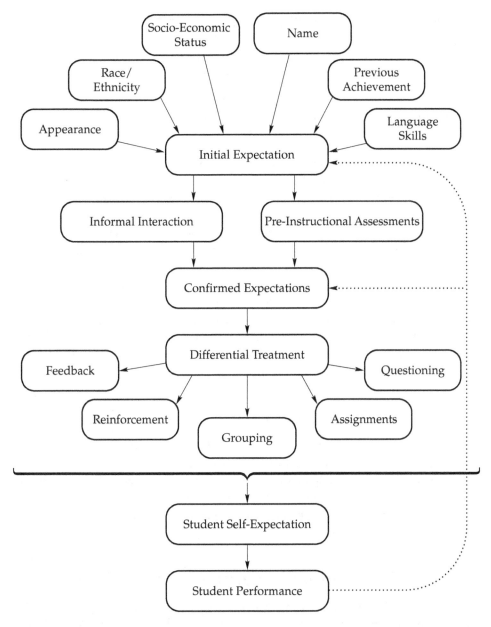

Figure 4.5 A Model of the Formation and Effect of Teacher Expectations

In their worst form, teacher expectations can be self-fulfilling and detrimental. Students become what is expected of them. According to Good and Brophy (2003), the process looks like this:

1. Early in the year, the teacher forms expectations.

2. The teacher interacts differently with the students, consistent with these expectations.

3. This treatment informs students about what they may achieve or what behaviour is appropriate for them.

4. If the teacher's treatment is consistent over time and students do not resist, it will affect students' self-concept and classroom conduct.

5. Subsequent student behaviour reinforces the teacher's initial expectations.

6. Eventually, student achievement is affected: high-expectation students will achieve at their potential; low-expectation students will achieve less than their potential.

Teachers must obtain as much information as possible about their students so that their expectations are accurate. Classroom observation and classroom performance of students are what teachers use most to form initial expectations. Standardized tests and other external sources of information are helpful because they are independent of a teacher's sometimes unconsciously biased perceptions. If anything, teachers tend to dismiss low test scores in their evaluations of students. This is a safe approach; if you are going to err, err toward more positive expectations. It is better, however, to have realistic expectations of students. This will allow you to target instruction more accurately, and it will help to provide appropriate evaluations of student performance. For example, should you give similar feedback to two students who perform the same when one student has high ability and the other low ability? Probably not. Your feedback will depend on how the performance is related to ability. If your perception of the student's ability is inaccurate, your feedback will be less helpful than it could be.

HIGH-QUALITY PRE-INSTRUCTIONAL ASSESSMENT

Teacher assessments of students before instruction form the foundation of many instructional decisions and influence the nature of subsequent interactions between the teacher and students. So it is very important to employ certain procedures and approaches to enhance the quality of these assessments. Not surprisingly, these procedures, summarized in Table 4.1, can be organized around the more general points made in Chapter 3 regarding high-quality assessments.

Clear and Appropriate Learning Expectations

Before you examine information about your students, establish or identify clear learning expectations that are not too specific. These targets should include some idea of the criteria that you will use to evaluate student learning. My suggestion is to begin with expectations for units. Consider different types of expectations as well. Once you identify the expectations, you can design pre-instructional assessments to give you information that will have a direct influence on your modification of the expectations. Perhaps the emphasis you originally intended for certain expectations needs to be changed to better meet the needs of your students. For example, suppose you have mostly reasoning and

Table 4.1 Criteria for Ensuring High-Quality Pre-Instructional Assessments

Criterion	Description
Clear and Appropriate Learning Expectations	Base pre-instructional assessments on initial learning expectations for the unit.
Appropriateness of Assessment Methods	Match the method of assessment with the learning expectation.
Validity	Strengthen the validity of your inferences by using multiple methods over time and looking for discrepancies.
Reliability	Reduce error in pre-instructional assessment by using multiple methods and giving students the benefit of the doubt.
Fairness	Avoid inappropriate perceptions of students by using procedures that reduce bias.
Positive Consequences	Consider the effect of the pre-instructional assessments. Will they promote student learning?
Alignment	Check to make sure that pre-instructional assessments align with knowledge and skills needed and those that will be taught.
Practicality and Efficiency	Use assessments that are familiar and not too time-consuming.

skill expectations before the class begins. If it appears that your class will contain a high percentage of low-ability students, you may need to rethink this emphasis. It may be more appropriate to include more knowledge expectations to provide students with the prerequisite skills they need.

Clarity in learning expectations also focuses your attention on the right areas. Otherwise, it is easy to form more general opinions that may be stereotypes. Initial impressions are strong and influence subsequent observations and decisions.

Appropriateness of Assessment Methods

Your methods of pre-instruction assessment need to match the type of information you need. Generally, the strengths of pre-instructional assessment methods are similar to those in Chapter 3. For knowledge and simple understanding expectations, examine test scores from previous years and ask knowledge questions during the first week. Assess deep understanding, reasoning, and skill expectations using aptitude test scores, informal observation, and performance on structured exercises. You can assess product expectations by looking at student work from the previous year (portfolios are good for this type of assessment). Affect expectations will depend on your informal observations of the students and their interactions with each other.

Validity

Pre-instruction assessments are valid if the inferences you make about your students are accurate. To enhance validity, use multiple assessment methods for each learning expectation and look for consistency with these results. We cannot stress enough how important it is to *never rely on a single source of information*. Be careful not to allow inferences about some learning expectations to influence inferences about other expectations. For example, you may infer that a particular student has weak writing skills. Before you conclude that the student also has weak reading skills and a poor vocabulary, gather information about each of these areas. It would be invalid to conclude that the student had poor reading skills by examining only his or her writing skills.

Look for consistency across time. Once you have formulated an initial impression, examine further student behaviour for evidence that is inconsistent with this impression. Give the student opportunities to demonstrate behaviour that is inconsistent with your impression. Given such opportunities, consistent behaviour would provide evidence for valid inferences.

The validity of your impressions will also be influenced by your general beliefs and philosophy of education, which form a lens through which your observations are filtered. For example, interpretations of knowledge and skill may be affected by whether you believe all students can succeed, or whether you believe in maximizing the learning of each student.

Reliability

Remember that reliability is concerned with how much error is present in the assessment. Multiple assessments reduce the overall error, as do longer assessments. That is, standardized test scores are more reliable than your informal observations over a day or two. Keep a proper perspective about error. Realize that any single assessment may be determined more by error than anything else, and give students the benefit of pre-instructional assessments that are borderline. Schedule a sufficient number of observations to establish a pattern of behaviour or response. Treat initial evaluations as tentative judgments that are confirmed with additional information. When in doubt, ask other teachers for their judgments.

Fairness

A fair pre-instructional assessment provides an equal opportunity to all students. This means that your interpretation of the information is not influenced by race, gender, ethnic background, disability, or other factors unrelated to what is being assessed. It is important to remain unbiased. Sometimes teachers will interpret cultural differences as deficits, forming lower expectations of students because of race or ethnicity. It is also difficult not to form expectations based on student socio-economic status. Students from poor families are often believed to know less and be less capable than students from affluent homes. Keep the focus on student performance and behaviour and suspend judgments made on the basis of cultural or economic differences.

Positive Consequences

You will want to conduct pre-instructional assessment so that the results will have positive consequences for you and your students. If the information is viewed as helpful, this attitude will facilitate positive consequences. You should feel more confident about your teaching as you plan instruction based on an assessment foundation. If you use the information to form realistic expectations, your behaviour toward the students will communicate positive, realistic messages about what they will achieve.

Alignment

To accurately determine the best instructional strategies, you must determine the extent to which pre-instructional assessments align with the knowledge and skills students need. Typically, norm-referenced standardized tests have the least amount of alignment. Provincial large-scale tests generally align well, but the test scores can be several months old and may not provide you with diagnostic information. Teacher-made assessments usually have the strongest alignment, though there may be a trade-off with technical quality. Investigate the cognitive level demanded in pre-instructional assessments, and match it with cognition needed to successfully attain learning expectations.

Practicality and Efficiency

Like all assessments, those done before instruction need to be practical and efficient. Use information that is familiar and not too time-consuming. For example, you may find that the specific skills listed on standardized test reports for your students are too numerous to consider individually. It is helpful to look for specific grades or teacher comments in cumulative files, making note of unusual or conflicting information that you will need to investigate further. During the first week, keep your assessments simple and direct, providing sufficient information but not more than you need for planning. Whatever methods and approaches you use, be as clear as possible about how you will use the information *before* you collect it. It is easy to assess with the thought that the results may be useful, but without carefully considering its specific use, information is collected but often never used.

SUMMARY

Assessment occurs before instruction, to facilitate instructional planning. Some information is available before school begins, though the most relevant information is gathered by the classroom teacher after school begins. Major points in the chapter for effective use of pre-instructional assessment include the following:

- Before school begins, information is contained in school records, standardized tests, provincial large-scale assessments, and information cards. School records contain grades, teacher comments, and other data. Teachers should carefully review this information to learn as much as possible about their students so that they can form accurate yet flexible expectations.

- Combine information in school records with teacher observations and other direct assessments.

- Different types of large-scale tests provide important information.

- Proper interpretation of scores from norm-referenced standardized tests depends on the nature of the norm group and on understanding relative standing as indicated by percentile rank and grade equivalent.

- Test batteries can indicate strengths and weaknesses.

- Criterion-referenced and standards-based tests measure performance on clearly defined skills or areas.

- Aptitude and readiness tests measure the capacity to learn.

- During the first week of school, teachers use informal observation, structured exercises, and pretests to supplement existing information.

- Pretests should be short and should not interfere with establishing a positive classroom climate.

- Informal observation consists of observing student behaviour, interpreting it, synthesizing, and naming the trait or characteristic. Nonthreatening, informal exercises are used to assess specific skills.

- Teacher expectations are teacher beliefs about what students are capable of achieving.

- Expectations are formed from many sources of information before instruction. These expectations should be realistic and avoid negative self-fulfilling prophecies.

- Eight criteria for high-quality pre-instructional assessment were presented.

SELF-INSTRUCTIONAL REVIEW EXERCISES

1. Summarize the advantages and disadvantages of using information in school records to learn about students before school starts. Do you agree that it is best to know as much as possible about your students? Why or why not?

2. What kind of information would lead a teacher to conclude that a student has clear weaknesses in a particular skill?

3. How is it possible for all school districts in a province to be above the 50th percentile on a standardized norm-referenced test?

4. Indicate whether each of the following characteristics refers to a norm-referenced (NR), criterion-referenced (CR), aptitude (A), or provincial large-scale (S) test. More than one may apply to each characteristic.

   a. reports scores as percentage of items correct

   b. shows capacity to learn

   c. reports grade equivalents

   d. reports percentile scores

   e. readiness test

5. Using Figure 4.5 as a general guide, draw a diagram that illustrates a teacher expectation that has applied to you or one that you have observed. Label each part of the diagram so you can identify each step of the expectation process.

SUGGESTIONS FOR ACTION RESEARCH

1. Ask for access to school records to review the contents. For several students, determine if the information is consistent. For example, are standardized test scores and grades consistent? Compare the composite picture of some students, as determined from a review of their records, observations of them in the classroom, and teachers' comments.

2. Interview several teachers about how they use information about their students before instruction. Ask them what data they use, and why and how they gain access to it. If they do not use specific sources of information, such as pretests, ask them why they do not. Ask them if they like to have special information about all their students, and on what they base their expectations of their students.

3. Observe some students informally in a classroom and make some judgments about their academic strengths and weaknesses. Then compare your judgments with those of the teacher or school records. Ask the teacher what you could do to make more accurate judgments.

4. Locate a standardized test manual to determine the definition of some of the knowledge and skills assessed. Through a review of the objectives and sample items, compare what the test is assessing with what is taught in a local school curriculum.

Chapter 5

Formative Assessment: Assessing and Promoting Student Progress *during* Instruction

Formative Assessment
- During instruction
- Instructional changes

Instructional Tools
- Homework
- In-class assignments
- Quizzes

Using Questions
- Purposes
- Effective questions
  — are clear
  — match with targets
  — involve entire class
  — use appropriate wait time
  — encourage appropriate responses
  — extend initial answers
  — are in sequence
  — inform the teacher

Informal Observation
- Nonverbal behaviour
  — facial expressions
  — body language
  — gestures
- Voice-related cues
- Sources of error

ASSESSING STUDENT PROGRESS

Student Self-Assessment
- Involvement in assessment
- Self-evaluation
- Reflection
- Metacognition
- Activities

Praise and Feedback
- Effective praise
  — is specific
  — is spontaneous
  — relates to standard
  — focuses on attributions
  — shows progress
- Effective feedback
  — relates performance to standards
  — relates performance to strategies
  — indicates progress
  — indicates corrective action
  — is given frequently
  — is given immediately
  — is specific and descriptive
  — focuses on errors
  — focuses on effort attributions

Based on assessments done before school and during the first week, you have set your learning expectations and planned your lessons. Now is the time for instruction. As we have seen, teaching is fast-paced and hectic. Many different tasks and events occur simultaneously, and decisions must be made quickly. Research has shown that in this complex environment, effective teachers employ a process of beginning instruction, assessing student progress, making decisions about what to do next, responding to students, and revising planned instruction as appropriate. During instruction, assessment takes place simultaneously to inform teacher decision making. Instruction and assessment are woven seamlessly together and are essentially indistinguishable.

A key element in this process is continuous monitoring by teachers to ascertain their students' reactions to instruction and their progress toward understanding the content or accomplishing the skill. Carlson, Humphrey, and Reinhardt (2003) describe the process as *continuous assessment*. How is the flow of activities? How are students responding to the activities? Are they interested and attentive? Should I speed up or slow down? Should I give more examples? Here is where good assessment is essential to effective teaching and where it drives instruction. You need to know what to look for in your students during instruction, how to interpret what you see and hear, how to respond to the students, and then how to adjust your teaching. Strickland and Strickland (1998) point out that effective teachers are "always searching for patterns, supporting students as they take risks and move forward, and watching in order to better facilitate student learning . . . and try to understand how each student is progressing" (p. 31).

FORMATIVE ASSESSMENT

Formative assessment has become a buzzword in the field of educational measurement. Based on comprehensive reviews of studies and subsequent research (Black & Wiliam, 1998, 2004; Brookhart, 2005), we know that when teachers employ effective formative assessment strategies, student achievement is enhanced for both classroom and large-scale tests.

You may begin to see the term *benchmark* used interchangeably with *formative* in the commercial testing market, but there are important differences between the two terms. **Benchmark assessments** are formal tests that often do not provide the kind of detail needed for appropriate instructional correctives. Many teachers find them restrictive, burdensome, and unnecessary. For students, such testing tends to interrupt instruction and provide minimal meaningful feedback. Benchmark assessments are best used as indicators or "early warnings" of possible student deficiencies *that require further evidence to confirm*.

The quality of benchmark assessments can vary. Some districts may develop their own benchmark assessments with little evidence of reliability and validity, and testing companies and other organizations are eager, perhaps too eager, to provide such assessments quickly (at a cost, of course!).

The goal of formative assessment is the *improvement of student motivation and learning*. To reach this goal, teachers must employ a circular, continuing process involving their evaluations of student work and behaviour, feedback to students, and instructional correctives (Figure 5.1). Thus, after teachers gather evidence of students' knowledge, understandings, and skills by monitoring students and asking questions, they interpret that evidence (evaluation) and provide appropriate specific feedback. This feedback, which either supports and extends proper understandings or targets deficiencies, is followed by activities (correctives) that build on understandings to broaden and expand learning or correct misconceptions (Guskey, 2005; Shepard, 2004). Correctives must contain new strategies and approaches, and include a message that *making errors or being wrong is a part of learning*. It isn't very effective to simply repeat an unsuccessful activity.

Rather, correctives must be qualitatively different from the initial teaching. Following student involvement with the correctives, teachers conduct additional evaluations of student learning, and the cycle is repeated.

Using students' judgments about what more is needed is particularly helpful in motivating students (Harlen, 2003). Formative assessment techniques are judged by the extent to which they are embedded within instruction and promote learning. *Assessment without the use of instructional changes is not formative.* Teachers often give quizzes each Friday, grade them, and return the tests on Monday with a grade. By itself, this is not formative assessment. Instead, it is a short assessment. Formative assessment does document student learning to some extent after instruction, but it does so in small increments as corrective instructional practices are employed.

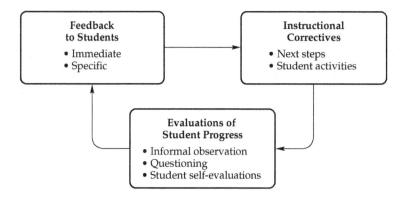

Figure 5.1 Formative Assessment Cycle

Teachers have always had to determine how well students are doing. For this role, formative assessment provides a more formal structure in which their decisions about next steps (correctives) are based on carefully gathered and interpreted evidence. This process is consistent with cognitive theories that emphasize the importance of actively constructing meaning with what is learned. As students relate new ideas and knowledge to existing understandings, formative assessment helps them see the connections and clarify meaning in small, successive steps.

The next two sections of this chapter concern how teachers can gather information from students during instruction through observation and questioning for formative assessment. As Matese (2005) points out, teachers must know how to create assessment opportunities to informally gather evidence of student learning.

INFORMAL OBSERVATION

For most teachers, no assessment activity is more pervasive than informal observation of student behaviour. These observations are made to determine such factors as the following:

- the nature of student participation in class discussion
- the interpersonal skills used in cooperative groups
- the correctness of student responses to questions
- the verbal skills demonstrated in expressing thoughts
- whether more examples are needed
- which students to call on
- the interest level of the students
- the degree of understanding demonstrated in student answers

This list could go on and on. Informal observation is unstructured in the sense that there is no set format or procedure, but it is not random. For example, effective teachers learn to observe key students in each class who show their reactions more clearly than others. Some of these students are vocal and stand out, and others are quiet leaders.

We will first consider the observation of nonverbal behaviour, and then we will look at vocal cues such as pauses and tone of voice.

Assessing Nonverbal Behaviour

Teachers rely greatly on students' body language, facial expressions, and eye contact to accurately observe and interpret their behaviour. These actions are called *nonverbal* because the message is communicated by something about students other than the content of their speech. These nonverbal cues are often more important than what is said. According to Mehrabian (1981), as much as 93 per cent of a message is communicated by nonverbal factors. Some is communicated through general appearance and behaviour such as body language, gestures, and facial expressions, and some is communicated by vocal cues that accompany what is said, such as tone of voice, inflection, pauses, and emphasis.

Nonverbal behaviours help you to assess both meaning and emotion. For instance, we rely on facial and bodily expressions to determine the intent of the message. Nonverbal cues punctuate verbal messages in much the same way that exclamation points, question marks, boldface, and italics focus the meaning of written language. Knapp (1996) suggests that this punctuation occurs in the following ways:

- *Confirming or Repeating.* When nonverbal behaviour is consistent with verbal content, the message is confirmed or repeated. For instance, when Yvonne gave the correct answer to a question, her eyes lit up (facial expression), she sat up straight in her chair and her hand was stretched up toward the ceiling (body motion), and her answer was animated and loud (voice quality). She indicated nonverbally as well as verbally that she knew the answer.

- *Denying or Confusing.* Nonverbal and verbal messages are often contradictory, suggesting denial or confusion. For example, Ms. Batiste has just asked her class if they are prepared to begin their small-group work. The students say yes, but at the same time they look down with confused expressions on their faces. The real message is that they are not ready, despite what they have said.

- *Strengthening or Emphasizing.* Nonverbal behaviour can punctuate what is said by adding emotional colour, feelings, and intensity. These emotions strengthen or emphasize the verbal message. Suppose Mr. Terrell suggests to Teresa that she take the lead in the next school play. Teresa responds by saying, "No, I wouldn't want to do that," while she shakes her head, avoids eye contact, and becomes rigid. Teresa doesn't just mean no, she means NO! If she really wanted to take the lead, her nonverbal behaviour would deny her verbal response.

- *Controlling or Regulating.* Nonverbal behaviour can be used to control others and regulate the nature of the interaction. In a cooperative learning group, you may observe that when Noah goes to ask David for some help, David controls the conversation by looking away.

Emotions and feelings are often communicated more clearly and accurately by nonverbal than by verbal cues. Not only are nonverbal cues the richest source of information on affect, but they are also the most stable and consistent. Because most nonverbal behaviour is not consciously controlled, the messages are relatively free of distortion and deception. When you consciously attend to appropriate nonverbal behaviour, it is not difficult to determine mood, mental state, attitude, self-assurance, responsiveness, confidence, interest, anger, fear, and other affective and emotional dispositions. Attending to nonverbal behaviour is especially helpful when the nonverbal and verbal messages conflict. That is, *how* students say something through their nonverbal behaviour is as important, if not more so, than *what* they say. Think about a student who answers a question but does so in a slow, low voice, while looking away. Even if the answer is correct, these nonverbal cues may tell you something important about the student's level of confidence. Your interpretation would be different for a student who looks directly at you, speaks with authority, and whose face displays excitement. In this section we look at how specific nonverbal behaviours communicate different meanings and emotions, and how teachers respond to these cues.

Facial Expressions. The face is the most important source of nonverbal information because it is the primary outlet for emotions and it rarely distorts meaning. The face projects a great variety of messages, in part because of its complex and flexible set of muscles. To know what to look for, focus on three areas: the brows and forehead; the eyes, lids, and nose; and the lower face. The upper portion of the face is more likely to indicate concern and anger (e.g., the brows are lowered and drawn together in anger). The lower area, particularly the mouth, will communicate happiness and amusement. It is fairly obvious what smiles, frowns, twisted lips, a raised chin, a clenched mouth, and other expression communicate.

Let's see how you do with a short test of facial meaning (The Facial Meaning Sensitivity Test, Leathers, 1997). Figure 5.2 shows 10 photographs of different facial expressions. Match the emotional states listed on the next page with the pictures below before looking at the correct answers.

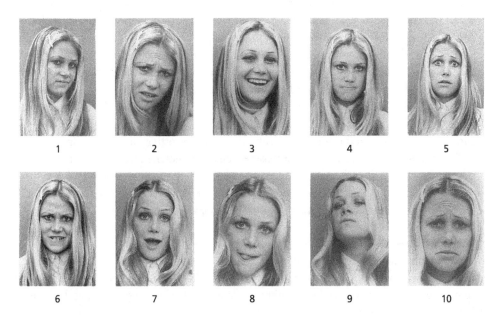

Figure 5.2 The Facial Meaning Sensitivity Test

Source: D.G. Leathers (1997), *Successful nonverbal communication: Principles and applications,* 3rd edition, p. 36. All rights reserved. Reprinted by permission of Nancy Leathers.

Facial Meaning	Photograph # (from Figure 5.2)	Facial Meaning	Photograph # (from Figure 5.2)
Disgust	_____	Contempt	_____
Happiness	_____	Surprise	_____
Interest	_____	Anger	_____
Sadness	_____	Determination	_____
Bewilderment	_____	Fear	_____

The correct choices are disgust = 1, happiness = 3, interest = 8, sadness = 10, bewilderment = 2, contempt = 9, surprise = 7, anger = 6, determination = 4, and fear = 5.

For the purposes of teaching, be especially careful to attend to facial expressions of bewilderment and interest. Teachers use these emotions extensively to gauge student understanding and motivation. Emotions similar to bewilderment are confusion, doubt, frustration, and puzzlement. Obviously, these cues suggest that the student does not understand or is not progressing. Interest conveys anticipation and excitement. These emotions are important indications of attention.

The most informative aspect of the face is the eye, and the nature of eye contact is very important. Eye contact indicates a readiness to communicate, and continued direct eye contact signifies confidence and competence. Students who use positive eye contact, who look directly at you and watch your movements, are probably attentive and interested.

Averted eyes often suggest an unwillingness to respond, a lack of confidence, or a general sense of apathy. For example, if a student looks down before responding, looks away from teachers when interacting with them, keeps eyes downcast, or looks at the ceiling, a reasonable interpretation is that the student may lack confidence, knowledge, or skills, and may have other negative emotions. When most of the students in a class start looking around the room, at each other, and out the window, they have lost interest and are not involved. The students may not understand well enough, or they may be bored. (However, in some cultures the lack of eye contact may indicate respect for an authority figure or older person, and not a lack of self-confidence or other negative feeling.)

The pupils of the eyes convey the intensity of emotion shown more generally in the face. They tend to enlarge as we become more interested in something, more emotionally aroused, and happier with positive anticipation. Pupils contract as we become less interested and experience more negative emotions, such as sadness, sorrow, and indifference.

Body Language. Like facial expressions and voice, body language, movement, and posture communicate messages. The meaning associated with different bodily cues is best understood by considering five categories of nonverbal behaviour, each of which has a different function or purpose: emblems, illustrators, affect displays, regulators, and adapters (Ekman & Friesen, 1969).

An *emblem* is a body cue that has a direct one- or two-word verbal translation. Emblems are used to consciously communicate a particular message, such as holding up your hand with your palm facing the other person (which means "wait"), putting your finger to your puckered lips ("quiet"), and waving toward yourself ("come over"). Most of these emblems are substitutes for words.

Although not much research has been done on emblems in schools, you should be aware of possible cross-cultural differences. For example, nodding your head in Canada means that you agree, but in Japan it acknowledges only that you have received the other person's message.

An *illustrator* is used to increase clarity and awareness and to augment what is being said. It reinforces the strength of the emotional message. For example, holding your fingers close together augments "small," and pointing to an object clarifies what you intend to communicate about. If a student's fist is clenched, it may indicate anger in association with what the student has verbalized.

The third type of bodily communication is the *affect display*. These cues show emotion through the position and posture of the body and certain gestures. If the student has a rigid, tense, slumped body with arms and legs crossed, the affect is negative and defensive. Students with open, relaxed bodies who lean toward the teacher and do not fidget or tap something communicate positive affect, attention, and confidence. Suppose you notice that a student is slumped in her chair and has one hand to her mouth and the other arm clenched to her body. How would you interpret this body language? The student is probably not very confident about the lesson or assignment and generally has negative emotions that will interfere with learning.

Regulators indicate the initiation, length, and termination of verbal messages. Students use these cues to inform the teacher about whether they want to initiate a response, are finished with a comment or thought, or want to continue speaking. An obvious initiation regulator is to raise the hand or index finger. Other initiation regulators include eye contact, head nodding, smiles, and raised eyebrows. When students do not want to make a comment, they may use such "turn-denying" behaviours as staring at something (especially looking down at the desk) and slumping in the chair. Students who want to continue speaking may lean toward you, use gestures to punctuate their thoughts, and display an enthusiastic, expectant face.

The final category is the *adapter*. Adapters are a rich source of information about attitudes, levels of confidence, and anxiety. They include behaviours such as picking at oneself, chewing nails, and fidgeting (these indicate nervousness, anxiety, and concern). Covering the face with one's hands indicates that a message is undesirable, painful, or unpleasant.

Gestures. Gestures are hand and arm movements that individuals use to communicate; they either supplement verbal messages or act as the sole means through which meaning is conveyed. Gestures play an important role in child development and learning. For example, young children often point to answers or use some kind of gesture to indicate understanding. Students often use gestures as part of an explanation or as an answer. Gesturing allows students to express learning in a simple and direct way, often demonstrating understanding that is not apparent through language.

By paying attention to gestures, teachers can confirm whether students have a complete or partial understanding of something. Understanding is partial when there is discord between gestures and speech. It is more complete when gestures and speech are in concordance. Some research suggests that gesture–speech mismatches indicate a readiness for learning (Roth, 2001).

Assessing Voice-Related Cues

Voice-related cues include tone of voice, loudness, intensity, pauses, silences, voice level, inflection, word spacing, emphases, and other aspects of voice that add colour to the content of what is said. The potential of vocal cues to provide information about a student's level of understanding, confidence, and emotional state is exceeded only by facial expressions.

A summary of research on the relationship between vocal cues and messages is presented in Table 5.1 (Leathers, 1997). Although this research has not been conducted with teacher/student dyads or groups, the findings do have important implications. For example, on the basis of vocal cues, you would expect students who are confident in their knowledge or skill to speak relatively loudly rather than quietly, in a high pitch, rapidly, and fluently with few pauses, "ahs," sentence changes, throat clearings, word repetitions, and incomplete sentences. Students who are unsure of their knowledge or ability to perform a skill are likely to speak quietly, in a low pitch with little variety, and slowly with many pauses and frequent throat clearings. A student who lacks confidence will speak nonfluently and with a flat voice—monotonously instead of with variety in pitch and rate. Research has also determined that people who demonstrate little variation in pitch and rate tend to be viewed as introverts, lacking assertiveness and dynamism. Voices that are clear, articulate, and confident are viewed as positive.

Be careful not to infer lack of knowledge, confidence, anxiety, or motivation *solely* on the basis of vocal cues. Like nonverbal behaviour, voice is one of many pieces of evidence that you need to consider before making an accurate assessment.

Table 5.1 Vocal Cues and Messages

Vocal Cue	Message
Loudness	*Loud*—competent, enthusiastic, forceful, self-assured, excited *Quiet*—anxious, unsure, shy, indifferent
Pitch (musical note voice produces)	*High*—excited, explosively angry, emotional *Low*—calm, sad, stunned, quietly angry, indifferent *Variety*—dynamic, extroverted
Rate	*Fast*—interested, self-assured, angry, happy, proud, confident, excited, impulsive, emotional *Slow*—uninterested, unsure, unexcited, unemotional
Quality (combination of attributes)	*Flat*—sluggish, cold, withdrawn *Nasal*—unattractive, lethargic, foolish

The challenge is observing these nonverbal and verbal cues, making appropriate interpretations, and then taking corrective action when needed. To help you with this, we have prepared a table that combines different types of nonverbal behaviours and vocal cues in relation to particular messages students send (Table 5.2).

Table 5.2 Messages Students Convey through Nonverbal Behaviour and Vocal Cues

Message	Facial Expressions	Body Language	Vocal Cues
Confident	Relaxed, direct eye contact; pupils enlarged	Erect posture; arms and legs open; chin up; hands waving; forward position in seat	Fluent; few pauses; variety in tone; loud
Nervous	Tense; brows lowered; pupils contracted	Rigid; tense; tapping; picking	Pauses; "ah" sounds; repetition; shaky; soft; fast; quiet
Angry	Brows lowered and drawn together; teeth clenched	Fidgety; hands clenched; head down	Loud or quiet; animated
Defensive	Downcast eyes; pupils contracted; eyes squinted	Arms and legs crossed; leaning away; leaning head on hands	Loud; animated
Bored	Looking around; relaxed; pupils contracted	Slumped posture; hands to face	Soft; monotone; flat
Frustrated	Brows together; eyes downcast; squinting	Tense; tapping; picking; placing fingers or hands on each side of head	Pauses; low pitch
Happy	Smiling, smirking; relaxed; brows natural; pupils enlarged	Relaxed; head nodding; leaning forward	Animated; loud; fast
Interested	Direct eye contact; brows uplifted	Leaning forward; relaxed; opening arms and legs; nodding; raising hand or finger	Higher pitch; fast
Not understanding	Frowning; biting lower lip; squinting eyes; looking away	Leaning back; arms crossed; head tilted back; hand on forehead; fidgeting; scratching chin; leaning head on hands	Slow; pauses; "ah," "um," "well" expressions; low pitch; monotone; quiet; soft

We also asked some teachers to summarize the nonverbal behaviour and vocal cues they attend to, how they interpret what they see and hear, and the action they take following their observation and interpretation. Examples of the teachers' responses include the following:

Nonverbal Behaviour	Interpretation	Action
Students start to look around the room and at each other.	Some students are not understanding; some may be bored.	Refocus students; review previous lesson; reteach lesson; regroup students.
Room quiets; students are writing in their notebooks.	Students are motivated and on-task.	Keep going—it may not last long!
Students pull materials from their desks quickly.	Students understand the assignment.	Begin monitoring individuals.
Many students wave their hands eagerly.	Students are confident of their answers.	Ask students to write answers so most will participate, or call on lower-ability students.
Students slump in chairs, look down, and avoid eye contact when questions are asked.	Students seem to be losing contact or no longer understanding.	Use a "mind capture" to refocus student attention. Cautiously, encourage students to ask questions.
Some students are sleeping in class.	This may be boredom or fatigue.	Check to see which students have jobs and how much they work.
Students squint and adjust the focus of their eyes.	This indicates a lack of understanding, frustration, or boredom.	Rephrase the question or ask the students what it is that they do not understand.

Sources of Error in Informal Observation

In a busy classroom, it's difficult to make continuous informal observations that are accurate, whether of individual students or of groups. Some of the more common errors that teachers make in their informal observations and interpretations are presented in Table 5.3. To make accurate, reliable observations, learn what to look for and listen to. Next, be aware of the types of errors that are possible and consciously monitor yourself to avoid making these errors. Finally, use a few of the following simple procedures:

■ Ask yourself if the verbal message is consistent with the nonverbal behaviour. Is this behaviour normal or unusual?

■ Plan time to make informal observations while you are not actively teaching a lesson to the entire class (e.g., during seat work, small-group work, and individual interactions).

Table 5.3 Sources of Error in Informal Observation

1. Leniency or generosity	Teachers as observers tend to be lenient or generous.
2. Primacy effects	Teacher's initial impressions have a distorting effect on later observations.
3. Recency effect	Teacher's interpretations are unduly influenced by his or her most recent observation.
4. Logical generalization errors	Teacher makes assumptions that some nonverbal behaviour generalizes to other areas (e.g., lack of confidence in math means lack of confidence in English).
5. Failure to acknowledge self	Teacher fails to take into account his or her influence on the students.
6. Unrepresentative sampling	Teacher erroneously interprets behaviours that do not accurately reflect the student or do not occur frequently enough to provide a reliable measure.
7. Observer bias	Teacher's preconceived biases and stereotypes distort the meaning of what is observed.
8. Failure to consider student perspective	Teacher fails to obtain student interpretations that would clarify the teacher's impressions.
9. Student reactions to being observed	Some students get nervous or uneasy when observed by teachers (e.g., students would behave differently if the teacher were not present).
10. Lack of consideration for the rapid speed of relevant action	Teacher may miss critical behaviours because of the speed of what occurs in the classroom.
11. Lack of consideration for the simultaneity of relevant action	Teacher may fail to account for more than one message being sent at the same time.
12. Student faking	Teacher may fail to realize that students are faking (e.g., eye contact and nodding does not always indicate engagement); as students become more sophisticated they develop strategies to make themselves appear to be on-task.

Source: Adapted from G. Evertson & J. Green (1986). Observation as inquiry and method (p. 183). In M.C. Wittrock (ed.), *Handbook of research on teaching*, 3rd ed. (pp. 162–213). New York: Gale Group. Reprinted by permission of The Gale Group.

- Keep a list of possible errors from Table 5.3 where you can refer to it easily, such as in your desk. Make a habit of referring to the list frequently.

- When possible during the school day, write down informal observations, your interpretations, and the action you took. Be sure to keep the interpretations separate from the observations. The brief, written descriptions of behaviour are essentially **anecdotal observations** or *notes*. These notes will provide accurate records of what transpired and will help make observations more accurate. In addition, you can use anecdotal records to document personal insights and student reactions that otherwise are easily forgotten or distorted (see Hill, Ruptic, & Norwick, 1998, for a more extensive discussion of anecdotal notes).

- At the end of the day, set aside a few minutes to briefly record important informal observations. Refer to your notes each week to look for patterns and trouble spots that need attention.

- If you are unsure about what a nonverbal behaviour may mean, and if the implications are serious, investigate further during an individual conference with the student. For example, if you are picking up from nonverbal behaviour that a student does not understand a procedure, even though the student's answers are correct on worksheets, ask the student directly about how he or she felt about the procedure and inquire about his or her confidence. You may discover that the student was concerned with other things at the time, and that this affect was being displayed.

- Consciously think about informal observations of behaviour in relation to student's understanding and performance of learning expectations. Those that directly relate to the expectations are most important.

- Don't be fooled by students who appear to be on-task and interested but aren't.

Remember, do not base an interpretation solely on the basis of a single nonverbal behaviour or vocal cue.

USING ORAL QUESTIONING TO ASSESS STUDENT PROGRESS

Good instruction involves much more than simply presenting information and giving students assignments to work on. Effective teaching requires constant monitoring of your students' understanding during instruction. Along with observing nonverbal behaviour, teachers rely heavily on how students answer questions during instruction to know if they understand what is presented or can perform skills. Thus, the questions teachers ask in the classroom and subsequent teacher–student interaction are essential components of effective instruction. Oral questioning, therefore, is the predominant method of assessing student progress during instruction. Most teachers ask hundreds of questions each day (Morgan & Saxton, 1991). Except for lecturing, questioning during student–teacher interactions is the most frequently used instructional strategy.

Questioning typically occurs in four formats: teacher-led reviews of content, discussions, recitations, and interactions with individual students. The review may be a fast-paced drill designed to cover specific knowledge. Discussions are used to promote student questioning and exchange ideas and opinions to clarify issues, promote thinking, generate ideas, or solve a problem. In a recitation, the teacher asks questions while presenting the material to engage students in what they are learning. Teachers question students individually to obtain information that is specific to each student. This allows teachers to individualize assessment and target suggested next steps.

Purposes of Questioning

Teachers use questions for five major purposes: to involve students in the lesson, to promote students' thinking and comprehension, to review important content, to control students, and to assess student progress. We will review the first four purposes briefly, then discuss in greater depth the use of questioning for formative assessment.

First, questions can conveniently and efficiently grab students' attention and engage them in the lesson. Questions can challenge beliefs and get students to think about the topic under discussion by creating a sense of cognitive dissonance, imbalance, or disequilibrium. McTighe and Wiggins (2005) describe "essential" questions as those that provoke and engage students in inquiry and argument about plausible responses. Second, questions can promote student reasoning and comprehension by helping them think through and verbalize their ideas. Actively thinking through answers to questions enhances student understanding. Learning is also enhanced by listening to the answers of other students; their answers may be expressed in ways that make more sense to the student than the way the teacher explains things.

Third, questions signal to students important content to be learned and provide an opportunity for students to assess their own level of understanding in these areas. The types of questions asked also indicate how students should prepare to demonstrate their understanding. For instance, asking questions that compare and contrast (e.g., How were Prime Ministers Trudeau and Chrétien similar?) will cue students that they need to learn about how these prime ministers were similar and different, not just consider characteristics of each one. If you ask simple recall questions (e.g., What three major legislative initiatives occurred during the Trudeau years?), you will tell your students that they need to memorize the names of these initiatives.

Fourth, questions are used to control student behaviour and manage the class. Questions requiring brief answers that are asked at random of different students maintain student attention. Teachers often ask a specific question of a student who is not paying attention to stop inappropriate behaviour. Conversely, questions can be used to reinforce good behaviour. Questions are also used to refocus students and to remind them of the classroom rules and procedures. Through the use of good questions, students will keep actively involved in learning, preventing opportunities for student misbehaviour.

The final purpose of questioning is to obtain information about student understanding and progress. You can accomplish this if the questions are effective and elicit helpful information. We will review characteristics of good questions and questioning skills in relation to this purpose.

Characteristics of Effective Questioning to Assess Student Progress

Your goal is to ask questions during instruction that will provide you with accurate information about what students know, understand, and can do. With this goal in mind, the following suggestions and strategies will help you.

1. State Questions Clearly and Succinctly So That the Intent of the Question Is Understood. Students understand the question if they know how they should respond. Questions are vague if there are too many possible responses or if the question is too general. With such questions, students wonder, "What does she mean?" Because they are unsure of what you intend, they are less willing to answer the question, and you are less likely to find out what they know. This is true for a single vague question and for run-on questions (those in which two or more questions are asked together). For example, if a grade 4 teacher wants to determine current student understanding of noun–verb agreement in sentences, an inappropriately vague question might be:

> What is wrong with the sentences on the board?

It would be better to ask the following:

> Read each of the three sentences on the board. In which sentence or sentences is there agreement between the noun and the verb? In which one or ones is there disagreement? How would you correct the sentence(s) in which the verb and noun do not agree?

Other questions that are too vague include the following:

> What did you think about this demonstration?
> What about the early explorers of Canada?
> Can you tell me something about what you learned?
> What do you know about the solar system?

2. Match Questions with Learning Expectations. The questions you ask should reflect your learning expectations, the degree of emphasis on different topics that will be assessed more formally in a unit test, and the difficulty of learning expectations. Ask more questions and spend more time questioning with difficult learning expectations. Doing so will give you sufficient information to make sure students understand. Ask questions in rough proportion to how you will eventually test for student learning. We have all been in classes where we spent much class time discussing something that was covered only lightly on the test. Try to avoid this.

Matching questions to learning expectations requires that the questions be phrased to elicit student responses required by those learning expectations. For this purpose, most oral questions will correspond to either knowledge or reasoning expectations. Knowledge expectations focus on remembering and understanding. Questions that assess knowledge expectations often begin with *what, who, where,* and *when.* For example, "What is the definition of *exacerbate?*" "What is the sum of 234 and 849?" "When did Jacques Cartier discover the St. Lawrence River?" "Who are Banting and Best?" These are examples of knowledge questions that require factual recall or rote memorization of dates, names, places, and definitions.

Other knowledge questions go beyond simple factual recall and assess student understanding and comprehension. Students must show that they grasp the meaning of something by answering questions that require more than rote memory, for example, "What is the major theme of this article?" "What is an example of a metaphor?" "Explain what is meant by the phrase *opposites attract?*" and "How do you find the area of a parallelogram?" More thinking is required than simple rote memory. These types of questions are effective when you want to assess more than one student in whole-group instruction because each student uses his or her own words for the answer. If there is only one way to state the correct answer, only one student can answer it correctly.

Students need more time to respond to reasoning questions. These questions are generally *divergent,* in that more than one answer can be correct or satisfactory. In a reasoning question, the teacher asks students to mentally manipulate what they know in order to analyze, synthesize, problem solve, create, and evaluate. Reasoning questions will include words or intents such as *distinguish, contrast, generalize, judge, solve, compare, interpret, relate,* and *predict.* Examples include "Relate the causes of World War I to the causes of World War II. How are they the same, and how are they different?" "What was the implication of the story for how we live our lives today?" "What would happen if these two liquids were mixed?" As you might imagine, reasoning questions are excellent for promoting student thinking and discussion, but they are relatively inefficient for assessing student progress.

An effective approach to engaging students in reasoning is to have a one-on-one conversation with the student in which questions are specific to that student. Asking students to "think out loud" when responding or when solving a problem can reveal their ability to employ appropriate thinking strategies and steps (Stiggins, 2005).

Teachers should balance knowledge with reasoning questions to keep student attention and enhance a broad range of student abilities.

3. Involve the Entire Class. Ask questions of a range of different types of students in your class, rather than allowing a few students to answer most questions. Balance is needed between those who volunteer and those who don't, high- and low-ability students, males and females, and students near and far from you. It is easy to call on the same students most of the time, so be aware of who has and who has not participated. If you are judging the progress of the class as a whole, you should obtain information from different students. However, if your better students are confused or having difficulty, chances are good that the rest of the class is as well. If slower students respond correctly, then most students are ready to move on.

You can enhance involvement by supporting everyone's responses. One technique for engaging most students is to address the question to the class as a whole, allow students time to think about a response, and then call on specific students. This encourages all the students to be responsible for an answer, not just the student whose name you call first. Teachers who restrict their questioning to a small group of students probably communicate inappropriate expectations. Also, it is most fair if all students have the opportunity to benefit from the practice of answering questions.

4. Allow Sufficient Wait Time for Student Responses. You can more accurately assess what students know if they have sufficient time to think about and then respond to each question. Students need this time to process their thoughts and formulate their answers. Research shows that some teachers have difficulty waiting more than a single second before cuing a response, calling on another student, or rephrasing a question. When teachers wait three to five seconds, the quality and quantity of student responses are enhanced. This includes an increase in the length of responses, unsolicited but appropriate responses, speculative responses, and the number of responses to reasoning questions, and a decrease in failures to respond (Good & Brophy, 2003). It follows from these findings that longer wait times will result in better assessment, but only if the questions engage students in thinking. A longer wait time for a simple recall question is not nearly as effective as a question that engages students to deepen their understanding. This point is illustrated nicely by the following teacher comments:

> Not until you analyze your own questioning do you realize how poor it can be. I found myself using questions to fill time and asking questions which required little thought from the students . . . it is important to ask questions which get them thinking about the topic and will allow them to make the next step in the learning process. Simply directing them to the "correct answer" is not useful. (Black & Wiliam, 2004, p. 26)

It may be difficult for you to wait more than a couple of seconds because the silence may seem much longer. Tell students directly that such wait time is not only expected, but also required, so that immediate responses do not take opportunities away from students who need a little more time. This will help alleviate your own insecurity about having so much silence during a lesson. Reasoning questions will naturally require more wait time than knowledge questions.

5. Give Appropriate Responses to Student Answers. Your responses to student answers will be very important for gathering valid information about student progress, because your style and approach—the climate and pattern of interaction that is established—will affect how and if students are likely to answer your questions. Each student's response should be acknowledged with some kind of meaningful, honest feedback. Feedback is part of ongoing assessment because it lets students know, and confirms for you, how much progress has been made. During a class recitation or discussion, this feedback is usually a short, simple phrase indicating correctness, such as answering, for example, "Right," "Correct," "No," or maybe nodding your head. We will consider more about feedback later in this chapter.

6. Avoid Questions Answered by a Yes or No. There are two reasons to avoid yes/no questions or other questions that involve a choice between stated alternatives. First, if there are two alternatives, such as those available when answering a yes/no or true/false question, students can guess the correct answer 50 per cent of the time. After a while, students tend to key into teacher behaviours or the way such a question is phrased to guess correctly. You will also need to ask a lot of such questions to assess student progress accurately.

Second, these types of questions do not reveal much about a student's understanding of the content. They are not very diagnostic in nature. If you want to use such questions, do so sparingly and as a warm-up to questions that are better able to assess student learning. Adding a simple "Why?" after an answer to a yes/no question will increase its diagnostic power considerably. It is better to use these types of questions with students individually rather than in groups.

7. Extend Initial Answers. Probes are specific follow-up questions. Use them to better understand how students arrived at an answer, their reasoning, and the logic of their response. Examples of probes include phrases such as the following:

- Why did you think that was the correct answer?
- How did you arrive at that conclusion?
- Explain why you think you are correct.
- Explain how you arrived at that solution.
- Give another example.
- Could you argue that that is not the best solution?

Essentially, you are asking students to extend their understanding and to think about what they have learned. When students are asked to explain their answers, their learning improves

(Black & Wiliam, 1998). Another benefit of this technique is that it shows students that thinking about what they are learning is as important as giving the right answer.

8. Avoid Tugging, Guessing, and Leading Questions. Asking these types of questions makes it difficult to obtain an accurate picture of student knowledge and reasoning. Tugging questions ask students to answer more without indicating what they should focus on. They are usually vague questions or statements that follow what the teacher judges to be an incomplete answer. For example, "Well? . . ." "And? . . ." and "So? . . ." are tugging questions. Instead, use a specific probe. For example, if the question is "Why were cities built near water?" and a student answered, "So the people could come and go more easily," a tugging question would be, "And what else?" A better probe would be, "How did coming and going affect the travel of products and food?"

Guessing questions obviously elicit guessed answers from students; for example, "How many small computer businesses are there in this country?" This type of question is useful in getting students' attention and getting them to think about a problem or area, but it is not helpful in assessing progress.

Leading questions, like rhetorical questions, are more useful for pacing a lesson than for obtaining information about student knowledge. Therefore, these types of questions ("That's right, isn't it?" or "Let's go on to the next chapter, okay?") should be avoided.

9. Avoid Asking Students What They Think They Know. It is not usually helpful to ask students directly if they know or understand something. The question might be, "Do you know how to divide fractions?" or "What do you know about Samuel de Champlain?" or "Is everyone with me?" Students may be reluctant to answer such questions in class because of possible embarrassment, and if they do answer, they often say they know and understand when they really don't. If your relationship with your students is good, asking them if they understand or know something may work well.

With older students, you can distribute a sheet at the beginning of class that lists all the subject areas you plan to teach. Ask the students to check off the subjects they know about, or to indicate how confident they are in their knowledge of a specific content area. Assure them that their answers will remain anonymous. Like oral questions, however, this strategy is generally not as good as asking direct questions that require the student to demonstrate understanding, knowledge, or skills.

10. Ask Questions in an Appropriate Sequence. Asking questions in a planned sequence will enhance the information you receive to assess student understanding. Good sequences begin with knowledge questions to determine if students know enough about the content to consider reasoning questions. For example, consider the following situation. After having her students do an Internet search on Canada's peacekeeping role in Kosovo, Mrs. Headly asks the question, "Should Canada have committed 1300 peacekeepers to Operation Kinetic?" Students give some brief opinions, but it's clear that this reasoning question is premature. She then asks some knowledge questions to determine whether students understand enough from their Internet searches to ask other reasoning questions, such as "What were the main goals of this peacekeeping mission?" "Historically, what happened in Yugoslavia to warrant Canadian and NATO involvement?" and "How did the people of Kosovo receive the Canadian soldiers?" Such questions also serve as a review for students to remind them about important aspects of the mission. Once students show that they understand the conditions and history, then divergent questions that require reasoning are appropriate.

Table 5.4 summarizes the do's and don'ts of using effective questioning to assess student progress toward meeting learning expectations.

USING HOMEWORK, IN-CLASS ASSIGNMENTS, AND QUIZZES

In addition to oral questioning and observation, you will probably use homework, in-class assignments, and quizzes as instructional tools. Student performance on these assessments and exercises is used both to check student understanding and to extend and solidify their understanding and application of knowledge and skills. These teaching strategies show how assessment and instruction are integrated.

Homework

The primary purpose of homework for most teachers is to provide extra practice in applying knowledge and skills. Homework can extend, expand, and elaborate student learning. A third purpose is to check on student learning; homework enables teachers to determine whether students, individually and as a group, are demonstrating correct performance. In this sense, teachers use homework diagnostically to determine which specific areas of knowledge and skill need further instruction. Teachers can use the information to give further assignments, group students, and provide individualized help.

Of course, there are well-known limitations of homework—most importantly, differential input and assistance from parents, siblings, and friends. Research suggests that the

Table 5.4 Do's and Don'ts of Effective Questioning

Do	Don't
State questions clearly and succinctly.	Ask yes/no questions.
Match questions with learning expectations.	Ask tugging questions.
Involve the entire class (all students).	Ask guessing questions.
Allow sufficient wait time for students to respond.	Ask leading questions.
Give appropriate responses to student answers.	Ask students what they know.
Extend initial answers.	
Sequence questions appropriately.	
Ask questions of all students, not just those you know will answer correctly.	

learning benefits to students on average are minimal (Cooper, Lindsay, Nye, & Greathouse, 1998). Because of this, homework that provides good diagnostic information should require students to complete, in their own writing, answers to constructed-response questions and assignments that show, where appropriate, work that led to their answers (e.g., with math problems). By reviewing students' work in small steps, you can provide more specific feedback and instructional correctives to help students. Simply giving correct answers and having students check their work, without any prescriptive information, is not very helpful. Students need to know why they do not understand or have not correctly applied a skill. Knowing this increases their sense of self-determination and intrinsic motivation. Directions to students about the help they can receive should be clear. Younger students should receive short assignments to avoid stress. There are also interesting issues about how homework is included in grading, which will be discussed in Chapter 12.

In-Class Assignments

Through a variety of in-class student assignments, teachers can obtain feedback about student learning from multiple perspectives, thereby increasing the validity of their inferences about what students know, understand, and can do. With seat work and other individualized activities, teachers can circulate, monitor student performance, and provide immediate, specific feedback. Although the use of worksheets is discouraged, more direct models of teaching, which are becoming more popular, often use seat work to give students practice. Seat work can be used to provide formative information as long as there is close monitoring, frequent feedback, and opportunities for students to self-assess according to the rubrics and criteria provided. To use seat work as formative assessment, the teacher must be actively involved; students should not simply be on their own. At the very least, they should be required to come to the teacher to have their work checked and to receive meaningful feedback.

Group activities are also used frequently, especially cooperative group learning. Johnson and Johnson (2004) show how observation, checklists, tests, and interviewing can be adapted to cooperative group learning for both formative and summative assessment. From a formative assessment perspective, both group and individual student learning can be monitored by keeping groups small, by ensuring ongoing teacher observation, by using random questions to check progress, by having students complete short self-assessments and/or assessments of the group as a whole, by calling out students individually to give private oral reports to the teacher, and by giving students checkpoint quizzes as they complete sequential steps in the learning process.

Quizzes

Teachers use quizzes for both formative and summative purposes. From a formative standpoint, the quiz is a structured procedure to check on student learning of specific skills, outcomes, or objectives that are part of more general goals for major units of instruction.

Often objective in nature, quizzes quickly provide the teacher with an indication of current knowledge and skills. This information is then used immediately to individualize instruction, form small groups, and provide instructional correctives that will address learning deficits and move students (as appropriate) to the next level of learning.

The influence of large-scale assessment on quizzes and summative tests has been dramatic. Some teachers now use multiple-choice items for most of their assessments, and textbook and test publishers provide multiple-choice item test banks that allow teachers to select items for "diagnosing" student knowledge and understanding. This is an entirely new development in assessment, one that will become more and more popular because it is relatively easy to draw on large banks of items electronically and give students online quizzes.

Increasingly, testing agencies are exploring methods to provide formative assessments to teachers. For example, Educational Testing Service (ETS) now has the Formative Assessment Item Bank, which includes more than 11 000 standards-based questions. Teachers can select items or can have tests formed automatically. CTB McGraw-Hill has I-know, an online system that can be accessed to use *benchmark* assessments designed to diagnose student strengths and weaknesses. Pearson Education has the Progressive Assessment Series for grades 3–8. Harcourt Assessment, Inc., has Stanford Learning First, a formative instructional assessment system for grades 3–8. While none of these companies has developed anything yet for the Canadian market, CastleRock has piloted computerized adaptive formative assessments in Alberta. What remains to be seen is whether such services can actually provide formative information in an efficient and targeted way. Research suggests that the most helpful diagnostic information is from constructed-response assessments. Here is how one teacher views these assessments:

> The assessments where students actually have to show me some work or write are most valuable for informing me about how much students know. Because it's then that you know that they understood every process. That tells you more about a student than just grading a sheet of answers. (McMillan & Workman, 1999, p. 25)

PROVIDING FEEDBACK AND PRAISE

As we already noted, an essential component of assessment is use of the information gathered. By using assessment information, teachers know how to respond to students after they demonstrate their knowledge, reasoning, skill, or performance. The teacher's response is called **feedback**—the transfer of information from the teacher to the student following an assessment. Thus, one purpose of assessment while teaching is instructional; another purpose is to provide information to make decisions about the frequency and nature of feedback to students. In one sense, feedback is also provided in the form of grades on unit tests and report cards, though normally grades offer very limited feedback. Our discussion will focus on the characteristics of effective feedback that is provided both during and after instruction. In Chapter 12, feedback in the form of grades is discussed in greater detail.

Research literature, as well as commonsense experience, has confirmed that the right kind of feedback is essential for effective teaching and learning. Corrective feedback is needed for learning and motivation, and assessment is needed to provide the feedback. The key is that the feedback must be *useful*. A simple definition of feedback is confirming the correctness of an answer or action; that is, whether it is right or wrong. We do this with most tests—tell students what they got right and what they missed; it is also the extent of the feedback many teachers give to a student's answers to oral questions—"Good," "That's right," "Close," and so on. Feedback of this nature is only part of what students need to improve their learning. Students also need to know *why* their performance was graded as it was and what *corrective procedures* will improve their performance. When feedback is presented as information that can guide the student's meaningful construction of knowledge and understanding, learning and intrinsic motivation are enhanced (Mayer, 2002).

To further illustrate the importance of effective feedback, consider the following example. Ryann, a gymnast, had a goal to earn a score of 10. After she completed a routine, the judges gave her a score of 8.5. This is analogous to a teacher giving a student a score or grade. But simply knowing the score didn't help Ryann know how to improve her score. When the judge indicated specifically why certain points were deducted, then she knew what to work on. Furthermore, if the judge or coach told Ryann how she could correct the skill, she had the corrective procedures needed. Similarly, a student who receives a grade of 70 per cent on a test knows that he or she has not done well, but unless otherwise indicated, this information alone does not tell the student what to do next. Or suppose you are just starting to learn golf. You miss the ball. Your skill level is obviously low. But knowing that is not enough. You need to get feedback about *why* you missed it. Is it because of your stance, your hand grip, the position of your head, your backswing, or some other aspect of your swing? When the teacher tells you precisely what you did wrong, what you need to correct, how you can correct it, and how you can advance, he or she has provided you with effective feedback.

Characteristics of Effective Feedback

Feedback is helpful when it has the following eight characteristics (Elawar & Corno, 1985; Kindsvatter, Wilen, & Ishler, 1996; Mayer, 2002; Wiggins, 1993, 1998):

1. relates performance to outcomes
2. relates performance to strategies
3. indicates progress
4. indicates corrective procedures
5. is given frequently and immediately

6. is specific and descriptive

7. focuses on key errors

8. focuses on effort attributions

1. Relate Performance to Outcomes. The first of these essential components is that feedback shows how the performance compares to an outcome, exemplar, or goal. As we emphasized previously, students should know the outcomes they will be judged against before learning and assessment. This information makes it much easier for you to show students how their performance compares to this outcome and for students to self-assess their work. To make this process more efficient, write outcomes on the board, show exemplars of student work, and reinforce the meaning of scores and grades. Word your feedback to refer to these outcomes; for example, "Kennedy, your paper did not include an introductory paragraph, as shown here on our exemplar" or "Your answer is partially correct but, as I said in my question, I am looking for an example of a sentence with both adjectives and adverbs." Promote student self-assessment by asking students to critique their work according to the examples that you provide.

Research shows that when the goal is specific, moderately difficult, and attainable, student motivation is enhanced (Pintrich & Schunk, 2002). For low-achieving students, you may need to set goals that provide initial success before moving to more difficult goals.

2. Relate Performance to Strategies. A particularly effective technique is to give students feedback about how well they are applying specific thinking strategies or steps. When students know that their approach to learning is correct, self-efficacy and motivation are enhanced (Pintrich & Schunk, 2002). Teachers should link successful outcomes to the strategies employed; for example, "Swana, your answer to the problem is correct. I can see that you used the right three steps in solving the problem."

3. Indicate the Progress Students Have Made. Indicate progress by placing the feedback in the context of previous and expected performance. This encourages the student and helps to define what needs to be done next; for example, "Maria, your division has improved by showing each step you have used in your work. Now you need to be more careful about subtraction."

4. Indicate Corrective Action That Students Can Take. Corrective action is pragmatic and possible. It gives students specific actions they can take to improve. For example, "You have made seven errors in the use of commas in your paper. Please refer to Chapter 3 in your text and review the rules for using commas," or, "You can improve your understanding of how to use adverbs if you work through a computer program that is available." Such feedback explains how to correct the performance. Often, you can do this most effectively by asking the student what actions he or she could take to improve. Doing this without judgment is a key to effective teaching. Judgments about the current level of achievement, especially those that compare students, are not helpful in showing students the next steps they can take to improve.

We should also point out that students who are mastering a concept or skill still need feedback to tell them what actions they should take to extend and deepen their understanding. Though not "corrective" in the sense that a deficit is addressed, such feedback keeps students on-task and teaches them the importance of diagnosing what they have learned and what else they could learn.

5. Give Feedback Frequently and Immediately if Possible. The best kind of feedback is given continually as we perform. Constant feedback is not usually possible in classrooms, except with the help of recent computer programs, but frequent and timely feedback is much better than feedback given only after the performance is completed. When Ryann does gymnastics, her coach gives her feedback on how well she is performing as she does her routine, not just after she has finished ("Straighten your legs, point your toes, lift your chin, smile"). It is more difficult for students to change what they have learned than it is for them to adjust their current behaviour or when learning something for the first time. Consequently, you will not want to have long periods of teaching and learning time without feedback. This is one reason for recommending frequent testing, even though testing alone does not ensure adequate feedback. Of course, tests should be returned promptly if you want to use the results as feedback to improve learning.

You provide more frequent, immediate feedback when you (1) develop or select activities with built-in opportunities for feedback; (2) circulate to monitor individual work, making comments to students; (3) provide exemplars and directions to students so that they can self-assess; (4) use examples of ongoing student work to show all students' mistakes and corrections; and (5) use techniques during recitation to monitor the progress of all students. You can achieve the last suggestion by having students complete practice exercises individually; then give the answer and ask for a show of hands of those answering correctly. At the elementary level, ask students to close their eyes and raise their hands if they got the answer correct or if a particular choice was correct; for example, "Close your eyes. If you think A was correct, raise your hand."

6. Give Specific and Descriptive Feedback. Be as specific and descriptive as possible when giving feedback. If the feedback is vague or general, it will not be helpful to the student; it will communicate only a sense that the performance was good or bad. If feedback is comparative rather than descriptive, there is little to gain by it. For example, saying to a student "you did better than most students in the class" is comparative, and as feedback it indicates nothing about what was correct or incorrect or how the student can improve.

A descriptive statement specifies in exact terms the nature of the performance; for example, "Your speech was delivered too quickly. It will help you to pronounce each word more slowly and to pause between each sentence," or "I really liked the way you read your story this morning. You pronounced the words very clearly and spoke enthusiastically." How often have you received feedback like "Good work," "Nice job," "Excellent," "Awkward," and "OK"? What did these vague messages mean? Feedback like this, if you can call these phrases feedback, provides very little that is helpful.

Research shows that middle and high school students find written teacher comments on assignments and papers most helpful when the comments provide constructive criticism. You should make specific, descriptive comments on errors or incorrect strategies, and you should balance this criticism with comments about progress and positive aspects of the student's work.

We emphasize two additional points about specificity. First, feedback must be individualized. The same feedback may be meaningful to one student but not helpful to another. Second, make sure that the feedback is provided in language that the student can understand and act on. Just because feedback is specific does not mean that the student can internalize the message and take steps to improve.

7. Focus Feedback on Key Errors. It is not practical to provide detailed and specific feedback to every student on homework and other assignments. You will need to make some choices about what to focus on; determine what the most significant error is or what changes will be most helpful to the student. For example, it is relatively easy to comment on misspellings and grammatical errors on student papers, but is this the most important aspect of the paper the student needs feedback about? A study of grade 6 teachers demonstrated that feedback can be improved dramatically when teachers use four questions as a guide (Elawar & Corno, 1985). The first question helps the teacher focus on significant errors; the remaining questions summarize, in a different way, the other characteristics of effective feedback:

1. What is the key error?
2. What is the probable reason the student made this error?
3. How can I guide the student to avoid this error in the future?
4. What did the student do well that I could note?

8. Focus on Effort Attributions. When students complete a learning task, they think about why they were successful or unsuccessful. These messages are called **attributions**, and it is important for teachers to help students internalize the appropriate reasons. Motivation will be enhanced if students believe they were successful because of the effort they put forth (Pintrich & Schunk, 2002). Effort attributions are helpful because they help establish positive self-efficacy that communicates an ability to do the work successfully. Hence, teachers can point out how students' specific effort was responsible for their being correct. Effort attributions are especially important for low-performing students. Too often these students develop attributions that their success is linked to external reasons (luck or teacher help), rather than to internal attributes such as effort.

Characteristics of Effective Praise

Praise is ubiquitous in the classroom. Though it can be thought of as a type of feedback to the student, teachers frequently use it to control student behaviour and for classroom management. In general, research shows that teachers use too much praise and use it inappropriately as positive reinforcement (Good & Brophy, 2003).

Like effective feedback, praise can be helpful to students if it draws attention to student progress and performance in relation to outcomes. Praise is also a good message to accompany other types of feedback, particularly when it focuses on student effort and other internal attributions so that students know that their efforts are recognized, appreciated, and connected to their performance.

Praise is most effective when it is delivered as a spontaneous but accurate message, giving the teacher's genuine reaction to student performance, and when it includes a specific description of the skill or behaviour that is commended. You should praise students simply and directly, in natural language, without gushy or dramatic words. Use a straightforward, declarative sentence. For example, say: "Good; you did a wonderful job of drawing the vase; your lines are clear and the perspective is correct," not "Incredible!" or "Wow!" Try to be specific about what you are praising, and include your recognition of the student's effort. For example, say "You did an excellent job of paraphrasing the story. It is well organized, and you have captured each of the major elements of the story. I like the way you kept at this assignment and worked hard to provide the detail you did." Call attention to progress and evidence of new skills. For instance, say, "I notice that you have learned to move sentences around with the blocking feature on your computer. Keep learning new ways to improve your computer and writing skills."

CASE STUDY FOR REFLECTION

Ms. Watson, a grade 10 French teacher at East River Collegiate, recently attended a professional development workshop. The presenter addressed the characteristics of appropriate feedback for high school students. He said that it should, among other things, be given frequently and immediately. Ms. Watson argued that her students were old enough to wait for feedback from the teacher. She said that high school student tests could be quite lengthy and that sometimes it could take her a couple of weeks to get them all graded and returned to the students. She assured the presenter that her grade 10 students never complained about her assessment practices.

Questions for Consideration

1. What advice could you give Ms. Watson to convince her that her assessment practice is not in the best interest of her students?

2. Do younger elementary students need more feedback than older students?

Try to use as many different phrases as you can when praising. If you say the same thing over and over again, a student may perceive praise as insincere and think that little serious attention is being paid to the performance. This is especially true if the phrase is a vague generality such as "Good" or "Nice job." Keep your verbal praise consistent with your nonverbal behaviour. Students quickly and accurately pick up teachers' nonverbal messages. If the performance really is good and the student demonstrates progress, give praise with a smile, using a voice tone and inflection that communicates warmth and sincerity.

Additional useful guidelines for effective praise are given in Table 5.5.

Table 5.5 Do's and Don'ts of Effective Praise

Do	Don't
Focus on specific accomplishments.	Focus on general or global achievement.
Attribute success to effort and ability.	Attribute success to luck or others' help.
Praise spontaneously.	Praise predictably.
Refer to prior achievement.	Ignore prior achievement.
Individualize and use variety.	Give the same praise to all students.
Give praise immediately.	Give praise much later.
Praise correct strategies leading to success.	Ignore strategies and focus only on outcomes.
Praise accurately with credibility.	Praise for undeserving performance.
Praise privately.	Praise publicly.
Focus on progress.	Focus solely on current performance.

Student Self-Assessment

One of the most effective ways teachers can integrate assessment with instruction in a formative manner is to use student self-assessment continually, on a daily basis. The purpose of self-assessment is to involve students deeply in evaluating their work so that immediate feedback can be incorporated and used to improve learning. The emphasis is on progress and mastery of knowledge and understanding, which increases confidence and motivation. Students learn to use assessment information to set performance goals, to make decisions about how to improve, to describe quality work, to communicate their progress toward meeting learning expectations, and to develop metacognitive skills (Chappuis & Stiggins, 2002).

A good example of work showing how student self-assessment can improve learning is reported by Frederikson and White (2004). In their work, students use a process the researchers called *reflective assessment*. The purpose of reflective assessment is to develop students' metacognitive science inquiry knowledge. Students were taught to evaluate their work according to criteria representing "higher-level" cognitive skills, such as reasoning, being inventive, and being systematic. Students evaluated the scientific research they had conducted using these criteria on a five-point scale. They also wrote justifications for their ratings. Based on this approach, experiments comparing students using reflective assessment to a control group showed that reflective assessment was effective in developing the students' thinking skills and in providing higher-quality products.

A key element in self-assessment is the development of students' reflective habits and skills. To accomplish this, you will need a clear idea of what the habits and skills are and specific instruction in these dispositions. Be very clear to students about your expectations that they monitor their work and thinking and be reflective about their work, describing what you expect them to do in terms they can understand. Examples that illustrate the dispositions are helpful. This may need to be very simple. For example, students can be introduced to self-assessment by asking them to say whether answers to questions are correct or incorrect, then answering: Why is the answer incorrect? What tells you specifically that it is incorrect? What can be done to obtain a correct answer? As students respond to these questions, focus on whether their answers reflect a willingness to apply what they know; simply showing this kind of engagement needs to be recognized and rewarded.

At a more sophisticated level, self-assessment includes the ability to monitor and evaluate thinking skills and strategies. This aspect of metacognition develops students' abilities to form internal questions about their learning and performance, to make decisions about what other learning is needed, and to be aware if they are not making appropriate progress with projected learning plans. The power of becoming a self-directed learner is evident in motivation, engagement, and a positive attitude toward learning. These dispositions provide a set of skills and habits that will serve students in many situations. Figures 5.3 and 5.4 illustrate rubrics that can be used periodically to remind students about the metacognitive skills they should be using.

The goal of self-assessment is to empower students so that they can guide their own learning and internalize the criteria for judging success. This occurs when students understand the criteria to evaluate their progress toward attaining specific achievement expectations as they learn, and know what further learning is needed to reach the expectations. Students give themselves meaningful formative feedback during instruction. This process is individualized for each student, allowing them to obtain specific information, rather than relying on general evaluative feedback for the class as a whole. Assessment is integrated with learning and instruction, and when students judge their own performance, the responsibility for learning lies more with them than with the teacher.

There are many kinds of self-assessment activities. Some examples are summarized, and activities are listed by when they occur—either before, during, or after instruction (Chappuis & Stiggins, 2002; Costa & Kallick, 2004; Stiggins, 2005).

Before **instruction, students**

- review the table of specifications with the teacher to discuss what it means
- examine samples of student performance in the past to show how criteria can be used to evaluate the samples with reference to the learning goals
- suggest how samples of student performance could be improved to meet the targeted performance
- share scoring criteria with exemplars of student work illustrating different levels of performance
- analyze examples of student work using the scoring criteria
- develop a table of specifications
- develop assessments and scoring criteria

Self-Monitoring, Self-Modifying, and Self-Managing				
Criteria	4	3	2	1
Sets goals for work.	Independently sets work goals that are realistic and appropriate to the task at hand.	Requires reminders to set work goals. Goals are realistic and appropriate to the task at hand.	Requires reminders. Sets work goals that include some unrealistic expectations for the task at hand.	Requires reminders. Sets minimal goals that indicate minimal expectations for the task at hand.
Monitors progress toward goals.	Independently revises and adjusts time-management plans throughout the work process.	Requires reminders to make adjustments to the work process.	Requires continual reminders to maintain a well-balanced work process.	Requires frequent reminders and shows evidence of poor time management.
Monitors for clarity and understanding.	Independently revises work for depth of meaning. Solicits outside readers to confirm clarity of communication.	Requires suggestion to revise work. Responds to suggestions for outside reader to confirm clarity of communication.	Requires continual reminders to revise work and check for understanding.	Requires frequent reminders and resists revisions and feedback for clarity and meaning.
Monitors for accuracy.	Independently checks for accuracy.	Requires suggestion to check for accuracy.	Requires continual reminders to check for accuracy.	Requires frequent reminders and resists checking for accuracy.

Figure 5.3 Rubric for Metacognition

Source: A.L. Costa & B. Kallick (2004). *Assessment strategies for self-directed learning.* Thousand Oaks, CA: Corwin Press.

■ develop practice test items

■ match test items to the table of specifications

■ transform criteria into checklists and other methods of keeping track of progress

During **instruction, students**

■ keep track of the match between what is covered and target criteria

■ keep a log of growth toward meeting the expectation

Metacognitive Skill	I *Rarely* Do This	I Do This *Some* of the Time	I Do This *Most* of the Time	I *Always* Do This
I make sure I know the criteria for judging my performance before I begin.				
I am willing to share with others and the teacher when I don't understand something.				
I learn from my mistakes.				
I strive for more learning.				
I check my work for mistakes and completeness.				
I know how to evaluate the work of other students.				
I think about what I need to do to perform better.				

Figure 5.4 Checklist for Metacognitive Skills

- signal the teacher when milestones are accomplished
- evaluate their own and others' work at the end of each day, and show progress toward meeting the expectation
- make predictions about how well they will perform in the summative assessment
- ask questions that encourage self-evaluation (e.g., How does your work compare to the exemplars? Have you met the expectation completely? What additional learning is needed? What can you do to improve your learning? Are you sure that is correct? How do you know? What areas are you having trouble learning? What rating do you

deserve? Why? How much more time will you need to reach this expectation? What are some ways you can learn to reach the expectation? What do you need to work on?)

- rate each other during discussions
- predict how well they will perform and the areas in which they will need further learning
- identify expectations that have been difficult to learn
- self-evaluate understanding every 15 to 20 minutes
- engage in peer tutoring
- maintain learning portfolios
- check work in progress
- list the steps needed to learn the material

After **instruction, students**

- design practice tests
- evaluate the quality of practice test items
- participate in scoring the assessments
- make suggestions about how to improve the assessment
- construct test items and justify how they will measure student performance in relation to learning expectations
- evaluate their own work and/or others' work according to provided criteria
- rate themselves and others
- interview each other to judge performance
- conduct student-led parent–teacher conferences
- provide their own explanations for grades they have received

Although you won't be able to use all these suggestions, you will need to find and be comfortable using activities that will use and promote student self-assessment. It's largely a matter of the commitment you make to self-assessment, and whether it's something that you are aware of when planning and carrying out instruction and end-of-instruction assessments.

Student self-assessment is not without limitations. Perhaps the biggest challenge is to get students used to doing it. This will take time, because most students are accustomed to receiving only teacher feedback and appraisal. Some students will self-assess better than others; these students will require some individual attention from the teacher. It may also be so time-consuming to have students involved in self-assessment that valuable instructional time is lost.

You should provide students with worksheets, checklists, sentence completion, rating scales, and other prepared material to give structure to self-assessment. Especially for younger students, concepts such as self-assessment, self-monitoring, and self-rating are abstract and difficult to comprehend. Figures 5.5 and 5.6 show examples of the kinds of forms you can prepare and use with your students.

Self-Assessment for Essay Question/Assignment

Student Name: _____

Date: _____

Directions: Check (X) appropriate criteria.

Pre-Writing State:

- Have I read the question carefully? _____
- Did I highlight the key words or phrases? _____
- Did I construct an outline that includes the key words and the main ideas? _____

The Essay

A. Introduction

- Did I make sure the topic of my essay is included in the introductory paragraph? _____
- Did I say what my point of view or theme was in a clear manner? _____

B. Body of Essay

- Does each of my paragraphs link back to my introduction? _____
- Is each of my ideas or details in the introduction followed up on in the body of my essay? _____
- Do I have a enough proof to support my reasoning? _____

C. Conclusion

- Do I have a concluding paragraph that supports what I have already stated? _____
- Have I been careful to avoid putting in new data that I have not already reported? _____

Post-Writing State:

- Did I read over my final copy to look for possible changes and improvements of such things as spelling and sentence structure? _____

Figure 5.5 Student Self-Assessment for Essay Question

Source: A. Ryan (1991). *Student evaluation: A teacher handbook.* Saskatchewan Education, www.sasked.gov.sk.ca/docs/policy/studeval/index.html.

Teacher's Corner

Michelle Prytula

Through our professional learning communities, we created an exemplar wall for our students' writing goals. This was needed so that all teachers had a consistent system of assessment across all grades, based on curriculum learning outcomes. Although it was initially created so that teachers could consistently measure student progress from week to week, month to month, and year to year, it quickly became an excellent tool for self-assessment. Teachers posted the writing exemplars for all levels of writing at their different grade levels, students compared their work with the exemplars, and students discussed similarities and discrepancies with their teachers. This provided an invaluable, explicit, and motivating tool for students, as they knew exactly where they needed to go, and, with their teacher, were able to build their skills to get there.

Reading Progress Report

Student Name: _____

Teacher Name: _____

Date: _____

I am able to do the following:

	Yes, Let's Go On	Not Quite Yet	Not Yet
Explain the author's purpose.			
Pick out fact from fantasy.			
Describe how the setting is important to the story.			
Describe how the language used is important to the story.			
Pick out the main characters of the story.			

Figure 5.6 Self-Assessment Rating Form for Reading

SUMMARY

This chapter focused on what you can do to improve instruction by obtaining appropriate information from students as they learn. Key points in the chapter include the following:

- Assessing student progress consists of a teacher monitoring students and their academic performances to inform instructional decision making and the nature of feedback given to students.

- Formative assessment provides ongoing feedback from students to teachers and from teachers to students; summative assessment measures student learning at the end of a unit of instruction.

- Informal observation includes the teacher "reading" nonverbal behaviour such as facial expressions, eye contact, body language, and vocal cues. These behaviours indicate student emotions, dispositions, and attitudes.

- Emotion is communicated best through facial expression. Eye contact is key to assessing attentiveness, confidence, and interest.

- Body language includes gestures, emblems, illustrators, affect displays, regulators, adapters, body movement, and posture.

- Voice-related cues such as pitch, loudness, rate, and pauses indicate confidence and emotions.

- Errors in informal observation are often associated with when the observations are made, sampling of student behaviour, and teacher bias.

- Teachers use oral questioning to involve students, promote thinking, review, control students, and assess student progress. Effective questions are clear, matched with learning expectations, involve the entire class, and allow sufficient wait time. Avoid yes/no, tugging, guessing, and leading questions, and keep questions in the proper sequence.

■ Homework, in-class assignments, and quizzes can be used effectively for formative assessment as long as they are sufficiently specific, targeted, and diagnostic.

■ Effective feedback relates performance to outcomes, progress, and corrective procedures. It is given frequently and immediately, and it focuses specifically and descriptively on key errors.

■ Effective praise is sincere, spontaneous, natural, accurate, varied, and straightforward. It focuses on progress, internal attributions, specific behaviours, and corrective actions.

■ Student self-assessment can be used to help students understand learning expectations, evaluate their own work, monitor progress, and know what needs to be done to improve their learning.

SELF-INSTRUCTIONAL REVIEW EXERCISES

1. To sharpen your interpretation of facial expressions, match the pictures shown below to the 10 emotions listed on page 118.

2. Identify each of the following examples of body language as an emblem (E), illustrator (I), affect display (AD), regulator (R), or adapter (A).

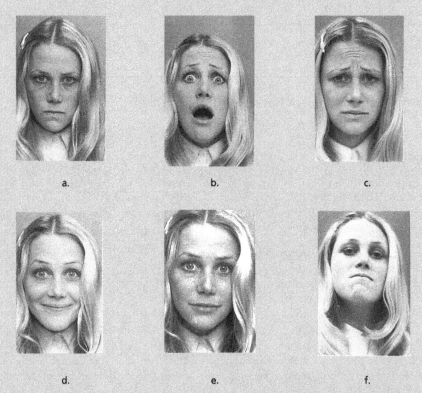

a.   b.   c.

d.   e.   f.

Source: D. G. Leathers (1997). *Successful nonverbal communication: Principles and applications* (3rd ed.) (pp. 38–39.). New York: Macmillan. Reprinted by permission of Nancy Leathers.

a. A student leans toward you and raises both hands immediately after you ask a question.

b. A student points to the pencil sharpener as if to ask, "May I sharpen my pencil?"

c. It seems that Jason is always chewing on the end of his pencil.

d. You notice that Julie is picking at her nail polish.

e. Cally is sitting upright in her chair, arms on desk, chin up, with an expectant expression on her face.

f. Sam uses his hands to show how large the fish was.

3. Match the messages most likely to be conveyed with the descriptions provided. Each message may be used once, not at all, or more than once.

_____ **(1)** Pauses when speaking; eyes downcast

_____ **(2)** Eyebrows uplifted; speaks fast; raises hand

_____ **(3)** Looks around room; slumped in chair with head resting in one hand

_____ **(4)** Direct eye contact; speaks clearly with few pauses; uses variety in tone

_____ **(5)** Enlarged pupils; chin up; arms open

_____ **(6)** Taps pencil; rigid body; pupils contracted

_____ **(7)** Loud; eyebrows lowered; hands make fists

_____ **(8)** Arms and legs crossed; leans away

a. Confident

b. Nervous

c. Angry

d. Defensive

e. Bored

f. Frustrated

g. Happy

h. Interested

4. Mr. Ozomoto observed Trent carefully over the past few days because he was concerned that Trent would revert to his old pattern of cheating by looking at others' papers. What observation error was Mr. Ozomoto most susceptible to, and why?

5. Mrs. Rafferty saw Renée staring out the window, obviously not concentrating on her work. Because Renée is a good student and this is not very typical of her, Mrs. Rafferty ignored the behaviour. What type of observation error was Mrs. Rafferty careful *not* to make in this situation? What error is possible in her interpretation?

6. Why is it important to match the type of question you ask students in class with your learning expectations?

7. How would a teacher preface a question to make sure students take sufficient time to think about the answer before responding?

8. What type of question—convergent or divergent—would best determine whether students know how to find the area of a rectangle?

9. What are the do's and don'ts for effective use of homework, in-class assignments, and quizzes as formative assessments?

10. Evaluate each of the following forms of feedback on the basis of the eight characteristics in the chapter.

a. "Lanette, that was a great job you did yesterday!"

b. "Jeff, your writing is improving. Your *b*s are much better because you are making a straighter line and not a loop."

c. "Andrew, you have a good report. Your grammar is excellent, although you have some problems with sentence structure. The conclusion is incomplete. Work harder to provide more detail."

11. Indicate whether each of the following is characteristic of effective praise (EP) or ineffective praise (IP). If ineffective, indicate why.

　　a. "Keira, you did the best in the class!"

　　b. "Jon, I can see by your work that you are really good in math."

　　c. "This shows that you did the report well because you worked hard and because you are a good writer."

　　d. "Good work. This time you doubled the length and width before adding them to find the perimeter of the rectangle."

　　e. "You typed 35 words a minute with seven mistakes. This was among the best in the class."

12. What are some strengths and limitations of using student self-assessment as a means of providing formative information?

SUGGESTIONS FOR ACTION RESEARCH

1. While in a classroom, informally observe students' nonverbal behaviour. It would be best if another observer could also observe in the class so that you could compare notes. Take a sheet of paper and draw a line down the middle. On the left-hand side, record a description of the nonverbal behaviour—such as a facial expression, body language, or vocal cue—and on the right side, summarize your interpretation of each one. It would be interesting to check these out with the teacher for accuracy.

2. Ask a teacher about the kinds of questions he or she asks and what kinds of student responses are typical. Compare the teacher's comments to the suggestions for effective questioning presented in Table 5.4. If possible, observe the teacher and record examples of effective and ineffective questioning.

3. Ask a group of students about the kind of feedback they get from teachers. Ask questions about how the feedback affects them.

4. Observe how teachers in two or three different classrooms use praise. What kind of praise is given by each teacher? What is the effect of the praise on the students? How could the praise you observe be improved?

5. Ask a group of students about self-assessment. What do they think about the idea? Do they think it would motivate them? Give them some specific examples of student self-assessment. Would they be interested in doing them? What do the students see as strengths and weaknesses? Do they think they have the skills to do self-assessment?

Chapter 6

Objectively Scored Assessments of Knowledge and Simple Understanding

Completion, Short-Answer, and Selected-Response Items

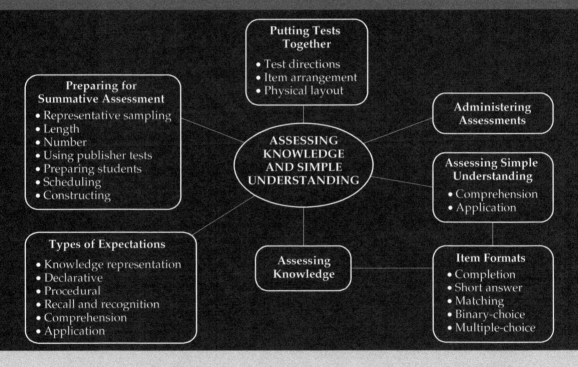

Putting Tests Together
- Test directions
- Item arrangement
- Physical layout

Preparing for Summative Assessment
- Representative sampling
- Length
- Number
- Using publisher tests
- Preparing students
- Scheduling
- Constructing

Administering Assessments

Assessing Simple Understanding
- Comprehension
- Application

ASSESSING KNOWLEDGE AND SIMPLE UNDERSTANDING

Types of Expectations
- Knowledge representation
- Declarative
- Procedural
- Recall and recognition
- Comprehension
- Application

Assessing Knowledge

Item Formats
- Completion
- Short answer
- Matching
- Binary-choice
- Multiple-choice

You have taught your students using assessment to inform your instructional decision making. Now you need to see how much your students have really learned and whether there are patterns of errors that require additional instruction. It's time for the unit, chapter, or semester test or quiz. These are **summative assessments** that all of us have had to take in order to demonstrate our knowledge about specified subject matter, or to exhibit acquired skills. Results of these assessments have important consequences for students because they affect grades, placement in special classes or groups, and conferring of honours.

In this chapter and the next three, we will see how different learning expectations can be conceptualized and how appropriate assessment methods are used to measure each type of learning. The logic here is that *the nature of the learning expectation is what should influence which assessment method is used*. That is why chapter titles refer to type of expectation as well as type of assessment. As we pointed out in Chapter 3 (Table 3.1), some assessment methods measure certain expectations better than others. Your job is to first refine your learning expectations, select the most appropriate type of assessment, prepare the assessment so that it will meet the criteria of high quality, administer it, and then score and interpret the results.

Knowledge and understanding learning expectations are the ones most commonly assessed in summative tests. As you can probably confirm from your own experience, most tests require students to remember facts, definitions, concepts, places, and so on, usually by either recall or recognition. Some tests go beyond simple memorization and assess understanding. In this chapter, we examine different types of knowledge and simple understanding expectations and the assessment methods that do the best job of measuring them. The following chapters will examine reasoning, skills and products, and affect expectations, which are best measured with different assessment methods. We will begin, though, with some important considerations for preparing for any type of summative assessment.

PREPARING FOR SUMMATIVE ASSESSMENT

As you think about how to construct a summative assessment, a number of preliminary steps will be helpful. First, review what you want to do while considering the criteria for ensuring high-quality assessments that were presented in Chapter 3:

1. Do I have clear and appropriate learning expectations?
2. What method of assessment will best match the expectations?
3. Will I have good evidence that the inferences from the assessments will be valid?
4. How can I construct an assessment that will minimize error?
5. Will my assessment be fair and unbiased? Have students had the opportunity to learn what is being assessed?
6. Will the assessment be practical and efficient?
7. Will my assessment be aligned with instruction?
8. Are the consequences of the assessment positive?

Additional considerations include how you will obtain a representative sample of what has been learned, the length and number of assessments, whether you should use tests provided by publishers, how students should be prepared for the assessment, when the assessment should be scheduled, and when you should construct the assessment.

Representative Sampling

Most assessments *sample* what students have learned. It is rare, except for quizzes about short lessons, to assess everything that is included in your learning expectations. There simply is not enough time to assess each fact or skill. Rather, you will select a sample of what students should know and then assume that how they respond to assessments of this sample is typical of how they would respond to additional assessments of the entire unit.

As we pointed out in Chapter 3, an important step in representative sampling is preparing a test blueprint or outline. This set of specifications is helpful because it indicates what students are responsible for learning. When you base assessment items on this outline, it is more likely that the sampling will be reasonable. You will literally be able to look at the blueprint to see how the sampling came out. Without a test blueprint or some type of outline of content, you tend to oversample areas that you particularly like and to overload the assessment with a disproportionately large number of questions about simple facts (since these questions are much easier to write).

Another consideration when preparing a representative sample is constructing or selecting the appropriate number of items. Suppose you are preparing a test for a six-week social studies unit on early civilizations, and you want to assess how much knowledge the students retained. How many items will be needed? Thirty? Sixty? Eighty? In the absence of any hard-and-fast rules, a couple of rules of thumb will help determine how many items are sufficient. First, a minimum of ten items is needed to assess each knowledge learning expectation that encompasses the unit. Thus, if one learning expectation is that "students will identify the location of 25 ancient cities on a map," a test that asks them to identify 10 of the 25 would be reasonable. But which 10? You can select randomly if all the cities are equally difficult to locate. Normally, however, your sampling will be purposeful, so that a good cross-section of difficulty is selected (in this case, different types of cities).

With more specific learning expectations, as few as five items can provide a good assessment. For example, you can usually determine if a student knows how to multiply three-digit numbers by requiring answers to five problems.

Number and Length of Assessments

Knowing how many items or questions are needed, you then decide how many separate assessments you will give and the length of each one. This decision will depend on several factors, including the age of the students, the length of classes, and the types of questions. One rule of thumb, though, is that the time allocated for assessment is sufficient for all students to answer all the questions. We generally do not want to use *speeded* tests in school to obtain a fair assessment of what students know and can do. This is because **speeded tests**, which require students to answer as quickly as possible to obtain a high score, increase the probability that other factors, such as anxiety and test-taking skills, will influence the result.

There is an obvious relationship between the number and length of assessments. Many short assessments can provide the same, if not better, information than a single long assessment. You should focus on length first without regard to the number of assessments. This will indicate what is needed to obtain a representative sample. Then you can decide whether your assessments are best given in one large block of time, three smaller tests, weekly assessments, or another combination. If you wait until the end of a unit to begin constructing your assessment, you may find that there is insufficient time to administer the test so that other high-quality criteria are met.

The age of students and the length of their classes are other important considerations. Kindergarten and grade 1 students have relatively short attention spans, so summative assessments usually last only five to ten minutes. Attention spans and stamina increase with age, but it is still best to use many short assessments rather than one or two long ones for elementary students. Thus, in later elementary grades, summative assessments typically should last between fifteen and thirty minutes.

Ironically, when students are old enough to have longer attention spans, they are in middle or high schools where the length of the class usually determines the maximum length of the assessment. Consequently, most teachers plan unit and other summative assessments to last one class period, or approximately forty-five minutes in many schools. In this situation, you need to provide time for directions and student questions, so you have to be careful not to end up with a speeded test. With block scheduling and other innovations, more time is available for assessment.

Another important influence on the length of time it takes students to complete an assessment is the type of item used. Obviously, essay items require much more time to complete than objective items. Students also take longer to complete short-answer items than multiple-choice or true/false questions. The nature of the subject is also important. For example, in a test of simple knowledge in a content area, students can generally answer as many as two to four items per minute. For more difficult items, one per minute is a general rule of thumb. In math, students may need as long as three or four minutes for each item. Experience will be your best guide. Initially, try some assessments that are short, in order to determine how long it takes students to complete each item. Using practice questions will also give you an idea of the number of items that would be reasonable in a unit test. The best practice is to give your students too much time rather than too little time to complete the assessment.

Use of Assessments Provided by Textbook and Test Publishers

You will receive ready-made tests from textbook and instructional packages that can be used for summative assessments. These tests are prepared by the publisher for chapters and units. Some of these tests are adequate and may be useful if you remember a few key points. First, you can't assume that just because a test is provided that the results will be reliable or valid. Review the test carefully to make sure that fundamental principles of good assessment are followed. Second, a decision to use *any* type of assessment—whether provided in instructor's materials, by other teachers, or by you—is always made *after* you have identified the learning expectations that you will assess. The prepared test may be technically sound, but if there is not a good match between what it tests and what you need tested, it should not be used in its entirety. Also, because these tests are often prepared by someone other than the textbook author(s), some sections may be stressed much more than others. Third, check the test carefully to make sure the language and terminology are appropriate for your students. The author of the test may use language that is inconsistent with the text or the way you have taught the material. The vocabulary and sentence complexity may not be at the right level for your students. Fourth, the number of items for each expectation needs to be sufficient to provide a reliable measure.

The obvious advantage of using these "prepared" tests is that they can save time, especially when the test is provided in a format that can be simply copied. Feel free, however, to use only part of the test and to modify individual questions. Often the best use of prepared items is to provide a good starting point for you to prepare your own test.

Preparing Students for Summative Assessments

Your objective in summative assessment is to obtain a fair and accurate indication of student learning. You need to take some simple, yet often neglected, steps to prepare your students to demonstrate what they know, understand, and can do (see Figure 6.1).

First, ensure that all your students have adequate test-taking skills, such as paying attention to directions, reading each item in its entirety before answering it, planning and outlining responses to essay questions, and pacing themselves while answering the questions. (As one teacher told me, "When I first gave math tests, students would include the item number with the problem; for example, if item 2 was 3 + 4, they would answer 9—incorrect answer, but they knew how to add!") Students should be directed to answer all questions (guessing is rarely penalized in classroom tests, though you don't want to encourage mindless guessing). If there is a separate sheet for recording responses, teach students to check the accuracy of their answers.

- Teach test-taking skills.
- Familiarize students with test length, format, and types of questions.
- Teach to the test (do not teach *the* test).
- Review before the test.
- Tell students when the test is scheduled.

Figure 6.1 Preparing Students for Summative Assessments

Second, ensure students are familiar with the format and type of question and response that will be needed on the test. This is accomplished by giving students practice test items. If time is available, have students practise writing test items themselves. This is good for review sessions. Familiarity with the type of question lessens test anxiety. Of course, you don't want to teach the test, use examples in class that are identical to the test items, or give students practice on the test items before they take the test. It's fine to teach to the test, in the sense of instructing students about what they will eventually be tested on. It's also helpful to students if they know the length of the test and how much the test will count in their grade.

Although multiple-choice formats are common, especially in large-scale standardized tests, your primary objective is to increase student learning, and this will rarely be achieved if only one type of test item is used. *Use the type of item that maximizes student engagement and learning.* Students need to demonstrate their knowledge and understanding in different ways, and constructed-response items are often the best kind of assessment for detecting errors.

A review of the unit or chapter learning expectations is both fair and helpful. There are several purposes of the review: to reacquaint students with material taught early in the unit, to allow students an opportunity to ask questions for clarification, to re-emphasize the important knowledge and skills that students should focus on, and to provide an opportunity for students to check their understanding of what will be tested.

Finally, tell students, as soon as possible after beginning the unit, when the test is scheduled. This gives students an adequate period of time to prepare for the test. Lack of time to prepare and review for the test contributes to student anxiety and lessens the validity of the results.

Scheduling the Summative Assessment

To give students the best opportunity to show what they have learned, be careful about when you schedule the test. Try to avoid giving a test on days that make it difficult for students to perform to their capability (e.g., right after spring break). Also, try to schedule the test when you know you will be present, and not when the class has a substitute.

When Summative Assessments Should Be Constructed

Summative assessments need to be planned well in advance of the scheduled testing date. A good procedure is to construct a general outline of the test before instruction, based on your learning expectations and a table of specifications. This does not include developing or selecting specific items, but it provides enough information to guide you in instruction. As the unit proceeds, you can make decisions about the format of the test and begin to construct individual items. Determine the final form of the test no later than the review session. Don't try to finalize the test too soon. You will likely find that as you teach, your learning expectations will change somewhat, or that the emphasis you place on certain topics is not as you planned. These expected instructional variations should be reflected in the test. Consequently, allow the test and instruction to influence each other while teaching the content or skills.

With this summary of considerations for preparing any type of summative assessment, we now turn to knowledge and simple understanding expectations.

TYPES OF KNOWLEDGE AND SIMPLE UNDERSTANDING EXPECTATIONS

The phrase "what students should know" frequently includes important learning outcomes and standards. But this phrase is also vague. We need to be much more specific about what we mean by "know" and "knowledge." Then we can select appropriate assessment methods to foster and measure the desired type of learning.

Knowledge Representation

Until recently, Bloom's taxonomy provided a definition of *knowledge* for many educators. In this scheme, knowledge is the first and "lowest" level of categories in the cognitive domain, in which knowledge is defined as remembering something. Students are required only to recall or recognize facts, definitions, terms, concepts, procedures, principles, or other information.

In the revision of Bloom's taxonomy (Anderson & Krathwohl, 2001), the original knowledge category is divided into two categories: a knowledge dimension, and remembering as a cognitive process. There is a distinction between "factual knowledge" that is remembered and other types of knowledge (conceptual, procedural, and metacognitive). Factual knowledge encompasses basic elements about a discipline, including knowledge of terminology (specific verbal and nonverbal labels and symbols such as words, numerals, pictures, and signs) and knowledge of specific details and elements (events, locations, sources of information, dates, and other pertinent information). Further details with examples of factual knowledge remembering are shown in Tables 6.1 and 6.2. These correspond to the nature of learning that is the focus of this chapter. Regardless of the classification scheme, the important point is that when students are required to remember something, whether a fact, concept, or procedure, this represents the most basic and elementary form of learning. For our purposes here, *knowledge* will be used in the same way as it was defined in the original taxonomy—as the process of simply remembering something.

The contemporary view of knowledge is that remembering is only part of what occurs when students learn. You also need to think about how the knowledge is represented in the mind of the student. *Knowledge representation* is how information is constructed and stored in long-term and working memory (Gagne, Yekovich, & Yekovich, 1993). We will examine two types of knowledge representation that have direct application to

Table 6.1 Part of Knowledge Dimension of New Taxonomy

Major Types	Definition	Subtypes	Examples
Factual Knowledge	Basic elements of a discipline	Knowledge of terminology	Vocabulary; symbols
		Knowledge of specific details and elements	Major facts important to good health
Conceptual Knowledge	Interrelationships among basic elements that enable them to function together	Knowledge of classifications and categories	Forms of business ownership
		Knowledge of principles and generalizations	Law of supply and demand
		Knowledge of theories, models, and structures	Theory of evolution
Procedural Knowledge	How to do something, methods of inquiry, and skills, algorithms, and methods	Knowledge of subject-specific skills and algorithms	Painting skills; division algorithm
		Knowledge of subject-specific techniques and methods	Scientific method
		Knowledge of criteria for determining when to use appropriate procedures	Knowing when to apply Newton's second law

Source: Adapted from L. W. Anderson & D. R. Krathwohl (2001). *A taxonomy for learning, teaching, and assessing: A revision of Bloom's taxonomy of educational objectives.* Boston: Allyn and Bacon. Copyright © 2001 Pearson Education. Reprinted by permission of the publisher.

assessment: declarative and procedural. These are major types of knowledge in the revision to Bloom's taxonomy (Table 6.1).

Declarative Knowledge and Understanding

Declarative knowledge is information that is retained about something, knowing that it exists. The information learned can be ordered hierarchically, depending on the level of generality and degree of understanding that is demonstrated (Marzano, Pickering, & McTighe, 1993; Marzano, 1996) and the way the knowledge is represented. At the "lowest" level, declarative knowledge is similar to Bloom's first level—remembering or recognizing specific facts about persons, places, events, or content in a subject area. The knowledge is represented by simple association or discrimination, such as rote memory. At a higher level, declarative knowledge consists of concepts, ideas, and generalizations that are more fully understood and applied. This type of knowledge involves *understanding* in the form of comprehension or application, the next two levels in Bloom's original taxonomy.

Table 6.2 Part of Cognitive Process Dimension of New Taxonomy

Major Types	Definition	Subtypes	Illustrative Verbs	Examples
Remember	Retrieval of knowledge from long-term memory	Recognizing	Identifying	Recognize dates of important events.
		Recalling	Retrieving	Recall dates of important events.
Understand	Construct meaning from oral, written, and graphic communication	Interpreting	Representing, translating	Paraphrase meaning in important speeches.
		Exemplifying	Illustrating	Give examples of painting styles.
		Classifying	Categorizing, subsuming	Classify different types of rocks.
		Summarizing	Abtracting, generalizing	Write a summary of a story.
		Inferring	Concluding, predicting	Draw a conclusion from data presented.
		Comparing	Contrasting, mapping	Compare historical events to contemporary events.
		Explaining	Constructing models	Show cause-and-effect of pollution affected by industry.
Apply	Carry out a procedure	Executing	Carrying out	Divide whole numbers.
		Implementing	Using	Apply procedure to an unfamiliar task.

Source: Adapted from L. W. Anderson & D. R. Krathwohl (2001). *A taxonomy for learning, teaching, and assessing: A revision of Bloom's taxonomy of educational objectives.* Boston: Allyn and Bacon. Copyright © 2001 Pearson Education. Reprinted by permission of the publisher.

In the revision of Bloom's taxonomy, understanding and application are cognitive process categories that are differentiated from remembering (Table 6.2). We believe it is best to use the term *understand* as different from *remember*, and that simple understanding involves either comprehension or application. Comprehension understanding would be similar to what is called *understand* in the revised taxonomy and *comprehension* in the original taxonomy. Application understanding is the same as *application* in Bloom's original taxonomy and *apply* in the revision. Thus, for our purposes here, declarative knowledge can exist as recall, recognition, or simple understanding, depending on the intent of the instruction and how the information is learned. Assessments of procedural knowledge likewise measure recall, recognition, or understanding.

The nature of the representation moves from rote memorization and association of facts to generalized understanding and usage. This is a critical distinction for both learning and assessment. As we pointed out in Chapter 1, constructivists contend that students learn most effectively when they meaningfully connect new information to an existing network of knowledge. Constructivists believe that new knowledge is acquired through a process of seeing how something relates, makes sense, and can be used in reasoning. This notion is quite different from the memorized learning that can be demonstrated for a test. Although we don't want to suggest that some rote memorization is inappropriate, we do want to point out that your learning expectations can focus on recall or understanding types of declarative knowledge, and that your choice of assessment method and test items will be different for each of these.

Let's look at an example of different types of declarative knowledge. One important type of information students learn about is geometric shapes. Each shape is a concept (mental structures that use physical characteristics or definitions to classify objects, events, or other things into categories). If students learn the concept of "rectangle" at the level of *recall* or *recognition*, then they simply memorize a definition or identify rectangles from a set of different shapes that look like the ones they studied in class. If students *understand* the concept of rectangle, however, they will be able to give original examples and identify rectangles of different sizes, shapes, and colours they have never seen before. Each of these levels of learning is "knowing something," but the latter is much closer to true student mastery and what constructivists advocate. Also, because these levels are hierarchical, understanding requires recall. Thus, it may be better to state learning expectations that require understanding but to also teach and test for recall, since one is a prerequisite to the other.

Procedural Knowledge and Understanding

Procedural knowledge is knowing how to do something. It is knowledge that is needed to carry out an action or solve a problem. What is demonstrated is knowledge of the strategies, procedures, and skills students must engage in; for example, how to tie shoes, how to divide fractions, or how to check out library books. Like declarative knowledge, procedural knowledge can be demonstrated at different levels. At the level of recall, students simply identify or repeat the needed steps. Simple understanding is indicated as students summarize in their own words (comprehension) and actually use the steps in executing a solution (application).

Definitions of the two major types of knowledge are presented in Table 6.3; examples are provided in Table 6.4. We will use these learning expectation categories to present

Table 6.3 Definitions of the Levels of Declarative and Procedural Knowledge and Simple Understanding

Level	Declarative	Procedural
Knowledge	Remembers, restates, defines, identifies, recognizes, names, reproduces, or selects *specific facts, concepts, principles, rules, or theories.*	Remembers, restates, defines, identifies, recognizes, names, reproduces, or selects *correct procedure, steps, skills, or strategies.*
Simple Understanding: Comprehension	Converts, translates, distinguishes, explains, provides examples, summarizes, interprets, infers, or predicts in own words *essential meanings of concepts and principles.*	Converts, translates, distinguishes, explains, provides examples, summarizes, interprets, infers, or predicts in own words *correct procedure, steps, skills, or strategies.*
Simple Understanding: Application	Uses existing knowledge of concepts, principles, and theories in new situations to solve problems, interpret information, and construct responses.	Uses existing knowledge of correct procedures, steps, skills, or strategies in new situations to solve problems, interpret information, and construct responses.

examples of test items throughout the remainder of this chapter. The most effective methods for assessing knowledge are conveniently grouped into measuring recall or understanding. We now consider how different types of objective items can be used to assess the various knowledge expectations, beginning with knowledge.

Table 6.4 Examples of Declarative and Procedural Knowledge and Simple Understanding

Declarative

Knowledge	Is able to define the word *democracy*
Simple Understanding: Comprehension	Is able to give three examples of countries that are democracies
Simple Understanding: Application	Is able to determine by its description whether a new country is a democracy

Procedural

Knowledge	Is able to identify in correct order steps in the scientific method
Simple Understanding: Comprehension	Is able to explain whether a set of procedures follows the scientific method
Simple Understanding: Application	Is able to demonstrate in writing the correct use of the scientific method to solve a novel problem

Leslie Gross

Leslie is a middle-school social studies teacher and former Teacher of the Year for her school.

> In assessing knowledge a student has acquired, I most often use multiple choice questions. Students need to be very familiar and comfortable with these types of questions because many standardized and/or provincial large-scale assessments are based on multiple choice questions. This, however, is not the only type of question I include on my tests. A variety of question types is important in order to accommodate the various learning styles and patterns of all students. I also use matching, true/false, and short answer questions in order to assess a student's simple understanding of the curriculum.

ASSESSING KNOWLEDGE

Knowledge is best assessed with completion, short-answer, and selected-response items. This section presents suggestions for using these types of items and tests, along with examples. You will determine which of these methods to use based on their strengths and weaknesses in relation to your teaching situation and your personal preferences. You need to be comfortable with whatever method you use, and this is probably more important than other factors, such as ease of construction and scoring. The suggestions for writing each type of item are applicable to assessing both understanding and reasoning.

Completion and Short-Answer Items

The most common and effective way to assess knowledge is simply to ask a question and require students to answer it from memory. Items in which the student responds to an incomplete statement are *completion items*; a brief response to a question is a *short-answer item*.

Completion Items. The completion item offers the least freedom of student response, calling for one answer at the end of a sentence. Responses may be in the form of words, numbers, or symbols. If properly constructed, completion items are excellent for measuring how well students can recall facts because of these strengths: (1) they are easy to construct, (2) their short response time allows a good sampling of different facts, (3) guessing contributes little to error, (4) scorer reliability is high, (5) they can be scored more quickly than short-answer or essay items, and (6) they provide more valid results than a test with an equal number of selected-response items (e.g., multiple-choice). There are only two limitations of using completion items to measure knowledge. First, consider scoring. It takes a little more time to score completion items than selected-response items. Second, if the sentence is not well written, more than one answer may be possible.

The following suggestions for constructing completion items use examples that measure either declarative or procedural knowledge. The suggestions are summarized in the form of a checklist in Figure 6.2.

1. Paraphrase Sentences from Textbooks and Other Instructional Materials. It is tempting to lift a sentence verbatim from materials the students have studied, and replace a word or two with blanks. However, statements in textbooks, when taken out of context, are often too vague or general to be good completion items (Frey et al., 2005). Also, you don't want to encourage students to memorize phraseology in the text. Consistent with constructivist principles, you want students to connect what they learn with what they already know, even when it is recall. Thus, you want to paraphrase or restate facts in words that are different from those the students have read.

Examples

> The textbook statement is "In 1885, the imposition of Canadian sovereignty was resisted by the Métis people."
>
> *Poor:* In 1885, the imposition of Canadian sovereignty was resisted by _____.
>
> *Improved:* The group of people that resisted the imposition of Canadian sovereignty in 1885 was _____.

2. Word the Sentence So That Only One Brief Answer Is Correct. The single greatest error in writing completion items is to use sentences that can be legitimately completed with more than one response. This occurs if the sentence is too vague or open-ended.

Examples

> *Poor:* Saskatchewan became _____.
>
> *Improved:* Saskatchewan became a province in _____.
>
> *Better:* Saskatchewan became a province in the year _____.

In the first example, students could logically provide correct answers having nothing to do with the year. In the improved version, an answer like "1905" would be correct.

✓ Is verbatim language from instructional materials avoided?
✓ Is knowledge being assessed?
✓ Is a single, brief answer required?
✓ Is the blank at the end of the sentence?
✓ Is the length of each blank the same?
✓ Is the precision of a numerical answer specified?
✓ Is it worded to avoid verbal clues to the right answer?

Figure 6.2 Checklist for Writing Completion Items

3. Place One or Two Blanks at the End of the Sentence. If blanks are placed at the beginning or in the middle of the sentence, it may be more difficult for students to understand what response is called for. It is easier and more direct to first read the sentence and then determine what will complete it correctly. (That's why it's called a *completion* item!)

Examples

> *Poor:* Canada's Food Guide has _____ different food groups.
>
> *Improved:* The number of food groups in Canada's Food Guide is _____.

You also will not want to use several blanks in a single sentence. This will confuse students and measure reasoning skills as much as, if not more than, knowledge.

Example

> *Poor:* Canada's Food Guide _____ has _____ different _____ _____ to choose from.

4. If Answered in Numerical Units, Specify the Unit Required. For completion items that require numerical answers, the specific units or the degree of precision should be indicated.

Examples

> *Poor:* The distance between the moon and the earth is _____.
>
> *Improved:* The distance between the moon and the earth is _____ kilometres.

5. Do Not Include Clues to the Correct Answer. Test-wise students will look for clues in the way sentences are worded and the length of blanks that may indicate a correct answer. The most common wording errors are using single or plural verbs and wording the sentence so that the blank is preceded by "a" or "an." These clues can be eliminated by avoiding verb agreement with the answer, by using "a(n)," and by making all blanks the same length.

Examples

> *Poor:* The basic unit of matter is an _____.
>
> *Improved:* The basic unit of matter is a(n) _____.

Short-Answer Items. Short-answer items, in which the student supplies an answer consisting of one word, a few words, or a sentence or two, are generally preferred to completion items for assessing knowledge expectations. First, this type of item is similar to how teachers phrase questions and direct student behaviour during instruction, so the item is more natural for students. Students are familiar with answering questions and providing responses to commands that require knowledge (e.g., "Write the definition of each of the words on the board"). Second, it is easier for teachers to write these items to more accurately measure knowledge.

Short-answer items are usually stated in the form of a question (e.g., "Which province is bordered on the western side by the Rocky Mountains?"). They can also be stated in general directions (e.g., "Define each of the following terms"), and they can require responses to visual stimulus materials (e.g, "Name each of the countries identified with arrows A–D").

Like completion items, short-answer items are good for measuring knowledge because students can respond to many items quickly, a good sample of knowledge is obtained, guessing is avoided, scoring is fairly objective, and results are generally more valid than those obtained from selected-response formats. The main disadvantage of short-answer items is that scoring takes longer and is more subjective than completion or selected-response items. Figure 6.3 summarizes the following suggestions in a checklist format.

1. State the Item So That Only One Answer Is Correct. Be sure that the question or directions are stated so that what is required in the answer is clear to students. If more than one answer is correct, the item is vague and the result is invalid. If you are expecting a one-word answer, use a single short blank.

Examples

> *Poor:* Where is the Eiffel Tower located?
>
> *Improved:* In what country is the Eiffel Tower located? *or* Name the country in which the Eiffel Tower is located.

Obviously, in the first item, students could give several responses—Europe, Paris, or France—each of which would be technically correct.

2. State the Item So That the Required Answer Is Brief. Remember that short-answer items have answers that are *short!* Keep student responses to a word or two, or a short sentence or two if necessary, by properly wording the item, offering clear directions, and providing space or blanks that indicate the length of the response. In the directions, state clearly that students should not repeat the question in their answer.

Examples

> *Poor:* What does the term *reptile* mean?
>
> *Improved:* Name three characteristics of reptiles.
>
> 1. _____
>
> 2. _____
>
> 3. _____

✓ Is only one answer correct?
✓ Are questions from textbooks avoided?
✓ Is it clear to students that the answer is brief?
✓ Is the precision of a numerical answer specified?
✓ Is the item written as succinctly as possible?
✓ Is the space designated for answers consistent with the length required?
✓ Are words used in the item too difficult for any students?

Figure 6.3 Checklist for Writing Short-Answer Items

3. Do Not Use Questions Verbatim from Textbooks or Other Instructional Materials. Most textbooks include review questions and questions for study. Don't use these same questions on tests because it encourages rote memorization of answers.

4. Designate Units Required for the Answer. Students need to know the specific units and the degree of precision that should be used in their answer. Then students won't need to use up time figuring out what is required (such as asking a question for clarification during the test), and it will mitigate scoring difficulties.

Examples

> *Poor:* When was Louis Riel executed?
>
> *Improved:* In what year was Louis Riel executed?

5. State the Item Succinctly with Words Students Understand. State questions or sentences as concisely as possible, and avoid using words or phrases that may be difficult for some students to understand.

Examples

> *Poor:* What is the name of the extensive and binding agreements between the government of Canada and First Nations people that began before Confederation and continue to this day?
>
> *Improved:* What is the name of the binding agreements between First Nations people and the government of Canada?

Matching Items

Matching items effectively and efficiently measure the extent to which students know related facts, associations, and relationships. Some examples of such associations include terms with definitions, persons with descriptions, dates with events, and symbols with names.

The major advantage of matching is that the teacher can obtain a good sampling of a large amount of knowledge. Matching is easily and objectively scored. Constructing good matching items is more difficult than creating completion or short-answer items, but it is not as difficult as preparing multiple-choice items. However, poor matching items result when there is insufficient material in the item and when irrelevant information (which is unrelated to the major topic being assessed) is added.

In a matching item, the items on the left are called the *premises* or stems. In the right-hand column are the *responses* or answers. The student's task is to match the correct response with each of the premises. As long as the suggestions below are followed, matching items are excellent for measuring knowledge that includes associations.

1. Make Sure Directions Are Clear to Students. Even though matching items are familiar to students, it is helpful to indicate in writing (or orally for young students) the basis for the matching and where and how student responses should be recorded. Generally, letters are used for each response in the right-hand column, and students are asked to write the selected letter next to each premise. Younger students can be asked to draw lines to connect the premises to the responses. Indicate in the directions that *each response may be used once, more than once, or not at all*. This lessens the probability that, through a process of elimination, guessing will be a factor in the results.

2. Include Homogeneous Premises and Responses. Avoid putting information from different lessons in the same matching item. You wouldn't want to include recent scientists, early Canadian prime ministers, and sports figures in the same item. Even though what is homogeneous varies from one person to another, this principle is the one that is most violated. For example, it makes good sense to use matching to test student knowledge of important dates during the formation of democracy in Canada. It would not be a good idea to contain both dates and names as responses. Testing homogeneous material with matching is effective for fairly fine discriminations among facts. For example, matching dates with events in a specific World War I battle (e.g., Vimy Ridge, Passchendaele, etc.) provides greater discrimination than simply matching dates with major battles.

3. Use Four to Eight Premises. You do not want to have too long a list of premises. A relatively short list will probably be more homogeneous and will be perceived by students as more fair.

4. Keep Responses Short and Logically Ordered. Usually the responses include a list of one- or two-word names, dates, or other terms. Definitions, events, and descriptions are in the premise column. Students will be more accurate in their answers if the responses are in logical order. Thus, if responses are dates, they should be rank ordered by year; words or names should be alphabetized. Like premises, keep the number of responses to less than 7 for elementary students and less than 17 for secondary students (Frey et al., 2005). Longer lists waste students' time and contribute to error by including reasoning abilities as part of what is needed to answer the item correctly.

5. Avoid Grammatical Clues to Correct Answers. As with completion items, be careful that none of your matches are likely because of grammatical clues, such as verb tense agreement.

6. Put Premises and Responses on the Same Page. Students shouldn't have to flip back and forth between two pages to answer the items. This is distracting and only contributes to error.

7. Use More Responses Than Premises. Using more responses than premises (Frey et al., 2005) provides greater coverage of information and is a better indicator of knowledge. This technique reduces guessing of some correct answers that occurs if the same number of premises and responses are used and each response is used only once.

Example

> The following is an example of a good matching set. Notice the complete directions, responses on the right in logical order, and homogeneous content (grammar definitions).
>
> *Directions:* Match the definition in column A with the grammar term in column B. Write the letter of the grammar term on the line next to each number. Each term in column B may be used once, more than once, or not at all.

Column A		Column B
_____	1. Description of a person, place or thing	**A.** Noun
_____	2. Person, place or thing	**B.** Adverb
_____	3. Joins two parts of a sentence	**C.** Verb
_____	4. Action word	**D.** Adjective
		E. Conjunction

Suggestions for writing matching items are summarized in Figure 6.4.

True/False and Other Binary-Choice Items

When students select an answer from only two response categories, they are completing a **binary-choice item**. This type of item may also be called *alternative response, alternate response,* or *alternate choice*. The most popular binary-choice item is the true/false question; other types of options can be right/wrong, correct/incorrect, yes/no, fact/opinion, agree/disagree, and so on. In each case, the student selects one of two options.

Binary-choice items are constructed from propositional statements about the knowledge. A *proposition* is a declarative sentence that makes a claim about content or relationships among content. Simple recall propositions include the following:

> Winnipeg is the capital of Manitoba.
> Peru is in the southern hemisphere.
> The area of a square is found by squaring the length of one side.

These propositions provide the basis for good test items because they capture an important thought or idea. Once the proposition is constructed, it is relatively easy to keep it as is, rephrase and keep the same meaning, or change one aspect of the statement and then use it for a binary-choice test item. As such, the items provide a simple and

---

✓ Is it clear how and where students place their answers?
✓ Is it clear that each response may be used once, more than once, or not at all?
✓ Is the information included homogeneous?
✓ Are there more responses than premises?
✓ Are the responses logically ordered?
✓ Are grammatical clues avoided?
✓ Is there only one feasible answer for each premise?
✓ Is the set of premises or responses too long?
✓ Are premises and responses on the same page?

Figure 6.4 Checklist for Writing Matching Items

direct measure of one's knowledge of facts, definitions, and the like, as long as there is no exception or qualification to the statement. That is, one of the two choices must be *absolutely* true or false, correct or incorrect, and so on (Frey et al., 2005). Some subjects, such as science and history, lend themselves to this type of absolute proposition better than others.

Using binary-choice items has several advantages. First, the format of such questions is similar to questions asked in class, so students are familiar with the thinking process involved in making binary choices. Second, short binary items provide an extensive sampling of knowledge because students are able to answer many items in a short time (two to five items per minute). Third, these items can be written in short, easy-to-understand sentences. Compared to multiple-choice items, binary-choice questions are relatively easy to construct. Finally, scoring is objective and quick.

The major disadvantage of binary-choice items is that students are likely to guess at the answers, particularly if the items are poorly constructed, and often test-wise students can find clues to the correct answer. Thus, a combination of some knowledge, guessing, and poorly constructed items that give clues to the correct answer will allow some students to score well even though their level of knowledge may be weak.

Writing good binary-choice items begins with propositions about major knowledge expectations. In converting the propositions to test items, keep the items short, simple, direct, and easy to understand. Avoid ambiguity and clues. The following suggestions, summarized in Figure 6.5, will help accomplish this.

1. Write the Item So That the Answer Options Are Consistent with the Logic in the Sentence. The way the item is written will suggest a certain logic to what type of response is most appropriate. For example, if you want to test spelling knowledge, it doesn't make much sense to use true/false questions; instead, use correct/incorrect as options.

2. Include a Single Fact or Idea in the Item. For assessing recall knowledge, avoid two or more facts, ideas, or propositions in a single item. This is because one idea or fact may be true and the other false, which introduces ambiguity and error.

Examples

> *Poor:* T   F   More things can be dissolved in sulfuric acid and saltwater than in water.
>
> *Improved:* T   F   More things can be dissolved in sulfuric acid than in water.

✓ Does the item contain a single proposition or idea?

✓ Is the type of answer logically consistent with the statement?

✓ Are the statements succinct?

✓ Is the item stated positively?

✓ Is the length of both statements in an item about the same?

✓ Do the correct responses have a pattern?

✓ Are unequivocal terms used?

✓ Does the item try to trick students?

✓ Is trivial knowledge being tested?

✓ Are about half the items answered correctly with same response?

Figure 6.5 Checklist for Writing Binary-Choice Items

3. Avoid Long Sentences. Try to keep the sentences as concise as possible. This allows you to include more test items and reduces ambiguity. Longer sentences tend to favour students who have stronger reading comprehension skills.

Examples

> *Poor:* T F A cup with hot water that has a spoon in it will cool more quickly than a similar cup with the same amount of hot water that does not have a spoon in it.
>
> *Improved:* T F Hot water in a cup will cool more quickly if a spoon is placed in the cup.

4. Avoid Insignificant or Trivial Facts and Words. It is relatively easy to write "tough" binary-choice items that measure trivial knowledge. Avoid this by beginning with what you believe are significant learning expectations.

Examples

> *Poor:* T F Charles Darwin was 22 years old when he began his voyage of the world.
>
> *Poor:* T F An elephant spends about 15 hours a day eating and foraging.

5. Avoid Negative Statements. Statements that include the words *not* or *no* are confusing to students and make items and answers more difficult to understand. Careful reading and sound logic become prerequisites for answering correctly. If the knowledge can be tested only with a negatively worded statement, be sure to highlight the negative word with boldface type, underlining, or all caps.

Examples

> *Poor:* T F Members of Parliament are not elected in elections.
>
> *Improved:* T F Members of Parliament are elected in elections.

6. Avoid Clues to the Answer. Test-wise students will look for specific words that suggest that the item is false. When adjectives and adverbs such as *never, all, every, always,* and *absolutely* are used, the answer is usually false. Also, avoid any kind of pattern in the items that provides clues to the answer, such as all true items being longer, alternating true and false answers, tending to use one type of answer more than the other, or all the items being either true or false. It is best to write questions so that about 50 per cent of the answers are true.

7. **Do Not Try to Trick Students.** Items that are written to "trick" students by including a word that changes the meaning of an idea or by inserting some trivial fact should be avoided. Trick items undermine your credibility, frustrate students, and provide less valid measures of knowledge.

8. **Avoid Using Vague Adjectives and Adverbs.** Adjectives and adverbs such as *frequent, sometimes, occasionally, typically,* and *usually* are interpreted differently by each student. It is best to avoid these types of words because the meaning of the statement is not equivocal.

Multiple-Choice Items

Multiple-choice items are used widely in schools, even though they may *not* be the best method for assessing recall knowledge (see Table 3.1). Multiple-choice items have a **stem**, in the form of a question or incomplete statement, and three or more **alternatives**. The alternatives contain one correct or best answer and two or more **distractors**. It is usually best to use a question as the stem and to provide one correct answer. A direct question is preferred for several reasons: it is easier to write, it forces you to state the complete problem more clearly in the stem, its format is familiar to students, it avoids the problem of grammatically tailoring each alternative to the stem, and it places less demand on reading skills to understand the problem. Questions are clearly better for younger students. Items that assess the "best" answer allow for greater discrimination and are very effective for measuring understanding. In this type of item, each alternative may have some correct aspect, but one answer is better than the others.

Multiple-choice questions offer several advantages. Like other select-response items, they can provide a broad sampling of knowledge. Scoring is easy and objective, and the questions give students practice on the type of items they are likely to encounter on high-stakes provincial accountability tests. Compared with binary-choice items, multiple-choice are typically more reliable. There is much less of a guessing factor, and they are free from response set. Multiple-choice items also usually have more diagnostic power because selection of certain distractors can pinpoint an error in knowledge.

However, there are also disadvantages. Multiple-choice questions take longer to answer than other types of objective items, and consequently they do not sample as well. Also, it is relatively difficult to write multiple-choice items, especially good distractors. Many teachers find that it isn't too hard to come up with one or two good distractors, but the third or fourth ones are often giveaways to students. This increases the probability that students will guess the right answer. Students learn that the way to study for multiple-choice items is to read and reread the material to focus on recognition. Much less energy is spent on recalling information. Thus, like other selected-response items, the type of mental preparation prompted by knowledge of multiple-choice items is inconsistent with more contemporary theories of learning and information processing.

Suggestions for writing multiple-choice items are summarized in the following points and in Figure 6.6 in the form of questions. When you write the items, begin with the stem, then the correct response, and, finally, the distractors.

1. Write the Stem as a Clearly Described Question or Task. You want the stem to be meaningful by itself. It should clearly and succinctly communicate what is expected. If the stem makes sense only by reading the responses, it is poorly constructed. Put as much information as possible in the stem and not the responses, but make sure the stem does not become too wordy. The general rule is this: Use complete stems and short responses. This reduces the time students need to read the items and

---

✓ Is the stem stated as clearly, directly, and simply as possible?
✓ Is the problem self-contained in the stem?
✓ Is the stem stated positively?
✓ Is there only one correct answer?
✓ Are all the alternatives parallel with respect to grammatical structure, length, and complexity?
✓ Are irrelevant clues avoided?
✓ Are the options short?
✓ Are complex options avoided?
✓ Are options placed in logical order?
✓ Are the distractors plausible to students who do not know the correct answer?
✓ Are correct answers spread equally among all the choices?

FIGURE 6.6 Checklist for Writing Multiple-Choice Items

reduces redundant words. Do not include unnecessary words in the stem; the stem should be longer than the alternatives but still as succinct as possible. A good indicator of an effective stem is if students have a tentative answer in mind quickly, before reading the options.

Examples

Poor: Validity refers to

    a. the consistency of test scores.
    b. the inference made on the basis of test scores.
    c. measurement error as determined by standard deviation.
    d. the stability of test scores.

Improved: The inference made on the basis of test scores refers to

    a. reliability.
    b. stability.
    c. validity.
    d. measurement error.

Poor: What is the length of the table?

    a. 1 metre
    b. 3 metres
    c. 75 centimetres
    d. 200 centimetres

Improved: What is the length of the table in metres?

    a. 1.0
    b. 2.0
    c. 3.0
    d. 4.0

2. Avoid the Use of Negatives in the Stem. Using words such as *not* and *except* will confuse students and create anxiety and frustration. Often students simply overlook the negative, which leads to invalid results. It also takes longer to respond to such items. So try to word the stem positively. In cases in which knowing what not to do is important, as in knowing rules of the road for driving, the negative stem is fine as long as the negative word is emphasized by boldface or underlining.

Examples

Poor: Which of the following is not a mammal?

    a. Bird
    b. Dog
    c. Horse
    d. Whale
    e. Cat

Improved: Which of the following is a mammal?

   a. Bird
   b. Frog
   c. Whale
   d. Fish
   e. Lizard

3. Write the Correct Response with No Irrelevant Clues. There should not be any difference between the correct answer and distractors that would clue the student to respond on some basis other than the knowledge being tested. Common mistakes include making the correct response longer, more elaborate or detailed, more general, or more technical. Qualifiers such as *usually, some,* and *generally* are clues to the correct answer.

4. Write the Distractors to Be Plausible Yet Wrong. The distractors are useless if they are so obviously wrong that students do not even consider them as possible answers. The intent of a multiple-choice item is to have students *discriminate* among apparently *plausible* answers. Distractors should appear to be possibly correct to poorly prepared students. Distractors are intended to appeal to the uninformed and should not result in tricking students. To determine good distractors, identify common misunderstandings or errors by students and then write distractors that appeal to students who show these misunderstandings. Other ways to write good distractors include the use of words that have verbal associations with the stem, the use of important words (e.g., *enduring, major,* or *noteworthy*), length and complexity that matches the stem, and the use of qualifiers such as *generally* and *usually.* Poor distractors contain content that is plainly wrong, grammatical inconsistencies, or qualifiers such as *always* and *never,* or they state the opposite of the correct answer.

The number of distractors depends on several factors. Most multiple-choice items have two, three, or four distractors. Other things being equal, an item with two or three distractors is best when measuring more depth of knowledge. More questions are possible with only two distractors, which may provide better coverage. Questions for young children often have only two distractors. But don't add obviously wrong distractors just to get to three or four. Once you have had some experience with writing distractors, do an **item analysis** to determine whether the distractors are being selected with equal frequency. If a particular distractor is rarely selected, then it should be modified to be more plausible. (Item analysis is also done to see if the item *discriminates* between high and low performers on the test, i.e., whether most high performers answered it correctly and most low performers missed it, and to determine item difficulty.) A good rule of thumb is two or three distractors per item.

Examples

   Poor: Which of the following is the largest city in Canada?

   a. Toronto
   b. Vancouver
   c. New York
   d. Berlin

Improved: Which of the following is the largest city in Canada?

    a. Toronto
    b. Vancouver
    c. Montreal
    d. Calgary

5. Avoid Using "All of the Above," "None of the Above," or Other Special Distractors. These phrases are undesirable for a number of reasons. "All of the above" is the right answer if only two of the options are correct, and some students may select the first item that is correct without reading the others. Only when students need to know what *not* to do would "none of the above" be appropriate. Be sure to avoid options such as "A and C but not D" or other combinations. Items with this type of response tend to measure reasoning ability as much as knowledge, and, especially for measuring knowledge, they take far too long to answer.

6. Use Each Alternative as the Correct Answer about the Same Number of Times. If you have four possible choices, about 25 per cent of the items should have the same letter as the correct response (20 per cent if there are five choices). This avoids a pattern that can increase the chance that students will guess the correct answer. Perhaps you have heard the old admonition from test-wise students, "when in doubt, pick C." There is some truth to this for test writers who are not careful to use all the responses equally as the correct one.

ASSESSING SIMPLE UNDERSTANDING: COMPREHENSION AND APPLICATION

As stated earlier, comprehension and application are two types of knowing through which students demonstrate their understanding of something. We will consider each with some examples, using the aforementioned objective test methods. Other methods of assessment, such as essays, interpretive items, and performance assessments, are also good for measuring simple understanding but are even better for assessing deep understanding. We will consider these methods in Chapters 7 and 8.

Assessing Comprehension

Comprehension is demonstrated when students understand, in their own words, the essential meaning of a concept, principle, or procedure. They show this by providing explanations and examples, by converting and translating, and by interpreting and predicting.

Test items that assess knowledge can be changed easily to assess comprehension. To tap into translation, simply change the words used to describe or define something so that it is not verbatim from the instructional materials. Higher levels of comprehension require more work. Suppose that as a student you have learned that "photosynthesis is the process by which plants use light to make glucose." The following examples show how to measure this as knowledge or comprehension.

Examples

Knowledge (short-answer): Define photosynthesis: _____

_____

Comprehension (completion): Sunlight is used by plants to make energy in a process called _____.

Comprehension (short-answer): Explain how plants get energy from the sun.

_____

_____

Comprehension (short-answer): What would happen to plants if they did not receive any sunlight for a long time? _____

_____

Comprehension (binary-choice): T   F   Plants that receive 50 hours of light will produce more glucose than plants that receive 10 hours of light.

Knowledge (multiple-choice): Which of the following is the process by which plants use light to make glucose?

   a. respiration
   b. photosynthesis
   c. energizing
   d. growing

Comprehension (multiple-choice): In plants, sugar is made by energy from the sun through which of the following?

   a. respiration
   b. photosynthesis
   c. energizing
   d. growing

Comprehension (multiple-choice): Which of the following is most consistent with the process of photosynthesis?

   a. Plants that get light do not need to make glucose.
   b. Plants that get less light make less glucose.
   c. Glucose is produced from plants before photosynthesis.
   d. Energy is stored in plants as glucose.

Other examples of items that assess comprehension are illustrated in Figure 6.7.

Assessing Application

Understanding is demonstrated through application when students are able to use what they know to solve problems in a *new* situation. This is a more sophisticated type of understanding than comprehension, and it includes the ability to interpret new information

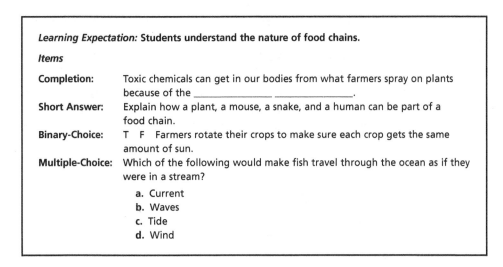

Learning Expectation: **Students understand the nature of food chains.**

Items

Completion: Toxic chemicals can get in our bodies from what farmers spray on plants because of the _____ _____.

Short Answer: Explain how a plant, a mouse, a snake, and a human can be part of a food chain.

Binary-Choice: T   F   Farmers rotate their crops to make sure each crop gets the same amount of sun.

Multiple-Choice: Which of the following would make fish travel through the ocean as if they were in a stream?

    a. Current
    b. Waves
    c. Tide
    d. Wind

Figure 6.7 Examples of Items That Assess Comprehension

with what is known and to apply rules, principles, and strategies to new problems and situations. Obviously, this is a very important type of learning expectation, because we want students to apply what they learn in school to new situations outside of school. Knowing something well enough to apply it successfully to new situations is called learning for *transfer*. The goal is to have sufficient understanding to transfer knowledge to different situations.

Perhaps the best example of learning for application is mathematics. At one level, students can memorize the steps for solving certain kinds of math problems—that is, what to do first, second, and so forth. They may even show some comprehension by being able to explain the steps in their own words. But if they cannot apply the steps to new problems and get the right answer, we conclude that they really don't *understand* the process. That's why we give math tests with new problems. Students learn procedural knowledge in math, preferably at the application level. In many ways, understanding mathematics is demonstrated by successful application. Likewise, much of language arts instruction is focused on understanding at the application level. Students learn rules for grammar, sentence structure, how to write drafts before a final copy, and reading skills. We conclude that they actually understand how to read and write by demonstrating their skill with new material.

To assess application, construct items that contain new data or information that the student must work with to obtain the answer, or create new problems or applications in which students must extend what they know in a novel way. The extent of newness determines, to some extent, item difficulty and degree of understanding demonstrated. Items that contain completely new material are generally more difficult than items in which there are only small differences between what was learned and the content of the question. This is why students may be able to solve new mathematics computational problems well, but have trouble applying the same procedures to word problems that put the question in a new context.

The key feature of application items, then, is presenting situations that the students have not previously encountered. There are several strategies for constructing such items. One approach is to present a fictional problem that can be solved by applying appropriate procedural knowledge. For example, if students have learned about electricity and resistance, the following objective questions would test at the application level.

Examples

Application

1. Shaunda has decided to make two magnets by wrapping wire around a nail and attaching the wires to a battery so that the electric current can create a magnetic force. One magnet (A) uses thin wire and one magnet (B) uses thick wire. Which magnet will be the strongest?

    a. A
    b. B
    c. A and B will be the same
    d. Cannot be determined from the information provided

2. T F Other things being equal, an electric stove with greater resistance will be hotter than a stove with less resistance.

3. To increase the heat produced from his electric iron, Mr. Jones would _____ the resistance.

Other examples of objective application items include the following.

Examples

1. What happens to water pollution when farmers use less fertilizer?

_____

2. A researcher investigated whether a new type of fertilizer would result in greater growth of corn plants. What is the independent variable?

    a. Growth of corn plants
    b. The researcher
    c. Type of fertilizer
    d. Amount of sunlight

3. William is given a $2.00 allowance each week. He wants to save enough money to go to a movie, which costs $4.00, and buy some candy and a soft drink at the movie. The candy will cost $1.50 and the drink will cost $2.50. How many weeks will William have to wait before he can go to the movie and buy the candy and soft drink?

    a. 2
    b. 3
    c. 4
    d. 5

Mr. Marshall, a grade 5 teacher, has been teaching a multidisciplinary unit on the life cycle of a pond. This unit covered science content, mathematics, geography, reading, writing, research skills, and computer skills. He has decided that part of his unit assessment needs to consist of "objective" items. He is considering completion, short-answer, and selected-response items.

Questions for Consideration

1. What are some examples of learning expectations that would be appropriate for the kinds of items Mr. Marshall wants to use?
2. Which unit topics and skills would be best assessed with each type of item? Why?
3. Which unit topics and skills would be better assessed using different kinds of items? Why?

PUTTING TESTS TOGETHER

Once you have developed test items, they need to be put together in the form of a test. The following guidelines, which include suggestions for directions, arranging items, and the physical layout of tests, should be followed.

Preparing Test Directions

According to Linn and Miller (2005), test directions should include the following:

1. purpose
2. time allowed for completing the test
3. basis for responding
4. procedures for recording answers
5. what to do about guessing
6. how constructed-response items will be scored

The purpose of the test should be made clear to students well in advance of the testing date. This is usually done when the test is announced. Students need to know why they are taking the test and how the results will be used.

Students need to know *exactly* how much time they will have to complete the test, even if the test is not speeded. It is helpful to indicate to students how they should distribute their time among various parts of the test. Allow plenty of time so that they do not feel rushed. As indicated earlier, students can be expected to complete at least one multiple-choice and two binary-choice items per minute, but the actual time will depend on the difficulty of the items and student preparation. Obviously, elementary students will need more time than high school students. Your judgments about how many items to include will improve with experience. In the beginning, err on the side of allowing too much time.

The basis for responding simply refers to what students should do to answer the question—that is, how to respond. This should be a simple and direct statement (e.g., "Select the correct answer," or "Select the best answer"). The procedure for responding indicates how students show their answers, whether they circle the answer, write the answer next to the item, write the word in the blank, and so on. If computations are to be shown, tell the students where they should write them.

In a test on which all the items are of the selection type, students may ask whether there is a penalty for guessing. In classroom tests it is very rare to find a correction for guessing. Be very clear that students should try to answer each item (e.g., "Your score is the total number of correct answers, so answer every item").

The final suggestion for directions concerns the scoring criteria for constructed-response items. For these items, clearly indicate the basis on which you will grade the students' answers. We will explore this in Chapter 7.

Arranging Items

Arranging items by level of difficulty (e.g., easy items first, then difficult ones) has little effect on the results. If you think your students gain confidence by answering the easiest items first, it's fine to order the items by increasing difficulty. The most important consideration in arranging items is item type. *Keep all the items that use the same format together.* Keep all the multiple-choice items in one section, all the matching items in another, and so on. This reduces the number of times students need to shift their response mode. It also minimizes directions and makes scoring easier. Generally it is best to order items in sections determined by type, based on how quickly students can answer. Items answered more quickly, such as completion and binary-choice, generally come first, followed by multiple-choice and short-answer items. If possible, group the items according to learning expectations, and keep assessments of the same expectation or content together.

Physical Layout of the Test

Objective test items need to be formatted so that they are easy to read and answer. A few commonsense suggestions help to achieve this goal. First, all the information needed to answer an item should be on the same page. Avoid having part of an item on one page and the rest of the item on another page. Second, do not crowd too many items onto a page. Although we all need to be careful about wasting paper, a crowded test probably contains more errors than one that has reasonable spacing and white space. Multiple-choice options should not be listed horizontally on the same line; they should be listed vertically below the item.

Examples

> *Poor Format:* What is the movement of animals from one environment to another between summer and winter called? (a) conditioning (b) hibernation (c) territorial reflex (d) migration

> *Improved Format:* What is the movement of animals from one environment to another between summer and winter called?
>
> **a.** conditioning
> **b.** hibernation
> **c.** territorial reflex
> **d.** migration

Finally, the format of the test should enhance scoring accuracy and efficiency. For older students, use a separate answer sheet that can be designed for scoring ease. Simply repeat the directions and list the items by number. Students circle or write in their answers. If you have students answer on the same piece of paper that contains the questions, leave blanks to the left of each binary-choice, multiple-choice, or matching item, and blanks on the right-hand side of the page for completion items. For younger students, minimize transfer of answers by having them circle or underline the correct answer or write the answer in the space provided in the item.

ADMINISTERING CLASSROOM ASSESSMENTS

When administering tests and other classroom assessments, several procedures are desirable. First, the environment during testing must be conducive to student performance. This means that there is sufficient light, the temperature is appropriate, and efforts are made to ensure quiet with no interruptions. Put a sign on your door—Testing, Do Not Disturb. Special arrangements will need to be made for students with exceptionalities (see Chapter 11). In essence, the physical environment should not interfere with students' demonstrating what they know, understand, and can do.

Second, students should not be overly anxious about taking the test or completing the assessment. Although some anxiety is good, too much inhibits students so that their performance will not reflect their actual level of attainment. Your challenge is to find the correct balance between too much and too little anxiety. Anxiety is increased when successful student performance depends on comparisons with other students in the class, when there is insufficient time to complete the test or assessment, when negative contingencies are attached if students do not do well, when the stakes are raised, and when the purpose is to audit learning.

Third, arrange an assessment to both discourage and prevent cheating. Research summarized by Cizek (1999, 2003) indicates that many, if not most, students cheat or know that others cheat. This includes looking at other students' test answers, using crib notes or a cheat sheet, plagiarism, getting others to do the students' work, obtaining copies of a test or correct answers, collusion, and using prohibited materials (Cizek, 2003). Of special note is plagiarism. With increased access to the Internet, students have access to prepared text on just about any topic. In addition to simply using such text, students may claim that they did not understand what constitutes plagiarism.

Cheating can be prevented by providing clear guidelines for students about cheating and the importance of providing honest answers to improve learning, by formatting tests and answer sheets to make cheating difficult, by careful and continuous close monitoring of students during tests, by using special seating arrangements, and by using more than one form of the test (e.g., different item order) (Linn & Miller, 2005). If plagiarism is possible, special precautions should be made, including providing examples to students and explaining how the information could be presented so that it is not plagiarized. Show students how you can use the Internet to detect papers that have been purchased or otherwise obtained from the Internet.

SUMMARY

This chapter examined the nature of knowledge and simple understanding learning expectations and selected-response and brief constructed-response test items used to assess students on these expectations. Suggestions for preparing summative assessments and assembling a test were also presented. Major points include the following:

- Preparation for summative assessment includes appropriately sampling what students are responsible for knowing, having the appropriate length and number of assessments, carefully using the tests provided by publishers, preparing students, properly scheduling the assessment, and allowing instruction to influence the final makeup of the test.

- Knowledge can be classified as declarative or procedural.

- Declarative knowledge often emphasizes memorization of facts, concepts, and principles.

- Declarative understanding involves greater generalization and connection with existing knowledge.

- Procedural knowledge emphasizes memorization of skills, steps, and procedures.

- Procedural understanding emphasizes the application of process skills to new problems and situations.

- Understanding varies in degree, from simple to deep.

- Simple understanding is defined by comprehension and application.

- Completion and short-answer items are effective if memorization is avoided, a single brief answer is correct, wording is understood by all students, and the specific nature and length of the answer is clearly implied.

- Matching items are effective for assessing simple understanding of related facts or concepts as long as responses are short, premises and responses are homogeneous, lists are logically ordered, no grammatical clues are given, and no more than 10 premises are in one matching item.

- Binary-choice items, such as true/false items, are effective if they are clearly, succinctly, and positively stated as single propositions or statements.

- Multiple-choice items are effective if they are clearly and directly stated with one correct answer, include plausible distractors, and do not provide clues to the correct answer.

- Simple understanding for application is assessed with objective items for application when previously learned facts or skills are used to solve problems in novel situations.

- Objective tests are put together by considering the directions, proper arrangement of the items, and correct formatting of the contents of the test.

- When administering tests, establish an appropriate physical environment and amount of student anxiety, and prevent cheating.

SELF-INSTRUCTIONAL REVIEW EXERCISES

1. Match the descriptions in part A with the criteria for constructing summative assessments in part B. Each criterion may be used once, more than once, or not at all.

Part A

_____ **(1)** Revision of a test provided in instructional materials

_____ **(2)** Use of test blueprint

_____ **(3)** Teaching test-taking skills

_____ **(4)** Using an adequate number of items for each area

_____ **(5)** Providing time for student questions

_____ **(6)** Chapter review

Part B

a. Representative sampling

b. Length of assessment

c. Number of assessments

d. Use of publisher's test

e. Preparing students

f. Scheduling assessments

2. Identify each of the following items as declarative (D) or procedural (P), and as demonstrating knowledge (K) or simple understanding (SU).

a. Define procedural knowledge.

b. What is the sequence of steps in preparing an objective test?

c. Give an example of a multiple-choice item that measures application.

d. List three suggestions for constructing matching items.

e. Predict whether students will have questions about how to answer the items in the test.

f. Review the strategy a teacher has used to construct binary-choice test items to determine if they can be improved.

3. Match the suggestions or descriptions from part A with the type(s) of objective items in part B. Each type of item may be used once, more than once, or not at all; each suggestion or description may have more than one correct match.

Part A

_____ **(1)** Generally more time-consuming to construct

_____ **(2)** Scoring may be a problem

_____ **(3)** Effectively measures relations

_____ **(4)** Conveniently constructed from instructional materials

_____ **(5)** Responses ordered logically

_____ **(6)** Correct answers spread equally among all possible choices

_____ **(7)** Verbatim language from textbooks is avoided

_____ **(8)** Uses clear, concise statements

_____ **(9)** Uses blanks of equal length

Part B

a. Completion

b. Short answer

c. Matching

d. Binary choice

e. Multiple choice

4. Using the checklists for writing objective items, evaluate each of the following items and revise it so that it will be improved.

(1) _____ _____ are sloping ledges that are formed underwater next to most continents such as Australia and North America.

(2) How does energy from the sun affect the earth?

(3) Match the provinces or territories with the characteristics.

_____ Manitoba

_____ Prince Edward Island

_____ British Columbia

_____ Nunavut

_____ Saskatchewan

_____ Quebec

_____ Nova Scotia

_____ Yukon

_____ Ontario

_____ New Brunswick

  a. Smallest province

  b. Contains capital of Canada

  c. Whitehorse

  d. Saint John

  e. Montreal

  f. Halifax

  g. Newest territory

  h. Saskatoon

  i. Bordered by Pacific Ocean

  j. Winnipeg

(4) T   F   Students do not construct their own answers to every type of item except multiple choice.

(5) Circle the best answer.

Ontario is (a) bordered by Hudson Bay, (b) a province in which the Rocky Mountains are located, (c) an example of a province that is west of Alberta, (d) none of the above.

(6) Circle the correct answer.

Biodegradable substances are

  a. nonrenewable resources.

  b. materials that can be broken down into substances that are simpler and do not result in environmental pollution.

  c. becoming less popular.

  d. like fossil fuels.

SUGGESTIONS FOR ACTION RESEARCH

1. Collect some examples of test items. Analyze the items and the format of the test in relation to the suggestions provided in the chapter. Show how you would improve the items and the format of the test.

2. Find ten examples of items that measure different types of knowledge expectations (e.g., declarative, procedural, simple understanding). Change items that measure knowledge to ones that measure simple understanding.

3. Conduct an interview with two teachers and ask them how they construct test items. Ask them if they use each of the test preparation guidelines (sampling, using publisher's tests, and so on). Ask them to give you some advice about putting together a test, and see if their advice is consistent with the suggestions in the chapter.

4. With another student, make up a knowledge test of the content of this chapter that could be taken in one hour. Begin with a table of specifications or outline and indicate the learning expectations. Include knowledge and simple understanding items. Give the test to four other students for their critique, and then revise the test as needed. Show the original test and the revised one to your supervisor or teacher for a critique and further suggestions. Keep a journal of your progress in making up the test. What was difficult? How much time did it take? What would have made the process more efficient?

Chapter 7
Selected-Response, Short-Answer, and Essay Items
Assessing Deep Understanding and Reasoning

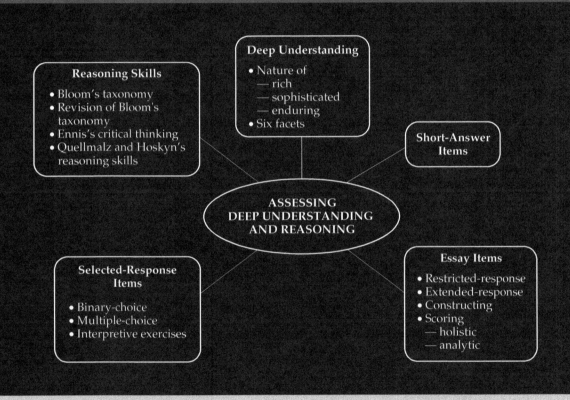

In this chapter, we examine the assessment of deep understanding and reasoning—how students use their knowledge for more complex thinking. As we will see, there are different ways to conceptualize cognitive skills such as thinking and reasoning. Two methods, the interpretive exercise and the essay question, are emphasized as the preferred approaches when using a paper-and-pencil test to assess these skills and accompanying deep understanding. In Chapter 8, we will see how performance assessments also provide an excellent way to assess deep understanding and reasoning.

WHAT IS DEEP UNDERSTANDING?

In this book, we have distinguished between *simple* and *deep* understanding. The difference is a matter of degree. With simple understanding, you can make sense out of something, and with further involvement and more detailed information, you deepen your understanding to eventually use information in new ways; you can think about what is known in a systematic, integrated, and holistic manner; and you can explain relationships. This continuum is represented in Figure 7.1 with terms that are associated with knowledge and different levels of understanding. The terms describe the nature of knowledge and the relative degree of understanding that is demonstrated, showing the spectrum from shallow to sophisticated.

Don't get too concerned about the usage of words such as *apply*, *interpret*, and *explain*, or quibble about whether these terms refer to different levels in Bloom's taxonomy of higher-order thinking skills or other listings of cognitive skills. Each typology or way of presenting the concepts will be different. The main point is that deep understanding implies that students know the "essence" of something: they can think about and use knowledge in new and sophisticated ways, and grasp the idea of relativity and significance (McTighe & Wiggins, 2004; Wiggins, 1998; Wiggins & McTighe, 2005); they can discover and interpret new

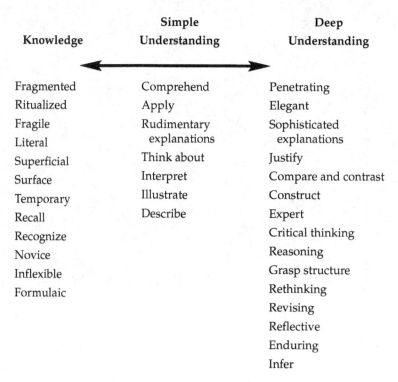

| | Simple Understanding | Deep Understanding |
Knowledge		
Fragmented	Comprehend	Penetrating
Ritualized	Apply	Elegant
Fragile	Rudimentary	Sophisticated
Literal	explanations	explanations
Superficial	Think about	Justify
Surface	Interpret	Compare and contrast
Temporary	Illustrate	Construct
Recall	Describe	Expert
Recognize		Critical thinking
Novice		Reasoning
Inflexible		Grasp structure
Formulaic		Rethinking
		Revising
		Reflective
		Enduring
		Infer

Figure 7.1 The Knowledge/Understanding Continuum

Source: Adapted in part from McTighe & Wiggins (2004), Perkins (1993), and Bruner (1960).

relationships, construct novel explanations, and reason using what they comprehend. They are able to understand the complexity of knowledge. As pointed out by Borich and Tombari (2004), when we initially learn about something, our understanding is undeveloped and unsophisticated. As we have more experience with it, our understanding deepens. For example, you may have had a surface or simple understanding of the meaning of the term *performance assessment* before reading this book. Initially, you may be able to provide a definition and simple understanding by recognizing performance assessments. Your understanding will be richer and more developed after you study performance assessments, use some in the classroom, and discuss their strengths and weaknesses with others.

Deep understanding expectations are needed to help students internalize what they are able to do with their knowledge and construct meaningful connections with what they already know. For example, Grant Wiggins, who has focused extensively on the nature of understanding and its importance in assessment, does not distinguish between simple and deep understanding in his recent work (McTighe & Wiggins, 2004). Rather, he emphasizes six *facets* of understanding (Table 7.1).

Table 7.1 Six Facets of Understanding

Facet	Description	Example
Explanation	Sophisticated explanations and theories that justify reasoning and conclusions	Explain how informal observation can be used to detect student understanding.
Interpretation	Narratives, translations, and other meanings derived	Come to a conclusion about what the standardized test scores indicate about the student's strengths and weaknesses.
Application	Use of knowledge in new situations and contexts	Construct appropriate classroom assessments for new learning expectations.
Perspective	Criticism and insightful thinking to justify or warrant ideas	Why would the public be concerned about the use of authentic assessments in the classroom?
Empathy	Ability to understand how others think and their perspectives	Describe how students feel when taking a high-stakes, large-scale exam.
Self-knowledge	Wisdom of knowing limitations of understandings and learning strategies that are most effective	What further understanding about performance assessments is needed? How will it be best to learn this information?

Source: Adapted in part from McTighe & Wiggins (2004). *Understanding by design.* Alexandria, VA: Association of Supervision and Curriculum Development.

At the very least, distinguish between surface recall and recognition knowledge, and deep understanding. Use the examples of how understanding can be operationalized in this chapter to match your provincial or school division learning standards. Even if these standards do not emphasize deep understanding, frame your classroom learning expectations and instruction so that these very important learning outcomes are stressed. As we will see, the implication for assessment is significant. Assessments that work well for knowledge and simple understanding are different from those that should be used for deep understanding.

WHAT ARE REASONING SKILLS?

In Chapter 2, reasoning expectations were defined as the use of knowledge for reasoning and problem solving. This suggests that reasoning is something students do with their knowledge, a kind of cognitive or mental operation that employs their understanding to some end. Of course, knowledge and simple understanding, like reasoning, involve some type of thinking skill. Thinking occurs in the most fundamental process of remembering something, just as it does in demonstrating understanding and reasoning. It is in the nature of the thinking, however, that knowledge is distinguished from reasoning.

Reasoning, as we have conceptualized it here, involves some kind of mental manipulation of knowledge. The task is to *employ* knowledge to interpret and draw inferences, solve a problem, make a judgment or decision, or engage in creative or critical thinking. Thinking is not normally content-free. Thus, it is helpful to identify three ingredients in reasoning. The first is the mental skill needed to perform the task; a second is the declarative or procedural knowledge or simple understanding needed; and the third is the task itself. These ingredients differentiate cognitive skills such as analysis, comparison, and discrimination from the problem-solving or interpretation task (see Figure 7.2). The mental skills are used in conjunction with knowledge to perform the task. Even though we are sometimes interested in teaching and assessing students on their ability to perform certain types of mental operations, such as analysis or deductive logic, we don't normally test these skills directly. Rather, we are usually interested in the *use* of these skills to demonstrate deep understanding or to perform a problem-solving task in subject-matter domains.

Assessing reasoning skills is challenging because the expectation is difficult to define. It is one thing to note the importance of teaching and testing *higher-order thinking* skills or *reasoning* skills, but operationalizing these general ideas into specific assessment expectations is far from straightforward. The literature on thinking and reasoning identifies three distinct conceptualizations, each based in a different academic discipline. Educators have emphasized mental skills, as illustrated by Bloom's taxonomy. Psychologists have focused on the application of problem-solving strategies and processes. Philosophers have contributed to our understanding of deductive and inductive logic and to "critical thinking." Each discipline has had a different focus, but all are discussing thinking skills or reasoning in a broad sense. We briefly present four thinking skill/reasoning frameworks that have been developed based on these perspectives. Each represents a different way to organize, label, and define thinking skills.

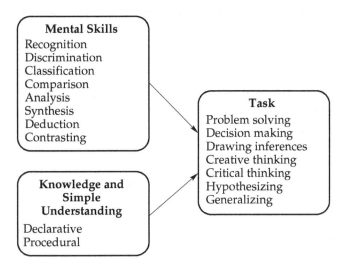

Figure 7.2 Major Components of Reasoning

We emphasize that selecting a way to operationalize thinking skills is up to you—there is no single right or best way. But assessing reasoning or thinking skills, no matter how one defines them, requires close attention to the nature of the specific mental operation involved. The following four frameworks are provide suggestions and examples for developing reasoning expectations.

Bloom's Taxonomy of the Cognitive Domain

Bloom's taxonomy has been described and, as previously noted, is both the most-used and the most-dated conceptualization of thinking. This taxonomy has popularized the term *higher-order thinking skills* because the six levels are interpreted by most as hierarchical (some are considered higher than others). However, considering the taxonomy as hierarchical does not make much practical sense. The third level, application, is considered to be lower than analysis, whereas comprehension, as measured by making an inference, is at the second level. Is the ability to make an inference a prerequisite for analysis? Our experience is that trying to teach and test as though the taxonomy is a hierarchy is unrealistic. It makes more sense to first identify the task, then examine the cognitive skills needed to complete it, rather than to delay evaluation until skills in other levels are demonstrated. Furthermore, Bloom's taxonomy has now been incorporated into more contemporary conceptualizations.

Revision of Bloom's Taxonomy

In the revision of Bloom's taxonomy (Anderson & Krathwohl, 2001), three cognitive processes apply to deep understanding and reasoning: analyze, evaluate, and create. Analyze is essentially the same as *analysis* in other frameworks, whereas evaluate is similar to critical thinking and problem solving. Create is similar to *inquiry* and emphasizes synthesis of information and problem solving. The three cognitive processes, with definitions and examples, are summarized in Table 7.2.

Table 7.2 Deep Understanding and Reasoning Parts of the Revision of Bloom's Taxonomy

Cognitive Process	Definition	Subtypes	Illustrative Verbs	Examples
Analyze	Break material into its constituent parts and determine how the parts relate.	Differentiating	Discriminating, distinguishing, focusing, selecting	Distinguish between relevant and irrelevant numbers in a math word problem.
		Organizing	Finding coherence, integrating, outlining	Structure historical evidence for and against a particular historical explanation.
		Attributing	Deconstructing	Determine the point of view of an author based on his or her political perspective.
Evaluate	Make judgments based on criteria and standards.	Checking	Coordinating, detecting, monitoring, testing	Determine if conclusions follow from observed data.
		Critiquing	Judging	Judge which of two methods is the best way to solve a problem.
Create	Pull elements together to form a whole; reorganize elements into a new structure or pattern.	Generating	Hypothesizing	Generate a hypothesis to account for observed phenomenon.
		Planning	Designing	Plan a research paper.
		Producing	Constructing	Build habitats for a specific purpose.

Source: Adapted from L.W. Anderson & D.R. Krathwohl (2001). *A taxonomy for learning, teaching, and assessing: A revision of Bloom's taxonomy of educational objectives.* Boston: Allyn and Bacon. Copyright © 2001 Pearson Education. Reprinted by permission of the publisher.

Ennis's Taxonomy of Critical Thinking Dispositions and Abilities

Critical thinking is defined by Ennis as "reasonable reflective thinking that is focused on deciding what to believe or do" (1987, p. 10). Ennis notes that critical thinking *involves* higher-order thinking skills, but the act of thinking critically must include a decision or judgment about a belief, action, or answer. Critical thinking means being able to carefully analyze a knowledge claim or information to judge its merit and worth in relation to the action or belief that results. It is the ability to evaluate and weigh information and evidence to make an informed judgment. These descriptions are similar to how Wiggins (1998) defines deep understanding. In the end, some judgments are better than others.

To promote "reasonable" thinking in making judgments, Ennis lists several abilities that should be employed. The "best" judgment results from being able to successfully apply these abilities. From a practical standpoint, the abilities are organized in a series of steps that are employed in the process of critical thinking. By following the steps and using the abilities, students are able to reason effectively.

Table 7.3 presents the steps involved in critical thinking, along with the critical thinking abilities required and practical examples. Assessment of critical thinking as reasoning begins with identifying the task—the judgment that the student needs to make. Students are presented with information formulated to assess specific critical thinking abilities. Thus, you may purposefully include some illogical arguments or unreliable sources of information

Table 7.3 Critical Thinking Steps and Abilities

Steps	Abilities	Examples
Clarify problem	Identify or formulate a question; put the problem in context; ask questions or seek information to clarify the problem	Which medication should Troy choose? What background factors would affect Troy's choice? Does Troy have any other options?
Gather information	Distinguish verifiable facts from value claims; determine the credibility of a source; distinguish relevant from irrelevant information, claims, or reasons; detect bias	What information is based on opinion about the medications and what is based on objective evidence? Should the information from drug companies be used? Is it important to know that a medication tastes good? Would a company representative be biased about the company's medication?

(continued)

Table 7.3 (Continued)

Make inferences	Recognize logical inconsistencies in deductive reasoning; recognize unwarranted claims or generalizations from inductive reasoning	The medication worked well with adults, but will it work as well with children? If the medication should not be used with adults, does this mean it shouldn't be used with children?
Conduct advanced clarification	Identify unstated assumptions; identify ambiguous or illogical arguments; determine the strength of an argument; detect fallacy labels such as *straw person, name-calling,* and *non sequitur;* detect inconsistencies; detect stereotypes; consider alternative judgments; distinguish cause and effect from relationships	How good is the evidence that a particular medication will be effective? Is a particular argument for a medication reasonable? Is calling one of the medications silly and insignificant important? What are the advantages and disadvantages of each medication?
Make a judgment	Decide on an answer, solution, or course of action	Select a medication and provide reasons for the decision.

Sources: Adapted from R.H. Ennis (1987). A taxonomy of critical thinking dispositions and abilities. In J. Boykoff Baron and R.J. Sternberg, *Teaching thinking skills: Theory and practice.* © 1987 W. H. Freeman and Company. Used with permission; S.P. Norris & R.H. Ennis (1995). *Evaluating critical thinking.* Pacific Grove, CA: Midwest Publications; and Beyer, B. K. (1985). Critical thinking: What is it? *Social Education, 22,* 270–276.

to see if students are able to recognize these and use them appropriately in defending their judgments. We will see that essay-type test questions are best for this type of assessment because students can be asked to defend their judgments or answers.

Quellmalz and Hoskyn's Framework for Reasoning Strategies

Quellmalz (1987) and Quellmalz and Hoskyn (1997) conducted an analysis of the different ways of conceptualizing thinking and reasoning skills as presented in the literature. They concluded that the various frameworks contained four common elements that made sense for teaching and assessment: analysis, comparison, inference and interpretation, and evaluation.

Analysis is used in essentially the same way as it is in Bloom's taxonomy. In this operation, students divide a whole into component parts. This includes identification of the parts, the relationships among different parts, and the relation of parts to the whole. With this skill, students are able to break down, differentiate, categorize, sort, or subdivide.

The second element, comparison, is concerned with reasoning about similarities and differences; the student compares, contrasts, and relates. Simple comparisons are done by pointing out one or several similarities and differences; for example, by asking "How are two sentences the same or how are they different?" More complex comparisons require reasoning about many attributes or components.

Inference and interpretation require deductive or inductive thinking. In a deductive task, students are asked whether one thing follows from another. Often, students are given a generalization or principles and are asked to identify or construct a correct conclusion. For example, giving students a fact like "Étienne is taller than Shuanda, and Shuanda is taller than Giselle," then asking, "Is Étienne taller or shorter than Giselle?" requires deductive thinking. Inductive reasoning involves reaching a reasonable conclusion or generalization from information provided. Other thinking skills that require inference include hypothesizing, predicting, and synthesizing.

In the final kind of reasoning, evaluation, students express or defend an opinion, judgment, or point of view. This is essentially the same as critical thinking. Students justify, explain, argue, and criticize.

The appeal of Quellmalz and Hoskyn's work is that the types of reasoning are easily applied to different subjects. Table 7.4 presents examples of what are labelled reasoning strategies.

The various frameworks that have been presented provide different ways to think about deep understanding and reasoning. Through the verbs they use and through examples, you

Table 7.4 Applications of Quellmalz and Hoskyn's Framework of Reasoning Strategies

Cognitive Strategy	Domain		
	Literacy	Social Science	Science
Analyze	Narrative Story, plot, and character elements; setting; style	Elements of an event, features of a culture, features of a historical period	Components of a process, features of animate and inanimate objects, evolution of species
	Persuasive issue Position, reasons, evidence, conclusion		
	Expository Main idea, support and elaboration, organization and coherence, style		

(continued)

Table 7.4 (Continued)			
Compare	Narrative elements, themes, points of view, evidence, accuracy, organization	Leaders, cultures, political systems, ideologies, time periods, accounts of an event	Regions, climates, scientific processes, energy sources, habitats, ecosystems
Infer and Interpret	Themes, motivation, mood, bias, predict cause and effect	Causes and influences, predict future effects, infer consequences	Test hypotheses, draw conclusions, infer consequences, link cause and effect, interdependencies
Evaluate	Significance, coherence, clarity, style, believability	Significance of contributions, practicality, credibility of arguments, alternative interpretations	Soundness of scientific procedures, credibility of conclusions, significance of findings, feasibility, impact

Source: Adapted from E.S. Quellmalz & J. Hoskyn (1997). Classroom assessment of reasoning strategies. In G. Phye (ed.), *Handbook of classroom assessment: Learning, adjustment, and achievement* (p. 108). San Diego, CA: Academic Press. Reprinted with permission from Elsevier Science.

can determine which framework is most closely related to the deep understanding and reasoning expectations in your discipline or classroom. You should also feel free to adapt one or more frameworks for your teaching. It's fine to pick and choose, mix and match, and modify as appropriate.

ASSESSING DEEP UNDERSTANDING AND REASONING

Before we consider several effective methods of assessing deep understanding and reasoning skills, two points should be emphasized. First, remember that each of the assessment methods we discuss in this book can be used to measure any learning expectation. Reasoning can be measured by selected-response items, and knowledge can be evaluated in student essays or performance products. However, some methods are better than others for assessing particular types of expectations. Second, normally when we assess reasoning, we are also measuring how much students understand. This is clearly illustrated in the scoring criteria for many essay items, in which students are graded for demonstrating an understanding of certain concepts or principles. But there is an important trade-off—items that assess reasoning and deep understanding well cannot even begin to sample the *amount* of knowledge and simple understanding that can be tested with simple objective items.

We will look at how the selected-response and short-answer items discussed in Chapter 6 work for assessing deep understanding reasoning, and then we will review two paper-and-pencil test methods that are better suited for assessing reasoning, but aren't as good for assessing knowledge—interpretive exercises and essays. In Chapter 8, we will examine performance assessment and its potential for measuring knowledge, reasoning, and skills.

Michelle Prytula

One of the things we do to ensure deep understanding in math is to use a four-quadrant form for assessing concept attainment. These quadrants appeal to different ways of knowing for one question—through a picture, manipulatives, an algorithm, and a description. Here's how it works: suppose students working in the algebra strand were asked a simple question, such as "$2A = 8$." Students would complete the first quadrant with a drawing or picture depicting two of something being eight. In the second quadrant, they would use manipulatives (such as algtiles, bingo chips, or whatever the students had used in class). With respect to the problem, students might put eight chips on one side and then divide the total chips into two sets, to show that it was solved using the manipulatives. In the third quadrant, students would solve the problem algebraically, using the algorithm for solving for "A" that they learned in class. In the last quadrant, which tends to be the most difficult, students would use fluid prose to explain how they solved the problem, and how it made sense to them. The variance in explanations is high, but authentic. We find that there is a direct relationship between how well the students complete the fourth quadrant, which is built from the previous three, and how well they understand and can solve the problem.

Short-Answer and Selected-Response Items

We will consider some examples of how short-answer and selected-response items can be used to measure the isolated thinking skills required for reasoning tasks, but there are far too many thinking skills to cover all of them with each type of item. The suggestions in Chapter 6 for writing items are also applicable here.

Short-Answer Items. Short-answer items can assess thinking skills when students are required to supply a brief response to a question or situation understood only by the use of the targeted thinking skills. Reasoning tasks, such as decision making and critical thinking, are not assessed very well with short-answer items.

Examples

(*Comparing*) List three ways the recession of the 1980s was like the depression of the 1930s.

(*Comparing*) How does a pine tree differ from an oak tree?

(*Comparing*) Name one difference between vertebrate and invertebrate animals.

(*Deductive reasoning*) Coach Liu substitutes his basketball players by height, so that the first substitute is the tallest player on the bench, the next substitute is the next tallest, and so forth. Reginald is taller than Sam, and Juan is taller than Reginald. Which of these three players should Coach Liu play first?

(*Credibility of a source*) The principal needs to decide if the new block schedule allows teachers to go into topics in greater detail. He can ask a parent, a teacher, or a principal from another school. Whom should he ask to get the most objective answer?

(*Analysis/prediction*) Shoppers want to be environmentally friendly, but they don't want to have to pay for plastic bags at the grocery store. The grocery store has decided to charge shoppers 5 cents for every plastic bag used. What action by the shoppers is most likely?

(*Investigating*) Several paper towel companies claim that their product absorbs more liquid than the other brands. Design an experiment to test the absorbency of each brand of paper towel.

(*Analysis*) List the anatomical structures of the kidney, explain the function of each part, and describe how they all work together.

McTighe and Wiggins show how sentence completion items can assess deep understanding (2004, p. 156):

What are the implications of _____?

What are other possible reactions to _____?

What are different points of view about _____?

What might happen if _____?

What is the meaning of _____?

Binary-Choice Items. Binary-choice items can be used to assess reasoning skills in several different ways. Students can be asked to indicate whether a statement is a fact or an opinion:

Examples

If the statement is a fact, circle F; if it is an opinion, circle O.

F   O   Literature is ancient Rome's most important legacy.
F   O   Ottawa is the capital of Canada.
F   O   The best way to wash a car is with a sponge.

Additional reasoning skills can be assessed using the same approach by developing some statements that are examples of the skill and some statements that are not examples. This can be done with many of the critical thinking skills (e.g., identifying stereotypes, biased statements, emotional language, relevant data, and verifiable data).

Examples

If the statement is an example of a stereotype, circle S; if it is not a stereotype, circle N.

S   N   Quebecois people are good musicians.
S   N   Women live longer than men.

If emotional language is used in the statement, circle E; if no emotional language is used, circle N.

E   N   Health care in Canada needs to be reformed so that people with serious health problems do not need to wait a long time for important tests.
E   N   Health care reform is going to cost a lot of money.

Logic can be assessed by asking if one statement follows logically from another:

Examples

> If the second part of the sentence explains why the first part is true, circle T for true; if it does not explain why the first part is true, circle F for false.
>
> T F Food is essential *because* it tastes good.
> T F Plants are essential *because* they provide oxygen.
> T F Michael is tall *because* he has blue eyes.

Multiple-Choice Items. Simple multiple-choice items can be used to assess reasoning in two ways. The first way is to focus on a particular skill, like the binary-choice items, in order to determine whether students are able to recognize and use that skill. The second way is to assess the extent to which students can use their knowledge and skills in performing a problem-solving, decision-making, or other reasoning task. The first use is illustrated with the following examples:

Examples

> (*Distinguishing fact from opinion*) Which of the following statements about our solar system is a fact rather than an opinion?
>
> **a.** The moon is made of attractive white soil.
> **b.** Stars can be grouped into important clusters.
> **c.** A star is formed from a white dwarf.
> **d.** Optical telescopes provide the best way to study the stars.
>
> (*Identifying assumptions*) When Lester B. Pearson said, "Of all our dreams today there is none more important—or so hard to realize—than that of peace in the world. May we never lose our faith in it or our resolve to do everything that can be done to convert it one day into reality," his assumption was that
>
> **a.** everyone would agree with him.
> **b.** Canadians would be impressed by the speech.
> **c.** there is no goal more important than peace.
> **d.** his words would be taught to students for years.
>
> (*Recognizing bias*) Peter told the group that "the ill-prepared, ridiculous Member of Parliament/MP has no business being involved in this important debate." Which words make Peter's statement biased?
>
> **a.** important, Member of Parliament
> **b.** important, business
> **c.** ill-prepared, ridiculous
> **d.** debate, involved
>
> (*Comparison*) One way in which insects are different from centipedes is that
>
> **a.** they are different colours.
> **b.** one is an arthropod.
> **c.** centipedes have more legs.
> **d.** insects have two body parts.

(*Analysis*) Ganesh decided to go sailing with a friend. He took supplies with him so he could eat, repair anything that might be broken, and find where on the lake he could sail. Which of the following supplies would best meet his needs?

a. bread, hammer, map
b. milk, bread, screwdriver
c. map, hammer, pliers, screwdriver
d. screwdriver, hammer, pliers

(*Synthesis*) What is the main idea in the following paragraph?

Julie picked a pretty blue boat for her first sail. It took her about an hour to understand all the parts of the boat and another hour to get the sail on. Her first sail was on a beautiful summer day. She tried to go fast but couldn't. After several lessons she was able to make her boat go fast.

a. Sailing is fun
b. Julie's first sail
c. Sailing is difficult
d. Going fast on a sailboat

The next few examples show how multiple-choice items can be used to assess students' ability to perform a reasoning task.

Examples

(*Hypothesizing*) If there were a significant increase in the number of hawks in a given area,

a. the number of plants would increase.
b. the number of mice would increase.
c. there would be fewer hawk nests.
d. the number of mice would decrease.

(*Problem solving*) Farmers want to be able to make more money for the crops they grow, but too many farmers are growing too many crops. What can the farmers do to make more money?

a. Try to convince the public to pay higher prices.
b. Agree to produce fewer crops.
c. Reduce the number of farmers.
d. Work on legislation to turn farmland into parks.

(*Critical thinking*) Robert is deciding which car to buy. He is impressed with the sales representative for the Ford, and he likes the colour of the Buick. The Ford is smaller and gets more kilometres per litre of gas. The Buick takes larger tires and has a smaller trunk. More people can ride in the Ford. Which car should Peter purchase if he wants to do everything he can to ensure that his favourite lake does not become polluted?

a. Ford
b. Buick
c. either car
d. can't decide based on the information provided

(*Predicting*) Suppose that the Canadian prairies, the source of most of Canada's wheat, suffered a drought for several years and produced much less wheat than usual. What would happen to the price of wheat?

a. The price would rise.
b. The price would fall.
c. The price would stay the same.
d. People would eat less wheat.

Interpretive Exercises. The best type of short-answer or selected-response item for assessing reasoning skills is the interpretive exercise. It consists of information or data followed by several questions. The questions are based on the information or data, which can take the form of maps, paragraphs, charts, figures, a story, a table of data, or pictures. This form makes it possible to ask questions that require interpretation, analysis, application, critical thinking, and other reasoning skills.

Interpretive exercises have four major advantages over other types of items. First, because there are several questions about the same information, you can measure more reasoning skills in greater depth. Second, because information is provided, you can separate the assessment of the reasoning skills from content knowledge of the subject. If content is not provided in the question, as with most multiple-choice items, then providing a poor answer could be attributed to either the student's lack of knowledge or lack of reasoning skill. In the interpretive exercise, students have all or most of the information needed as part of the question, so successful performance provides a more direct measure of reasoning skill. Clearly, the intent of the exercise is to assess how students use the information provided to answer questions. If students know ahead of time that the information will be provided, then they can concentrate their study on application and other uses of the information.

A third advantage of the interpretive exercise is that it consists of relatively easy-to-use items that students will encounter in everyday living, such as maps, newspaper articles, and graphs. Consistent with constructivist learning theory, this connects the material better to the student, increasing meaningfulness and relevance. Finally, because interpretive exercises provide a standard structure for all students and are scored objectively, the results tend to be more reliable. Students are unable to select a reasoning skill they are most proficient with, as they can do with essay questions. They must use the one called for in each question. Like all objective items, the scoring is efficient, especially if the answers are not of the short-answer type. This is an important consideration in comparing interpretive exercises with essays and performance products, which are also used extensively for assessing reasoning skills.

Interpretive exercises have three limitations. First, they are time-consuming and difficult to write. Not only do you need to locate or develop new information or data at the right difficulty level, which could take considerable time, but you also need to construct the objective questions (multiple-choice ones will take longest). The information you first identify may need to be modified, and most teachers are not accustomed to writing several objective items for a single passage or example.

A second limitation is that you can't assess how students organize their thoughts and ideas or know whether they can produce their own answers without being cued. Third, many interpretive exercises rely heavily on reading comprehension, which puts poor readers at a distinct disadvantage. It takes them longer to read the material for understanding, let alone to reason about it. This disadvantage holds for other types of items that require extensive reading as well, but it is especially troublesome in interpretive exercises.

Whether you develop your own interpretive exercises or use ones that have already been prepared, the following suggestions will help ensure high quality (see Figure 7.3 for a checklist summary).

1. Identify the Reasoning Skills to Be Assessed Before Selection or Development of the Interpretive Exercise. The sequence you use is important; you want the exercise to fit your learning expectations, not have your learning expectations determined by the

---

✓ Are reasoning expectations clearly defined before writing the exercise?
✓ Is introductory material brief?
✓ Is introductory material new to the students?
✓ Are there several questions for each exercise?
✓ Does the exercise test deep understanding and reasoning (and not just simple understanding)?

Figure 7.3 Checklist for Writing Interpretive Exercises

exercise. This is especially important given the number of different conceptualizations of thinking and reasoning skills. What may be called "critical thinking" or "analysis" in a teacher's manual may not coincide with what you think the expectation is. You need a clear idea of the skill to be assessed and then to select or develop the material that best fits your definition.

2. Keep Introductory Material as Brief as Possible. Keeping the introductory material brief minimizes the influence of general reading ability. There should be just enough material so that the students can complete the reasoning task.

3. Select Similar but New Introductory Material. Reasoning skills are best measured with material that is new to the students. If the material is the same as that covered in class, you will measure rote memory or simple understanding rather than reasoning. Find or develop examples that are similar to what students have already studied. The material should vary slightly in form or content, but it should not be completely new. To accomplish this, take passages, examples, and data students have been exposed to and alter them sufficiently so that correct answers cannot be given by memory.

4. Construct Several Test Items for Each Exercise. The test items can be short-answer, multiple-choice, or binary-choice. Asking more than one question for each exercise obtains a better sample of the proficiency of students' reasoning skills. It is particularly inefficient to have a very long introductory passage and a single question. One common approach to asking questions is to give the students a key of possible answers and have them apply the key to selected aspects of the introductory material (key-type item). For example, if after reading a passage, students are asked to judge the relevance of different parts of the passage, the key could simply be as follows:

Key: A   if the statement is relevant

        B   if the statement is irrelevant

Or, if you are testing student ability to distinguish facts from opinions:

Key: A   if the statement is a fact

        B   if the statement is an opinion

If you use a key, do not mix different types of reasoning tasks in the same key (e.g., you wouldn't want to put relevant, irrelevant, fact, and opinion in the same key). Like a matching item, the choices should be homogeneous.

5. Construct Items to Assess Deep Understanding and Reasoning. Don't use questions that can be answered without even reading the introductory material. This happens when students' general knowledge is such that they can determine the correct answer from the question alone.

Interpretive exercises are illustrated in the following three examples. Note that many different formats can be used for the items. The reasoning skills that are assessed are indicated in parentheses next to the name of each example.

Example 1. Interpretive exercise[1] (drawing inferences, analyzing perspectives)

Two citizens spoke at the city council meeting. Here are their statements. Use the information to help you answer questions 10–13.

CITIZEN A: The Bélenger House should be restored and used as a museum. A museum would help the people of the community learn about their heritage and would attract tourists to La Lange. We should not sell the property to the Opti Company. La Lange has grown too quickly, and a factory would bring even more people into the area. In addition, a factory's industrial waste would threaten the quality of our water.

CITIZEN B: La Lange needs the Opti factory. The factory would provide needed jobs. The tax money it would bring into the community would help improve our streets, schools, and other city services. A museum, on the other hand, would hurt our local economy. Taxes would have to be raised to pay for the restoration of the Bélenger House. A museum would not create enough jobs to solve our unemployment problem.

Key: Write the letter A next to each statement that Citizen A would most likely agree with. Write the letter B next to each statement that Citizen B would most likely agree with.

_____ **(10)** Jobs are the foundation of a community.
_____ **(11)** Pollution problems will multiply.
_____ **(12)** We are in danger of losing the history of our community.
_____ **(13)** Hanging on to the past hurts the future.

Example 2. Interpretive exercise (recognizing the relevance of information)

Cally lost her pencil on her way to school. It was red and given to her by her grandmother. She wanted the teacher to ask the class if anyone found the pencil.

Key: Circle *yes* if the information in the sentence will help the class find the pencil. Circle *no* if the information in the sentence will not help the class find the pencil.

yes   no   **1.** The pencil was new.
yes   no   **2.** Cally rides the bus to school.
yes   no   **3.** The pencil is red.
yes   no   **4.** The pencil was a present from Cally's grandmother.
yes   no   **5.** The pencil had a new eraser.
yes   no   **6.** The teacher knows Cally's grandmother.

Example 3. Interpretive exercise (analysis, inference, error analysis)

Based on Figure 7.4, circle T if the statement is true and F if the statement is false.

T   F   Persons with disabilities account for a greater percentage of Saskatchewan urban poor than visible minorities.

T   F   Recent immigrants have the highest poverty rate.

T   F   Overall, the population of visible minorities is larger than the population of recent immigrants.

T   F   Persons of Aboriginal identity represent the largest distribution of Saskatchewan poor.

Statistical Profile of Urban Poverty in Saskatchewan					
	Total	Poor	Distribution of total	Distribution of poor	Poverty rate
Population groups (all persons)*	930 500	170 500	100%	100%	18%
Recent immigrants	7 700	3 500	1%	2%	45%
Visible minorities	26 600	8 000	3%	5%	30%
Aboriginal identity	70 900	37 600	8%	22%	53%
With disabilities	100 400	27 000	11%	16%	27%

* Population groups not mutually exclusive.
Note: A margin of error may be present due to rounding of figures. Percentages based on unrounded figures.

Figure 7.4 Profile of Saskatchewan's Urban Poor

Source: Adapted from the Canadian Council on Social Development (2000). Retrieved May 12, 2009: www.ccsd.ca/pubs/2000/up/b1-9.htm.

Answer each of the following questions:

What percentage of Saskatchewan's urban poor are visible minorities?
_____

Which population groups demonstrate the greatest poverty? _____

To effectively foster deep understanding, ask students to justify and explain their answers. This is best accomplished by providing opportunities to examine different responses and to evaluate these responses according to scoring criteria and/or a rubric. Students can be asked to determine which criteria are met, and they can examine inadequate responses and explain why. By critiquing responses and making suggestions for improvements, understanding is richer and more complete (Parke, Lane, Silver, & Magone, 2003).

An example of an interpretive item that assesses deep understanding in mathematics is illustrated in Figure 7.5. The expectation is student understanding of the concept "average." Students know in advance that they will need to explain their answer. The scoring criteria are summarized in Table 7.5, and examples of responses are shown in Figures 7.6 and 7.7. Can you match the answers with the scoring criteria?[2] (See Endnote 2 to check your evaluation.)

Essay Items

Essays can tap complex thinking by requiring students to organize and integrate information, interpret information, give arguments, give explanations, evaluate the merit of ideas,

Anita has four 20-point projects for science class. Anita's scores on the first three projects are shown below.

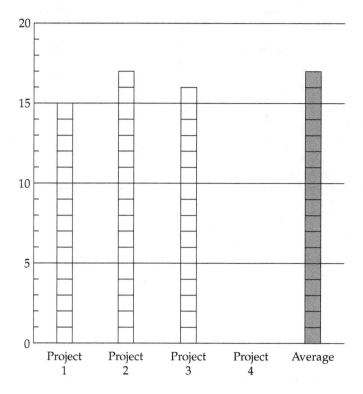

A. What score must Anita get on project 4 so that her average for the four projects is 17?

Answer: _____ . You may draw your answer on the graph.

B. Explain how you found your answer.

Figure 7.5 Example of Interpretive Item

Source: C.S. Parke, S. Lane, E.A. Silver, & M.E. Magone (2003). *Using assessment to improve middle-grades mathematics teaching and learning: Suggested activities using QUASAR tasks, scoring criteria, and students' work* (p. 96). Reston, VA: National Council of Teachers of Mathematics. Copyright © 2003 the National Council of Teachers of Mathematics. Reprinted with permission. All rights reserved.

Table 7.5 Bar Average Task Scoring Criteria

Level 4	Explanation, work, or drawing on the graph shows a correct and complete understanding of the concept of average in the context of the problem. The strategy used to obtain the correct answer is appropriate and is implemented completely and correctly. (Various solution strategies are provided in the task description.)
Level 3	Explanation, work, or drawing on the graph shows a good understanding of the concept of average in the context of the problem; however, the implementations of the strategy contain a minor error or omission. For example, in finding the total of the first three scores, the student may make a calculation error, which leads to an incorrect answer for the fourth score.
Level 2	Explanation, work, or drawing on the graph shows some understanding of the concept of average in the context of the problem, but the use of a strategy to obtain the answer is somewhat incomplete, unclear, or incorrect. For instance, the work may show a correct answer but provide only a general explanation that states that the scores were added to find an answer that worked.
Level 1	A beginning understanding of the concept of average in the context of the problem is revealed. The strategy used to obtain the answer is unclear or incorrect, or no strategy is apparent. The answer may be correct, but no explanation is provided, or possibly, the average of the first three scores is found.
Level 0	No understanding of the concept of average in the context of the problem is evident. Calculations are meaningless and no explanation is provided, or the explanations are meaningless and no explanation is provided, or the explanation simply restates the problem.

and conduct other types of reasoning. Although more objective formats are clearly superior for measuring knowledge, the essay is an excellent way to measure deep understanding and mastery of complex information. Research on student learning habits shows that when students know they will face an essay test, they tend to study by looking for themes, patterns, and relationships, and how information can be organized and sequenced. In contrast, when studying for objective tests, students tend to fragment information and memorize each piece.

Essay items that assess knowledge and simple understanding require relatively brief answers. These may be called *short essay* or *restricted-response essay* to distinguish them from short-answer items, even though the length of the answer does not necessarily indicate the type of expectation being measured. We will focus here on both *restricted-response* and *extended-response* essay items. The extended-response format is the best one for assessing deep understanding and reasoning expectations.

Anita has four 20-point projects for science class. Anita's scores on the first three projects are shown below.

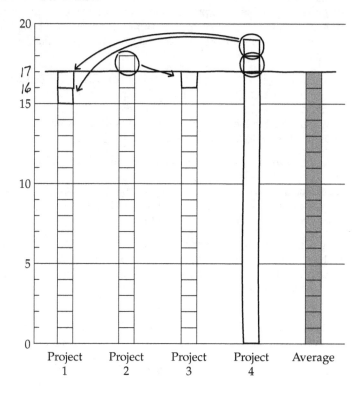

A. What score must Anita get on project 4 so that her average for the four projects is 17?

Answer: _____19_____ . You may draw your answer on the graph.

B. Explain how you found your answer.

I drew a line where the average should be then I put 17 on project 4. placed all the extras over the ones who needed it then drew 2 more that I needed on project 4 and the answer was 19.

Figure 7.6 Student A Response to Bar Average Task

Source: C.S. Parke, S. Lane, E.A. Silver, & M.E. Magone (2003). *Using assessment to improve middle-grades mathematics teaching and learning: Suggested activities using QUASAR tasks, scoring criteria, and students' work* (p. 96). Reston, VA: National Council of Teachers of Mathematics. Copyright © 2003 the National Council of Teachers of Mathematics. Reprinted with permission. All rights reserved.

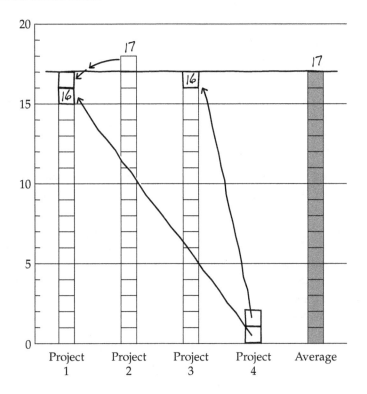

Anita has four 20-point projects for science class. Anita's scores on the first three projects are shown below.

A. What score must Anita get on project 4 so that her average for the four projects is 17?

Answer: _____2_____ . You may draw your answer on the graph.

B. Explain how you found your answer.

Because you would have to average out the other scores, and you would have to add points.

Figure 7.7 Student B Response to Bar Average Task

Source: C.S. Parke, S. Lane, E.A. Silver, & M.E. Magone (2003). *Using assessment to improve middle-grades mathematics teaching and learning: Suggested activities using QUASAR tasks, scoring criteria, and students' work* (p. 96). Reston, VA: National Council of Teachers of Mathematics. Copyright © 2003 the National Council of Teachers of Mathematics. Reprinted with permission. All rights reserved.

Examples: Restricted-Response Essay Questions

> Why are tornadoes more likely to strike Alberta than Nova Scotia?
> Why are tomatoes better for your health than potato chips?
> What is the effect on inflation of raising the prime interest rate?

Examples: Extended-Response Essay Questions

> Explain how the fertilizer that farmers use to grow crops may pollute our lakes and streams.
> Describe the major events that led to the beginning of World War I, showing how the events are related.
> Give an example, new to me and not one from class, of how the law of supply and demand would make prices of some products increase.

Advantages and Disadvantages. The major advantage of using essay questions is that deep understanding, complex thinking, and reasoning skills can be assessed. Essays motivate students to adopt better study habits and provide students with flexibility in their response. Written responses allow you to evaluate the ability of students to communicate their reasoning. Compared to developing selected-response items that measure reasoning, essay items are less time-consuming to construct. However, constructing a *good* essay question may take considerable time.

The major disadvantages of essay items are related to scoring student responses. Reading and scoring answers is very time-consuming, especially if done conscientiously to give students meaningful feedback. From a practical standpoint, most teachers find that they can give only a few essay items. Scoring essays is also notoriously unreliable.

In most classrooms, only a single individual—the teacher—judges the answers, and variations in mood, halo effects, expectations, the order in which students are evaluated, and other factors affect professional judgments. This does not imply that it is inappropriate to use subjective judgments in scoring. You *want* to be able to make judgments; that's one reason for using the essay format. When done appropriately, these judgments are professional, not intuitive. We will review guidelines for ensuring high-quality scoring shortly.

A final shortcoming of essay items is that they do not provide a very good sampling of content knowledge. The essay cannot sample well because relatively few questions are asked. Sampling is also limited to the reasoning skills that are assessed. For example, a single extended-response essay item that asks students to make a decision based on information provided may give you a good indication of one or two reasoning skills, but several shorter items could sample different types of skills.

Constructing Essay Items. Essay items are strengthened by adhering to the following suggestions, summarized in Figure 7.8. In the next section we will review important principles for scoring student answers.

1. Construct the Item to Elicit Skills Identified in the Learning Expectation. Once the reasoning skill is identified, the wording in the question needs to elicit the

✓ Is the targeted reasoning skill measured?
✓ Is the task clearly specified?
✓ Is there enough time to answer the questions?
✓ Are choices among several questions avoided?

Figure 7.8 Checklist for Writing Essay Items

specific skill(s) needed to answer the question. This is easier with restricted-response items that focus on a single reasoning skill. With extended-response items, the scoring criteria can be matched to the skills assessed. To write the item to match the expectation, start with a standard stem, then modify it as needed for the subject and level of student ability. Some examples of such items are illustrated in Table 7.6.

2. Write the Item So That Students Clearly Understand the Specific Task. After reading an essay item, students ask, "What does the teacher want in my answer?" If the assessment task is described ambiguously, so that different students interpret what is required differently, many responses will be off target. Such responses lead to flawed interpretations by teachers. When students misinterpret the task, you don't know if they have the targeted skill or not, leading to invalid conclusions.

To clearly set forth the nature of the task, try to make the essay question as specific as possible. Don't be hesitant about stating the desired response explicitly.

Examples

> *Poor:* Why do Haitian farmers have trouble making a living?
>
> *Improved:* Describe how the weather, soil, and poverty in Haiti contribute to the plight of farmers. Indicate which of these three factors contributes most to the difficulties farmers experience, and give reasons for your selection.
>
> *Poor:* How was World War I different from World War II?
>
> *Improved:* How were the social and political factors in Germany leading up to World War I different from those leading up to World War II? Focus your answer on the 10-year period that preceded the beginning of each war.

You can see that each of the "poorly" worded items gives students too much freedom to write about any of a number of aspects of either Haiti or the differences between the wars.

Another way to clarify for students the nature of the task is to indicate the scoring criteria in the question. This can be labelled a *scoring plan, scoring criteria,* or *attributes to be scored.* It essentially tells the students what you will be looking for when grading their answers. This is particularly important if the organization of the response or writing skills are included as criteria.

Table 7.6 Sample Item Stems for Assessing Reasoning Skills

Skill	Stem
Comparing	Describe the similarities and differences between . . . Compare the following two methods for . . .
Relating cause and effect	What are major causes of . . . ? What would be the most likely effects of. . . . ?
Justifying	Which of the following alternatives do you favour and why? Explain why you agree or disagree with the following statement.
Summarizing	State the main points included in . . . Briefly summarize the contents of . . .
Generalizing	Formulate several valid generalizations from the following data. State a set of principles that can explain the following events.
Inferring	In light of the facts presented, what is most likely to happen when . . . ? How would Member of Parliament X be likely to react to the following issue?
Classifying	Group the following items according to . . . What do the following items have in common?
Creating	List as many ways as you can think of for . . . Make up a story describing what would happen if . . .
Applying	Using the principle of . . . as a guide, describe how you would solve the following problem. Describe a situation that illustrates the principle of . . .
Analyzing	Describe the reasoning errors in the following paragraph. List and describe the main characteristics of . . .
Synthesizing	Describe a plan for proving that . . . Write a well-organized report that shows . . .
Evaluating	Describe the strengths and weaknesses of . . . Using the given criteria, write an evaluation of . . .

Source: R.L. Linn & M.D. Miller (2005). *Measurement and assessment in teaching* (9th ed.) (p. 235). Adapted by permission of Pearson Education, Inc., Upper Saddle River, New Jersey.

Examples of Scoring Criteria

(For Scoring Writing Skills)

- Organization
- Clarity
- Appropriateness to audience
- Mechanics

(For Scoring an Argument)

- Distinguishing between facts and opinions
- Judging credibility of a source
- Identifying relevant material
- Recognizing inconsistencies
- Using logic

(For Scoring Decision Making)

- Identifying goals or purpose
- Identifying obstacles
- Identifying and evaluating alternatives
- Justifying the choice of one alternative

3. Indicate Approximately How Much Time Students Should Spend on Each Essay Item. You should have some idea of how much time students will need to answer each item. For restricted-response questions, the amount of time needed is relatively short and easy to estimate. For extended-response items, estimating is more difficult. You can get some idea by writing draft answers, and, as you gain more experience, previous student responses to similar questions will help. Take into consideration the writing abilities of your students, and ensure that even your slowest writers can complete their answers satisfactorily in the time available. (You want to assess reasoning, not writing speed!) If you are unsure about the time needed, err by providing more time rather than less.

4. Avoid Giving Students Options as to Which Essay Questions They Will Answer. Many teachers offer students a choice of questions to answer. For example, if there are seven questions, the teacher may tell students to answer their choice of three. Students love such questions because they can answer the items they are best prepared for. They will especially like this approach if they know before taking the test that they will have a choice. Then they can restrict their study to part of the material, rather than to all of it (you can avoid this by telling students *you* will select the items they will write on).

Giving students a choice of questions, however, means that each student may be taking a different test. Differences in the difficulty of each question are probably unknown. This makes scoring more problematic, and your inferences of student ability less valid. It is true that you can't measure every important expectation, and giving students a choice does provide them an opportunity to do their best work. However, this advantage is outweighed by difficulties in scoring and making sound inferences.

Scoring Essays. Scoring essay question responses is difficult because each student writes a unique answer and many distractions affect scoring reliability. Obviously, scoring is subjective, so practise a few procedures to ensure that your professional judgments are accurate. The following guidelines will help (see Figure 7.9).

✓ Is the answer outlined before testing students?

✓ Is the scoring method—holistic or analytic—appropriate?

✓ Is the role of writing mechanics clarified?

✓ Are items scored one at a time?

✓ Is the order in which the papers are graded changed?

✓ Is the identity of the student anonymous?

Figure 7.9 Checklist for Scoring Essays

1. Outline What Constitutes a Good or Acceptable Answer as a Scoring Key. This should be completed before administering or scoring student responses. If done before the test is finalized, an outline provides you with an opportunity to revise the stem or question based on what you learn by delineating the response. Specify the points before reading student answers so that you are not unduly influenced by the initial papers you read. These papers can set the standard for what follows. The scoring key provides a common basis for evaluating each answer. An outline lessens the influence of other extraneous factors, such as vocabulary or neatness.

2. Select an Appropriate Scoring Method. Essays are scored in two ways: holistically or analytically. In **holistic** scoring, the teacher makes an overall judgment about the answer, giving it a single score or grade. The score can be based on a general impression or on several specific scoring criteria used to come up with a single score for each essay. This is often accomplished by placing essays in designated piles that represent different degrees of quality. The holistic method is most appropriate for extended-response essays (in which the responses are not limited and are generally long). Table 7.7 shows an example of a holistic scoring guide for an extended-response essay item.

Teacher's Corner

Joshua Cole

The type of test questions that I use to assess students' deep understanding and reasoning skills are generally open-ended essay-type questions. These test questions are directly related to the curriculum, but have a sense of creativity that allows the students to expand on the basic information that they have been taught. For instance, some open-ended essay test questions will include different scenarios so that the students will be able to think critically in their attempt to answer them. Ultimately, these types of questions challenge my students to think beyond the content and give answers that truly have meaning to them.

Analytic scoring is achieved by giving each of the identified criteria separate points. Thus, there would be several scores for each essay, and probably a total score that results from adding all the component scores. Analytic scoring is preferred for restricted-response questions (for which there is a limit to the amount of response the student provides). The advantage of analytic scoring is that it provides students with more specific feedback (though this should not replace individualized teacher comments). However, analytic scoring can be very time-consuming, and sometimes adding scored parts does not do justice to the overall student response. To avoid excessive attention to specific factors, keep the number of features to be scored analytically to three or four. The holistic scoring guide used in Table 7.7 is transformed into an analytic guide in Table 7.8.

3. Clarify the Role of Writing Mechanics. Suppose you are a biology teacher and you use essay questions. Does it matter if students spell poorly or use bad sentence structure? Such writing mechanics can certainly influence your overall impression of an answer, so decide early about whether and to what extent these factors are included as scoring criteria. Regardless of how you decide to incorporate writing mechanics, it is generally best to give students a separate score for these skills (as long as they were among your expectations) and not add this score into the total.

Table 7.7 Example of Essay Holistic Scoring Guide

Item: Compare and contrast the first and second Iraq wars. Show how they were similar and how they were different along geographic, political, and natural resource dimensions.

Level of Performance	Description
Exceptional (5)	Thorough and detailed understanding of both wars; provides justifications for all points; complete listing of similarities and differences for all dimensions; provides additional insights
Excellent (4)	Complete understanding of both wars; justifications for most points; lists similarities and differences for all dimensions
Very Good (3)	Mostly complete understanding of both wars; justifications for some points; most similarities and differences for two dimensions
Acceptable (2)	Incomplete understanding of one or both wars; justifications provided for some points, though incomplete; similarities and differences listed with some attention to dimensions
Poor (1)	Incomplete understanding of both wars; justifications inadequate or not present; similarities and differences not correct

Table 7.8 Example of Essay Analytic Scoring Guide

Item: Compare and contrast the first and second Iraq wars. Show how they were similar and how they were different along geographic, political, and natural resource dimensions.

Facet	Inadequate	Adequate	Very Good	Excellent	Points
	1	*2*	*3*	*4*	
Understands both wars	Clearly does not under-stand	Demonstrates minimal understanding	Demonstrates complete understanding of most aspects	Demonstrates complete understanding of all aspects	
Similarities	Does not address	Shows one correct similarity	Shows two correct similarities	Shows at least three correct similarities	
Differences	Does not address	Shows one correct difference	Shows two correct differences	Shows at least three correct differences	
Inclusion of dimensions	Fails to include any dimensions	Includes one correct dimension	Includes two correct dimensions	Includes at least three correct dimensions	
TOTAL POINTS					

4. Use a Systematic Process in Scoring Many Essays at the Same Time. When faced with a pile of papers to grade, it's tempting to simply start with the first paper, grade all the questions for that student, and then go on to the next student. To lessen the influence of order and your own fatigue, however, score one item at a time for all students, and change the order of the papers for each question. Reliability will increase if you read all responses to question 1 in one order, all responses to question 2 in a different order, and so on. This technique discourages you from allowing the answer a student gives to the first question to influence your evaluations of the remaining answers. Score all answers to each item in one sitting, if possible. This helps you to be consistent in applying criteria to the answers.

5. If Possible, Keep the Identity of the Student Anonymous. It is best not to know whose answer you are grading. Then you will not be influenced by impressions of the student from class discussion or other tests. This source of error, which is probably the most serious one that influences results, is difficult to control because most teachers get to know the writing of their students. You can have students put their names on the back of the papers, but the best way to minimize the potential bias is to be consciously aware of it.

SUMMARY

This chapter focused on the assessment of deep understanding and reasoning skills. The following points summarize the chapter:

- Reasoning is mental manipulation of knowledge for some purpose. Many different thinking skills are involved.

- Bloom's taxonomy represents a popular, though dated, framework for identifying reasoning skills. New categories are suggested in the revision of Bloom's taxonomy.

- Deep understanding is in-depth, rich, detailed, reflective, and sophisticated to facilitate complex mental representations and reasoning.

- Critical thinking involves the application of evaluative thinking skills, such as identifying irrelevant information, analyzing an argument, detecting bias, and using deductive logic to decide what to do or believe.

- Quellmalz and Hoskyn's framework combines other conceptualizations to result in five major types of reasoning: recall, analysis, comparison, inference, and evaluation.

- Deep understanding and reasoning expectations are best assessed by interpretive exercises and essay items, though selected-response and brief constructed-response questions can be used effectively to measure specific thinking skills.

- Binary-choice items are good for assessing a student's ability to discriminate among differences such as fact or opinion, relevant or irrelevant, and biased or unbiased.

- Multiple-choice items can be used to assess deep understanding and reasoning skills, but they are difficult to write.

- Interpretive exercises include information or data followed by objective questions that require students to reason about what was presented, providing a good measure of understanding and reasoning.

- Good interpretive items are difficult to write and may penalize students who are not good readers.

- Each interpretive item should have relatively short, familiar, but new introductory material and several questions that do not measure recognition of the introductory material.

- Essay items allow students to show their understanding reasoning skills by constructing an answer.

- Extended-response essays are best for assessing complex reasoning skills such as decision making and problem solving, and restricted-response items are better for assessing specific thinking skills, comprehension, and application.

- The major disadvantage of essays is in the scoring, which is time-consuming and fraught with many potential sources of error.

- Good essay questions clearly define the task to students, specifically in terms of the skills that will be assessed. Students should know how much time to spend on each essay item, and the option to choose items should be avoided.

- Scoring essays is enhanced when an outline of an acceptable answer is made before testing students; when the correct method of scoring is used (holistic or analytical); when the scoring is done by question, not by student; when the order of papers is changed; and when students are anonymous.

SELF-INSTRUCTIONAL REVIEW EXERCISES

1. Identify the thinking or reasoning skill illustrated by each of the following examples, using this key:

   A analysis
   S synthesis
   C critical thinking
   D decision making
   P problem solving
   I inference
   E evaluation

   a. Suppose you were the prime minister and had to decide whether to send more troops to Afghanistan. What would you do? Why would you do it?

   b. State your reasons for agreeing or disagreeing with the following statement: Religious people are more likely to help others.

   c. Given what you know about sailing, what would most likely occur if a novice sailor tried to sail directly into the wind?

   d. Examine three different human cultures. What is common in all three cultures, and what principle about being human does this suggest?

   e. Examine four recent speeches by the prime minister. Is any part of the speeches the same?

   f. How can Canada reduce its rate of teenage pregnancy?

   g. Suppose you had to choose between increasing taxes to reduce the Canadian budget deficit or decreasing federal spending to reduce the deficit. Which would you choose? Why? How would your choice affect retired persons?

   h. Examine the data on birth rates. What is likely to happen to the birth rate by the year 2010? Why?

2. Indicate whether each of the following would be best measured by an objective item (O), an interpretive exercise (I), or an essay question (E).

   a. Discerning the meaning of a series of pictures

   b. Asking students about the validity of an argument used in a debate tournament

   c. Analyzing a passage to identify irrelevant information and opinions

   d. Being able to construct a logical argument

   e. Knowing the sequence of steps involved in problem solving

   f. Giving examples of the principle of tropism

   g. Being able to distinguish critical thinking from decision making

   h. Determining whether Michelangelo would be regarded as a great artist if he lived today and, if so, why

   i. Identifying several valid generalizations from the data presented

3. Based on the food web presented in Figure 7.10, evaluate the following questions:

   a. What must the perch eat to get energy generated from the sun?

   b. What happens to the food for perch if some chemicals spilled into the water kill the pond grass?

   c. What happens to the valve snail population if the pond grass is fertilized?

   d. What happens to the valve snail and mosquito larva populations if all the yellow perch are caught by fishermen?

4. Evaluate the following essay question. What learning expectations does it appear to assess? How could it be improved?

   Do you think that Aboriginal residential school settlements should be available only to those individuals who are still alive, or should the settlements extend to the families of the victims? Justify your answer.

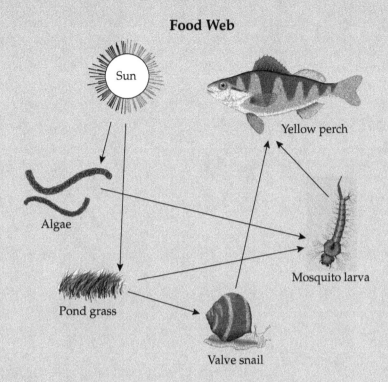

Food Web

Sun

Algae

Pond grass

Valve snail

Yellow perch

Mosquito larva

Figure 7.10 Food Web

Source: Virginia Department of Education Released Test Items. Retrieved November 2005: www.pen.k12.va.us/VDOE/Assessment/
Release2004/5SciCorr1WEB.pdf.

SUGGESTIONS FOR ACTION RESEARCH

1. Devise some deep understanding and reasoning learning expectations for this chapter or one of the previous chapters. Then construct four objective and two essay items to assess these expectations.

2. Provide examples of five of Quellmalz and Hoskyn's reasoning skills from the discipline you teach. Share your examples with two other students, and ask for their critique.

3. Write an essay question with criteria for analytic or holistic scoring and examples of responses that would be graded A, B, and C. Give the question, scoring criteria, and examples of responses with grades deleted to four other students

for them to grade. Compare their judgments with the grades you assigned.

4. Examine two or three textbooks written for the area in which you teach, either teachers' editions or the ones students use, and identify examples of the deep understanding, reasoning, or thinking skills that are assessed. Then match the skills in the textbooks with the frameworks presented in the chapter.

5. Ask a teacher how he or she conceptualizes deep understanding or reasoning skills and how these are measured in the classroom. Compare the teacher's responses to the checklists presented in the chapter.

6. Observe some students as they take a test that assesses deep understanding. How long does it take them to formulate an answer? How much time does it take to write an answer? If possible, examine their responses. How would you evaluate their work?

ENDNOTES

1. Adapted from California Achievement Test 5, Performance Assessment Component, CTB/Macmillan/McGraw-Hill, 1993, p. 39.

2. Student A's answer was at level 4; student B's answer was at level 2 (incorrect answer although some understanding of levelling is demonstrated by the drawing on the graph; an error is made in using data from other projects to obtain an answer).

Chapter 8
Performance Assessments
Assessing Deep Understanding, Reasoning, and Skills

Characteristics
- Strengths
  — authentic
  — integrated with instruction
  — engaging
  — no single correct answer
  — specific criteria
- Limitations
  — reliability
  — sampling
  — time

Performance Tasks and Contexts
- Restricted
- Extended
- Description
- Question or prompt
- Suggestions
  — essential
  — authentic
  — engaging
  — feasible
  — open
  — constraints

PERFORMANCE ASSESSMENT

Rubrics
- Characteristics
- Rating scales
  — holistic
  — analytic
- Developing criteria rubrics

Learning Expectations
- Deep understanding
- Reasoning
- Skills
  — communication and presentation
  — psychomotor
- Products
  — papers
  — reports
  — projects
  — presentations

I n Chapters 6 and 7, we examined what are often called conventional *paper-and-pencil* methods of assessment. These techniques have been used effectively for many years to assess knowledge and understanding expectations and, to a lesser extent, to assess reasoning and skill expectations. With greater emphasis on reasoning and being able to apply learning to real-life situations and problems, there has been extensive interest in assessments that require students to *do* something, not simply know it or know how to do it. It is one thing to demonstrate written knowledge about how to give a speech, but actually giving the speech represents a different kind of learning expectation. Students are required to show what they can do, not simply tell what they know or would do.

WHAT IS PERFORMANCE ASSESSMENT?

Simply put, a **performance assessment** is one in which the teacher observes and makes a judgment about the student's demonstration of a skill or competency in creating a product, constructing a response, or making a presentation. There are two parts to a performance assessment—a task and a systematic procedure for evaluation (using scoring criteria and rubrics). The term *performance* is shorthand for performance-based or *performance-and-product*. The emphasis is on the students' ability to perform tasks by producing their own work with their knowledge and skills. In some cases this is a presentation, such as singing, playing the piano, or performing gymnastics. In other cases, this ability is expressed through a product, such as a completed paper, project, or solution. Over the past two decades, educators have taken the best principles of performance-and-product assessment and used them to assess learning expectations that used to be measured mostly by conventional objective tests. In doing this, however, the field has been deluged by confusing terms and definitions (Palm, 2008). Other terms, such as *alternative assessment* and *authentic assessment*, are sometimes used interchangeably with performance assessment, but they actually mean something different. An **alternative assessment** is any method that differs from conventional paper-and-pencil tests, particularly objective tests. Examples of alternative assessments include observations, exhibitions, oral presentations, experiments, portfolios, interviews, and projects. Some think of essays as a type of alternative assessment because they require students to construct responses.

Authentic assessment involves the direct examination of a student's ability to use knowledge to perform a task similar to what is encountered in real life. Authenticity is judged in the nature of the task completed and in the context of the task (e.g., in the options available, constraints, and access to resources). Like any performance assessment, students plan, construct, and deliver an original response, and explain or justify their answers. The students are aware of the criteria and standards by which the work will be judged before beginning their work.

Performance assessment may or may not be authentic. In fact, we find that authenticity in terms of the real-world use of knowledge is one of several characteristics of performance assessment that is a matter of degree. Some performance assessments are more authentic than others.

Figure 8.1 summarizes the characteristics of performance assessments. Most of these characteristics are typically present to some extent in a performance assessment. But be careful: Because the term *performance assessment* is so popular, some use it as a label for constructed-response, interpretive exercises, and essay items. There is an ideal for what a performance assessment should look like, and many variations in practice.

- Students perform, create, construct, produce, or do something.
- Deep understanding and/or reasoning skills are needed and assessed.
- Involves sustained work, often days and weeks.
- Calls on students to explain, justify, and defend.
- Involves engaging ideas of importance and substance.
- Relies on trained assessor's judgments for scoring.
- Multiple criteria and standards are prespecified and public.
- There is usually no single "correct" answer.
- If authentic, the performance is grounded in real-world contexts and constraints.

Figure 8.1 Characteristics of Performance Assessments

STRENGTHS AND LIMITATIONS OF PERFORMANCE ASSESSMENTS

The major benefits of performance assessments are tied closely to instruction. This explains much of the appeal of the approach. Learning occurs while students complete the assessment. Teachers interact with students as they do the task, providing feedback and prompts that help students learn through multiple opportunities to demonstrate their learning. Teachers have the opportunity to assess the reasoning processes students use in their work. Because the assessments are usually tied to real-world challenges and situations, students are better prepared for such thinking and performance once out of school. Students justify their thinking and learn that often no single answer is correct. In this way, the assessments influence the instruction to be more meaningful and practical. Students value the task more because they view it as rich rather than superficial, engaging rather than uninteresting, and active rather than passive.

As pointed out in Chapter 1, much instruction is now based on constructivist principles of learning, with an emphasis on applied reasoning skills and integrated subject matter. Performance assessments are better suited than selected-response tests to measure these kinds of expectations. Students are more engaged in active learning as a part of the assessment because they need it to perform successfully. Because the emphasis is on what students *do*, teachers assess skills more directly and have more opportunities to observe the process students use to arrive at answers or responses. Students who traditionally do not perform well on paper-and-pencil tests have an opportunity to demonstrate their learning in a different way.

Another advantage of performance assessments is that teachers identify multiple, specific criteria for judging success. Teachers share these criteria with students before the assessment so that the students can use them as they learn. In this way, students learn how to evaluate their own performance through self-assessment. They learn how to ask questions and, in many assessments, how to work effectively with others.

Wiggins (1993) makes the point that performance assessment is simply applying the teaching/learning methods used successfully for years in the adult world. Musicians, artists, athletes, architects, and doctors all learn by obtaining feedback on what they do, and the important goal is not what they know, but how what they know is demonstrated in practice. Thus, an important advantage of performance assessment is that this same approach can be applied to learning all content areas. It helps instruction target more important outcomes.

Finally, performance assessment motivates educators to explore the purposes and processes of schooling (Jamentz, 1994; Wiggins, 1998). Because of the nature of the assessments, teachers revisit their learning goals, instructional practices, and learning outcomes. They explore how students will use their classroom time differently and whether there are adequate resources for all students.

Bill Hadley, a high school mathematics teacher, illustrates how performance assessment can transform the classroom:

> In my general math classes this past year I decided not to give separate stand-alone tests but to assess my students' growth and understanding of mathematics through the use of performance assessments. . . . I assigned groups or pairs of students certain tasks to perform. Then by coaching, observing, and interviewing the students as they worked on these tasks, I was able to assess their knowledge and growth. The information I received was much more comprehensive and complete, and I found that I was able to give the students grades that I thought very accurately reflected their progress. . . . This positive experience with alternative assessment forms and with integrating assessment and instruction will enable me to employ similar methods more often in my other classes. I have discovered that tests do not have to be a primary or necessary type of assessment . . . traditionally structured tests seem to be an impediment to effective instruction. (Stenmark, 1991, p. 12)

The limitations of performance assessment lie in three areas: reliability, sampling, and time. Unfortunately, performance assessments are subject to considerable measurement error, which lowers reliability. Like essay items, the major source of measurement error in performance assessments is in scoring. Because scoring requires professional judgment, there will be variations and error due to bias and other factors, similar to what affects evaluating essay answers. Although some procedures can minimize scoring error—such as carefully constructed criteria, tasks, and scoring rubrics; systematic scoring procedures; and using more than one rater—rating reliability is probably lower than what is achieved with other types of assessment. Inconsistent student performance also contributes to error. That is, student performance at one time may differ noticeably from what the student would demonstrate at another time (this might occur, for example, if the student is ill on the day of the performance).

Because it takes a lot of time for students to do performance assessments, you will have relatively few samples of student achievement and ability. Furthermore, we know that performance on one task may not provide a very good estimate of student proficiency on other tasks. If you intend to use the results of performance assessment to form conclusions about capability in a larger domain of learning expectations, you need to accumulate information from multiple tasks. It also helps to select tasks that can optimize generalization to the learning expectations. Suppose the learning expectation is concerned with skills associated with making a PowerPoint presentation. If the task is relatively restricted (e.g., using only a few PowerPoint features with a short presentation, making a two-minute speech), generalization is more confined than when the task encompasses more of the skills (e.g., the PowerPoint presentation is longer and contains many features, making a fifteen-minute speech). Your choice is to use many restricted tasks of limited generalizability or few tasks that have greater generalizability.

The third major limitation of performance assessment concerns time. First, it is very time-consuming to construct good tasks, develop scoring criteria and rubrics, administer the task, observe students, and then apply the rubrics to student performance. For performances that cannot be scored later, teachers must take adequate time with each student as he or she performs the task. Second, it is difficult, in a timely fashion, to interact with all students and give them meaningful feedback *as they learn* and make decisions. Finally, it is difficult to estimate the amount of time students will need to complete performance assessments, especially if the task is new and if students are unaccustomed to the format and/or expectations.

The strengths and weaknesses of performance assessments are summarized in Figure 8.2. The weaknesses are usually outweighed by the strengths, but only if the

Strengths	Weaknesses
Integrates assessment with instruction.	Reliability may be difficult to establish.
Learning occurs during assessment.	Measurement error due to subjective nature of the scoring may be significant.
Provides opportunities for formative assessment.	Inconsistent student performance across time may result in inaccurate conclusions.
Tends to be more authentic than other types of assessments.	Few samples of student achievement.
More engaging; active involvement of students.	Requires considerable teacher time to prepare and student time to complete.
Provides additional way for students to show what they know and can do.	Difficult to plan for amount of time needed.
Emphasis on reasoning skills.	Limited ability to generalize to a larger domain of knowledge.
Forces teachers to establish specific criteria to identify successful performance.	
Encourages student self-assessment.	
Emphasis on application of knowledge.	
Encourages re-examination of instructional goals and the purpose of schooling.	

Figure 8.2 Strengths and Weaknesses of Performance Assessments

teacher's approach is thoughtful, reflective, and rigorous. Performance assessment is complex and demanding. Time, energy, and resources must be invested to meet goals identified in the strengths listed.

LEARNING EXPECTATIONS FOR PERFORMANCE ASSESSMENTS

Performance assessments are primarily used for four types of learning expectations: deep understanding, reasoning, skills, and products. Deep understanding and reasoning involve in-depth, complex thinking about what is known and application of knowledge and skills in novel and more sophisticated ways. Skills include student proficiency in reasoning, communication, and psychomotor tasks. Products are completed works, such as term papers, projects, and other assignments in which students use their knowledge and skills. Teachers in some fields have been using performance assessments for years, such as in art, music, typing, athletics, and writing. More recent applications of performance assessment have focused on knowledge and simple understanding expectations, though the emphasis on objective high-stakes tests has mitigated this application.

Deep Understanding

The essence of performance assessment includes the development of students' deep understanding of something. The idea is to involve students meaningfully in hands-on activities for extended periods of time so that their understanding is rich and more extensive than what they can attain by more conventional instruction and traditional paper-and-pencil assessments. Deep understanding in performance assessments focuses on the *use* of knowledge and skills. Students construct responses in unique ways to demonstrate depth of thought and subtleties of meaning in novel situations. Students are asked to demonstrate what they understand through the application of knowledge and skills.

Reasoning

Like deep understanding, reasoning is essential in performance assessment. Students will use reasoning skills as they demonstrate skills and construct products. Typically, students are given a problem to solve or are asked to make a decision or other outcome, such as a letter to the editor or school newsletter, based on information that is provided. Reasoning expectations delineated in Chapter 7 are needed for students to be successful. They must use cognitive processes such as analysis, synthesis, critical thinking, inference, prediction, generalizing, and hypothesis testing. You should delineate the specific reasoning skills that will be demonstrated, with scoring criteria related to these skills.

Note that having reasoning expectations, as well as deep understanding expectations, does not necessarily mean that the measure of student success is a performance assessment.

There are many ways of assessing these types of expectations. Teachers can assess critical thinking, for example, by using short-answer questions asking students to evaluate the credibility of an argument. This is quite different from having students develop a mock trial in which both prosecution and defence "lawyers" (students) present arguments, some of which are credible and some of which aren't. We can call just about anything students do "performance," but that's not the same as implementing a systematic performance assessment as discussed here.

Skills

In addition to reasoning skills, students are required to demonstrate communication, presentation, and psychomotor skills. These expectations are ideally suited to perform-ance assessment. We'll consider each one.

Communication and Presentation Skills. Learning expectations focused on communication skills involve student performance of reading, writing, speaking, and lis-tening. For reading, expectations can be divided into process—what students do before, during, and after reading—and product—what students get from the reading. Reading expectations for elementary students progress from process skills such as being able to han-dle a book appropriately (e.g., holding it right side up and turning pages), to expectations such as phonemic awareness skills (e.g., decoding, phonological awareness, and blending), to skills needed for comprehension and understanding (such as discrimination, contextual cues, inference, blending, sequencing, and identifying main ideas). For effective perform-ance assessment, each of these areas needs to be delineated as a specific expectation. For instance, a word identification expectation may include naming and matching upper case and lower case letters, recognizing words by sight, recognizing sounds and symbols for con-sonants at the beginnings and ends of words, and sounding out three-letter words. For older students, reading expectations focus on comprehension products and strategies and on reading efficiency, including stating main ideas; identifying the setting, characters, and events in stories; drawing inferences from context; and reading speed. More advanced read-ing skills include sensitivity to word meanings related to origins, nuances, or figurative meanings; identifying contradictions; and identifying possible multiple inferences. All reading expectations should include the ability to perform a specific skill for novel reading materials. A variety of formats should also be represented.

Writing skill expectations are also determined by a student's grade level. The empha-sis for young students is on their ability to construct letters and copy words and simple sentences legibly. For writing complete essays or papers, elaborate delineations of skills have been developed. Typically, important dimensions of writing are used as categories, as illustrated in the following writing expectations:

Purpose	Clarity of purpose; awareness of audience and task; clarity of ideas
Organization	Unity and coherence

Details	Appropriateness of details to purpose and support for main point(s) of writer's response
Voice/Tone	Personal investment and expression
Usage, Mechanics, and Grammar	Correct usage (tense formation, agreement, and word choice), mechanics (spelling, capitalization, and punctuation), grammar, and sentence construction

Other dimensions can be used when the writing skill being measured is more specific, such as writing a persuasive letter, a research paper, or an editorial. Writing expectations, like reading expectations, should include the ability to perform the skill in a variety of situations or contexts. That is, if a student has been taught persuasive writing by developing letters to editors, he or she may write a persuasive advertisement or speech to demonstrate the skill.

Oral communication skill expectations can be generalized to many situations or focused on a specific type of presentation, such as giving a speech, singing a song, speaking a foreign language, or competing in a debate. When the emphasis is on general oral communication skills, the expectations typically centre on the following three general categories (Airasian, 2005):

Physical expression	Eye contact, posture, facial expressions, gestures, and body movement
Vocal expression	Articulation, clarity, vocal variation, loudness, pace, and rate
Verbal expression	Repetition, organization, summarizations, reasoning, completeness of ideas and thoughts, selection of appropriate words to convey precise meanings

A more specific set of oral communication skill expectations is illustrated in the following guidelines for high school students:[1]

A. Speaking clearly, expressively, and audibly
   1. Using voice expressively
   2. Speaking articulately and pronouncing words correctly
   3. Using appropriate vocal volume

B. Presenting ideas with appropriate introduction, development, and conclusion
   1. Presenting ideas in an effective order
   2. Providing a clear focus on the central idea
   3. Providing signal words, internal summaries, and transitions

C. Developing ideas using appropriate support materials
   1. Being clear and using reasoning processes
   2. Clarifying, illustrating, exemplifying, and documenting ideas

D. Using nonverbal cues
   1. Using eye contact
   2. Using appropriate facial expressions, gestures, and body movement

E. Selecting language to a specific purpose
   1. Using language and conventions appropriate to the audience

For specific purposes, the skills are more targeted. For example, if a presentation involves a demonstration of how to use a microscope, the expectation could include such criteria as clarity of explanations, understanding of appropriate steps, appropriateness of examples when adjustments are necessary, dependency on notes, and whether attention is maintained, as well as more general features such as posture, enunciation, and eye contact.

Psychomotor Skills. There are two steps in identifying psychomotor skill learning expectations. The first step is to describe clearly the physical actions that are required. These may be developmentally appropriate skills, or skills that are needed for specific tasks. We have divided the psychomotor area into five categories in Figure 8.3 to help you describe the behaviour: fine motor skills (such as holding a pencil, focusing a microscope, and using scissors), gross motor actions (such as jumping and lifting), more complex athletic skills (such as shooting a basketball or playing golf), some visual skills, and verbal/auditory skills for young children.

The second step is to identify the level at which the skill will be performed. One effective way to do this is to use an existing classification of the psychomotor domain (Simpson, 1972). This system is hierarchical. At the most basic level is *perception*, the ability to use sight, smell, hearing, and touch to be aware of a stimulus. The second level is *set*, which is a state of readiness to take action. The next level is *guided response*, which involves imitating a behaviour or following directions. The fourth level is reached when an action becomes

Fine Motor	Gross Motor	Complex	Visual	Verbal and Auditory
Cutting paper with scissors	Walking	Performing a golf swing	Copying	Identifying and discriminating sounds
Drawing a line	Jumping	Operating a computer	Finding letters	Imitating sounds
Tracing	Balancing	Driving a car	Finding embedded figures	Pronouncing carefully
Eye–hand coordination	Throwing	Dissecting a frog	Identifying shapes	Articulating
Penmanship	Skipping	Performing back walkover on balance beam	Discriminating on the basis of attributes such as size, shape, and colour	Blending vowels
Colouring	Pull-ups	Operating a microscope		Using proper lip and tongue placement to produce sounds
Drawing shapes	Hopping	Sailing a boat		
Connecting dots	Kicking	Operating a drill press		
Pointing				
Buttoning				
Zippering				

Figure 8.3 Examples of Psychomotor Skills

habitual and is done correctly with confidence. This is called *mechanism*. *Complex overt response* is the fifth level and involves correct actions comprising complex skills. The sixth level is *adaptation*, through which students can make adjustments to suit their needs. The final and highest level is *origination*, which refers to creating new actions to solve a problem. You can use the levels to determine the nature of the expectation for the skills identified from step 1. For instance, suppose you are interested in assessing your students' abilities to write capital letters correctly. At one level, students need to be able to identify the letter, perhaps by locating an example of it on the wall (the perception level). Then they need to be physically prepared to write correctly by sharpening their pencils and placing their papers in the correct position (set), followed by being able to copy letters from the board (guided response). Then they can demonstrate their skill when drafting paragraphs (mechanism) and alter the shapes to accommodate different widths between lines (adaptation).

Products

Performance assessment products are completed works that include most of the characteristics in Figure 8.1 to some degree. For years, students have done papers, reports, and projects. What makes these products different when used for performance assessment is that they are more engaging and more authentic, and are scored more systematically with public criteria and standards. For example, rather than having sixth graders report on a foreign country by summarizing its history, politics, and economics, students write promotional materials for the country that would help others decide if it would be an interesting place to visit. In chemistry, students are asked to identify an unknown substance. Why not have them identify the substances from a local landfill, river, or body of water?

In music, students can demonstrate their proficiency and knowledge by creating and playing a new song. Table 8.1 presents some other examples, varying in authenticity.

As a learning expectation, each product needs to be clearly described in some detail so that there is no misunderstanding about what students are required to do. It is insufficient to say, for example, "Write a report on one of the planets and present it to the class." Students need to know about the specific elements of the product (e.g., length, types of information needed, nature of the audience, context, materials that can be used, and what can be shown to the audience) and how they will be evaluated. To do this, show examples of completed projects to students. These are not meant to be copied, but they can be used to communicate outcomes and expectations. In other words, show examples of the expectation to the students. If the examples demonstrate different levels of proficiency, so much the better. To generate products, think about what people in different occupations do. What does a city planner do? What would an expert witness produce for a trial? How does a map-maker create a map that is easy to understand? What kinds of stories does a newspaper columnist write? How would an advertising agent represent state parks to attract tourists?

CONSTRUCTING PERFORMANCE TASKS

Once you have identified learning expectations and decided that a performance assessment is the method you want to use, three steps remain in constructing the complete performance task. The first is to identify the performance task in which students will

Table 8.1 Performance Products and Skills Varying in Authenticity

Relatively Inauthentic	Somewhat Authentic	Authentic
Indicate which parts of a garden design are accurate.	Design a garden.	Create a garden.
Write a paper on zoning.	Write a proposal to change fictitious zoning laws.	Write a proposal to present to city council to change zoning laws.
Answer a series of questions about what materials are needed for a trip.	Defend the selection of supplies needed for a hypothetical trip.	Plan a trip with your family, indicating needed supplies.
Explain what you would teach to students learning to play basketball.	Show how to perform basketball skills in practice.	Play a basketball game.
Listen to a tape and interpret a foreign language.	Hold a conversation with a teacher in a foreign language.	Hold a conversation with a person from a foreign country in his or her native language.

be engaged; the second is to develop descriptions of the task and the context in which the performance will be conducted; and the third is to write the specific question, prompt, or problem the students will receive (Figure 8.4).

The performance task is what students are required to do in the performance assessment, either individually or in groups. The tasks can vary by subject and by level of complexity. Some performance tasks are specific to a content area; others integrate several subjects and skills. Regarding level of complexity, it is useful to distinguish two types: restricted and extended.

Restricted- and Extended-Type Performance Tasks

Restricted-type tasks target a narrowly defined skill and require relatively brief responses. The task is structured and specific. These tasks may look similar to short essay questions and interpretive exercises that have open-ended items. The difference is in the relative emphasis on characteristics listed in Figure 8.1. Often the performance task is structured to elicit student explanations of their answer. Students may be asked to defend an answer; indicate why a different answer is not correct; tell how they did something; draw a diagram; construct a visual map, graph, or flow chart; or show some other aspect of their reasoning. In contrast, short essay questions and interpretive exercises are designed to infer reasoning from correct answers. Although restricted-type tasks require relatively little time for administration and scoring in comparison with extended-type tasks (providing greater reliability and sampling), they usually include fewer of the important characteristics of authentic performance assessments. Further examples of restricted-type performance tasks are listed in Figure 8.5.

Extended-type tasks are more complex, elaborate, and time-consuming. These tasks often include collaborative work with small groups of students. The assignment usually requires that students use a variety of sources of information (e.g., observations, a library, and interviews). Judgments will need to be made about which information is most relevant. Products are typically developed over several days or even weeks, with opportunities for revision. This allows students to apply a variety of skills and makes it easier to integrate different content areas and reasoning skills.

It is not too difficult to come up with ideas for an engaging extended-type task. As previously indicated, you can think about what people do in different occupations.

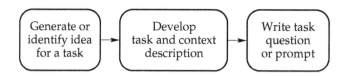

Figure 8.4 Steps in Constructing Performance Tasks

Another way to generate ideas is to check curriculum guides and teachers' editions of textbooks, because most will have activities and assignments that tap student application and reasoning skills. Perhaps the best way to generate ideas is by brainstorming with others, especially members of the community. They can help you in thinking about authentic tasks that involve reasoning and communication skills. Some ideas that could be transformed into extended-type tasks are included in Figure 8.5. Once you have a general idea for the task, develop it into a more detailed set of specifications.

Performance Task Descriptions and Contexts

The performance task needs to be specified so that it meets the criteria for good performance assessment and is clear to students. To do this, prepare a *task description*. The purpose of the task description is to provide a blueprint or listing of specifications to ensure that essential criteria are met, that the task is reasonable, and that it will elicit desired student performance. The task description is not the same as the actual format

Restricted-Type	Extended-Type
Construct a bar graph from data provided.	Construct a PowerPoint presentation.
Talk in French about what is on a menu.	Design a playhouse and estimate the cost of materials and labour.
Read an article from a newspaper and answer questions.	Plan a trip to another country; include the budget and itinerary.
Review a zoning map of a city and indicate changes that would encourage more commercial development.	Conduct a historical re-enactment (e.g., Red River Rebellion).
Flip a coin 10 times. Predict what the next 10 flips would be. Explain why.	Diagnose and repair a car problem.
Listen to CBC News and explain whether you believe the stories are biased.	Design an advertising campaign for a new or existing product.
Construct a poster that explains the parts of flowers.	Publish a newspaper.
Sing a song.	Design a park.
Type at least 35 words per minute with five or fewer mistakes.	Create a commercial.
Using scissors, cut outlined figures from a page.	Write and perform a song.
Recite a poem.	Prepare a plan for dealing with waste materials.
Write a paper about the importance of protecting forests from being converted to farmland.	Design and carry out a study to determine which grocery store has the lowest prices.
Write examples of good and poor multiple-choice questions.	Plan and install a new car stereo system.

Figure 8.5 Restricted- and Extended-Type Performance Assessment Tasks

and wording of the question or prompt that is given to students; it is more like a lesson plan. The task description should include the following:

- Content and skill expectations to be assessed
- Description of student activities
    - Group or individual
    - Help allowed
- Resources needed
- Teacher role
- Administrative process
- Scoring procedures

Clearly describe the specific expectations to be assessed, to make certain that the activities and scoring are well matched to ensure both valid and practical assessments. Think about what students will actually do to respond to the question or solve the problem by specifying the context in which they will work:

- Will they consult other experts, use library resources, or do experiments?
- Are they allowed to work together, or is it an individual assignment?
- What types of help from others are allowed?
- Is there sufficient time to complete the activities?

Once you describe the activities, identify the resources needed to accomplish them:

- Are needed materials and resources available for all students?
- What needs to be obtained before the assessment?

Describe your role in the exercise:

- Will you consult your students or give them ideas?
- Are you comfortable with and adequately prepared for what you will do?
- What administrative procedures are required?

Finally, identify scoring procedures:

- Will scoring match the learning expectations?
- Is adequate time available for scoring?
- Do you have the expertise needed to do the scoring?
- Is it practical?

To design the task, think about what you have done instructionally (Smith, Smith, & De Lisi, 2001). Structure the assessment task to mirror the nature of classroom instruction so that what you are asking students to do is something that they are already somewhat familiar with.

Once you complete the task description and you are satisfied that the assessment will be valid and practical, you are ready to prepare the specific performance task question or prompt.

Performance Task Question or Prompt

The actual question, problem, or prompt that you give to students is based on the task description. It must clearly identify what the final outcome or product is, outline what students are allowed and encouraged to do, and explain the criteria that will be used to judge the product. A good question or prompt also provides a context that helps students understand the meaningfulness and relevance of the task. A good performance task is illustrated in Figure 8.6.

Because considerable time is required to construct good performance tasks, use or adapt ones that have already been developed. Several professional organizations have organized networks and other resources for developing performance tasks. Many of the

---

Comparison Task

Grade-level range: Upper Elementary–Middle

Working in pairs, list as many insects as possible. Come up with a classification system that focuses on key characteristics of the insects and place the insects from your list in the appropriate categories. Do the same classification procedure two more times, but from the following perspectives: **[Nature of Final Product]**

- An exterminator (sample categories: insects found in homes, flying insects, crawling insects, insects commonly found in kitchens, insects that prefer dark basements).
- A frog (sample categories: insects that fly above water, insects that can swim, insects that would make a big meal, insects that would make a little meal).

You will have to consult various resources (materials in the classroom, peers, adults, and so on) to obtain the information necessary to classify the insects accurately. When you turn in your three classification systems, include a list of the resources you used and explain in a short paragraph which were most and least useful. Be ready to share with the class some interesting things you discovered as a result of doing these classifications. You will be assessed on and provided rubrics for the following: **[What Students Are Required to Do]**

1. Your understanding of the characteristics of insects.
2. Your ability to specify important defining characteristics of the categories. **[Criteria Used to Judge the Product]**
3. Your ability to accurately sort the identified elements into the categories.
4. Your ability to effectively use a variety of information-gathering techniques and information resources.

Figure 8.6 Performance Task Prompt

Source: Adapted from R.J. Marzano, D. Pickering, & J. McTighe (1993). *Assessing student outcomes: Performance assessment using the dimensions of learning model* (p. 51). Alexandria, VA: Association for Supervision and Curriculum Development. Adapted by permission of McREL. © 1993.

provincial ministries of education, such as the British Columbia Ministry of Education, provide examples of performance assessment tasks on their websites. Subject-oriented professional organizations, such as The Canadian Association of Second Language Teachers, have good resources for identifying performance tasks. The Internet can also be used to tap into a vast array of examples that can be modified to fit your context.

Whether you develop your own tasks or use intact or modified existing ones, you should evaluate the task based on the suggestions summarized in Figure 8.7 and characteristics summarized in Figure 8.8, which shows how they are defined and contrasted with what occurs in more traditional assessment.

1. The Performance Task Should Integrate the Most Essential Aspects of the Content Being Assessed with the Most Essential Skills. Performance assessment is ideal for focusing student attention and learning on the "big ideas" of a subject—the major concepts, principles, and processes that are important to a discipline. If the task encourages learning of peripheral or tangential topics or specific details, it is not well suited to the goal of performance assessment. Tasks should be broad in scope. Similarly, reasoning and other skills essential to the task should represent essential processes. The task should be written to integrate content with skills. For example, it would be better to debate important content or contemporary issues rather than something relatively unimportant. A good test of whether the task meets these criteria is whether what is assessed could be done as well with more objective, less time-consuming measures.

Examples

> *Poor:* Estimate the answers to the following three addition problems. Explain in your own words the strategy used to give your answer.

> *Improved:* Sam and Tyron were planning a trip to a nearby province. They wanted to visit as many different major cities as possible. Using the map, estimate the number of major cities they will be able to visit on a single tank of gas (sixty litres) if their car's fuel economy is 7 litres/100 km.

✓ Are essential content and skills expectations integrated?
✓ Are multiple expectations included?
✓ Is the task authentic?
✓ Is the task teachable?
✓ Is the task feasible?
✓ Are multiple solutions and paths possible?
✓ Is the nature of the task clear?
✓ Is the task challenging and stimulating?
✓ Are criteria for scoring included?
✓ Are constraints for completing the task included?

Figure 8.7 Checklist for Writing Performance Tasks

2. The Task Should Be Authentic. This suggestion lies at the heart of authentic performance assessment. Grant Wiggins has developed a set of six standards for judging the degree of authenticity in an assessment task (Wiggins, 1998). He suggests that a task is authentic if it:

A. *Is realistic.* The task replicates the ways in which a person's knowledge and abilities are "tested" in real-world situations.

B. *Requires judgment and innovation.* The student has to use knowledge and skills wisely and effectively to solve unstructured problems, and the solution involves more than following a set routine or procedure or plugging in knowledge.

C. *Asks the student to "do" the subject.* The student has to carry out exploration and work within the discipline of the subject area, rather than restating what is already known or what was taught.

Essential	• The task fits into the core of the curriculum. • It represents a "big idea."	vs. Tangential
Authentic	• The task uses processes appropriate to the discipline. • Students value the outcome of the task.	vs. Contrived
Rich	• The task leads to other problems. • It raises other questions. • It has many possibilities.	vs. Superficial
Engaging	• The task is thought-provoking. • It fosters persistence.	vs. Uninteresting
Active	• The student is the worker and decision maker. • Students interact with other students. • Students are constructing meaning and deepening understanding.	vs. Passive
Feasible	• The task can be done within school and homework time. • It is developmentally appropriate for students. • It is safe.	vs. Infeasible
Equitable	• The task develops thinking in a variety of styles • It contributes to positive attitudes.	vs. Inequitable
Open	• The task has more than one right answer. • It has multiple avenues of approach, making it accessible to all students.	vs. Closed

Figure 8.8 Criteria for Performance Tasks

Source: Reprinted with permission from Jean Kerr Stenmark (1991). *Mathematics assessment: Myths, models, good questions, and practical suggestions.* National Council of Teachers of Mathematics. All rights reserved.

D. *Replicates or simulates the contexts in which adults are "tested" in the workplace, in civic life, and in personal life.* Contexts involve specific situations that have particular constraints, purposes, and audiences. Students need to experience what it is like to do tasks in workplace and other real-life contexts.

E. *Assesses the student's ability to efficiently and effectively use a repertoire of knowledge and skill to negotiate a complex task.* Students should be required to integrate all knowledge and skills needed, rather than to demonstrate competence of isolated knowledge and skills.

F. *Allows appropriate opportunities to rehearse, practise, consult resources, and get feedback on and refine performances and products.* Rather than rely on secure tests as an audit of performance, learning should be focused through cycles of performance-feedback-revision-performance, on the production of known high-quality products and standards, and learning in context. (pp. 22, 24)

A similar set of standards has been developed by Fred Newmann (1997). In his view, authentic tasks require the following:

Construction of meaning (use of reasoning and higher-order thinking skills to produce meaning or knowledge)
1. Organization of information
2. Consideration of alternatives

Disciplined inquiry (thinking like "experts" searching for in-depth understanding)
3. Disciplinary content
4. Disciplinary process
5. Elaborated written communication

Value beyond school (aesthetic, utilitarian, or personal value apart from documenting the competence of the learner)
6. Problem connected to the world
7. Audience beyond the school

Newmann summarizes these standards by saying that authentic tasks "demand construction of knowledge through disciplined inquiry and result in discourse, products, and performance that have value or meaning beyond success in school" (p. 366).

Examples

Poor: Compare and contrast different kinds of literature.

Improved: You have volunteered to help your local library with its literacy program. Once a week after school, you help people learn how to read. To encourage your students to learn, you tell them about the different kinds of literature you have read, including poems, biographies, mysteries, tall tales, fables, and historical novels. Select three types of literature and compare them, using general characteristics of literature and the specific characteristics of each genre that you think will help your students see the similarities and differences among the types of literature. Create a table or chart to visually depict the comparison.[2]

Notice also how the improved version integrates content and language arts with two skills, comparison and communication.

3. Structure the Task to Assess Multiple Learning Expectations. As pointed out in the first suggestion, the task should assess both content and skill expectations. Within each of these areas, there may be different types of expectations. For instance, assessing content may include both knowledge and understanding and, as in the example above, reasoning and communication skills. It is also common to include different types of communication and reasoning skills in the same task (e.g., students provide both a written and an oral report, or need to think critically and to synthesize in order to arrive at an answer).

4. Structure the Task So That You Can Help Students Succeed. Good performance assessment involves the interaction of instruction with assessment. The task needs to be something that students learn from, which is most likely when you have opportunities to increase proficiency by asking questions, providing resources, and giving feedback. In this kind of active teaching, you are intervening as students learn, rather than simply providing information. Part of teachability is being certain that students have the prerequisite knowledge and skills needed to succeed.

5. Think through What Students Will Do to Be Sure That the Task Is Feasible. Imagine what you would do if given the task. What resources would you need? How much time would you need? What steps would you take? It should be realistic for students to implement the task. This depends both on your own expertise and willingness, and on the

---

Teacher's Corner

Elizabeth O'Brien

In the strand Geometry and Measurement in Math, when studying volume I have students bring in products from home that come in double containers. For example, toothpaste comes in a tube and then is packaged in a box, and most pills come in a bottle and then are packaged in a box. Students are asked to find the volume of the outer package using the formulas we have studied, and then find the volume of the inner package by displacement. When they find the difference between the volumes we discuss how companies could save money on packaging and why they might use the double-package method. To conclude the unit, students are asked to write a letter to the manufacturer of the product describing their findings and what and why they think changes should be made.

Overall, students enjoy this project. It allows them to use geometry for something they see as useful. They also love taking a side and using their data to argue for or against a change. The letters allow me to see a depth of understanding that a typical problem does not allow for.

costs and availability of equipment, materials, and other resources, so that every student has the same opportunity to be successful.

6. The Task Should Allow for Multiple Solutions. If a performance task is properly structured, more than one correct response is not only possible, but also desirable. The task should not encourage drill or practice for which there is a single solution. The possibility of multiple solutions encourages students to personalize the process and makes it easier for you to demand that students justify and explain their assumptions, planning, predictions, and other responses. Different students may take different paths in responding to the task.

7. The Task Should Be Clear. An unambiguous set of directions that explicitly indicates the nature of the task is essential. If the directions are too vague, students may not focus on the learning expectations or may waste time trying to figure out what they should be doing. A task such as "give an oral report on a foreign country" is too general. Students need to know the reason for the task, and the directions should provide sufficient detail so that students know how to proceed. Do they work alone or with others? What resources are available? How much time do they have? What is the role of the teacher? Here is an example of a clearly defined task:

> We will be reading George Orwell's 1984, which could be described as a work of projective investigation. We will also be studying what was happening in the world around the time this book was written, the decade of the 1940s.
>
> First, working in small groups, your task is to select specific events, ideas, or trends from the 1940s and show how Orwell projected them into the future. You'll be given a chart on which you can graphically depict these connections.
>
> Second, each person is to select a field of study that interests you (economics, science and technology, health care, fashion, sports, literature, the arts, politics, sociology) and select current events, ideas, and trends in that field, with an emphasis on areas where there is some controversy or disagreement.
>
> Finally, using your knowledge of the field, construct a scenario for the future that makes sense and is a plausible extension of the present. Present your scenario in any way you wish (written prose or poetry, art form, oral or video presentation, etc.). In your presentation, clearly communicate your predictions and how they plausibly extend the present. (Marzano, Pickering, & McTighe, 1993, p. 61)

8. The Task Should Be Challenging and Stimulating to Students. Your hope is that students will be motivated to use their skills and knowledge to be involved and engaged, sometimes for days or weeks. You also want students to monitor themselves and think about their progress. This is more likely to occur when the task is something students can get excited about or can see the relevance of, and when the task is neither too easy nor too difficult. Persistence is fostered if the task is interesting and thought-provoking. This is easier if you know your students' strengths and limitations, and are familiar with the topics that would motivate them. One approach is to blend what is familiar with what is novel. Tasks that are authentic are not necessarily stimulating and challenging.

9. Include Explicitly Stated Scoring Criteria as Part of the Task. By now you are familiar with this admonition. Specifying criteria helps students understand what they need to do and communicates learning priorities and your expectations. Students need to know about the criteria *before* beginning work on the task. Some criteria are individually tailored to each task; others are more generic for several different kinds of tasks. The criteria you share with students as part of the task, however, may not be the same instrument or scale you use when evaluating their work. For example, for the task in suggestion 7, the following contains part of what you might share with students:

> You will be assessed on and provided rubrics for the following:
>
> **A.** Your understanding of the extent to which the present can inform the future
>
> **B.** Your depth of understanding of major events, ideas, and trends from a field of study
>
> **C.** Your ability to accurately identify what is already known or agreed upon about the future event
>
> **D.** Your ability to construct a scenario for some future event or hypothetical past event for which a scenario is not readily available or accepted
>
> **E.** Your ability to express ideas clearly
>
> **F.** Your ability to communicate effectively in a variety of ways (Marzano, Pickering, & McTighe, 1993, p. 61)

The identification of scoring criteria, and how you translate those criteria into a scale for evaluation, is discussed in the next section. From a practical perspective, the development of the task and scoring criteria is iterative: one influences the other as both are developed.

10. Include Constraints for Completing the Task. One of the hallmarks of authentic thinking and decision making is that such performance is done under constraints defined by context, rules, and regulations that are similar to conditions outside the classroom. According to Borich and Tombari (2004), these constraints include:

> *Time.* How much time should a learner or group of learners have to plan, revise, and finish the task?
>
> *Reference material.* What resources (dictionaries, textbooks, class notes, CD-ROMs) will learners be able to consult while they are completing the assessment task?
>
> *Other people.* Will your learners be able to ask for help from peers, teachers, and experts as they take a test or complete a project?
>
> *Equipment.* Will your learners have access to computers, calculators, spell checkers, or other aids or materials as they complete the assignment?
>
> *Scoring criteria.* Will you inform your learners about the explicit standards that you use to evaluate the product or performance? (p. 220)

The intent of considering such constraints is to realistically define the nature of the situation in which the performance or product is demonstrated. It allows students to more closely associate what they are doing with real-life contexts.

CRITERIA AND RUBRICS

After students have completed the task, you must evaluate their performance. Because students construct responses, evaluation is always a matter of reviewing their work and making a professional judgment about the performance or product. Rather than relying on unstated rules for making these judgments, performance assessments include *performance criteria*, which is what you use to determine student proficiency.

Performance Criteria

Performance criteria (or *scoring criteria* or simply *criteria*) are what you look for in student responses to evaluate their progress toward meeting the learning expectation. In other words, performance criteria are the dimensions or traits in products or performance that are used to illustrate and define understanding, reasoning, and proficiency. Explicitly defined performance criteria help to make a subjective process clear, consistent, and defensible (Arter & McTighe, 2001).

Determining defensible criteria begins with identifying the most important dimensions or traits of the performance. This is a summary of the essential qualities of student proficiency. These dimensions should reflect your instructional goals as well as teachable and observable aspects of the performance. Ask yourself this question: "What distinguishes an adequate from an inadequate demonstration of the expectation?"

One of the best approaches to identifying criteria is to work backward from examples of student work (Moskal, 2003). You can analyze these exemplars to determine what descriptors distinguish them. You can also use them as **anchor** papers for making judgments, and give them to students to illustrate the dimensions. The dimension is the trait you are looking for. For a speech, that dimension might be content, organization, and delivery. Delivery may be divided further into posture, gestures, facial expressions, and eye contact. For a singing performance, you could include pitch, rhythm, diction, and tone quality, and each of these can be further delineated. As you might imagine, you can go into great detail describing dimensions. But to be practical, you need to balance specificity with what is manageable (the next section includes some examples of what is reasonable).

The following is an example of criteria for a specific learning expectation.

Learning expectation:	Students will be able to write a persuasive paper to encourage the reader to accept a specific course of action or point of view.
Criteria:	Appropriateness of language for the audience
	Plausibility and relevance of supporting arguments
	Level of detail presented
	Evidence of creative, innovative thinking
	Clarity of expression
	Organization of ideas

Sometimes criteria are listed with an indication of how the traits contribute to the overall evaluation. This is illustrated in the following example of criteria used to evaluate a PowerPoint presentation:

1. The topic has been extensively and accurately researched.

2. A storyboard, consisting of logically and sequentially numbered slides, has been developed.

3. The introduction is interesting and engages the audience.

4. The fonts are easy to read and point size varies appropriately for headings and text.

5. The use of italics, bold, and underline contributes to the readability of the text.

6. The background and colours enhance the text.

7. The graphics, animation, and sounds enhance the overall presentation.

8. Graphics are of proper size.

9. The text is free of spelling, punctuation, capitalization, and grammatical errors. (Lantz, 2004, p. 10)

When the performance assessment includes both understanding and skill expectations, these should be listed separately so that students receive feedback on each. (A good example of how this could be accomplished is illustrated later in Figure 8.14.) Once all the criteria have been identified, a rating scale is used to show different levels of performance in relation to the traits.

Rating Scales

A rating scale is used to indicate the degree to which a particular dimension is present. It provides a way to record and communicate qualitatively different levels of performance. Several types of rating scales are available; we will consider three: numerical, qualitative, and numerical/quantitative combined.

The numerical scale uses numbers on a continuum to indicate different levels of proficiency in terms of frequency or quality. The number of points on the scale can vary, from as few as two to ten or more. The number of points is determined based on the decision that will be made. If you are going to use the scale to indicate low, medium, and high, then three points are sufficient. More points on the scale permit greater discrimination, provide more diagnostic information, and permit more specific feedback to students.

Here are some examples of numerical scales:

Complete Understanding of the Problem	5 4 3 2 1	No Understanding of the Problem
Little or No Organization	1 2 3 4 5 6 7	Clear and Complete Organization
Emergent Reader	1 2 3	Fluent Reader

A qualitative scale uses verbal descriptions to indicate student performance. There are two types of qualitative descriptors. One type indicates the different gradations of the dimension. The simplest form is the checklist. This lists different dimensions and provides a way to check each dimension. An example of a checklist is illustrated in Figure 8.9 for the PowerPoint presentation criteria.

More complex scales summarize different levels of the dimensions. There is no indication of or reference to a standard in any of these scales. The idea is to describe the performance accurately, without indicating whether any particular point on any of the scales is considered passing or failing, or without indicating some other type of judgment about what the description means or how it is used. Typically, language provides the basis for the scale, including words such as:

minimal, partial, complete
never, seldom, occasionally, frequently, always
consistently, sporadically, rarely
none, some, complete

Some examples of more descriptive qualitative scales include the following:

Complete understanding	*Nearly complete understanding*	*Some understanding*	*Limited understanding*
Uses capital letters appropriately most or all of the time	*Uses capital letters appropriately some of the time*	*Rarely uses capital letters appropriately*	
Always speaks clearly	*Speaks clearly most of the time*	*Speaks clearly some of the time*	*Rarely speaks clearly*

A second type of qualitative scale includes gradations of the criteria and some indication of the worth of the performance. That is, the evaluative component is

---

Yes No

____ ____ **1.** The topic has been extensively and accurately researched.

____ ____ **2.** A storyboard, consisting of logically and sequentially numbered slides, has been developed.

____ ____ **3.** The introduction is interesting and engages the audience.

____ ____ **4.** The fonts are easy to read and point size varies appropriately for headings and text.

____ ____ **5.** The use of italics, bold, and underline contributes to the readability of the text.

____ ____ **6.** The background and colours enhance the text.

____ ____ **7.** The graphics, animation, and sounds enhance the overall presentation.

____ ____ **8.** Graphics are of proper size.

____ ____ **9.** The text is free of spelling, punctuation, capitalization, and grammatical errors.

Figure 8.9 Checklist for Evaluating a PowerPoint Presentation

incorporated in the rating. This is the most frequently used type of rating scale for performance assessments. Descriptors such as the following are associated with different points on the scale:

novice, emergent, proficient, advanced
novice, intermediate, advanced, superior
inadequate, needs improvement, good, excellent
excellent, proficient, needs improvement
absent, developing, adequate, fully developed
limited, partial, thorough
emerging, developing, achieving
not there yet, shows growth, proficient
excellent, good, fair, poor

Rubrics

When scoring criteria are combined with a rating scale, we have the foundation for a complete *scoring guideline*, or a *rubric*. A **rubric**, or *scoring rubric*, is a scoring guide that uses criteria to differentiate between levels of student proficiency. It organizes and clarifies the scoring criteria. Because rubrics are worded to communicate how teachers evaluate the essence of what is being assessed, they are especially useful in assessment for learning (Tierney & Simon, 2004). According to Wiggins (1998), rubrics answer the following questions:

By what criteria should performance be judged?

Where should we look and what should we look for to judge performance success?

What does the range in the quality of performance look like?

How do we determine validly, reliably, and fairly what score should be given and what that score means?

How should the different levels of quality be described and distinguished from one another?

A rubric uses descriptions of different levels of quality on each of the criteria. For example, one of the criteria in judging the persuasiveness of a paper in the earlier example is plausibility and relevance of supporting arguments. Different levels of quality for those criteria could be expressed as follows:

No supporting arguments
Few supporting arguments that have weak plausibility and relevance
Some supporting arguments that have acceptable plausibility and relevance
Many supporting arguments that are clearly plausible and relevant

In addition, many rubrics label each category with evaluative language, using gradations of descriptors (e.g., inadequate, minimal, adequate, superior; novice, developing, or developed).

Whether numbers, levels, or evaluative language is used in a rubric, the goal is to make criterion-referenced interpretations so that students are informed about specific deficiencies and strengths, and so that teachers are clearer about what they use in making their judgments. An example of an excellent rubric is shown in Figure 8.10.

9–8 The upper-range responses satisfy the following criteria:

  a. *Summary.* The summary should identify the main idea [of the reading].

  b. *Focus of agreement.* Agreement or disagreement may be complete or partial but writer must make clear what he/she is agreeing/disagreeing with. Specifically, 9–8 papers must address author's thesis, not substance abuse in general.

  c. *Support for agreement/disagreement.* Support should provide an analysis of argument and/or relevant and concrete examples.

  d. *Style and coherence.* These papers demonstrate clear style, overall organization, and consecutiveness of thought. They contain few repeated errors in usage, grammar, or mechanics.

  [The four phrases in italics represent the dimensions being scored. Two of the criteria are underlined.]

7 This grade is used for papers that fulfill basic requirements for the 9–8 grade but have less development, support, or analysis.

6–5 Middle-range papers omit or are deficient in one of these four criteria:

  a. *Summary.* Summary is absent or incomplete, listing only author's thesis.

  b. *Focus of agreement/disagreement.* What the writer is agreeing/disagreeing with is not clear or is unrelated to author's proposals. Example: writer doesn't use enough phrasing like "on the one hand . . . on the other hand . . . " [an indicator].

  c. *Support.* Writer only counterasserts; examples are highly generalized or not distinguishable from examples in the article. Analysis may be specious, irrelevant, or thin.

  d. *Style and coherence.* These papers are loosely organized or contain noticeable errors in usage, grammar, or mechanics.

4 This grade is used for papers that are slightly weaker than the 6–5 papers. Also, a student who writes his/her own parallel essay in a competent style should receive a 4.

3–2 These papers are deficient in *two* or more of the criteria. Typically they weakly paraphrase the article or they have serious organization/coherence problems. Papers with serious, repeated errors in usage, grammar, or mechanics must be placed in this range. [This whole paragraph, like all the previous ones, is a descriptor for this point on the scale.]

Figure 8.10 Exemplary Example of a Rubric: Assessing a High School Senior Essay on Substance Abuse

Source: Adapted from G.P. Wiggins (1998). *Educative assessment: Designing assessments to inform and improve student performance* (p. 155). San Francisco: Jossey-Bass. Reprinted by permission of John Wiley & Sons, Inc.

Developing Rubrics. Rubrics are best developed by combining several different procedures. Begin by clarifying how the discipline defines different levels of performance. This will give you an idea of the nature and number of gradations that should be used. You can also obtain samples of how others have described and scored performance in the area to be assessed.

Another approach is to gather performance samples and determine characteristics that distinguish effective from ineffective ones. The samples could be from students as well as so-called experts in the area. Start by putting a group of student samples into three qualitatively different piles to indicate three levels of performance. Then examine the samples to see what distinguishes them. The identified characteristics provide the basis for the dimensions of the rating scale. At this point, you can review your initial thinking about the scale with others to see whether they agree with you. With feedback from others, write the first draft of the descriptors at each point of the rating scale.

Use the first draft of the rubric with additional samples of student work to verify that it works as intended. Revise as needed, and try it again with more samples of student work until you are satisfied that it provides a valid, reliable, and fair way to judge student performance. Don't forget to use student feedback as part of the process. This entire process is repeated over and over to improve the rubric.

Four suggestions for developing criteria for rubrics are illustrated in Figure 8.11. Note how they combine your understanding of what is being assessed with others' opinions and actual student performances. See Arter and McTighe (2001) for a compendium of excellent examples of many different rubrics in different subjects. Subject-oriented professional organizations such as The Canadian Association of Second Language Teachers also provide examples of and links to existing rubrics.

An important decision is whether the rubric scale will be *holistic* or *analytic*. A **holistic scale** is one in which each category of the scale contains several criteria, yielding a single score that gives an overall impression or rating. Advantages of using a holistic scale are its simplicity and the ability to provide a reasonable summary rating. All the traits are efficiently combined, the work is scored quickly, and only one score results. For example, in gymnastics, a single holistic score between 1 and 10 is awarded, in which separate judgments for various dimensions (flexibility, balance, position, etc.) are combined. The disadvantage of a holistic score is that it reveals little about what needs to be improved. Thus, for feedback purposes, holistic scores provide little specific information about what the student did well and what needs further improvement.

When the purpose of the assessment is summative at the end of a unit or course, a holistic scale is appropriate. But even when used summatively, holistic scales can vary greatly in the specificity of what is used in the judgments. For example, the following holistic scale for reading is rather skimpy; very little is indicated about what went into the judgment.

Level 4: Sophisticated understanding of text indicated with constructed meaning.

Level 3: Solid understanding of text indicated with some constructed meaning.

Level 2: Partial understanding of text indicated with tenuous constructed meaning.

Level 1: Superficial understanding of text with little or no constructed meaning.

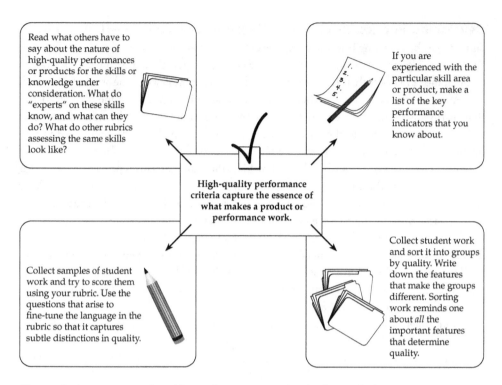

Figure 8.11 How to Identify Performance Criteria for Rubrics

Source: J. Arter & J. McTighe (2001). *Scoring rubrics in the classroom: Using performance criteria for assessing and improving student performance* (p. 34). Thousand Oaks, CA: Corwin Press. Copyright © 2001 Sage Publications, Inc. Reprinted by permission of Corwin Press, Inc.

Popham (2005) refers to this type of holistic rubric as *hypergeneral.* Such rubrics are so general and limited that there is little indication of the criteria that should be used to make judgments about student achievement. This leads to greater rater error and does not provide much instructional guidance or student awareness of criteria. Contrast this scale with the one in Table 8.2, which is also concerned with reading. This more developed and specific rubric provides a more detailed explanation of how the reading was judged and why each level was assigned. Even with this more specific scale, however, how do you judge a student who showed multiple connections between the text and the reader's ideas/experiences but had interpretations that were not directly supported by appropriate text references? This kind of problem, in which the traits being assessed do not all conform within a single category, is almost certain to exist with holistic scales for some students.

Another example of a holistic scale is illustrated in Table 8.3 for graphing data. Note how several criteria are included in each of the three levels.

An **analytic scale** (or *analytic-trait scale*) is one in which each criterion receives a separate score. If analytic scoring were used in gymnastics, each criterion such as flexibility, balance, and position would be scored separately. This kind of scale provides much better

Table 8.2 Example of Holistic Rating Scale and Rubric

	Reading Rubric
Rating Scale	*Evaluative Criteria*
4	Reader displays a sophisticated understanding of the text. There is substantial evidence of constructed meaning from the text. Meaningful and sophisticated interpretations are supported with text references. There is evidence of connections between the text and the reader's ideas/experiences. Reader takes a critical stance (e.g., analyzes the author's style of writing, questions the text, provides alternative interpretations, views the text from different perspectives).
3	Reader displays a solid understanding of the text. There is adequate evidence of constructed meaning. Some, but not many, connections are made between the text and the reader's ideas/experiences. Interpretations are generally supported by appropriate text references. There is some evidence of a critical stance toward the text.
2	Reader displays only partial understanding of the text. There is incomplete evidence of constructed meaning. While some connections are made between the text and the reader's ideas/expressions, these connections are superficial and not well developed. Interpretations are not displayed and/or not supported by appropriate text references. Reader shows little or no evidence of critical stance toward the text.
1	Reader displays a poor, superficial understanding of the text. There is very limited evidence of constructed meaning. There is no evidence of connections between the text and the reader's ideas/experiences. There are no interpretations or evidence of a critical stance.

Source: Adapted from J. McTighe & S. Ferrara (1998). *Assessing learning in the classroom* (p. 23). Washington, DC: National Education Association.

Table 8.3 Holistic Rubric for Graphic Display of Data

3	All data are accurately represented on the graph. All parts of the graph (units of measurement, rows) are correctly labelled. The graph contains a title that clearly tells what the data show. The graph is very neat and easy to read.
2	Data are accurately represented on the graph *or* the graph contains minor errors. All parts of the graph are correctly labelled *or* the graph contains minor inaccuracies. The graph contains a title that generally tells what the data show. The graph is generally neat and readable.
1	The data are inaccurately represented, contain major errors, or are missing. Only some parts of the graph are correctly labelled, or labels are missing. The title does not reflect what the data show, or the title is missing. The graph is sloppy and difficult to read.

Source: J. McTighe & G. Wiggins (2004). *Understanding by design: Professional development workbook.* Alexandria, VA: Association for Supervision and Curriculum Development. Reprinted by permission.

diagnostic information and feedback for the learner and is more useful for formative evaluation during instruction. Students can see their strengths and weaknesses more clearly. They are able to connect their preparation and effort with each evaluation. However, analytic scales take longer to create and score.

To the extent possible based on practical constraints, it is generally best to use analytic rating scales. Once established, good analytic scales will serve you well for many years. For that reason, and for the instructional advantages, it makes good sense to invest time in developing them. Two analytic scales and rubrics are illustrated in Table 8.4. The first example simply transforms the holistic scale in Table 8.3 about graphing data into an analytic one. In this example, four criteria are evaluated separately—title, labels, accuracy,

Table 8.4 Examples of Analytic Scales and Rubrics

Analytic-Trait Rubric for Graphic Display of Data[1]					
		Title	*Labels*	*Accuracy*	*Neatness*
Weight		*10%*	*20%*	*50%*	*20%*
Score	3	The graph contains a title that clearly tells what the data show.	All parts of the graph (units of measurement, rows) are correctly labelled.	All data are accurately represented on the graph.	The graph is very neat and easy to read.
	2	The graph contains a title that generally tells what the data show.	Some parts of the graph are inaccurately labelled.	Data representation contains minor errors.	The graph is generally neat and readable.
	1	The title does not reflect what the data show or the title is missing.	Only some parts of the graph are correctly labelled or labels are missing.	The data are inaccurately represented, contain major errors, or are missing.	The graph is sloppy and difficult to read.

[1] J. McTighe & G. Wiggins (2004). *Understanding by design: Professional development workbook.* Alexandria, VA: Association for Supervision and Curriculum Development. Reprinted by permission.

[2] J. McTighe & S. Ferrara (1998). *Assessing learning in the classroom* (p. 24). Washington, DC: National Education Association.

and neatness. The rubric also shows the weight that each criterion has in determining the overall score. Actually, an analytic scale can be as simple as a numerical scale that follows each criterion, such as the following, which could be used to evaluate creative writing:

	Outstanding		Competent		Marginal
Criterion	5	4	3	2	1
Creative ideas					
Logical organization					
Relevance of detail					
Variety in words and sentences					
Vivid images					

Oral Presentation Rubric[2]

Rating Scale	Evaluative Criteria		
	Organization	Delivery	Language Conventions
4	Coherent organization throughout; logical sequence; smooth transitions; effective introduction and conclusion	Excellent volume; fluent delivery with varied intonation; effective body language and eye contact	Highly effective use of language enhances the message; few, if any, grammatical mistakes
3	Good organization generally but with some break in the logical flow of ideas; identifiable introduction and conclusion	Adequate volume and intonation; generally fluent; generally effective body language and eye contact	Generally effective use of language supports the message; minor grammatical errors do not interfere with message
2	Flawed organization; ideas not developed; weak transitions; ineffective conclusion	Volume is too low or too high; delivery is not fluent; body language and eye contact do not enhance message	Use of language not always aligned with the message; grammatical errors may interfere with message
1	Lack of organization; flow of ideas difficult to follow; no evidence of transitions; no introduction or conclusion	Message cannot be understood due to low volume; strained delivery; ineffective body language; lack of eye contact	Major grammatical errors make the message very difficult or impossible to follow

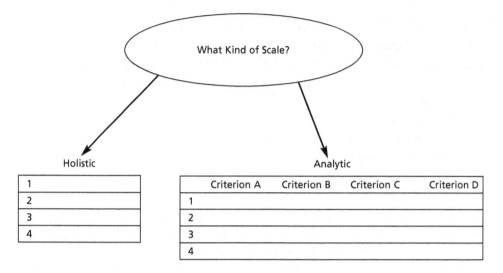

Figure 8.12 Differences between Holistic and Analytic Scales

Source: Adapted from J. Arter & J. McTighe (2001). *Scoring rubrics in the classroom: Using performance criteria for assessing and improving student performance* (p. 25). Thousand Oaks, CA: Corwin Press. Copyright © 2001 Sage Publications, Inc. Reprinted by permission of Corwin Press, Inc.

However, such scales still do not indicate much about why ideas were "competent" and not "outstanding" or why vivid images were rated "marginal." Analytic scales use language that is as descriptive as possible about the nature of the criterion that differentiates it from one level from the next. It will be much more helpful, for example, for students to know "that eye contact with the audience was direct and sustained for most of the presentation," rather than receiving feedback such as "excellent" or "completely." The difference between holistic and analytic scales is illustrated in Figure 8.12.

The following suggestions, summarized in Figure 8.13, will provide further help as you develop rubrics.

1. Be Sure the Criteria Focus on Important Aspects of the Performance. There are many ways to distinguish between different examples of student work. Use those criteria that are essential in relation to the learning expectations you are assessing. Because it is not feasible to include every possible way in which performances may differ, identify those that are most important. For example, if you are making judgments about writing and use mechanics as one of the criteria, it would not be practical to include every grammatical rule in characterizing the descriptions. Rather, you need to select a few of the most important aspects, such as tense formation, agreement, and punctuation.

2. Match the Type of Rating with the Purpose of the Assessment. If your purpose is more global and you need an overall judgment, use a holistic scale. If the major reason

✓ Do criteria focus on important aspects of the performance?
✓ Is the type of rating matched with purpose?
✓ Are the traits directly observable?
✓ Are the criteria understandable?
✓ Are the traits clearly defined?
✓ Is scoring error minimized?
✓ Is the scoring system feasible?

Figure 8.13 Checklist for Writing and Implementing Rubrics

for the assessment is to provide feedback about different aspects of the performance, an analytical approach is best.

3. The Descriptions of the Criteria Should Be Directly Observable. Try to keep the descriptions focused on behaviours or aspects of products or skills that you can observe directly. Use clearly visible, overt behaviours for which relatively little inference is required (e.g., behaviours such as loudness, eye contact, and enunciation are easily and reliably observed). Avoid high-inference criteria that are judged on the basis of behaviour, such as attitudes, interests, and effort, because the behaviours are easily faked and are more susceptible to rater error and bias. So when the expectation is affective, focus on behaviours that can be directly observed. Avoid the use of adverbs that communicate standards, such as *adequately, correctly,* and *poorly.* These evaluative words should be kept separate from what you observe.

Examples

> *Poor:* Demonstrates a positive attitude toward learning keyboarding skills.
>
> *Improved:* Voluntarily gives the teacher or other students two reasons why it is important to learn keyboarding skills.

4. The Criteria Should Be Written So That Students, Parents, and Others Understand Them. Recall that the criteria should be shared with students before instruction. The purpose of sharing them is to encourage students to incorporate the descriptions as standards in doing their work. Obviously, if the descriptions are unclear, students cannot apply them to their work, and the meaningfulness of your feedback is lessened. Consequently, pay attention to wording and phrases; write so that students easily comprehend the criteria. A simple approach to ensure understanding is often overlooked—ask the students! You can also provide examples of student work that illustrate different descriptions.

Perhaps the most effective way to ensure understanding of the criteria is to have students self-assess on the rubric. Two examples of rubrics designed for elementary student self-assessment are illustrated in Figure 8.14. Note that the language in the rubric needs to be at an appropriate level. Even at a young age, students can definitely incorporate criteria and levels of performance to know what they have learned and what they need to learn.

5. The Characteristics and Traits Used in the Scale Should Be Clearly and Specifically Defined. You need to have sufficient detail in your descriptions so that the criteria are not vague. If a few general terms are used, observed behaviours are open to different interpretations. The wording needs to be clear and unambiguous.

Exemplary Primary Science Rubric

Levels	Science Tools	Science Concepts	Reasoning Strategies	Communication
Getting Started (Novice)	I did not use tools yet.	I don't get it yet.	Mixed up steps.	I did not record or share.
Almost (Apprentice)	I tried to use some tools. Data started.	I get some of it.	Taking steps.	I started to record and share my ideas.
Got it! (Practitioner)	I did use tools. Most of my data was complete.	I get it.	Organized steps.	I did record and share my ideas.
Wow! (Expert)	Excellent use of all tools. Data complete. I can demonstrate.	My ideas shine! I can teach it to a friend.	I made more connections.	I did record details and asked questions.

Figure 8.14 Rubrics Designed for Student Self-Assessment

Source: © Exemplars, 2001, 271 Poker Hill, Underhill, Vermont 05489. www.exemplars.com

(continued)

Figure 8.14 (Continued)

Level	Understanding	Strategies, Reasoning, Procedures	Communication
Novice Makes an effort. No understanding.	I did not understand problem.	I was not sure how to do it.	I have no explanation. I am not sure how to draw the problem.
Apprentice OK, good try. Unclear.	I got started. I have part of the problem.	I am still thinking. It would help me to work with somebody. My answer doesn't look right to me.	I can explain some of what I did. I tried to use pictures, numbers, graphs, and words.
Practitioner Very good. Clear, strong.	I understood the problem, including all of the math required to solve it. I have the right answer.	I used a plan to solve the problem. I can tell you or show you how I got the answer.	I used mathematical terms, pictures, graphs, numbers, and words to tell you how I solved the problem.
Expert Wow! Awesome! Excellent!	I got it. I used important math ideas to solve the problem. I have the right answer.	I had a very efficient way of solving the problem. I checked to make sure my answer was right. I showed you some other ways that you can use this same plan to solve new problems, or I made a connection to another problem.	I showed you how I know my answer is right step by step. I clearly used words, pictures, numbers, graphs, and/or models to show my solution and mathematical thinking.

Examples (wood shop assignment to build a letter holder)

  Poor: Construction is sound.

  Improved: Pieces fit firmly together; sanded to a smooth surface; glue does not show; varnish is even.

  6. Take Appropriate Steps to Minimize Scoring Error. The goal of any scoring system is to be objective and consistent. Because performance assessment involves professional judgment, particular types of errors should be avoided to achieve objectivity and consistency. The most common errors are associated with the *personal bias* and *halo effects* of the person making the judgment. Personal bias results in three kinds of errors. **Generosity error** occurs when the teacher tends to give higher scores; **severity error** results when teachers use the low end of the scale and underrate students' performances. A third type of personal bias is **central tendency error**, in which students are rated in the middle.

CASE STUDY FOR REFLECTION

Here is how a high school teacher recently described the use of student suggestions in the development of a rubric for grading an action-research essay:

> So, we did the assessment brainstorming, and put all of the students' suggestions on the blackboard. Then, I asked them to lump the individual points into larger categories, and we arrived at these four: style, structure, quality of argument, and presentation. And then, I told them that they had 100 points to distribute among the four categories. We argued about that for a while, and eventually reached consensus (more or less) on this arrangement: 20, 20, 50, and 10, respectively. It's always interesting listening to the students' arguments about how to do this: The reasoning here was that the essay was content-driven, according to the kids, so most of the marks should be for content. I didn't really agree with that: I wanted the reflection, and therefore possibly the structure, to be worth more, but I lost. The whole exercise was quite democratic, especially for a school setting, and I didn't want to impose my values on their opinions. As well, this was not the first time that we had done this kind of negotiated assessment thing during the semester, and so the students knew how to play the game. (Strickland & Strickland, 1998, p. 86)

Questions for Consideration

1. From this example, what would you say are the advantages and disadvantages of using student suggestions to develop a scoring rubric?

2. Did the issue of grading seem to interfere in any way with the establishment of the criteria?

3. How does the teacher modify the suggestions to incorporate more criteria that he or she believes are important and should be included?

The **halo effect** occurs when the teacher's general impression of the student affects scores given on individual traits or performances. If the teacher has an overall favourable impression, he or she may tend to give ratings that are higher than what is warranted; a negative impression results in the opposite. The halo effect is mitigated if the identity of the student is concealed (though this is not possible with most performance assessments), by using clearly and sufficiently described criteria, and by periodically asking others to review your judgments. Halo effects can also occur if the nature of a response to one dimension, or the general appearance of the student, affects your subsequent judgments of other dimensions. That is, if the student does extremely well on the first dimension, you tend to rate the next dimensions higher, and you may rate students who look and act nice higher. To avoid the halo effect, be aware of its potential for affecting your judgment and monitor yourself so that it doesn't occur. Other sources of scoring error, such as order effects and rater exhaustion, should also be avoided.

To be consistent in the way you apply the criteria, rescore some of the first products scored after finishing all of the students, and score one criterion for all students at the same time. This helps avoid order and halo effects that occur because of performance on previous dimensions. Scoring each product several times, each time on a different criterion, allows you to keep the overall purpose of the rubric in mind.

7. The Scoring System Needs to Be Feasible. There are several reasons to limit the number and complexity of criteria that you judge. First, you need to be practical with respect to the amount of time it takes to develop the scoring criteria and do the scoring. Generally, five to eight different criteria for a single product are sufficient and manageable. Second, students will be able to focus only on a limited number of aspects of the performance. Third, if holistic descriptions are too complex, it is difficult and time-consuming to keep all the facets in mind. Finally, it may be difficult to summarize and synthesize too many separate dimensions into a brief report or evaluation.

SUMMARY

This chapter introduced performance assessment as a method to measure skill and product learning expectations, as well as knowledge and reasoning expectations. Important points made in the chapter include:

- In contrast to paper-and-pencil tests, performance assessment requires students to construct an original response to a task that is scored with teacher judgment.

- Authentic assessment involves a performance task that approximates what students are likely to have to do in real-world settings.

- Performance assessment integrates instruction with evaluation of student achievement and is based on constructivist learning theory. Multiple criteria for judging successful performance are developed, and students learn to self-assess.

- Major limitations of performance assessments include the resources and time needed to conduct them, bias and unreliability in scoring, and a lack of generalization.

- Performance assessment is used most frequently with deep understanding, reasoning, skill, and product learning expectations.

- Communication skill expectations include reading, writing, and speaking.

- Psychomotor skill expectations consist of physical actions (fine motor, gross motor, complex athletic, visual, and verbal/auditory) and the level to which the action is demonstrated (perception, set, guided response, mechanism, complex overt response, adaptation, and origination).

- Product expectations are completed student works, such as papers, written reports, and projects.

- Presentation expectations include oral presentations and reports.

- The performance task defines what students are required to do.

- Restricted-type tasks target a narrowly defined skill and have a brief response.

- Extended-type tasks target complex tasks and have extensive responses. These may take several days or even weeks to complete.

- The task description needs to clearly indicate the expectation, student activities, resources needed, teacher role, administrative procedures, and scoring procedures.

- Effective tasks have multiple expectations that integrate essential content and skills, are grounded in real-world contexts, rely on teacher help, are feasible, allow for multiple solutions, are clear, are challenging and stimulating, and include scoring criteria.

- Scoring criteria and rubrics are used to evaluate student performances.

- Criteria are narrative descriptions of the dimensions used to evaluate the students.

- Rating scales are used to indicate different levels of performance.

- Holistic rubrics contain several dimensions together; analytic rubrics provide a separate score for each dimension.

- Qualitative rating scales verbally describe different gradations of the dimension. Complete scoring rubrics include both descriptions and evaluative labels for different levels of the dimension.

- Scoring criteria are based on clear definitions of different levels of proficiency and samples of student work.

- High-quality scoring criteria focus on important aspects of the performance, match the type of rating (holistic or analytical) with the purpose of the assessment, are directly observable, are understandable, are clearly and specifically defined, minimize error, and are feasible.

SELF-INSTRUCTIONAL REVIEW EXERCISES

1. How does authentic assessment differ from performance assessment?

2. Explain how each of the following words is important in describing the nature of performance assessment: explain, reasoning, observable, criteria, standards, engaging, and prespecified.

3. Identify each of the following as an advantage (A) or disadvantage (D) of performance assessment.

   a. resource intensive
   b. integrates instruction with assessment
   c. student self-assessment
   d. scoring
   e. reasoning skills
   f. active learning
   g. use of criteria
   h. length

4. Identify each of the following skills as fine motor (FM), gross motor (GM), or complex (C), and use the hierarchy in Figure 8.3 to identify the level of the skill.

   a. making up new dives
   b. tracing a picture of a lion just as the teacher did
   c. making cursive capital letters easily

   d. changing running stride to accommodate an uneven surface

5. Classify each of the following as a restricted (R) or extended (E) performance task.

   a. tie shoes
   b. prepare a plan for a new city park
   c. construct a building from toothpicks
   d. interpret a weather map
   e. re-enact the Battle of the Plains of Abraham
   f. read a tide table

6. Evaluate the following performance task description. What is missing?

   You have been asked to organize a camping trip in Manitoba. There are seven campers. Indicate what you believe you will need for a three-day trip, and provide reasons for your answer. Include a detailed itinerary of where you will go while camping. You may use any library resources you believe are helpful, and you may interview others who have had camping experience. As your teacher, I will answer questions about how you gather information, but I will not evaluate your answer until you have something to turn in.

7. Create a scoring rubric for the task presented in question 6. Show how each of the elements of writing and implementing scoring criteria presented in Figure 8.13 is followed in your answer. Include reasoning skills in your rubric.

SUGGESTIONS FOR ACTION RESEARCH

1. Identify a teacher who is using performance assessments and observe students during the assessment. Are they actively involved and on-task? Do they seem motivated, even eager to get feedback on their performance? How "authentic" is the task? Can there be more than one correct answer? Is instruction integrated with the assessment? If possible, interview some students and ask them how they react to performance assessments. What do they like and dislike about them? How do they compare to more traditional types of assessment? How could they be more effective?

2. Devise a performance assessment for some aspect of this chapter. Include the performance task and scoring rubric, using the criteria in Figure 8.8. Critique the assessments through class discussion.

3. Try out some scoring rubrics with teachers. You will need to formulate learning expectations and the performance task. Construct exemplars of student work that illustrate different scores. Ask the teachers to give you some feedback about the scoring rubrics. Are they reasonable? Do they allow for meaningful differentiation between important dimensions of the tasks? Are they practical? Would students understand the rubrics? How could the scoring rubrics be improved?

4. In a small group with other students, do some research on three examples of performance tasks in your field. Do they appear to meet the criteria in Figure 8.8? How could they be improved? Be prepared to present your findings to the class for discussion.

ENDNOTES

1. From "District 214's speech assessment rating guide." (n.d.) Township High School District 214, Arlington Heights, IL.

2. A comparison task from Marzano, Pickering, & McTighe, 1993, p. 50.

Chapter 9

Portfolios: Assessing Understanding, Reasoning, Skills, and Products

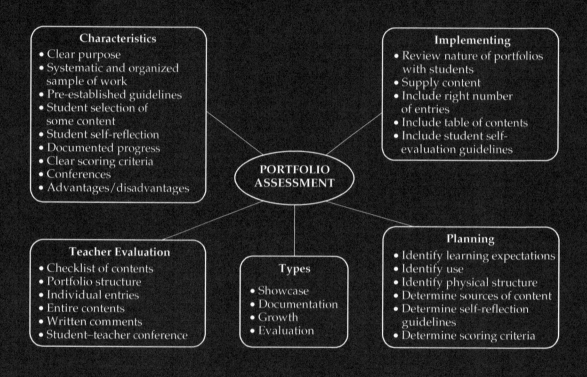

Characteristics
- Clear purpose
- Systematic and organized sample of work
- Pre-established guidelines
- Student selection of some content
- Student self-reflection
- Documented progress
- Clear scoring criteria
- Conferences
- Advantages/disadvantages

Implementing
- Review nature of portfolios with students
- Supply content
- Include right number of entries
- Include table of contents
- Include student self-evaluation guidelines

PORTFOLIO ASSESSMENT

Teacher Evaluation
- Checklist of contents
- Portfolio structure
- Individual entries
- Entire contents
- Written comments
- Student–teacher conference

Types
- Showcase
- Documentation
- Growth
- Evaluation

Planning
- Identify learning expectations
- Identify use
- Identify physical structure
- Determine sources of content
- Determine self-reflection guidelines
- Determine scoring criteria

Portfolios have emerged as a prominent type of alternative assessment, albeit with less emphasis due to extensive use of objectively scored high-stakes accountability tests. Although the term *portfolio assessment* is an evolving concept, some professional standards have been established. It is becoming increasingly clear that this method of collecting and evaluating student work over time has significant advantages over more conventional approaches to assessment. Portfolios are much more than large folders containing examples of student work. Using them requires some changes in how students are involved in assessment. In this chapter, we review essential characteristics of effective portfolios, show how they can be integrated with instruction, and illustrate, with examples, how portfolios are designed and implemented.

WHAT ARE PORTFOLIOS?

In many professions, *portfolio* is a familiar term. Portfolios are the primary method of evaluation in fields such as art, architecture, modelling, photography, and journalism. These professions have realized the value of documenting proficiency, skill, style, and talent with examples of actual work. In education, a **portfolio** is defined as a purposeful, systematic process of collecting and evaluating student products to document progress toward attaining learning expectations or to show evidence that a learning expectation has been achieved. Arter and Spandel (1992) point out that portfolios involve student participation in the selection of the portfolio's contents, specific and predetermined guidelines for selecting materials and criteria for scoring, and evidence of students' self-reflection about their accomplishments. By including student participation in selection and student self-reflection, the emphasis is on how portfolios are integrated with instruction. This is illustrated nicely by how two secondary teachers define *portfolio*:

> A collection of artefacts accompanied by a reflective narrative that not only helps the learner to understand and extend learning, but invites the reader of the portfolio to gain insight about learning and the learner. (Porter & Cleland, 1995, p. 154)

Defined in this way, then, a portfolio has several essential characteristics (Figure 9.1). First, a portfolio is *purposeful*. There is a clear reason why certain works are included and how the portfolio will be used. Second, rather than reflecting a haphazard collection of examples, the portfolio represents a *systematic* and *well-organized* collection of materials that make up a *sample*—not a comprehensive or exhaustive collection—of student work. Third, *pre-established guidelines* are set up so that it is clear what materials should be included. Fourth, students are engaged in the process by *selecting some of the materials* and by continually evaluating and *reflecting* on their work. Fifth, based on clear

---

- Clearly defined purpose and learning expectations
- Systematic and organized collection of student products
- Pre-established guidelines for what will be included
- Student selection of some of what is included
- Student self-reflection and self-evaluation
- Progress documented with specific products and/or evaluations
- Clear and appropriate criteria for evaluating student products
- Portfolio conferences between students and teachers

Figure 9.1 Characteristics of Portfolio Assessment

Source: Adapted with permission from J. Arter & V. Spandel (1992). Using portfolios of student work in instruction and assessment. *Educational Measurement: Issues and Practice, 11*, 36–44.

and well-specified *scoring criteria, progress* is documented with the evaluations. Finally, *conferences* are held between teacher and student to review progress, identify areas that need further improvement, and facilitate student reflection.

Although the precise nature of what is called *portfolio assessment* is unique to a particular setting, three models have developed (Valencia & Calfee, 1991). The *showcase* or *celebration* portfolio includes a student's selection of his or her best work. Because the student chooses the work, each profile of accomplishment is unique, and individual profiles emerge. This encourages self-reflection and self-evaluation, but makes scoring more difficult and time-consuming because of the unique structure and content of each portfolio. The *documentation* or *working* portfolio is like a scrapbook of information and examples. It may include observations, tests, checklists, and rating scales, in addition to selections by both teachers and students. It includes student self-reflection and external evaluation. The *growth* portfolio reveals change in student proficiency over time. Selections of student work are collected at different times to show how skills have improved. The same evaluative criteria should be used throughout the period that the portfolio is used. As pointed out by Stiggins, "The motivational power of a growth portfolio can be immense when students get to see their own improvement" (2005, p. 327). The *evaluation* portfolio is more standardized. The purpose is more to assess student learning than to enhance instruction, although student self-reflection may be included. Most of the examples are selected by teachers or are predetermined.

Burke (1999) lists the following as more specific types of portfolios.

- Writing—dated writing samples to show progress
- Process Folios—first and second drafts of assignments along with final product to show growth
- Literacy—combination of reading, writing, speaking, and listening pieces
- Best-Work—student and teacher selections of the student's best work
- Unit—one unit of study
- Integrated—a thematic study that brings in different disciplines
- Yearlong—key artifacts from entire year to show growth
- Career—important artifacts collected to showcase employability
- Standards—evidence to document meeting standards
- Working—collection of all student work before selections are made

Regardless of the specific type or label, portfolios have advantages and disadvantages that determine whether you will find them useful in your own teaching. Portfolios combine the strengths of performance assessments with the ability to provide a continuous record of progress and improvement. The advantages that result serve as compelling reasons to use portfolios if needed resources are provided. Like any method of assessment, limitations and trade-offs exist, so the choice depends on your overall goals and your philosophy of instruction and learning.

Advantages

Perhaps the most important advantage of using portfolios is that students are actively involved in self-evaluation and self-reflection (Borich & Tombari, 2004; Hebert, 1998; Wolf, 1989). Students become part of the assessment process. They reflect on their performance and accomplishments, critique themselves, and evaluate their progress. This leads to setting goals for further learning. Students learn that self-evaluation is an important part of self-improvement; portfolios encourage and support critical thinking through student self-reflection. Students also apply decision-making skills in selecting certain works to be included and providing justifications for inclusion. In this sense, portfolios are open and always accessible to the student. This is quite different from teachers maintaining a private record of student accomplishments.

Closely related to self-assessment is the notion that portfolios involve *collaborative assessment*. Students learn that assessment is most effective when it is done with others. In addition to self-reflections, students learn from peer reviews and teacher feedback. They may evaluate the work of others and interact with teachers to come to a better understanding of the quality of their performance.

Another important advantage of portfolios is that they promote an ongoing process wherein students demonstrate performance, evaluate, and revise to learn and produce quality work. Assessment is continuous and integrally related to learning. Rather than being only summative, systematic formative evaluation is conducted. This is different from the type of informal feedback teachers give to students, as summarized in Chapter 5. With portfolios, well-developed criteria are used to continually evaluate student progress.

Because portfolios contain samples of student work over time, they focus on self-improvement rather than comparison with others. The samples clearly document how students have progressed. This reinforces the idea that what is most important is how each student, as an individual, improves. This helps to focus the assessment on strengths and what is correct, rather than on weaknesses and what is wrong. Because each student has a unique set of materials in his or her portfolio, assessment and learning are individualized. Thus, portfolios easily accommodate individual differences among students, even though the overall learning expectations are the same, and can show unique capabilities and accomplishments. As we will see, however, this is also a disadvantage when it comes to scoring.

Motivation is enhanced as students see the link between their efforts and accomplishments and as they exert greater control over their learning. They become more engaged in learning because both instruction and assessment shift from being completely externally controlled by the teacher to being a mix of external and internal control. A grade 6 teacher relates this kind of impact on students: "With this portfolio, I saw better work than I had in the past. Students were more excited than they had ever been in my class. They were thrilled about what they had accomplished" (Martin-Kniep, 1998, p. 60). As Borich and Tombari (2004) point out, this enables teachers to focus on students' persistence, effort, and willingness to change.

A hallmark of portfolios is that they contain examples of student products. This emphasis on products is helpful in several ways. First, products reinforce the importance of performance assessment to students and parents. Products provide excellent evidence to help teachers diagnose learning difficulties, meet with students, and provide individualized feedback. Concrete examples provided by products are very helpful in explaining student progress to parents. It is much easier to clarify reasons for your evaluations in a parent conference when you have a set of examples.

Finally, portfolios are flexible. They can be adapted to different ages, types of products, abilities, interests, and learning styles. There is no single set of procedures, products, or grading criteria that you must use. You have the opportunity to customize portfolio requirements to your needs and capabilities, to different learning expectations, to available resources, and, most important, to differences among students.

Here is how one mathematics teacher describes student reactions to what was obviously a positive experience:

> The students liked the portfolio. They felt it allowed them to "mess up" and not be penalized. They liked being able to choose the quality of the work. A test is only one grade and is not always your best effort. They felt a combination of the two, test and portfolio, was a good measure of what they had learned. The portfolio really was an accumulation of everything I had been trying. It reflected a wide variety of assignments and assessments. It forced me to use and acknowledge the principles of learning that are being uncovered by researchers. The students liked it, and I did too! (Stenmark, 1991, p. 35)

Disadvantages

Some limitations to using portfolios must be considered. Like other performance assessments, scoring is the major drawback. Scoring is time-consuming, and research on reliability in scoring portfolios has shown that it is difficult to obtain high inter-rater reliability. Inconsistent scoring results from criteria that are too general, subject to different interpretations, or so detailed that raters are overwhelmed; it also results from raters who are inadequately trained. Usually, criteria are too general, and raters have not received much training.

A second disadvantage is that portfolio assessment takes considerable time and resources to do correctly. Many hours are needed to design the portfolios and scoring criteria, and many more hours will be spent reviewing, scoring, and conferencing with students and parents. You may need additional time to obtain the training you need to feel confident and to implement the portfolios properly. You need to decide if this amount of time is worth the effort. We emphasize that time and resources are needed to do portfolio assessment *correctly*. It's not the same as producing a folder of student work. Portfolio assessment, when done correctly, is very demanding; it requires time, expertise, and commitment.

A final limitation is the potential for limited generalizability. With portfolios, you generalize from the examples and demonstrated performance according to the criteria to broader learning expectations. In doing this, be careful that the generalization is justified, and that the portfolio's contents provides each student with a fair opportunity to demonstrate his or her level of competency on the general learning expectation. For example, if you are making judgments about the ability of a student to communicate by writing and the only types of writing in the portfolio are creative and expository, then the validity of the conclusion about writing in general is weak. Figure 9.2 summarizes the advantages and disadvantages of portfolio assessment.

Advantages	Disadvantages
• Promotes student self-assessment	• Scoring difficulties may lead to low reliability
• Promotes collaborative assessment	• Teacher training needed
• Enhances student motivation	• Time-consuming to develop criteria, score, and meet with students
• Systematic assessment is ongoing	• Students may not make good selections of which materials to include
• Focus is on improvement, not comparisons with others	• Sampling of student products may lead to weak generalization
• Focus is on students' strengths— what they can do	• Parents may find portfolios difficult to understand
• Assessment process is individualized	
• Allows demonstration of unique accomplishments	
• Provides concrete examples for parent conferences	
• Products can be used for individualized teacher diagnosis	
• Flexibility and adaptability	

Figure 9.2 Advantages and Disadvantages of Portfolio Assessment

PLANNING FOR PORTFOLIO ASSESSMENT

The process of planning and implementing portfolio assessment is illustrated in Figure 9.3. In this section of the chapter, we examine the planning phase of the process, which is represented in the first four steps. These steps are completed before implementation. Suggestions for planning are presented in the form of a checklist in Figure 9.4.

Purpose

Designing a portfolio begins with a clear idea about the purpose of the assessment. This involves both the specific learning expectations and the use of the portfolio.

Learning Expectations. As suggested by the title of this chapter, portfolios may be used to assess understanding but are ideal for assessing product, skill, and reasoning expectations. This is especially true for multi-dimensional skills such as writing, reading, and problem solving that are continually improved and demonstrated through products. With extensive self-reflection, critical thinking is an important expectation. Students also develop metacognitive and decision-making skills. As with other performance assessments, portfolios generally are not very efficient for assessing knowledge expectations.

It is important to distinguish between learning expectations for individual work samples and for the contents of the portfolio as a whole. Expectations that reflect all contents tend to be broader and more general, such as "development as a reader," "adapts writing to audience," "speaks clearly," and "adapts writing style to different purposes."

Uses. We have already discussed four primary uses for portfolios: documentation, showcasing, growth, and evaluation. Determine the degree to which each purpose is important, because this will influence the contents of the portfolio and the criteria used for evaluation. For example, if the primary purpose is to document typical student work

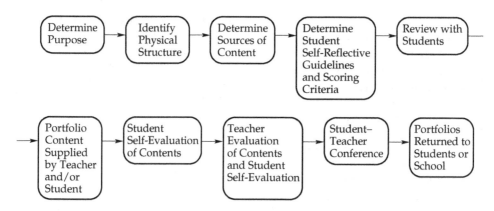

Figure 9.3 Steps for Planning and Implementing Portfolio Assessment

✓ Are learning expectations clear?

✓ Are uses of the portfolio clear?

✓ Is the physical structure for holding materials adequate and easily accessed?

✓ Are procedures for selecting the content clear?

✓ Does the nature of the content match the purpose?

✓ Are student self-reflective guidelines and questions clear?

✓ Are scoring criteria established?

Figure 9.4 Checklist for Planning Portfolio Assessment

and progress, the portfolio will be highly individualized. It will tend to be a relatively loosely organized collection of samples selected by both the teacher and the student, accompanied by both student and teacher evaluations. It will consist of many entries representing different levels of performance, because the goal is to show the student's typical (but not necessarily best) work.

If the primary purpose is to illustrate what students are capable of doing, then a showcase type of portfolio is appropriate. Only the student's best work is included. The portfolio emphasizes student selection, self-reflection, and self-assessment, rather than standardization for evaluation. This approach uses the portfolio to celebrate and show-case what each individual has achieved. Teachers often display the results in a book or folder. There may or may not be much indication of progress, but the emphasis is clearly on what the student has accomplished, rather than on improvement.

In a growth portfolio, improvement over time is shown by comparing early products or efforts with later ones. A good example could be a persuasive letter to the editor. At the beginning of the semester, students write such a letter. Later in the semester, after learning what is needed to be persuasive, students write another letter. Growth is demonstrated by comparing the two products using the same criteria.

If the portfolios are used primarily for evaluation, there will be greater standardization of what to include and how the portfolios are reviewed. The teacher selects most samples and emphasizes scoring.

Some portfolios are used to show parents and others what students have achieved. If this is the primary purpose, give more attention to what makes sense to parents, and somewhat less attention to student self-reflection. In contrast, if portfolios are used primarily diagnostically and with students to help them progress, then spend more time with student–teacher conferences during the school day. If the purpose is to help students self-reflect or conduct a peer review, then provide structure and support for these activities.

Most teachers implement portfolios for multiple purposes. Because your time and energy are limited, identify a *primary* purpose and design the portfolio based on that purpose. Wiggins (1998) points out that portfolio assessment is often implemented without sufficient attention to purpose and corresponding implications. He indicates, for example, that portfolios can serve primarily as instruction or assessment tools, focus on documentation or evaluation, be controlled by the teacher or student, and contain a sample of best work or show change over time. The specific nature of portfolio assessment differs depending on the importance of these various purposes. As a consequence, clearly determining primary purpose is critical.

Identify Physical Structure

Once your purpose has been clarified, think about some practical aspects of the portfolio. What will it look like? Most portfolios are contained in envelopes or folders. How large do the folders need to be? Where are they stored so that students can have easy access to them? Do you have boxes to put them in? Commonly used containers include cardboard boxes, file folders, file cabinets, cereal boxes, and accordion files. Putting folders on shelves where they are visible and accessible tells students the portfolios are important and should be used continuously. Your choices for these physical demands will influence the contents of the portfolios to some extent. In addition, think about the actual arrangement of the documents in the portfolio. Is it done chronologically, by subject area, or by type of document? What materials will be needed to separate the documents?

Determine Sources of Content

The content of a portfolio consists of work samples and student and teacher evaluations. Work samples are usually derived directly from instructional activities, so that products that result from instruction are included. The range of work samples is extensive, determined to some extent by the subject. For example, in English/Language Arts, you could use entries from student journals, book reports, audiotapes of oral presentations, workbook assignments, and poetry. In science, you might include lab reports, questions posed by students for further investigation, drawings, solutions to problems, and pictures of projects.

Select categories of samples that will allow you to meet the purpose of the portfolio. If you need to show progress, select tasks and samples that can show improvement. If you need to provide feedback to students on the procedures they use in putting together a report, include a summary of that process as part of the portfolio. Use work samples that capitalize on the advantages of portfolios, such as flexibility, individuality, and authenticity. The categories should allow for sufficient variation so that students can show individual work. This often means giving students choices about what they can include.

To give you a better idea of the types of work samples to include, refer to the examples in Figures 9.5 and 9.6. It is also helpful to consult other sources that include different kinds of portfolios. A number of books on portfolio assessment in specific content areas contain examples.

Language Arts[1]	Mathematics[2]
• Projects, surveys, reports, and units from reading and writing	• A solution to an open-ended question done as homework
• Favourite poems, songs, letters, and comments	• A mathematical autobiography
• Interesting thoughts to remember	• Papers that show the student's correction of errors or misconceptions
• Finished samples that illustrate wide writing skills: persuasive, letters, poetry, information, stories	• A photo or sketch made by the student of a student's work with manipulatives or with mathematical models of multidimensional figures
• Examples of writing across the curriculum: reports, journals, literature logs	• A letter from the student to the reader of the portfolio, explaining each item
• Literature extensions: scripts for drama, visual arts, written forms, webs, charts, timelines, murals	• A report of a group project, with comments about the individual's contribution
• Student record of books read and attempted	• Work from another subject area that relates to mathematics, such as an analysis of data collected and presented in a graph for social studies
• Audiotape of reading	
• Writing responses to literacy components: plot, setting, point of view, character development, links to life, theme, literary links and criticism	• A problem made up by the student
	• Artwork done by the student, such as string designs, coordinate pictures, and scale drawings or maps
• Writing that illustrates critical thinking about reading	• Draft, revised, and final versions of student work on a complex mathematical problem, including writing, diagrams, graphs, charts
• Notes from individual reading and writing conference	
• Items that are evidence of the development of style: organization, voice, sense of audience, choice of words, clarity	• A description by the teacher of a student activity that displayed understanding of a mathematical concept or relation
• Writing that shows growth in usage of traits—growing ability in self-correction, punctuation, spelling, grammar, appropriate form, and legibility	
• Samples in which ideas are modified from first draft to final product	
• Unedited first drafts	
• Revised first drafts	
• Evidence of effort—improvement noted on pieces, completed assignments	

Figure 9.5 Examples of Portfolio Work Samples

[1] R.J. Tierney, M.A. Carter, & L.E. Desai (1991). *Portfolio assessment in the reading-writing classroom* (pp. 72–74). Norwood, MA: Christopher-Gordon Publishers. Used with the permission of the publisher.

[2] Reprinted with permission from Jean Kerr Stenmark (1991). *Mathematics assessment: Myths, models, good questions, and practical suggestions* (p. 37). Copyright © 1991 by the National Council of Teachers of Mathematics. All rights reserved.

PRIMARY

LANGUAGE ARTS PORTFOLIO

Integrated Unit on Spiders

Table of Contents

1. Letter to parents about what students have learned
2. Book review of *Charlotte's Web*
3. Web of characteristics of spiders
4. Watercolour picture of spiders
5. Tape of student reading story about spiders
6. Original short story (first and final drafts) about a spider
7. Science report on "arachnids"
8. Spider rap song
9. Pictures of group project on spiders
10. Self-assessment using a criteria checklist

HIGH SCHOOL

BIOLOGY PORTFOLIO

Table of Contents

1. Reports on careers related to the field of biology
2. One lab report
3. One problem-solving log
4. Pamphlet on diabetes (group project)
5. Video of group presentation on the circulatory system.
6. Essay on germ warfare
7. Research paper on AIDS
8. Tape-recorded interview with college biology professor about AIDS
9. Self-evaluation of portfolio: using rubric
10. Goal-setting web

Figure 9.6 Examples of Portfolio Contents

Source: Kay Burke, *The mindful school: How to assess authentic learning*, 3rd edition © 1999, 1994, 1993 Skylight Training and Publishing Inc. Reprinted by permission of Sage Publications.

Determine Student Self-Reflective Guidelines and Scoring Criteria

Before implementing a portfolio assessment, establish guidelines for student self-reflection and the scoring criteria you will use when evaluating student performance. This needs to be done so that both the guidelines and criteria can be explained to students *before* they begin their work. In many cases, you can involve students in the development of self-reflective guidelines and scoring criteria. By working on these together, students will develop greater ownership of the process and will have experience in working collaboratively with you. However, as the teacher, you have ultimate responsibility to control the process to ensure integrity and high quality. You will also need to be prepared to tell students how their portfolios will be evaluated.

IMPLEMENTING PORTFOLIO ASSESSMENT

Planning is complete. Now you can begin the process of actually using the portfolios with your students. Start by explaining to students what portfolios are and how they will be used. The checklist in Figure 9.7 summarizes the suggestions for effective implementation and use.

✓ Are students knowledgeable about what a portfolio is and how it will be used?

✓ Do students know why portfolios are important?

✓ Are students responsible for or involved in selecting the content?

✓ Is there a sufficient number of work samples but not too many?

✓ Is a table of contents included?

✓ Are specific self-evaluation questions provided?

✓ Is the checklist of contents complete?

✓ Are scoring criteria for individual items and entire contents clear?

✓ Are individualized teacher-written comments provided?

✓ Are student–teacher conferences included?

Figure 9.7 Checklist for Implementing and Using Portfolios

Review with Students

Because many students will not be familiar with portfolios, explain carefully what is involved and what they will be doing. Begin with your learning expectations, show examples, and give students opportunities to ask questions. Try to provide just enough structure so students can get started without telling them exactly what to do. Put yourself in the student's place—if you had to do this new thing, what would your response be and what would you like to know?

Supplying Portfolio Content

Who selects the content of the portfolio—the student, teacher, or both? If both the student and teacher supply samples, what should the proportions be? Are the entries prescribed? Answers to these questions depend on the age and previous experience of students and the purpose of the portfolio. It is not advisable to have preschool and primary students assume sole responsibility for selecting all the samples for their portfolios, although they certainly can be consulted and play an active role in selection. Older students should assume more responsibility for selection, although even older students who are inexperienced with portfolios will initially need considerable structure. Even if students are primarily responsible for selecting the contents, you should provide guidelines about the nature of the works to be included. When the portfolios are used primarily for evaluation, teachers should make the selections or specifically prescribe what to include.

When deciding who will select the content, you need to consider somewhat conflicting goals. On the one hand, you want to foster student ownership and involvement, which is enhanced when students have input into what to include. On the other hand, you will probably need some degree of standardization in order to provide equitable evidence of student performance and improvement. You can accomplish this with greater teacher control. One effective compromise is for students and teachers to decide together, with non-restrictive guidelines, what to include. For example, students can select, in consultation with the teacher, three pieces they believe demonstrate their writing ability and progress for a semester. Another approach is to give students some restrictions and include student explanations of the choices. The teacher might prescribe the categories of writing samples, such as poem, persuasive essay, and technical report, and students would select within each of these categories (Arter & Spandel, 1992). Regardless of who makes the selections, however, provide clear guidelines for what is included, when it should be submitted, and how it should be labelled.

You will need to answer questions about the number of samples. Too many indiscriminate samples become overwhelming and difficult to organize, but too few items will not provide enough information to be useful. A portfolio with more complex products that take a longer time to create will have fewer samples than one that illustrates the growth of several relatively simple skills. A general rule of thumb for a documentation portfolio is to add one sample every week or two, for a total of 10 to 15 different items. For showcase portfolios, as few as 3 samples may be sufficient. Some teachers differentiate between a *working* portfolio, in which students keep most of their work, and a *display* or *final* portfolio, in which selections are made from the working portfolio. Haertel (1990) suggests a value-added approach, in which students include only those samples that contribute to understanding how the student has improved or progressed. That is, the student or teacher might ask, "What value is added by each piece of evidence?" If a piece doesn't contribute something new, it's not included. The fewest number of samples will be contained in an evaluation portfolio, in which only samples that illustrate final performance are included.

Teacher's Corner

Michelle Prytula

I think that the effects of portfolio assessment on students and parents are one of the portfolio's biggest strengths. Portfolios are exceptional for helping students recognize their progress, and how they have achieved according to the curriculum learning outcomes. When teachers provide students with exemplars and targeted learning outcomes at the outset, as students build and review their portfolios they are able to compile excellent information as to their own progress, understand that progress, and set direction and goals. When teachers then spend time with students, one on one, reviewing the portfolio, that direction and those goals are reinforced. Throughout the year and during reporting periods, through the portfolios parents also have information about the learning outcome goals, and evidence of their child's work at their fingertips so that the student, parent, and teacher can continue to move forward with the same information and goals.

To organize the portfolio, include a table of contents that can be expanded with each new entry. The table, which should be located at the beginning (some are pasted to the back of the front page of the folder), should include a brief description, date produced, date submitted, and date evaluated. You can provide a sample table of contents, but you will enhance ownership by providing students with some flexibility to develop their own table or overview. Directions to students could be something like, "Suppose some people who don't know you are looking at your portfolio and you are not there to tell them important things. What would you need to tell them so that they could follow and understand your portfolio?" (Collins & Dana, 1993, p. 17).

Student Self-Evaluations

One of the most challenging aspects of using portfolios is getting students to the point where they are comfortable, confident, and accurate in analyzing and criticizing their own work. These *reflective* or *self-evaluation* activities need to be taught. Most students have had little experience with reflection, so one of the first steps in using a portfolio is getting students comfortable with simple and nonthreatening forms of self-evaluation. To accomplish this, begin with teacher modelling and critiques. Once students understand what is involved (by seeing examples, such as an overhead of work from previous, unnamed students), they can engage orally in self-reflection with each other. After they have engaged in these elementary forms of reflection, will they be prepared to proceed to more complex self-evaluations? This can take several weeks.

A good way to introduce students to self-evaluation is to have them label various pieces as "Best Work," "Most Creative," "Most Difficult," "Most Effort," "Most Fun," "Most Improved," and so on.

Students are used to sentence completion exercises in which they are given a stem, so the next step could be the use of such items to structure student evaluations. For example:

> This piece shows that I've met the standard because . . .
>
> This piece shows that I really understand the process because . . .
>
> If I could show this piece to anyone, I would pick _____ because . . .
>
> The piece that was my biggest challenge was _____ because . . .
>
> One thing that I have learned from doing this piece is that I . . .

Finally, questions can be asked that give students less structure in how to respond:

> What did you learn from writing this piece?
>
> What would you have done differently if you had had more time?
>
> What are your greatest strengths and weaknesses in this sample?
>
> What would you do differently if you could do this over?
>
> What problems or obstacles did you experience when doing this? How would you overcome these problems or obstacles next time?

Is this your best work? Why or why not?

What will you do for your next work?

If you could work more on this piece of writing, what would you do?

Which sample would you say is most unsatisfying? Give specific reasons for your evaluation. How would you revise it so that it would be more satisfying?

How did your selection change from rough draft to final copy?

Such reflection is completed for each individual work sample, for groups of pieces, and then for the portfolio as a whole. Student responses are insights into how involved students have been in reaching the learning expectation, what the students perceive to be their strengths, and how instruction can be tailored to meet needs (sometimes a student's perceived strengths are inaccurate and need to be corrected). Figures 9.8 and 9.9 present examples of student responses to self-reflective prompts. In Figure 9.8, students were asked to select a piece of writing that "is important to them," and explain why they made the selection. This example indicates responses from the same three students, appearing in the same order. The answers, although varied, illustrate what students think about themselves and what they believe they need to work on in the future. Figure 9.9 shows how younger students—in this case, third graders—can be involved in self-reflection.

Students often are asked to engage in peer evaluations. These can be very helpful, especially when students are beginning to get used to the idea of self-reflection and the teacher is trying to establish a trusting environment. The focus of peer evaluations is on analysis and the constructive, supportive criticism of strategies, styles, and other concrete aspects of the product. Here are three examples of the type of feedback that you can provide to students. In this situation, students were asked to give advice to one another and to comment on "standout" selections:

When I looked at the portfolio selections with Shawn, I noticed a lot of things I could have done better on. For instance, on my problem-solving section I did not do so good because it was the beginning of the year and I had not really gotten into school yet.

I worked with Jeff today. He helped me see many things about my papers but most of all he helped me pick my best work. This is "How many books are in the library?" This work shows reasoning, estimation, observations, and many other things. This is why this work stands out so well. It shows what my work was. This was also challenging and exciting to me. Even though my estimation was 5600 and the actual was 19 000 I still think my reasoning and attitude towards this project was very good [sic].

Today I worked with Andrew. Helped me see the things I was doing wrong. I had a code cracker which didn't show a lot but he helped me see how to make it work.

He told me to add an explanation about it for it to fit. I think a standout piece is my million's project. It shows everything I need. It has the original problem plus it shows all my work. It has an explanation about the problem and what we did. (Lambdin & Walker, 1994, p. 322)

More comprehensive reflection is done on all the contents of the portfolio at the end of the semester or year. This evaluation focuses much more on the overall learning expectation.

Why did you select this particular piece of writing?

"I believe it's my best piece all year. I think it's a very strong piece."

"It's the most thoughtful piece I have written all year."

"I had to use more references to do this writing, and you can see this by how much more details [sic] are in it."

What do you see as the special strengths of this paper?

"It shows that I can write a unique piece, different from the rest of the crowd."

"The wording and the form."

"I sense a strong ability to spot details from the text."

What was especially important when you were writing this piece?

"I wanted to write something that would stand out, that people would notice. And it was."

"What I thought friendship was all about."

"My main goal was to defend a thesis with as much information as possible."

What have you learned about writing from your work on this piece?

"I can begin to write something, and end up with something totally different."

"Writing a poem wasn't as hard as it seems."

"I have learned that when you are writing you must always stick to the topic."

If you could go on working on this piece, what would you do?

"I would make it longer, taking off the end, making many more levels of anticipation."

"Be more descriptive."

"I would go into the different ways each of the boys handled their tribes."

What kind of writing would you like to do in the future?

"Short stories, POEMS!"

"Narrative."

"I have always wanted to write a murder mystery."

Figure 9.8 Middle and High School Student Responses to Self-Reflection Questions

Source: R. Camp (1992). Portfolio reflections in middle and secondary school classrooms. In K.B. Yancey (Ed.), *Portfolios in the writing classroom.* Urbana, IL: National Council of Teachers of English. Copyright © 1992 by the National Council of Teachers of English. Reprinted with permission.

Notice how the following questions are different from those about a single piece or sample in the portfolio:

What do you notice about your earlier work?

Do you think your writing has changed?

What do you know now that you did not know before?

```
LANGUAGE ARTS PORTFOLIO
STUDENT REFLECTION

Name: __Patricia__                              Date: _____

This piece was selected because:
                I was very happy with it
                My handwritting is good.
_____

This piece is good because:
                It shows that I can
                write.
_____

One thing I learned from doing this piece was that:
                If I try harder I can
                do well.
_____

What I would do to make the piece better:
                Make it longer.
_____
```

Figure 9.9 Elementary Student Self-Reflection

At what points did you discover something new about writing?

How do the changes you see in your writing affect the way you see yourself as a writer?

Are there pieces you have changed your mind about—that you liked before but don't like now, or didn't like before but do like now? If so, which ones? What made you change your mind?

In what ways do you think your reading has influenced your writing? (Camp, 1992, p. 76)

Here is how one grade 12 student answered these questions:

When I look back at my writing from the beginning of the year I realize that I have changed tremendously as a writer. My earlier work is not as explicit and does not seem like anything I would write now. . . . I know now that revising your work adds a great deal to the quality of the piece. If I may quote [my teacher], "Nothing is ever perfect the first time." Each piece of writing we did made me realize more and more things that could make my writing better. After these changes have been made I find that I look upon myself as a better and more sophisticated writer. At the beginning of this year I thought my "Lady and the Tiger" piece was the best I could ever do. When I look at it now I see a lot of places in which I could change it to make it 100% better. (Camp, 1992, pp. 77–78)

A more structured kind of self-reflection is illustrated in Figure 9.10 for a middle school social studies class.

Student self-reflection can also include comments or a review by parents. One of the advantages of using portfolios is that they are well-suited to parent involvement. At the beginning of the year, inform parents about what portfolios are and how they as parents can actively participate to be helpful. Students can consult their parents when selecting work samples, and parents can help students reflect on their work. Informally, parents can continuously provide advice and encouragement. More formally, they can complete a form or answer a specific set of questions. Students can then incorporate parent comments and suggestions into their own reflection.

Teacher Evaluation

Teachers evaluate portfolio contents in several different ways. These include checklists of contents, evaluations of the quality of the portfolio's structure, evaluations of individual entries, and evaluations of learning expectations as demonstrated by all the contents. We'll consider each of these types.

Checklists of Contents. You can provide a summary in the form of a simple checklist to ensure that the contents of the portfolio are complete. The checklist can vary according to the level of specificity desired and by the audience. Some checklists are relatively brief, and others are long and detailed. A student checklist is illustrated in Figure 9.11. Others can be designed for teachers, administrators, or parents. Student checklists tend to be brief, but those for teachers and schools are typically more comprehensive.

Portfolio Structure Evaluation. You can evaluate portfolios according to how well students have demonstrated skill in completing the structural requirements, such as the selection of samples, thoroughness, appearance, self-reflection, and organization. Evaluate these aspects by assigning points to each aspect according to a scale (e.g., 5 = excellent, 1 = poor), by making written comments, or both. When evaluating selections, consider the diversity of the samples, the time periods represented, and overall appropriateness. You can judge the quality of student reflection by the clarity and depth of thought, the level of analysis, and the clarity of communication. Evaluate organization by using a checklist to indicate whether required components are included, properly sequenced, and clearly labelled.

Personal Assessment of Portfolio

Dear Student: Your portfolio consists of all the writing assignments you have completed in social studies thus far. This form will assist you in monitoring your portfolio and determining the strengths and weaknesses of your writing.

Part I: Read the statements below. Write the number that most honestly reflects your self-assessment. (Scale 1–5: 5=strong, 4=moderately strong, 3=average, 2=moderately weak, 1=weak)

_____ **1.** My portfolio contains all of the items required by my teacher.

_____ **2.** My portfolio provides strong evidence of my improvement over the course of the unit.

_____ **3.** My portfolio provides strong evidence of my ability to report factual information.

_____ **4.** My portfolio provides strong evidence of my ability to write effectively.

_____ **5.** My portfolio provides strong evidence of my ability to think and write creatively.

Part II: On the lines below, write the topic of each assignment. Rate your *effort* for each piece (5=strong effort, 1=weak effort). In the space below, write one suggestion for improving each piece.

_____ **1.** _____
_____

_____ **2.** _____
_____

_____ **3.** _____
_____

_____ **4.** _____
_____

_____ **5.** _____
_____

Part III: In assessing my overall portfolio, I find it to be (check one)

Very satisfactory   _____   Satisfactory   _____

Somewhat satisfactory _____   Unsatisfactory   _____

Part IV: In the space below, list your goal for the next marking period and three strategies you plan to use to achieve it.

Goal:

Strategies: 1.

      2.

      3.

Figure 9.10 Structured Student Assessment of Portfolio

Source: D.V. Goerss (1993). Portfolio assessment: A work in process. *Middle School Journal, 25*(2), 20–24. Reprinted with permission from National Middle School Association.

Portfolio Checklist
(For Language Arts Class Only)

Name ______________________________ Date ______________

By the end of the year, your portfolio must contain the original copies of the following items:

_______ Student Assessment Letter(s)

_______ Reading Log and Book Reviews

_______ Reading Attitude Survey

_______ Writing Samples

Figure 9.11 Example of Student Portfolio Checklist

Source: A. A. De Fina (1992). *Portfolio assessment: Getting started* (p. 79). New York: Scholastic Professional Books. Reprinted by permission of Scholastic.

Evaluations of Individual Entries. Each individual entry in the portfolio can be evaluated with the scoring criteria and rubrics that were discussed in Chapter 8, although often much less standardization is used with portfolios. Many teachers find that more individualized, informal feedback on work samples is effective and efficient, particularly when many items are included in the portfolio. Furthermore, not every entry will likely be evaluated in the same way. However, provide sufficient feedback so that students know what they have done well and what they need to improve.

Evaluation of Entire Contents. The learning expectations for the portfolio as a whole are different from those for individual entries. Likewise, the criteria for judging progress toward meeting learning expectations of the collective contents is different from criteria used for each entry. The language of the evaluation reflects the more general nature of the expectation. The words used also emphasize the developmental nature of learning because the focus is on student improvement and progress. Thus, phrases such as "students demonstrate the ability to understand increasingly complex software programs," "a greater number of self-evaluative criteria applied," "increased understanding of," or "increased ability to" are used. Be sure to include individualized written comments for each student. This descriptive summary of performance and progress should highlight changes that have occurred, strengths, and areas that need improvement. Point out the strengths and improvements first, and then address weaknesses in language that clearly explains what needs improvement but will not discourage students or cause a sense of futility. Words such as *improving, developing, partial*, and even *novice* are better than *unacceptable* or *inadequate.*

Overall evaluations can also address effort and the student's willingness to learn. Use a simple scale (e.g., very willing to learn, somewhat willing to learn, resistant to learning) or write individual comments.

Student–Teacher Conferences

The final step in implementing portfolios (before returning them to the student or school file) is conducting a conference with each student to review the contents, student reflections, and your evaluations of individual items and the collective work as related to learning expectations. Schedule conferences with students throughout the year; some suggest having one conference each month at the elementary level. Especially early in the year, the conferences can be used to clarify purposes and procedures, answer questions, and establish trust. Although scheduling and conducting these conferences takes time, the sessions provide an important link between students and teachers.

CASE STUDY FOR REFLECTION

Ms. Singh is really frustrated with the progress of her grade 9 English Language Arts classes. It's already March, and the provincial Alberta Achievement Test in English Language Arts is coming up soon. What if her students aren't ready? It seems as though all she has worked on this year has been the writing portfolios. Last year, when her school division required every student to have a portfolio, it sounded like a good idea. Who could have known how much time it would take? Teachers conferencing with students, students conferencing with each other, and students self-evaluating their progress has taken time away from teaching. She promises herself that next year she will develop some strategies to help the whole process run more smoothly.

Questions for Consideration

1. What mistakes with writing portfolios did Ms. Singh make this school year?
2. Could you help her formulate a list of strategies to try next year so that the process will run more smoothly?

Give students some guidelines to prepare for each conference. During the conference, allow the student to do most of the talking. Have students compare their reflections with your evaluations and make plans for subsequent work. Although weaknesses and areas for improvement need to be covered, show students their progress and the possibilities, rather than what is wrong. Make sure that at the end of the conference there is a plan of action for the future. Limit the conference to no more than 10 or 15 minutes. You may want to have students take notes about what you discussed in the conference and make your own brief notes. Focus on one or two major topics or areas at each conference. This helps ensure a full and thoughtful discussion, rather than a superficial treatment of several areas.

Unit	Semester	Yearlong
1. Collect items for three or four weeks.	5. Collect items the entire semester.	10. Collect one to two items each week.
2. Select and reflect on items two weeks prior to the end of the unit.	6. Select seven to ten final items four weeks before the end of the semester.	11. Review all items at the end of each quarter and select three or four items. Date all items.
3. Conduct conferences in the last week.	7. Allow one week for students to select, organize, and reflect on contents.	12. Repeat each quarter. Students write reflections at the end of each quarter.
4. Grade the last week.	8. Allow one week for conferences.	13. Select the final ten to twelve items four weeks before the end of school.
	9. Allow one week for grading.	14. Allow two to three weeks for reflection, organization, and conferencing.
		15. Allow one to two weeks for grading.

Figure 9.12 Portfolio Implementation Time Lines

Source: Adapted from Kay Burke, *The mindful school: How to assess authentic learning* (3rd ed.), © 1999, 1994, 1993, Skylight Training and Publishing Inc. Reprinted by permission of Sage Publications.

Figure 9.12 summarizes steps in implementing portfolio assessment with an emphasis on when certain activities take place and the time needed to complete them. Specific time lines will depend on the type of portfolio and the degree of student involvement.

SUMMARY

The essence of portfolios is to gather and evaluate, on a continual basis, student products that demonstrate progress toward specified learning expectations. By combining principles of performance assessment with student self-reflection, portfolios can be powerful tools to improve student learning. With the flexibility inherent in portfolios, you can individualize assessment to maximize meaningful feedback to each student. Other major points in the chapter include the following:

■ Portfolio assessment is systematic and purposeful.

■ Portfolio assessment includes student selection of contents and student self-reflection.

■ Different types of portfolios include showcase, documentation, growth, and evaluation.

■ Portfolios integrate assessment with instruction by focusing on improvement and progress.

■ Portfolios are adaptable to individual students.

■ Reliability of scoring is a limitation of portfolios.

■ Portfolios require considerable teacher time for preparation and implementation.

■ Portfolios may result in limited generalizability.

■ Planning for portfolio assessment includes identifying learning expectations and uses, physical structures, sources of content, guidelines for student self-reflection, and scoring criteria.

- Implementing portfolio assessment includes reviewing with students, supplying content, student self-evaluations, teacher evaluations, and student–teacher conferences.

- Students should be meaningfully involved in the selection of work samples.

- Just enough work samples need to be included to meet the purpose of the portfolio.

- A table of contents should be included in the portfolio.

- Student self-evaluation needs to be taught. Students progress to eventually become skilled at analyzing and critiquing their own and others' works.

- The teacher evaluates checklists of contents, the student's ability to put together the portfolio, individual items, and the content as a whole, among other things, which may include scores from rubrics and written comments.

- Student–teacher conferences should be held throughout the year to review progress and establish plans.

SELF-INSTRUCTIONAL REVIEW EXERCISES

1. Indicate whether each of the following is an advantage (A) or disadvantage (D) of using portfolio assessment:

    a. collaboration between student and teacher

    b. student selection of contents

    c. scoring

    d. continuous monitoring of student progress

    e. training the teacher to use portfolios

    f. generalizability

    g. student self-evaluation

2. Indicate whether it would be best to use a showcase (S), documentation (D), growth (G), or evaluation (E) portfolio for each of the following purposes:

    a. to show examples of all of a student's work

    b. for the student to demonstrate his or her best work

    c. to show what students in a class are capable of doing

    d. to indicate the progress of the class on an important expectation

    e. for grading

    f. to show a student's progress

3. Evaluate the planning that is illustrated by the teacher in the following example. Is what she has planned consistent with what a portfolio is all about? Why or why not? Is her planning adequate? What else does she need to do?

    Ms. Taylor has decided to implement a mathematics portfolio in her grade 6 classroom. She believes the portfolios will increase student learning. She provides manila folders for the students and tells them that they will keep all their math worksheets and tests in it. She tells the students that they will be talking to her periodically about what is in the folder.

4. Match the description or example with the appropriate step in implementing portfolio assessment. Each step can be used more than once or may not be used at all:

    _____ (1) rubric used to evaluate the sixth writing sample

    _____ (2) Mr. Lind meets with students once a week

    _____ (3) students ask questions about how to self-reflect

    _____ (4) teacher prepares an overhead that outlines the basics of portfolio assessment

    _____ (5) table of contents is prepared

_____ **(6)** students select three work samples

_____ **(7)** a checklist includes outline and self-reflection categories

a. review with students

b. supply content

c. student self-reflection

d. teacher evaluation

e. student–teacher conference

5. The following scenario describes how a junior high school social studies teacher in Manitoba goes about implementing portfolio assessment in his class. After reading the scenario, review the checklist in Figure 9.7. Use this checklist as criteria to evaluate how well Mr. Janzen does in using portfolios.

Matt Janzen has read a lot lately about portfolios and decides to use them with his grade 7 social studies classes. He spends the last week before school fine-tuning what he hopes his students can learn from doing the portfolios. Although he thinks he must give grades to ensure student motivation, he plans to use the portfolios to demonstrate to other teachers what his students are capable of achieving.

Matt decides to ask his students to bring something to class to hold the portfolio contents. He explains to his students that they will be selecting one example each week from their work in his class that shows their best effort. Every month students meet with each other to critique what was included, and after the meeting, students complete a self-evaluation worksheet. Throughout the semester, Matt plans to talk with each student at least once about his or her portfolio.

Near the end of the semester, Matt collects all the portfolios, grades them, and returns them to his students. He makes sure that each student receives individualized comments with the grade.

SUGGESTIONS FOR ACTION RESEARCH

1. Locate two or three examples of portfolios from different teachers. Review the contents of the portfolios carefully, looking for characteristics that have been discussed in this chapter. How are the portfolios alike, and how are they different? Are they being used for different purposes? Is the structure and content appropriate for the intended use?

2. Interview students who have had some experience with portfolios. Ask them what they like and don't like about doing portfolios, how much time it takes them to complete their work, and what the teacher does to help them. Focus on student self-reflection. Ask the students how they have self-evaluated themselves and what they think they have learned from the process.

3. Visit two or three classrooms and see how portfolios are organized and stored. If possible, talk with the teachers to get their views about how to organize portfolios so that they are practical.

4. Devise a student portfolio assignment for students. Include each of the steps in Figure 9.3, and include examples where possible. Then ask two or three teachers to review your assignment and give you feedback on how it could be improved, how much time it would take to implement, how realistic it would be, and what students would probably get out of it.

Chapter 10
Assessing Affective Traits and Dispositions

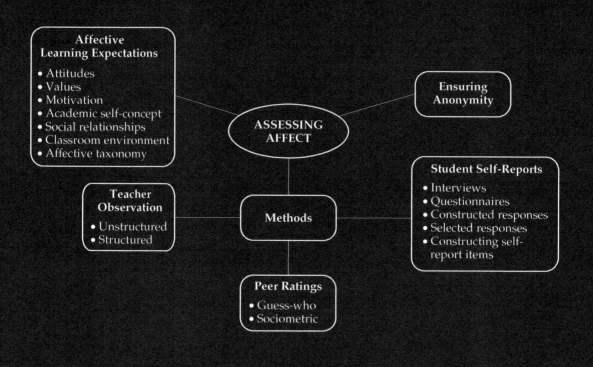

Affective Learning Expectations
- Attitudes
- Values
- Motivation
- Academic self-concept
- Social relationships
- Classroom environment
- Affective taxonomy

Ensuring Anonymity

ASSESSING AFFECT

Student Self-Reports
- Interviews
- Questionnaires
- Constructed responses
- Selected responses
- Constructing self-report items

Teacher Observation
- Unstructured
- Structured

Methods

Peer Ratings
- Guess-who
- Sociometric

C hapters 6 to 9 focused on what have traditionally been labelled *cognitive* learning expectations and skills. We now turn to a set of student dispositions and traits that many educators regard as equally important—what have become known as *affective* outcomes. We'll look at how to define affective learning traits and expectations and how, practically speaking, to assess these traits and expectations in the classroom in a way that improves instruction and student cognitive learning. These expectations, if well-conceptualized and assessed, are essential for providing students with the life skills they need.

ARE AFFECTIVE LEARNING EXPECTATIONS IMPORTANT?

Research has established clear linkages between affect and learning (Ormrod, 2004). Students are more proficient at problem solving when they enjoy what they are doing. Students who are in a good mood and emotionally involved are more likely to pay attention to information, remember it, rehearse it meaningfully, and apply it. Too much anxiety interferes with learning, and an optimum level of arousal is needed for maximum performance. Classrooms with more positive "climates" foster student well-being (Petegem, Aelterman, Van Keer, & Rosseel, 2008), engagement, and learning much more do than classrooms with negative climates (Fraser, 1994).

Despite this research, there is very little systematic assessment of affect in the classroom (McMillan, Workman, & Myran, 1998; Stiggins & Conklin, 1992). Teachers know that students who are confident about their ability to learn, like the school subjects they study, have a positive attitude toward learning, respect others, and show a concern for others are much more likely to be motivated and involved in learning. At the same time, however, most teachers do not rely on any kind of formal affective assessment procedures, nor do they set specific affective learning expectations for their students. Why? Two reasons seem plausible. First, especially in the higher grades, schooling is organized by subject matter. Cognitive subject matter expectations are agreed on as desirable for all students. This puts affect in the position of being important but still secondary to cognitive learning. It also makes coming to an agreement about which affective expectations are appropriate for all students difficult. That is, it simply isn't easy to define attitudes, values, and interests.

Second, assessing affective expectations is fraught with difficulties. The many potential sources of error in measuring affective traits often result in low reliability. Student motivation is a primary concern. Students need to take such assessments seriously to provide accurate results, yet many may be inhibited if their responses are not anonymous. They would find it easy to fake responses on self-report instruments if the results are to be used for grading or some other purpose. They may want to please the teacher with positive responses. Another source of error is that some affective traits are easily influenced by momentary or temporary moods. This is especially true for younger students, who may report much more negative affect after a bad day. Teacher bias can also have a significant influence on what may be recorded or perceived.

What are the advantages, then, to systematically setting and assessing affective expectations? Positive affective traits and skills are essential for

- effective learning,
- being an involved and productive member of society,
- preparing for occupational and vocational satisfaction and productivity (e.g., work habits, a willingness to learn, and interpersonal skills),
- maximizing the motivation to learn now and in the future, and
- preventing students from dropping out of school.

Most current school and school district mission statements include affective outcomes, and teachers constantly assess affect informally during instruction. The following sections discuss suggestions and techniques for taking affect to a more serious level. What better way can teachers signal to students that clearly defined positive affect is important than by systematically assessing it? This begins with identifying appropriate affect expectations, which we consider next.

WHAT ARE AFFECTIVE TRAITS AND LEARNING EXPECTATIONS?

The term **affective** has come to refer to a wide variety of traits and dispositions that are different from knowledge, reasoning, and skills (Hohn, 1995). The term **affect** has a technical meaning that is rather restrictive: the emotions or feelings we have toward someone or something. However, attitudes, values, self-concept, citizenship, and other traits usually considered to be noncognitive involve more than emotion or feelings. In fact, most kinds of student affect involve both emotion and cognitive beliefs. Nevertheless, the literature refers to a range of possible outcomes as affective (see Table 10.1).

Attitude Expectations

Attitudes are internal states that influence what students are likely to do. The internal state is some degree of positive/negative or favourable/unfavourable reaction to an object, situation, person, group of objects, general environment, or group of persons (McMillan, 1980). Attitudes do not refer to behaviours, what a student knows, right or wrong in a moral or ethical sense, or characteristics such as the student's ethnicity, age, or socio-economic status. Thus, we always think about attitudes *toward* something. In schools, that may be learning, subjects, teachers, other students, homework, and other objects or persons. Usually, then, you can identify the positive or negative attitudes that

Table 10.1 Affective Traits	
Trait	**Definition**
Attitudes	Predisposition to respond favourably or unfavourably to specified situations, concepts, objects, institutions, or persons
Interests	Personal preference for certain kinds of activities
Values	Importance, worth, or usefulness of modes of conduct and end states of existence
Opinions	Beliefs about specific occurrences and situations
Preferences	Desire or propensity to select one object over another
Motivation	Desire and willingness to be engaged in behaviour and intensity of involvement
Academic Self-Concept	Self-perceptions of competence in school and learning
Self-Esteem	Attitudes toward oneself; degree of self-respect, worthiness, or desirability of self-concept
Locus of Control	Self-perception of whether success and failure are controlled by the student or by external influences
Emotional Development	Growth, change, and awareness of emotions and ability to regulate emotional expression
Social Relationships	Nature of interpersonal interactions and functioning in group settings
Altruism	Willingness and propensity to help others
Moral Development	Attainment of ethical principles that guide decision making and behaviour
Classroom Environment	Nature of feeling tones and interpersonal relationships in a class

you want to foster or at least monitor because they are related to current and future behaviour. Some examples are:

Fostering A Positive Attitude Toward
learning
school
math, science, English, and other subjects
homework
classroom rules
teachers

working with others
staying on-task
taking responsibility for one's acts

Fostering A Negative Attitude Toward
cheating
drug use
fighting
skipping school
dropping out

Social psychologists, through extensive research, have found that attitudes consist of three elements or contributing factors (Forsyth, 1999):

1. an *affective* component of positive or negative feelings

2. a *cognitive* component describing worth or value

3. a *behavioural* component indicating a willingness or desire to engage in specific actions

The *affective* component consists of the emotion or feeling associated with an object or a person (e.g., good or bad feelings, enjoyment, likes, comfort, or anxiety). When we describe a student as liking math or enjoying art, we are focusing on the affective component. The *cognitive* component is an evaluative belief (such as thinking something is valuable, useful, or worthless, etc.). In school, students can think history is useless and mathematics is valuable. The *behavioural* component is actually responding in a positive way. Students show a strong and stable attitude when all three components are consistent. That is, when Nazeem likes science, thinks it's important, and reads *National Geographic* at home, he has a very strong positive attitude. But it's likely that, for many students, these components will contradict one another. Louise may not like English Language Arts very much but think that it's important. What would her attitude be, in a general sense, toward English Language Arts? That would depend on what components of the attitude you measure. If you measured only the affective component, the attitude would be negative; a measure of the cognitive component would reveal a positive attitude.

This tripartite conceptualization has important implications for identifying attitude expectations. Are you interested in feelings, thoughts, or behaviours? If you want to have a learning expectation such as "students will have a positive attitude toward school," include all three components in your assessment, because the general nature of the expectation needs to be consistent with the assessment. However, if your expectation is "students will like coming to school," then the assessment should focus on the affective component.

Value Expectations

Values generally refer either to end states of existence or to modes of conduct that are desirable or sought (Rokeach, 1973). End states of existence are conditions and aspects of ourselves and our world that we want, such as a safe life, world peace, freedom, happiness, social acceptance, and wisdom. Modes of conduct are reflected in what we believe is appropriate and needed in our everyday existence, such as being, honest, cheerful, ambitious, loving, responsible, and helpful. Each of these values can be placed into categories consistent with different areas of our lives. Thus, you can think about moral, political, social, aesthetic, economic, technological, and religious values.

We recommend that you focus on values that are relatively noncontroversial and that are clearly related to academic learning and school and district goals. Popham (2005) has suggested some values as being sufficiently meritorious and noncontroversial:

- *Honesty*. Students should learn to value honesty in their dealings with others.

- *Integrity*. Students should firmly adhere to their own code of values, for example, moral or artistic beliefs.

- *Justice*. Students should subscribe to the view that all citizens should be the recipients of equal justice from governmental law enforcement agencies.

- *Freedom*. Students should believe that democratic nations must provide the maximum level of freedom to their citizens. (p. 230)

Other relatively noncontroversial values include kindness, generosity, perseverance, loyalty, respect, courage, compassion, and tolerance. Popham also suggests that you should limit the number of affective traits targeted and assessed. It is better to do a sound job of assessing a few important traits than to try to assess many traits superficially.

Motivation Expectations

In the context of education, motivation can be defined as the extent to which students are involved in trying to learn. This includes the students' initiation of learning, intensity of effort, commitment, and persistence. In other words, *motivation* is the purposeful engagement in learning to master knowledge or skills; students take learning seriously and value opportunities to learn (Ames, 1990; McMillan & Forsyth, 1991). Much research on motivation can be organized according to what is called the *expectancy* x *value* framework (Brophy, 2004; Pintrich & Schunk, 2002). This model suggests that motivation is determined by students' expectations—their beliefs about whether they are likely to be successful—and the value of the outcome. Expectations refer to the *self-efficacy* of the student, which is the student's self-perception of his or her capability to perform successfully. Values are self-perceptions of the importance of the performance. That is, does the student see any value in the activity? Is it intrinsically enjoyable or satisfying? Will it meet some social or psychological need, such as self-worth, competence, or belonging, or will it help the student to attain an important goal? Students who believe that they are capable of achieving success, and that the activity holds value for them, will be highly motivated to learn. If they value the outcome but believe that no matter how hard they try they probably won't be successful, their motivation will be weak. Similarly, many very capable students are unmotivated because the activity holds no importance for them.

Motivation expectations should follow from the expectancy x value theory (McMillan, Simonetta, & Singh, 1994). But because it is impossible to pinpoint the source of the lack of effort and involvement, motivation expectations should focus on self-efficacy and value. The motivation expectations should also be differentiated by academic subject and type of learning (e.g., knowledge, understanding, and reasoning). Here are some examples:

- Students will believe that they are capable of learning how to multiply fractions. (self-efficacy)

- Students will believe that it is important to know how to multiply fractions. (value)

- Students will believe that they are capable of learning how the cardiovascular system functions. (self-efficacy)

- Students will believe that it is important to know how the cardiovascular system functions. (value)

Another important consideration in assessing motivation is why students are learning, and the reasons they provide for their actions. When students do something because it is inherently interesting, enjoyable, or challenging, they are intrinsically motivated. In contrast, extrinsic motivation is doing something because it leads to a separate outcome (e.g., reward or punishment) (Ryan & Deci, 2000). Similarly, students who are motivated by a need to understand and master the task (mastery orientation) demonstrate more positive behaviour and thinking than students who are doing something for the result or outcome (performance orientation). Mastery orientation students are more engaged, have a natural inclination to generate solutions to problems, and generate more positive attributions to success and failure (success attributed to ability and moderate effort; failure to lack of effort).

Academic Self-Concept Expectations

Extensive literature exists on self-concept and its cousin, self-esteem. Many educators refer to these characteristics when discussing students who have problems with school and learning (e.g., "Stefan has a low self-concept" or "Parminder has a low opinion of herself"). There is no question about the importance of these beliefs, even with the controversy over whether self-concept and self-esteem proceed or result from academic learning. According to our definition of motivation, some level of positive self-efficacy is needed for achievement. This aspect of self-concept is probably formed, at least in part, when children experience meaningful success with moderate effort.

When setting expectations, remember that self-concept and self-esteem are multidimensional (Marsh & Craven, 1997). There is a bodily self, an athletic self, a mathematics self, a social self, and so forth. Each of us has a self-description in each area, which is our self-concept or self-image. In addition, we also have a sense of self-regard, self-affirmation, and self-worth in each area (self-esteem). Thus, a student can have a self-concept that he is tall and thin but feel very comfortable with that and accept this description. Another student can have the same self-concept but feel inferior or inadequate, or have a low self-esteem.

Like attitudes and motivation, measuring general self-concept is simply not that helpful. This is because much of what makes up general self-concept comes from areas not directly related to academic learning. By specifying *academic* self-concept, you will obtain a more valid indication of what students think about themselves as learners. If you set expectations that are specific to subject areas, the resulting information will be more useful. Also, it's helpful to know where students draw the line between descriptions of themselves and whether they like those descriptions. From the standpoint of more serious psychological or emotional problems, a general measure may be needed, but you should leave that to a school psychologist or counsellor.

Social Relationship Expectations

Social relationships involve a complex set of interaction skills, including the identification of and appropriate responses to social cues. Peer relationships, friendship, functioning in groups, assertiveness, cooperation, collaboration, prosocial behaviour, empathy, taking perspective, and conflict resolution are examples of the nature of social relationships that can be specified as expectations. Many of these are required skills for academic achievement at the academic level. At the secondary level, interpersonal abilities are becoming more and more important as schools work with the business community to identify and promote the skills needed to be successful in the workplace. Furthermore, social interaction is a key element of knowledge construction, active learning, and deep understanding (Borich & Tombari, 2004). As interaction occurs, students are forced to adjust their thinking to accommodate alternative viewpoints, to defend their ideas, and to debate their opinions. These processes encourage a deep, rather than superficial, understanding and keep students engaged. Interaction also can promote good reasoning and problem-solving strategies through observation and the give-and-take that ensues.

For each of these broad social relationship areas, specific expectations need to be identified. For example, an expectation concerned with peer relationships might include showing interest in others, listening to peers, sharing, and contributing to group activities. Cooperative skills could include sharing, listening, volunteering ideas and suggestions, supporting and accepting others' ideas, taking turns, and criticizing constructively.

Collaborative skills needed to work in small groups could include four components: (1) basic interaction, (2) getting along, (3) coaching, and (4) fulfilling particular roles (Borich & Tombari, 2004; Hoy & Greg, 1994). Skills for each of the components are summarized in Table 10.2.

Our recommendation is similar to suggestions about identifying attitude, motivational, and self-concept expectations—be very specific about the expectation. A general expectation about "improved social relationships" or "improved collaboration skills"

Table 10.2 A Taxonomy of Collaborative Skills

Component	Definition	Skills
Basic Interaction	Students like and respect each other	Listening Making eye contact Answering questions Using the right voice Making sense Apologizing
Getting Along	Students sustain their respect and liking for one another	Taking turns Sharing Following rules Assisting Asking for help or a favour Using polite words
Coaching	Students both give and receive corrective feedback and encouragement	Suggesting an action or activity Giving and receiving compliments or praise Being specific Giving advice Correcting and being corrected
Role-Fulfilling	Fulfilling specific roles creates positive interdependency and individual accountability	Summarizer Checker Researcher Runner Recorder Supporter Troubleshooter

Source: M.L. Tombari & G.D. Borich (1999). *Authentic assessment in the classroom: Applications and practice* (pp. 191–192). Upper Saddle River, NJ: Pearson Education. Reprinted by permission of Pearson Education, Inc., Upper Saddle River, NJ.

simply does not provide the specificity needed to focus your instruction and assessment. Here are some examples of possible social relationship expectations:

- Students will contribute to small group discussions.
- Students will have sustained friendships with two or more other students.
- Students will demonstrate skills in helping other students solve a problem.
- Students will demonstrate that they are able to negotiate with others and compromise.

Classroom Environment Expectations

Every classroom has a unique climate and feel to it. You can sense the degree to which a class is comfortable, relaxed, and productive, and whether students seem happy, content, and serious. Some classes are warm and supportive; others seem very cold and rejecting. Together, such characteristics make up what is called **classroom environment, classroom climate** (Raviv, Raviv, & Reisel, 1990), or **classroom culture** (Gallego & Cole, 2001). Research indicates that a positive classroom environment that reduces student anxiety, encourages camaraderie, and promotes safe interactions increases academic achievement (Boreman & Overman, 2004). A positive classroom environment has also been identified as a factor that can foster the educational resilience of students who are at risk for academic failure (Dunn, 2004).

Classroom environment is made up of a number of characteristics that can be used as affective expectations. These include the following:

affiliation—the extent to which students like and accept each other

involvement—the extent to which students are interested in and engaged in learning

task orientation—the extent to which classroom activities are focused on the completion of academic tasks

cohesiveness—the extent to which students share norms and expectations

competition—the emphasis on competition between students

favouritism—whether each student enjoys the same privileges

influence—the extent to which each student influences classroom decisions

friction—the extent to which students bicker with one another

formality—the emphasis on enforcing rules

communication—the extent to which communication among students and with the teacher is genuine and honest

warmth—the extent to which students care about each other and show empathy

Fraser (1999) suggests that is useful to compare students' perspectives on classroom environment with those of teachers. For example, it has been demonstrated in many settings that students prefer a more positive classroom environment than they perceive is present, and that teachers thought that the environment was more positive than students did. Such a pattern of results informs teachers about what needs to be changed to enhance student learning.

Affective Domain of the Taxonomy of Educational Objectives

One of the earliest treatments of affective objectives was called the *Taxonomy of Educational Objectives, Handbook II: Affective Domain* (Krathwohl, Bloom, & Masia, 1964). It was a companion to Bloom's *Taxonomy* of the cognitive domain. Although the taxonomy was developed more than 40 years ago, it conceptualized attitudes, values, and other affective traits in a hierarchy, which is appealing from the standpoint of assessment.

The affective taxonomy arranges affective expectations along a five-stage continuum. These stages, with definitions and examples, are summarized in Table 10.3. Let's look at

Table 10.3 Affective Taxonomy of Educational Objectives

Category (Level)	Definition	Examples
Receiving (*Attending*)	Develops an awareness, shows a willingness to receive, shows controlled or selected attention	Student considers reading books for extra credit Student pays attention to teacher lecture about smoking
Responding	Shows a willingness to respond and finds some initial level of satisfaction in responding	Student asks questions about different books Takes pleasure in playing sports
Valuing	Shows that the object, person, or situation has worth Something is perceived as holding a positive value, a commitment is made	Student reads continually, asks for more books Asks for further help in improving writing skills Practices sports all the time
Organization	Brings together a complex set of values and organizes them in an ordered relationship that is harmonious and internally consistent	Student develops a plan for integrating reading and sports Weighs concerns for social justice with governmental size
Characterization	Organized system of values becomes a person's life outlook and the basis for a philosophy of life	Student develops a consistent philosophy of life Reading forms the basis for most everything in the student's life

Source: Adapted from D.R. Krathwohl, B.S. Bloom, & B.B. Masia (1964). *Taxonomy of educational objectives, handbook II: Affective domain.* Boston: Allyn and Bacon. Copyright © 1964 Pearson Education. Reprinted by permission of the publisher.

an example that refers to attitudes toward science. At the most basic level, students are merely aware of and perceive science (*receiving*). At the next level, students are able to pay attention to science (*responding*). Next, students indicate through their voluntary behaviour that science has value (*valuing*). Once science is valued, it can be organized with other subjects and other values (*organization*). The highest stage occurs when science is so highly valued that it becomes a determining tendency and influence on other aspects of the student's life (*characterization*).

The affective taxonomy for classroom assessment of affect helps you determine the standard or level of affect that is part of your expectation. It also provides good suggestions for using student behaviours as indicators of affect at each level. For example, suppose you want your students to develop an appreciation for classical music. At what level do you want your expectation? Will students simply be aware of what classical music is and what it sounds like (receiving)? Or do you want them to really *like* classical music (valuing)?

METHODS OF ASSESSING AFFECTIVE EXPECTATIONS

There are really only three feasible methods of assessing affective traits and dispositions in the classroom: teacher observation, student self-report, and peer ratings. Because affective traits are not directly observable, they must be inferred from behaviour or what students say about themselves and others. Some very sophisticated psychological measures can assess many affective traits, but these are rarely used by classroom teachers. As we will see, you need to rely on your own observation and some student self-reports.

Keep three considerations in mind whenever you assess affect. First, emotions and feelings can change quickly, especially for young children and during early adolescence. To obtain a valid indication of an individual student's emotion or feeling, conduct several assessments over a substantial length of time. You want to know what the dominant or prevalent affect is, and if you rely on a single assessment, what you measure may not be a good indication of the trait. Measure repeatedly over several weeks.

Second, try to use different approaches to measuring the same affective trait. Reliance on a single method is problematic because of limitations inherent in that method. For example, if you use only student self-reports, which are subject to social desirability and faking, these limitations may significantly affect the results. However, if student self-reports are consistent with your observations, then you can make a stronger case.

Finally, decide if you need individual student or group results. This is related to purpose and will influence the method you should use. If you are using assessment for making reports to parents, then obviously you need information on each student. In this case, use multiple methods of collecting data over time, and keep records to verify your judgments. If you are using the assessments to improve instruction, then you need results for the group as a whole. This is the more common and advisable use of affective assessment, primarily because you can rely more on anonymous student self-reports (Popham, 2005).

Teacher Observation

In Chapter 5, teacher observation was discussed as an essential tool for formative assessment. Here, we emphasize how teachers can make more systematic observations to record student behaviour that indicates the presence of targeted affective traits.

In using observation, determine in advance how specific behaviours relate to the expectation. Begin with a clear definition of the trait, followed by lists of student behaviours and actions that correspond to the trait's positive and negative dimensions. Let's consider attitudes. Identify the behaviours and actions initially by considering what students with positive and negative attitudes do and say. If we have two columns, one listing behaviours for positive attitudes and one listing behaviours for negative attitudes, we define what to observe. Suppose you are interested in attitudes toward learning. What is it that students with a positive attitude toward learning do and say? What are the actions of those with a negative attitude? Table 10.4 lists some possibilities. These behaviours provide a foundation for developing guidelines, checklists, or rating scales. The ones in the positive column

Table 10.4 Student Behaviours Indicating Positive and Negative Attitudes toward Learning

Positive	Negative
rarely misses class	is frequently absent
rarely late to class	is frequently tardy
asks lots of questions	rarely asks questions
helps other students	rarely helps other students
works well independently without supervision	needs constant supervision
laughs	is not involved in extracurricular activities
is involved in extracurricular activities	says he or she doesn't like school
says he or she likes school	rarely comes to class early
comes to class early	rarely stays after school
stays after school	doesn't volunteer
volunteers to help	often does not complete homework
completes homework	doesn't care about bad grades
tries hard to do well	never does extra credit work
completes extra credit work	never completes assignments before the due date
completes assignments before they are due	complains
rarely complains	sleeps in class
is rarely off-task	bothers other students
rarely bothers other students	stares out window

are referred to as *approach* behaviours; those in the negative column are *avoidance* behaviours. Approach behaviours result in more direct, frequent, and intense contact; avoidance behaviours are just the opposite, resulting in less direct, less frequent, or less intense contact. These dimensions—directness, frequency, and intensity—are helpful in describing the behaviours that indicate positive and negative attitudes.

How do you develop these lists of positive and negative behaviours? We have found that the best approach is to find time to brainstorm with other teachers. Published instruments are available that may give you some ideas, but these won't consider the unique characteristics of your school and students. The following characteristics were brainstormed by teachers to indicate a positive student attitude toward school subjects (e.g., mathematics, science, or English):

seeks corrective feedback
asks questions
helps other students
prepares for tests

reads about the subject outside of class

asks about careers in the subject

asks about universities that are strong in the subject

asks other students to be quiet in class

is concerned with poor performance

joins clubs

initiates activities

stays alert in class and on-task

Once you develop a fairly complete list of behaviours, decide if you want to use an informal, unstructured observation or one that is more formal and structured. These types differ in preparation and in what is recorded.

Unstructured Observation. Unstructured (anecdotal) observation is much like what was discussed in Chapter 5. In this case, however, your purpose is to make summative judgments.

An unstructured observation is usually open-ended; typically there is no checklist or rating scale for recording what you observe. However, you do know what affective trait you are focused on, and you have at least generated some guidelines and examples of behaviours that indicate the affective trait. Although you have determined in advance what to look for, be open to other actions that may reflect on the trait.

During the observation period, or just after it, record behaviours that reflect the affective trait. Some of what you record may correspond to the guidelines or a list of possible behaviours, but record other actions too—anything that may have relevance to the expectation. Keep your interpretations separate from descriptions of the behaviours. Take brief anecdotal notes and then make sense of them later; this is what teachers do regularly in their heads in a way that is even less systemic than these unstructured observations. The difference is in whether there is any predetermined list of behaviours, and whether teachers record their observations.

Avoid making conclusions or inferences in what you record. You want to describe what you saw or heard, not what it may mean. Words such as *unhappy*, *frustrated*, *sad*, *motivated*, and *positive* are your interpretations of observed behaviours. It is better to stick to simple descriptions, such as *frowned*, *asked question*, *stared out window*, and *kept writing the entire time*. Look for both positive and negative actions. The tendency is to be more influenced by bad or negative behaviour, especially if it interferes with other students. Once you record descriptions from several different times, look them over and make conclusions about the affective trait. Don't rely on a single observation.

The advantage of unstructured observation is that it is more natural and you are not constrained by what is in a checklist or rating scale. There is no problem if specific behaviours aren't displayed, and behaviours that were not previously listed can be included. A disadvantage is that it is not practical to record much about student behaviour on a regular basis. It's hard to find even 15 or 20 minutes at the end of the day, and it is virtually impossible to find any time during the school day.

Structured Observation. A structured observation differs from an unstructured one in the amount of preparation needed and the way you record what is observed. In structured observation, you need more time to prepare a checklist or rating form used for recording purposes. This form is generated from the list of positive and negative behaviours, to make it easy and convenient for you to make checks quickly and easily.

The format of the checklist is simple and straightforward. The behaviours are listed, and you make a single check next to each behaviour to indicate frequency. Frequency can be indicated by answering yes or no, observed or not observed; by the number of times a behaviour occurred; or by some kind of **rating scale** (*always, often, sometimes, rarely, never, occasionally, or consistently*). Rating scales are used to describe behaviour over an extended period of time.

Two examples of checklists for assessing attitude toward reading are illustrated in Figure 10.1. The first, labelled *frequency*, is used to record the number of times each behaviour was observed. The second type is a *rating* in which the teacher estimates how often each behaviour occurs as defined by a set scale. Another example is shown in Figure 10.2. In this example, the targeted affective trait is participation. A holistic rating scale is used to describe qualitatively different levels of participation. Notice that several behaviours are included in scores 2–5. This type of rating scale provides a general

---

Frequency Method

Student Name: _____   Date: _____   Time Frame: _____

Number of Occurrences	Behaviour
	1. Tells others that a book was good
	2. Reads for at least five minutes continuously
	3. Asks questions about what is read
	4. Goes through books on the table

Rating Method

Student Name: _____   Date: _____   Time Frame: _____

Behaviour	Never	Rarely	Sometimes	Most of the Time	Almost Always
Tells others that a book was good					
Reads for at least five minutes continuously					
Asks questions about what is read					
Goes through books on the table					

Figure 10.1 Checklists for Structured Observations of Reading Behaviour

Participation in Class		
Student: _____ Date: _____ Lesson:_____		
Criteria		**Score**
Always listens to instructions. Very actively involved from the beginning. Obviously intent on learning the skill. Leads others. Shares thoughts and ideas.		5
Listens to instructions. Once started, actively involved. Usually intent on learning the skill. Rarely distracted from the task. Often shares thoughts and ideas. Does not usually lead others.		4
Sometimes needs clarification about directions. Hard to get started and stay involved. More passive than active. Sometimes distracted from the task. Rarely shares thoughts and ideas.		3
Does not pay attention to instructions. Distracts others. Needs reminders to stay on task. Passive. Rarely shares thoughts and ideas.		2
Did not participate.		1

Figure 10.2 Scoring Criteria for Participation

overview of the trait being measured. Your choice of checklist or rating scale depends on the time frame (ratings are better for longer periods of time) and the nature of the behaviour. Some behaviours are better suited to a simple checklist, such as "follows instructions" and "completes homework." Our experience is that a simple scale, with only three descriptors to indicate frequency (e.g., *usually*, *sometimes*, and *rarely*), is usually sufficient. Additional rating scales are illustrated in Figure 10.3. If there are a large number of behaviours, organize them into major categories. This will make it easier to record and draw inferences from the results. Other suggestions are listed in Figure 10.4.

Student Self-Report

There are several ways in which students tell us about their affect using self-report methods. The most direct way is in the context of a personal conversation or interview. Students can also respond to a written questionnaire or survey about themselves or other students. First, we consider interviews.

Student Interviews. Teachers can use different types of personal communication with students, such as individual and group interviews, discussions, and casual conversations, to assess affect. This is similar to observation, but because you have an opportunity to be directly involved with the students, you can probe and respond in order to better understand. An important prerequisite for getting students to reveal their true feelings and beliefs is establishing trust. Without a sense of trust, students may not be comfortable expressing their feelings. They will tend to say what they think their teachers want to hear, say what is socially acceptable or desirable, or say very little. Younger students are usually pretty candid about themselves; older students may be more reserved. You enhance trust

PRIMARY

SOCIAL SKILLS CHECKLIST

ASSESSMENT OF SOCIAL SKILLS

Dates: 10/21
Class: 3rd Grade
Teacher: Forbes

Rating:
+ = Frequently
✓ = Sometimes
O = Not Yet

Skills: Listening, Using First Name, Taking Turns, Encouraging, Sharing

Who	Skill 1	Skill 2	Skill 3	Skill 4	Skill 5	Comments
1. Lois	✓	✓	O	✓	✓	
2. Connie	+	+	O	✓	+	Dropped in 2 areas
3. James	✓	✓	✓	✓	✓	
4. Juan	+	+	✓	+	+	
5. Beth	O	O	+	✓	✓	Improved in 2 areas
6. Michele	✓	✓	O	✓	✓	
7. John	✓	✓	O	✓	✓	
8. Charles	+	+	O	✓	+	
9. Mike	✓	✓	✓	✓	✓	Went from 50s to this in 2 months
10. Lana	+	+	✓	+	+	

Notes: Work with Lois on a regular basis. Change her seat and group.

MIDDLE SCHOOL

OBSERVATION CHECKLIST

Student: Denise   Class: Science   Date: 12/5
Type of Assignment: Work Habits

☐ Teacher   Date _____   Signed _____
☐ Peer   Date 12/5   Signed _____
☒ Self   Date 12/5   Signed Denise Smith

	Not Yet	Sometimes	Frequently
WORK HABITS:			
• Gets work done on time			X
• Asks for help when needed		X	
• Takes initiative		X	
STUDY HABITS:			
• Organizes work			X
• Takes good notes			X
• Uses time well			X
PERSISTENCE:			
• Shows patience		X	
• Checks own work	X		
• Revises work		X	
• Does quality work			X
SOCIAL SKILLS:			
• Works well with others		X	
• Listens to others		X	
• Helps others		X	

COMMENTS: _I always get my work done on time, and I am really organized. I just need to check my own work and help my group work._

FUTURE GOALS: _I need to be more patient with my group and try to work with them more. I worry about my own grades, but I don't do enough to help group members achieve their goals._

Figure 10.3 Examples of Rating Scales

Source: Kay Burke. *The mindful school: How to assess authentic learning* (3rd ed.). © 1999, 1994, 1993 Skylight Training and Publishing Inc. Reprinted by permission of Sage Publications.

✓ Determine behaviours to be observed in advance.
✓ Record student, time, date, and place.
✓ If unstructured, record brief descriptions of relevant behaviour.
✓ Keep inferences separate from descriptions.
✓ Record both positive and negative behaviours.
✓ Make several observations of each student.
✓ Avoid personal bias.
✓ Record as soon as possible following the observation.
✓ Use a simple and efficient system.

Figure 10.4 Checklist for Using Teacher Observation to Assess Affect

by communicating warmth, caring, and respect, and by listening attentively to what the students communicate.

An advantage of interviewing is that you can clarify questions, probe where appropriate to clarify responses, and note nonverbal behaviour. Students have an opportunity to qualify or expand on previous answers. These procedures help avoid ambiguity and vagueness, problems often associated with measuring affect.

It is difficult for some students, even when there is a trusting relationship, to articulate their feelings in a one-on-one interview. They may simply be unaccustomed to answering questions about attitudes and values. A group discussion or group interview is a good alternative for these students. People generally open up more in a group setting, as long as peer pressure and cliques don't interfere.

Another advantage of using groups is that it is much more efficient than individual interviews. Also, feelings and beliefs can become clearer as students hear others talk. Students can lead group interviews, as they may be better able to probe for deeper understanding because they are familiar with the language and lifestyles of their classmates. Respected student leaders will be highly credible.

Be prepared to record student responses and your interpretations. During an interview it is difficult to write very much, and it's not practical to tape record, transcribe, and analyze the transcription. We suggest that you prepare a brief outline of the major areas that will be covered, leaving space to make brief notes as you interview. As soon as possible after the interview, go back over your notes and fill in enough detail so that what the student said and communicated are clearly indicated. Like observation, be careful to keep your descriptions separate from your interpretations.

Questionnaires and Surveys. You have probably completed many self-report attitude questionnaires or surveys, so you have a general idea what they are like. However, teachers rarely use such instruments in the classroom (Stiggins & Conklin, 1992). This is primarily because of the time and expertise it takes to construct, administer, and score student responses. Most standardized instruments—there are hundreds of them—are not specific enough to help a teacher in a specific context. What is measured is conceptualized as a general trait, and this usually isn't relevant for teachers to use in planning or delivering instruction.

According to Stiggins (2005), one key to the successful use of student self-reports is to get students to take the questionnaires seriously. This will happen if students see that what you are asking about is relevant to them and that actions are taken as a result of the findings. You want to help students understand that they have nothing to lose and something to gain by being cooperative.

Another key is using questions to which students are willing and able to provide thoughtful responses. To accomplish this, ensure that the wording of the questions is precise, the format is easy to understand and respond to, and the response options make sense. These and other suggestions are discussed in reviewing the major types of attitude, value, and self-concept self-report instruments.

Constructed-Response Formats. A straightforward approach to asking students about their affect is to have them respond to a simple statement or question. Often, incomplete sentences can be used.

Examples

> I think mathematics is . . .
> When I have free time I like to . . .
> The subject I like most is . . .
> What I like most about school is . . .
> What I like least about school is . . .
> Science is . . .
> I think I am . . .

Essay items can be used with older students. These items provide a more extensive, in-depth response than incomplete sentences. You can ask students for reasons for their attitudes, values, or beliefs.

Example

> Write a paragraph on the subject you like most in school. Tell me why. Comment on what it is about the subject and your experience with it that leads you to like it the most. Describe yourself as a student. Are you a good student? What are you good at? How hard do you try to get good grades? Is learning easy or hard for you?

An advantage of the incomplete sentence format is that it taps whatever comes to mind from each student. You are not cueing students about what to think or suggesting how they should respond, so you get what is foremost and most salient in the student's mind. Of course, students need to be able to read, write, and take the task seriously. If you use this method, be sure to give them enough time to think and write, and encourage them to write as much as they can for each item.

Teacher's Corner

Elizabeth O'Brien

In the beginning of the year I always have students write a "mathography." I ask them to write about themselves, and their history and relationship with math. I learn a tremendous amount about my students that I would never learn otherwise. This helps to explain some students' attitudes and approaches to the material. It also enables me to understand the situations that students have dealt with in the past, which often affect how they deal with material in the present. In addition, I do a learning style inventory in the beginning of the year with students. I do this as much for them as for myself. Many students have not given any thought to how they learn best or why they often do better for one type of teacher versus another. This instrument allows me and the students to get a better picture of my classroom and the students in it and how I should adapt my teaching to them.

There are two disadvantages to constructed-response formats. First, even if you tell students that their answers are anonymous, they may think you'll recognize their handwriting; hence, faking is a concern. Second, scoring the responses takes time and is more subjective than more traditional objective formats. But this approach offers an excellent way to get a general overview of student perspectives, feelings, and thoughts.

Selected-Response Formats. There are many different types of selected-response formats to choose from when assessing affective expectations. We will examine a few commonly used scales. When you decide to create your own instrument and wonder which of these response formats would be best, try to match the format with the trait. There is no single best response format. Some work better with some traits, and some work better with others, depending on the wording and the nature of the trait. Your job will be to make the best match.

Most selected-response formats create a scale that is used with statements concerning the trait. A widely used format to assess attitudes, for example, is the **Likert scale**. This scale can be adapted to almost any type of affective trait, so it is very versatile. Students read statements and then record their agreement or disagreement with them according to a five-point scale (*strongly agree, agree, not sure, disagree, strongly disagree*). The statements are generated from your list of positive and negative behaviours or beliefs and are put in a form that fits the response scale. The statements indicate the direction of the attitude, as illustrated in the following examples. The response scale indicates intensity.

Examples

> Mathematics is boring.
> It is important to get good grades in school.
> It is important to complete homework on time.
> Class discussion is better than lectures.
> School is fun.
> I enjoy reading.
> Science is challenging.
> Presenting in front of an audience is difficult.

An advantage of this format is that many such statements can be presented on a page or two to assess a number of different attitudes efficiently (see Figure 10.5). Note that some negatively worded statements are included in the example. These should be used sparingly with younger children, with words such as *not*, *don't*, and *no* appropriately highlighted or underlined.

The responses to the Likert scale are scored by assigning weights from 1 to 5 for each position on the scale so that 5 reflects the most positive attitude and 1 the most negative attitude (SA = 5, A = 4, NS = 3, D = 2, SD = 1). The scores from all the items assessing the same attitude trait are then totalled, although the percentage of responses to each position is probably more important than summary statistics. In other words, you wouldn't add the scores from items 1, 7, and 8 in Figure 10.5 because they address different traits, though you could

Student Opinion Survey					
Directions: Read each statement carefully and indicate how much you agree or disagree with it by circling the appropriate letter(s) to the right.					

Key:
- SA – Strongly Agree
- A – Agree
- NS – Not Sure
- D – Disagree
- SD – Strongly Disagree

1. Science class is challenging.	SA	A	NS	D	SD
2. Reading is important.	SA	A	NS	D	SD
3. I like coming to school.	SA	A	NS	D	SD
4. I like doing science experiments.	SA	A	NS	D	SD
5. Homework is hard for me.	SA	A	NS	D	SD
6. Cheating is very bad.	SA	A	NS	D	SD
7. Learning about circles and triangles is useless.	SA	A	NS	D	SD
8. I do not like to work in small groups.	SA	A	NS	D	SD
9. Doing well in school is important.	SA	A	NS	D	SD
10. I believe that what I learn in school is important.	SA	A	NS	D	SD

Figure 10.5 Likert Scale for School Attitudes

add items 3, 9, and 10, which deal with attitudes toward school. When adding items and obtaining average scores of statements that are worded so that a "disagree" response refers to a more positive attitude or belief, the scoring needs to be reversed. Thus, the scoring for items 1, 5, 7, and 8 in Figure 10.5 should be reversed (SD = 5, D = 4, A = 2, SA = 1).

The reliability of overall scores is higher if several items assessing the same trait can be added together. You need to balance this with the practical limitation on the total number of items in the questionnaire, and with the response of students who feel that they don't need to answer questions that are nearly identical to items they have already responded to.

Use the principle of the Likert scale to construct any number of different response formats. For younger children, for example, the five-point scale is usually truncated to three responses (*agree, unsure, disagree*), or even two (such as *agree* or *disagree, yes* or *no, true* or *not true*). Many self-report instruments use a Likert-type scale that asks students to indicate *how often* they have engaged in specific behaviours or had particular thoughts. These scales are easier to respond to because they are less abstract. They are best for behaviours and cognitive components of attitudes.

Examples

How often do you believe that most of what you learn in school is important?

a. always
b. frequently

c. sometimes

d. rarely

e. never

How frequently do you *dislike* coming to this class?

a. all the time

b. most of the time

c. sometimes

d. rarely

e. never

How often do you find the classroom activities interesting?

a. almost always

b. often

c. occasionally

d. rarely if ever

Another frequently used variation of the Likert scale is to ask students whether something is true for them. You can use either a simple dichotomous item, such as a true/false statement, or a scale.

Examples

How true is each statement for you?
If I want, I can get good grades in science.

a. very true

b. somewhat true

c. not at all true

When I really try hard, I can do well in school.

a. true

b. untrue

Students are very competitive in this class.

a. true

b. false

I am a good student.

a. yes

b. no

Scales are mixed in some questionnaires so that there are different scales for different items. In these types of items, the response formats are dependent on the terminology and intent of each item. Sometimes the nature of the trait is named in the item; then the scale gives students choices. For other items, the scale defines the trait being measured.

Examples

How important is it for you to be a good reader?

a. extremely important   **c.** somewhat important

b. very important   **d.** not important

Science is

a. interesting

b. dull

c. difficult

Indicate how you feel about your performance on the test.

_____	_____	_____	_____
immense pride	some pride	some failure	immense failure

_____	_____	_____	_____
very happy	somewhat happy	somewhat sad	very sad

Indicate the extent to which you believe your performance on the project was a success or failure.

a. extreme success

b. somewhat successful

c. failure

d. extreme failure

Circle the statement that best describes your interest in learning *most of the time*.

a. I am pretty interested in what we learn.

b. This class is somewhat interesting, but I find my mind wandering sometimes.

c. I often find this class pretty boring.

For young students, the response format is often in the form of faces rather than words.

Examples

Learning about science

Reading books

For classroom climate and value expectations, self-report questionnaires often ask students to select from several options. The options refer to different traits or values, rather than showing a range of the same trait.

Examples

I did well on this test because I

a. studied hard.
b. got lucky.

Select one of the following:

a. Students in this class like to help each other out.
b. There is a lot of bickering between students in this class.

Select the statement that you agree with the most.

a. People should be required to volunteer to help those less fortunate.
b. People who find a wallet should give it to the police.

Interests are efficiently measured with checklists, ranking, or simple dichotomous choices.

Examples

Indicate whether you are interested (I) or uninterested (U) in learning about each of the historical topics listed.

_____ **a.** Northwest Rebellion
_____ **b.** World War II
_____ **c.** the Holocaust
_____ **d.** the Depression
_____ **e.** stock market crash

Rank the following from most liked (1) to least liked (5).

_____ history
_____ physical education
_____ science
_____ music
_____ art

Another common approach to measuring affective traits is to use variations of the **semantic differential**. These scales use adjective pairs that provide anchors for feelings or beliefs that are opposite in direction and intensity. The student would place a check between each pair of adjectives that describes positive or negative aspects of the trait. In the following examples, the traits are attitudes toward a test and a subject.

Examples

Science Test

| fair | _____ | _____ | _____ | _____ | _____ | unfair |
| hard | _____ | _____ | _____ | _____ | _____ | easy |

History

boring	_____	_____	_____	_____	_____ interesting
important	_____	_____	_____	_____	_____ useless
like	_____	_____	_____	_____	_____ hate

An advantage of selected-response formats is that they make it easy to assure anonymity. Anonymity is important when the traits are more personal, such as values and self-concept. It is also a more efficient way of collecting information. However, don't ask too many questions just because it is efficient; keep self-report questionnaires short. Although you need more than a single item to reliably assess an affective trait, if you have too many items, students may lose concentration and motivation. Select only those traits that you will take action on; don't use items simply because it would be interesting to know what students think. It's also not a good idea to include open-ended items such as "Comments" or "Suggestions" at the end of a selected-response questionnaire.

Constructing Self-Report Items. If you need to develop your own self-report items to assess affect expectations, begin by listing the behaviours, thoughts, and feelings that correspond to each affective trait, similar to what we suggested earlier for observations. Once you select a response format, write sentences that are clear and succinct, and write direct statements that students will easily understand. You are not trying to assess knowledge, intelligence, reading ability, or vocabulary, so keep items simple and short. Published instruments will provide some good ideas about how to word items, set up response formats, and lay out a questionnaire. An existing instrument may meet your purpose very well. Now we move to some specific suggestions, with examples, for those who will be constructing items.

In wording the items, avoid the use of negatives, especially double negatives.

Examples

> *Poor:* There isn't a student in this class who does not like to work with others.
>
> *Improved:* Students in this class like to work with each other.

If you are interested in present self-perceptions, which is usually the case, avoid writing in the past tense.

Examples

> *Poor:* I have always liked science.
>
> *Improved:* I like science.

Avoid absolutes such as *always, never, all,* and *every* in the item stem. Because these terms represent an all-or-none judgment, they may cause you to miss the more accurate self-perception.

Examples

> *Poor:* I never like science.
>
> *Improved:* I rarely like science.

Avoid items that ask about more than one thing or thought. Double-barrelled items are difficult to interpret because you don't know which of the two thoughts or ideas the student has responded to.

Examples

> *Poor:* I like science and mathematics.
>
> *Improved:* I like science.

These and other suggestions presented in this section are summarized in Figure 10.6. I should point out, however, that classroom teachers rarely have an opportunity to develop sophisticated instruments with strong and well-documented technical qualities. Thus, use locally developed items and instruments with caution and in conjunction with other evidence.

Peer Ratings

Peer appraisal is the least common method of assessing affect. This is due to the relatively inefficient nature of conducting, scoring, and interpreting peer ratings. However, two primary methods for obtaining peer ratings—the guess-who and sociometric techniques—represent approaches that can be used in conjunction with observation and self-reports to strengthen assessment of interpersonal and classroom environment expectations.

Guess-Who Approach. In this method, students are asked to list the students they believe best correspond to behaviour descriptions. The descriptions may be positive or negative, though usually they are positive to avoid highlighting undesirable behaviours or traits. Typically, this approach uses only a few items so that students can complete it quickly, and scoring is done by simply tallying the number of times each student is listed. One disadvantage is that some shy and withdrawn students may be overlooked, resulting in a lack of information about them. Figure 10.7 illustrates a guess-who form for assessing cooperative behaviour.

✓ Keep measures focused on specific affective traits.
✓ Establish trust with students.
✓ Match response format to the trait being assessed.
✓ Ensure anonymity if possible.
✓ Keep questionnaires brief.
✓ Keep items short and simple.
✓ Avoid negatives and absolutes.
✓ Write items in present tense.
✓ Avoid double-barrelled items.

Figure 10.6 Checklist for Using Student Self-Reports to Assess Affect

Student Survey

Directions: Write the names of students in this class who fit the descriptions. No other students will see your answers. Include students who are absent today. The same student can be named in more than one category.

Who is most willing to cooperate with others? ______________________

Who helps other students the most? ______________________

Who is asked most for help? ______________________

Which student is most concerned about others? ______________________

Which student enjoys working with others? ______________________

Figure 10.7 Example of a Guess-Who Form for Assessing Cooperative Behaviour

Sociometric Approach. Sociometric techniques are used to assess the social structure of the class and the interaction patterns among the students. This allows you to learn about the social acceptance and liking patterns of the students. The results can be used for forming small groups of students, targeting interventions with individual students, and identifying cliques, popular students, and social isolates.

Students are asked to nominate students they would like to work or play with. Although this is technically a self-report, the results are used as a way for students to rate each other. The questions would be like the following:

I choose these students to work with.
I would like to sit next to ______________________.
I would like to have the following students on my team.

Ask about general activities, such as who to work with or sit next to, rather than specific ones (e.g., walking to school or doing a report). Avoid asking negative items (e.g., "I would not like to sit next to . . .").

Once the students have made their choices, first tabulate the results listing all the students and indicating the number of times each student was selected. This provides a measure of general social acceptance. Then, create a matrix to identify students who have selected each other. Finally, as illustrated in Figure 10.8, construct a **sociogram.** This is a diagram that shows the social structure of the group. In this example, the number of times any student was selected is depicted by the concentric circles (students with more than nine choices in the middle, those with six to nine choices in the second circle, etc.). Not all choices are shown; lines are used for mutual choices and rejections.

Although sociograms are a very interesting and informative technique, constructing them takes considerable time. However, often teachers are surprised by the results, so if you intend to assess social adjustment and other interpersonal affect expectations in depth, a sociogram would be very beneficial.

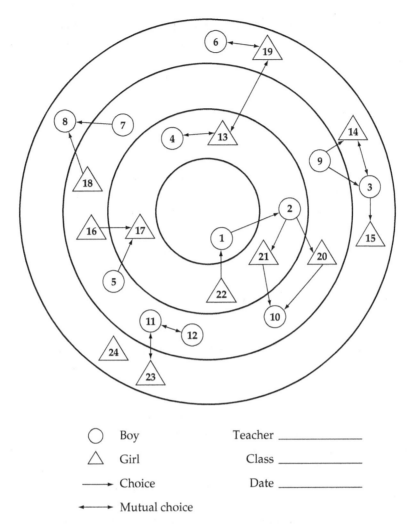

Boy ○
Girl △
→ Choice
↔ Mutual choice

Teacher _____
Class _____
Date _____

Figure 10.8 Example of a Sociogram

Which Method or Combination of Methods Should I Use?

We have covered three approaches to measuring affect—observation, student self-report, and peer ratings—and each method has advantages and disadvantages. Your choice of which of these to use depends on a number of factors. Consider the type of affect you want to assess. You can get a pretty good idea of a student's general reaction to something or someone through observation, but to diagnose attitude components, you'll need a self-report of some kind. You can follow observation with peer ratings to assess socially oriented affect. If you are interested in group responses and tendencies, which is generally recommended, then use a selected-response self-report because you can assure anonymity and it is easily scored. Finally, take into consideration how you will use the information. If you intend to use the results for grading, (which is not recommended), then you may need multiple approaches, and you should be especially careful about faking on self-reports and even peer judgments. In the end, the choice of method depends most on your context, expectations, and comfort level in using any particular approach.

Ensuring Anonymity

Anonymity has been mentioned several times as a desirable feature when assessing affect. Popham (2005) makes the argument that anonymity is not only desirable but also essential to obtaining valid results. He has pointed out that you can use several techniques to enhance perceived anonymity when you are interested in results for the class as a whole:

1. Direct students not to write their names or in any way identify themselves on their self-reports.
2. Use selected-response item formats.

CASE STUDY FOR REFLECTION

Mrs. Williams is a grade 2 teacher at James Elementary School who has had difficulty in her classroom this semester. She has had to spend ever-increasing amounts of time and energy to keep students from verbally or physically abusing each other. She has noticed that many of these students also make disparaging remarks about themselves and call themselves "dumb" or "stupid." She has used anecdotal records and feedback from talking with the school counsellor about the situation to help her assess the situation. She has decided to take a 15-minute block of time every day next term to teach appropriate social skills and to allow time for students to air their complaints in a nonviolent atmosphere. The counsellor has assured her that these students have low self-esteem, but through classroom discussion and role-play, they can learn to appreciate themselves and others. Mrs. Williams also plans to introduce a behaviour modification plan for students, which will help her track student progress with improved social behaviour. Mrs. Williams is concerned that the principal and parents of her students will not understand her attempts to assess student affective traits to improve the classroom environment.

Questions for Consideration

1. What should Mrs. Williams do before classes start next term?
2. What strategies could she use to appropriately assess students to provide data that will be reassuring to the principal and parents?

3. Inform students that their responses will be anonymous.

4. Position yourself in the class so that students know you cannot see their answers.

5. Direct students not to write anything other than checking or circling, to avoid your recognizing handwriting.

6. Provide a procedure for collecting self-reports so that you won't be able to identify responses (e.g., in a container at the back of the room, not on your desk).

7. Tell students why anonymity is important.

8. Use a response format that minimizes the likelihood that responses can be seen by other students.

SUMMARY

This chapter considered student affect, an important but often neglected area. Sound assessment of affect begins with clear and specific affective expectations. We made suggestions for conceptualizing affective traits that are usually considered essential for successful learning. Two methods are used most frequently for measuring affect in the classroom: teacher observation and student self-reports. Observation can be structured or unstructured, and there are many different formats for self-reports. In the end, you'll need to customize the assessment of affect for your students, school, and curriculum. Pick a few of the most important traits, do a good job of assessing them, and then use the results to improve instruction. Other essential points made in the chapter include:

■ Positive affective traits influence motivation, involvement, and cognitive learning.

■ Although the term *affect* refers to emotions and feelings, affective expectations include cognitive and behavioural traits.

■ Attitudes are predispositions to respond favourably or unfavourably. They include cognitive, affective, and behavioural components.

■ Values are end states of existence or desired modes of conduct.

■ Motivation is the purposeful engagement to learn. It is determined by self-efficacy (the student's beliefs about his or her capability to learn) and the value of learning.

■ Academic self-concept is the way students describe themselves as learners. Self-esteem is how students feel about themselves. Both are multi-dimensional; avoid general measures of self-concept or self-esteem.

■ Social relationship expectations involve interpersonal interaction and competence.

■ Classroom environment is the climate established through factors such as affiliation, involvement, cohesiveness, formality, friction, and warmth.

■ The affective domain of Bloom's taxonomy defines different levels of affect in a hierarchical fashion, from attending to something to using something as a determining factor in one's life.

■ Three methods are used to assess student affect: teacher observation, student self-report, and peer ratings.

■ Teacher observation can be structured or unstructured. Several observations should be made, and recording behaviour should occur as soon as possible after the observation. Inferences are made from what was observed.

■ Student self-reports include interviews, questionnaires, and surveys. Trust between the students and the teacher is essential.

■ Interviews allow teachers to probe and clarify in order to avoid ambiguity, though they cannot be anonymous and are time-consuming.

- Questionnaires are time-efficient and can be anonymous. Proper student motivation to take the questions seriously is essential.

- Constructed-response questionnaires tap traits without cueing students, which indicates what is most salient to students.

- Selected-response formats, such as the Likert scale, are efficient to score and can be anonymous when assessing groups.

- In constructing questionnaires, keep them brief, write in the present tense, and avoid negative and double-barrelled items.

- Peer ratings can be used to assess interpersonal traits. Frequencies of nominations and sociograms are used to analyze the results.

- Use appropriate techniques for ensuring anonymity.

SELF-INSTRUCTIONAL REVIEW EXERCISES

1. What are some reasons that most teachers don't systematically assess affective expectations?

2. Match the nature of the learning with the affective expectation. Each expectation may be used more than once or not at all.

   _____ **(1)** cooperation and conflict resolution

   _____ **(2)** student expectations and need to do well

   _____ **(3)** honesty and integrity

   _____ **(4)** character education

   _____ **(5)** cognitive and affective components

   _____ **(6)** responding and organization

   _____ **(7)** warmth in the classroom

   _____ **(8)** thinking math is important but not liking it

   _____ **(9)** engagement and involvement

   _____ **(10)** kindness, respect, tolerance

   a. attitude
   b. value
   c. motivation
   d. academic self-concept
   e. social relationships/collaboration
   f. classroom environment
   g. affective taxonomy

3. Critique the efforts of the teachers in the following two scenarios to assess affect. What have they done well and how could they improve?

   Scenario 1: Mr. Talbot

   Mr. Talbot decided that he wanted to assess his grade 5 class on their attitudes toward social studies. He asks students to complete the sentence, "Social studies is. . . ." Also, at the end of each week, he summarizes how much students liked the social studies units. He writes a brief description for each student, then gives each a rating of 1 to 5.

   Scenario 2: Ms. Chorny

   Ms. Chorny teaches art to junior high school students. Because all the students in the school come through her class, she wants to be sure that students leave the class with a positive attitude toward art and strong aesthetic values. She decides to develop and administer a survey of art attitudes and values at the beginning and end of each semester. She consults other teachers to generate a list of thoughts and behaviours that are positive and negative. She uses a response format of "like me" and "not like me" with the 50 items. Ms. Chorny instructs the students not to put their names on the surveys.

4. Identify each of the following as a characteristic of observation (O), constructed-response self-report (CRSR),

selected-response self-report (SRSR), or peer rating (PR).

a. can take into account nonverbal behaviours

b. relatively easy to administer but difficult to score

c. subject to teacher bias

d. can be anonymous

e. very time-consuming to gather data

f. student explanations for answers can be provided

g. the method of choice for checking which students are leaders

h. can be done without students' knowledge or awareness

SUGGESTIONS FOR ACTION RESEARCH

1. Identify some affective expectations for students and construct a short questionnaire to assess the expectations. If possible, find a group of students who could respond to the questionnaire. After they answer all the questions, ask them about their feelings toward the questions and the clarity of the wording. What do the results look like? Would the teacher agree with the results? How difficult was it to develop the questionnaire?

2. Interview several teachers about affective expectations in the classroom. Ask them how they arrived at their expectations and whether there is any systematic approach to assessing them. Ask what the advantages and disadvantages would be to using different kinds of assessment techniques, such as observation and student self-reports.

Chapter 11

Assessing Students with Exceptionalities in Inclusive Settings

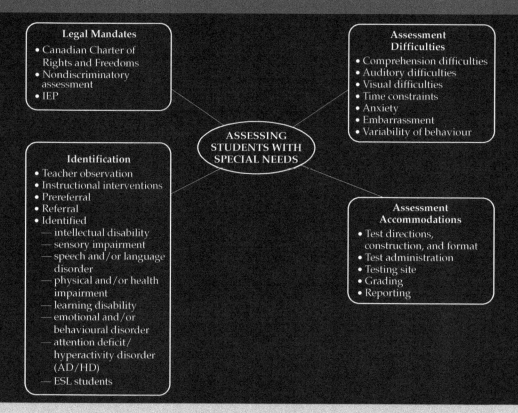

Legal Mandates
- Canadian Charter of Rights and Freedoms
- Nondiscriminatory assessment
- IEP

Assessment Difficulties
- Comprehension difficulties
- Auditory difficulties
- Visual difficulties
- Time constraints
- Anxiety
- Embarrassment
- Variability of behaviour

ASSESSING STUDENTS WITH SPECIAL NEEDS

Identification
- Teacher observation
- Instructional interventions
- Prereferral
- Referral
- Identified
  - intellectual disability
  - sensory impairment
  - speech and/or language disorder
  - physical and/or health impairment
  - learning disability
  - emotional and/or behavioural disorder
  - attention deficit/hyperactivity disorder (AD/HD)
  - ESL students

Assessment Accommodations
- Test directions, construction, and format
- Test administration
- Testing site
- Grading
- Reporting

One of most significant changes for Canadian teachers since the advent of inclusion has been accommodating students with exceptionalities into regular classrooms. **Inclusion**, which was introduced in the early 1980s in Canada, emphasized that students with exceptionalities should be fully included in all school programs and activities (Smith, Polloway, Patton, Dowdy, McIntyre, & Francis, 2009). Students with mild disabilities are now routinely included with other students in the same class, and the regular classroom teacher is responsible for both instructing and evaluating these students. Teachers are also responsible for using assessment information to identify those students who may be eligible for special education services. In this chapter, we review the role of the classroom teacher in identifying and adapting assessment practices so that they are fair and unbiased for students with exceptionalities. First, we look briefly at the implications of the legal mandates in this area.

LEGAL MANDATES

In 1982, with the adoption of the Constitution Act and the Canadian Charter of Rights and Freedoms, Canada became the first country in the world to guarantee the rights and freedoms of persons with exceptionalities. Although all provinces and territories must abide by the Charter, the pathway to inclusive classrooms differs by location in Canada. The differences are rooted in the fact that education (and special education) is the jurisdiction of the provinces and territories. Each province and territory in Canada has established its own policy documents, and all adhere to the inclusion model to various degrees. However, students with exceptionalities are defined differently in different provinces and territories. In Saskatchewan, students are defined as having exceptional needs if they have "physical, intellectual and learning disabilities, sensory impairments, social, emotional or behavioural challenges, and language delays and disorders" (Saskatchewan Learning, 2000). In contrast, no definition of exceptionality is included in the Northwest Territories policy documents, but the Education Act (1995) focuses on the rights of all students to an inclusive education and support services to meet their needs.

As a result of the inclusion movement, most classroom teachers must now be familiar with how students are identified as having "special needs" and how assessment procedures used in the course of regular classroom instruction need to be modified to ensure that these students are evaluated fairly.

When parents and teachers express concerns about a child as a result of their observations and interactions with the student, a review process is initiated. This review process usually includes a referral to special education services. Once a referral has been made, the student is formally evaluated to determine whether he or she has an exceptionality, and, if so, which special education services would be most beneficial and appropriate. The results of the formal evaluation (including the results of any assessments conducted) are then translated into a specific educational plan for the student. Such a plan is generally termed an **individualized education plan (IEP)**. The IEP may also be termed a *Personal Program Plan* (PPP) or an *Individualized Program Plan* (IPP), depending upon the province or territory. The IEP is a written plan, developed by a team of individuals (IEP committee), that specifies the student's present level of knowledge and skills (educational performance), measurable annual goals, and short-term learning objectives (Smith et al., 2009). The teacher plays a major role in identifying children for referral, developing and implementing the IEP, and monitoring progress toward mastery of the goals and objectives. Assessments used by teachers provide the information necessary to determine whether students are making satisfactory progress toward meeting learning objectives as specified in the IEP. The selection and administration of materials and procedures used for evaluation and placement should be **nondiscriminatory**. At a minimum, it is required that

1. Trained personnel administer validated tests and other evaluation materials and provide and administer such materials in the child's native language or other mode of communication.

2. Tests and other evaluation materials include those tailored to assess specific areas of educational need and not merely those designed to provide a single general intelligence quotient.

3. Trained personnel select and administer tests to reflect accurately the child's aptitude or achievement level without discriminating against the child's disability.

4. Trained personnel use no single procedure as the sole criterion for determining an appropriate educational program for a child.

5. A multidisciplinary team assess the child in all areas related to the suspected disability. (Wood, 2002, p. 11)

Essentially, these provisions mean that assessment must be planned and conducted so that the disability does not contribute to the score or result. That is, it would be unfair to use a test written in English to determine that a student whose primary language is French has an intellectual disability, just as it would be unfair to conclude that a student with a fine-motor disability did not know the answer to an essay question because there was insufficient time to write the answer.

With respect to writing and implementing the IEP, teachers have several responsibilities. As a member of an IEP committee, the classroom teacher provides important information because the plan must be based on a clear and accurate documentation of the present level of educational functioning. This includes identifying a student's deficits and weaknesses, as well as the student's strengths.

Another teacher responsibility is setting short- and long-term learning objectives and specifying the criteria and evaluation procedures that will be used to monitor progress toward meeting the objectives (McLoughlin & Lewis, 2005). Here, it is important to set truly *individualized* goals. Every student needs a customized set of realistic objectives that takes into account identified strengths and weaknesses and preferred learning modes and styles. Appropriately delineated evaluation criteria and procedures need to reflect the degree of difficulty in the tasks, the variety of methods that should be employed, and a reasonable timetable.

Finally, teachers are responsible for ensuring that the student will participate in regular classroom activities to the maximum extent possible. This includes both formal and informal classroom assessments. Here, your understanding of what is required with each type of assessment and your knowledge of the specific student disabilities are used to ensure that, whenever possible, assessment procedures are not modified.

ASSESSING STUDENTS FOR IDENTIFICATION

Although, the exact steps used to identify a student as having an exceptionality will differ by province, the general steps leading to identifying a student as having an exceptionality are summarized in Figure 11.1. To examine your role in the assessment process, we consider two major categories of steps: those done before identification, and the actual identification of various exceptionalities.

Steps before Identification

Initially, the teacher observes and evaluates students, and then tries intervention strategies to attempt to improve student performance. In effect, you need to be certain that relatively simple changes in teaching methods or materials are insufficient for improving the student's performance.

If the student continues to have difficulties after you make instructional interventions, you must closely analyze the student's ability to perform as expected. This usually includes performing a diagnostic assessment of specific learning difficulties or deficits using routine, teacher-made assessments. An analysis of errors may pinpoint these difficulties and suggest specific remediation strategies.

Some schools have a formal process of prereferral review for students with continuing difficulties. This may be called the prereferral committee, the child study team, or the student assistance team. This group provides both an external review of your tentative diagnosis and feedback concerning instructional interventions that have been tried. The group usually includes other teachers, school administrators, the school counsellor, and special education teachers. Sometimes members of the committee may observe the student in class or conduct individual assessments. Often, the committee will recommend additional interventions that may effectively address the problem, or a specific plan will be developed. In the event that the student still struggles, a comprehensive educational assessment is usually requested.

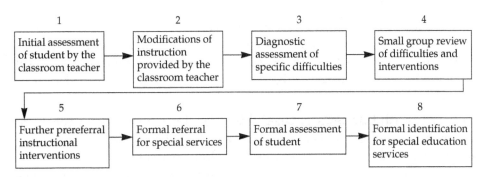

Figure 11.1 Typical Steps for Used in Identifying Students for Special Education Services

Formal referral is a serious step because it suggests that the student may be eligible for special education services. Consequently, you should have specific documentation of the learning or behaviour difficulties, interventions that have been tried, and the results of these interventions. It would be inadequate to simply say, for example, that "Derek is always causing trouble in class. He likes to bother other students by poking and provoking them. We have tried several different approaches with Derek, each with limited success. He has a lot of trouble with mathematics." Rather, the information needs to be specific. For example, you might say the following:

> Derek touched, hit, or poked other students an average of 15 times per day in a way that disturbed or bothered the students. He talks without raising his hand in class discussions 75 per cent of the time. Time out, individual contracts, and sessions with the counsellor have been used with limited success that soon dissipates. Derek has turned in homework only 20 per cent of the time. In class, he is unable to complete mathematics assignments that deal with the addition and subtraction of complex fractions. He is off-task with mathematics assignments 50 per cent of the time.

A screening committee may review the written referral and will contact the student's parents. Suggestions for additional instructional interventions may be made. If the committee concludes that a formal assessment is needed, they will secure parental permission and begin a comprehensive evaluation. This process includes the assessment of all areas of suspected difficulty and/or disability, which is administered and interpreted by specialists in different areas (e.g., a school psychologist to administer intelligence, personality, and projective tests; a physical therapist to evaluate gross-motor skills; and an audiologist to evaluate hearing acuity). Students are tested by a variety of methods, which may include additional informal observation by the regular classroom teacher. Identification is confirmed when classroom teacher evaluations and specialists' evaluations coincide.

Identification

Following formal assessment, the student may be identified as having one or more specific educational disabilities. Each of the disabling conditions is confirmed by applying specific criteria. We will review the assessment criteria and implications of several common mild learning deficits because students with these deficits are the ones most likely to be included in regular classes.

Students with Intellectual Disabilities. Students with intellectual disabilities demonstrate some degree of impaired mental abilities and difficulty in coping with the social demands of the environment. Usually, students are identified on the basis of low scores on a standardized intelligence test and consistent deficits of what are termed *adaptive behaviours* that adversely affect educational performance for their age and/or grade. **Adaptive behaviours** are those required for normal functioning in daily living situations—for example, expressive and receptive communication, daily living skills such as personal hygiene and eating habits, coping skills, and motor skills. The severity of the disability is indicated in degrees: severe, moderate, and mild.

Although school psychologists will conduct IQ testing, it may be up to you and the special education teacher to provide much of the information about adaptive behaviours. You can accomplish this with the help of established adaptive behaviour scales, such as the Vineland Adaptive Behavior Scale, the Adaptive Behavior Scale, and the Adaptive Behavior Inventory for Children. Teachers and primary caregivers are interviewed with these types of instruments to document the student's behavioural competence. In addition, you should confirm findings from these instruments with more informal observations. Keep in mind that some of these instruments may not have Canadian norms and thus results should be interpreted with caution.

Keep two cautions in mind when assessing adaptive behaviour. First, no single adaptive behaviour instrument covers all areas of behaviour, and the data for these instruments are usually gathered from third-party observers. Thus, you should select the instrument that will provide the most valid inferences for the situation and keep in mind that third parties may be biased. Second, be careful that a student's cultural or linguistic background does not cause the student to be inappropriately labelled as having inadequate adaptive behaviour. Some students who are perfectly capable of functioning in their day-to-day living environments may have difficulty functioning in the classroom because of cultural or language differences. Thus, adaptive behaviour is best evaluated relative to the context in which it occurs (Witt, Elliot, Daly, Gresham, & Kramer, 1998).

Sensory Impairment. Students who have vision or hearing deficits may be identified as sensory impaired. This could include visual difficulties, even with correction, including eye–hand coordination; or a hearing problem that interferes with educational performance. One of the first things you should do with students experiencing difficulty in learning is to check for visual and hearing acuity. Obviously, students who have trouble seeing or hearing will have trouble academically. Your close and careful observation of students will provide clues to these types of impairments.

Speech and/or Language Difficulties or Disorders. Students may have speech disorders such as difficulties with articulation (i.e., mispronouncing speech sounds), fluency (i.e., stuttering), or voice (i.e., pitch disorders). They may also have receptive language difficulties (i.e., understanding multi-step directions or vocabulary words) and/or expressive language difficulties (i.e., using vocabulary appropriately in conversational speech). If you are concerned with a student's speech and/or language skills, contact the speech-language pathologist in your school district.

Physical and/or Health Impairments. Physical disabilities include conditions such as an orthopaedic impairment (cerebral palsy or amputations) or a physical illness such as epilepsy, diabetes, or muscular dystrophy. Generally, these conditions will be obvious, and resources will be provided to make appropriate accommodations.

Learning Disability. No one definition for learning disabilities exists. In 2002, the Learning Disabilities Association of Canada (LDAC) defined **learning disabilities** as "a number of disorders which may affect the acquisition, organization, retention, understanding, or use of verbal or nonverbal information. As such, learning disabilities are distinct from global intellectual deficiency." Learning disabilities range in severity and result from impairments in perceiving, thinking, remembering, and/or learning. Students with a learning disability may have problems with oral language, reading, writing, and/or mathematics. You may need to comment on data from the student's cumulative folder and classroom performance and behaviour. As before, the process depends on your careful observation and evaluation of the student.

Emotional and/or Behavioural Disorders. There is no single definition of emotional and/or behavioural disorders used in Canadian schools. In general, a student is identified with an **emotional or behavioural disorder** if he or she displays: (1) a behaviour that goes to an extreme and that is significantly different from the behaviour that is normally expressed; (2) a behaviour problem that is chronic and does not disappear; (3) behaviour that is deemed socially or culturally inappropriate; (4) behaviour that clearly interferes with learning; or (5) behaviour that cannot be explained by health, sensory, or social difficulties (Hallahan & Kauffman, 1997). You may be asked to make systematic observations of a student suspected of having an emotional or behavioural disorder. This could include, for example, noting each time the student displays inappropriate behaviour, such as crying or yelling, in normal circumstances for no apparent reason. When the inappropriate behaviour continues for an extended time under different conditions, a serious emotional problem may be found. However, final diagnosis will require consultation with a specialist, such as a counsellor or school psychologist.

Attention Deficit/Hyperactivity Disorder (AD/HD). Attention deficit/ hyperactivity disorder (AD/HD) is a complex and controversial condition with a large classroom impact. Students with this disorder are fairly easy to spot in the classroom (Smith et al., 2009). They are often unable to sustain attention, are easily distracted, have difficulties organizing, make careless mistakes, tend to lose things, and may be forgetful (McLoughlin & Lewis, 2005). Students who fidget excessively, have difficulty sitting, appear restless, and are constantly "on the go" to the extent that it affects their ability to learn and demonstrate what they understand may be identified as **hyperactive**. Although standardized instruments are used to confirm the presence of these disorders, teacher observations are critical.

Despite this, AD/HD is not primarily an educational diagnosis (Smith et al., 2009), and in Canada, AD/HD is not listed as a separate category of exceptionality by provincial educational jurisdictions (Friend, Busruck, & Hutchinson, 1998). In order to qualify for funding, children with AD/HD in Canada tend to receive services under other categories, such as emotional and behavioural disorders (Smith et al., 2009).

Tables 11.1 and 11.2 summarize the teacher's role in the assessment and identification processes. Table 11.1 summarizes responsibilities for different steps in the assessment

Table 11.1 Classroom Teacher's Role in the Assessment Process

Steps in the Assessment Process	Regular Classroom Teacher's Role
Before referral	Use informal assessment methods to monitor daily progress, curriculum-based assessment, and behavioural observations; consult with committee members
	Implement educational interventions
Diagnosis of specific disability	Recognize behaviours and characteristics of specific disabilities so that students can be identified, evaluated, and served if appropriate
	Recognize behaviours and characteristics that indicate cultural or linguistic differences and that do not warrant special education services
Referral	Document through data collection of student work samples, behavioural observations, teacher-made tests, and other informal measures to identify educational strengths and weaknesses
	Consult with committee members
	Consult with parents
	Complete necessary referral forms
	Attend child study committee meeting and present appropriate data collected on student progress and behaviours
	Participate during development and implementation of identification and IEP for students in the regular class setting

Source: Adapted from J. Wood (2002). *Adapting instruction to accommodate students in inclusive settings* (4th ed.) (p. 36). Upper Saddle River, NJ: Pearson Education. Copyright © 2002. Adapted by permission of Pearson Education, Inc.

process, and Table 11.2 shows a teacher's responsibilities for identification in major categories. Generally, your observations of the student will be used to corroborate the specialists' findings.

Students for Whom English is a Second Language

Students who are learning English as a second language are not classified as having a specific disability but may exhibit signs of language disorders. However, such language errors are likely part of the normal process of acquiring a new language (Roseberry-McKibbin & Brice, 2002). Regardless, these students are often included in regular classrooms, and teachers must modify instruction and assessment in ways that are similar to how English-language students with exceptionalities are taught and assessed.

Table 11.2 Classroom Teacher's Role in the Identification Process

Disability	Teacher's Role	Questions
Intellectual disability	Document adaptive behaviours; meet with the child study committee	How well does the student function with daily life skills? Do deficits in daily living skills affect academic performance? Does cultural or linguistic background contribute to deficits in daily living skills?
Sensory impairment	Document visual or auditory impairments; meet with the child study committee	Can the student see well enough? Is there adequate eye–hand coordination? Does the student have a hearing problem? Is there a speech problem of some kind?
Speech and/or language disorders	Document speech and language difficulties; meet with the child study committee	Is there a speech problem of some kind? Is there a language problem of some kind?
Physical and/or health impairments	Observe effect of disability on academic performance; meet with the child study committee	Does the disability adversely affect academic performance?
Learning disability	Document learning problems and achievement; interpret information in the cumulative folder; meet with the child study committee	Is there a large discrepancy between ability and achievement? Are sensory, physical, and mental disabilities ruled out?
Emotional and/or behavioural disorders	Document inappropriate behaviours and feelings; meet with the child study committee	Does the student have average or above-average intelligence? Is the behaviour extreme for the circumstances? Is the behaviour fleeting or consistent? Are any other disabilities responsible for the poor performance? How well does the student interact with others? Is the student unhappy, depressed, or withdrawn much of the time?

(continued)

Table 11.2 (Continued)

Disability	Teacher's Role	Questions
Attention deficit/ hyperactivity disorder (AD/HD)	Observe and record instances of failing to pay attention and record instances of inappropriate hyperactivity	Does the student repeatedly, in many circumstances, demonstrate significant inattention?
		Is the student easily distracted?
		Does the student make careless mistakes?
		Is the student constantly restless?
		Does the student fidget excessively?
		Is the student always on the go or "wired"?

ASSESSMENT PROBLEMS ENCOUNTERED BY STUDENTS WITH EXCEPTIONALITIES

Your goal in assessing student learning is to obtain a fair and accurate indication of performance. Because disabilities may affect test-taking ability, you will need to make accommodations or changes in assessments when needed so as to ensure valid inferences and consequences. There are many justifiable ways to alter assessments for students with exceptionalities. Before we consider these, it will be helpful to review the problems encountered by students with exceptionalities in testing situations. These difficulties are summarized in Table 11.3.

Table 11.3 Problems Encountered by Students with Exceptionalities That Affect Classroom Assessment

Problem	Impact on Assessment
Comprehension difficulties	Understanding directions; completing assessments requiring reasoning skills
Auditory difficulties	Understanding oral directions and test items; distracted by noises
Visual difficulties	Understanding written directions and test items; decoding symbols and letters; visual distractions
Time-constraint difficulties	Completing assessments
Anxiety	Completing assessments; providing correct information
Embarrassment	Understanding directions; completing assessments
Variability of behaviour	Completing assessments; demonstrating best work

Comprehension Difficulties

Many students with mild disabilities have difficulty with comprehension. They may not understand verbal or written directions very well. If there is a sequence of steps in the directions, they may not be able to remember the sequence or all the steps, particularly if the directions are verbal. Lengthy written directions may be too complicated, and the reading level may be too high. There may be words or phrases that the student does not understand. If the directions include several different operations, the student may be confused about what to do. Obviously, without a clear understanding of how to proceed, it will be difficult for these students to demonstrate their knowledge or skills.

Students with mild disabilities have even more difficulty understanding directions or test items that require reasoning skills. These students may respond well to knowledge and understanding questions and deal well with concrete ideas, but they may not respond very well to abstractions. For example, it would be relatively easy for such students to respond to a straightforward short-answer question such as "What are the characteristics of a democratic government?" but much harder to respond to a more abstract question such as "How is the government of Canada different from a socialistic government?"

Auditory Difficulties

Students with auditory disabilities have trouble quickly and accurately processing information they hear. This makes it especially hard for these students to follow and understand verbal directions.

These students may also be sensitive to auditory distractions in the classroom. Distractions could include sound from the hallway or an adjoining classroom, talking among students, outside noise, desk movement, pencil sharpening, questions asked by students, teacher reprimands, school announcements, and so on. Although these sounds may seem "normal" and do not bother most students, those with auditory disabilities will be distracted, and their attention will be diverted from the task at hand.

Visual Difficulties

Students with visual disabilities have difficulty processing what they see. These students may copy homework assignments or test questions from the board incorrectly by transposing numbers or interchanging letters. Often the student has difficulty transferring information to paper. A cluttered board that requires visual discrimination may also cause problems. Visual disabilities can also be a disadvantage on some handwritten tests if the test is not legible and clearly organized. Some students with a visual disability have difficulty decoding certain symbols, letters, and abbreviations, such as $+$, $-$, b and d, $<$ and $>$, and n and m. One symbol may be confused with another, and these students may take a long time to understand test problems with many symbols.

Some types of objective test items are a problem because of visual perceptual difficulties. For example, lengthy matching items pose particular problems because the student may take a long time to peruse the columns, searching for answers and identifying the correct letters to use. Multiple-choice items that run responses together on the same line make it hard to discriminate among the possible answers.

Visual distractions can also interfere with test taking. For some students, a single visual cue—such as students moving in the classroom when getting up to turn in papers, student gestures, teacher motions, or something or someone outside—disrupts their present visual focus and makes it difficult for them to keep their concentration.

Time-Constraint Difficulties

Time can pose a major problem for many students with exceptionalities. Frequently, visual, auditory, motor coordination, and reading difficulties make it hard for some students to complete tests in the same time frame as other students. Thus, students should not be penalized for being unable to complete a test, especially timed tests that are constructed to reward speed in decoding and understanding questions and writing answers.

Anxiety

Although most students experience some degree of anxiety when completing tests, students with exceptionalities may be especially affected by feelings of anxiety because of fear that their disability will make it difficult to complete the test. Some students are simply unable to function very well in a traditional test setting because the length or format of the test overwhelms them.

To reduce unhealthy anxiety, make sure that students have learned appropriate test-taking skills. They need to know what to do if they do not fully understand the directions and how to proceed in answering different types of items (e.g., looking for clue words in multiple-choice, true/false, and completion items; crossing out incorrect alternatives in multiple-choice items; crossing out answers used in matching items). They should also skip difficult items and come back to them when they have answered all other questions.

Embarrassment

Students with exceptionalities may be more sensitive than other students to feelings of embarrassment. They often want to hide or disguise their problems so that they are not singled out or labelled by their peers. As a result, they may want to appear to be "normal" when taking a test by not asking questions about directions and handing in the test at the same time as other students do, whether or not they are finished. They don't want to risk embarrassment by being the only one to have a question or by being the last one to complete their work. Students with exceptionalities may also be embarrassed if they take a different test than others.

Variability of Behaviour

The behaviour of students with exceptionalities varies greatly. Their disabilities may affect their behaviour one day and not the next, and it may be difficult to predict this variability, especially for students with emotional or behavioural disorders. For example, a student with a conduct disorder may be very disruptive one day and seem normal the next. Consequently, you will need to be tolerant and flexible in your assessments, realizing that, on a particular day, the disability may pose extreme difficulties for the student.

ASSESSMENT ACCOMMODATIONS

Once you understand how disabilities can interfere with valid assessment, take steps to adapt the test or other assessment to accommodate the disability. These accommodations can be grouped into three major categories: adaptations in test construction, test administration, and testing site (Wood, 2002).

Adaptations in Test Directions, Construction, and Format

The first component to adapt is the test directions. You can do this for all students, or you can provide a separate set of directions for students with exceptionalities. Here are some ways to modify test directions:

1. Read written directions aloud, slowly, and give students ample opportunity to ask questions about the directions. Reread directions for each page of questions.
2. Keep directions short and simple.
3. Give examples of how to answer questions.
4. Focus attention by underlining verbs.

5. Provide separate directions for each section of the test.

6. Provide one direction for each sentence (list sentences vertically).

7. Check the students' understanding of the directions.

8. During the test, check student answers to be sure that the students understand the directions.

The general test format should simplify the amount of information that is processed at one time. Leave plenty of white space on each page so that students are not overwhelmed. The printing should be large with adequate space between items; this results in a smaller number of items per page. The test should be separated into clearly distinguished short sections, and only one type of question should be on each page. The printing should be dark and clear. If bubble sheets are used for objective items, use larger bubbles. Be sure multiple-choice items list the alternatives vertically, and do not run questions or answers across two pages. Number each page of the test. Some students may be aided by a large sheet of construction paper that they can place below the question or cut out to allow a greater focus on a particular section of the test. If possible, design the adapted test to look as much as possible like the test the other students are writing.

Other accommodations to the format of the test depend on the type of item, as illustrated in the following examples.

Short-Answer and Essay Items. Students with exceptionalities may have extreme difficulty with short-answer items because of the organization, reasoning, and writing skills required. For these reasons, you should avoid complicated essay questions requiring long responses. If you use an essay question, be sure students understand terms such as *compare*, *contrast*, and *discuss*. Use a limited number of essay questions, and allow students to use outlines for their answers. Some students may need to record their answer rather than writing it; all students will need to have sufficient time.

Examples

> *Poor:* Compare and contrast the Canadian and United States governments.
>
> *Improved:* Compare and *contrast* the Canadian and United States governments.
>
> I. *Compare* by telling how the governments are *alike*. Give two examples.
> II. *Contrast* by telling how the governments are *different*. Give two examples.

If the short-answer question focuses on recall, adapt it in ways that will help students to organize their thoughts and not be overwhelmed.

Example (adapted from *Creating a Learning Community at Fowler High School*, 1993)

> *Poor:*
>
> Directions: On your own paper, identify the following quotations. Tell (1) who said it, (2) to whom it was said or if it was a soliloquy, (3) when it was said, and (4) what it means.

But soft, what light through yonder window breaks?
It is the east, and Juliet is the sun.
Arise, fair sun, and kill the envious moon.
(Include a series of several more quotes.)

Improved:

Directions: In the space provided, identify the following for each quotation.

Tell   **1.** Who said it

            2. To whom it was said or if it was a soliloquy

            3. When it was said

            4. What it means

Who said it; to whom
it was said   *When it was said*

Juliet   When Tybalt kills Mercutio
Romeo   When Juliet waits for news from Romeo
Paris   The balcony scene
Mercutio   When Paris discusses his marriage with Friar
The Prince

1. But soft, what light through yonder window breaks?
   It is the east, and Juliet is the sun.
   Arise, fair sun, and kill the envious moon.

Who said it   *To whom*   *When*   *What it means*

_____ _____ _____ _____

_____ _____ _____ _____

_____ _____ _____ _____

Multiple-Choice Items.

Multiple-Choice Items. If the test contains multiple-choice questions, have students circle the correct answer rather than writing the letter of the correct response next to the item or transferring the answer to a separate sheet. Arrange response alternatives vertically, and include no more than four alternatives for each question. Keep the language simple and concise, and avoid wording such as "a and b but not d," or "either a or c," or "none of the above" that weights the item more heavily for reasoning skills. Limit the number of multiple-choice items, and give students with exceptionalities plenty of time to complete the test. Other students may easily be able to answer one item per minute, but it will take exceptional students longer. Follow the suggestions listed in Chapter 6, and realize that poorly constructed and formatted items are likely to be more detrimental to students with exceptionalities.

Binary-Choice Items. State true/false and other binary-choice items clearly and concisely. Answers should be circled. Avoid negatively stated items. Sometimes students are asked to change false items to make them true, but this is not recommended for students with exceptionalities. Limit the number of items to from 10 to 15.

Completion Items. Modify these items to reduce the student's dependence on structured recall by providing word banks that accompany the items. The word bank is a list of possible answers that reduces dependence on memory. Print the list on a separate sheet of paper so that the student can move it up and down on the right side of the page. Also, provide large blanks for students with motor control difficulties.

Performance Assessments. The first accommodation in performance assessments may concern directions. Students with exceptionalities may need directions that clearly specify what is expected; provide examples and a reasonable time frame. Because these assessments involve thinking and application skills, be certain that students with exceptionalities are able to perform the skills required. The steps may need to be clearly delineated. Obviously, if some aspect of the performance requires physical skills or coordination that the disability prevents or makes difficult, you will need to provide assistance. If the performance requires group participation, closely monitor the interactions.

Portfolios. In some ways, this type of assessment is ideal for students with exceptionalities because you can individualize the assignments and products to show progress. You may need to adapt the portfolio requirements to fit the student's capabilities. In the portfolio, you could include your reflection on how the student made progress despite the disability, to demonstrate how he or she was responsible for success.

Adaptations in Test Administration

Adaptations during test administration involve changes in procedures that lessen the negative effect of disabilities while the student is taking the test. Most of these procedural accommodations depend on the nature of the disability or difficulty, as summarized in Table 11.4, and are based on common sense. For example, if the student has a visual problem, give directions orally and check carefully to determine whether he or she has understood the questions. For students who are hindered by time constraints, provide breaks and make sure they have sufficient time to complete the test. Divide a long test into sections, and spread the testing over several days, although you should avoid providing unlimited time to complete tests. A good rule of thumb is to provide students with exceptionalities 50 per cent more time to complete a test (Reynolds, Livingston, & Willson, 2006).

Place a "Testing—Do Not Disturb" sign on your classroom door to discourage visitors and other distractions. Monitor students with exceptionalities closely as they take the test and encourage them to ask questions. It is also helpful to encourage them to use dark paper to underline the items they are currently working on (Lazzari & Wood, 1994).

Adaptations in Testing Site

Students with exceptionalities may need to take the test in a different location than the regular classroom. This alternative test site is often the resource room in the school or some other room that is quiet with fewer distractions. As long as someone can monitor

Table 11.4 Adaptations in Test Administration

Disability or Problem	Adaptations
Poor comprehension	1. Give test directions both orally and in writing. 2. Double-check student understanding. 3. Avoid long talks before the test. 4. Allow students to tape-record responses to essay questions or the entire test. 5. Correct open-ended responses for content only and not for spelling or grammar. 6. Provide examples of expected correct responses. 7. Remind students to check for unanswered questions. 8. Allow the use of multiplication tables or calculators for math tests. 9. Read the test aloud for students with reading comprehension difficulties. 10. Give an outline for essay-question responses. 11. Give students an audio recording of instructions and questions. 12. Use objective items.
Auditory difficulties	1. Use written rather than oral questions. 2. Go slowly for oral tests, enunciating and sounding out distinctly. 3. Seat students in a quiet place for testing. 4. Stress the importance of being quiet to all students.
Visual difficulties	1. Give directions orally as well as in writing. 2. Give exam orally or tape recorded on audiotape. 3. Allow students to take the test orally. 4. Seat the student away from visual distractions (e.g., windows and doors). Use a carrel or place desk facing wall. 5. Avoid having other students turn in papers during the test. 6. Meet classroom visitors at the door and talk in the hallway.
Time-constraint difficulties	1. Allow more than enough time to complete the test. 2. Provide breaks during lengthy tests. 3. Give half the test one day, half the second day. 4. Avoid timed tests. 5. Give students with slow writing skills oral or tape-recorded tests.
Anxiety	1. Avoid adding pressure by admonishing students to "Hurry and get finished" or by saying "This test will determine your final grade." 2. Do not threaten to use test results to punish students. 3. Do not threaten to use tests to punish students for poor behaviour. 4. Give a practice test or practice items. 5. Allow students to retest if needed. 6. Do not threaten dire consequences if students do not do well. 7. Emphasize internal attributions for previous work. 8. Avoid having a few major tests; give many smaller tests. 9. Avoid norm-referenced testing; use criterion-referenced tests.

(continued)

Table 11.4 (Continued)

Disability or Problem	Adaptations
Embarrassment	1. Make the modified test closely resemble the regular test; use the same cover sheet. 2. Avoid calling attention to students with exceptionalities as you help them. 3. Monitor all students the same way. 4. Do not give students with exceptionalities special attention when handing out the test. 5. Confer with students privately to work out accommodations for testing. 6. Do not single out students with exceptionalities when returning tests.
Variability of behaviour	1. Allow retesting. 2. Allow student to reschedule testing for another day. 3. Monitor closely to determine if behaviour is preventing best work.

Source: Adapted from J. Wood (2002). *Adapting instruction to accommodate students in inclusive settings* (4th ed.) (pp. 567–569). Upper Saddle River, NJ: Pearson Education. Copyright © 2002. Adapted by permission of Pearson Education, Inc.

CASE STUDY FOR REFLECTION

Mr. Ashcraft is a grade 7 social studies teacher in a predominantly working-class school. He is a 12-year veteran who has been recognized by fellow teachers, administrators, and parents as a good teacher. At the beginning of the school year, Mr. Ashcraft was confronted with four special education students in his fourth-period class. All were boys; one was bilingual, and two were diagnosed as having attention deficit/hyperactivity disorder and learning disabilities. The fourth boy had an emotional disorder, and this was his first time in an inclusive classroom. Although Mr. Ashcraft had no experience with any special population, he was selected to take these students because of his reputation as a good teacher and classroom manager.

Each of the four students posed unique assessment problems. With the help of one of the special education teachers and a counsellor, Mr. Ashcraft learned some ways of adapting assessment instruments for these students. These methods included giving fewer problems, deleting a choice on multiple-choice tests, providing a word bank for fill-in-the-blank questions, and allowing students to skip certain sections altogether. He was also told he could give students oral tests and allow them to take tests before or after school.

Mr. Ashcraft was very concerned about this situation and felt he was in an awkward position. With no training in this area, he felt unqualified to make assessments about these new students. He questioned the legitimacy of what he was doing. When he shared his concerns with the head of the special education department, he was told that the inclusion of students with exceptionalities was the way things were going, and he might as well get used to it.

Questions for Consideration

1. Are Mr. Ashcraft's assessment accommodations appropriate?
2. What additional assessment accommodations would you suggest to Mr. Ashcraft?
3. What can Mr. Ashcraft do to feel more confident in assessing these students?

the testing, the student will have more opportunities to ask questions and will feel less embarrassed when asking for clarification or further explanation.

If you are unsure about how you should accommodate students with exceptionalities, check with the special education teacher in your school. This individual can help you more fully understand the strengths and limitations of each student, as well as the appropriateness of specific adaptations.

GRADING AND REPORTING ACCOMMODATIONS

The purpose of grading is to provide an accurate indication of what students have learned. For students with exceptionalities in inclusive settings, consider some adaptations to the grading procedures used for all students so that student disabilities do not unduly influence the determination of the grade. This may present a dilemma for teachers. On the one hand, is it fair to use different grading standards and procedures for some students? On the other hand, is it fair to possibly penalize students by forcing an existing grading scheme on them that may have detrimental impacts? The ideal solution would be a grading system for students with exceptionalities that is the same as that for other students, with appropriate accommodations in assessment strategies to ensure that the information on which the

Teacher's Corner

Michelle Prytula

We use Personal Program Plans (PPPs) because a child with exceptionalities is often not assessed using all standards stated in the curriculum. For such a student, the PPP describes his or her modified program. It is imperative that the parents, teacher, and learning assistance teacher (and also support staff, if possible) collaborate on the PPP so that it results in a well-designed and appropriate instructional and measurement tool. The PPP reports on the child's strengths, areas needing improvement, goals set, strategies that will be followed, and the leads on those strategies. Because students with exceptionalities are on modified programs, the curriculum is not always appropriate, and so the PPP holds everyone accountable.

grade is determined is not adversely affected by the disability. However, depending on the student's IEP, it may be necessary to adapt the grading system that is used.

Grading Accommodations

Several types of grading accommodations are appropriate for students with exceptionalities (Mehring, 1995). These include IEP grading, shared grading, and contract grading.

IEP Grading. The IEP grading system bases grades on the achievement of the goals and objectives stated in the student's IEP. The criteria needed to obtain satisfactory progress are stated in the IEP. It is problematic, however, to translate success in reaching IEP objectives to grades. One approach is to use the school district's performance standards to determine grades. For example, if the student has performed at the 90 per cent proficiency level as required by the IEP to demonstrate competence, and 90 per cent translates to a B letter grade, then the student is assigned a B for that assessment. Another approach is to review the criteria in the IEP and match levels of performance with what other students need to demonstrate for different grades. If you decide, for instance, that the level of mastery an exceptional student demonstrates by achieving but not exceeding all IEP objectives is about the same level as that demonstrated by other students receiving Cs, then the grade for the exceptional student would also be a C. If the student exceeds stated IEP objectives, then a B or A may be appropriate.

Because the goal of inclusion is to make the educational experience of students with exceptionalities like that of other students, grading procedures should reflect the same criteria. You should avoid determining the grade based merely on the percentage of IEP objectives obtained because there is a tendency to inadvertently set low or easier objectives to help students obtain good grades (Cohen, 1983).

Shared Grading. In shared grading, the regular classroom and special education or resource room teachers determine the grade together. The weight that each teacher provides for the grade should be agreed on at the beginning of the marking period and reflects to what extent each teacher is responsible for different areas of learning. Typically, the classroom teacher will have the most influence on the grades.

One advantage of this type of grading is that the special education or resource room teacher may be able to provide some insight to explain bad grades and other mitigating circumstances related to the student's disability. Using this team approach also helps the classroom teacher determine appropriate criteria and standards for grading.

Contracting. A contract is a written agreement between the regular classroom teacher and the student that specifies the nature of the work that the student must complete to achieve a particular grade. Teachers frequently use contracts for students with exceptionalities because they can integrate IEP objectives and clearly state for the student and parents the type and quality of work to be completed. For older students, the contract should include options for achieving different grades. Contracts for elementary-level students should be simpler, with more general outcomes at a single level, as illustrated in Figure 11.2. Include several components in a contract, such as the following:

- a description of the work to be completed
- a description of criteria by which work will be evaluated
- signatures of the student, teacher, and other involved parties
- a timeline for completion of the work

Reporting Accommodations

Regardless of the grading system you use, you will probably need to supplement the regular progress report with additional information. Typically, you would use a checklist or a narrative summary that interprets achievement in light of the student's disability. A checklist is convenient for showing progress in developmentally sequenced courses, and you can easily integrate IEP with course objectives to give a more complete report. The teacher indicates if each objective on the checklist has been mastered or needs further work.

My Contract

If I . . .

- take my belongings from my backpack and put them in my desk without being asked,
- come to my reading group the first time it is called,
- clean off my desk after a snack and put all the garbage in the trash can,
- raise my hand each time I want to answer, and
- put all my finished papers in the "done" basket before lunch,

. . . then I will receive a "plus" for the morning's work.

If I . . .

- line up on the playground the first time the whistle is blown,
- put all the classroom supplies back in the supply boxes after project time,
- put all my finished papers in the "done" basket before I go home,
- put my homework papers in my portfolio to take home, and
- put my belongings in my backpack, get my coat from the cubby, and line up before my bus is called,

. . . then I will receive a "plus" for the afternoon's work.

_____   _____
Student   Teacher

                 _____
                 Date

Figure 11.2 Sample Contract for Elementary-Level Students

Source: J. Wood (2002). _Adapting instruction to accommodate students in inclusive settings_ (4th ed.) (p. 597). Upper Saddle River, NJ: Pearson Education. Copyright © 2002. Adapted by permission of Pearson Education, Inc.

A narrative summary helps you to give the student a still more personalized evaluation. Although such a report takes some time, it more fully explains why the teacher believes the student demonstrated certain skills, which skills were not mastered, and which need special attention. You can also use the narrative to report on behavioural performance, emotions, and interpersonal skills, as well as academic performance. You can describe specific incidents or examples. The following is an example of a progress report for a grade 8 student with a learning disability. Notice that the teacher has indicated areas of improvement, accommodations (typing), and areas that will be stressed in the future.

> Alphonso has improved his ability to recognize and correct spelling errors. He has mastered the recognition and capitalization of proper nouns, names, titles, and buildings. He is not yet consistent in his capitalization of cities. Punctuation, especially the use of commas, is also an area in which Alphonso needs improvement. He has been using the computer to prepare drafts of his written products. This has made it easier for him to edit since his handwriting is laborious and illegible at times. The overall quality and length of his creative writings has improved significantly since the last reporting period. We will continue to focus on capitalization and punctuation throughout the next grading period. In addition, we will begin working on recognizing and correcting sentence problems (fragments, run-ons, unclear pronoun reference, and awkward sentences). (Mehring, 1995, p. 17)

By focusing a supplemental progress report on the learning process, you will give students a better idea of how they need to change to improve their performance. Students and parents need to know if a specific approach to learning needs to be modified or if something else needs to be further investigated.

SUMMARY

The purpose of this chapter was to introduce you to the assessment adaptations needed to accommodate students with exceptionalities in inclusive settings. Suggestions made in other chapters apply to these students, but keep some additional considerations in mind. It is important to make sure that a student's disability does not influence his or her performance on tests and other types of assessments. Major points in the chapter include the following:

■ Regular classroom teachers are responsible for gathering information to identify students for special education services.

■ The evaluation of students for identification must be non-discriminatory—in the student's native language and not racially or culturally biased.

■ Teacher observation is a major component in identification and in writing the student's IEP.

■ Teachers are responsible for setting individualized learning objectives with appropriate assessments.

■ Teachers are responsible for providing specific assessment information for referral and possible identification.

■ Students are identified as having one or more educational disabilities, based in part on careful teacher observation.

■ Teachers are responsible for assessing the adaptive behaviours of students referred and identified as having intellectual disorders.

- Comprehension difficulties require adaptations in test directions.
- Auditory and visual difficulties require a minimum of distractions.
- Time-constraint difficulties require longer testing time and frequent breaks in testing.
- Anxiety and embarrassment need to be minimized for students with exceptionalities.
- The behaviour of students with exceptionalities varies from day to day; this variation needs to be considered when observing and evaluating student behaviour.

- Adaptations may need to be made to test directions, the format of the test, and the construction of different types of items.
- Adaptations may be needed during test administration and to the testing site.
- Grading students with exceptionalities should include consideration of IEP objectives, opinions of other teachers working with the student, and contracting.
- Supplemental reports and feedback are helpful for focusing attention on IEP and learning process objectives.

SELF-INSTRUCTIONAL REVIEW EXERCISES

1. Indicate whether each of the following statements represents non-discriminatory assessment (Y for yes, N for no):

   a. A single procedure may be used for identification.

   b. The assessment is conducted by a multidisciplinary team.

   c. Assessments are conducted in English.

   d. The disability may not affect the scores students receive.

   e. Racial and cultural discrimination must be avoided.

2. Read the following scenario and indicate whether the teacher has properly followed the steps necessary to refer a student for identification.

   Mrs. Albert was immediately suspicious of Julie, thinking that she might have a learning disability. Julie did not achieve very well on written tests and seemed to have trouble concentrating. She was also distracted very easily. Mrs. Albert tried Julie in another reading group, but this did not seem to help. After looking at Julie's previous test scores, Mrs. Albert decided to refer her for further assessment.

3. Indicate whether each of the descriptions listed is characteristic of students with intellectual disability (ID), emotional

   or behavioural disorder (EBD), sensory impairment (SI), speech or language disorder (SL), physical impairment (PI), attention deficit/hyperactivity disorder (AD/HD), or learning disability (LD).

   a. diabetes

   b. language deficit

   c. discrepancy between ability and achievement

   d. poor adaptive behaviours

   e. poor eyesight

   f. slow learning

   g. restless

   h. easily distracted

4. Indicate whether each of the difficulties listed is characteristic of students with comprehension difficulties (C), sensory difficulties (SD), time-constraint difficulties (TCD), anxiety (A), embarrassment (E), or variability of behaviour (VB).

   a. gets sequence of steps wrong

   b. worries excessively about performance

   c. hands in an incomplete test with other students

   d. has trouble one day finishing a test, but no trouble the next day

   e. takes longer to complete a test

5. Indicate whether each of the following test administration adaptations is considered good practice (Y for yes, N for no).

   a. making tests with fewer items

   b. closely monitoring students while they are taking a test

   c. modifying tests

   d. giving special attention when handing out tests

   e. using norm-referenced testing

   f. emphasizing internal attributions

   g. giving practice tests

   h. allowing students to take a written test orally

   i. using objective rather than essay items

   j. using normal seating arrangements

   k. checking student understanding of directions

6. Read the following scenario and indicate what was correct and what was incorrect or lacking in the teacher's assessment accommodations.

Mr. Parvin was careful to read all the directions aloud, and he gave examples of how the students should answer each item. He prepared a separate set of directions for his students with exceptionalities. He designed the test to make sure as many questions as possible were included on each page. He underlined key words in the short-answer questions and wrote objective items so that the students corrected wrong answers. Mr. Parvin did not permit questions once students began the test. He told students that they had to complete the test in 30 minutes, and he placed a sign on the door indicating that testing was taking place.

7. Ms. Ramirez has a student with a learning disability in her classroom. His name is Tyron. Ms. Ramirez has decided to use a contract grading procedure, and she wants to be able to report progress on the contract to Tyron's parents. How would Ms. Ramirez begin to develop her contract, and how would she report progress to his parents?

SUGGESTIONS FOR ACTION RESEARCH

1. Interview two or three regular classroom teachers about the accommodations they make for students with exceptionalities who are in their classes. Ask about their experience in gathering information for identification and setting learning objectives, as well as about the assessment accommodations they have made. Compare their responses to suggestions in the chapter.

2. Interview two special education teachers. Ask them what they believe regular classroom teachers need to know to accommodate students with exceptionalities in inclusive settings. In their work with regular classroom teachers, what do they see as the teachers' greatest weaknesses when making assessment accommodations?

3. Interview school division central office personnel who are responsible for students with exceptionalities. What is the district's approach toward assessing students with exceptionalities? What kind of support is provided for the teachers?

4. In a team with one or two other students, devise a plan for how you would accommodate the assessment of one or two students with exceptionalities who have been placed in regular classrooms. You will need as much information about the students as possible, and it would be best if you could observe the students. Once the plan is complete, review it with the students' teacher(s) for feedback and suggestions.

Chapter 12

Grading and Reporting Student Performance

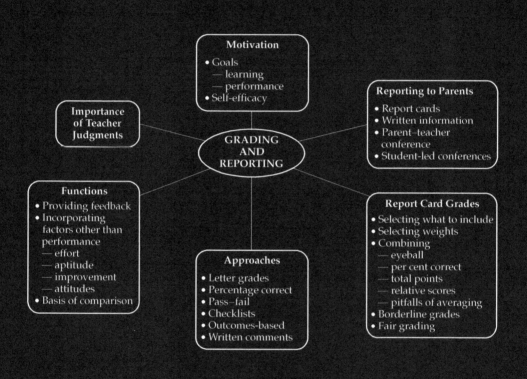

I n the past few chapters, we have seen how teachers can assess students on a variety of
learning expectations. As we pointed out in the model of classroom assessment presented in Chapter 1, now you need to *do* something with the assessments. Specifically,
you must make professional judgments about the quality of student work and translate
those judgments into grades and reports. We begin with a discussion of the importance of
a teacher's professional judgment in the use of assessment; we then consider some specific
approaches to marking, grading, and reporting.

TEACHERS' JUDGMENTS IN GRADING

You are probably aware of several different objective approaches to grading, such as grading on the curve and assigning grades based on percentage scores. But these approaches don't begin to capture the complexity and difficulty of grading. In practice, teachers make a number of professional judgments about how to evaluate and grade students. They make judgments before assessment (e.g., the difficulty of test items, what is covered on the assessment, and whether extra credit items will be included), as well as after assessments are completed (e.g., scoring short-answer and essay items). Teachers make further judgments in combining scores of different assessments to determine grades (e.g., how assessments are weighted and how to handle borderline scores). Here are some typical questions teachers ask that are answered by using their judgment:

Should effort and improvement be included in the grade?
How should different assessments be weighted and combined?
What distribution of grades should I end up with?
What do I do if most of my students fail the test?
Are my grades supposed to mean the same thing as other teachers' grades?
Am I grading students too hard or too easy?
What do I do with students who test well but don't hand in homework?
Should student participation be included in the grade?

There are no straightforward, necessarily correct answers to these questions, and while several provinces and school districts have developed policies around grading, these are often not much more than general guidelines and a grading scale. Consequently, grading practices vary considerably, even within the same school.

As well, unforeseen, unique situations may arise with students. These individual situations require teachers to use professional judgments. Consider the following scenarios:

> In your seventh grade social studies class, report card grades were based on quizzes, tests, and an out-of-class project which counted as 25% of the grade. Terry obtained an A average on his quizzes and tests but has not turned in the project despite frequent reminders.

> You are a biology teacher of a high school class which consists of students with varying ability levels. For this class you give two exams in each term. As you compute Bernie's grade for this term, you see that on the first exam, he obtained a score equivalent to a B, and on the second exam, a low A. (Brookhart, 1993, pp. 131, 133)

What grades would you give? Should Terry get a low grade even though he scores so high on tests? Should Bernie get an A because he showed improvement?

The evaluating and grading process requires you to make many *professional* decisions. These decisions are based on your personal value system regarding a number of different issues. In the end, grading is more a reflection of this value system, of perceived importance or perspective, than it is based on following specific correct guidelines or rules. Essentially, you develop a philosophy of grading that translates into what you do. To develop your own personal grading plan, consider and answer for yourself the following questions:

What meaning should each grade symbol carry?
What should "failure" mean?
What elements of performance should be incorporated in a grade?
How should the grades in a class be distributed?
What should the components that go into a grade be like?
How should the components of the grade be combined?
What method should be used to assign grades?
Should borderline cases be reviewed?
What other factors can influence the philosophy of grading? (Frisbie & Waltman, 1991, p. 210)

These questions are best answered by understanding the different purposes or functions grades serve and the types of comparison standards that are used. In the end, you should use methods and comparisons that best meet your major purpose. As we will see, grades often serve several purposes, which makes matters more complicated.

Let us make one point clear concerning professional judgments. These are *subjective* and *intuitive* in the sense that no single correct procedure or set of rules can take professional decision making out of the process. There is no completely objective procedure, nor should there be. You can use a grading scale, score student tests and performances, and mathematically calculate grades, but even though this procedure appears to be objective, it is not necessarily correct. Think for a moment about a physician deciding whether a patient is strong enough to endure an operation. In a sense, this is like grading. The doctor takes many measures and examines them *in the light of his or her experience and knowledge* before giving a yes or no judgment. Could two physicians differ in their opinions about whether to operate, given the same information? Absolutely. Likewise, two teachers can differ about the meaning of students' performances. One teacher might look at the tests and conclude that the student has mastered a skill, while another teacher might conclude the opposite. In the end, your value system makes the difference; to be an effective teacher you need to understand the issues, make some informed judgments, and have confidence in your decisions. Your goal is to use unbiased, thoughtful reasoning (Guskey & Bailey, 2001).

In Chapter 1 we pointed out that teachers' assessment and grading decisions are heavily influenced by teacher beliefs and values about enhancing student learning, and that these beliefs and values often conflict with external pressures such as mandated statewide testing, parental concerns, and district policies (McMillan, 2002b, 2004; McMillan & Workman, 1999). Teacher internal values and beliefs are essential because they provide a rationale for using grading practices consistent with the most important aspects of the teaching/learning process. Thus, because teachers want all students to succeed, they may give extra credit to enable students to "pull up" low grades. Because of individual differences in students, teachers may use different types of assessments so that everyone has a chance of obtaining a good grade. Teachers may use performance assessments because they motivate and engage students more effectively than multiple-choice tests and allow teachers to grade participation. Note in the following teacher responses how grading decisions are based on more encompassing beliefs and values about learning:

> Grades are extremely secondary to the whole process of what we do. We have goals to what we want to teach, and we use assessment so that we know what we need to work on, what students have mastered, and what they haven't.

> We should always be trying to find some ways so that all the children can find success, not just Johnny and Suzy getting the A but also Sally and Jim can get an A also. It is not about the amount of work that students have handed in or completed. The real question is to what extent the students have met the learning expectations.

External factors pressure teachers to adopt certain grading practices that focus on auditing and reporting student achievement, rather than promoting learning. Although teacher beliefs and values stress what is best for learning, these external pressures are usually more oriented to auditing student learning. Provincial large-scale testing has had some impact on classroom assessment, making it more aligned with the format of the provincial tests, with consequences for grading as well. Teachers want "objective" evidence of student performance to defend grades to parents, and district policies may restrict the nature and use of different grading procedures. Practical constraints limit what teachers can realistically accomplish. Although teachers might want to use many different samples of student performance for grades, doing so might not be feasible in light of other instructional needs. Consider these external factors with your own beliefs and values about teaching and learning in mind. Recognize that tension may exist, but keep your grading decision making based primarily on what promotes student learning.

Teacher's Corner

Dawn Leger

I can remember so well my high school teachers telling me that "participation" is an "easy A." In other words, if you pay attention, take notes, make an occasional comment or two during a marking period, another "A" test grade would be factored into your overall grade. This seemed easy enough from a student's point of view. From a teacher's point of view, or from my point of view anyway, it is much harder and often not fair. These are subjective grades and they are not directly addressed in the learning expectations listed in the curriculum. I labour over effort too, because it may differ so dramatically from child to child. They are, in a sense, my opinion, and I find it so easy to confuse effort with attentiveness and behaviour. I am now working harder to check that my grades reflect a student's achievement of the curricular expectations, rather than my opinion about their effort and participation.

FUNCTIONS OF MARKING AND GRADING

What do you want your grades to mean to your students? How do you want students to be affected? Do you want to motivate students to improve? Do you want to point out strengths and weaknesses? How do you want your students to interpret the grades they receive on tests, papers, and projects? The vast majority of teachers want marks and grades to have a positive impact on student learning, motivation, affect, and other outcomes. Yet many use grading practices that do not have that effect. Suppose Mr. Wren decides to be "fair" to students by using the top score on a test as 100 and adjusts the percentage correct for all other students accordingly (this actually has occurred). Would it be fair if the class happened to have one or two exceptionally bright students? What might happen to student motivation in that class? This example illustrates one of many factors that will determine how grades are interpreted and thus affect students. Some other important influences include the level of detail communicated in the grade or mark about the student performance, whether factors other than performance are included, and the basis of comparison of the grades. We'll consider these with the assumption that the primary use of grades should be to inform and motivate students.

Providing Feedback

One decision you will make about grading students is the nature and amount of feedback they will receive about their performance. Consider the example of Dr. McMillan's daughter, Ryann. He recalls that "when Ryann was in the sixth grade a few years ago, she spent several weeks putting together a report on Italy. In looking over the report, I thought she did an excellent job (of course there may be just a little bias here!). She got the paper back with a B+ on it and a short comment, "good work." She was somewhat disappointed, but more important, didn't know why she did not get a higher grade." There was no information about how the teacher had come to this conclusion. How did this affect her? The effect was negative; she was sad and bewildered. The teacher could have provided her with a detailed summary of how each section of the paper was evaluated so that she could better understand the strengths and weaknesses.

This example demonstrates the importance of providing appropriate feedback. Whether you give grades or numbers, you have the option of either giving a single indication or giving enough detail so that students know where they have made mistakes, where to improve, and what they have done well. Used properly, this more detailed feedback can have a positive effect on motivation, and it allows students to make more accurate connections between how they studied or prepared and their performance. At least when you return a conventional test with each item marked correct or incorrect, students can see which questions they missed and figure out their strengths and weaknesses. Unfortunately, for much student work, the level of detail is minimal. What students need is specific information based on the learning expectations.

Incorporating Factors Other Than Performance

It's fairly obvious that the primary determinant of a mark or grade is the performance of the student. The more a student knows, understands, and can do, the better the grade. However, it's not as simple as it seems. First, there is the issue of whether high means in comparison to other students or in comparison to a well-defined learning expectation or outcome. We'll consider this factor in a later section. Second, when grades are determined solely on performance, teachers tend to emphasize knowledge and simple understanding, in part because measures for these expectations are easier to develop, and grades based on such measures are easier to defend. This may mean that deep understanding, reasoning, and production are overlooked. Third, what do you do with factors such as student effort, aptitude, improvement, and attitude? These aspects of student performance are important to most teachers, particularly when doing whatever they can to encourage and motivate students. In fact, many studies have documented that teachers tend to award a "hodgepodge" grade of attitude, effort, and achievement (Brookhart, 1993, p. 36; Cross & Frary, 1996; McMillan, 2001b, 2002a; McMillan, Workman & Myran, 1998). A look at each of these factors is warranted. Let's begin with student effort.

Effort. There is a commonsensical logic to why student effort should be considered when grading. Aren't students who try harder learning more, even if it doesn't show up on a test, paper, or project? Isn't it good to reward low-achieving students who try hard? Don't we need to find something to praise low-achieving students for, in order to keep them engaged? Isn't it true that we value effort as a society, so children should learn the importance of effort by seeing it reflected in their grades?

These may be compelling reasons to include effort in determining grades, but there are also some good reasons not to do so. First, different teachers operationalize effort differently, so there is variation from one teacher to another. Second, we don't have a satisfactory way to define and measure effort. We could define effort as "completing homework," "participating in class discussion," or "being on-task," but each of these definitions is problematic. Although completing homework could be easily and accurately measured, using this as a measure of effort is pretty shallow. Participation in class discussion is influenced by many factors, only one of which is controlled by each student. How do you know if a student is on-task? Sometimes it seems obvious, though students can fake this pretty well, and most of the time we either can't tell or can't systematically observe and record sufficiently to get a good measure. If students know they will be graded on effort, will they try to make you think that they are trying by how they act, when they're actually bluffing and not really trying?

Third, does including effort tend to favour more assertive students? What about students who are quiet? Could gender or racial/ethnic characteristics be related to the value of effort or expectations about showing effort? Does effort doubly reward students who are doing well while doubly penalizing those who are not? We certainly would not want our grades to be affected by these characteristics. Fourth, how much would effort count? What amount of a grade or percentage of a score would be reasonable? We really don't know, and how would you keep the level of contribution the same for each student? Finally, are we sending students the wrong message if they learn that they can get by just by trying hard, even if the performance is less than satisfactory?

So what is the resolution? There seem to be some pretty good reasons for and against including effort. Grading policies in most Canadian provinces state that effort should not be used to calculate a student's grade. Rather, most report card systems provide a space for the teacher to comment on each student's work habits. Hence, effort is reported separately from performance. Do this often and allow students opportunities to disagree with your assessment. Try to define effort as clearly as possible, and stick to your definition. Share the definition, using examples, with students. Figure 12.1 summarizes arguments for and against the use of effort in grading.

Aptitude. A second factor that can easily influence grades and marks is student aptitude or ability. This reflects the student's potential or capability for learning. The argument for including aptitude goes something like this: if we can tailor assignments and grading to each student's potential, all students can be motivated, and all students can experience success. Rather than grading only on achievement, which favours students who have a higher aptitude for learning, grades reflect how well each student has achieved in relation to his or her potential. That is, each student is graded by comparing achievement to aptitude. Using this approach, we can better identify when students are over- or underachieving. High-aptitude students will be challenged, and low-aptitude students will have realistic opportunities for good grades.

However, this argument is based on knowing what aptitude is and being able to assess it. There has never been an agreed-upon definition of aptitude, though it is often used synonymously with general intelligence. Work by Sternberg (1986) and Gardner (1985) has challenged traditional definitions of intelligence and has shown that we are still a long way from adequately understanding something as complex as aptitude for learning. Furthermore, measuring aptitude is fraught with difficulties, not the least of which concerns cultural bias. Even if we had a proper definition and a good measure, there are insurmountable practical

For	Against
• Students who try hard learn more	• Teachers operationalize effort differently
• Rewards motivation and engagement	• Hard to define and measure
• Rewards lower-achieving students for something	• Can be faked
	• Favours more assertive students
• Rewards an internal attributional factor that learning is within the student's control	• Lack of consistency in how effort is weighted
• Leads to higher grades	• Teaches students that they can get by with effort and not performance
	• Takes focus away from performance

Figure 12.1 Arguments for and against Using Effort in Grading

difficulties in trying to assess aptitude for each student and to grade accordingly. Then there is the issue of explaining to high-aptitude students and their parents how they can get a higher score than low-aptitude students yet obtain a lower grade. Would you like to explain that? Some teachers essentially adopt two grading systems—one for low-aptitude students that emphasizes improvement and one for high-aptitude students that emphasizes absolute achievement. The problem with this approach is that the meaning of the grades is different.

Although students unquestionably have different levels of ability, and you should use this knowledge for both instruction and giving feedback, you don't want to factor it into grades and marks. The only exception might be for borderline situations. Even then, you should use prior achievement instead of aptitude. Using prior achievement avoids the conceptualization and measurement problems associated with aptitude. This suggests that another factor, improvement, could be used for grading.

Improvement. Because learning is defined as a change in performance, why not measure how much students know both before and after instruction? Students who show the most improvement—hence learning—would get the highest grades. Again, there are some serious limitations to this approach. What happens when students score high on the pretest and don't have an opportunity to show improvement? What about student faking, in which students intentionally score poorly on the pretest to more easily show improvement? Like trying to incorporate aptitude, keeping track of pre- and postinstruction scores for each student would not be very practical. But like aptitude and effort, improvement can be a positive motivator in borderline situations.

Attitudes. A final factor to consider in classroom grading and marking is student attitudes. Shouldn't students with positive attitudes be rewarded? Suppose two students perform about the same and are between two grades. If one or both students have a very positive attitude, would that mean that they should get the higher grade? Like student effort, attitudes are important, and it would be nice if we could efficiently and accurately include them in grading. However, attitudes are difficult to define and measure

Teacher's Corner

Marguerite Cole

I use "nonachievement" factors such as effort and participation in terms of providing ongoing formative feedback to students, helping my students to understand the importance of these aspects of classroom behaviour as a significant part of their improvement. If it is evident to me that a student is increasingly demonstrating some of these "nonachievement" factors, such as effort and participation, I make sure that I tell the student how this is helping to improve their achievement of the learning expectations. I also make several comments about each student's effort and participation in my report cards to parents, making sure to note my appreciation for any improvements. One other thing that I do when grading is to carefully look at my students' most recent marks on their assignments and summative assessments. If these marks are showing improvement, I will give them more weight than earlier marks.

and are susceptible to student faking. So like the other "nonacademic" factors we have considered, you should generally not try to use attitudes in grading. Grades and marks should be predominately determined by student performance in relation to learning expectations. Some curricula do identify specific attitudes as part of the learning expectations. In these cases, try to develop objective measures of attitudes in relation to the learning expectations, rather than attitudes towards the subject as a whole.

Basis of Comparison

A major consideration in determining the meaning and method of grading is whether grades communicate comparisons with others or to predefined standards or levels of performance. Grading by comparison to the achievement of other students is referred to as **norm-referenced** or *relative*. So the function of each student's grade is to indicate how the student performed in comparison with the other students in the class (or several classes in middle and high schools). This method is known popularly as *grading on the curve*. Certain proportions of students are given designated grades, regardless of the level of performance of the students. That is, a certain percentage of the class will receive As, Bs, Cs, Ds, and Fs. There is no indication of how much students master or the overall percentage score on tests and assignments. A student can answer 70 per cent of the items on one test correctly, and if that is the highest score, it will be an A. On another test, a 70 might be relatively low, receiving a C or D. It's also possible for a student to get a C for getting a 95 on a test if others received even higher scores.

In norm-referenced grading, the standard is a relative one that changes depending on the composition of the class. It is done by rank ordering student performances from highest to lowest and then assigning grades based on a predetermined curve (e.g., the top 10 per cent will receive As, the next 30 per cent Bs, the next 40 per cent Cs, the next 10 per cent Ds, and the bottom 10 per cent Fs). If you are in a high-ability class, it's usually more difficult to get a good grade.

Because norm-referenced grading is based on comparing students to each other, its major function is to show who the highest- or best-performing students are. It sorts students, and because many educators still believe this is a purpose of schooling, some variation of norm-referencing is often incorporated in grading. (Indeed, a definition of grades that includes C as average and B as above average is a norm-referenced type of comparison). Variations can be made by adjusting curves based on student ability (e.g., honours-track classes have a higher percentage of As than general track classes), by how difficult teachers make their tests, and by how tough teachers are in grading papers, projects, and other products.

One of the myths about norm-referenced grading is that you try to obtain a *curve* of student scores, usually something that looks like a normal curve (Figure 12.2a). Actually, this type of curved scores is undesirable; at each cut point between different grades, you have a maximum number of students at the borderline between the grades. If your purpose is to conclude that some students clearly know more than others, you would want to obtain a sculpted curve of scores that looks like a wave in Figure 12.2b. Each cut point at the bottom of the

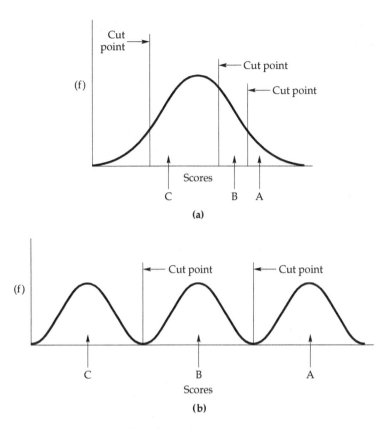

Figure 12.2 Normal and Sculpted Grading Curves

waves minimizes borderline scores, and you will be more accurate in your conclusions. Although you probably won't be able to get scores that look like those in Figure 12.2b, look for naturally occurring breaks. For example, if seven students scored above 80 on a test of knowledge and the next few students scored between 60 and 70, those two groups of students likely have different amounts of knowledge. However, using this *gap* method of identifying grading categories is fairly arbitrary, and it is likely that the breaks might be at different locations if the data were re-collected. Thus, use clear, distinct breaks that are relatively large.

Norm-referenced grading often fosters student competitiveness. When students know that their grade depends on how others perform, a very competitive environment can be created, which in turn usually has a negative impact on student effort, motivation, interpersonal relationships, and teacher communication. The motivation of students who continually score near the bottom is undermined. Student cooperation is reduced. For these reasons, as well as because of the capriciousness with which some teachers set curves, all grading policies in Canadian education now direct teachers to grade student performance relative to absolute levels of expected performance, without any comparison to how others performed. Grading that is determined by the level of performance obtained is commonly called **criterion-referenced** or **absolute grading**. There is no comparison with other students, so it is possible for all students to get the same grade. As an example, the British Columbia Ministry of Education states that "Criterion-referenced letter grades in Grades 4 to 12 indicate students' level of performance in relation to the prescribed learning outcomes set out in provincial curriculum guides for each subject or course and grade" (2009, p. 7).

The most common method of using absolute levels of performance is called *percentage-based* grading. This is typically used for tests, in which teachers assign a grade to a specific percentage of items answered correctly. However, it can also be found in many provincial policies related to report cards. Schools typically use the same scale developed by their provincial ministry of education. The grading scales used in Alberta and British Columbia are detailed below.

Percentages Associated with Letter Grades

Alberta		British Columbia	
A	80–100	A	86–100
B	65–79	B	73–85
C	50–64	C+	67–72
F	0–49	C	60–66
		C–	50–59
		F	0–49

The criterion is supposedly set by the percentage of learning expectations met or the proportion of correct responses. As you can see, these two provinces use slightly different grading structures, although both are based on percentages. One might conclude the scale in British Columbia, in which 86–100 is an A, is more stringent or tougher than the scale in Alberta, with an A range of 80–100. This is largely a myth, due to variation in item difficulty and the reality of ongoing attempts to sort students. Let's examine item difficulty first.

Simply put, a score of 70 on a hard test or assignment means something different from a 70 on an easy test or assignment. Consequently, what is important is not only the percentage of correct items, but also how hard it is to get those items correct. Two teachers, given the same learning expectation, can easily come up with assessments that differ in terms of difficulty. Suppose you are assessing student knowledge of different regions of Canada using a test. One way to assess the expectation is to ask which provinces are in a region; you might ask, for example, "Name the three prairie provinces." Another approach is to give a multiple-choice question:

Which of the following is a province in the prairies?
a. British Columbia
b. Nova Scotia
c. Ontario
d. Saskatchewan

The expectation is the same, but the completion item is more difficult. How do you know how difficult a test is going to be before you give it to your students? This is a common situation that teachers must deal with. Estimating difficulty before using any assessment instrument depends on how others have performed and the capabilities of those students. For example, if you have a high-aptitude class that works hard to learn the content but then gets a low score on the assessment, then the assessment is probably pretty tough. On the other hand, if your low-aptitude class exerts minimum effort and does well, it's probably an easy assessment.

What happens when you don't have any prior experience, you give a test, and most students get a very low grade? In this circumstance, either the students didn't know much or the test was not a fair assessment. Because you can't be sure which of these is true, you can justifiably make adjustments so that the distribution of scores reflects the range of likely student performance (but be cautious of adjusting high scores downward). As we already indicated, some teachers do this by using the top score to signify 100 per cent and recalculating all the students' scores with this new maximum number of possible correct answers. This is actually too arbitrary because the performance of a single student is too influential, but some adjustment may be needed. Yes, this is *subjective*, but no more so than your choice of item difficulty. Remember, your goal is to evaluate student performance fairly. A single test or assessment might not be fair, and relying on the scores would be an injustice to students. In any event, it's not difficult for teachers to tailor item difficulty to their students so that a final distribution of grades meets normative standards or guidelines.

Although theoretically all students can master learning expectations and receive As, most teachers simply can't do this. Because we still use school to indicate to others which particular students from the entire group have performed best, normative expectations continue to affect teacher practice. Hence, teachers (especially middle and high school teachers) will give some As, a lot of Bs and Cs, and even some Fs. Teachers are often unaware that their assessment practices lead to this sorting. For example, tests are typically devised so that not all students will do really well. That is, enough difficulty is built into the test that not all students will get As. One way or another, most teachers combine absolute performance and sorting when assigning grades. Even though provincial grading policies outline the use of criterion-referenced assessment, the underlying norm-referenced framework needs to be acknowledged for what it is so that whatever methods are used are fair to students. Sorting is still a function of schooling we need to deal with.

Another type of criterion-referenced performance standard is to spell out, in some detail, the specific behaviours students must perform to obtain a grade. This standard is used with performance assessments of skills and products and, increasingly, with reporting. The scoring rubric and exemplars define the behaviours, and, based on the teacher's observations, a grade is assigned to indicate which behaviours were demonstrated and hence which grade is received. In these systems, students' performances are compared only to the rubrics and exemplars, not to each other. A grade may be assigned to different levels, but it is more common to simply indicate the level achieved. As we will see in a later section, this leads to a different type of reporting system than traditional letter grades.

Table 12.1 summarizes differences between norm- and criterion-referenced approaches to assessment for marking and grading students.

Table 12.1 Characteristics of Norm- and Criterion-Referenced Assessment

	Norm-Referenced	Criterion-Referenced
Interpretation	Score compared to the performances of other students	Score compared to predetermined standards and criteria
Nature of Score	Percentile rank; standard scores; grading curve	Percentage correct; descriptive performance standards
Difficulty of Test Items	Uses average to difficult items to obtain spread of scores; very easy and very difficult items not used	Uses average to easy items to result in a high percentage of correct answers
Use of Scores	To rank order and sort students	To describe the level of performance obtained
Effect on Motivation	Dependent on comparison group; competitive	Challenges students to meet specified learning target
Strengths	Results in more difficult assessments that challenge students	Matches student performance to clearly defined learning targets; lessens competitiveness
Weaknesses	Grades determined by comparison to other students; some students are always at the bottom	Establishing clearly defined learning targets; setting standards that indicate mastery

Motivation

One way or another, your grading practices will motivate students. Depending on your practices, student motivation can be enhanced or diminished. Let's assume that you want grades to motivate students to be active learners (would anyone not want this?). To successfully accomplish this, make sure that grades communicate specific information that is relevant to each student. According to recent research in student motivation, a few key areas of information can be identified that fit well with certain theories of motivation (Brookhart, 2004). Let's take a look at some important ones.

It is well established that student motivation is enhanced when students believe that their success is due to internal, controllable attributions or beliefs about what caused the success. Did they succeed because of something they did (e.g., effort), that they can control in the future? Or did they succeed because of something they can't control, such as luck or help from others? Teachers can help students see the connection between their efforts and the grades they receive to reinforce their self-conception about their ability to be successful. This helps establish a well-grounded belief that they are able to do well—that they have internalized explanations for success. Students who know that they are capable have positive *self-efficacy*. Self-efficacy is enhanced when grades connect meaningfully to internal reasons for success, primarily the belief that students are able to be successful. One implication of this is that grades should not be used to reward mere participation unless participation is a specific learning expectation identified in the curriculum document (e.g., drama and physical education). Rather, grades should be tied to achievement students obtain through effort exerted to be successful with moderately challenging tasks. When students receive grades for tasks that are perceived as very easy, it simply verifies already established self-perceptions, with little new information about the ability to do well. This results in lower motivation. The old adage of "making sure students work for their grades" to motivate them is supported by research.

The role of goals in motivating students is well established (Elliot & Thrash, 2001). Students tend to have one of two types of goals—mastery or performance. As previously discussed, a **mastery** or **learning goal** involves students' conceptions of their competence to perform a task or complete a test. The focus is on self-improvement, on being able to demonstrate successfully the knowledge, understanding, or skill. There is an intrinsic reason for learning, for wanting to learn because demonstrating the knowledge or skill is what is important. Students with a mastery goal orientation learn more, prefer more challenging tasks, have more positive attitudes, become more success-oriented (rather than failure-avoiding), and believe that success depends on internal attributions such as effort and ability (Brookhart, 2004). With a **performance goal**, students are motivated not because of learning for its own sake, but for demonstrating competence, getting a high grade, passing the test, or scoring higher than other students. The motivation is to do well to achieve an extrinsic reward, regardless of the learning that occurs. Good grades are used to impress others, avoid failure, or obtain privileges.

When grades are perceived as feedback pertaining to mastery goals, students are more motivated than when grades are extrinsic rewards. As a classroom teacher, you must relate grades to mastery goals, especially with the increasing emphasis on large-scale accountability tests. If the meaning of the grade is mostly about "getting a good score" rather than "demonstrating understanding," motivation is transient and less powerful. When grades indicate feedback related to learning, intrinsic motivation results. The implication is that giving grades without accompanying feedback fosters extrinsic motivation. Grades need to be accompanied by specific feedback that students can use to both verify learning and to further develop their knowledge, understanding, or skill.

Finally, grades affect motivation most when they are presented while students learn (formatively), not just after they learn (summatively). When grades are used to support formative feedback, students are encouraged to be *self-monitoring* and *self-reflecting*, which enhances self-efficacy and intrinsic motivation. When grades are used as a summative judgment, the focus is on extrinsic rewards and management of student behaviour (compliance).

APPROACHES TO MARKING AND GRADING

There are several ways to mark and grade student performance. We will consider the most common types of symbols or scores that are used, including letter grades, percentage correct, pass–fail grades, checklists, outcomes-based, and written descriptions. Most teachers use a combination of these in the classroom.

Letter Grades

One of the more common methods teachers use to mark student performance on products other than tests is to give a letter grade. Traditionally, letter grades correspond to different adjectives, such as excellent or outstanding, good, average or acceptable, poor, and unsatisfactory, and often plus and minus symbols are used to provide finer distinctions. Letter grades provide a convenient, concise, and familiar approach to marking. In addition, grades are readily understood by students and parents to provide an overall indication of performance.

The major limitation of letter grades is that they provide only a general indication of performance. There is nothing wrong with giving students an overall, summary judgment in the form of a grade. However, such a general mark alone does not indicate what the student did correctly or incorrectly. It doesn't communicate strengths and limitations. Teachers also tend to be influenced by factors other than performance in determining a grade on papers, projects, and presentations (e.g., effort, work habits, and attitude). Furthermore, because teachers differ in their value systems, the proportion of students getting each grade can vary. In one class, most students can get As and Bs, while in another class, most students receive Bs and Cs.

You should make clear to your students what each letter means so that their interpretation is accurate, appropriate, and helpful. Does getting an A mean that I did outstanding work, or does it mean that I did best in the class? Does it mean that the teacher thinks I worked hard on this, or that I can do it really well? Does getting a C mean that I did about as well as most students, or that I did satisfactory work? One approach used in some Canadian provinces (for example, Ontario) is to use letter grades for report cards, but to use achievement charts containing overall performance descriptors for specific assessments. Rather than providing students with a percentage or letter grade score, the achievement chart in Ontario is a standard province-wide guide that enables teachers to make judgments about student work that are based on clear performance standards. These achievement charts are similar to scoring rubrics but are more general. Rather than using letter grades, students receive a level representing their achievement on a specific assessment (Level 1 = "below expectations," Level 2 = "minimally meets expectations," Level 3 = "meets expectations," and Level 4 = "exceeds expectations").

Be clear in your own mind about what each letter grade or performance standard means and communicate this to students. Make sure you are aware of the factors other than performance that affect your letter grade decisions (norm- or criterion-referenced).

Without careful thought and communication on your part, students will be unaware if their grades represent effort, achievement, improvement, achievement in comparison to aptitude (some teachers grade high-aptitude students more severely), relative standing, or level of mastery. Table 12.2 presents different interpretations of grades.

Table 12.2 Different Interpretations of Letter Grades

Grade	Criterion-Referenced (Standards-Based)	Norm-Referenced	Combined Norm- and Criterion-Referenced	Based on Improvement
A	Outstanding or advanced: complete knowledge of all content; mastery of all targets; exceeds standards	Outstanding: among the highest or best performance	Outstanding: very high level of performance	Outstanding: much improvement on most or all targets
B	Very good or proficient: complete knowledge of most content; mastery of most targets; meets most standards	Very good: performs above the class average	Very good: better than average performance	Very good: some improvement on most or all targets
C	Acceptable or basic: command of only basic concepts or skills; mastery of some targets; meets some standards	Average: performs at the class average	Average	Acceptable: some improvement on some targets
D	Making progress or developing: lacks knowledge of most content; mastery of only a few targets; meets only a few standards	Poor: below the class average	Below average or weak: minimum performance for passing	Making progress: minimal progress on most targets
F	Unsatisfactory: lacks knowledge of content; no mastery of targets; does not meet any standards	Unsatisfactory: far below average; among the worst in the class	Unsatisfactory: lacks sufficient knowledge to pass	Unsatisfactory: no improvement on any targets

Notice that it is possible to combine or mix norm- and criterion-referenced approaches (Terwilliger, 1989). Higher grades could be norm-referenced and the lower ones criterion-referenced. That is, to get an A, students need to perform better than most, but a failure judgment tends to be based on absolute standards. If a purely relative scale was used, and the norming group was the class itself, some students would always fail, despite what might be a high level of performance (a better procedure is to use data from previous classes to set the norm from a larger group). As well, some students would always succeed. It is only with absolute scales that all students can either succeed or fail. While such practices are not condoned in any provincial jurisdiction in Canada, the often fuzzy separation between criterion- and norm-referenced assessments allows these practices to occur.

Percentage Correct

For classroom tests, the most common approach to reporting performance is to indicate the percentage of items answered correctly. Thus, we often characterize our achievement as, say, getting a 75 or a 92 on a test. These numbers refer to the percentage of items or points obtained out of a possible 100. These scores are easy to calculate, record, and combine at the end of the grading period. Usually, letter grades are associated with ranges of scores, so this is really a letter-grade system that gives students a finer discrimination in their performance. It is possible, although becoming less common, to grade everything with percentage correct, even papers and essay items.

One limitation of using percentage correct in marking and grading is that, like a letter grade, only a general indication of performance is communicated. Another disadvantage is that the discriminations that are suggested by a scale from 1 to 100 are much finer than what can be reliably assessed. Because of error in testing, there is no meaningful difference between scores differentiated by one or two points. That is, scores of 92 and 93 suggest the same level of student performance. In other words, the degree of precision suggested by percentage correct is not justified given the error that exists.

A third limitation is the tendency to equate percentage of items correct with percentage mastered. As we have pointed out, items can differ tremendously in level of difficulty, so when students obtain a high percentage of correct answers, mastery may or may not be demonstrated, depending on the difficulty level of the assessment. Thus, it is probably incorrect to conclude that when a student obtains a 100, he or she knows 100 per cent of the learning expectations, or that a score of 50 corresponds to mastery of half of the expectations. This continues to be one of the biggest challenges for teachers who are expected to work in a criterion-referenced grading framework while equating percentages with letter grades.

Pass–Fail

The idea of making a simple dichotomous evaluation, such as pass versus fail or satisfactory versus needs improvement, is consistent with mastery learning. In these approaches to learning and instruction, students are assessed on each learning outcome. The judgment is criterion-referenced and results in a mastery–no mastery decision. Typically, students work on each outcome until they demonstrate mastery and then move on.

There is a certain appeal to this approach, especially at the early elementary level, but it doesn't accurately reflect the actual levels of performance that students demonstrate. Basically, a two-category system is too simple. Most teachers find that at least three categories are needed, such as fail, pass, and excellent, or N (needs improvement), S (satisfactory), and O (outstanding). A related limitation is that when we use a dichotomous system, we communicate even less information to students than when we use grades. It is also difficult to keep standards high with a pass–fail system. The tendency is to relax the standards so that most students will not fail. This tells students clearly what they need to do to avoid failure, but it doesn't tell them very much about what excellent or outstanding performance is like.

Checklists

A variation of the pass–fail approach is to give students a checklist of some kind to indicate their performance on each aspect of the learning target. The checklist has two or more categories. In a simple dichotomous checklist, the teacher might prepare a series of statements that describes aspects of the performance that students need to include. The teacher places a check mark next to each one the student demonstrates. To indicate student affect, checks can be placed next to each one demonstrated. This shows what the student both has and has not done.

A more elaborate approach provides students with scales of performance. The teacher makes checks on the scale to indicate the level of performance. The rubric that describes the scoring is used as the checklist. The advantage of this type of grading is that the students receive more detailed feedback about what they did well and what needs improvement. The detail in the rubric helps students understand more precisely where they need to improve. The difficulty of this approach is developing the checklists and keeping the system practical. However, once you develop detailed lists, they are fairly efficient because you only make check marks. Even if there are several such statements for each student product, this approach is certainly more efficient than writing comments on papers, though some individualized comments are important as well.

Outcomes-Based

With the continuing focus on curricular expectation and learning outcomes, standards-based (or outcomes-based) grading has emerged as a new and highly effective form of providing feedback to students and parents. Guskey and Bailey (2001) identify four steps in the development of standards-based grading:

1. Identify major learning goals and outcomes (expectations).
2. Establish performance indicators for the outcomes.

3. Identify benchmarks that indicate graduated levels of proficiency.

4. Develop reporting forms that indicate progress and final achievement toward meeting the outcomes.

As Brookhart (2004) pointed out, this form of grading is a direct descendant of criterion-referenced grading. Both emphasize the idea of an absolute, established level of performance in a carefully defined domain. In outcomes-based grading, however, the "criterion" tends to be broad, at a high level, and the same for all students. Typically, Canadian educators do not differentiate between the two.

The challenge of identifying the learning outcomes and expectations is to get them at the right level of specificity. Overly detailed and numerous learning expectations make reporting cumbersome and time-consuming for teachers, and too complex for parents to understand. Learning expectations that are too general do not provide enough information to show strengths or weaknesses. Most provincial curricular documents provide some guidance here. For example, curriculum documents in Ontario identify broad *overall learning expectations* and then list the *specific learning expectations* within these overall expectations. In other jurisdictions, the teacher may have to develop the broader expectations and outcomes based on the specific outcome provided in the curriculum documents (see Figure 12.3). This allows parents and students to see overall performance, as well as strengths and weakness.

The performance indicators are descriptors that indicate the status of student achievement in relation to the expectation. The most common form is to use four descriptors: *not yet meeting expectations, approaching expectations, meeting expectations,* and *exceeding expectations.* When the outcome or expectation is behaviourally oriented, descriptors that indicate how often the outcome was reached could be used, such as *seldom, sometimes, frequently,* or *consistently.* Descriptors should show graduated levels of proficiency to facilitate reporting progress as well as current status. However, broad quantitative descriptors can be problematic. It can be difficult to distinguish between sometimes and seldom, or frequently and consistently. Nor do specific numerical values solve this problem. Secondly, learning is often not graduated in terms of quantity, but rather in terms of differences in how a beginning learner and an accomplished learner complete the task. When you are proficient at doing something, the manner in which you complete a task is *qualitatively* different from the way in which a beginner completes it. Regardless of the method used, these progress indicators help students and parents gauge the amount of learning that has been demonstrated over the marking period. This is key information for understanding the link between student motivation and performance.

Written Comments

An alternative to giving only a grade or score is to mark students' work with written comments. The advantage of this approach is that the comments can be highly individualized, pointing out unique strengths and weaknesses, and can focus attention on important issues.

Overall Expectation

By the end of Grade 5, the student will read and demonstrate an understanding of a variety of literary, graphic, and informational texts, using a range of strategies to construct meaning.

Specific Expectations

Read a variety of texts from diverse cultures, including literary texts.

Identify a variety of purposes for reading and choose reading materials appropriate for those purposes.

Identify a variety of reading comprehension strategies and use them appropriately before, during, and after reading to understand texts.

Demonstrate understanding of a variety of texts by summarizing important ideas and citing supporting details.

Use stated and implied ideas in texts to make inferences and construct meaning.

Extend understanding of texts by connecting the ideas in them to their own knowledge, experience, and insights, to other familiar texts, and to the world around them.

Analyze texts and explain how various elements in them contribute to meaning.

Make judgments and draw conclusions about the ideas and information in texts and cite stated or implied evidence from the text to support their views.

Identify the point of view presented in texts, ask questions to identify missing or possible alternative points of view, and suggest some possible alternative perspectives.

Figure 12.3 Elementary Curriculum Illustrating Overall and Specific Learning Expectations

Source: Ontario Ministry of Education (2006). *The Ontario curriculum: Grades 1–8: Language.* Toronto: Queen's Printer for Ontario.

Students appreciate the effort of teachers who take the time to make these comments. Of course, the time needed is a major disadvantage. Most teachers simply do not have sufficient time to give this level of feedback. Then there is the added complication of parents trying to equate these descriptions with grades. A more common approach is to use a combination of letter grades and written comments. The comments are designed to support the students' learning, identifying strengths and weaknesses along with suggestions for continued improvement and learning.

Recently, assessment experts have focused attention on how marking and grading can improve instruction and student learning (Brookhart, 2004; Guskey, 1994; Guskey & Bailey, 2001). Detailed checklists, narratives, and marking based on prespecified criteria are preferred. To enhance student motivation, grading needs to be specific. You should avoid relative comparisons among students. But from a realistic perspective, your marking and grading also must be practical and result in accurate summaries for report cards. When marking each piece of student work, your challenge is to incorporate as much detail and reference to learning expectations as possible without being overwhelmed. Then you'll need to combine the marks into a final grade for the term or year.

The advantages and disadvantages of the different types of grading discussed are summarized in Table 12.3.

Table 12.3 Advantages and Disadvantages of Different Types of Grading

Approach	Advantages	Disadvantages
Letter Grades	Convenient; concise; familiar	Broad, sometimes vague indication of performance; often includes a hodgepodge of factors including effort and improvement
Percentage Correct	Easy to calculate, record, and combine; familiar	Broad, sometimes vague indication of performance; false sense of difference between close scores; mastery not necessarily indicated by high scores
Pass–Fail	Simple; consistent with mastery learning	Little discrimination in performance; less emphasis on high performance
Checklists	Provides specific feedback on discrete areas of knowledge and/or skills	Difficult to construct; may become too time-consuming
Standards-Based	Focus on high standards for all students; pre-established performance levels	May not reflect student learning in many areas; does not include effort or improvement
Written Comments	Provides individualized feedback to inform and motivate students	Time-consuming; difficult to convert to grades

DETERMINING REPORT CARD GRADES

At one or more time periods during the school year, you must review your students' achievement in each subject you teach, and use this information to determine a single measure of overall performance for each student. Teachers give these unit and term grades to provide a single indicator of student performance over a unit of study or period of time. Teachers are expected to keep students informed about their educational progress throughout the school year. These grades are also used to complete report cards that will be used to keep an ongoing record of your students' progress and inform their parents (or guardians). Provincial ministries of education may require teachers to provide a specific number of both "interim" and formal report cards. In British Columbia, for example, teachers must provide two interim reports and three formal reports on each child over the course of the school year. The last report card of the year (or semester in some high schools) contains the final grades, which are used to make important decisions for the following school year. Recognizing that professional judgment is essential for determining report card grades, as well as marks and grades for individual assessments, you will make some important decisions. These decisions can be summarized in the form of three steps:

1. Select what to include in the report card grade.
2. Select weights for each individual assessment.
3. Combine weighted scores to determine a single grade.

Let's examine each of these steps.

Select What to Include in the Grade

This is where you will have a fair amount of leeway. To some extent, it is up to you to determine which assessments will contribute to the grade. You should base grades primarily on academic performance linked to learning outcomes or expectations. But which performances should be included? Tests? Participation in class? Papers? Quizzes? Homework? Before selecting the assessments, think again about your overall learning goals. Your selection of what goes into the reported grade should provide the most accurate information in relation to these goals. If you have done a good job of basing your formal assessments on the learning expectations, then each of these assessments will contribute meaningfully to the grade. It is less clear if pop quizzes, participation, and homework should be included.

Certainly, pop quizzes, participation, and homework do focus on student performance, but can they legitimately serve as documentation of student learning and understanding? If they are primarily formative to give students practice and feedback, they may be viewed more as instruction than assessment and should not be included in a final grade. Some teachers argue that pop quizzes are not fair to students, and some also contend that homework may not have been completed by the student. Many teachers realize that participation in class is influenced by group dynamics and personality. Other teachers view pop quizzes, participation, and homework as indicators of how much students are paying attention and learning in class and will use them to calculate final grades. The school district or province in which you work may give you little choice about whether to include these student performances or not. If you do have the choice, carefully consider the purposes of these quiz, participation, and homework marks. If these assessments were intended to provide formative assessment information throughout the unit or term, do not include them in the grade. Always consider fairness and accuracy in your decision to use assessment information.

You will rarely consider factors such as attendance, effort, and personal/social characteristics such as cooperativeness, participation, and work habits in determining grades. Nonacademic factors, which probably have little relationship to academic learning, should not have much influence on the reported grade. Suppose a student is absent from school and misses a test. Does that mean a zero is appropriate? Even if the student has been expelled, giving a zero for not being present, and then inferring that the grade ultimately received reflects academic learning, is clearly a mistake. What about a student who, while in a cooperative learning group, doesn't participate very much or contribute to others' learning? Should that student be penalized for displaying weak cooperative skills? Do you evaluate the quality or quantity of the participation? Should a student who continually says silly things be penalized? These work habits are typically reported separately through either written comments or a separate reporting scale (needs improvement, satisfactory, good, and excellent).

If a grade is for academic performance in areas such as reading, science, mathematics, history, and the like, you should determine the grade primarily by student academic performance on major assessments. This is essentially a matter of maintaining appropriate validity so that your inferences about academic performance are reasonable. If cooperativeness and participation are important learning expectations described in the curriculum (performing arts, physical education, and music), you may include the relevant work habits in the reported grade. However, be careful your decisions do not doubly penalize those students who participate (cooperate) less while over-rewarding those who do participate regularly.

Finally, in planning the assessments that you will include, carefully consider how many are needed to give an accurate overall judgment of each student's performance. Would it be reasonable to base a grade on a single exam? How about a nine-week grade—would two tests and a paper be sufficient? Probably, most would agree that a single assessment is definitely insufficient. In the words of Grant Wiggins, "A single grade hides more than it reveals" (1998, p. 248). Three assessments for a nine-week grade is much better, but even that may not be enough. The rule of thumb with respect to the number of assessments needed is the more, the better, as long as assessment time does not interfere significantly with instructional time. So, although one or two assessments would probably be too few, you wouldn't want to give a test every day! Once again, your professional judgment is needed. For some subjects, at least one fairly major test or other assessment is needed about every two weeks. The structure and format of your major assessments must take into consideration your school timetable and the age and experience of your students. A major test may require over an hour of testing time. Children have limited attention spans, and if students lose interest or find it hard to concentrate, error is introduced into the assessment. Similarly, if your school timetable does not provide the uninterrupted time for a major test, look for alternative assessment methods.

Select Weights for Each Assessment

Not only do you need to identify the assessments, you also need to decide how much each one will count in the reported grade. Obviously, more important assessments are given greater weight. What determines if an assessment is important? You probably guessed it—more professional judgment! The most significant assessments are those that (1) correspond most closely to the learning outcomes and expectations (content-related evidence for validity), (2) reflect instructional time, (3) are most reliable, and (4) are most current.

Because there are multiple learning expectations in a unit or term, you need to break down the percentage that each expectation contributes to the whole. This is illustrated

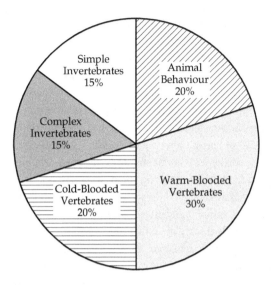

Figure 12.4 Percentage of Each Topic That Contributes to the Final Grade

in Figure 12.4 in the form of a pie chart for a unit on the animal kingdom. Different percentages correspond to each topic. In this case, the overall goal is determined mostly by vertebrate animal characteristics and behaviours. You should weigh your assessments to match these percentages so that the overall grade reflects the relative contribution of each topic. This will provide good content-related evidence for validity, which is a primary concern. We'll look at some examples of how to do that in the next section. In this example, about 50 per cent of what determines the final grade should be the assessments on vertebrates. This percentage is independent of the length of the book chapters, assessments, or instructional time devoted to each topic. What you are determining is solely the value of each of the topics.

Even though instructional time is not a factor in the first consideration of weights, it's still an important barometer of the amount of emphasis given to each topic. For that reason, it's only fair to factor in time devoted to instruction. As we have already emphasized, students need to know what will be covered before an assessment is taken. This may include topics or concepts that have not been discussed in class. Although there is nothing wrong with testing students on material they learn on their own, the weights should reflect instructional focus. If you spent 50 per cent of your term studying simple invertebrates, it probably wouldn't be fair to weight this topic at only 15 per cent. Similarly, although you *intended* to weight vertebrates at 50 per cent, when you look back over the weeks you might notice that students spent only 25 per cent of their time learning about vertebrates. A more appropriate weight would be 30–35 per cent, at most. Obviously, you don't know for sure how much time you will take until the instruction is completed. This means that your final determination of weights must be finalized close to the end of instruction. Weights should not be set in stone at the beginning of the unit.

Reliability is a factor in weighting because, *other things being equal*, especially validity, we want to put more weight on more accurate assessments. This will reduce the overall amount of error that is included in determining the grade. Generally, reliability increases with a greater number of items for each expectation and for objective items. The most important concern is validity, however; highly reliable assessments should never be given more weight than is appropriate given the validity of the assessment.

If you test the same content more than once, as you would with a cumulative final exam, put more weight on the most current assessment. In fact, a later assessment on the same material might mean that the earlier assessment should be dropped. In Ontario, the grading policy states that marks should be determined using the most recent and most consistent evidence. Since your goal is to communicate accurately the nature of a student's current performance, wouldn't the more recent assessment be better? From a practical standpoint, however, you may find that it is difficult to simply discard an earlier test score, especially if the more recent assessments cover different learning expectations, or assess the expectations in less depth. A good compromise is to weigh the cumulative exam more than each of the preceding ones so that final performance outweighs what students demonstrate at the beginning or middle of the unit.

Given these considerations, you now need to combine the assessments properly to obtain the term or final grade to be reported.

Combining Different Scores and Grades

The three basic approaches to combining scores and grades are the eyeball method, the per cent correct method, and the total points method.

Eyeball Method. The first method is called the *eyeball* method because the teacher simply reviews the scores and grades and estimates an average for them, without performing any calculations, to come up with what seems to be the correct grade. This has obvious disadvantages, not the least of which is the lack of objectivity. This method isn't recommended, but it does have one redeeming quality. With eyeballing, the teacher asks, "All things considered and looking at the whole as more than the sum of each part, what is the most valid grade for this student?" The notion that it is important to consider everything together has some merit because it recognizes that a teacher's professional judgment is needed to give grades. However, consider the other extreme: teachers who mindlessly calculate averages without any consideration of factors that might be important, such as student absenteeism, effort, and possible testing error. Just because a numeric average comes up with a certain grade doesn't mean that that grade is a valid indicator of student achievement. Just because a test says it's so, does that mean that it *is*?

Per Cent Correct Method. Because most teachers need to show some "objective" methods in their grading, scores and grades are typically combined into a single score that converts to a grade. Ensure that the calculations you use to combine the assessments are done correctly. Because most provinces require teachers to use a per cent correct scale in grading, especially in secondary school, we'll focus on combining scores to obtain a composite *percentage score*, which is readily converted to a grade.

Consider the example about a unit on animals (see Figure 12.4). If all you had for the final grade was a test for each of the topics, you would simply multiply the percentage of correct scores obtained by the percentages indicated in the chart, and then add the five products. To make matters simple, let's assume that you gave five 100-point tests, one for each topic. Here are the scores of two students on the five tests:

Test	LaKeith	Dion
1	70	85
2	65	90
3	80	88
4	75	93
5	83	95

You decide to weight each of the tests by the percentage indicated in the pie chart in Figure 12.4. To do this, multiply each test score by the percentage expressed as a decimal (e.g., 15 per cent, .15; 20 per cent, .20), and then add the resulting products. In this example, LaKeith's composite score would be 75:

$$(70 \times .15) + (65 \times .15) + (80 \times .20) + (75 \times .30) + (83 \times .20) = 75.35.$$

Dion's composite score would be 91:

$$(85 \times .15) + (90 \times .15) + (88 \times .20) + (93 \times .30) + (95 \times .20) = 90.75.$$

These composite scores would then be converted to grades, depending on the grading scale.

In reality, most teachers have a variety of different types of assessments and tests with different numbers of items and total scores, so keeping track of these and doing the calculations can get fairly complex. One important principle in doing this is to first *convert each score or grade to the same scale*. If you are using the per cent correct scale, this means converting each score or grade or other assessment to a per cent correct score. For a test with 50 items, multiply the raw score obtained by 2. For a test with 10 items, multiply the raw score by 10. Be careful to ensure that these tests are weighted appropriately. Do you want the 10-item test to have the same weight as the 50-item test? What about grades for papers, essays, performance assessments, and portfolios? You now have to convert the levels from the scoring rubrics into a percentage score. If you have given students a set of scores using different rubrics for different aspects of their performance, you could add these levels, considering weights, to obtain a total score that you then convert to a percentage score. A second option is to develop predetermined percentages for each of the levels. For example, a Level 4 paper is given an 85, a Level 3 paper a 75, a Level 2 paper a 65, and so forth. However, if there are only four levels of performance, the percentage scores may be quite different even if the differences in performance are relatively small. This has led to teachers identifying High, Medium and Low 4s, High, Medium and Low 3s, and so forth, and then assigning specific percentages to each of these. If you are including checklists, find a way to convert these to result in a number between 0 and 100. You might divide the number of checks obtained by a student by the total number of possible checks that could have been obtained.

Let's look at an example of how this might look in practice. Figure 12.5 illustrates part of Ms. Bryce's gradebook. The gradebook is a record of student accomplishments and performances throughout the grading period. In this case, you can see that there were two quizzes, a mid-term exam, a final exam, a paper, and homework. For each test, Ms. Bryce records the raw score, records grades for papers, and places a check mark beneath each homework assignment completed. Ms. Bryce has decided that the final grade will be determined as follows:

Final exam, 40 per cent
Mid-term exam, 30 per cent
Quizzes, 5 per cent each
Paper, 15 per cent
Homework, 5 per cent

This means that the unit quizzes together will count for 10 per cent. She has set up her gradebook to efficiently convert the raw scores to the per cent correct, weight them, and then add them to arrive at composite scores. You may find it convenient to prepare your own gradebook, although they are readily available commercially.

The first quiz had 25 items, so Ms. Bryce multiplied each raw score by 4 to obtain the percentage correct. The second quiz had 20 items, so she multiplied the raw scores by 5. Each mid-term had 50 items, so she multiplied the scores for each by 2. The final exam had 100 points, so it did not need to be converted. She worked out a score for each grade that could be given to the papers, and she gave each completed homework check a 100. To obtain a grade for the homework, she added the scores (either 100 or 0) and then divided by the total number of homework assignments, in this case 2 (this number is small for space reasons; typically much more homework would be recorded). After she calculated all the weighted scores, she added them to determine the final unit grade for each student, using a common grading scale (A = 86–100, B = 73–85, C+ = 67–72, C = 60–66, P = 50–59, F = below 50).

In Figure 12.6, the calculations are shown from the scores of two students in Ms. Bryce's class (see Figure 12.5), Eric and Ali. In these cases, the final unit grades are fairly clear, but what about Parvinder? As you can see in Figure 12.5, Parvinder is a borderline student, and you will need to be prepared to deal with such cases. In Shayla's case, she's so close to an A (85.3), shouldn't the teacher "give" it to her? You would need to think about the strongest information you have about Shayla's understanding of plant biology. Her final was an 84, just under an A, but her mid-term was an A, and her paper was in the high B range. Normally, these would be your best indicators that

Student	Quiz 1 (5%)			Quiz 2 (5%)			Mid-term (30%)		Final Exam (40%)			Paper (15%)		Homework (5%)				Total Score	Final Grade
	Raw Score	% Correct	Weighted Score	Raw Score	% Correct	Weighted Score	% Correct	Weighted Score	% Correct	Weighted Score	Level	% Correct	Weighted Score	#1	#2	Average	Weighted Score		
Alex	23	92	4.6	19	95	4.75	94	26.2	88	35.2	4-	85	12.75	✓	✓	100	5	90.5	A
Eric	20	80	4	17	85	4.25	84	25.2	82	32.8	3	80	12	✓	✓	100	5	83.3	B
Stacey	24	96	4.8	16	80	4	86	25.8	80	32	2+	68	10.2		✓	50	2.5	79.5	B
Isaac	18	72	3.6	15	75	3.75	74	22.2	72	28.8	3-	75	11.25	✓		50	2.5	72.1	C+
Parvinder	22	88	4.4	18	90	4.5	82	24.6	85	34	3	80	12	✓	✓	100	5	84.5	B
Shayla	21	84	4.2	17	85	4.25	86	25.8	84	33.6	3+	83	12.45	✓	✓	100	5	85.3	B
Rebecca	25	100	5	18	90	4.5	90	27	98	39.2	4	90	13.5	✓	✓	100	5	94.2	A
Ali	19	76	3.8	18	90	4.5	68	20.4	72	28.8	3-	75	11.25		✓	50	2.5	71.3	C+

Figure 12.5 Part of Ms. Bryce's Gradebook

	Quiz 1	Quiz 2	Mid-term	Final	Paper	Homework
Composite						
Eric	20×4=80	17×5=85	42×2=84	82	3(80)	✓✓(100)
	80×.05=4.0	85×.05=4.25	84×.3=25.2	82×.4=32.8	80×.15=12.0	100×.05=5
	4.0 +	4.25 +	25.2 +	32.8 +	12.0 +	5 = 83.3
Ali	19×4=76	18×5=90	34×2=68	72	3-(75)	✓ (50)
	76×.05=3.8	90×.05=4.5	68×.3=20.4	72×.4=28.8	75×.15=11.25	50×.05=2.5
	3.8 +	4.5 +	20.4 +	28.8 +	11.25 +	2.5 = 71.3

Figure 12.6 Calculation of Unit Final Grades

she understands the content, so from one perspective it would be justifiable to leave her final grade as a B. On the other hand, if she had gotten only a couple more questions correct on any of the exams, her composite score would have been over 85. Isn't there enough error in those tests to justify giving her the benefit of the doubt and raising her grade to an A? This is also a reasonable response. In such cases, think about your classroom interaction with Shayla and students who obtained an A as a final grade. Was she as knowledgeable as the other students who received an A? If so, it would be reasonable to raise her grade. Were there any extenuating circumstances that would have influenced her work?

In recent years, computerized grading software programs and electronic gradebooks have become very popular. The spreadsheet formats and database management systems make it easy and efficient to enter scores and calculate final grades and they simplify record keeping, especially for middle and high school teachers who have large numbers of students. Many programs offer flexibility in combining and weighting different entries. Some school districts mandate the use of a specific grading software program. Guskey (2002) points out, however, that the mathematical precision that is achieved does not necessarily bring greater objectivity, accuracy, or fairness. He notes that these programs do not lessen the challenges teachers face when making decisions about what will be included and how each score or grade contributes to the final grade (e.g., how to handle zeros, averaging, improvement).

Total Points Method. If you don't like to calculate percentages, give each assessment a number of points and add the points obtained for all the assessments to get a total. The points should be assigned to each assessment to reflect their weight in determining the total. For example, Ms. Bryce could use points rather than percentages. If the final is to count as 40 per cent of the grade, then 40 per cent of the total number of points should be allocated to the final exam. If the final had 100 questions, and each item counted for one point, then there would need to be a grand total of 250 points possible. The remaining points could be allocated to each assessment based on the percentage times 250. Thus, each quiz would have 12.5 points, the mid-term would have 75 points, and the paper would have 37.5 points.

You can see the disadvantage of this approach. Either you have to adjust the number of items to equal the points each assessment should provide, or you have to change the score of an assessment to reflect the points. In this case, each quiz would have a maximum of 12.5 points, regardless of the number of items. Obviously, this is pretty cumbersome, so if the total points method is used, the assessments are carefully designed to avoid recalculating any individual assessment so that they can simply be added. However, this tends to constrain the nature of the assessments. Rather than have the method of combining scores drive the assessments, let each assessment be constructed to provide the best measure of student performance, and then combine them. The per cent correct approach is much better than total points for this reason.

Whether you use the per cent correct or total points method, when you include many different assessments and mathematically combine them, you are essentially taking the average of all the performances. While averaging is justified as a way to include all the assessments (and to keep students motivated), there is a danger that *mindless* averaging will distort the student's true capabilities. For example, when a student evaluation system is designed to move students from novice to expert on an appropriate skill continuum, it may not make good sense to average performances during the entire period of learning (Wiggins, 1998). If a student begins as a novice and obtains a low score, should that score be averaged with a final "expert" performance to result in an average grade? What is critical is reporting student attainment of the skill in relation to the rubric and scoring criteria at the time of the report, regardless of earlier performances.

Combining Relative Scores and Grades. If you happen to be one of a small percentage of teachers who grade using a norm-referenced approach, you have an additional step to take when combining scores. Because the emphasis is on relative standing, take into account the degree or amount of difference between students on each assessment. You need to do this because the contribution of each assessment is a function of the difference between students, as well as the score. For example, suppose you give a mid-term and all students obtain the same score. On the final, the scores are pretty well distributed. You want the mid-term to count for 50 per cent, so you weight it appropriately, multiply by the score, and then add the product to the final exam. In reality, the final exam is weighted at 100 per cent. Because all students obtained the same score on the mid-term, what is added to the final is the same for each student. Thus, the only variability is provided by the final exam. Although you are unlikely to have a situation in which all students score the same on a test, differences in variation will affect the actual contribution of each assessment to the total.

There isn't enough space here to provide detailed examples of how to combine relative scores into a final grade. The suggested approach is to calculate linear transformations of each raw score to a standard score. You first figure the standard scores, weight them, and then add them together. Make the final determination of grades based on what percentage of students should receive each grade.

Borderline Grades

One of your most difficult challenges in grading is what to do with students whose composite grades are borderline—that is, just below the next grade. Perhaps you have experienced this as a student—getting a 79.4 but needing 79.6 to be rounded up to 80 to get an A! (Borderline grades that just make the higher grade are not a problem, though; with some of these, the students' true knowledge and understanding may be at a B level.) It's the grades that just aren't quite high enough that are troublesome. Research suggests that teachers want students to get the highest grade possible (McMillan, 2001b), and that nonacademic factors such as effort, participation, and improvement often are the basis for awarding a higher grade.

However, Stiggins (2005) stresses that the only credible information to consider in borderline cases is that which relates directly to academic performance. Getting a higher grade based on cooperative class participation is not nearly as credible as obtaining it because the preponderance of evidence suggests that the higher grade is a more valid indicator of student academic performance.

Suggestions for Fair Grading

Teachers have an overriding concern for grading students fairly (Brookhart, 1993, 2004). This is good, and we have discussed many factors teachers need to consider in fair grading practices. These suggestions, and some new ones, are summarized in Table 12.4 as do's and don'ts. A couple of issues deserve some additional attention.

One issue that many teachers disagree about is how to handle the zeros that students obtain when they do not hand in an assignment or are absent from class for some reason. To clarify the issue, consider the effect of a zero on an average. If you have a zero for 20 per cent of your grade because you didn't hand in any homework, you could have a 60 per cent average on all the tests and fail the class ($60 \times .80 = 48$; $20 \times 0 = 0$; $48 + 0 = 48$). Would this grade be a fair representation of what you knew and how you performed? We think not! One of the worst offences in grading is the indiscriminate use of zeros. In this situation, first consider the fairness of using homework to help determine grades. Even if the assignment has not been completed, does it mean zero achievement or learning? Perhaps a score of 40 would be more appropriate, rather than a zero. You may think that a 40 would encourage students to not do their work because the penalty is not very severe. However, this is a motivational problem that should not be solved by grading practices. Increasingly, provincial policies are developing procedures to address the issue of incomplete work. These policies reflect an attitude that students must have the opportunity to demonstrate their achievement of the learning expectations. This does not mean that

Table 12.4 Do's and Don'ts of Effective Grading

Do	Don't
Use well-thought-out professional judgments.	Depend entirely on number crunching.
Try everything you can to score and grade fairly.	Allow personal bias to affect grades.
Grade according to pre-established learning outcomes and expectations.	Grade on the curve using the class as the norm group.
Provide multiple opportunities for students to demonstrate they have met the learning expectations.	Use single indicators of achievement of the learning expectations.
Clearly inform students and parents of grading procedures at the beginning of the year or term.	Keep grading procedures secret.
Base grades on student performance with respect to the curricular expectations.	Use effort, improvement, attitudes, and motivation for borderline students.
Rely most on current and consistent information.	Penalize poorly performing students early in the year.
Mark, grade, and return assessments to students as soon as possible and with as much feedback as possible.	Return assessments weeks later with little or no feedback.
Review borderline cases carefully; when in doubt, assign the higher grade.	Be inflexible with borderline cases.
Convert scores to the same scale before combining.	Use zero scores indiscriminately when averaging grades.
Consider the relative importance of each assessment to the overall determination of the grade, and weight scores before combining.	Include extra credit assignments that are not related to the learning expectations.
Use a sufficient number of assessments.	Rely on one or two assessments for a term grade.
Be willing to change grades when warranted.	Lower grades for cheating, misbehaving, tardiness, or absence.

students should be given indefinite timelines to finish missing assignments. Rather, teachers should obtain alternative evidence to determine if the students have met the learning expectations. Grades should primarily reflect performance in relation to learning expectations, not non-completion. Many assessment experts, notably Brookhart (2004), contend that only academic performance should be used to determine grades, and this belief is reflected in most provincial grading policies. Another problem of averaging zeros is that student motivation may be negatively affected if it becomes impossible to achieve a passing grade. In this circumstance, the student may simply give up.

A second approach to zeros is to use them only for assessments that have a minuscule effect on the final grade. You can do this by giving the assessment very little weight. However, a better policy is to avoid zeros altogether.

Another issue is lowering grades in response to student cheating (Cizek, 1999, 2003). Obviously, cheating is a very serious offence, and appropriate disciplinary action is warranted. However, lowering grades is not appropriate discipline if there is an extremely negative impact on the grade. Suppose you give a zero to a student when he or she is caught cheating on a major test. Does this score accurately represent the student's knowledge and performance? You are using grades to punish the student. It would be better to find another kind of punishment and retest the student instead.

One of the most difficult challenges teachers face, especially when they first start to teach and test students, is to write tests at the appropriate level of difficulty and emphasis. Suppose you prepare a test and the majority of students do very poorly. There are two primary considerations here. One is that the students just didn't understand. The other is that the test is unfair—that the emphasis on some areas does not match instruction. Sometimes when students do poorly, it reflects more on the inadequacies of your teaching than it does on student achievement! Be open to this possibility and make appropriate changes to reflect student achievement more fairly. One option is to give an improved makeup test.

Finally, be willing to change grades when it is justified. In the first place, mistakes are made in calculating grades. A possible hint of this occurs when a final grade for a student doesn't seem right. In this circumstance, go back over the calculations to be sure there are no mistakes. Second, students sometimes have legitimate arguments about a grade. It is possible to overlook things. In fact, this is probable when you grade a lot of assessments. Be willing to admit that you were wrong and record the best, most accurate score or grade.

By the end of the first term, Ms. Byrd, a new middle school English teacher, had collected and graded a substantial amount of student work, including nine weekly tests, twelve quizzes, nearly thirty homework assignments, a writing journal, a research project, and several in-class assignments. When the time came to turn in student grades, she calculated individual student averages based on all the assignments and tests, the journal, and the research project. She weighted each grade recorded in her gradebook the same, but wasn't confident about how to translate journal and research project grades into numbers to get the overall average. And as she did the grades, she found several students she thought should have done better and others who probably deserved a lower grade, but she went with the numbers.

Questions for Consideration

1. What suggestions do you have for Ms. Byrd to improve her grading practices?
2. What kind of parent reaction do you think she might get when the grades are sent home?

REPORTING STUDENT PROGRESS TO PARENTS

An important function of marks and grades is to provide information that can be shared with parents. Parents are critical to student learning, and effectively reporting student progress can help them better understand their children and know how to provide appropriate support and motivation. Reporting to parents can take many forms, including weekly or monthly reports, phone calls, letters, newsletters, conferences, and, of course, report cards. Although grades are the most common way by which parents keep abreast of student progress, what those grades communicate is usually limited.

Report Cards

The foundation for most reporting systems is the report card. This simple form is constructed to communicate to parents their children's progress. Typically, teachers provide grades, checklists, or numerical scores, along with comments or observations about effort, cooperation, and other behaviours. To effectively communicate, parents must understand what the grades and comments mean. The information needs to be accurately interpreted, and parents need to learn enough to guide improvement efforts. The report card briefly describes the letter grade system in use and provides space for the teacher to give grades and comments for each of the required subjects. Check boxes denote if the student is identified for special supports or programs. The third page has space for students and parents to comment and acknowledge that they have received the report card. They can also indicate if they would like to meet with the teacher to discuss the report.

Most report cards indicate only current status in different subjects, and they do not provide the detail needed for parents to know what to *do* with the information (for alternatives to traditional report cards see Azwell & Schmar, 1995; Brookhart, 2004; Guskey, 1996; Guskey and Bailey, 2001; and Wiggins, 1998). Consequently, you will probably be expected to supplement report cards with other forms of communication.

Written Information

One approach to reporting student progress is to provide some type of written report. You could do this weekly, biweekly, or monthly. In the progress report, include learning targets for the period, copies of rubrics and scoring criteria, student performances on individual assessments, descriptions of student motivation and affect, suggestions for helping the student, and grades if possible. Because this is time-consuming, have a standard form available on which you can quickly record information. School districts often have a common form for these *interim reports*, as they are sometimes called. Older students can be taught to calculate their current grade average in the class. Be sure to include some positive comments. It may be helpful to identify two or three areas that the parents could focus on until the next report. If possible, provide specific expectations of what parents should do at home to help. Be clear in asserting that parents need to be partners in the learning process. If you can individualize these expectations for each student, so much the better, but even a standard list of expectations is good.

Another type of written communication is the informal note or letter. Taking only a minute or two to write a personal note to parents about their child is much appreciated. It shows your concern and caring. Begin such a note with something positive, then summarize progress and suggest an expectation or two for improvements. However, do not use these personal notes to comment only about students who are struggling. A well-timed, honest, and positive note can both inspire and motivate a student, especially if the student is unaccustomed to receiving such positive feedback.

Parent–Teacher Conferences

The parent–teacher conference is the most common way in which teachers communicate with parents about student progress. This is typically a face-to-face discussion, although phone conferences and calls can also be used. In fact, brief phone calls by the teacher to talk with parents, like informal notes, are very well received and appreciated, especially when the calls are about positive progress and suggestions, rather than for disciplinary or other problems.

There are two types of parent–teacher conferences, based on two primary purposes. Group conferences, such as those that occur at back-to-school nights, are conducted in the beginning of the year to communicate school and class policies, class content, evaluation procedures, expectations, and procedures for getting in touch with the teacher. Individual conferences are conducted to discuss the individual student's achievement, progress, or difficulties. Parent–teacher conferences may be initiated by either the teacher or the parent based on these purposes.

Parent–teacher conferences are required in public schools in most provinces. Many schools have formal parent–teacher conference nights, typically after report cards have been distributed. Middle and high school teachers find conferences more difficult because of the number of students, but fewer parents tend to attend conferences for their secondary school students. The checklist provided in Figure 12.7 lists some guidelines for successfully completing parent–teacher conferences.

It is essential to plan the conference and to be prepared. Have all the information well organized in advance, and know what you hope to achieve from the conference. This will probably include a list of areas you want to cover and some questions to ask parents. If possible, find out what parents would like to review before the conference. Organize examples of student work to show progress and performance in relation to learning targets. The conference is an ideal time for pointing out specific areas of strength and weakness that report card grades cannot communicate.

The conference should be a conversation, not a lecture. Listening to parents will help you understand their child better. Even though it is natural to feel anxious about meeting with parents, take a strong, professional stance. Rather than being timid, take charge, but use a friendly and informal tone that encourages parents to participate. Be positive, but also be direct and honest about areas that need improvement. Keep the focus on academic progress rather than student behaviour.

It is always important that elementary teachers discuss student performance in language arts and mathematics. Communication skills are also important to discuss, regardless of the subject matter. These communication skills are essential and should be

---

✓ Plan each conference in advance.
✓ Conduct the conference in a private, quiet, comfortable setting.
✓ Begin with a discussion of positive student performances.
✓ Establish an informal, professional tone.
✓ Encourage parent participation in the conference.
✓ Be frank in reviewing student strengths and weaknesses.
✓ Review language skills.
✓ Review learning targets with examples of student performances that show progress.
✓ Avoid discussing other students and teachers.
✓ Avoid bluffing.
✓ Identify two or three areas to work on in a plan of action.

Figure 12.7 Checklist for Conducting Parent–Teacher Conferences

reviewed. Avoid discussing other students or teachers, and be willing to admit that you don't know an answer to a question. By the end of the conference, you should identify, in consultation with the parents, a course of action or steps to be taken at home and at school. Guskey and Bailey (2001) suggest additional recommendations based on whether the time frame is before, during, or after the conference (see Table 12.5).

Student-Led Conferences

Another kind of reporting to parents involves students acting as leaders in their own conferences (Stiggins, 2005). In a student-led conference, students lead parents through a detailed and direct review of their work. Teachers take the role of facilitator by creating a positive environment in which the conferences can take place, and by preparing students. For

Table 12.5 Recommendations for Effective Parent–Teacher Conferences

Before the Conference . . .	During the Conference . . .	After the Conference . . .
• Encourage parents to review student work at home, note concerns or questions, and bring those to the conference.	• Provide child care, refreshments, and transportation, if needed.	• Provide parents with a telephone number and schedule of specific times so they may call you with concerns.
• Schedule times that are convenient for both working and nonworking parents.	• Show multiple samples of student work and discuss specific suggestions for improvement.	• Follow up on any questions or concerns raised during the conference.
• Notify parents well ahead of scheduled conference times.	• Actively listen and avoid the use of educational jargon.	• Plan a time to meet again, if necessary.
• Provide staff development for new teachers on the purpose of conferences, preparation, and scheduling.	• Communicate expectations and describe how parents can help.	• Encourage parents to discuss the conference with their child.
• Consider alternative locations, such as churches or community centres, for parents' convenience.	• Develop a system for ongoing communication with each parent that recognizes parents as partners.	• Ask parents for written evaluation of the conference and encourage them to make suggestions.
• Print conference schedules and materials in multiple languages, if necessary.	• Provide resources or materials that parents might use at home to strengthen students' skills.	• Debrief with colleagues to look for ways to improve future conferences.

Source: T.R. Guskey & J.M. Bailey (2001). *Developing grading and reporting systems for student learning* (p. 188). Thousand Oaks, CA: Corwin Press. Copyright © 2001 Sage Publications. Reprinted by permission of Corwin Press, Inc.

students to take responsibility for leading a conference with their parents, they need to have reflected on and evaluated their performance, usually through some kind of portfolio assessment. In addition to promoting student responsibility, parents tend to be more involved.

In a student-led conference, students are essentially telling a story about their learning. This helps parents to see progress over time from the student's perspective. In preparing for the conference, students must learn to describe and evaluate their work. This self-reflection promotes additional learning and gives students confidence that they are able to understand their capabilities and achievements. A sense of pride and ownership is developed in the student. See Bailey and Guskey (2001) for more details about setting up and conducting student-led conferences.

SUMMARY

This chapter stressed the importance of a teacher's professional judgment when implementing a grading and reporting system. There is no completely objective procedure for grading. Grading is professional decision making that depends on the teacher's values and beliefs, experience, external pressures, and best subjective judgments. We reviewed the different functions of marking and grading and took a close look at how factors other than academic performance affect grades. The chapter examined the basis of comparison used in grading, as well as approaches to marking and grading. Approaches to combining assessments were presented, along with reporting procedures to parents. Important points include the following:

■ In the classroom, the major function of marking and grading is to provide students with feedback about their performance.

■ Teachers need to provide a sufficient level of detail for marking to be informative for students.

■ In general, report effort, student aptitude, improvement, and attitudes separately from grading.

■ Grades communicate comparison between student performance and the performance of other students (norm-referenced) or between student performance and predetermined standards (criterion-referenced).

■ The major function of norm-referenced systems is to rank and sort students. Student competitiveness is fostered; most teachers find they must do some degree of sorting.

■ The major function of criterion-referenced and outcomes-based systems is to judge students in relation to established levels of performance.

■ Percentage correct is still the most common type of criterion-referenced grading, but rubrics are now also being used for grading purposes. Percentage correct depends on item difficulty.

■ The goal in grading is to provide a fair and accurate record of student performance in relation to learning expectations.

■ Motivation is enhanced when grades are used formatively as well as summatively to communicate internal attributions, self-efficacy, progress on mastery goals, and intrinsic value.

■ Approaches to grading include using letters, percentage-correct measures, pass–fail tests, checklists, standards-based methods, and written descriptions.

■ Determining report card grades requires professional decisions about what to include, how to weight each assessment, and how weighted assessments are combined.

■ Clarify the role homework will play in determining grades; nonacademic factors should only be included for those curriculum that explicitly identify these factors as learning expectations.

- Provide a sufficient number of assessments to obtain a fair and accurate portrait of the student.

- Weight each assessment by the contribution to the goal, instructional time, reliability, consistency, and recency. Give more recent, comprehensive assessments more weight.

- Put all assessments on the same scale before weighting and combining. Weight before combining.

- Consider variation of each assessment if you are combining relative comparisons.

- Be flexible with borderline cases; don't let numbers make what should be professional, subjective decisions.

- Do not use zeros indiscriminately when averaging scores.

- Grades should not be determined by inappropriate student behaviour or cheating.

- Grades should be changed when warranted to reflect the most fair and accurate record of student performance.

- Borderline cases should be decided primarily based on academic performance.

- Reporting student progress to parents can be done by phone, with written materials, and in teacher–parent conferences.

- Reports to parents should be well prepared, with samples of student work to illustrate progress and areas that need further attention.

- Teacher–parent conferences are informal, professional meetings during which teachers discuss progress with parents and determine action steps to be taken.

- Student-led conferences with parents promote student self-evaluation and parent involvement.

SELF-INSTRUCTIONAL REVIEW EXERCISES

1. Indicate whether each of the following refers to norm-referenced (NR) or criterion-referenced (CR) grading.
   a. used to show which students are the worst in a group
   b. average test scores are typically lower
   c. easily adapted from scoring rubrics
   d. uses percentile rank
   e. uses percentage correct
   f. items tend to be easier
   g. determination of standards is subjective
   h. fosters student competitiveness

2. In what ways is teacher professional judgment important in determining the actual standard employed in grading and marking students?

3. What major limitation do most approaches to grading have in common? What can teachers do to avoid this limitation?

4. From the following scenario, summarize what Ms. Gallagher did wrong when she determined her report card grades.

Ms. Gallagher calculated term grades on the basis of a mid-term, a comprehensive final exam, and student participation, which consisted of homework, class participation, and effort. Each component was worth 100 points; they were added and then divided by three to obtain the composite score, which was then translated to a grade.

5. Using the following grading scale and scores, what percentage-correct grade would Ralph and Sally receive?

   80–100: A, 70–79: B, 60–69: C, 50–59: D, <50: F

   Mid-term #1, 20 per cent

   Mid-term #2, 20 per cent

   Final exam, 30 per cent

   Paper, 20 per cent (A = 90, A– = 85, B+ = 78, B = 75, B– = 72, C+ = 68, C = 65, C– = 62)

   Participation, 10 per cent (same scale as paper)

	Ralph	Sally
Mid-term #1, 40 possible points	30 points	35 points
Mid-term #2, 50 possible points	40 points	35 points
Final exam, 200 possible points	170 points	140 points
Paper	B+	C
Participation	A+	A

6. Shaunda is a sixth grader. She is the oldest in a low-income family of six. Because her parents are not home very much, Shaunda takes on responsibilities with her brothers and sisters. The family lives in a small home, so it's hard for Shaunda to get the privacy she needs to do her homework. Consequently, she often does not hand in any homework. She has a very positive attitude toward school, and she is very attentive in class and tries hard to do well. Your class uses the following grading policy: in-class work accounts for 25 per cent of the final grade; homework, 25 per cent; and tests and quizzes, 50 per cent. The grading scale in the school is 86–100, A; 73–85, B; 60–72, C; 50–59, D; <50, F. Shaunda's averages are in-class work, 80 per cent; homework, 30 per cent; and tests and quizzes, 75 per cent. What overall composite per cent correct would Shaunda have? What grade would you give her? Does the grade reflect her academic performance? Should the grading policy be changed?

7. Suppose Greg is a very capable student who does very well on tests (e.g., 90s) but very poorly on homework. He just doesn't want to do work he sees as boring. His homework scores pull his test scores down so that the overall average is B–. What final grade would you give? How is motivation affected?

SUGGESTIONS FOR ACTION RESEARCH

1. Create a grading plan that would make sense for a class you plan to teach. Include a statement of purpose and explain what would be included, how weights would be established, and the final grading scale. Then give the plan to other students and ask them to critique it. If possible, give the plan to a classroom teacher and see how realistic it is.

2. Interview teachers on the subject of grading. Do they use a norm-referenced or criterion-referenced approach or a combination? Ask them about the areas that require professional judgments, like what to do with borderline students, how zeros are used, how to apply extra credit, and the like. Ask them how they use grades to motivate students.

3. Observe a class when graded tests or papers are returned to students. What is their reaction? What do they seem to do with the information?

4. Conduct an experiment by giving some students just grades and other students grades with comments and suggestions for improvement. See if the students react differently. Interview the students to determine if the nature of the feedback affected their motivation.

5. Talk with some parents about their experiences with parent–teacher conferences. What did they get out of it? How could it have been improved? Were the suggestions in Figure 12.8 followed?

Chapter 13

Administering and Interpreting Standardized and Provincial Large-Scale Tests

Descriptive Statistics
- Frequency distribution
- Central tendency
  - mean
  - median
  - mode
- Variability
  - range
  - standard deviation
- Relationship
  - scatterplot
  - correlation

Types of Scores
- Raw scores
- Standard scores
- Grade equivalent scores
- Standards-based percentages

Interpretation
- Standard error of measurement
- Alignment
- Norm-referenced
- Criterion-referenced/outcomes-based

STANDARDIZED AND PROVINCIAL LARGE-SCALE TESTS

Administering
- Importance of following directions

Understanding Reports
- Types
- Interpretive guide

Parent Interpretations
- Preparation needed
- Parent conferences

Preparing Students
- Test-taking skills
- Motivation
- Test anxiety

We first considered standardized and provincial large-scale tests in Chapter 4 in the context of instructional planning. In that chapter, we reviewed different types of large-scale tests and scores to better understand students' initial levels of achievement and aptitude, strengths and weaknesses, and deficiencies, in order to establish learning targets and plan an effective instructional program. We also note that there are few examples of truly standardized testing in Canada. Rather, there are several examples of provincial large-scale tests that have standardized administration procedures. In this chapter, we focus on the other important uses of these provincial testing programs in Canada, including year-to-year system and school accountability and monitoring, inclusion of test results in grading, and interpreting test scores to parents. We will also discuss your role in administering provincial and other external tests. First, we need to review the statistical terms and numerical indices that are commonly used in creating and reporting these test scores. Although your reaction to the term *statistics* may include some anxiety, we emphasize a conceptual understanding that does not require advanced mathematical calculations.

FUNDAMENTAL DESCRIPTIVE STATISTICS

Descriptive statistics are used to describe or summarize a larger number of scores. The description can be in the form of a single number, such as an average score, a table of scores, or a graph. You have seen and read many of these kinds of descriptions (e.g., the average rainfall for a month, the median price of new homes, or a baseball batting average). Descriptive statistics efficiently portray important features of a group of scores to convey essential information for understanding what the scores mean. For standardized and large-scale tests, descriptive statistics are used as the basis for establishing, reporting, and interpreting scores.

Frequency Distributions

The first step in understanding important characteristics of a large set of scores is to organize the scores into a frequency distribution. This distribution simply indicates the number of students who obtained different scores on the test. In a simple **frequency distribution**, the scores are ranked from highest to lowest, and the number of students obtaining each score is indicated. If the scores are organized into intervals, a *grouped frequency distribution* is used. Suppose, for example, that a test had 80 items. Figure 13.1 illustrates the scores received by 20 students, as well as simple and grouped frequency distributions that show the number of students obtaining each score or interval of scores.

Often the scores are presented graphically as a frequency polygon or histogram to more easily explain important features (see Figures 13.2a and 13.2b). The **frequency polygon** is a line graph that is formed by connecting the highest frequencies of each score. The **histogram** is formed by using rectangular columns to represent the frequency of each score.

For a relatively small number of scores, a frequency polygon is usually jagged, as shown in Figure 13.2a. For a large number of scores and test items, the line looks more like a smooth curve. The curve can usually be described as being *normal, positively skewed, negatively skewed,* or *flat*. Typically, for large-scale tests, the curve very closely approximates a normal distribution (a symmetrical, bell-shaped curve) for a large group of students (e.g., for the norming group). If the distribution is **positively skewed**, or skewed to the right, most of the scores are piled up at the lower end, and there are just a few high scores. For a **negatively skewed** distribution, it is just the opposite—most of the scores are high, and there are few low scores (skewed to the left). Negatively skewed distributions are more common with criterion-referenced tests. In a flat distribution, each score is obtained with about the same frequency. Figures 13.3a–13.3d illustrate each of these types of curves.

Student	Score	Simple Frequency Distribution		Grouped Frequency Distribution	
		Score	f	Interval	f
Austin	96				
Tyler	94	96	1	92–96	3
Tracey	92	94	1	86–91	4
Karon	90	92	1	80–85	7
Hannah	90	90	2	74–79	3
Lanie	86	86	2	68–73	3
Allyson	86	84	3		
Felix	84	80	4		
Tryon	84	78	1		
Freya	84	74	2		
Mike	80	70	2		
Mark	80	68	1		
Ann	80				
Kristen	80				
Laura	78				
Megan	74				
Michelle	74				
Kathryn	70				
Don	70				
Jim	68				

Figure 13.1 Frequency Distributions of Test Scores

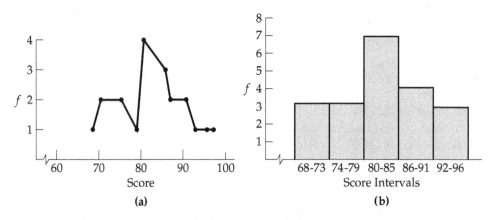

Figure 13.2 Frequency Polygon of Scores (a) and Histogram (b) from Figure 13.1

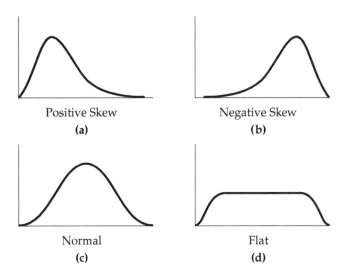

Figure 13.3 Types of Frequency Distributions

Measures of Central Tendency

A measure of central tendency is a single number that is calculated to represent the average or typical score in the distribution. There are three measures of central tendency commonly used in education: the mean, median, and mode. The **mean** is the arithmetic average. It is calculated by adding all the scores in the distribution and then dividing that sum by the number of scores. It is represented by $\bar{X}$ or M. For the distribution of scores in Figure 13.1, the mean is 82.

$$\bar{X} = \frac{\Sigma X}{N}$$

where

$\bar{X}$ = the mean
Σ = the sum of (indicates that all scores are added)
X = each individual score
N = total number of scores

So, for Figure 13.1:

$$\bar{X} = \frac{1640}{20}$$

$$\bar{X} = 82$$

The **median**, represented by *mdn*, is the midpoint, or middle, of a distribution of scores. In other words, 50 per cent of the scores are below the median, and 50 per cent of the scores are above the median. Thus, the median score is at the 50th percentile.

The median is found by rank ordering all the scores, including each score that occurs more than once, and locating the score that has the same number of scores above and below it. For our hypothetical distribution, the median is 82 ([84 + 80] ÷ 2; for an uneven number of scores, it will be a single existing score).

The **mode** is simply the score in the distribution that occurs most frequently. In our distribution, more students scored an 80 than any other score, so 80 is the mode. It is possible to have more than one mode; in fact, in education, distributions are often described as *bimodal*.

In a normal distribution, the mean, median, and mode are the same. In a positively skewed distribution, the mean is higher than the median (skewed positively), and in a negatively skewed distribution, the mean is lower than the median. This is because the mean, unlike the median, is calculated by taking the value of every score into account. Therefore, extreme values affect the mean, whereas the median is not affected by an unusually high or low score.

Measures of Variability

A second type of statistic that is essential in describing a set of scores is a measure of variability. Measures of variability, or dispersion, indicate how much the scores spread out from the mean. If the scores are bunched together close to the mean, then there is little or a small amount of variability. A large or great amount of variability is characteristic of a distribution in which the scores are spread way out from the mean. Two distributions with the same mean can have very different variability, as illustrated in Figure 13.4.

To more precisely indicate the variability, two measures are typically used—the range and standard deviation. The **range** is simply the difference between the highest and lowest score in the distribution (in our example 28; 96 – 68). This is an easily calculated but crude index of variability, primarily because extremely high or low scores result in a range that indicates more variability than is actually present.

A more complicated but much more precise measure of variability is standard deviation. The **standard deviation** (*SD*) is a number that indicates the *average* deviation of the

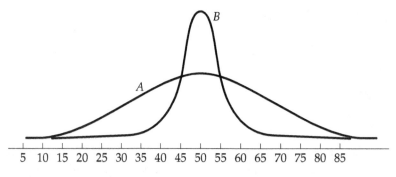

Figure 13.4 Distributions with the Same Mean, Different Variability

scores from the mean. It is calculated by employing a formula that looks difficult but is relatively straightforward. These are the essential steps:

1. Calculate the mean of the distribution.

2. Calculate the difference each score is from the mean (these are called deviation scores).

3. Square each difference score (this makes all the deviation scores positive).

4. Add the squared difference scores.

5. Divide by the total number of scores in the distribution.

6. Calculate the square root of the result of step 5.

These steps are illustrated with our hypothetical set of test scores in Figure 13.5. Essentially, you simply calculate the squared deviation scores, find the *average* squared deviation score, and then take the square root to return to the original unit of measurement. In this distribution, one standard deviation is equal to 7.92. Since most teachers now use a criterion-referenced

Score	(1) Deviation Score	(2) Deviation Score Squared	(3) Squared Deviation Scores Added	(4) Added Scores Divided by *N*	(5) Square Root
96	$96 - 82 = 14$	$14 \times 14 = 196$	+196		
94	$94 - 82 = 12$	$12 \times 12 = 144$	+144		
92	$92 - 82 = 10$	$10 \times 10 = 100$	+100		
90	$90 - 82 = 8$	$8 \times 8 = 64$	+ 64		
90	$90 - 82 = 8$	$8 \times 8 = 64$	+ 64		
86	$86 - 82 = 4$	$4 \times 4 = 16$	+ 16		
86	$86 - 82 = 4$	$4 \times 4 = 16$	+ 16		
84	$84 - 82 = 2$	$2 \times 2 = 4$	+ 4		
84	$84 - 82 = 2$	$2 \times 2 = 4$	+ 4		
84	$84 - 82 = 2$	$2 \times 2 = 4$	+ 4		
80	$80 - 82 = -2$	$-2 \times -2 = 4$	+ 4		
80	$80 - 82 = -2$	$-2 \times -2 = 4$	+ 4		
80	$80 - 82 = -2$	$-2 \times -2 = 4$	+ 4		
80	$80 - 82 = -2$	$-2 \times -2 = 4$	+ 4		
78	$78 - 82 = -4$	$-4 \times -4 = 16$	+ 16		
74	$74 - 82 = -8$	$-8 \times -8 = 64$	+ 64		
74	$74 - 82 = -8$	$-8 \times -8 = 64$	+ 64		
70	$70 - 82 = -12$	$-12 \times -12 = 144$	+144		
70	$70 - 82 = -12$	$-12 \times -12 = 144$	+144		
68	$68 - 82 = -14$	$-14 \times -14 = 196$	+196	1256/20 = 62.8	$\sqrt{62.8} = 7.92$
			= 1256		

Figure 13.5 Steps in Calculating Standard Deviation

grading system, standard deviation is not very helpful for classroom testing. However, because of the relationship between standard deviation and the normal curve, it is fundamental to understanding standardized and provincial test scores. In a normal distribution, the meaning of the term *one standard deviation* is the same in regard to percentile rank, regardless of the actual value of standard deviation for that distribution. Thus, +1SD is always at the 84th percentile, +2SD is at the 98th percentile, −1SD is at the 16th percentile, and −2SD is at the 2nd percentile in every normal distribution.

Standardized tests commonly use a norming group to obtain a score distribution that is approximately normal. These norming groups make it possible to compare student scores to the norm group distribution in terms of percentile rank and to compare your relative standing on different tests. For instance, suppose a norm group took a standardized test, and, based on their performance, a raw score of 26 items answered correctly was one standard deviation above the mean for the norm group (84th percentile). When a student in your class gets the same number of items correct (26), the percentile reported is the 84th. Obviously, if the norm group were different and 26 items turned out to be at +2SD, then the student's score would be reported at the 98th percentile. You would also know that a score at one standard deviation on one test is the same in terms of relative standing as one standard deviation on another test. Most important for standardized tests, standard deviation is used to compute standard scores and other statistics that are used for interpretation and analysis. A fundamental difference between provincial testing programs and other available standardized tests is the use of norming groups. It is important to know that provincial testing programs in Canada do not use norming groups in their provincial testing programs; however, norming groups are used in many of the standardized psychological tests or commercial external aptitude and achievement tests (e.g., Canadian Test of Basic Skills) that are available.

Measures of Relationship

It is often helpful, even necessary, to know the degree to which two scores from different measures are related. Typically, this degree of relationship is estimated by what is called a *correlation coefficient*. Correlations are reported in standardized-test technical manuals for validity and reliability. An important principle in interpreting test scores, standard error of measurement, is also determined from correlation.

Scatterplot. The **scatterplot**, or *scattergram*, is a graphic representation of relationship. When used in education, a scatterplot can give you a descriptive picture of relationship by forming a visual array of the intersections of students' scores on two measures. As illustrated in Figure 13.6, each measure is rank ordered from lowest to highest on a different axis. Use the two scores from each student to establish a point of intersection. When this is completed for all students, the resulting pattern provides a general indication of the direction and strength of the relationship. The direction of the pattern indicates whether there is a positive, negative, or curvilinear relationship, or no relationship. It is positive if scores on one variable increase with increases in the other scores, and it is negative (inverse) if scores on one variable increase as scores on the other measure decrease. If the

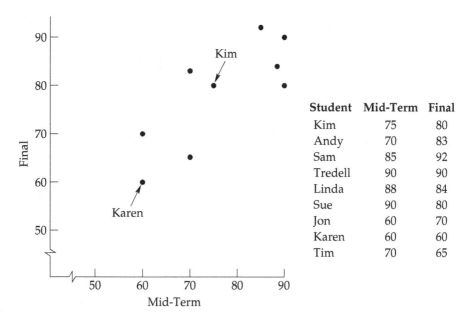

Student	Mid-Term	Final
Kim	75	80
Andy	70	83
Sam	85	92
Tredell	90	90
Linda	88	84
Sue	90	80
Jon	60	70
Karen	60	60
Tim	70	65

Figure 13.6 Scatterplot of Relationship between Two Tests

pattern looks like a U shape, it is curvilinear; and if it is a straight line or has no particular pattern at all, there is little if any relationship.

Scatterplots help to identify intersections that are not typical and that lower the correlation coefficient; they also help to identify curvilinear relationships. However, these scatterplots are rarely reported in test manuals. Typically, these manuals report the correlation coefficients.

Correlation Coefficient. The **correlation coefficient** is a number that is calculated to represent the direction and strength of a relationship. The number ranges between −1 and +1. A high positive value (e.g., +.85 or +.90) indicates a high positive relationship, a low negative correlation (e.g., −.10 or −.25) represents a low negative relationship, and so forth. The *strength* of the relationship is independent from the *direction*. Thus, a positive or negative value indicates direction, and the value of the correlation (from 0 to 1 or from 0 to −1) determines strength. A perfect correlation is designated by either +1 or −1. As the value approaches these perfect correlations, it becomes stronger, or higher. That is, a correlation is stronger as it changes from .2 to .5 to .6, and also as it changes from −.2 to −.5 to −.6. A correlation of −.8 is stronger (higher) than a correlation of +.7.

There are several different types of correlation coefficients. The most common is the Pearson product-moment correlation coefficient. This is the one most likely to be used in test manuals. It is represented by r.

We emphasize four cautions when interpreting correlations. First, correlation does not imply causation. Just because two measures are related, it does not mean that one *caused* the other. Other factors may be involved in causation, and the direction of the cause is probably unclear. Second, be alert for curvilinear relationships, because most correlation coefficients, such as the Pearson, assume that the relationship is linear. Third, also be alert to **restricted range**. If the values of one measure are truncated, with a small range, it will probably result in a low correlation. Given a full range of scores, the correlation would be higher. Fourth, relationships expressed as correlation coefficients generally are less precise than the number would suggest. That is, a very high correlation of .80 does not mean that 80 per cent of the relationship is accounted for. If you think of correlation as predicting one score from another score, you will see how relatively imprecise it can be. Examine the scatterplots of various correlations in Figure 13.7. You will see that in a moderate relationship (c), if you try to predict the value of variable B on the y axis, say, from a score of 10 for variable A, a range of approximately 5 to 20 is predicted.

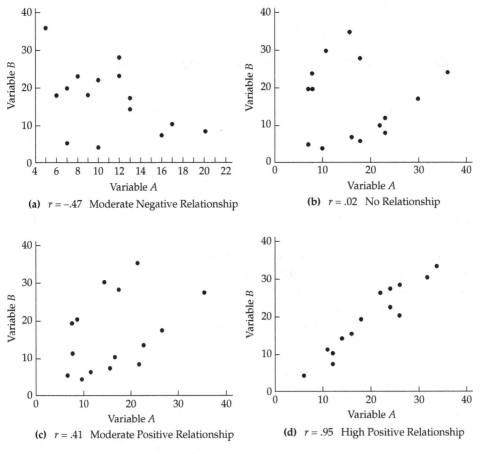

Figure 13.7 Scatterplots of Various Correlations

TYPES OF DERIVED STANDARDIZED TEST SCORES

Three kinds of standardized test scores were introduced in Chapter 4: raw scores, percentile rank, and grade equivalent. Raw scores are simply the number of items answered correctly. Raw scores alone are not as versatile as other scores that are *derived* or *transformed* from these raw scores. One easily understood derived score, for example, is per cent correct. Percentile rank and grade equivalent scores are also derived in the sense that they are computed from raw score distributions. Additional derived scores are commonly used with standardized tests and the provincial tests administered throughout Canada, and we will consider these in this chapter; we will also discuss percentile ranks and grade equivalents. Descriptions of the various types of test scores you will encounter are summarized in Table 13.1. Most provincial testing programs in Canada use either per cent correct or scale scores, or a modified scale score that has been categorized into a level of performance. Commercial external tests use one and more commonly, several, forms of standardized test scores.

Per Cent Correct. The simplest and most easily calculated score is the per cent correct score, which indicates the proportion of items each student has correctly answered. While common in classroom testing and assessment, per cent correct scoring is rarely used for

Table 13.1 Types of Derived Standardized Test Scores

Type	Description
Per Cent Correct	Number of points obtained, divided by the total number of points possible and multiplied by 100
Percentile Rank	Percentage of norm group examinees who scored at or below the given score
Grade Equivalent	Score that indicates the median score of students in the norm group at the same grade and month
Standard Scores	
z-score	Score based on a distribution with a mean of 0 and a standard deviation of 1
T-score	Score based on a distribution with a mean of 50 and a standard deviation of 10
NCE	Score based on a distribution with a mean of 50 and a standard deviation of 21.06
Stanine	Score based on dividing the normal distribution into nine parts; each score describes one part
Deviation IQ	Score based on a distribution with a mean of 100 and a standard deviation of 15 or 16
Scale	Unique scores to indicate growth over several years in relation to the norm group or standards-based results

standardized testing because the scores do not have any of the features of standard scores. In particular, the same percentage scores may have very different meanings depending on the difficulty of a specific test or on the distribution of test scores.

Percentile Rank. Percentile rank scores are a measure of the proportion of people who scored less than a given score. Hence, the actual score that a student receives is only used to determine the ranking of the student in comparison to all other students. A student who has a percentile rank of 95 did not necessarily score 95 per cent on the test. Rather, 95 per cent of the students who wrote the test received a lower score. Similarly, a percentile rank of 50 does not represent an actual score of 50 per cent. In this case, the student received the median score and 50 per cent of other students scored below this score.

Deviation IQ and Standard Age Scores. For many years, the results of IQ and general ability testing have been reported on a scale that has a mean of 100 and a standard deviation of 15 or 16. Originally, IQ scores were actual intelligent quotients, calculated by dividing mental age by chronological age and multiplying this ratio by 100. Today, IQ scores are determined like other derived standard scores. For each age group in a norming sample, the raw scores are converted to z-scores, then to deviation IQ scores by multiplying the z-score by 15 or 16 and adding that product to 100. Most test publishers use terms such as the student's *ability* or *aptitude*, or refer to *standard age* scores rather than to IQ because intelligence refers to many other traits besides academic ability or reasoning. Some of these tests have a standard deviation as small as 12 or as large as 20. This is one reason that it is inappropriate to compare the scores of two individuals who have taken different tests.

Grade Equivalent Scores. Grade equivalents (GEs) were also introduced in Chapter 4. These scores are much like scale scores, except that the unit is expressed in grade levels and months. As we pointed out earlier, GEs are useful only in indicating growth or progress; they should not be used for grade placement. In addition, most GEs are determined by interpolation. That is, a test may be given to beginning grade 4 students, and the median score for that group will be assigned a grade equivalent of 4.0. The same test might be given to beginning grade 5 students, with the median score given a GE of 5.0. No other tests are given, but scores are still reported in months (e.g., 4.2 or 4.8). If the students in grade 4 (month 2 and month 8) were not given the test, how was the median of each group determined? The answer is that the medians were interpolated or estimated from existing scores. This means that the reported scores of, say, 4.1 or 4.6, are only estimates. For some tests, GEs are extrapolated beyond the grade levels actually tested. Thus, a test may be given to students in grades 3, 4, and 5, but GEs may range from 2.0 to 7.0 and beyond. Extrapolated scores are less accurate than interpolated ones, and they should be interpreted cautiously.

Figure 13.8 shows a normal distribution with the corresponding standard deviation units, percentiles, and selected standard scores.

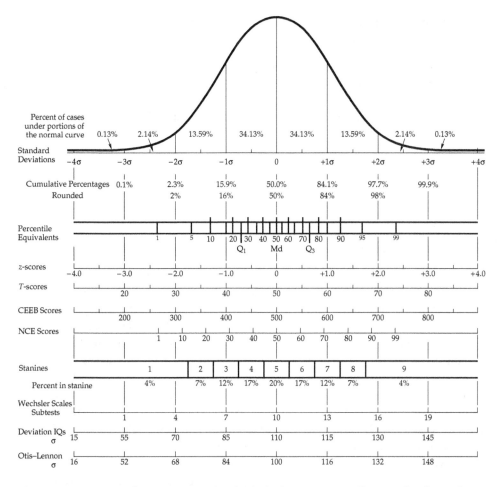

Figure 13.8 Normal Curve, Standard Deviations, Percentiles, and Selected Standard Scores

Source: Test service notebook no. 148 (p. 2). Used courtesy of The Psychological Corporation. Harcourt Brace Jovanovich, Publishers. Reproduced by permission. All rights reserved.

Standard Scores

Standard scores are derived from raw scores in units based on the standard deviation of the distribution. They are obtained by using a linear transformation, which simply changes the value of the mean and one standard deviation, or a nonlinear, normalizing transformation based on the percentiles of the normal curve. Most standard scores reported with standardized tests are normalized, though we will briefly review two common linear transformations, *z*-scores and *T*-scores. The term *standard* in this context does not mean a specific level of performance or expectation. Rather, it refers to the standard normal curve as the basis for interpretation. Standard scores have equal units between different values, which allows for additional statistical procedures.

z-Scores. The simplest and most easily calculated standard score is the **z-score**, which indicates how far a score lies above or below the mean in standard deviation units. Since $1SD = 1$, a z-score of 1 is one standard deviation unit above the mean. The formula for computing z-scores is relatively straightforward if you know the value of one standard deviation:

$$z\text{-score} = \frac{X - \bar{X}}{SD}$$

where

X = any raw score
$\bar{X}$ = mean of the raw scores
SD = standard deviation of the raw score distribution

For example, a z-score for 90 in our hypothetical distribution would be 1.01 ([90 − 82] ÷ 7.92). If the raw score is less than the mean, the z-score will be negative (e.g., the z-score for 70 in our distribution of 20 students would be −1.52 ([70 − 82] ÷ 7.92).

Most z-scores are calculated through the **linear transformation** given above, and the distribution of z-scores will be identical to the distribution of raw scores. It is also possible to *normalize* the raw score distribution when converting to z-scores. This transforms the distribution to a normal one, regardless of what the raw score distribution looked like. If the raw score distribution is normal, then using the formula will also result in a normal distribution of z-scores. For most standardized tests, the standard scores are normalized. Thus a z-score of 1 is at the 84th percentile, a z-score of 2 is at the 98th percentile, and so forth. This normalization is not done for provincial testing programs.

While z-scores are important for transforming scores into other types of scores, they are rarely used by themselves. It is very difficult for students, parents, and even educators to understand that a score of 0 is average. Negative scores are even more difficult to score. Thus, most standardized and large-scale tests report their results using other standard scoring systems. Because the z-score distribution has a standard deviation equal to 1, these scores can easily be transformed to other standard scores that will only have positive values (e.g., T-scores, NCEs, stanines, and scale scores).

T-Scores. **T-scores** are the same as z-scores except that the *T*-score distribution has a different mean, 50, and a different standard deviation, 10. *T*-scores are obtained by using a simple formula to convert from z-scores:

$$T\text{-score} = 50 + 10(z)$$

Thus, a *T*-score of 60 is the same as a z-score of 1; both are at the 84th percentile. Like z-scores, *T*-scores may be straight linear transformations from the raw score distribution, or normalized.

Normal Curve Equivalent. The **normal curve equivalent (NCE)** is a normalized standard score that has a mean of 50 and a standard deviation of 21.06. The reason for selecting 50 for the mean and 21.06 for the standard deviation was so that NCE scores, like percentiles, would range from 1 to 99. The percentiles of 1, 50, and 99 are equivalent to NCEs of 1, 50, and 99. However, at other points on the scale, NCEs are not the same as percentiles. For example:

NCE	Percentile
90	97
75	88
25	12
10	3

For someone unfamiliar with measurement principles, it is fairly easy to confuse NCEs with percentiles because they convert the same range of scores (1–99). Thus, be careful when explaining to parents what NCEs mean. So why are NCEs used at all? Because they are standard scores (percentiles are not), they can, like other standard scores, be used statistically for research and evaluation purposes.

Stanines. One historically popular type of standard score for standardized tests is the stanine. A **stanine** indicates approximately where a score lies in relation to the normal curve of the norming group. Stanines are reported as single-digit scores from 1 to 9. A stanine of 5 indicates that the score is in the middle of the distribution; stanines 1, 2, and 3 are considered below average; 7, 8, and 9 are above average; and stanines of 4, 5, and 6 are about average. Think of each stanine as representing a part of the normal curve, as illustrated in Figure 13.8. Although there is a precise, statistically determined procedure for determining stanines, it is practical to use the range from 1 to 9 as a simple, easily understood way to indicate relative standing. Each stanine covers a specific area of the normal curve in terms of percentiles:

Stanine	Percentile Rank	Stanine	Percentile Rank
9	96 or higher	4	23 to 39
8	89 to 95	3	11 to 22
7	77 to 88	2	4 to 10
6	60 to 76	1	Below 4
5	40 to 59		

Notice that there is a different percentage of scores in stanines 5, 6, 7, 8, and 9. This is because the width of the stanine is the same in relation to the curve of the normal distribution. You can think of stanines as having a mean of 5 with a standard deviation of 2. Because they are normalized, stanines from conceptually similar but different tests, such as aptitude and achievement tests, can be compared. Meaningful differences in performance are indicated when the scores differ by at least two stanines.

A disadvantage of the stanine is that even though you know the area of the normal curve the score lies in, you don't know what part of this area the score is in. In this sense, stanines are less precise than percentile rank. For example, percentile scores of 42 and 58 have the same stanine score of 5. However, when stanine scores differ by more than 1, there is probably also a meaningful difference in achievement.

Scaled Score. Most standardized tests use what is called a **scaled score** (also called the *scale level*, or *growth* score) to show year-to-year progress in achievement, to compare different levels of the same test, or to highlight a unique testing program. Each test publisher uses a different scale. When used to measure growth, the higher scores are normally associated with higher grade levels. For example, the Canadian Test of Basic Skills (CTBS) uses a score of 200 to indicate the median performance of grade 4 students, 150 as the median for grade 1 students, and 250 as the median for grade 8 students. The complete scale across grade levels is as follows:

Grade:	K	1	2	3	4	5	6	7	8	9
Scaled Score:	130	150	168	185	200	214	227	239	250	260

Thus, the median performance for grade 3 students is assigned a score of 185, and so on. These median and mean scores and associated standard deviations provide anchors against which a student's progress can be compared. This makes it possible to use developmental standard scores to plot performance from year to year. However, because they are more abstract than other scores, they are relatively difficult to interpret.

Other Scaled Scores. The advantage of standard scores—being able to convert raw scores to scores directly related to the normal curve and percentile rank—is also a disadvantage because there are so many different standard scores. None of the Canadian provincial testing programs use any of the standardized scores described above when reporting results. For example, the Ontario Secondary School Literacy Test (OSSLT) uses a unique scale ranging from 200 to 400, even though there are only about 50 questions on the test. The British Columbia scholarship scores are reported on a scale ranging from 200 to 800, with a mean of 500. The use of such scaled scores prevents students, teachers, and parents from making inappropriate comparisons with other similar scales, while creating a scale that can be used for reporting information. For example, if the OSSLT used a scale of 0 to 100, people would likely compare the reported scores to a percentage score, thinking that a score of 65 meant 65 per cent.

INTERPRETING STANDARDIZED AND PROVINCIAL LARGE-SCALE TESTS

Armed with a basic knowledge of important descriptive statistics and types of scores, you can more accurately understand, interpret, and use your students' standardized and provincial large-scale test scores. We begin our discussion with two more technical issues—standard error of measurement and alignment of the test with curriculum, teaching, and classroom assessments. Then we will look at issues involved in norm- and criterion-referenced based interpretation before examining some actual test score reports.

Standard Error of Measurement

As we have stressed throughout this book, every test has some degree of error. Chapter 3 introduced the relationship between error and reliability. Basically, as error increases, reliability decreases. But we can directly measure reliability only in a test; we cannot know what type or amount of error has influenced a student's score. Therefore, we estimate the degree of error that is probable, given the reliability of the test. This degree of error is estimated mathematically and is reported as the **standard error of measurement (SEM)**.

SEM is determined by a formula that takes into account the reliability and standard deviation of the test. If a student took a test many times, the resulting scores would look like a normal distribution. That is, sometimes the student would get "good" error, resulting in a higher score, and sometimes the student would get "bad" error, resulting in a lower score. If we assume that the student's *true* score is the mean of this hypothetical distribution, then we can use this as a starting point for estimating the *actual* true score. From our knowledge of the normal curve and standard deviation, 68 per cent of the time, the actual true score would be between one standard deviation of the student's normal curve of many testings; 96 per cent of the time, the actual true score would fall within two standard deviations of this distribution. We call the standard deviation of this hypothetical normal distribution the *standard error of measurement*.

For example, if a student's GE score on a test was 3.4, and the test had a standard error of measurement of .2, then we would interpret the student's true performance with 68 per cent confidence, to be 3.4 ± .2; with 96 per cent confidence, we would interpret the student's true score to be 3.4 ± .4. In other words, the standard error of measurement creates an interval, and we can be confident that the student's true score lies within this interval. Different degrees of confidence are related to the number of standard errors of measurement included; these intervals can be thought of as **confidence bands**. Of course, we do not know *where* in the interval the true score lies, so we are most accurate in interpreting the performance in terms of the interval, not as a single score.

The idea of interpreting single scores as bands or intervals has important implications. If you are drawing a conclusion about the performance of a single student, your thinking should be something like this: "Trevor's performance in mathematics places him between the 86th and 94th percentiles," rather than, "Trevor's score is at the 90th percentile." This will give you a more realistic and accurate basis for judging Trevor's real or actual level of performance. When comparing two scores from the same test battery, a meaningful difference in performance is indicated only when the intervals, as established by one standard error of measurement (68 per cent confidence interval) or two standard errors of measurement (95 per cent confidence interval), do not overlap. Thus, it would be wrong to conclude that a student's language achievement score of 72 is higher than the reading score of 70 if the standard error is two or more. The same logic is needed for comparing ability with achievement or for comparing the scores of different individuals on the same test. That is, if the bands overlap, then you should conclude that there is no difference between the scores.

Fortunately, major test publishers report standard errors of measurement to help you interpret the scores properly, and often they are displayed visually in the form of a shaded band surrounding the score. Often these errors of measurement are reported in a separate *technical manual*. Unfortunately, there is usually a slightly different standard error of measurement for each subtest and for different ranges of scores. Thus, in the technical manual, there are tables of standard errors of measurement. We don't want to suggest that you consult these tables for each student and for each score. However, it may be helpful to use this information when making decisions about referral for identification for special education and placement into special programs. Many standardized test reporting formats display the appropriate standard error of measurement on each student's report, although you will need to look at a key to know the exact nature of the band.

Alignment

One of the most critical aspects of interpreting standardized and large-scale test scores is to determine the extent to which the test content is aligned with the curriculum, with your teaching, and with your classroom assessments. Provincial testing programs in Canada are generally very well aligned with the curriculum because these tests are developed within the ministry of education, which is also responsible for provincial curriculum. Furthermore, practising teachers are often involved in developing these provincial assessments. Commercial standardized tests typically fit less well with the provincial curriculum.

If the content, emphasis, and cognitive level of the standardized or provincial test match well with your instruction, the curriculum, and classroom assessment, then there is strong alignment. With strong alignment, external test scores serve as a check on the effectiveness of instruction. With weak alignment, scores on external tests have some implications, but because of a lack of emphasis on the same content and cognitive level, these implications are not as clear. For example, if we know that there is a good match and the scores are low, there is reason to learn why. High test scores with a good match validate that students are indeed learning the content as intended.

Teacher's Corner

Dodie Whitt

I feel as though standardized testing has improved my teaching in so many ways. Not only am I accountable for my students' learning during the course of one academic year, but I am also accountable for long-term learning due to the data that are kept from the standardized tests. This is a challenge and one that keeps me constantly evaluating and re-evaluating my teaching methods and practices.

Interpretation of Norm-Referenced Standardized Tests

Most commercial standardized tests are designed to provide norm-referenced interpretations. You can compare performance to a well-defined *norming* or reference group and determine relative strengths and weaknesses of students. When comparing an individual's performance to the norm group, the overall competence of this group is critical in determining relative position. Ranking high with a low-performing group may indicate, in an absolute sense, less competence than ranking low in a high-performing group. Thus, the exact nature of the norming group is important, and several types of norms can be used.

Types of Standardized Test Norms. Norms are sets of scores. Each type of norm differs with respect to the characteristics of the students who comprise the norm group. The most commonly used type are **national norms**. These norms are based on a nationally representative sample of students. Generally, testing companies do a good job of obtaining national samples, but there is still variation from one test to another based on school cooperation and the cost of sampling. As well, most testing companies oversample minorities and other underrepresented groups. Thus, one reason that national norms from different tests are not comparable is that the sampling procedures do not result in equivalent norm groups. For example, you should never conclude that one student has greater knowledge or skill than another because her reading score on the Canadian Test of Basic Skills is at the 90th percentile, compared to another student who scored at the 80th percentile on the Canadian Achievement Test (there would also be differences in the content of the items). On the other hand, most testing companies use the same norm group for both achievement and aptitude batteries, which allows direct achievement/aptitude and subtest score comparisons.

There are also many different *special group norms*. These types of norms comprise subgroups from the national sample. For example, special norms may be available for large cities, school districts of high or low socio-economic status, suburban areas, special grade levels, norms for tests given at different times of the year (usually fall and spring), and other specific subgroups. Whenever a special group norm is used, the basis for comparison changes, and the same raw score on a test will probably be reported as a different percentile rank. For instance, because both achievement and aptitude are related to socio-economic status (higher socio-economic status equals higher achievement), school districts that contain a larger percentage of students of high socio-economic status than is true for the entire population (and hence, the national norm group) almost always score above the mean with national norms. Conversely, districts with a high percentage of students of low socio-economic status typically have difficulty scoring above the mean. However, if the district of high socio-economic status is compared to suburban norms, the percentile ranks of the scores will be lower; for districts of low socio-economic-status, the percentiles will be higher if the norm group is from districts of low socio-economic status. Understandably, then, suburban districts almost always want to use national norms. However, if these districts are compared to a norm sample of other high-income districts, their percentile will be much lower and may be below the mean. Hence, it is always important to consider the norming sample that is being used for comparison.

One common misconception is that students who test in the spring of the year obtain a higher percentile rank than students who test in the fall. However, each of these testing times has a separate norm group, so that a student is compared only to those in the norming group who took the test at the same time during the year. However, a grade equivalency or developmental score would be higher for students taking the spring test because they would have greater knowledge than students in the same grade level in the fall.

Another type of norm is one that is for a single school district. These are called *local norms*. Local norms are helpful in making intraschool comparisons and in providing information that is useful for student placement in appropriate classes. If you use commercial norm-referenced standardized tests to support your teaching, it is very important for you to examine standardized test reports and know the type of norm that is used to determine percentile rank and standard scores.

Using Test Norms. Once you clearly understand the type of norm group that is used, you will be in a position to interpret the scores of your students more accurately. In making these interpretations and using the norms correctly, adhere to the following suggestions (summarized in Figure 13.9):

1. Remember That Norms Are Not Outcomes or Expectations. Norm-referenced test scores show how a student compares to a reference group. The scores do not tell you how much the student knows in terms of specific learning expectations, or how much students should know. Students who score below the norm (that is, below the mean score) may or may not be meeting your learning outcomes and expectations. That determination is criterion-referenced.

2. Match Your Intended Use of the Scores with the Appropriate Norm Group. As we have discussed, there are many different types of norms. Determine your intended use, and then use the norm group that will provide you with the most valid comparison. For determining general strengths and weaknesses and aptitude/achievement discrepancies, national norms are appropriate. If you want to use the scores to select students for a special class, local norms are probably best. When you counsel a student regarding a career, national norms will not be as helpful as norms more specific to the field.

3. Sampling for the Norm Group Should Be Representative and Well Described. Supplement the test publisher's description of the norming group with an examination of the specific nature of the sampling that was used. This can be found in the technical manual for the test. Often, we need to be sure that specific subgroups are represented in the proper proportion. You can determine this only if the sampling procedures are clearly

---

✓ Are norms differentiated from outcomes and expectations?

✓ Is the type of norm matched with the intended use?

✓ Is the norm group sampling representative and well described?

✓ Are the test norms current?

Figure 13.9 Checklist for Using Norm-Referenced Test Scores

described and relevant characteristics of the sample are provided, such as gender, age, race, socio-economic status, and geographic location.

4. If Possible, Use the Most Recently Developed Test Norms. Standardized test norms are developed based on sampling one year, and this serves as the reference group for several more years. Thus, you may well use the same test that was normed in, say, 2003 with your students in 2010. The performance of your students in 2010 is compared to how well students performed on the test in 2003. Over the years between the norming and current testing, the curriculum can change to be more consistent with the test, and your student population can change. These factors affect the current scores and make it possible for all school divisions to be rated above average. For the norming group, 50 per cent of the students are below average. This distribution is set so that in the future more than 50 per cent of the students could obtain a raw score higher than the mean raw score of the norming group. In general, the most current norms provide the most accurate information. Be wary of using old test norms that have not been updated.

The SAT Reasoning Test in the U.S. provides an interesting illustration of how the date of the norming group makes an impact. Until 1995, the norming group for the SAT consisted of 10 000 college-bound students tested in 1941. Every year between 1941 and 1995, each student who took the SAT was compared to the 1941 norm group. This resulted in a decline in SAT averages because the population of students taking the SAT more recently had a much larger percentage of lower-ability students. The decline was a function of a population of students taking the SAT that was different from the original norming group. Today, the SAT has been *renormed* to more adequately reflect the population of students who currently take the test.

Criterion-Referenced/Outcomes-Based Interpretations

As we previously discussed, criterion-referenced/outcomes-based interpretations compare student performance to established expectations for student performance, rather than to other students. Some standardized tests and almost all of the provincial large-scale tests are only criterion-referenced (they may also be called objectives-based, absolute, domain-referenced, or content-referenced tests, though the technical meaning may differ). These tests are designed to provide a valid measure of skills and knowledge in specific areas. Most norm-referenced tests also provide criterion-referenced information by indicating the number of items answered correctly in specific areas, but because the primary purpose of these tests is to compare individuals, they typically do not provide information as meaningful as what criterion-referenced/outcomes-based tests provide. Keep in mind that there is a difference between a criterion-referenced/outcomes-based standardized *test* and criterion-referenced/outcomes-based *interpretations*.

Whether the test is norm- or criterion-referenced, each skill or area for which a score is reported must be described in detail. With delimited and well-defined learning expectations, the score can more easily be interpreted to suggest some degree of mastery.

Without a clearly defined expectation, such interpretation is questionable at best. Typically, criterion-referenced/outcomes-based tests do the best job of this because it is essential to their primary purpose.

Your judgment concerning the degree of a student's mastery is usually based on the percentage of correctly answered items that measure a specific expectation. For provincial assessments, the meaning that is given to the percentage of correct answers is generally made by a group of teachers who have been selected to participate in a *standard setting* panel. Standard setting is a formal process in which teachers conduct a review of the definition of the expectations and the difficulty of the items, and, based on this review and the panel's professional judgment, test scores are aligned with levels of expected test performance. Individual teachers may also use a similar process to identify their own levels of expected performance for students, and, in some districts, a team, a group of educators, or parents may set standards. An important aspect of making this decision is having a sufficient number of items to adequately measure the trait. Criterion-referenced/outcomes-based tests are designed to have enough items for each score, but norm-referenced tests may or may not have enough items.

Although results are not reported as percentile ranks or standard scores, there may be information in the technical manual about the difficulty of items or average scores of various groups. This information is helpful when determining the correspondence between the percentage of items answered correctly and mastery of the skill or content area. One approach to doing this is to set in your mind a group of "minimally competent" students in reference to the target, then see how many items these students answer correctly. If the mean number of correct answers is, say, seven of ten, then your "standard" becomes 70 per cent of the items. It may be that the level is set in relation to a goal for students by the end of the year, or you may set standards based on how others have performed in the past. Regardless of your approach, your interpretation is largely a matter of professional judgment, so think carefully about the criteria that are used.

Due to the external accountability and monitoring that is attached to most provincial testing programs in Canada, provincial test results are often reported simply by indicating the percentage of students that "passed" or "met or exceeded" established provincial expectations. For example, if students need to obtain a scaled score of 300 to pass, which is used in the Ontario Secondary School Literacy Test (OSSLT) in Ontario, the result reported for a specific class or school is the percentage of students tested that scored 300 or above. This simple statistic is helpful for general reporting, but it is not very helpful to teachers, especially if the result is for an extensive amount of material. Thus, obtaining a "pass" or "proficient" score is outcomes-based in the sense that an established standard has been used to report results, but such information is not diagnostic. To fully interpret the results, teachers need to know how the test was designed, what subscales are used, and how the standard of expected performance was determined. Disaggregating results to specific outcomes provides information most likely to be used by teachers in their instruction. Unfortunately, most provincial tests do not have enough test items to provide accurate scores about student performance on specific learning outcomes.

A very recent development that has implications for teachers is that some testing companies now offer specialized tests that they claim will assess knowledge and skills that align with the provincial tests. Online assessments tied directly to provincial outcomes are becoming increasingly popular, and many also have instructional resources integrated with the results. But beware! These companies have rushed to provide these services, sometimes with little attention to quality indicators such as reliability and validity. Review the test items and blueprints carefully for proper use and interpretation.

School districts may require teachers to use external assessments on a regular schedule—for example, monthly or every nine weeks. The idea is to provide more formative data to pinpoint instructional resources. Examples of such assessments include the Comprehension, Attitude, Strategies and Interests (CASI) test from Nelson and the Developmental Reading Assessment (DRA) from Pearson. As with other commercially available tests, however, the psychometric qualities of these tests may not be established. Once again, your own judgments are needed.

With these recommendations, keep the following suggestions in mind when making criterion-referenced/outcomes-based interpretations from standardized tests (summarized in Figure 13.10):

1. Determine the Primary Purpose of the Test—Is It Norm- or Criterion-Referenced/Outcomes-Based? Criterion-referenced/outcomes-based tests are designed for criterion-referenced/outcomes-based interpretations. As long as the descriptions of the traits match your learning expectations, these types of tests will provide the best information. Be wary of using norm-referenced tests for criterion-referenced/outcomes-based interpretations.

2. Examine the Clarity and Specificity of the Definitions and Traits Measured. For each score that is reported, you require an adequate definition of what is being measured. Norm-referenced tests tend to define what is measured more broadly, while criterion-referenced/outcomes-based tests define what is measured specifically. You may need to consult the technical manual to get sufficient detail of the definition to make a valid judgment about the match between what the tests says it is measuring and what you want measured. There should be good content-related evidence of validity to demonstrate an adequate sampling of content or skills from a larger domain.

3. Be Sure There Is a Sufficient Number of Items to Make a Valid Decision. The general rule is to have at least six to eight different test items for each outcome or

---

✓ Is the primary purpose of the test norm- or criterion-referenced/outcomes-based?
✓ Are measured targets delimited and clearly defined?
✓ Are there enough items to measure each expectation adequately?
✓ Is the difficulty level of the items matched with the learning expectation?

Figure 13.10 Checklist for Using Criterion-Referenced/Outcomes-Based Test Scores

expectation. For learning expectations that are less specific, more than ten items may be needed. In some norm-referenced tests you may see skills listed with as few as three or four items. This is too few for making definite conclusions, though this may suggest a need for further investigation.

4. Examine the Difficulty of Items and Match This to Your Expectations. Norm-referenced tests may not use easy items because they do not discriminate among students, whereas criterion-referenced/outcomes-based tests tend to have somewhat easier items so that students who have met the expectation will do well on the items. This means that the difficulty of the items may differ considerably with the same definition for the target. Inspect the items carefully and use your knowledge of their difficulty in setting standards.

Figure 13.11 summarizes differences between norm- and criterion-referenced/outcomes-based interpretations.

Norm-Referenced	Criterion-Referenced/Outcomes-Based
• Based on how an individual compares to others	• Based on performance compared to absolute levels or standards of proficiency
• Nature of comparison or "norm" group critical	• Needs clearly defined learning expectations and standards of performance
• Provides percentile rank and standard scores	• How absolute levels are determined and who sets them are critical
• Allows comparisons between different subjects and different years	• Provides percentage correct and categorical designation (e.g., pass–fail)

Figure 13.11 Norm- and Criterion-Referenced/Outcomes-Based Interpretations

UNDERSTANDING STANDARDIZED TEST SCORE REPORTS

When you first look at some standardized test score reports, they may seem to be very complicated and difficult to understand. This is because they are designed to provide as much information as possible on a single page. For a comprehensive battery, scores are often reported for each skill as well as each subskill. The best approach to understanding a report is to consult the test manual and find examples that are explained. Most test publishers do a very good job of showing you what each part of the report means.

There are also many different types of reports. Each test publisher and provincial ministry of education has a unique format for reporting results and usually includes different kinds of scores. In addition, there are typically different formats to report the same scores. Thus, the same battery may be reported as a list of students in your class, the class as a whole, a skills analysis for the class or individual student, individual profiles, profile charts, growth scale profiles, and other formats. Some reports include only scores for major tests; others include subskill scores and item scores. Different norms may be used. All of this means that each report contains somewhat different information, organized and presented in dissimilar ways. First, identify what type of report you are dealing with, and then find an explanation for it in an interpretive guide. After you have become acquainted with the types of standardized tests and reports used in your school and province, you will be in a position to routinely interpret them in accurate and helpful ways.

Figure 13.12 illustrates a student report for the Canadian Test of Basic Skills Performance Profile. Various norm-referenced scores are summarized in the upper box for this grade 3 student. The SS is the CTBS standard score, GE refers to grade equivalent, NPR is the Student National Percentile, and S is the stanine. With a composite score of 196, you can see that Matthew is somewhat above average overall, compared to the national norm group (NPR = 80 and stanine = 7). He is weaker in most literacy measures, but he is scoring higher than his peers in reading comprehension, mathematics, science, and reference materials. The main body of the report provides more detailed information, showing how many items were attempted, the percentage correct, the average percentage correct for the nation, and graphs showing differences from the national average, including the standard error of measurement for Matthew's scores. This is a more criterion-referenced type of information and can be used to better understand overall performance. Figure 13.13 provides a sample school report for the Reading portion of the Foundation Skills Assessment School Report from the British Columbia Ministry of Education. The report gives results for all of the students who completed the assessment, along with results for important subgroups. Subgroups with very small numbers are masked from the report in order to protect the identity of these students (MSK).

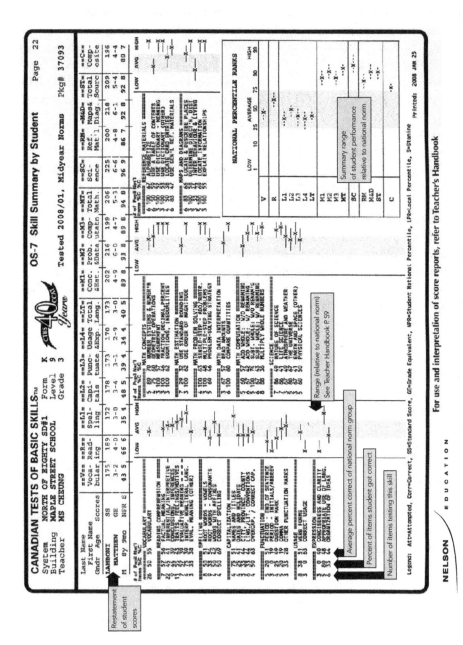

Figure 13.12 Individual Performance Profile

Source: Nelson Education Ltd. (2008). *Canadian tests of basic skills: Teacher's handbook: Instructional resource and activities, forms K & L, levels 9–14* (p. 58).

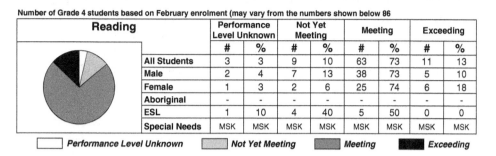

Figure 13.13 Foundation Skills Assessment School Report

Source: Adapted from the British Columbia Ministry of Education (2009). www.bced.gov.bc.ca/assessment/fsa/results.

INTERPRETING TEST REPORTS FOR PARENTS

Most teachers interpret the results of standardized, and, more commonly, provincial tests for parents, although research has shown that nearly half of our teachers feel unprepared to do this (Nolen, Haladyna, & Haas, 1989). Because you are in contact with students daily and are aware of their classroom performance, you are in the best position to communicate with parents regarding the results of standardized or provincial tests. You can determine what level of detail to report and how the results coincide with classroom performance. You can communicate most effectively face-to-face, in the context of a teacher–parent conference, although many provinces send written reports directly to students' homes. In a conference, point out important cautions and discuss the results in a way that will make sense to parents. Before the conference, review available information and prepare it to show student progress and areas of strength and weakness that may need specific action at home and school. In addition to the test results, include other examples of student work to lessen the tendency to place too much value on test scores.

In preparing for the conference, keep in mind that most parents are interested in particular types of information. These include some indication of relative standing, growth since earlier testing, performance compared to expectations, weaknesses, and strengths. For each of these areas, present the relevant numbers, but include a clear and easy-to-understand narrative—using plain, everyday language—that explains the numbers. If applicable, always include some explanation of norms, standards, and the standard error of measurement. It is important for parents to realize that for most reports, the scores do not represent comparisons with other students in the class. Parents obviously don't need an extended explanation of error, but they should understand that the results represent *approximate* and not absolute or precise performance.

Of the different types of scores to report to parents, percentiles from norm-referenced tests are most easily understood, even though some parents will confuse percentile with percentage correct. They may also think that percentile scores below 70 are poor because they are accustomed to grading systems in which 70 or below may mean below provincial expectations. In fact, for most standardized tests, students will score in the average range if they answer 60 to 70 per cent of the items correctly. Grade equivalents are commonly reported but easily misunderstood. Parents often think that GEs indicate the grade in which a student should be placed. This is one of the main reasons that GEs are rarely used in Canadian education. Be diligent in pointing out that GEs are only another way of comparing performance to the norm group.

Most provincial tests have special reports that are prepared for parents. Although these are very informative, supplement the scores with a note from the teacher or school indicating your willingness to confer with the parents, by phone or in person, to answer any questions and clarify the meaning of the results.

In summary, the following suggestions will help you interpret standardized test reports confidently and in a way that will accurately inform parents and help the student:

1. **Understand the Meaning of Every Score Reported to Parents.** It is embarrassing, not to mention unprofessional, not to know how to interpret each score on the report.

2. **Examine Individual Student Reports Comprehensively before a Conference with Parents.** This will prevent you from trying to understand and explain at the same time.

3. **Gather Evidence of Student Performance in the Classroom That Can Supplement the Test Scores.** This demonstrates your commitment to the preparation and careful analysis of each student's performance, and it provides more concrete examples of performance that parents can easily understand.

4. **Be Prepared to Address Areas of Concern Most Parents Have, Such as Standing, Progress, Performance Compared to Standards, Strengths, and Weaknesses.** This may require you to review the student's previous performance on other standardized or classroom tests.

5. **Be Prepared to Distinguish between Ability and Achievement.** Many parents want to know whether their child is performing "up to their ability." You might even have a short written description of the difference between ability and achievement to supplement your verbal explanation.

6. **Explain the Importance of Norms and Error in Testing for Proper Interpretation.** This could include your knowledge of any extenuating circumstances that may have affected the student's performance.

7. **Summarize Clearly What the Scores Mean.** Don't simply show the numbers and expect the parents to be able to understand. You will need to summarize in language that parents can comprehend.

8. **Try to Create a Discussion with Parents, Rather Than Making a Presentation to Them.** Ask questions to involve parents in the conference and to enhance your ability to determine whether they in fact understand the meaning of the scores.

CASE STUDY FOR REFLECTION

Mrs. Jones called right after the provincial test score reports were sent home. She wanted to know how her daughter, Ellen, could be scoring so high, yet not be getting very good grades. In reviewing Ellen's scores, it turns out that she obtained a Level 4 on the Ontario grade 6 literacy test, but her Language Arts grades were Cs and Bs.

Questions for Consideration

1. How would you explain the meaning of Ellen's provincial test scores to her mother?

2. How would you explain the discrepancy between her grades and test score? What other information might be important in providing a reasonable explanation?

3. How would you prepare for a meeting with Mrs. Jones to discuss the scores and Ellen's grades?

PREPARING STUDENTS TO TAKE LARGE-SCALE TESTS

You want your students to perform as well as possible on large-scale tests, and with high-stakes testing accompanying increased demands for accountability, every student should have a fair opportunity to do his or her best work. This can be accomplished if students are properly prepared before taking the test, and this preparation will probably be your responsibility.

One area to address is ensuring that students have good test-taking skills. These skills help to familiarize the students with item formats and give them strategies that improve the validity of the results. Students should be proficient in the test-taking skills listed in Figure 13.14.

Set an appropriate classroom climate or environment for taking the test. This begins with your attitude toward the test. If you convey to students that you believe the test is a burden or an unnecessary or even unfair imposition, then students will also adopt such an attitude and may not try their best. Be positive about the test; convey an attitude of challenge and opportunity. Discuss the purpose and nature of the test with your students. Emphasize how important it is for students to try to do their best, not just to obtain a high score. Tell the students how the tests will be used in conjunction with other information; this will reduce anxiety. Enhance confidence by giving students short practice tests. Most provincial websites do provide sample tests for students to practise. These tests help to acquaint students with the directions and the types of items they will answer.

Student motivation is an important factor. Motivate your students to put forth their best effort by helping them understand how the test results will benefit them. Show them

1. Listen carefully to directions; ask questions if directions are not clearly understood.
2. Read directions and all items slowly and carefully.
3. Look for key words.
4. Follow directions carefully.
5. Understand the concept of "best answer."
6. Establish a pace in answering items so that no items are unanswered.
7. Skip difficult items and return to them if time permits.
8. Do not omit items as long as guessing is not penalized; make an educated guess.
9. If you do not know or you are unsure of the answer to a multiple-choice test item, eliminate alternatives.
10. Check to make sure answers and items match.
11. Check items if there is extra time.

Figure 13.14 Important Test-Taking Skills

how results can be used to improve learning and essential life skills, their knowledge of themselves, and planning for the future. Avoid comments that might make students concerned or anxious.

Some of your students may be so anxious about the test that their anxiety seriously interferes with their performance. If you suspect that a student's performance is adversely affected by test anxiety, even after you have done all you can to alleviate the fears, you may consider having the student examined by a counsellor to determine the extent of the problem. If necessary, appropriate counselling and desensitization exercises can be explored. At the very least, incorporate your awareness of the anxiety when interpreting the test results. See Cizek and Burg (2006) for further detail on test anxiety.

Of course, be sure that the physical environment for taking the test is appropriate. There should be adequate work space and lighting, as well as good ventilation. The room should be quiet, without distractions, and you should schedule the test to avoid events that may disturb the students. Seat students to avoid distractions and cheating. Morning testing is preferred. Remove any visual aids that could assist students, and place a sign on the outside of the door, such as "Testing—Do Not Disturb."

Figure 13.15 lists some do's and don'ts regarding test preparation practices.

ADMINISTERING STANDARDIZED TESTS

Because most standardized and provincial tests are given in the classroom, you will probably be responsible for administering them to your students. The most important part of administering these tests is to *follow the directions carefully and explicitly*. This point cannot be overstated. You must adhere strictly to the instructions that are given by the test

Do	Don't
Improve student test-taking skills.	Use the standardized test format for classroom tests.
Establish a suitable environment.	
Motivate students to do their best.	Characterize tests as an extra burden.
Use released items.	Tell students important decisions are made solely on the basis of test scores.
Explain why tests are given and how results will be used.	Use previous forms of the same test.
Give practice tests.	Teach the test.
Tell students they probably won't know all the answers.	Have a negative attitude about the test.
Tell students not to give up.	Limit instruction and classroom assessments to be aligned only with the test.
Allay student anxiety.	
Have a positive attitude about the test.	

Figure 13.15 Do's and Don'ts of Test Preparation

publisher. The procedures are set to ensure standardization in the conditions under which students in different classes and schools take the test. The directions indicate what to say, how to respond to student questions, and what to do as students are working on the test. Familiarize yourself with the directions before you read them, word for word, to your students. Don't try to paraphrase directions or recite them from memory, even if you have given the test many times.

During the test you may answer student questions about the directions or procedures for answering items, but you should not help students in any way with an answer or discuss what is meant by a question on the test. Although you may be tempted to give students hints or tell them to "answer more quickly" or "slow down and think more," these responses are inappropriate and should be avoided. Suspend your role as classroom teacher for a while and assume the role of test administrator. This isn't easy, and you may well catch yourself deviating slightly from the directions.

While observing students as they take the test, you may see some unusual behaviour or events that could affect the students' performance. Record these behaviours and events for use in subsequent interpretation of the results. Interruptions should also be recorded.

If the test directions specify time limits for subtests, follow these strictly, including the instruction to collect completed answer sheets and tests promptly. Once the test is over, you must account for all copies to ensure test security. Some tests require that you write down the exact beginning and ending times. Most provincial testing programs provide adequate time for students to complete the test. There are also policies and procedures to support those students who have been identified as requiring special supports or accommodations to help them complete the test.

SUMMARY

The purpose of this chapter was to introduce you to the principles of standardized and provincial large-scale testing, to enable you to administer such tests and interpret your students' scores. Canadian teachers are most likely be involved at some time with a provincial testing program. Although such external tests may not directly influence your day-to-day teaching, you have a professional responsibility to interpret the scores from these types of tests accurately for yourself, students, and parents. The results of provincial tests, when used correctly, provide helpful information concerning the effectiveness of your instruction and the progress of your students. Important points in the chapter include the following:

■ Frequency distributions show you how scores are arrayed: normal, positively skewed, negatively skewed, or flat.

■ Measures of central tendency include the mean, median, and mode.

■ Measures of variability, such as the range and standard deviation, provide numerical values for the degree of dispersion of scores from the mean.

■ Standard scores, such as z-scores, T-scores, normal curve equivalent (NCE), the developmental scale, and deviation IQ scores, are converted from raw scores into units of standard deviation.

■ Grade equivalency scores indicate performance related to norming groups and should be cautiously interpreted.

■ Scatterplots show relationships graphically as being positive, negative, or curvilinear.

■ Correlation coefficients are numbers from 1 to 1 that indicate direction and strength of a relationship.

■ Correlation does not imply causation.

■ Standard error of measurement (SEM) expresses mathematically the degree of error to be expected with individual test scores; test results are best interpreted as intervals defined by the SEM.

■ Percentile rank, standard scores, and grade equivalents for students are based on comparisons with the norming group.

■ Alignment of the content, emphasis, and cognitive level of a test with instruction is needed for proper interpretation.

■ Norm-referenced test scores provide external measures and help identify relative strengths and weaknesses.

■ Different types of norms, such as national norms, special group norms, or local norms, influence the reported percentile ranks and other comparative scores.

■ Norms are not standards or expectations; they should be recent, appropriate to your use, and based on good sampling.

■ Criterion-referenced/outcomes-based interpretations depend on the difficulty of the items and professional judgments to set standards.

■ Good criterion-referenced/outcomes-based judgments depend on well-defined targets and a sufficient number of test items to provide a reliable result.

■ Standardized and provincial test reports vary in format and organization; consult the interpretive guide to aid in understanding.

■ Adequate interpreting of standardized and provincial test scores to parents depends on your preparation, your full understanding of the meaning of the scores, your ability to translate the numerical results into plain language, and your placement of the scores in the context of classroom performance.

■ Prepare your students for taking external tests by establishing a good environment, lessening test anxiety, motivating students to do their best, avoiding distractions, and giving students practice tests and exercises.

SELF-INSTRUCTIONAL REVIEW EXERCISES

1. For the following set of numbers, calculate the mean, median, and standard deviation. Also determine linear z- and T-scores for 18, 20, and 11.

   10, 17, 18, 15, 20, 16, 15, 21, 12, 11, 22

2. If you have a normal distribution of scores with a mean of 80 and a standard deviation of 6, what is the approximate percentile rank of the following scores: 86, 68, 83, and 71?

3. Given the following standardized test scores for Mary, a grade 8 student, her mother believes that Mary is in the wrong grade. She believes Mary would be better off in grade 9. She also believes that the test scores seem to indicate that Mary is stronger in science than in language arts, mathematics, or social science. How would you respond to Mary's mother?

Test	NATL PR	Stanine	GE
Mathematics	75	6	9.2
Science	87	7	9.7
Social studies	80	7	9.4
Language arts	63	6	8.5
Study skills	72	6	9.0

4. Indicate whether each of the following suggested activities helps or hinders student performance on a provincial test:

   a. Tell students their futures depend on their scores.

   b. To avoid making students anxious, do not tell them very much about the test.

   c. Make sure the room temperature is about right.

   d. Arrange desks so that students face each other in groups of four.

   e. Give students a practice test that is very similar in format.

   f. Tell students they probably won't be able to answer many of the questions.

   g. Teach to the test.

   h. Tell students you think the test is taking away from class time and student learning.

SUGGESTIONS FOR ACTION RESEARCH

1. Observe a class in which students take a provincial test. If possible, take a copy of the test administration guidelines with you and determine how closely the teacher follows the directions. What has the teacher done to motivate the students and set a proper environment? Observe the students as they are taking the test. Do they seem motivated and serious? How quickly do they work?

2. Sit in on two or three teacher–parent conferences that review the results of provincial tests. Compare what occurs with the suggestions in the chapter. How well, in your opinion, does the teacher interpret the scores? Is the teacher accurate?

3. Interview some parents about provincial tests. What did they get from the reports? Which types of scores were most meaningful to them? Did the results surprise them? Were the results consistent with other performance, such as grades?

4. Interview some teachers about provincial testing. Ask them how they use the results of provincial tests to improve their instruction. Ask them to recall situations in which parents did not seem to understand the results of the test very well. Looking back, what could the teacher have done differently to enhance parent understanding?

APPENDIX A Answers to Self-Instructional Review Exercises

CHAPTER 1

1. Complex classroom environments influence the nature of teacher decision making, and assessment is needed to make good decisions.

2. "Add-on" means assessment that occurs at the end of an instructional unit, for example, the mid-term or final exam. However, the teacher also assesses students before and during instruction. Assessment should not be thought of as testing only at the end of instruction.

3. A test is only one part of assessment. Assessment refers to measuring something, evaluating what is measured, and then using the information for decision making. A test is one way to measure.

4. a. og, b. post, c. og, d. og, e. pre, f. og, g. pre.

5. a. E, b. P, c. E, d. M, e. U.

6. Expectations are set by the nature of the standards and criteria used in the assessments and the way teachers provide feedback and otherwise respond to students.

7. Recent learning research has shown the importance of connecting new to existing information, of applying knowledge, and of thinking skills. Performance assessments foster these behaviours by relating content and processes to problem solving in meaningful contexts.

CHAPTER 2

1. a. E, b. G, c. E, d. LO.

2. Criteria are part of what would be included in a learning outcome. Criteria, in contrast to outcomes, contain descriptions of different levels of performance.

3. b.

4. You could have selected from communicating goals and different levels of work to parents, documenting judgments, helping students evaluate their own work, and motivating students.

5. Criteria are needed to completely understand the nature of the expectation and what it takes to achieve different levels of performance. Without criteria, students don't understand the expected level of performance.

6. a. S, b. K, c. R, d. K, e. A, f. P.

7. Bloom's taxonomy is not aligned very well with more recent research on learning and motivation.

8. For example,

   Knowledge and Simple Understanding: Students are able to recall and write accurately 80 per cent of the definitions of key terms in the chapter.

   Deep Understanding and Reasoning: Students are able to analyze five examples of learning expectations and modify them in writing so that they correspond better to the criteria in the chapter.

   Skill: Students will use the library computer system to locate critiques of three published tests.

   Product: Students can construct learning expectations after receiving an instructional unit on teaching fractions. The expectations are judged by the extent to which criteria are included. Or, students can construct a multiple-choice test that corresponds to the criteria in the book.

   Affect: Students increase the importance they give to constructing criteria for learning outcomes.

9. Learning outcomes describe the nature of the material to be learned, whereas performance standards indicate levels of achievement that must be met concerning the content.

10. Responses will vary by province and curriculum. For example, based on the Saskatchewan curriculum, a *general* learning outcome (foundational objective) for grade 6 English Language Arts (Writing) would be: "Write fluently and confidently for a variety of purposes and audiences, employing appropriate formats." An example of a *specific* learning outcome would be: "Write to convince and to persuade (e.g., support a position on a topic)."

CHAPTER 3

1. Yes, but not in the way psychometricians do with published, standardized tests. Validity and reliability are essential to fairness, proper interpretation of assessments, and teacher decision making. Unless statistics are easily found, validity and reliability are best estimated by teacher judgment and logical analysis.

2. (1) d, (2) f, (3) a, (4) c, (5) b, (6) e.

3. a. OB, b. OR, c. S, d. E, e. SR, f. S.

4. a. Yes; if the score is not consistent or stable, the inference will likewise not be consistent or stable and hence, inaccurate and invalid. b. Yes; a measure of the circumference of your big toe is very reliable but not very valid for measuring your ability to read. c. No; tests are not valid or invalid; only inferences are.

5. a.

6. Not very reliable. Germaine scored highest on Test A, but near the bottom on Test B; Robert scored at the bottom on Test A, but near the top on Test B. A reliable assessment would result in nearly the same rank ordering for both tests.

7. a. Student knowledge of assessment. b. Student knowledge of assessment. c. Opportunity to learn. d. Biased content. e. Alignment.

8. Probably not. For bias to exist, it needs to be fairly obvious. In this example, a minority group name is used, but it would be unlikely to elicit negative affect from Pakistani members of the class. There is no content that is clearly biased.

9. Because your time is limited, set your priorities so that you balance instruction with assessment.

CHAPTER 4

1. Refer to Figure 4.1 for the advantages and disadvantages of using school records. The major issue related to knowing as much as possible about the students before you meet them is your confidence about forming appropriate expectations. As long as you keep in mind the need to be flexible in your expectations, more information is better than less.

2. Your conclusion should be based on the following: information from several different sources that suggests the same conclusion, a pattern of performance over several years, and your own informal assessment that coincides with what is in school records.

3. This is possible because norms are established in one year (e.g., 2008) and then used for several more years, and current scores (2010) are compared to the 2008 norms. Before new norms are established, all the school districts may target skills assessed on the test.

4. a. clearly CR, some NR, and S; b. A; c. NR; d. NR, A, maybe S; e. A.

5. The answer to this question will vary depending on the individual student, but it should correspond to the figure. Remember that expectations do not influence students unless there is differential teacher behaviour. In other words, fully operational expectations include both the teacher's belief about students and the teacher's behaviour toward the students.

CHAPTER 5

1. a. anger, b. fear, c. sadness, d. happiness, e. interest, f. determination.

2. a. R, b. E, c. A, d. A, e. AD, f. I.

3. (1) f, (2) h, (3) e, (4) a, (5) a, (6) b, (7) c, (8) d.

4. Mr. Ozomoto is using previous behaviour to motivate his informal observations, so his initial impressions may distort what he finds (primacy effect). He may also have a preconceived idea about what Trent would do (observer bias).

5. At least Mrs. Rafferty recognized that this was not a common occurrence and did not commit the error of unrepresentative sampling. However, her interpretation that Renée was not thinking about her lesson may be inaccurate. If this type of behaviour became frequent and extensive, Mrs. Rafferty should ask Renée about it to get her perspective.

6. Matching questions with learning expectations (1) helps to clarify to students what is important, (2) allows you to check student understanding of expectations, (3) reinforces learning, and (4) balances emphasis given to each expectation.

7. The easiest way is the most direct—simply tell the students to wait a certain number of seconds before answering (e.g., 15 or 30 seconds). You can also ask them to write their answer and think about it before responding orally.

8. Convergent; only one or two possible ways are correct.

9.

	Do	**Don't**
Homework	Make it clear how much help, from whom, is permitted. Use constructed-response exercises. Have students show their work. Give instructional correctives with feedback. Give younger students shorter assignments.	Allow any kind of help. Use primarily selected-response items. Give only correct answers. Use homework for motivation, without feedback or correctives. Simply check for correct answers.
In-class assignments	Monitor student engagement and performance. Give private correctives. Give frequent, immediate, specific, and individualized feedback. Use observation, checklists, and individual accountability for cooperative group learning. Use checkpoint quizzes.	Sit at a desk while students complete assignments. Give general feedback to all students. Wait until all students have completed the work to give feedback. Use only group achievement accountability for cooperative learning.
Quizzes	Keep quizzes short. Use them frequently. Use results to provide individualized instructional correctives. Use primarily constructed-response items. Be wary of quizzes from test item banks.	Use long quizzes. Use them infrequently. Surprise students. Fail to connect results with instructional correctives. Use mostly selected-response items. Rely solely on items prepared by others.

10. **a.** This is poor in almost all respects. Feedback is not specific or descriptive, it is unrelated to learning outcomes, and it does not focus on key errors. It is not given immediately, and no corrective actions are suggested.

    b. This is pretty good feedback as praise. It is specific, descriptive, and focuses on improvement. However, include areas to improve as well.

    c. This feedback seems okay at first; you may well have received something similar many times. But when you look closely at it, the feedback is weak. The teacher does not indicate how Andrew can improve, nor does the teacher identify Andrew's specific mistakes or problems in sentence structure, conclusion, or providing detail. The teacher has indicated there is "improvement," but this is not a clear indication of progress. The teacher also does not say how Andrew can improve his difficulties, only that he has them.

11. **a.** IP; too general, compares performance only to others.

    b. IP; too general, and attributes success only to ability.

    c. EP; although general, still attributes success to both effort and ability (internal factors).

    d. EP; specific, shows progress.

    e. Both EP and IP; on the one hand, the praise is specific, but on the other hand, success is indicated by comparison to others.

12. Strengths include the following: promotes better student understanding of expectations and scoring criteria; promotes student self-reflection and self-evaluation; provides immediate, specific, and individualized feedback; leads to an awareness of progress; and increases motivation. Limitations include the following: self-assessment skills need to be taught; time is needed for self-evaluation; differences between students require individualized instruction; may not be supported because of other initiatives or alignment requirements; and instructional time may be lost.

CHAPTER 6

1. (1) d, (2) a, (3) e, (4) a, (5) b, (6) e.

2. a. DK, b. PK, c. DSU, d. DK, e. DSU, f. DSU.

3. (1) e; (2) a and b; (3) c; (4) a and d; (5) c and e; (6) d and e; (7) a, b, c, d, and e; (8) a, b, c, d, and e; (9) a.

4. **(1)** This may be lifted verbatim from the instructional material, requiring memorization of a definition. The blanks are not at the end of the sentence. The length of the blanks gives a clue to the correct answer. It is not a concise statement that includes only what is needed to answer the item.

    Revision: The sloping ledge formed underwater next to most continents is the _____ _____.

(2) This is poorly worded because many answers could be correct. There is no indication of how long the answer should be, and it is possible that a "correct" answer could be several sentences long—hardly short-answer!

Revision: Name two sources of energy from the sun that affect the earth.

(3) There are probably too many items in one list. Additional responses should be included as distractors. Provinces should be listed on the right. The directions are inadequate, and the format is difficult to score. The premises are not homogeneous. Do not mix cities with geographic descriptions.

Revision: On the line next to each number in column A, write the letter of the province or territory from column B that matches the geographic description. Each province or territory may be used once, more than once, or not at all.

Column A

_____ (1) Contains the capital of Canada

_____ (2) Contains Lake Winnipeg

_____ (3) Is bordered by the Pacific Ocean

_____ (4) Is an island in the Atlantic Ocean

_____ (5) Contains Ellesmere Island

Column B

a. Saskatchewan

b. Nunavut

c. British Columbia

d. New Brunswick

e. Prince Edward Island

f. Northwest Territories

g. Quebec

h. Manitoba

i. Ontario

(4) The negatives in this item make it very hard to understand. State more directly the proposition to be tested. Include directions.

Revision: If the statement is true, circle T; if it is false, circle F.

T F Students construct answers to multiple-choice items.

(5) The directions should indicate "correct" answer, not "best" answer. The alternatives should be listed vertically under the stem. The stem should be long, the alternatives short. Option (c) does not fit grammatically and is not concise. "None of the above" should be avoided. It would be better to use a question.

Revision: Circle the correct answer.

Which of the following is a characteristic of Ontario?

a. It is bordered by Hudson Bay.

b. It contains the Rocky Mountains.

c. It is a single island.

d. It borders the Atlantic Ocean.

(6) The correct answer, b, is obvious because of the complexity of the sentence in relation to the others. Fossil fuels are also biodegradable, so more than one correct answer is possible. The stem is short and the correct alternative long. It is more clearly stated as a question.

Revision: Circle the correct answer.

What type of material is broken down by decomposers into simpler substances that do not pollute the environment?

a. Nonrenewable

b. Biodegradable

c. Fossil fuel

d. Decomposition

CHAPTER 7

1. a. D, b. C, c. I, d. S, e. A, f. P, g. C, h. I.

2. a. I, b. I or E, c. I, d. E, e. O, f. E, g. O; h. E, i. I.

3. The general format of the question is appropriate, and it is good to have several questions about the material presented. Introductory information is kept to a minimum. Presumably, students have been studying food chains or webs; this one should be new. Clearly, the questions cannot be answered correctly unless the student can understand the food web. The format of the questions could be improved so that students check or circle correct answers, rather than taking time to write their answers. (For example, in response to "What must the perch do to get energy generated from the sun?" students could circle a. live in warmer areas, b. eat pond grass, c. swim on the surface of the water, or d. eat mosquito larva and valve snail). This would reduce the time needed to answer the questions and the time needed for scoring. The reasoning target assessed by the question is primarily inference and deductive reasoning. Application and understanding targets are also assessed. The assessment could be improved by asking additional "what if" questions, especially about things that indirectly affect the food web. For example, "What if there is cloudy weather?" and "What would happen to the amount of algae if fishermen were allowed to catch more perch?"

4. This essay question assesses evaluation and critical thinking skills. A decision must be made with reasonable justification. It also assesses constructing support and deductive reasoning. The item could be improved by indicating how much time students should take in answering it, by indicating scoring criteria, and by providing more specific information about what is expected. Including a reference to both the victims and the families gives students a clear indication that the teacher wants the student to pick either the victim or the family. Phrases such as "justify your answer" give students some direction but are vague. What level of detail is expected? How many reasons are adequate? What is meant by justify? There should also be an indication of the total points for the item.

CHAPTER 8

1. Authentic assessment refers to the nature of the task that approximates a real-world example. Performance assessment involves the construction of responses by students—it may or may not be authentic.

2. Students are required to explain their responses as well as to produce them; reasoning expectations are usually assessed; students use reasoning skills to demonstrate their proficiency; student performance is judged by what is directly observable; criteria are used to judge the adequacy of the performance on the basis of prespecified standards that relate a description of the performance to a statement of worth; good performance tasks are those that engage students.

3. a. D, b. A, c. A, d. D, e. A, f. A, g. A, h. D.

4. a. C, origination; b. FM, guided response; c. FM, mechanism; d. GM, adaptation.

5. a. R, b. E, c. E, d. R, e. E, f. R.

6. As a performance prompt, this isn't too bad, but as a performance task description it could be improved considerably. There is no indication of the learning expectations, whether this is an individual or group project, and the administrative process. Most importantly, there is no indication of the scoring criteria. It is a fairly authentic task that integrates different subjects. It does say something about the role of the teacher and resources, but more detail about both of these aspects could be provided.

7. There will be individual answers to this question, so review each other's work by applying the questions in Figure 8.13. We would begin with an analysis of the essential understandings and skills needed to plan the trip. This analysis comprises the dimensions that are evaluated (e.g., the ability to use maps, the ability to understand the impact of terrain and time of year on supplies needed, the extent to which plans follow from assumptions, and the logic and soundness of reasons stated). We would then employ a scale to indicate the extent to which each of these dimensions is present (e.g., inadequate, adequate, more than adequate, or absent; developing, proficient, or advanced). For example, for the extent to which plans follow from assumptions, you might note the following:

Absent There is no indication of assumptions or how plans are based on assumptions.

Developing Assumptions are not clearly stated but implied; plans are not explicitly related to assumptions but are implied.

Proficient Some assumptions are clearly stated, and plans are explicitly related to the assumptions.

Advanced A comprehensive and well-thought-out list of assumptions is used; assumptions are explicitly related to plans.

CHAPTER 9

1. a. A, b. A or D (a disadvantage if students are not provided with sufficient direction and supervision), c. D, d. A, e. D, f. D, g. A.

2. a. D, b. S, c. S, d. G, e. E, f. G.

3. This is not really portfolio assessment, at least not in the way portfolios have been discussed in this chapter. Neither the teacher nor the students select anything (everything is included), and there is no indication that any performance products are included. The teacher doesn't specify the purpose of the portfolio. Folders will be used, but we don't know where they will be placed. There is no indication that student self-reflection guidelines and scoring criteria have been developed.

4. (1) d, (2) e, (3) c, (4) a, (5) b, (6) b, (7) d.

5. Matt is right to use portfolios, but he needs to be more specific and systematic in a number of areas. It's good that he takes time to plan what he wants to do. However, the stated purpose is not one of the major reasons that portfolios should be used. There is only a brief reference to learning expectations and no indication that he has prepared specific scoring criteria or student self-reflection guidelines. Simply asking students to select one example of their work per week is probably too vague. Matt needs to be more specific about what kinds of work should be included and about the physical structure of the portfolio. Because he has several classes, it may not be feasible to store each portfolio in the room. It's not clear that students know enough about portfolios for the procedure to work. It's good that students select the content, and Matt is on target in emphasizing student self-reflection. There may be too many work samples by the end of the term, making Matt's grading process difficult. It might be better to have students select one work example per week; at the end of the term, they could choose a few items from these to demonstrate achievement. Matt's plan to meet with students at least once informally is okay, but there is no provision for a more formal conference near the end of the semester. It's good that he includes individualized written comments.

CHAPTER 10

1. Three reasons were given in the chapter: affect takes second place to cognitive outcomes; assessing affect is difficult to do well; and teachers do not want to tolerate controversy.

2. (1) e, (2) c, (3) b, (4) b, (5) a, (6) g, (7) f, (8) a, (9) c, (10) b or e.

3. **Scenario 1.** On the positive side, Mr. Talbot has used more than one method to assess attitudes, and he has a fairly narrow trait in mind. It's good that he isolates the affective component of attitudes (likes) and that his observation notes are brief. On the negative side, his sentence is too broad and may not elicit much information about attitudes. There is no indication that he has generated examples of approach and avoidance behaviours. Students could easily respond with answers such as "short" or "in the morning," which wouldn't be much help. He should try to summarize more frequently than once a week, even though trying to write descriptions for each student is time-consuming. He records his interpretations rather than student behaviour.

   Scenario 2. For the most part, this is an example of good affective assessment. Ms. Chorny took the time to first list behaviours, establish a response format that would work, and develop the items. She ensured anonymity, and she looked at attitudes and values before and after her course. However, the survey is pretty long, and she is dependent on a single assessment method. Her bias could be perceived by students, and it might encourage them to provide positive answers at the end of the semester.

4. a. O and CRSR (interview), b. PR, c. O and CRSR, d. SRSR, e. O and CRSR, f. CRSR, g. PR, h. O.

CHAPTER 11

1. a. N, b. Y, c. N, d. Y, e. Y.

2. Mrs. Albert did some things right but in general did not do enough to justify formal referral. She seems to have targeted behaviours that are characteristic of students with a learning disability, and she did try one instructional intervention. However, more instructional interventions are needed to ensure that the problems could not be ameliorated in the class without referral. There is no indication that the teacher made any more structured diagnostic assessments, and there is no evidence of any type of prereferral review. A serious oversight is that Mrs. Albert didn't request that outsiders review the situation. She should also speak to Jane's parents.

3. a. PI, b. SL, c. LD, d. ID, e. SI, f. none, g. AD/HD, h. AD/HD.

4. a. C, b. A, c. E, d. VB, e. TCD.

5. a. N, b. Y, c. Y, d. N, e. N, f. Y, g. Y, h. Y, i. Y, j. N, k. Y.

6. Correct procedures included reading the directions aloud, giving examples, underlining key words, and placing a sign on the door. Incorrect procedures, from an adaptation perspective, included giving students with exceptionalities a separate set of directions (which may cause embarrassment), putting too much on each page of the test, asking students to correct wrong answers for objective items, not permitting questions during the test, and giving students what seems like a short time limit.

7. Begin with a clear indication of the work to be completed and how different grades will be assigned. A specific timeline for completing the work should be included.

Signatures of the student and parents are needed to indicate that they understand. The teacher's report should include not only what grades are achieved, but also personalized comments and suggestions.

CHAPTER 12

1. a. NR, b. NR, c. CR, d. NR, e. CR, f. CR, g. CR, h. NR.

2. The standard is set by how difficult the teacher makes the assessment items; scores essay, short-answer, and performance-based assessments; and sets the criterion level (e.g., the percentage correct).

3. The major limitation of letter grades, per cent correct, and pass–fail approaches is that they provide only a general overview of performance. Supplemental information that details the strengths and weaknesses of the students is needed.

4. Ms. Gallagher made several significant errors. There are too few assessments to determine a semester grade; many more are needed. The three components should not be weighted equally. Because the final is comprehensive, it should count the most. The participation grade is weighted too heavily and should not combine academic work (homework) with nonacademic factors. The weighting makes it possible for students who have poor performance to do satisfactorily in the course. There is no indication of how much each of the separate participation components counts for.

5. First, convert all scores to the same 100-point scale. Because the first mid-term is worth 40 points, the score would be multiplied by 2.5, the second mid-term score by 2, and the final exam divided by 2. Each of these scores is multiplied by the appropriate weight and then added.

   Ralph: $(30 \times 2.5 \times .2) + (40 \times 2 \times .2) + (170/2 \times .3) + (78 \times .2) + (85 \times .1)$
   $= 15 + 16 + 25.5 + 15.6 + 8.5 = 80.6 = A$

   Sally: $(35 \times 2.5 \times .2) + (35 \times 2 \times .2) + (140/2 \times .3) + (65 \times .2) + (90 \times .1)$
   $= 17.5 + 14 + 21 + 13 + 9 = 74.5 = B$

6. Shaunda's composite score would be figured as $(80 \times .25) + (30 \times .25) + (75 \times .5)$ $= 20.0 + 7.5 + 37.5 = 65.0$. According to the grading scale, she would receive a C. This reflects the relatively high contribution of homework and the fact that she was not able to get much of it finished. However, her class work and performance on tests tell a different story, and a more accurate grade would be a B. Suppose homework was 10 per cent instead of 25 per cent and class work was 40 per cent. Then her composite would be a 73, almost 8 points higher. Given her home situation, she certainly should not receive a C, and the grading scale should be changed to put more weight on academic performance. The relatively high percentage for in-class work, 25 per cent, is subject to teacher bias and should be reduced.

7. Actual test performance should not be affected negatively by nonacademic factors such as effort and compliance. We'd use a policy that homework won't hurt a grade (but could improve it) and give the student an A. Motivation is negatively affected because homework is obviously too easy and does not help Greg learn. The final grade has little meaning with respect to his self-efficacy. The goal orientation is on performance rather than mastery, and the final grade of B– does not accurately indicate his level of competence. There is no indication that grades have been used formatively.

CHAPTER 13

1. $\bar{X} = 161/11 = 16.09$; $mdn = 16$. Rounding the mean to 16, the SD is 3.83. The z- and T-scores are as follows: 18: $z = 18 - 16/3.83 = .53$; $T = 50 + 10(.53) = 55.3$; 20: $20 - 16/3.83 = 1.05$; $T = 50 + 10(1.05) = 60.5$; 11: $11 - 16/3.83 = -1.31$; $T = 50 + 10(-1.31) = 36.9$.

2. The score of 86 is one standard deviation above the mean, so the percentile is the 84th; 68 is two standard deviations below the mean, so the percentile is the 2nd; 83 is one half of a standard deviation above the mean, so the percentile rank is between 50 (mean) and 84 (one SD); because 34 per cent of the scores lie in this range, one half of 34 is 17, so 83 is at about the 67th percentile (50 + 17). (Actually, it would be a little greater than 17 because of the curve of the distribution, but 67 is a good approximation.) Using the same logic, 71, which is one and one-half standard deviations below the mean, would be at approximately the 8th percentile (50 − 34 + 8).

3. Mary's mother is probably looking at the GEs and thinking that this means Mary should be in grade 9. This is not true. It's very possible that most of the students in grade 8 have GEs of 9 or higher. It's true that Mary's science score is her highest, but, given a normal standard error of measurement of about 6 percentile points, the confidence interval overlaps suggest that there is no meaningful difference between science (81–93) and social studies (74–86), but it could be concluded that the science score is definitely higher than the language arts (57–69). The stanines give you the impression that the scores on all the tests are about the same, which is somewhat misleading. Yes, they are all well above the norm, but the science percentile score is at the top of stanine 7, whereas the language arts percentile is at the bottom of stanine 6. Refer to examples of reports in Chapter 4 for interpretation. Give examples of some test scores.

4. a. hinder, b. hinder, c. help, d. hinder, e. help, f. hinder, g. help, h. hinder.

Principles for Fair Student Assessment Practices for Education in Canada

The *Principles for Fair Student Assessment Practices for Education in Canada* was developed by a Working Group guided by a Joint Advisory Committee. The Joint Advisory Committee included two representatives appointed by each of the following professional organizations: Canadian Education Association, Canadian School Boards Association, Canadian Association for School Administrators, Canadian Teachers' Federation, Canadian Guidance and Counselling Association, Canadian Association of School Psychologists, Canadian Council for Exceptional Children, Canadian Psychological Association, and Canadian Society for the Study of Education. In addition, the Joint Advisory Committee included a representative of the Provincial and Territorial Ministries and Departments of Education.

Financial support for the development and dissemination of the *Principles* was provided principally by the Walter and Duncan Gordon Charitable Foundation, with additional support provided by various Faculties, Institutes, and Colleges of Education and Provincial and Territorial Ministries and Departments of Education in Canada. This support is gratefully acknowledged.

The following professional organizations have endorsed the *Principles*: Canadian School Boards Association, Canadian Association for School Administrators, Canadian Teachers' Federation, Canadian Guidance and Counselling Association, Canadian Association of School Psychologists, Canadian Council for Exceptional Children, Canadian Psychological Association, and Canadian Society for the Study of Education.

The Joint Advisory Committee invites users to share their experiences in working with the with *Principles* and to submit any suggestions that could be used in revise and improve *Principles*. Comments and suggestions should be sent to the Joint Advisory Committee at the address shown below.

The *Principles for Fair Student Assessment Practices for Education in Canada* is not copyrighted. Reproduction and dissemination are encouraged. Please cite the *Principles* as follows:

Principles for Fair Student Assessment Practices for Education in Canada. (1993). Edmonton, Alberta: Joint Advisory Committee. (Mailing address: Joint Advisory Committee, Centre for Research in Applied Measurement and Evaluation, 3–104 Education Building North, University of Alberta, Edmonton, Alberta, T6G 2G5).

Principles for Fair Student Assessment Practices for Education in Canada

The *Principles for Fair Student Assessment Practices for Education in Canada* contains a set of principles and related guidelines generally accepted by professional organizations as indicative of fair assessment practice within the Canadian educational context. Assessments depend on a professional judgment; the principles and related guidelines presented in this document identify the issues to consider in exercising this professional judgment and in striving for the fair and equitable assessment of all students.

Assessment is broadly defined in the *Principles* as the process of collecting and interpreting information that can be used (i) to inform students, and their parents/guardians where applicable, about the progress they are making toward attaining the knowledge, skills, attitudes, and behaviors to be learned or acquired, and (ii) to inform the various personnel who make educational decisions (instructional, diagnostic, placement, promotion, graduation, curriculum planning, program development, policy) about students. Principles and related guidelines are set out for both developers and users of assessments. Developers include people who construct assessment methods and people who set policies for particular assessment programs. Users include people who select and administer assessment methods, commission assessment development services, or make decisions on the basis of assessment results and findings. The roles my overlap, as when a teacher or instructor develops and administers an assessment instrument and then scores and interprets the students' responses, or when a ministry or department of education or local school system commissions the development and implementation of an assessment program and scoring services and makes decisions on the basis of the assessment results.

The *Principles for Fair Student Assessment Practices for Education in Canada* is the product of a comprehensive effort to reach consensus on what constitutes sound principles to guide the fair assessment of students. The principles and their related guidelines should be considered neither exhaustive nor mandatory; however, organizations, institutions, and individual professionals who endorse them are committing themselves **to endeavor to follow their intent and spirit** so as to achieve fair and equitable assessments of students.

Organization and Use of the Principles
The principles and their related guidelines are organized in two parts. Part A is directed at assessments carried out by teachers at the elementary and secondary school levels. Part A is also applicable at the post-secondary level with some modifications,

particularly with respect to whom assessment results are reported. Part B is directed at standardized assessments developed external to the classroom by commercial test publishers, provincial and territorial ministries and departments of education, and local school jurisdictions (boards, boroughs, counties, and school districts).

Five general principles of fair assessment practices are provided in each Part. Each principle is followed by a series of guidelines for practice. In the case of Part A where no prior sets of standards for fair practice exist, a brief comment accompanies each guideline to help clarify and illuminate the guideline and its application.

The Joint Advisory Committee recognizes that in the field of assessment some terms are defined or used differently by different groups of people. To maintain as much consistency in terminology as possible, an attempt has been made to employ generic terms in the *Principles*.

A. CLASSROOM ASSESSMENTS

Part A is directed toward the development and selection of assessment methods and their use in the classroom by teachers. Based on the conceptual framework provided in the *Standards for Teacher Competence in Educational Assessment of Students* (1990), it is organized around five <u>interrelated</u> themes:

- I.   Developing and Choosing Methods for Assessment
- II. Collecting Assessment Information
- III. Judging and Scoring Student Performance
- IV. Summarizing and Interpreting Results
- V. Reporting Assessment Findings

The Joint Advisory Committee acknowledges that not all of the guidelines are equally applicable in all circumstances. However, consideration of the full set of principles and guidelines within Part A should help to achieve fairness and equity for the students to be assessed.

I. Developing and Choosing Methods for Assessment

Assessment methods should be appropriate for and compatible with the purpose and context of the assessment.

Assessment method is used here to refer to the various strategies and techniques that teachers might use to acquire assessment information. These strategies and techniques include, but are not limited to, observations, text- and curriculum-embedded questions and tests, paper-and-pencil tests, oral questioning, benchmarks or reference sets, interviews, peer-and self-assessments, standardized criterion-referenced and norm-referenced tests, performance assessments, writing samples, exhibitions, portfolio assessment, and project and product assessments. Several labels have been used to describe subsets of these alternatives, with the most common being "direct assessment," "authentic assessment," "performance assessment," and "alternative assessment." However, for the purpose of the *Principles*, the term assessment method has been used to encompass all the strategies and techniques that might be used to collect information from students about their progress toward attaining the knowledge, skills, attitudes, or behaviors to be learned.

▶ 1. Assessment methods should be developed or chosen so that inferences drawn about the knowledge, skills, attitudes, and behaviors possessed by each student are valid and not open to misinterpretation.

Validity refers to the degree to which inferences drawn from assessments results are meaningful. Therefore, development or selection of assessment methods for collecting information should be clearly linked to the purposes for which inferences and decisions are to be made. For example, to monitor the progress of students as proofreaders and editors of their own work, it is better to assign an actual writing task, to allow time and resources for editing (dictionaries, handbooks, etc.), and to observe students for evidence of proofreading and editing skill as they work than to use a test containing discreet items on usage and grammar that are relatively devoid of context.

▶ 2. Assessment methods should be clearly related to the goals and objectives of instruction, and be compatible with the instructional approaches used.

To enhance validity, assessment methods should be in harmony with the instructional objectives to which they are referenced. Planning an assessment design at the same time as planning instruction will help integrate the two in meaningful ways. Such joint planning provides an overall perspective on the knowledge, skills, attitudes, and behaviors to be learned and assessed, and the contexts in which they will be learned and assessed.

▶ 3. When developing or choosing assessment methods, consideration should be given to the consequences of the decisions to be made in light of the obtained information.

The outcomes of some assessments may be more critical than others. For example, misinterpretation of the level of performance on an end-of-unit test may result in incorrectly holding a student from proceeding to the next instructional unit in a continuous progress situation. In such "high-stake" situations, every effort should be made to ensure the assessment method will yield consistent and valid results. "Low stake" situations, such as determining if a student has correctly completed an in-class assignment, can be less stringent. Low stake assessments are often repeated during the course of a reporting period using a variety of methods. If the results are aggregated to form a summary comment or grade, the summary will have greater consistency and validity than its component elements.

▶ 4. More than one assessment method should be used to ensure comprehensive and consistent indications of student performance.

To obtain a more complete picture or profile of a student's knowledge, skills, attitudes, or behaviors, and to discern consistent patterns and trends, more than one assessment method should be used. Student knowledge might be assessed using completion items; process or reasoning skills might be assessed by observing performance on a relevant task; evaluation skills might be assessed by reflecting upon the discussion with a student about what materials to include in a portfolio. Self-assessment may help to clarify and add meaning to the assessment of a written communication, science project, piece of art work, or an attitude. Use of more than one method will also help minimize inconsistency brought about by different sources of measurement error (for example, poor performance because of an "off-day"; lack of agreement among items included in a test, rating scale, or questionnaire; lack of agreement among observers; instability across time).

▶ 5. Assessment methods should be suited to the backgrounds and prior experiences of students.

Assessment methods should be free from bias brought about by student factors extraneous to the purpose of the assessment. Possible factors to consider include culture, developmental stage, ethnicity, gender, socio-economic background, language, special interests, and special needs. Students' success in answering questions on a test or in an oral quiz, for example, should be not be dependent upon prior cultural knowledge, such as understanding an allusion to a culture tradition or value, unless such knowledge falls within the content domain being assessed. All students should be given the same opportunity to display their strengths.

▶ 6. Content and language that would generally be viewed as sensitive, sexist, or offensive should be avoided.

The vocabulary and problem situation in each test item or performance task should not favour or discriminate against any group of students. Steps should be taken to ensure that stereotyping is not condoned. Language that might be offensive to particular groups of students should be avoided. A judicious use of different roles for males and females and for minorities and the careful use of language should contribute to more effective and, therefore, fairer assessments.

▶ 7. Assessment instruments translated into a second language or transferred from another context or location should be accompanied by evidence that inferences based on these instruments are valid for the intended purpose.

Translation of an assessment instrument from one language to another is a complex and demanding task. Similarly, the adoption or modification of an instrument developed in another country is often not simple and straightforward. Care must be taken to ensure that the results from translated and imported instruments are not misinterpreted or misleading.

II. Collecting Assessment Information

Students should be provided with a sufficient opportunity to demonstrate the knowledge, skills, attitudes, or behaviors being assessed.

Assessment information can be collected in a variety of ways (observations, oral questioning, interviews, oral and written reports, paper-and-pencil tests). The guidelines which follow are not all equally applicable to each of these procedures.

▶ 1. Students should be told why assessment information is being collected and how this information will be used.

Students who know the purpose of an assessment are in a position to respond in a manner that will provide information relevant to that purpose. For example, if students know that their participation in a group activity is to be used to assess cooperative skills, they can be encouraged to contribute to the activity. If students know that the purpose of an assessment is to diagnose strengths and weaknesses rather than to assign a grade, they can be encouraged to reveal weaknesses as well as strengths. If the students know that the purpose is to assign a grade, they are well advised to respond in a way that will maximize strength. This is especially true for assessment methods that allow students to make choices, such as with optional writing assignments or research projects.

▶ 2. An assessment procedure should be used under conditions suitable to its purpose and form.

Optimum conditions should be provided for obtaining data from and information about students so as to maximize the validity and consistency of the data and information collected. Common conditions include such things as proper light and ventilation, comfortable room temperature, and freedom from distraction (e.g., movement in and out of the room, noise). Adequate work-space, sufficient materials, and adequate time limits appropriate to the purpose and form of the assessment are also necessary. For example, if the intent is to assess student participation in a small group, adequate work space should be provided for each student group, with sufficient space between subgroups so that the groups do not interfere with or otherwise influence one another and so that the teacher has the same opportunity to observe and assess each student within each group.

▶ 3. In assessments involving observations, checklists, or rating scales, the number of characteristics to be assessed at one time should be small enough and concretely described so that the observations can be made accurately.

Student behaviors often change so rapidly that it may not be possible simultaneously to observe and record all the behavior components. In such instances, the number of components to be observed should be reduced and the components should be described as concretely as possible. One way to manage an observation is to divide the behavior into a series of components and assess each component in sequence. By limiting the number of components assessed at one time, the data and information become more focused, and time is not spent observing later behavior until prerequisite behaviors are achieved.

▶ 4. The directions provided to students should be clear, complete, and appropriate for the ability, age, and grade level of the students.

Lack of understanding of the assessment task may prevent maximum performance or display of the behavior called for. In the case of timed assessments, for example, teachers should describe the time limits, explain how students might distribute their time among parts for those assessment instruments with parts, and describe how students should record their responses. For a portfolio assessment, teachers should describe the criteria to be used to select the materials to be included in a portfolio, who will select these materials, and, if more than one person will be involved in the selection process, how the judgments from the different people will be combined. Where appropriate, sample material and practice should be provided to further increase the likelihood that instructions will be understood.

▶ 5. In assessment involving selection items (e.g., true–false, multiple-choice), the directions should encourage students to answer all items without threat of penalty.

A correction formula is sometimes used to discourage "guessing" on selection items. The formula is intended to encourage students to omit items for which they do no know the answer rather than to "guess" the answer. Because research evidence indicates that the benefits expected from the correction are not realized, the use of the formula is discouraged. Students should be encouraged to use whatever partial knowledge they have when choosing their answers, and to answer all items.

▸ 6. When collecting assessment information, interactions with students should be appropriate and consistent.

Care must be taken when collecting assessment information to treat all students fairly. For example, when oral presentations by students are assessed, questioning and probes should be distributed among the students so that all students have the same opportunity to demonstrate their knowledge. While writing a paper-and-pencil test, a student may ask to have an ambiguous item clarified, and, if warranted, the item should be explained to the entire class.

▸ 7. Unanticipated circumstances that interfere with the collection of assessment information should be noted and recorded.

Events such as a fire drill, an unscheduled assembly, or insufficient materials may interfere in the way in which assessment information is collected. Such events should be recorded and subsequently considered when interpreting the information obtained.

▸ 8. A written policy should guide decisions about the use of alternate procedures for collecting assessment information from students with special needs and students whose proficiency in the language of instruction is inadequate for them to respond in the anticipated manner.

It may be necessary to develop alternative assessment procedures to ensure a consistent and valid assessment of those students who, because of special needs or inadequate language, are not able to respond to an assessment method (for example, oral instead of written format, individual instead of group administered, translation into first language, providing additional time). The use of alternate procedures should be guided by a written policy developed by teachers, administrators, and other jurisdictional personnel.

III. Judging and Scoring Student Performance

Procedures for judging or scoring student performance should be appropriate for the assessment method used and be consistently applied and monitored.

Judging and scoring refers to the process of determining the quality of a student's performance, the appropriateness of an attitude or behavior, or the correctness of an answer. Results derived from judging and scoring may be expressed as written or oral comments, ratings, categorizations, letters, numbers, or as some combination of these forms.

▶ 1. Before an assessment method is used, a procedure for scoring should be prepared to guide the process of judging the quality of a performance or product, the appropriateness of an attitude or behavior, or the correctness of an answer.

To increase consistency and validity, properly developed scoring procedures should be used. Different assessment methods require different forms of scoring. Scoring selection items (true–false, multiple-choice, matching) requires the identification of the correct or, in some instances, best answer. Guides for scoring essays might include factors such as the major points to be included in the "best answer" or models or exemplars corresponding to different levels of performance at different age levels and against which comparisons can be made. Procedures for judging other performances or products might include specification of the characteristics to be rated in performance terms and, to the extent possible, clear descriptions of the different levels of performance or quality of a product.

▶ 2. Before an assessment method is used, students should be told how their responses or the information they provide will be judged or scored.

Informing students prior to the use of an assessment method about the scoring procedures to be followed should help ensure that similar expectations are held by both students and their teachers.

▶ 3. Care should be taken to ensure that results are not influenced by factors that are not relevant to the purpose of the assessment.

Various types of errors occur in scoring, particularly when a degree of subjectivity is involved (e.g., marking essays, rating a performance, judging a debate). For example, if the intent of a written communication is to assess content alone, the scoring should not be influenced by stylistic factors such as vocabulary and sentence structure. Personal bias errors are indicated by a general tendency to rate all students in approximately the same way (e.g., too generously or too severely). Halo effects can occur when a rater's general impression of a student influences the rating of individual characteristics or when a previous rating influences a subsequent rating. Pooled results from two or more independent raters (teachers, other students) will generally produce a more consistent description of student performance than a result obtained from a single rater. In combing results, the personal biases of individual raters tend to cancel one another.

▶ 4. Comments formed as part of scoring should be based on the responses made by the students and presented in a way that students can understand and use them.

Comments, in oral and written form, are provided to encourage learning and to point out correctable errors or inconsistencies in performance. In addition, comments can be used to clarify a result. Such feedback should be based on evidence pertinent to the learning outcomes being assessed.

▶ 5. Any changes made during scoring should be based upon a demonstrated problem with the initial scoring procedure. The modified procedure should then be used to rescore all previously scored responses.

Anticipating the full range of student responses is a difficult task for several forms of assessment. There is always the danger that unanticipated responses or incidents that are relevant to the purpose of the assessment may be overlooked. Consequently, scoring should be continuously monitored for unanticipated responses and these responses should be taken into proper account.

▸ 6. An appeal process should be described to students at the beginning of each school year or course of instruction that they may use to appeal a result.

Situations may arise where a student believes a result incorrectly reflects his/her level of performance. A procedure by which can appeal such a situation should be developed and made known to them. This procedure might include, for example, checking for addition or other recording errors or, perhaps, judging or scoring by a second qualified person.

IV. Summarizing and Interpreting Results

Procedures for summarizing and interpreting assessment results should yield accurate and informative representations of a student's performance in relation to the goals and objectives of instruction for the reporting period.

Summarizing and interpreting results refers to the procedures used to combine assessment results in the form of summary comments and grades which indicate both a student's level of performance and the valuing of that performance.

▸ 1. Procedures for summarizing and interpreting results for a reporting period should be guided by a written policy.

Summary comments and grades, when interpreted, serve a variety of functions. They inform students of their progress. Parents, teachers, counsellors, and administrators use them to guide learning, determine promotion, identify students for special attention (e.g., honours, remediation), and to help students develop future plans. Comments and grades also provide a basis for reporting to other schools in the case of school transfer and, in the case of senior high school students, post-secondary institutions and prospective employers. They are more likely to serve their many functions and those functions are less likely to be confused if they are guided by a written rationale or policy sensitive to these different needs. This policy should be developed by teachers, school administrators, and other jurisdictional personnel in consultation with representatives of the audiences entitled to receive a report of summary comments and grades.

▸ 2. The way in which summary comments and grades are formulated and interpreted should be explained to students and their parents/guardians.

Students and their parents/guardians have the "right-to-know" how student performance is summarized and interpreted. With this information, they can make constructive use of the findings and fully review the assessment procedures followed.

It should be noted that some aspects of summarizing and interpreting are based upon a teacher's best judgment of what is good or appropriate. This judgment is derived from training and experience and may be difficult to describe specifically in advance. In such circumstances, examples might be used to show how summary comments and grades were formulated and interpreted.

▶ 3. The individual results used and the process followed in deriving summary comments and grades should be described in sufficient detail so that the meaning of a summary comment or grade is clear.

Summary comments and grades are best interpreted in the light of an adequate description of the results upon which they are based, the relative emphasis given to each result, and the process followed to combine the results. Many assessments conducted during a reporting period are of a formative nature. The intent of these assessments (e.g., informal observations, quizzes, text-and-curriculum embedded questions, oral questioning) is to inform decisions regarding daily learning, and to inform or otherwise refine the instructional sequence. Other assessments are of a summative nature. It is the summative assessments that should be considered when formulating and interpreting summary comments and grades for the reporting period.

▶ 4. Combining disparate kinds of results into a single summary should be done cautiously. To the extent possible, achievement, effort, participation, and other behaviors should be graded separately.

A single comment or grade cannot adequately serve all functions. For example, letter grades used to summarize achievement are most meaningful when they represent only achievement. When they include other aspects of student performance such as effort, amount (as opposed to quality) of work completed, neatness, class participation, personal conduct, or punctuality, not only do they lose their meaningfulness as a measure of achievement, but they also suppress information concerning other important aspects of learning and invite inequities. Thus, to more adequately and fairly summarize the different aspects of student performance, letter grades for achievement might be complemented with alternate summary forms (e.g., checklists, written comments) suitable for summarizing results related to these other behaviors.

▶ 5. Summary comments and grades should be based on more than one assessment result so as to ensure adequate sampling of broadly defined learning outcomes.

More than one or two assessments are needed to adequately assess performance in multi-facet areas such as Reading. Under-representation of such broadly defined constructs can be avoided by ensuring that the comments and grades used to summarize performance are based on multiple assessments, each referenced to a particular facet of the construct.

▶ 6. The results used to produce summary comments and grades should be combined in a way that ensures that each result receives its intended emphasis or weight.

When the results of a series of assessments are combined into a summary comment, care should be taken to ensure that the actual emphasis placed on the various results matches the intended emphasis for each student.

When numerical results are combined, attention should be paid to differences in the variability, or spread, of the different sets of results and appropriate account taken where such differences exist. If, for example, a grade is to be formed from a series of paper-and-pencil tests, and if each test is to count equally in the grade, then the variability of each set of scores must be the same.

▶ 7. The basis for interpretation should be carefully described and justified.

Interpretation of the information gathered for a reporting period for a student is a complex and, at times, controversial issue. Such information, whether written or numerical, will be of little interest or use if it is not interpreted against some pertinent and defensible idea of what is good and what is poor. The frame of reference used for interpretation should be in accord with the type of decision to be made. Typical frames of reference are performance in relation to pre-specified standards, performance in relation to peers, performance in relation to aptitude or expected growth, and performance in terms of the amount of improvement or amount learned. If, for example, decisions are to be made as to whether or not a student is ready to move to the next unit in an instructional sequence, interpretations based on pre-specified standards would be most relevant.

▶ 8. Interpretations of assessment results should take account of the backgrounds and learning experiences of the students.

Assessment results should be interpreted in relation to a student's personal and social context. Among the factors to consider are age, ability, gender, language, motivation, opportunity to learn, self-esteem, socio-economic background, special interests, special needs, and "test-taking" skills. Motivation to do school tasks, language capability, or home environment can influence learning of the concepts assessed, for example. Poor reading ability, poorly developed psycho-motor or manipulative skills, lack of test-taking skills, anxiety, and low self-esteem can lead to lower scores. Poor performance in an assessment may be attributable to a lack of opportunity to learn because required learning materials and supplies were not available, learning activities were not provided, or inadequate time was allowed for learning. When a student performs poorly, the possibility that one or more factors such as these might have interfered with a student's response or performance should be considered.

▶ 9. Assessment results that will be combined into summary comments and grades should be stored in a way that ensures their accuracy at the time they are summarized and interpreted.

Comments and grades and their interpretations, formulated from a series of related assessments, can be no better than the data and information upon which they are based. Systematic data control minimizes errors which would otherwise be introduced into a student's record or information base, and provides protection of confidentiality.

▶ 10. Interpretations of assessment results should be made with due regard for limitations in the assessment methods used, problems encountered in collecting the information and judging or scoring it, and limitations in the basis used for interpretation.

To be valid, interpretations must be based on results determined from assessment methods that are relevant and representative of the performance assessed. Administrative constraints, the presence of measurement error, and the limitations of the frames of reference used for interpretation also need to be accounted for.

V. Reporting Assessment Findings

Assessment reports should be clear, accurate, and of practical value to the audiences for whom they are intended.

▶ 1. The reporting system for a school or jurisdiction should be guided by a written policy. Elements to consider include such aspects as audiences, medium, format, content, level of detail, frequency, timing, and confidentiality.

The policy to guide the preparation of school reports (e.g., reports of separate assessments; reports for a reporting period) should be developed by teachers, school administrators, and other jurisdictional personnel in consultation with representatives of the audiences entitled to receive a report. Co-operative participation not only leads to more adequate and helpful reporting, but also increases the likelihood that the reports will be understood and used by those for whom they are intended.

▶ 2. Written and oral reports should contain a description of the goals and objectives of instruction to which the assessments are referenced.

The goals and objectives that guided instruction should serve as the basis for reporting. A report will be limited by a number of practical considerations, but the central focus should be on the instructional objectives and the types of performance that represent achievement of these objectives.

▶ 3. Reports should be complete in their descriptions of strengths and weaknesses of students, so that strengths can be build upon and problem areas addressed.

Reports can be incorrectly slanted towards "faults" in a student or toward giving unqualified praise. Both biases reduce the validity and utility of assessment. Accuracy in reporting strengths and weaknesses helps to reduce systematic error and is essential for stimulating and reinforcing improved performance. Reports should contain the information that will assist and guide students, their parents/guardians, and teachers to take relevant follow-up actions.

▶ 4. The reporting system should provide for conferences between teachers and parents/guardians. Whenever it is appropriate, students should participate in these conferences.

Conferences scheduled at regular intervals and, if necessary, upon request provide parents/guardians and, when appropriate, students with an opportunity to discuss assessment procedures, clarify and elaborate their understanding of the assessment results, summary comments and grades, and reports, and, where warranted, to work with teachers to develop relevant follow-up activities or action plans.

▶ 5. An appeal process should be described to students and their parents/guardians at the beginning of each school year or course of instruction that they may use to appeal a report.

Situations may arise where a student and his/her parents/guardian believe the summary comments and grades inaccurately reflect the level of performance of the student. A procedure by which they can appeal such a situation should be developed and made known to them (for example, in a school handbook or newsletter provided to students and their parents/guardians at the beginning of the school year).

▶ 6. Access to assessment information should be governed by a written policy that is consistent with applicable laws and with basic principles of fairness and human rights.

A written policy, developed by teachers, administrators, and other jurisdictional personnel, should be used to guide decisions regarding the release of student assessment information. Assessment information should be available to those people to whom it applies—students and their parents/guardians, and to teachers and other educational personnel obligated by profession to use the information constructively on behalf of students. In addition, assessment information might be made available to others who justify their need for the information (e.g., post-secondary institutions, potential employers, researchers). Issues of informed consent should also be addressed in this policy.

▶ 7. Transfer of assessment information from one school to another should be guided by a written policy with stringent provisions to ensure the maintenance of confidentiality.

To make a student's transition from one school to another as smooth as possible, a clear policy should be prepared indicating the type of information to go with the student and the form in which it will be reported. Such a policy, developed by jurisdictional and ministry personnel, should ensure that the information transferred will be sent by and received by the appropriate person within the "sending" and "receiving" schools respectively.

B. ASSESSMENTS PRODUCED EXTERNAL TO THE CLASSROOM

Part B applies to the development and use of standardized assessment methods used in student admissions, placement, certification, and educational diagnosis, and in curriculum and program evaluation. These methods are primarily developed by commercial test publishers, ministries and departments of education, and local school systems.

The principles and accompanying guidelines are organized in terms of four areas:

    I.   Developing and Selecting Methods for Assessment
    II.   Collecting and Interpreting Assessment Information
    III. Informing Students Being Assessed
    IV. Implementing Mandated Assessment Programs

The first three areas of Part B are adapted from the *Code of Fair Testing Practices for Education* (1988) developed in the United States. The principles and guidelines are modified in these three sections are intended to be consistent with the *Guidelines for Educational and Psychological Testing* (1986) developed in Canada. The fourth area has been added to contain guidelines particularly pertinent for mandated educational assessment and testing programs developed and conducted at the national, provincial, and local levels.

I. Developing and Selecting Methods for Assessment

Developers of assessment methods should strive to make them as fair as possible for use with students who have different backgrounds or special needs. Developers should provide the information users need to select methods appropriate to their assessment needs.

Users should select assessment methods that have been developed to be as fair as possible for students who have different backgrounds or special needs. Users should select methods that are appropriate for the intended purposes and suitable for the students to be assessed.

Developers should:

▶ 1. Define what the assessment method is intended to measure and how it is to be used. Describe the characteristics of the students with which the methods may be used.

▶ 2. Warn users against common

Users should:

▶ 1. Determine the purpose(s) for assessment and the characteristics of the students to be assessed. Then select an assessment method suited to that purpose and type of student.

▶ 2. Avoid using assessment methods for

misuses of the assessment method.

▶ 3. Describe the process by which the method was developed. Include a description of the theoretical basis, rationale for selection of content and procedures, and derivation of scores.

▶ 4. Provide evidence that the assessment method yields results that satisfy its intended purpose(s).

▶ 5. Investigate the performance of students with special needs and students from different backgrounds. Report evidence of the consistency and validity of the results produced by the assessment method for these groups.

▶ 6. Provide potential users with representative samples or complete copies of questions or tasks, directions, answer sheets, score reports, guidelines for interpretation, and manuals.

▶ 7. Review printed assessment methods and related materials for content or language generally perceived to be sensitive, offensive, or misleading.

▶ 8. Describe the specialized skills and training needed to administer an assessment method correctly, and the specialized knowledge to make valid interpretations of scores.

purposes not specifically recommended by the developer unless evidence is obtained to support the intended use.

▶ 3. Review available assessment methods for relevance of content and appropriateness of scores with reference to the intended purpose(s) and characteristics of the students to be assessed.

▶ 4. Read independent evaluations of the methods being considered. Look for evidence supporting the claims of developers with reference to the intended application of each method.

▶ 5. Ascertain whether the content of the assessment method and the norm group(s) or comparison group(s) are appropriate for the students to be assessed. For assessment methods developed in other regions or countries, look for evidence that the characteristics of the norm group(s) or comparison group(s) are comparable to the characteristics of the students to be assessed.

▶ 6. Examine specimen sets, samples or complete copies of assessment instruments, directions, answer sheets, score reports, guidelines for interpretation, and manuals and judge their appropriateness for the intended application.

▶ 7. Review printed assessment methods and related materials for content or language that would offend or mislead the students to be assessed.

▶ 8. Ensure that all individuals who administer the assessment method, score the responses, and interpret the results have the necessary knowledge and skills to perform these tasks (e.g., learning assistance teachers, speech and language pathologists, counsellors, school psychologists, psychologists).

9. Limit sales of restricted assessment materials to persons who possess the necessary qualifications.

10. Provide for periodic review and revision of content and norms, and, if applicable, passing or cut-off scores, and inform users.

11. Provide evidence of the comparability of different forms of an instrument where the forms are intended to be interchangeable, such as parallel forms or the adaptation of an instrument for computer administration.

12. Provide evidence that an assessment method translated into a second language is valid for use with the second language. This information should be provided in the second language.

13. Advertise an assessment method in a way that states it can be used only for the purposes for which it was intended.

9. Ensure access to restricted assessment materials is limited to persons with the necessary qualifications.

10. Obtain information about the appropriateness of content, the recency of norms, and, if applicable, the appropriateness of the cut-off scores for use with the students to be assessed.

11. Obtain information about the comparability of interchangeable forms, including computer adaptations.

12. Obtain evidence about the validity of the use of an assessment method translated into a second language.

13. Verify advertising claims made for an assessment method.

II. Collecting and Interpreting Assessment Information

Developers should provide information to help users administer an assessment method correctly and interpret assessment results accurately.

Users should follow directions for proper administration of an assessment method and interpretation of assessment results.

Developers should:

1. Provide clear instructions for administering the assessment method and identify the qualifications that should be held by the people who should administer the method.

Users should:

1. Ensure that the assessment method is administered by qualified personnel or under the supervision of qualified personnel.

▸ 2. When feasible, make available appropriately modified forms of assessment methods for students with special needs or whose proficiency in the original language of administration is inadequate to respond in the anticipated manner.

▸ 2. When necessary and feasible, use appropriately modified forms of assessment methods with students who have special needs or whose proficiency in the original language of administration is inadequate to respond in the anticipated manner.

Ensure that instruments translated from one language to another are administered by persons who are proficient in the translated language.

▸ 3. Provide answer keys and describe procedures for scoring when scoring is to be done by the user.

▸ 3. Follow procedures for scoring as set out for the assessment method.

▸ 4. Provide score reports or procedures for generating score reports that describe assessment results clearly and accurately. Identify and explain possible misinterpretations of the scores yielded by the scoring system (grade equivalents, percentile ranks, standard scores) used.

▸ 4. Interpret scores taking into account the limitations of the scoring system used. Avoid misinterpreting scores on the basis of unjustified assumptions about the scoring system (grade-equivalents, percentile ranks, standard scores) used.

▸ 5. Provide evidence of the effects on assessment results of such factors as speed, test-taking strategies, and attempts by students to present themselves favourably in their responses.

▸ 5. Interpret scores taking into account the effects of such factors as speed, test-taking strategies, and attempts by students to present themselves favourably in their responses.

▸ 6. Warn against using published norms with students who are not part of the population from which the norm or comparison sample was selected or when the prescribed assessment method has been modified in any way.

▸ 6. Interpret scores taking account of major differences between the norm group(s) or comparison group(s) and the students being assessed. Also take account of discrepancies between recommended and actual procedures and differences in familiarity with the assessment method between the norm group(s) and the students being assessed.

Examine the need for local norms, and, if called for, develop these norms.

▸ 7. Describe how passing and cut-off scores, where used, were set and provide evidence regarding rates of

▸ 7. Explain how passing or cut-off scores were set and discuss the appropriateness of these scores in terms of rates of misclassification.

misclassification.

Examine the need for local passing or cut-off scores and, if called for, reset these scores.

▶ 8. Provide evidence to support the use of any computer scoring or computer generated interpretations. The documentation should include the rationale for such scoring and interpretations and their comparability with the results of scoring and interpretations made by qualified judges.

▶ 8. Ensure that any computer administration and computer interpretations of assessment results are accurate and appropriate for the intended use. If necessary, ensure that relevant information not included in computer reports is also considered.

▶ 9. Observe jurisdictional policies regarding storage of and subsequent access to the results. Ensure that computer files are not accessible to unauthorized users.

▶ 10. Ensure that all copyrights and user agreements are observed.

III. Informing Students Being Assessed

Direct communication with those being assessed may come from either the developer or the user of the assessment method. In either case, the students being assessed and, where applicable, their parents/guardians should be provided with complete information presented in an understandable way.

Developers or Users should:

▶ 1. Develop materials and procedures for informing the students being assessed about the content of the assessment, types of question formats used, and appropriate strategies, if any, for responding.

▶ 2. Obtain informed consent from students or, where applicable, their parents/guardians in the case of individual assessments to be used for identification or placement purposes.

▶ 3. Provide students or, where applicable, their parents/guardians with information to help them decide whether to participate in the assessment when participation is optional.

▶ 4. Provide information to students or, where applicable, their parents/guardians of alternate assessment methods where available and applicable.

Control of results may rest with either the developer or user of the assessment method. In either case, the following steps should be followed.

Developers or Users should:

▶ 1. Provide students or, where applicable, their parents/guardians with information as to their rights to copies of instruments and completed answer forms, to reassessment, to rescoring, or to cancellation of scores and other records.

▶ 2. Inform students or, where applicable, their parents/guardians of the length of time assessment results will be kept on file and of the circumstances under which the assessment results will be released and to whom.

▶ 3. Describe the procedures that students or, where applicable, their parents/guardians may follow to register concerns about the assessment and endeavor to have problems resolved.

IV. Implementing Mandated Assessment Programs[1]

Under some circumstances, the administration of an assessment method is required by law. In such cases, the following guidelines should be added to the applicable guidelines outlined in Sections I, II, and III of Part B.

Developers or Users should:

▶ 1. Inform all persons with a stake in the assessment (administrators, teachers, students, parents/guardians) of the purpose(s) of the assessment, the uses to be made of the results, and who has access to the results.

▶ 2. Design and describe procedures for developing or choosing the methods of assessment, selecting students where sampling is used, administering the assessment materials, and scoring and summarizing student responses.

▶ 3. Interpret results in light of factors that might influence them. Important factors to consider include characteristics of the students, opportunity to learn, and comprehensiveness and representativeness of the assessment method in terms of the learning outcomes to be reported on.

▶ 4. Specify procedures for reporting, storing, controlling access to, and destroying results.

▶ 5. Ensure reports and explanations of results are consistent with the purpose(s) of the assessment, the intended uses of the results, and the planned access to the results.

▶ 6. Provide reports and explanations of results that can be readily understood by the intended audience(s). If necessary, employ multiple reports designed for different audiences.

---

[1]The Joint Advisory Committee wishes to point out it has not taken a position on the value of mandated assessment and testing programs. Rather, given the presence of these programs, the intent of the guidelines presented in Section IV, when combined with applicable guidelines in the first three sections of Part B, is to help ensure fairness and equity for the students being assessed.

References

Code of Fair Testing Practices for Education. (1988). Washington, D.C.: Joint Committee on Testing Practices.

Guidelines for Educational and Psychological Testing. (1986). Ottawa, Ont.: Canadian Psychological Association.

Standards for Teacher Competence in Educational Assessment of Students. (1990). Washington, D.C.: American Federation of Teachers, National Council on Measurement in Education, and National Educational Association.

The membership of the Working Group (WG) that developed the *Principles for Fair Student Assessment Practices for Education in Canada* and of the Joint Advisory Committee that oversaw the development was as follows:

Allan Bacon	Michael Jackson	Jean Pettifor
Marvin Betts	Michel Laurier (WG)	Sharon Robertson
Gary Broker	Tom Maguire (WG)	Don Saklofske
Clement Dassa (WG)	Romulo Magsino	Marvin Simner
Dick Dodds	Linda McAlpine	Marielle Simon (WG)
Tom Dunn (WG)	Stirling McDowell	Ross Traub (WG)
Bob Gilchrist	Allan McDonald	Sue Wagner
Nicholas Head	Craig Melvin	Kim Wolff
Douglas Hodgkinson	Kathy Oberle (WG)	Todd Rogers (Chair, Working
Barbara Holmes (WG)	Frank Oliva	Group and Joint Advisory
		Committee)

APPENDIX C The Scope of a Teacher's Professional Role and Responsibilities for Student Assessment

The scope of a teacher's professional role and responsibilities for student assessment may be described in terms of the following activities. These activities imply that teachers need competence in student assessment and sufficient time and resources to complete them in a professional manner.

Activities Occurring Prior to Instruction

a. Understanding students' cultural backgrounds, interests, skills, and abilities as they apply across a range of learning domains and/or subject areas
b. Understanding students' motivations and their interests in specific class content
c. Clarifying and articulating the performance outcomes expected of pupils
d. Planning instruction for individuals or groups of students

Activities Occurring During Instruction

a. Monitoring pupil progress toward instructional goals
b. Identifying gains and difficulties pupils are experiencing in learning and performing
c. Adjusting instruction
d. Giving contingent, specific, and credible praise and feedback
e. Motivating students to learn
f. Judging the extent of pupil attainment of instructional outcomes

Activities Occurring After the Appropriate Instructional Segment (e.g., lesson, class, semester, grade)

a. Describing the extent to which each pupil has attained both short- and long-term instructional goals
b. Communicating strengths and weaknesses based on assessment results to students and parents or guardians
c. Recording and reporting assessment results for school-level analysis, evaluation, and decision making
d. Analyzing assessment information gathered before and during instruction to understand each student's progress to date and to inform future instructional planning
e. Evaluating the effectiveness of instruction
f. Evaluating the effectiveness of the curriculum and materials in use

Activities Associated with a Teacher's Involvement in School Building and School District Decision Making

a. Serving on a school or district committee examining the school's and district's strengths and weaknesses in the development of its students
b. Working on the development or selection of assessment methods for school building or school district use
c. Evaluating school district curriculum
d. Other related activities

Activities Associated with a Teacher's Involvement in a Wider Community of Educators

a. Serving on a state committee asked to develop learning goals and associated assessment methods
b. Participating in reviews of the appropriateness of district, state, or national student goals and associated assessment methods
c. Interpreting the results of state and national student assessment programs

Source: Standards for Teacher Competence in Educational Assessment of Students (1990). American Federation of Teachers, National Council on Measurement in Education, National Education Association.

Standards for Teacher Competence in Educational Assessment of Students

Standard	Skills
1. Teachers should be skilled in *choosing* assessment methods appropriate for instructional decisions	**a.** Use concepts of assessment error and validity. **b.** Understand how valid assessment supports instructional activities. **c.** Understand how invalid information can affect instructional decisions. **d.** Use and evaluate assessment options considering backgrounds of students. **e.** Be aware that certain assessment activities are incompatible with certain instructional goals. **f.** Understand how different assessment approaches affect decision making. **g.** Know where to find information about various assessment methods.
2. Teachers should be skilled in *developing* assessment methods appropriate for instructional decisions.	**a.** Be able to plan the collection of information needed for decision making. **b.** Know and follow appropriate principles for developing and using different assessment methods.

Standard	Skills
	c. Be able to select assessment techniques that are consistent with the intent of the instruction.
	d. Be able to use student data to analyze the quality of each assessment technique used.
3. The teacher should be skilled in administering, scoring, and interpreting the results of both externally produced and teacher-produced assessment methods.	**a.** Be skilled in interpreting informal and formal teacher-produced assessment results, including performances in class and on homework.
	b. Use guides for scoring essay questions, projects, response-choice questions, and performance assessments.
	c. Administer standardized achievement tests and interpret reported scores.
	d. Understand summary indexes, including measures of central tendency, dispersion, relationships, and errors of measurement.
	e. Analyze assessment results to determine student strengths and weaknesses.
	f. Use results appropriately and do not increase students' anxiety levels.
4. Teachers should be skilled in using assessment results when making decisions about individual students, planning teaching, developing curriculum, and making recommendations for school improvement.	**a.** Use accumulated assessment information to organize a sound instructional plan.
	b. Interpret results correctly according to established rules of validity.
	c. Use results from local, regional, state, and national assessments for educational improvement.
5. Teachers should be skilled in developing valid pupil grading procedures that use pupil assessments.	**a.** Devise, implement, and explain a procedure for developing grades.
	b. Combine various assignments, projects, in-class activities, quizzes, and tests into a grade.
	c. Acknowledge that grades reflect their own preferences and judgments.
	d. Recognize and avoid faulty grading procedures.
	e. Evaluate and modify their grading procedures.
6. Teachers should be skilled in communicating assessment results to students, parents, other lay audiences, and other educators.	**a.** Understand and be able to give appropriate explanations of how to interpret student assessments as moderated by student background factors such as socioeconomic status.
	b. Explain that assessment results do not imply that background factors limit a student.

(continued)

Standard	Skills
	c. Communicate to parents how they may assess a student's educational progress. **d.** Explain the importance of taking measurement errors into account when making decisions based on assessment. **e.** Explain the limitations of different types of assessments. **f.** Explain printed reports of assessments at the classroom, school district, state, and national levels.
7. Teachers should be skilled in recognizing unethical, illegal, and otherwise inappropriate assessment methods and uses of assessment information.	**a.** Understand laws and case decisions that affect their classroom, school district, and state assessment programs. **b.** Understand the harmful consequences of misuse or overuse of various assessment procedures such as embarrassing students or violating a student's right to confidentiality. **c.** Understand that it is inappropriate to use standardized student achievement test scores to measure teaching effectiveness.

Source: *Standards for Teacher Competence in Educational Assessment of Students* (1990). American Federation of Teachers, National Council on Measurement in Education, National Education Association.

Glossary

Absolute grading a criterion-referenced type of grading in which grades are based on performance compared to set standards.

Adaptive behaviour being able to meet independence and social responsibility expectations for the age and context in which the behaviour occurs.

Affect *see* Affective.

Affective emotional feelings.

Alignment extent to which instructional activities and classroom assessments cover tested material.

Alternative assessment refers to a number of different kinds of assessments that are not traditional paper-and-pencil tests, such as performance and portfolio assessments.

Alternatives refers to possible answers in a multiple-choice item.

Analytic scale type of scoring in which separate scores are provided for each criterion used.

Anchor examples of student responses, products, and performances that illustrate specific points on a scoring criteria scale.

Anecdotal observation brief written notes or records of student behaviour.

Aptitude test type of standardized test that measures cognitive ability, potential, or capacity to learn.

Assessment the process of gathering, evaluating, and using information.

Attention deficit/hyperactivity disorder (AD/HD) a classification of special needs in which the student is inattentive, hyperactive, and/or impulsive.

Attitude a predisposition to respond favourably or unfavourably to something; consists of affective, cognitive, and behavioural components.

Attributions students' beliefs about the nature of the factors they believe caused achievement outcomes.

Authentic assessment assessments that mirror tasks carried out in actual, naturally occurring settings.

Authenticity describes instruction and assessment that are characterized by tasks that are similar to what is done or accomplished in real life.

Benchmark content standard for particular grade levels or developmental levels.

Benchmark assessment regular testing of students during the school year to monitor progress toward achieving end-of-year standards.

Binary-choice item type of selected-response item in which the respondent selects one of two possible answers.

Central tendency error scoring bias in which students tend to be rated in the middle of the evaluation scale.

Classroom assessment the collection, evaluation, and use of information for teacher decision making.

Classroom climate *see* Classroom environment.

Classroom culture *see* Classroom environment.

Classroom environment feeling tones and nature of interpersonal interactions in a classroom.

Cognitive mental processing that includes knowing, understanding, and reasoning.

Confidence bands show the standard error of measurement for obtained scores.

Constructed-response format type of item in which students create or produce their own answer or response.

Construct-related evidence type of evidence for validity that focuses on the meaning and definition of constructs that are assessed.

Content-related evidence type of evidence for validity in which judgments are made about the representativeness of a sample of items from a larger domain.

Content standards describe what students should know and be able to do.

Correlation coefficient a number between -1 and $+1$ that indicates the direction and strength of the relationship between two measures.

Criteria categories of specific behaviours or dimensions used to evaluate students.

Criterion-referenced type of test score interpretation in which performance is compared to levels of established criteria.

Criterion-related evidence type of evidence for validity in which scores from an assessment are related to other measures of the same trait or future behaviour.

Developmental standards describe what students should know and be able to do at each grade level.

Distractors incorrect alternatives in a multiple-choice item.

Educational goal a general statement of what students should know and be able to do.

Emotional or behavioural disorders consistent, inappropriate behaviours and feelings not attributed to other disabilities that interfere with academic work.

Essay type of item in which students provide an extended or restricted written response to a question.

Evaluation interpretation of gathered information to make the information meaningful.

Exemplar *see* Anchor.

Expectation level of performance communicated to others.

Extended-type task a performance assessment task that may last days or weeks in which students provide extensive answers to tasks.

Feedback indicating verbally or in writing the correctness of an action, answer, or other response.

Formative assessment assessment that occurs during instruction to provide feedback to teachers and students.

Frequency distribution indicates the number of individuals receiving each score.

Frequency polygon shows the number of individuals receiving each score as a line graph.

Generosity error scoring bias in which teachers rate students higher than their performance deserves.

Grade equivalent (GE) type of standardized test score that indicates performance in units of year and month of school as compared to the norm group.

Grade-level standards describe age-appropriate standards that reflect changes over time.

Halo effect general impression that influences scores or grades on subsequent assessments.

High-stakes tests tests that students must perform adequately on for graduation, promotion in grade, school accreditation, and other important implications.

Histogram graphic illustration of a frequency distribution using bars to represent the frequency of each score or groups of scores.

Holistic scale type of scoring in which a single score is given for overall performance.

Hyperactive excessively active behaviour sustained in many situations.

Impulsivity responding quickly, without time for reflection.

Inclusion educational approach in which students with exceptionalities are taught in classrooms with students who do not have exceptionalities.

Individualized education plan (IEP) plan for providing appropriate services to students with exceptionalities.

Instructional validity judgment of the extent of the match between what is taught and what is assessed.

Item analysis review of pattern of responses to an objective item to determine the quality of distractors, discrimination, and difficulty.

Learning disability mental-processing deficit that manifests as a significant discrepancy between aptitude and achievement.

Learning expectations, outcomes, and objectives descriptions of performance that include what students should know and be able to do and what criteria are used to judge the performance.

Learning goal student desire to understand and learn with positive self-conceptions of competence.

Linear transformation derived scores that are consistent with the raw score distribution.

Likert scale rating scale in which a respondent indicates the extent to which there is agreement or disagreement among a series of statements.

Mastery goal *see* Learning goal.

Mean arithmetic average of all scores in a distribution.

Measurement a systematic process of differentiating traits, characteristics, or behaviour.

Median the midpoint of a distribution, dividing it into an equal number of scores.

Mode the most frequently occurring score in a distribution.

National norms the range of test scores that represent the usual performance in a sample from across Canada (or another nation).

Negatively skewed a distribution in which the mean is lower than the median.

Nondiscriminatory assessment in which the nature of the materials, questions, and procedures do not influence the results.

Normal curve equivalent (NCE) derived normalized score with a mean of 50 and a standard deviation of 21.06.

Norm-referenced a type of test interpretation in which relative standing is identified by comparing performance to how others (norm group) performed.

Oral questioning type of assessment in which the teacher asks questions orally.

Percentile rank indicates the percentage of scores at or below the specified score.

Performance assessment type of assessment in which students perform an activity or create a product.

Performance criteria *see* Criteria.

Performance goal motivation for doing well is to pass or obtain a score rather than primarily to understand.

Performance standard a set of criteria designated to signify qualitatively different levels of performance.

Personal communication student interactions with the teacher to provide assessment information.

Portfolio a systematic collection of student products to assess progress.

Positively skewed a distribution in which the mean is higher than the median.

Range the difference between the highest and lowest score in a distribution.

Rating scale a scale that contains gradations of the trait being assessed.

Readiness test type of standardized aptitude test that identifies strengths and weaknesses of specific skills.

Reasoning mental operation in which cognitive skills are combined with knowledge to solve a problem, make a decision, or complete a task.

Reliability the consistency, stability, and dependability of scores.

Restricted range a small range of scores.

Restricted-type task performance assessment task in which the student provides a limited response to a task that is completed within a day, hour, or minutes.

Rubric a scoring guide that uses criteria to differentiate between levels of student proficiency on a rating scale.

Scaled score derived scores used in standardized testing to indicate growth in years.

Scatterplot visual array of scores from two measures that illustrates possible relationships.

Selected-response format type of item for which students select a response from possible responses that are provided.

Semantic differential rating scale in which opposite adjectives are used and respondents check appropriate spaces between the adjectives.

Severity error scoring bias in which teachers rate students lower than they should.

Sociogram pictorial graph that shows how members of a group relate to one another.

Speeded tests type of test in which students have a set, minimal amount of time to answer all questions.

Standard deviation a number that indicates the average distance of scores from the mean.

Standard error of measurement (SEM) estimate of the degree of error in obtained scores.

Standards *see* Performance standards *or* Content standards.

Stanine derived score that indicates the approximate location of a score on the normal distribution.

Stem question or phrase in a multiple-choice item that is answered by selecting from given alternatives.

Student self-assessment students reporting on or evaluating themselves.

Summative assessment assessment that occurs at the end of an instructional unit to document student learning.

Table of specifications *see* Test blueprint.

Teacher expectations beliefs about what students are capable of knowing, understanding, and doing.

Teacher observation method of gathering assessment information in which the teacher systematically or informally observes students.

Teaching objective a description of the instructional plan.

Test battery several standardized tests that are normed on the same sample.

Test blueprint systematic presentation of the learning targets and nature of items in an assessment.

Test-retest a stability estimate of reliability in which a group answers the same questions twice.

T-**score** derived score with a mean of 50 and a standard deviation of 10.

Validity the appropriateness and legitimacy of the inferences, claims, and uses made from test scores.

Values end states of existence or desirable modes of conduct.

z-**score** derived scores with a mean of 0 and a standard deviation of 1.

References

Airasian, P.W. (2005). *Classroom assessment: Key concepts and applications* (5th ed.). New York: McGraw-Hill.

American Educational Research Association. (2003). Standards and tests: Keeping them aligned. Research Points, 1(1), 1–4.

Ames, C.A. (1990). Motivation: What teachers need to know. *Teachers College Record, 91,* 409–421.

Anderson, L.W. (1981). Assessing affective characteristics in the schools. Boston: Allyn & Bacon.

Anderson, L.W., & Krathwohl, D.R. (2001). A taxonomy for learning, teaching, and assessing: A revision of Bloom's taxonomy of educational objectives. Boston: Allyn and Bacon.

Arter, J., & McTighe, J. (2001). Scoring rubrics in the classroom: Using performance criteria for assessing and improving student performance. Thousand Oaks, CA: Corwin Press.

Arter, J., & Spandel, V. (1992). Using portfolios of student work in instruction and assessment. *Educational Measurement: Issues and Practice, 11,* 36–44.

Arter, J.A. (1996). Establishing performance criteria. In R.E. Blum & J.A. Arter (Eds.), *Handbook for student performance assessment in an era of restructuring* (pp. VI-1:1–VI-2:8). Alexandria, VA: Association for Supervision and Curriculum Development.

Azwell, T., & Schmar, E. (1995). *Report card on report cards: Alternatives to consider.* Portsmouth, NH: Heinemann.

Bailey, J.M., & Guskey, T. R. (2001). *Implementing student-led conferences.* Thousand Oaks, CA: Corwin Press.

Beyer, A., et al. (1993). *Alternative assessment: Evaluating student performance in elementary mathematics.* Ann Arbor Public Schools. Palo Alto, CA: Dale Seymour Publications.

Beyer, B.K. (1985). Critical thinking: What is it? *Social Education, 22,* 270–276.

Billups, L.H., & Rauth, M. (1987). Teachers and research. In V. Richardson-Koehler (Ed.), *Educator's handbook.* White Plains, NY: Longman.

Black, P., & Wiliam, D. (1998). Assessment and classroom learning. *Assessment in Education, 5*(1), 103–110.

Black, P., & Wiliam, D. (2004). The formative purpose: Assessment must first promote learning. In M. Wilson (Ed.), *Towards coherence between classroom assessment and accountability.*103rd Yearbook of the National Society for the Study of Education. Chicago: University of Chicago Press.

Bloom, B.S. (Ed.) (1956). Taxonomy of educational objectives: The classification of educational goals. Handbook 1. Cognitive Domain. New York: David McKay.

Boreman, G., & Overman, L. (2004). Academic resilience in mathematics among poor and minority students. *Elementary School Journal, 104,*177–197.

Borich, G.D., & Tombari, M.L. (2004). *Educational assessment for the elementary and middle school classroom* (2nd ed.). Upper Saddle River, NJ: Pearson Education Inc.

British Columbia Ministry of Education (2006). *Social Studies K to 7: Integrated Resource Package.* www.bced.gov.bc.ca/irp/ssk7.pdf.

British Columbia Ministry of Education (2009). *Reporting Student Progress: Policy and Practice.* www.bced.gov.bc.ca/reportcards/09_report_student_prog.pdf.

Brookhart, S.M. (1993). Teachers' grading practices: Meaning and values. *Journal of Educational Measurement, 30,* 123–142.

Brookhart, S.M. (1997). A theoretical framework for the role of classroom assessment in motivating student effort and achievement. *Applied Measurement in Education, 10,* 161–180.

Brookhart, S.M. (2001). Successful students' formative and summative uses of assessment information. *Assessment in Education, 8*(2), 153–169.

Brookhart, S.M. (2004). *Grading.* Upper Saddle River, NJ: Pearson Education Inc.

Brookhart, S.M. (2005). *Research on formative classroom assessment: State-of-the-art.* Paper presented at the annual meeting of the American Educational Research Association, Montreal.

Brophy, J.E., & Alleman, J. (1991). Activities as instructional tools: A framework for analysis and evaluation. *Educational Researcher, 20,* 9–23.

Brophy, J. (1981). Teacher praise: A functional analysis. *Review of Educational Research, 51,* 5–32.

Brophy, J.E. (2004). *Motivating students to learn* (2nd ed.). Boston: McGraw-Hill.

Bruner, J.S. (1960). *The process of education.* New York: Random House.

Burke, K. (1999). *The mindful school: How to assess authentic learning* (3rd ed.). Arlington Heights, IL: SkyLight Professional Development.

Camp, R. (1992). Portfolio reflections in middle and secondary school classrooms. In K. B. Yancey (Ed.), *Portfolios in the writing classroom.* Urbana, IL: National Council of Teachers of English.

Canadian Council on Social Development (2000). *Urban Poverty in Canada, Statistical Profile: Saskatchewan.*www.ccsd.ca/pubs/2000/up/b1-9.htm

Carlson, M.O., Humphrey, G.E., & Reinhardt, K.S. (2003). Weaving science inquiry and continuous assessment: Using formative assessment to improve learning. Thousand Oaks, CA: Corwin Press.

Chappuis, S., & Stiggins, R.J. (2002). Classroom assessment for learning. *Educational Leadership, 60*(1), 40–44.

Cizek, G.J. (1999). Cheating on tests: How to do it, detect, and prevent it. Mahwah, NJ: Lawrence Erlbaum.

Cizek, G.J. (2003). Detecting and preventing classroom cheating: Promoting integrity in assessment. Thousand Oaks, CA: Corwin Press.

Cizek, G.J., & Burg, S.S. (2006). Addressing test anxiety in a high-stakes environment: Strategies for classrooms and schools. Thousand Oaks, CA: Corwin Press.

Cohen, S.B. (1983). Assigning report card grades to the mainstreamed child. *Teaching Exceptional Students, 15,* 86–89.

Collins, A., & Dana, T.M. (1993). Using portfolios with middle grades students. *Middle School Journal, 25,* 14–19.

Conley, M.W. (2005). Connecting standards and assessment through literacy. Boston: Allyn & Bacon.

Cooper, H., Lindsay, J.J., Nye, B., & Greathouse, S. (1998). Relationships among attitudes about homework, amount of homework assigned and completed, and student achievement. *Journal of Educational Psychology, 90,* 70–83.

Costa, A.L., & Kallick, B. (2004). *Assessment strategies for self-directed learning.* Thousand Oaks, CA: Corwin Press.

Cross, L.H., & Frary, R.B. (1996). *Hodgepodge grading: Endorsed by students and teachers alike.* Paper presented at the annual meeting of the National Council on Measurement in Education, New York.

CTB Macmillan/McGraw-Hill (1003). California Achievement Test 5 Performance Assessment Component, p. 39.

Davis, M.M.D. (1995). The nature of data sources that inform decision making in reading by experienced second grade teachers. Doctoral dissertation, Old Dominion University.

De Fina, Alan A. (1992). *Portfolio assessment: Getting started. New York:* Scholastic Professional Books.

Doyle, W. (1986). Classroom organization and management. In M.C. Wittrock (Ed.), *Handbook of research on teaching* (3rd ed.). New York: Macmillan.

Dunn, T. (2004). Enhancing mathematics teaching for at-risk students: Influences of a teaching experience in alternative high school. *Journal of Instructional Psychology, 31*(1), 46-52.

Earl, L.M. (2003). Assessment as learning: using classroom assessment to maximize student learning. Thousand Oaks, CA: Corwin Press.

Ekman, P., & Friesen, W.V. (1969). The repertoire of nonverbal behavior: Categories, origins, usage, and coding. *Semiotica, 69,* 49–97.

Elawar, M.C., & Corno, L. (1985). A factorial experiment in teachers' written feedback on student homework: Changing teacher behavior a little rather than a lot. *Journal of Educational Psychology, 77,* 162–173.

Elliot, A.J., & Thrash, T.M. (2001). Achievement goals and the hierarchical model of achievement motivation. *Educational Psychology Review, 13*(2), 139–156.

Ennis, R.H. (1987). A taxonomy of critical thinking dispositions and abilities. In J. B. Baron & R.J. Sternberg (Eds.), *Teaching thinking skills: Theory and practice*. New York: W. H. Freeman.

Evertson, C., & Green, J. (1986). Observation as inquiry and method. In M.C. Wittrock (Ed.), *Handbook of research on teaching* (3rd ed., pp. 162–213). New York: Gale Group.

Forsyth, D.R. (1999). *Our social world* (3rd ed.). Belmont, CA: Wadsworth.

Fraser, B.J. (1994). Research on classroom and school climate. In D. Gabel (Ed.), *Handbook of research on science teaching and learning*. New York: Macmillan.

Fraser, B.J. (1999). Using learning environment assessments to improve classroom and school climates. In H. J. Freiberg (Ed.), *School climate: Measuring, improving and sustaining health learning environments*. London: Falmer Press.

Frederiksen, J.R., & White, B.Y. (2004). Designing assessments for instruction and accountability: An application of validity theory to assessing scientific inquiry. In M. Wilson (Ed.), *Toward coherence between classroom assessment and accountability*.103rd Yearbook of the National Society for the Study of Education. Chicago: University of Chicago Press.

Frey, B.B., Petersen, S.E., Edwards, L.M., Pedrotti, J.T., and Peyton, V. (2005). Item-writing rules: Collective wisdom. *Teaching and Teacher Evaluation, 21*, 357-364.

Friend, M., Busruck, W., & Hutchinson, N. (1998). *Including Students with Special Needs: A Practical Guide for Classroom Teachers* (3rd edition). Boston: Allyn & Bacon.

Frisbie, D.A., & Waltman, K.K. (1992). Developing a personal grading plan. *Educational Measurement: Issues and Practice, 11*, 35–42.

Gagne, E.D., Yekovich, C.W., & Yekovich, F.R. (1993). *The cognitive psychology of school learning* (2nd ed.). New York: HarperCollins.

Gallego, M.A., & Cole, M. (2001). Classroom cultures and cultures in the classroom. In V. Richardson (Ed.), *Handbook of research on teaching* (4th ed.). Washington, DC: American Educational Research Association.

Gardner, H. (1985). *Frames of mind: The theory of multiple intelligences*. New York: Basic Books.

Glatthorn, A.A. (1998). *Performance assessment and standards-based curricula: The achievement cycle*. Larchmont, NY: Eye on Education.

Goerss, D.V. (1993). Portfolio assessment: A work in process. *Middle School Journal, 25*(2), 20–24.

Gold, S.E. (1992). Increasing student autonomy through portfolios. In K.B. Yancey (Ed.), *Portfolios in the writing classroom*. Urbana, IL: National Council of Teachers of English.

Good, T.L., & Brophy, J.E. (2003). *Looking in classrooms* (9th ed.). New York: Longman.

Gordon, M. (1987). *Nursing diagnosis: Process and application*. New York: McGraw-Hill.

Gronlund, N.E. (1995). *How to write and use instructional objectives* (5th ed.). New York: Macmillan.

Gullickson, A.R. (2003). *The student evaluation standards*. Thousand Oaks, CA: Corwin Press.

Guskey, T.R. (1994). Making the grade: What benefits students? *Educational Leadership, 52*, 14–20.

Guskey, T.R. (Ed.). (1996). *Communicating student learning: 1996 ASCD Yearbook*. Alexandria, VA: Association for Supervision and Curriculum Development.

Guskey, T.R. (2002). Computerized gradebooks and the myth of objectivity. *Phi Delta Kappan, 83*(10), 775–780.

Guskey, T.R. (2005). *Formative classroom assessment and Benjamin S. Bloom's theory, research, and implications*. Paper presented at the annual meeting of the American Educational Research Association, Montreal.

Guskey, T.R., & Bailey, J.M. (2001). *Developing grading and reporting systems for student learning*. Thousand Oaks, CA: Corwin Press.

Haertel, E. (1990). *From expert opinions to reliable scores: Psychometrics for judgment-based teacher assessment*. Paper presented at the annual meeting of the American Educational Research Association, Boston.

Hallahan, D.P., & Kauffman, J.M. (1997). *Exceptional Learners: Introduction to Special Education* (7th edition). Boston: Allyn & Bacon.

Hanna, G.S. (1993). *Better teaching through better measurement*. Orlando, FL: Harcourt Brace Jovanovich.

Harlen, W. (2003). *Enhancing inquiry through formative assessment*. San Francisco: Institute for Inquiry, Exploratorium.

Hebert, E.A. (1998). Lessons learned about student portfolios. *Phi Delta Kappan, 79*, 583–585.

Hein, G.E., & Price, S. (1994). Active assessment for active science: A guide for elementary school teachers. Portsmouth, NH: Heinemann.

Herman, J.L., Aschbacher, P.R., & Winters, L. (1992). The National Center for Research on Evaluation, Standards and Student Testing (CRESST). *A Practical Guide to Alternative Assessment*. Alexandria, VA: Association for Supervision and Curriculum Development.

Heubert, J.P., & Hauser, R.M. (Eds.). (1999). *High stakes testing for tracking, promotion, and graduation*. Washington, DC: National Academy Press.

Hill, B.C., Ruptic, C., & Norwick, L. (1998). *Classroom based assessment*. Norwood, MA: Christopher-Gordon.

Hohn, R.L. (1995). *Classroom learning and teaching*. White Plains, NY: Longman.

Hoy, L., & Greg, M. (1994). *Assessment in special education*. Pacific Groves, CA: Brooks/Cole.

Inclusive Education Project (1993). *Creating a Learning Community at Fowler High School*. Syracuse, NY: Syracuse University.

Jackson, P.W. (1990). *Life in classrooms*. New York: Holt, Rinehart, and Winston.

Jamentz, K. (1994). Making sure that assessment improves performance. *Educational Leadership, 51*, 55–57.

Johnson, D.W., & Johnson, R.T. (2004). Assessing students in groups: Promoting group responsibility and individual accountability. Thousand Oaks, CA: Corwin Press.

Kendall, J.S., & Marzano, R.J. (1997). *Content knowledge: A compendium of standards and benchmarks for K–12 education*. Aurora, CO: Mid-continent Regional Educational Laboratory.

Kindsvatter, R., Wilen, W., & Ishler, M. (1996). *Dynamics of effective teaching* (3rd ed.). White Plains, NY: Longman.

Kissock, C., & Iyortsuun, P.T. (1982). *A guide to questioning: Classroom procedures for teachers*. London: Macmillan Press.

Klinger, D.A., DeLuca, C., & Miller, T. (2008). The evolving culture of large-scale assessments in Canadian education. *Canadian Journal of Educational Administration and Policy, 76*. www.umanitoba.ca/publications/cjeap/articles/klinger.html.

Knapp, M.L. (1996). *Nonverbal communication in human interaction* (4th ed.). New York: Holt.

Krathwohl, D.R., Bloom, B.S., & Masia, B.B. (1964). *Taxonomy of educational objectives, handbook II: Affective domain*. Boston: Allyn & Bacon.

Lambdin, D.V., & Walker, V.L. (1994). Planning for classroom portfolio assessment. *The Arithmetic Teacher, 41*, 318–324.

Lantz, H.B. (2004). Rubrics for assessing student achievement in science grades K–12. Thousand Oaks, CA: Corwin Press.

Lazzari, A.M., & Wood, J.W. (1994). *Test right: Strategies and exercises to improve test performance*. East Moline, IL: LinguiSystems.

Learning Disabilities Association of Canada. (2002). *Official Definition of Learning Disabilities*. www.ldac-taac.ca/defined/defined_new-e.asp.

Leathers, D.G. (1997). Successful nonverbal communication: Principles and applications (3rd ed.). New York: Macmillan.

LeMahieu, P.G., & Reilly, E.C. (2004). Systems of coherence and resonance: Assessment for education and assessment of education. In M. Wilson (Ed.), *Toward coherence between classroom assessment and accountability*. 104th Yearbook of the National Society for the Study of Education. Chicago: National Society for the Study of Education.

Lickona, T. (1993). The return of character education. *Educational Leadership, 51*, 6–11.

Linn, R.L., & Miller, M.D. (2005). *Measurement and assessment in teaching* (9th ed.). Upper Saddle River, NJ: Pearson Education Inc.

Marsh, H.W., & Craven, R. (1997). Academic self-concept: Beyond the dustbowl. In G. D. Phye (Ed.), *Handbook of classroom assessment: Learning, adjustment, and achievement*. San Diego, CA: Academic Press.

Martin-Kniep, G.O., & Cunningham, D. (1998). *Why am I doing this? Purposeful teaching through portfolio assessment*. Portsmouth, NH: Heinemann.

Marzano, R.J. (1992). *A different kind of classroom: Teaching with dimensions of learning*. Alexandria, VA: Association for Supervision and Curriculum Development.

Marzano, R.J. (1996). Understanding the complexities of setting performance standards. In R.E. Blum & J.A. Arter (Eds.), *Handbook for student performance assessment in an era of restructuring* (pp. 1:6-1–1:6-8). Alexandria, VA: Association for Supervision and Curriculum Development.

Marzano, R.J., Brandt, R., & Hughes, C.S. (1988). *Dimensions of thinking: A framework for curriculum and instruction*. Alexandria, VA: Association for Supervision and Curriculum Development.

Marzano, R.J., & Kendall, R.S. (1996). *A comprehensive guide to designing standards-based districts, schools, and classrooms*. Aurora, CO: Mid-continent Regional Educational Laboratory.

Marzano, R.J., Pickering, D., & McTighe, J. (1993). *Assessing student outcomes: Performance assessment using the dimensions of learning model*. Alexandria, VA: Association for Supervision and Curriculum Development.

Matese, G. (2005). *Cognitive factors affecting teachers' formative assessment practices*. Paper presented at the annual meeting of the American Educational Research Association, Montreal.

Mayer, R.E. (2002). The promise of educational psychology: Vol. II. Teaching for meaningful learning. Upper Saddle River, NJ: Merrill/Prentice Hall.

McLoughlin, J.A., & Lewis, R.B. (2005). *Assessing students with special needs* (6th ed.). Upper Saddle River, NJ: Pearson Education, Inc.

McMillan, J.H. (1980). Attitude development and measurement. In J.H. McMillan (Ed.), *The social psychology of school learning*. New York: Academic Press.

McMillan, J.H. (2001a). *Essential assessment concepts for teachers and administrators*. Thousand Oaks, CA: Corwin Press.

McMillan, J.H. (2001b). Secondary teachers' classroom assessment and grading practices. *Educational measurement: Issues and Practice, 20*(1), 20–32.

McMillan, J.H. (2002a). Elementary school teachers' classroom assessment and grading practices. *Journal of Educational Research, 95*(4), 203–214.

McMillan, J.H. (2002b). *The impact of high-stakes external testing on classroom assessment decision-making*. Paper presented at the annual meeting of the American Educational Research Association, New Orleans.

McMillan, J.H. (2003). Understanding and improving teachers' classroom assessment decision making. *Educational Measurement: Issues and Practices, 22*(4), 34–43.

McMillan, J.H., & Forsyth, D.R. (1991). What theories of motivation say about why learners learn. In R.J. Menges & M.D. Svinicki (Eds.), *College teaching: From theory to practice*. San Francisco: Jossey-Bass.

McMillan, J.H., Simonetta, L.G., & Singh, J. (1994). Student opinion survey: Development of measures of student motivation. *Educational and Psychological Measurement, 54*, 496–505.

McMillan, J.H., & Workman, D. (1999). *Teachers' classroom assessment and grading practices: Phase 2*. Richmond, VA: Metropolitan Educational Research Consortium.

McMillan, J.H., Workman, D., & Myran, S.M. (1998). *Teachers' classroom assessment and grading practices: Phase 1*. Richmond, VA: Metropolitan Educational Research Consortium.

McTighe, J., & Ferrara, S. (1998). *Assessing learning in the classroom*. Washington, DC: National Education Association.

McTighe, J., & Wiggins, G. (2005). *Understanding by design: Professional development workbook*. Alexandria, VA: Association for Supervision and Curriculum Development.

Mehrabian, A. (1981). *Silent messages* (2nd ed.). Belmont, CA: Wadsworth.

Mehrens, W.A., & Lehmann, I.J. (1987). *Using standardized tests in education* (4th ed.). New York: Longman.

Mehring, T.A. (1995). Report card options for students with disabilities in general education. In

T. Azwell & E. Schmar (Eds.), *Report card on report cards: Alternatives to consider.* Portsmouth, NH: Heinemann.

Morgan, N., & Saxton, J. (1991). *Teaching, questioning, and learning.* New York: Routledge.

Moskal, B.M. (2003). Recommendations for developing classroom performance assessments and scoring rubrics. *Practical Assessment, Research & Evaluation, 8*(14). Accessed June 1, 2005, from http://PAREonline.net/getvn.asp?v=8,n=14.

National Council on Measurement in Education. (1995). *Code of professional responsibilities in educational measurement.* Washington, DC. www.natd.org/Code_of_Professional_Responsibilities.html.

National Forum on Assessment. (1995). *Principles and indicators for student assessment systems.* Cambridge, MA: National Center for Fair and Open Testing (FairTest).

National Research Council. (2001). Knowing what students know: The science and design of educational assessment. Washington, DC: National Academy Press.

National standards for civics and government. (1994). Calabasas, CA: Center for Civic Education.

National standards for United States history: Exploring the American experience. (1994). Los Angeles, CA: National Center for History in the Schools.

Nelson Education Ltd. (2008). Canadian tests of basic skills: Teacher's handbook: Instructional resource and activities, forms K and L, levels 9–14, 58. Toronto: Nelson Education Ltd.

Newmann, F.M. (1997). Authentic assessment in social studies: Standards and examples. In G. D. Phye (Ed.), *Handbook of classroom assessment: Learning, adjustment, and achievement.* San Diego, CA: Academic Press.

Nolen, S.B., Haladyna, T.M., & Haas, N.S. (1989). *A survey of Arizona teachers and administrators on the uses and effects of state-mandated standardized achievement testing* (Tech. Rep. No. 89–2). Phoenix, AZ: Arizona State University, West Campus.

Norris, S.P., & Ennis, R.H. (1995). *Evaluating critical thinking.* Pacific Grove, CA: Midwest Publications.

Ontario Ministry of Education (2005). *The Ontario Curriculum: Mathematics.* Toronto: Queen's Printer for Ontario.

Ontario Ministry of Education (2006). *The Ontario Curriculum: Grades 1–8: Language.* Toronto: Queen's Printer for Ontario.

Ontario Ministry of Education (2009). *Ontario Report Card for Grades 1–6 (Public).* www.edu.gov.on/ca/eng/document/forms/report/1998/ep16.pdf.

Oosterhof, A.C. (1987). Obtaining intended weights when combining students' scores. *Educational measurement: Issues and practices, 6,* 29–37.

Ormrod, J E. (2004). *Human learning* (4th ed.). Upper Saddle River, NJ: Merrill/Prentice Hall.

Overton, T. (2003). *Assessing learners with special needs: An applied approach.* Upper Saddle River, NJ: Merrill/Prentice Hall.

Palm, T. (2008). Performance assessment and authentic assessment: A conceptual analysis of the literature. *Practical Assessment, Research & Evaluation, 13*(4), 1–11.

Parke, C.S., Lane, S., Silver, E.A., & Magone, M.E. (2003). Using assessment to improve middle-grades mathematics teaching and learning: Suggested activities using QUASAR tasks, scoring criteria, and students' work. Reston, VA: National Council of Teachers of Mathematics.

Perkins, D. (1993). *Smart schools.* New York: Simon and Schuster.

Phye, G.D. (1997a). Classroom assessment: A multidimensional perspective. In G.D. Phye (Ed.), *Handbook of classroom assessment: Learning, adjustment, and achievement.* San Diego, CA: Academic Press.

Phye, G.D. (Ed.). (1997b). Handbook of classroom assessment: Learning, adjustment, and achievement. San Diego, CA: Academic Press.

Pintrich, P.R., & Schunk, D.H. (2002). *Motivation in education: Theory, research, and applications.* Upper Saddle River, NJ; Columbus, OH: Merrill/Prentice Hall.

Popham, W. J. (1994). *Anonymity-enhancement procedures for classroom affective assessment.* Paper presented at the annual meeting of the American Educational Research Association, New Orleans.

Popham, W.J. (2005). *Classroom assessment: What teachers need to know* (4th ed.). Boston: Allyn & Bacon.

Porter, C., & Cleland, J. (1995). *The portfolio as a learning strategy*. Portsmouth, NH: Boynton/Cook.

The Psychological Corporation. *Test service notebook no. 148*. New York: Harcourt Brace Jovanovich.

Quellmalz, E. (1987). Developing reasoning skills. In J.B. Baron & R.J. Sternberg (Eds.), *Teaching thinking skills: Theory and practice*. New York: W. H. Freeman.

Quellmalz, E.S., & Hoskyn, J. (1997). Classroom assessment of reasoning strategies. In G.D. Phye (Ed.), *Handbook of classroom assessment: Learning, adjustment, and achievement*. San Diego, CA: Academic Press.

Raviv, A., Raviv, A., & Reisel, E. (1990). Teachers and students: Two different perspectives: Measuring social climate in the classroom. *American Educational Research Journal, 27*, 141–157.

Reynolds, C.R., Livingston, R.B., & Willson, V. (2006). *Measurement and assessment in education*. Boston: Pearson Education Inc.

Rodriguez, M.C. (2005). Three options are optimal for multiple-choice items: A meta-analysis of 80 years of research. *Educational Measurement: Issues and Practice, 24*(2), 3–13.

Rokeach, M. (1973). *The nature of human values*. New York: Free Press.

Roseberry-McKibbin, C., & Brice., A. (2002) Choice of languages in instruction: One language or two? *Teaching Exceptional Children, 33*(4) 10–36.

Roth, W.M. (2001). Gestures: Their role in teaching and learning. *Review of Educational Research, 71*(3), 365–392.

Ryan, A. (1991). *Student Evaluation: A Teacher Handbook*. Saskatchewan Education. www.sasked.gov.sk.ca/docs/policy/studeval/index.html.

Ryan, A.M., & Deci, E.L. (2000). Self-determination theory and the facilitation of intrinsic motivation, social development, and well-being. *American Psychologist, 55*, 68–78.

Saskatchewan Ministry of Education (January, 2000). Directions for diversity: "Enhancing supports to children and youth with diverse needs." Final report of the Saskatchewan special education review committee. Regina, SK. www.publications.gov.sk.ca/details.cfm?p=10114.

Salvia, J., & Ysseldyke, J.E. (2001). *Assessment* (8th ed.) Boston: Houghton Mifflin.

Schunk, D.H. (2004). *Learning theories: An educational perspective* (4th ed.). Upper Saddle River, NJ: Pearson Education Inc.

Scruggs, T.E., & Mastropieri, M.A. (1992). *Teaching test-taking skills: Helping students show what they know*. Cambridge, MA: Brookline Books.

Shepard, L.A. (2000). The role of assessment in a learning culture. *Educational Researcher, 29*(10), 4–14.

Shepard, L.A. (2004). Curricular coherence in assessment design. In M. Wilson (Ed.), *Towards coherence between classroom assessment and accountability*. 103rd Yearbook of the National Society for the Study of Education. Chicago: University of Chicago Press.

Simpson, E.J. (1972). The classification of educational objectives in the psychomotor domain. *The psychomotor domain* (vol. 3). Washington, DC: Gryphon House.

Smith, T.E.C., Polloway, E.A., Patton, J.R., Dowdy, C.A., McIntyre, L.J., & Francis, G.C. (2009). *Teaching Students with Special Needs in Inclusive Settings* (3rd ed.). Toronto: Pearson Education.

Smith, J.K., Smith, L.F., & De Lisi, R. (2001). *Natural classroom assessment: Designing seamless instruction & assessment*. Thousand Oaks, CA: Corwin Press.

Spinelli, C.G. (2002). Classroom assessment for students with special needs in inclusive settings. Upper Saddle River, NJ: Merrill/Prentice Hall.

Stenmark, J.K. (1991). Mathematics assessment: Myths, models, good questions, and practical suggestions. Reston, VA: National Council of Teachers of Mathematics.

Sternberg, R.J. (1986). The future of intelligence testing. *Educational measurement: Issues and practice, 5*, 19–22.

Stiggins, R.J. (1993). Teacher training in assessment: Overcoming the neglect. In S. Wise (Ed.), *Teacher training in assessment and measurement skills*. Lincoln, NE: Buros Institute.

Stiggins, R.J. (2002). Assessment crisis: The absence of assessment for learning. *Phi Delta Kappan*, 83(10), 758–765.

Stiggins, R.J. (2005). *Student-involved assessment FOR learning*. Upper Saddle River, NJ: Pearson Merrill Prentice Hall.

Stiggins, R.J., & Conklin, N.F. (1992). *In teachers' hands: Investigating the practices of classroom assessment*. Albany, NY: State University of New York Press.

Strickland, K., & Strickland, J. (1998). Reflections on assessment: Its purposes, methods, and effects on learning. Portsmouth, NH: Heinemann.

Terwilliger, J.S. (1989). Classroom standard setting and grading practices. *Educational Measurement: Issues and Practice*, 8, 15–19.

Tierney, R. & Simon, M. (2004). What's still wrong with rubrics: Focusing on the consistency of performance criteria across scale levels. *Practical Assessment, Research & Evaluation*, 9(2), 1–11.

Tierney, R.J., Carter, M.A., & Desai, L.E. (1991). *Portfolio assessment in the reading-writing classroom*. Norwood, MA: Christopher-Gordon Publishers.

Tittle, C.K., Hecht, D., & Moore, P. (1993). Assessment theory and research for classrooms: From *Taxonomies* to constructing meaning in context. *Educational Measurement: Issues and Practices*, 12, 13–19.

Tombari, M.L., & Borich, G.D. (1999). *Authentic assessment in the classroom: Applications and practice*. Upper Saddle River, NJ: Pearson Education Inc.

Valencia, S.W., & Calfee, R. (1991). The development and use of literacy portfolios for students, classes, and teachers. *Applied Measurement in Education*, 4, 333–345.

Van Petegem, K., Aelterman, A., Van Keer, H., & Rosseel, Y. (2008). The influence of student characteristics and interpersonal teacher behaviour in the classroom on student's wellbeing. *Social Indicators Research*, 85(2), 279–91.

Virginia Department of Education Released Test Items. Accessed November 2005. www.pen.k12.va.us/VDOE/Assessment/Release2004/5SciCorr1WEB.pdf.

Volante, L., & Ben Jaafar, S. (2008). Educational Assessment in Canada. *Assessment in Education: Principles, Policy and Practice*, 15, 201–210.

Wiggins, G.P. (1993). Assessing student performance: Exploring the purpose and limits of testing. San Francisco: Jossey-Bass.

Wiggins, G.P. (1998). Educative assessment: Designing assessments to inform and improve student performance. San Francisco, CA: Jossey-Bass.

Wiggins, G.P., & McTighe, J. (2005). *Understanding by design* (2nd ed.). Washington, DC: Association for Supervision and Curriculum Development.

Witt, J.C., Elliott, S.N., Daly, E.J., III, Gresham, F.M., & Kramer, J.J. (1998). *Assessment of at-risk and special needs children* (2nd ed.). Boston: McGraw-Hill.

Wolf, D.P. (1989). Portfolio assessment: Sampling student work. *Educational Leadership*, 46, 35–39.

Wood, J.W. (2002). *Adapting instruction to accommodate students in inclusive settings* (4th ed.). Upper Saddle River, NJ: Pearson Education Inc.

Wurtz, E. (1993). *Promises to keep: Creating high standards for American students*. Report on the Review of Education Standards from the Goals 3 and 4 Technical Planning Group to the National Education Goals Panel, Washington, DC.

Wylie, R.C. (1989). *Measures of self-concept*. Lincoln: University of Nebraska Press.

Index